The New GEORGIA GUIDE

A Project
of the
Georgia
Humanities
Council

The New GEORGIA GUIDE

The
University of
Georgia Press
Athens
and London

© 1996 by the University of Georgia Press
Athens, Georgia 30602
and the Georgia Humanities Council
Atlanta, Georgia 30303
All rights reserved

Designed by Sandra Strother Hudson
Cartography by Georgia State University
Cartography Research Laboratory
Set in Berkeley Old Style by Books International
Printed and bound by Maple-Vail
The paper in this book meets the guidelines for
permanence and durability of the Committee on
Production Guidelines for Book Longevity of the
Council on Library Resources.

Printed in the United States of America
00 99 98 97 96 C 5 4 3 2 1
00 99 98 97 96 P 5 4 3 2 1

Library of Congress Cataloging in
Publication Data

The new Georgia guide.
p. cm.
"A project of the Georgia Humanities
Council"—t.p.
ISBN 0-8203-1798-5 (hardcover : alk. paper).
— ISBN 0-8203-1799-3 (pbk. : alk. paper)
1. Georgia—Tours.
F284.3.N49 1996   95-46800
917.5804'43—dc20   CIP

British Library Cataloging in Publication Data
available

CONTENTS

STATE OF GEORGIA
OFFICE OF THE GOVERNOR
Atlanta, Georgia 30334-0900

Zell Miller

GOVERNOR

It was a pleasure for me to take part in the response to the groundswell of interest in the new version of the WPA guide to Georgia.

As a student and teacher of Georgia's history and as an active participant in its contemporary life, I was delighted that the people of this state assembled the talent and resources to produce the *New Georgia Guide*. While the WPA guide inspired this project, the *New Georgia Guide* charts a new course of the modern and traditional. It reflects the thought of our most recent residents as well as those who have lived in our state for many years.

We have produced a clear-eyed look at the state we love—the achievements and adversities, the unpleasant and the beautiful. So here is Georgia: its land, its people, its past, and the challenges of its future.

Sincerely,

Zell Miller

THE NEW GEORGIA GUIDE EDITORIAL BOARD

BENEFACTORS

The State of Georgia

The Joseph B. Whitehead
Foundation

The Georgia Humanities Council

The Atlanta Journal-Constitution

The Georgia Power Company
Foundation

The Coca-Cola Company

Fieldale Farms

The *New Georgia Guide* is made possible in part through the support of The Atlanta Committee for the Olympic Games Cultural Olympiad.

ACKNOWLEDGMENTS

The introduction to this volume speaks to the genesis of the *New Georgia Guide* and to those people and organizations that played vital roles in the beginnings of this project. The credits that follow are directed to those who were important to the actual production of the book beyond the staffs of the project and the University of Georgia Press.

As the concept of the Guide took shape, there was an initial decision to look at and write about Georgia in terms of its obvious regional characteristics. Following a prolonged drawing and redrawing of map lines, the scheme represented here was determined, and the Georgia Humanities Council set about helping identify regional coordinators to assist the writers of the tours and essays for these regions. These coordinators arranged for publicity for the project, contacted interested citizens for possible information and assistance, arranged community meetings to bring together residents, writers, and staff, and in the draft stages of production gave a critical reading to both the essays and tours for their respective regions. The coordinators were chosen for their knowledge of the regions and their ability to smooth the way for the writers. The following people have been a most significant cadre of foot soldiers for the *New Georgia Guide*:

Dr. Alice Taylor-Colbert, associate professor of history and director of the Shorter College Museum and Archives (Northwest); Dr. Ray C. Rensi, professor of history, North Georgia College (Northeast); Dr. Kathryn W. Kemp, historian (Metropolitan Atlanta); Dr. Edward J. Cashin, professor of history and department chairman, Augusta College (East Central); Kaye Lanning Minchew, director, Troup County Archives (West Central); Dr. Bernadette Loftin, professor of history emerita, Middle Georgia College (Central); Dr. Mariella Glenn Hartsfield, chair, Humanities Division, Bainbridge College (Southwest); Dr. Delma E. Presley, director, Georgia Southern University Museum (Southeast); and Linda O. King, executive director, Coastal Georgia Historical Society (Coast). Additionally, the participants who attended regional meetings made outstanding contributions to the body of information collected for the Guide.

Several state organizations and agencies were strong institutional supporters in the production of the Guide, notably the Georgia Department of Archives and History of the Office of Secretary of State, the Georgia Humanities Council, the Georgia Department of Transportation, the Georgia Department of Industry, Trade and Tourism (ITT), and the Office of the Governor. Jeff McMichael and Ran Young of Georgia State University's Department of Geography expertly created maps. Photographs by the score were shared through the good offices of Robert W. Busby Jr., head of audio-visual for ITT, and his staff, especially Greg Knobloch. Lisa Dosie of the governor's staff and Paul R. Weimer of the Humanities Council were helpful time and again. The Vanishing Georgia Collection in the State Archives was a major source of historic images thanks to the help of Gail DeLoach, and the effort of securing photograph copies under the constraints of time was eased by George Whiteley of the Archives staff.

Several contributions took the form of meeting places, work places, and staff. The Georgia Department of Archives and History donated an office for the more than two years of the production schedule. Because the project was housed at the Archives, Dr. Edward Weldon and the reference and support staff gave daily aid. Gainesville College, thanks to the early and sustained enthusiasm of Pres. J. Foster Watkins, furnished staff assistance and space throughout the project.

Particular thanks are due the University of Georgia, which contributed resources and personnel to the project as it did in the publication of the WPA guide. The Institute of Community and Area Development provided consultation in the project's early stages. Vice President for Services S. Eugene Younts put the resources of his office behind the project in late 1992 and gave both personnel and other forms of support. Special thanks are due Mrs. Jeanette Stroer of Dr. Younts's office. She gave much-needed secretarial and organizational support for the project always with consummate professional skill and personal courtesy. In addition, the project has been cheerfully supported by the secretarial staff of the Institute of Higher Education at the University.

Public officials at every level willingly provided helpful directions, details, and suggestions all along the way. Writers' visits to historic sites, state and national parks, courthouses, city halls, local and regional libraries, and the halls of state government were always rewarded with generous help. Anne P. Smith, library director of the Georgia Historical Society, and Dr. Elizabeth Lyon, Carole Griffith, Carole Moore, and Kenneth Thomas Jr. of the Historic Preservation Division, Georgia Department of Natural Resources, gave sound advice, and their colleagues provided reference materials and assistance. Among the state's various networks of regional support, the seventeen Regional Development Centers were valuable resources to which writers, regional coordinators, and staff frequently turned, especially to the regional historic preservation planners. Hanna Ledford, head of tourism for the state, offered advice and staff cooperation.

The Guide owes a special debt to two friends of the project, G. Kimbrough Taylor and Thompson H. Gooding Jr., whose guidance came at a time when it was much needed. The editorial board thanks in particular Leslie Gordon, Wyatt Ware, and Mark Allio of the Atlanta Committee for the Olympic Games Cultural Olympiad for their interest, support, and courtesy.

In the private sector individuals and businesses enthusiastically encouraged our efforts. Wherever we went, the general public seemed interested in what we were doing and proud that we were including their particular part of the state in our coverage. Staffs and volunteers of chambers of commerce, convention and visitors' bureaus, and historical societies supplied literature and arranged meetings, site visits, and interviews. Local media publicized both the meetings and the project.

Organizations supplying space for various regional and staff functions were the Museum of Arts and Sciences in Macon, Columbus Museum, Middle Georgia College, Chattooga County Library, Dougherty County Library, Fitzgerald Main Street Association, Gordon County Chamber of Commerce, White County Chamber of Commerce, the Georgia Humanities Council, Georgia Archives, Emory University, and the Jimmy Carter Library.

The University System of Georgia provided support through the talent of personnel in the system schools. Albany State, Fort Valley State, North Georgia, Gainesville, Augusta, Bainbridge, Georgia, Middle Georgia, and Columbus Colleges; the University of Georgia; Georgia State University; Georgia Tech; and Georgia Southern University took part, as did private institutions including Clark Atlanta University, Emory University, and Shorter College.

As the staff began to draft these acknowledgments, we jokingly referred to what we called "omni-thanks," a category that included the broad array of individuals and groups that don't easily fit into the usual categories, the everywoman and everyman across Georgia who helped us, cheered us on, told us their stories, and sometimes put us back on course. They are legion, and all their names were never even really known. Some who were known are listed below. We thank these and all unnamed who helped make possible this *New Georgia Guide*:

Rick Allen, Leroy Alman, Hulda Baker, Buddy Baxley, Rita Bumgarner, Carole Chambers, Louise and Edward Chubb, Kenneth Coleman, Dale Couch, Thomas Daniel, Ogden Doremus, Charles F. Douglas, Mary Jo Dudley, Betty Bevins Edwards, Anne S. Floyd, Virginia Anne Franklin, Janice Gorham, Rebecca Gurr, Patricia Hall, Bradley Hill, Katherine Rogers Hood, Harvey H. Jackson III, Gayle Kimble, Ulf Kirchdorfer, Jeff McCord, Kemp Mabry, James H. Mackay, Tommy Maloof, Pauline Milhouse, Mike Miller, Matthew Moye, Carole Mumford, Robin Nail, Myron B. Parker, T. E. Parker, Linda and Stanley

Poore, Gladys Moss Powers, William S. Price Jr., Jo Ann Ray, Marvin Robertson, Fred Sanchez, Carolyn and Rick Segers, Claudell Smith Family, Virginia Snell, Steve Storey, Patricia Suhrcke, Gladys Tavenner, Rev. Charles Walker, Richard Waterhouse, Regina Wheeler, Robert E. White Jr., Stanley Whonic, Fort Frederica National Monument, Georgia Building Authority, Georgia Council for the Arts, Georgia State Parks, Department of Natural Resources, Glen-Ella Springs Inn and Conference Center and the Aycock Family, National Park Service, Savannah Visitors Center, Seabrook Foundation, Sea Island Company.

Thomas G. Dyer # INTRODUCTION

This is a book about the contours of Georgia, about its lands, waters, culture, and people. It strives to outline the shapes and patterns of this state and convey them in essays and tours. The book is the harvest of a project stretching over several years. The project organizers have organized and the project writers have written for the people of Georgia and for those who visit this state in person or vicariously. The *New Georgia Guide* is a book filled with deep affection and appreciation for Georgia and its people. It is also a book brimming with candor and free of the braggadocio often associated with travel guides. At times it is pensive, humorous, colorful, entertaining, and even provocative. We hope that it is never dull. To American visitors and to our friends from abroad who come here for the first time: Do not be surprised at the frankness that characterizes this volume. It is marked by what some see as a hard-edged honesty that is typical of Georgians. Such candor in writing about our home, we believe, should reassure our visitors that they have come to a state that is full of pride in itself but one that values honesty over bombast.

The roots of the *New Georgia Guide* reach back to the days of the Great Depression. In 1935, during the administration of Pres. Franklin D. Roosevelt, the Federal Writers' Project of the Works Progress Administration, a New Deal agency, began the American Guide Series. For the next seven years, thousands of out-of-work writers produced cogently written and critically acclaimed guides to all forty-eight states and a number of American cities, blending knowledge derived from many academic fields with insight and stylish prose. Some of the most gifted writers of the twentieth century worked on these literary monuments to the people and places of the depression-era United States of America. Conrad Aiken, Saul Bellow, John Cheever, Loren Eiseley, Ralph Ellison, and Studs Terkel all were eligible for relief and thus qualified to participate in the project.

The distinguished series of guides is a testament not only to the talent of those involved but also to the manner in which this massive federal project was conceived and implemented. As the American historian Bernard Weisberger has observed, critics both then and now have praised the project. Alfred Kazin described the guides as "an extraordinary American epic." Lewis Mumford thought them "the finest contributions made to American patriotism" in a long while.

Van Wyck Brooks wrote to the project director in strong praise of the "skill, taste, and judgment" of the series and unerringly predicted that many of the guides would "still be going strong when most of our current books are dead and forgotten." In recent times, the journalist-critic Edwin Newman wrote in the *New York Times Book Review* that the guides were "infused with quiet pride and some sense of the astonishing richness and variety of this nation, and some sense of what it could be." The Book-of-the-Month Club had every reason to be happy about the guides, since the series provided that organization with its "largest dividend ever."

Not everyone felt as positively about the guides as the critics and the book clubs. Because the series was a federal project, politicians inevitably found much to criticize in the management of the project and the content of the guides. Despite a heedful, circumspect approach to topics that would be politically sensitive, the guides encountered animosity from both conservative Republicans and Democrats. As Weisberger has observed, the New Deal–era Congress "as a whole reflected a deep Babbitt-like national distrust of the arts, especially under taxpayer sponsorship." In some instances, censorship occurred, and there were "hunts for real and imaginary Communists."

The production of the Georgia volume apparently included no dramatic witch hunts, but as the distinguished Georgia historian Phinizy Spalding discovered, *Georgia: The WPA Guide to Its Towns and Countryside*, like the guides to the other forty-seven states, did not spring fully formed from the federal bureaucracy. The state of Georgia was in desperate straits in 1935, "*in extremis*," as Spalding observed, ravaged by depression and boll weevil and saddled with a governor who "chose to fight the ameliorative measures of the New Deal tooth and nail." The election of 1936 produced a new governor, Eurith D. Rivers, who recognized the need for reform and adopted a cooperative attitude toward federal officials and such projects as the Federal Writers' Project. The administrator of New Deal programs in Georgia was Gay B. Shepperson, a tough-minded Virginian who oversaw the creation of the Georgia Writers' Project and who soon clashed with its supervisor, William O. Key. Eventually, Shepperson dismissed Key and replaced him with another project official who also left, disenchanted with the performance of the employees and discouraged by the literary products of the writers, many of whom were unqualified.

The project was saved by the efforts of Samuel Tupper Jr., an Atlanta novelist who became the project director. Although Tupper encountered difficulties with the state's Department of Education, the principal state sponsor of the guide, he found support in Governor Rivers, who protected the project from the state superintendent of education. Soon Tupper had the assistance of truly able writers and editors, who pieced together the research and the drafts of "steady estimable young men and women who came from shops and offices with neither talent nor special training for writing." When the federal government divested the Federal Writers' Project in 1939, the project continued as the Georgia Writers' Project under state sponsorship. The University of Georgia became a sponsor, and under the new arrangements, a number of offices across the state that had been responsible for gathering information were closed, leaving a streamlined program with offices in Atlanta, Augusta, and Savannah. According to Spalding, the "hardest work had been done; it was now up to the University of Georgia Press to cap the climax with publication."

When the press issued the guide in the spring of 1940, it received a strongly positive response from critics including Harold Martin of the *Atlanta Constitution*, who praised it for including "a history that moves with the swift pace of a mountain stream" and for dealing with the lovely and the unlovely in Georgia. "The splendor and the sordidness of 200 years of Georgia history are in it," Martin wrote, noting that the guide did not flinch from including either those things that make Georgians proud or those that give shame.

The guide swiftly became a favorite of thoughtful readers and achieved a considerable fame throughout the state, leading to a reissue of the volume in 1954—shorn, however, of the frank history that Martin so admired. In the late 1980s, when Phinizy Spalding agreed to help bring out a new edition of the guide, he unhesitatingly restored the dismissed history. And when the University of South Carolina Press reissued *Georgia: The WPA Guide to Its Towns and Countryside* in 1990, a new generation of Georgians lugged along the 578-page book with its updated highway guides on motor trips or settled in with it for more leisurely armchair travel.

Among those taken by the guide was Colin Campbell, a journalist with roots in Georgia and a direct descendant of Henry Grady, late-nineteenth-century spokesman for the New South and editor of the *Atlanta Constitution*. Campbell joined the staff of the *Constitution* in 1987 and set out to reacquaint himself with Georgia, wandering around the state with a worn-out copy of the 1954 reprint edition of the *Guide* by his side. He discovered the riches of the old volume and found it fascinating to compare the contemporary scene to depression-era Georgia, as presented in the book. He also mentally compared the book to modern travel literature, noting with pleasure the contrast between the conventional tourist manual (replete with directions to curio "shoppes" and fast-food restaurants) and the *Guide*, with its intelligent commentary on the state and its people.

A year later, while rummaging around in a bookstore in Columbia, South Carolina, Campbell discovered the reprint edition of the *Guide* that Phinizy Spalding had shepherded to publication. Campbell noted with pleasure the reintroduction of the material that had been excised from the 1954 version. Then he had an inspiration: Georgia should have a new guide, done along the lines of the classic depression-era version.

"I have a proposal for Gov. Zell Miller," Campbell wrote in his column during the spring of 1991. "Since there really is a need for a totally updated and sophisticated guide to Georgia, and since Miller knows and cares about the history of the state, why doesn't he help organize an all new Georgia guidebook?" Campbell then sketched out a rough blueprint for the project: A university or two might become involved; "also students, historians, agricultural experts, journalists, publishers, etc." How would such an undertaking be financed? Campbell had no idea, and he also confessed that he was unsure about another essential: how such a "complicated project would keep its literary zip and intellectual integrity in a commercialized, bureaucratized, politicized environment." But Zell Miller would know all that, Campbell concluded; after all, the governor had written his master's thesis in history at the University of Georgia on Eurith D. Rivers, the governor who had protected the New Deal–era project from its critics.

Within a short time, Campbell telephoned the governor about another matter. During the conversation, he brought up the prospect of a new WPA-type guide. He summarized the conversation with the governor in a column impishly entitled "Guidebook mania seizes state!" published in July 1991. "I love the idea," Zell Miller told Campbell; "It's an excellent idea." The governor then offered a few suggestions for getting the project underway and invited Campbell to "pay him a visit" to talk about the proposal. "He loves traveling around this large and infinitely curious state," Campbell wrote. Campbell also heard from Phinizy Spalding and other readers who shipped him guides and pamphlets dealing with one aspect or another of Georgia.

Four months later, Campbell ventured farther out on the guidebook limb with another column in which he mentioned that he had had discussions about the guide with Malcolm Call, director of the University of Georgia Press. Campbell had been impressed by the quality of the press's list and its production of "superior books." Call also liked the idea, but he repeatedly asked a nettlesome question: "Who will pay for it?"

By the spring of 1992, Campbell had also heard from the Georgia Humanities Council. Over the previous ten years or so, the council had won a statewide reputation for sponsoring outstanding public programs dealing with literature, history, and allied fields. Council-sponsored programs reached into every nook and cranny of Georgia and included some publishing ventures, but nothing of the size or complexity of what Campbell envisioned. Earlier in the process, Campbell had talked with Patricia Suhrcke, then assistant director of the council, who had independently come up with the same idea. As early as 1991, she had urged the Humanities Council to undertake the project.

Now Campbell had a letter from Ronald Benson, president of the council, who told Campbell that he was going to convene a small group of Georgians to talk about producing a new guide. Benson enlisted the aid of the director of the Carter Presidential Library, Donald Schewe, who provided the group with a room for the meeting. Campbell attended and so did Call; Benson; Edward Weldon, director of the Georgia Department of Archives and History; Betsey Weltner of the Georgia Council for the Arts; Alexa Henderson, chairperson of the Humanities Council and a professor of history and associate dean at Clark-Atlanta University; Hanna Ledford of the Georgia Department of Industry, Trade and Tourism; and Steve Wrigley, senior executive assistant to the governor and a trained historian with a Ph.D. from Northwestern University.

Colin Campbell professed astonishment and delight that so distinguished a group had been gathered to discuss "this crazy project." When Campbell asked who would be in charge of the project, Benson responded that the Humanities Council would take responsibility. Malcolm Call told the group that the project would need an editor, perhaps even a board of scholarly editors. Ed Weldon said that he saw the guide as "a snapshot of Georgia around 1995." Inevitably the discussion turned to money. Call's earlier persistent questioning of who would pay came up again. A figure of twenty thousand dollars was mentioned as a reasonable sum to see the project through the preliminary planning. Steve Wrigley said that he hoped that the state might find a way to provide some support.

Indeed it did. Governor Miller underwrote the preliminary planning, which stretched over a period of approximately six months. Benson foresaw a planning period of four months during which one or two persons would assemble information, study the prospect for a new guide, consult with others across the state, and recommend whether the project seemed feasible.

From hindsight, the optimism of the early planners seems overly enthusiastic. Large publishing ventures managed by volunteers, involving significant numbers of collaborators, and (in keeping with the mission of the Humanities Council) requiring multiple opportunities for citizen participation need a great deal of time to come together. Moreover, university presses typically need at least one year for the preparation and publication of such a large manuscript. And there was the desire by Campbell, the governor, and others that the volume be organized, written, and published in time for the arrival of hundreds of thousands of visitors from here and abroad who would descend upon Atlanta in 1996 for the Olympics.

The preliminary planners did a splendid job. Energetic and thorough, Sarah Brown and Jennifer Wewers talked to people across the state and helped to organize meetings of citizens who would give their suggestions. They gathered pamphlets, brochures, statistics, and other travel guides. They began files on each county and collected information from chambers of commerce. They carefully laid out possible organizational approaches for both the project and the resultant book. They carved up the state into regions that made conceptual sense and could be dealt with thematically by essayists. And they made arrangements for a group of Georgia's leading scholars to sit down and talk about the project. Specifically, the scholars were asked to think about how such a book might maintain the intellectual honesty that Colin Campbell had pointed to as a sine qua non of a new guide.

The list of scholars invited reads like a who's who of American history in Georgia. It included Numan Bartley, the E. Merton Coulter Professor of History at the University of Georgia; Donnie D. Bellamy, Regents Professor of History at Fort Valley State College; Dan T. Carter, Andrew Mellon Professor of History at Emory University; Edward J. Cashin Jr. of Augusta College; Steve Gurr of Gainesville College; John S. Lupold of Columbus College; John M. Matthews of Georgia State University; Robert C. McMath of the Georgia Institute of Technology; R. Frank Saunders of Georgia Southern University; Alexa Henderson; and Malcolm Call.

They talked about the issues that should be considered when drawing a portrait of Georgia in the 1990s. They also talked about content and format. Should the format follow that of the 1940 guide? Should there be a group of essays by various authors? If so, what topics should be written about? Should there be essays on major cities? Should there be an essay on each region? What fields or disciplines should the writers represent? Should the tours be regionally based? Would there be a project staff? an advisory committee? How would writers be chosen and persuaded to take part in such a project? Could the universities provide support? Who would the readers be? How could community involvement effectively contribute to the editorial objectives of the publication? And where would the money come from to pay for the project?

After a freewheeling discussion, the group decided that a new Georgia guide was a good idea. Enthusiastic concurrence in the concept was one thing; how to carry out the project was quite another. The group did not minimize the difficulty of the task; it recommended that a small professional staff be engaged at some point and that an editorial board made up of scholars and other citizens be assembled as volunteer stewards of the project. They would have to be chosen carefully to ensure that a variety of views were represented and, even more important, to be certain that they would give the necessary time.

Governor Miller liked the idea of an independent editorial board, and by mid-autumn he had written to twelve Georgians and asked them to join in the venture. They all said yes. Doug Bachtel was a sociologist and expert on Georgia statistics at the University of Georgia. Donnie Bellamy from Fort Valley had participated in the early planning, and so had Alexa Henderson, Dan Carter, and Edward Cashin. Melissa Fay Greene was an Atlanta author whose prizewinning book, *Praying for Sheetrock*, had just come out. John Burrison, professor of English at Georgia State University, was the author of *Brothers in Clay* and an expert on Georgia folklore. Virginia Spencer Carr, head of the Department of English at Georgia State, was an internationally known biographer. Stanley Lindberg was editor of the distinguished literary magazine, the *Georgia Review*, based at the University of Georgia. Steve Wrigley, who had temporarily left the governor's office, was also at Georgia State University. Thomas G. Dyer was a professor of higher education and history at the University of Georgia and for seven years editor of the *Georgia Historical Quarterly*. And, not surprisingly, the governor also appointed Colin Campbell, who had been present from the beginning.

Governor Miller invited four others to serve as ex-officio members of the board. They were Ronald Benson, Malcolm Call, Steve Gurr, and Edward Weldon. Later, Karen Orchard, new director of the University of Georgia Press, joined the board as an ex-officio member.

With time in short supply and the 1996 deadline for publication looming, the board met for the first time in Room 107 of the State Capitol just before Christmas 1992. Zell Miller came to the meeting and spoke eloquently about his vision for the guide. Colin Campbell later wrote of the governor's comments: "Miller thanked us and said go to it. He said he envied us, and that we should be doing this great book even if the Olympics *weren't* coming. He seemed wonderfully clear. And then he left, saying he'd help all he could but that we'd have to do it."

The board thanked the governor and got to work. It elected a chairman and appointed a project director, Steve Gurr, the vice president for academic affairs at Gainesville College and co-editor of the *Dictionary of Georgia Biography*. Foster Watkins, president of Gainesville College, and H. Dean Propst, chancellor of the University System of Georgia, had agreed to release one-third of Gurr's time for work on the project.

Over the next year, the board met nearly every month, sometimes in Atlanta, hosted by Edward Weldon and the staff of the State Archives; sometimes in Athens at the University of Georgia. The meetings were always cordial and collegial; everyone knew that the project had to be organized quickly. But these were independent-minded Georgians, and healthy debates ensued about directions for the project. Everyone, however, agreed on one matter. There could be no project without funds.

Steve Wrigley chaired the committee that found the support needed to underwrite the project. In this, as in most critical phases of the effort, the *New Georgia Guide* had the strong support of Governor

Miller. Put simply, the project might never have succeeded without Miller and his vigorous backing. In the end, the public and private sectors joined hands to support the guide. The Joseph B. Whitehead Foundation, in keeping with its long record of interest in the people of Georgia, provided generous backing for the project. The Georgia Power Company Foundation, the Coca-Cola Company, the *Atlanta Journal-Constitution* and Fieldale Farms did likewise. The board of the Georgia Humanities Council provided significant cash support in addition to its already substantial contribution of staff time and effort. In time, the Cultural Olympiad of the Atlanta Committee on the Olympic Games would provide valuable financial assistance.

The manner of financing the project contrasted sharply with the earlier guide that had been wholly sponsored by the federal and (to a lesser extent) the state governments. It reflected the emphasis of the 1990s on private and public cosponsorship of endeavors.

At an early meeting, the board adopted its "Statement of Editorial Principles" that sets out straightforwardly the purposes of the project and the principles undergirding it. The board wanted to be sure that the statement would be included in the guide so that readers could be clear about the conceptual foundations of the book. The entire text follows.

> Taking as our model the spirit informing the WPA state guides of the 1930s and 1940s, the editorial board of the "New Georgia Guide" has adopted as its primary objective the creation and publication of a comprehensive guide to the state of Georgia as it exists now in all its diversity. Although we expect the final product to draw extensively upon the most reliable demographics of the state's population, as well as statistics regarding its industry, agriculture, and other vital concerns, we do not envision the final product as attempting to present an encyclopedic gathering of such statistical data. Similarly, while we expect the guide to examine the natural, historical, political, economic, and other cultural forces that have and are shaping the state, we do not envision it as a reference book to cover any of these individual areas in detail. Most specifically our objective is not to celebrate or to promote the state with an image-boosting document, nor do we see this book as advocating any specific social agendas. We seek to provide an objectively informed but genuinely engaging portrait of Georgia that catches the spirit of this place and time in such a way as to guide both citizens and visitors to a better understanding of who we are, where we have come from, and where we are heading as we approach a new century.

The board oversaw the organization, writing, and production of the book and worked for more than three years to bring the task to closure. By the early spring of 1993, the membership had adopted a format for the guide, deciding on a combination of regional essays and tours that would seek to give coverage to as much of the state as possible. The board also decided that the earlier guide's emphasis upon Georgia history should be continued and commissioned an overview historical essay.

By the early fall of 1993, contracts had been issued to authors who would write on nine regions of the state, somewhat arbitrarily drawn and sure to please almost no one completely. Regional coordinators had been hired who would help the writers in assembling materials and who would take suggestions from the public concerning the guide. By the late fall, writers had also been signed on who would produce tours that would follow and complement the essays. And the board had induced Jane Powers Weldon, a superbly experienced and professionally astute editor, to become the project coordinator, working with the equally able Steve Gurr, who worked half-time as project director after his retirement from Gainesville College in July 1994.

All but two writers completed their tasks, and there were only minor slippages of deadlines. The two who failed to deliver were replaced by William Hedgepeth, who wrote the essay on Central Georgia, and Buddy Sullivan, who wrote the coastal tour. The board owes a special debt of thanks to these two writers.

By late January 1995, the manuscript was in hand, and it was approved by the editorial board on February 3, 1995. By late March, it had been delivered to the University of Georgia Press, whose editorial board had officially accepted it for publication on February 23, 1995. Numerous editing and production tasks awaited Steve Gurr and Jane Weldon, but the volunteers who comprised the board heaved a collective and audible sigh of relief, secure in the knowledge that the challenge and charge laid out by Governor Miller on December 17, 1992, had been accomplished. There was considerable satisfaction and considerable hope that those who read and used the guide would value it.

Early in the process and almost incidentally, the board had adopted the official title of the volume. It would be the *New Georgia Guide*. Some wondered whether the emphasis should fall upon *New* or whether it might fall upon *New Georgia*. There have been many New Souths, of course, and perhaps an equal number of New Georgias, but those who liked the idea of stressing the "New Georgia" portion of the title pointed to the striking contrasts that existed between contemporary Georgia and the state at the time of publication of the first guide. In education, in cultural life, in commerce and finance, in the development of an indigenous philanthropy, in confidence, and most important of all, in race relations, the Georgia of the 1990s offers a hopeful contrast to the state reflected in the WPA guide.

There have been trade-offs, of course, and several of the essayists in this volume point clearly to those. For example, the pace and style of living in the 1990s are quite different. The 1940 guide described a way of life that was rural and poor; the *New Georgia Guide* has been written in a time of sprawling urbanization and increasing affluence. In contemporary Georgia, there is still wretched, grinding poverty, but there is also a booming economy that has brought an infinitely higher standard of living to Georgians as a whole than would have been dreamed possible in the 1930s when the first guide was being written. Increasingly, the emphasis falls upon building the state's economy from within, with less attention given to the industry-chasing that characterized an earlier era. Much of the economic drama that has unfolded over the past five decades has resulted from the activities of a cadre of hard-nosed financiers and business people who value and protect the "business friendly" climate of the state. Sometimes they are hailed as visionaries; sometimes they are derided as boosters; but it is hard to imagine contemporary Georgia having developed as it has without the vigor and resilience that characterize business people and commerce in the state today.

Most significant for the health of Georgia's economy, however, was the revolution in race relations that accompanied the hard-fought, hard-won gains of the modern civil rights movement. No state's population has benefited so greatly from the expanded opportunities that stemmed from this liberating force that was beginning to build when the first guide was being written. More generally speaking, perhaps no state has been so dramatically freed, transformed, and invigorated by the moral, social, and political force of the civil rights revolution.

In 1940, Georgia had slightly over three million people; now there are over seven million. Georgia is now the eleventh most populous of the United States—that surprises many who do not know the state well—and demographers predict that it will soon become tenth. Much of that growth results from an explosion in immigration since the late 1960s. Immigrants have come from virtually every section of the United States, many seeking economic opportunity more difficult to find elsewhere. Others have come from all over the world. The population of Georgia today is infinitely more cosmopolitan than in the 1930s and 1940s. If Georgia was largely a black-and-white state then, today it is multi-hued and multi-ethnic and shows every prospect of becoming even more so.

The indigenous folklife of Georgia persists in the 1990s in ways that might please the generation of the 1930s. In some ways, the traditions of music, art, and culture that characterized the state in the 1930s are stronger than ever, carefully preserved by performers, scholars, and citizens. Perhaps the most striking change in the state's cultural life since the 1930s has been in the fine arts. The internationally acclaimed Atlanta Symphony Orchestra, recently having celebrated its fiftieth anniversary, is younger than the 1940 guide. Vibrant symphonies exist in Augusta, Columbus, Savannah, and other cities, and there are at least three lively opera companies in the state. Moreover, the state's libraries and museums are a growth industry with literally hundreds scattered throughout the state.

In education, the picture in 1990s Georgia differs dramatically. A racially segregated system of elementary, secondary, and higher education was the norm in the 1930s. Georgia education was hopelessly underfunded and mired in an ethos that placed a low social value on education. Although serious problems still exist, particularly in elementary and secondary education, gigantic strides have been taken in those areas and in technical and adult education as well. In particular, there is great strength in Georgia higher education; the state's universities and colleges have soared to national and international recognition in the span of the last forty years.

Georgia's natural beauty endures. Mountains, marshes, rivers, islands, plains, swamps, hammocks, embayments, and swales: The variety and beauty of the great and small landforms are limitless and persisting despite the environmental devastation wrought by natural forces and poor conservation practices in the 1930s (and previous decades) and the often untrammeled, rapid-paced development of later times. Few travelers will fail to marvel at the startling variety of the land and the diversity of the floral and faunal inhabitants—great live oaks, longleaf pine, peerless rhododendron, *Spartina alterniflora*, the mysterious *Franklinia* tree, alligators, azaleas, egrets, sea turtles, armadillos, gallinules, the majestic osprey, and the fecund deer that sometimes pose hazards to travelers.

The late Phinizy Spalding, who understood Georgia better than most, wrote in his introduction to the 1990 edition of the WPA guide that travelers in Georgia would discover that Georgians in the small towns and byways are "friendly, curious as to your intentions, straightforward, and scrupulously honest." And in the cities, he wrote, "they usually are, after a period of hesitation, basically the same." Spalding was right. Civility endures in Georgia and can have only a positive effect upon the evolution of the culture of this state. At a time when courtesies decline and comity disappears in much of America, travelers to Georgia will find abundant and plentiful evidence that Georgians persist in the high value that they have historically placed upon consideration and civil kindness. To be sure, the state has plenty of problems, and there is ample attention to them in these pages, but there is also in this book a profound affection for Georgia and Georgians that needs no apology and offers none. It is an affection for a people of pride and persistence, of tradition and vision.

Welcome to Georgia.

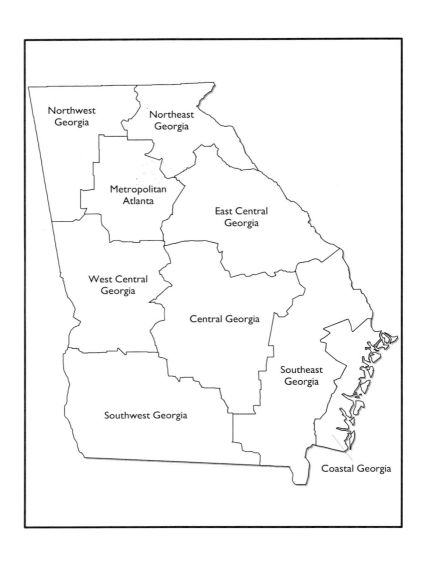

Northwest
Georgia

Northeast
Georgia

Metropolitan
Atlanta

East Central
Georgia

West Central
Georgia

Central Georgia

Southeast
Georgia

Southwest Georgia

Coastal Georgia

Steve Gurr and
Jane Powers Weldon

AN INTRODUCTION TO THE TOURS

Travelers using this book should keep in mind that the regional tours inevitably reflect the varying interests of individual writers and are limited by the number of pages assigned to those writers. Each writer was asked to take the traveler to sites that would convey the history and spirit of the region. Just as the writers did, readers are urged to look beyond the tours to discover even more attractions—and peculiarities—that make up this state. These tours may be only the first step on a much longer journey through Georgia.

The *New Georgia Guide* is a product of the mid-1990s; its predecessor was a product of the late 1930s. Much has changed in those intervening years, much will change during the life of this book, and much is changing even as the guide goes to press. As recently as the day this introduction was written, newspapers announced that Savannah's Waving Girl would be temporarily moved because of riverwalk construction, to be returned to her customary place in June of 1996; and that Lexington's 116-year-old jail had burned. Structures rise and fall, trees and hilltops succumb to bulldozers, lakes appear and disappear, all seemingly inescapable consequences of the dynamic advancement of nature and humankind.

As the traveler negotiates this changing state, the way will be eased by well-maintained state and federal highways. Though amenities may be sparse in rural areas, paved roads smooth the way in finding them. A Georgia Department of Transportation (DOT) highway map is an essential addition to the maps in this book, which are intended to be used as tour indicators only.

Governmentally, Georgia is composed of 159 units known as counties. The county is the local framework for education, schools, libraries, roads, water and power, and the increasing problems attendant to the protection of the environment. Frequently it is the focal point of local identification and pride. The county courthouse, an oft-mentioned feature in the tours that follow, is a fitting symbol of the significance of these units of local identification.

In courthouse towns during the week, information will be readily available from chambers of commerce, historical societies, and libraries with personnel who agreeably will provide help for the traveler. Near the courthouse there usually is a restaurant where government officials and merchants enjoy a midday meal. These cafes provide a welcome change from fast-food fare, and their waiters and cashiers are likely to know local sites.

The traveler will in all likelihood approach Georgia from a roadway. In Georgia at the close of the twentieth century, roadways are, in descending order of magnitude: interstate highways, federal highways, state highways (either two- or four-laned), county roads, and country roads (sometimes dirt or gravel or otherwise improved to only a limited degree). You will get to know the state best by traveling these roadways in reverse order of development, from unimproved to multi-laned interstate. It is on the back road that you will find the Georgia likely to be least homogenized into the mainstream amalgam that may be called contemporary America, i.e., consolidated, franchised, uniform, and standardized as much beyond local peculiarities as is possible. Real towns with real people occupy the old main streets, not the bypass highways.

International visitors may be shocked to discover that there is no significant passenger rail system. Distances may seem great to the international traveler, but air travel within the state, while available, has little to recommend it. Likewise there is nothing much in the way of intrastate bus transportation. Mass transport is best found in Atlanta, on MARTA (Metropolitan Atlanta Rapid Transit Authority). In some of Georgia's other urban areas, there is limited intercity bus service.

Other than highway signs or markers or the personal responses your questions bring, you may find formal sources that help reveal a place: the local weekly newspaper; regional and city magazines; brochures printed by regional development commissions, local chambers of commerce, official visitors' centers, and tourism bureaus. The Georgia Department of Industry, Trade, and Tourism publishes the annual *Georgia on My Mind*, a helpful guide to a number of the state's accommodations and sites.

No matter where these tours point, travelers will discover their own versions of Georgia. Remember that it is more than you will see, smell, hear, or feel; that it is changing; that it has changed; and that your being here has been a part of that process of change, we hope for the better.

TIPS FOR THE TRAVELER

Here are several things to keep in mind as you travel Georgia. In the appendix you will find more specific information about regulations, sources of information, state facilities, and addresses and telephone numbers.

1. Georgia is a large state, in square miles the largest east of the Mississippi River. It is 322 miles on I-75 from Dalton, in the northwest, to Valdosta, near the Florida line. The trip east to west from Savannah to Columbus is 255 miles.

2. Georgia's land forms move from barrier islands and Coastal Plains in the south, across the fall line to the Piedmont Plateau, to Ridge and Valley in the northwest and Appalachian Mountains in the northeast. This variety of terrain, like distance, should be considered in planning travel time.

3. The state of Georgia is a state of flux. Sites mentioned as under construction or planned for 1996 may be complete or defunct by the time this book, which went to press in the spring of 1995, appears.

4. Newer or remodeled sites are required to conform to federal regulations for visitors with disabilities, but older sites may present problems of accessibility. The best way to assure physical access is to call ahead.

5. Sites that are described but not designated "private" were open to the public when these tours were researched, though hours may vary for days of the week and season, and admission charge policies may change. Many places are staffed by volunteers or part-time personnel. State welcome centers and local tourist information bureaus distribute literature and information, including phone numbers, on nearby attractions.

6. The bed-and-breakfast inns and hostels common in Europe are seldom available in Georgia in their familiar form. There are B&Bs, but they are largely designed for the upscale market rather than the budget-minded traveler. Hostels are rare.

7. Road symbols used in these tours are I- (for interstate), U.S. (for federal), Ga. (for state), Alt. (alternate), Bu. (business), C (connector), Sp. (spur), Lp. (loop), and E, W, N, and S (east, west, north, and south). They correspond with most symbols on highway signs and DOT maps.

8. Practical guidance for the traveler may be missing at the most inopportune time. Where do you find a restroom? Interstate highways have rest stops (but some have no facilities); fast-food restaurants have restrooms; food markets/gasoline stations are not always cheerful about allowing the use of their facilities. In a real emergency, you might try the public library, local hospital, or other public agency building.

Finally, the traveler in Georgia should remember that the state's towns are connected by more than a network of roads and rails. There are many networks of people, and by inquiring about their interests, you will find a rich lode of local and statewide lore.

The New GEORGIA GUIDE

James C. Cobb # GEORGIA ODYSSEY

Not many of today's Georgians are likely
to recognize themselves in the first few pages of the 1940 Works
Progress Administration's *Georgia: A Guide to Its Towns and Countryside*:
"The average Georgian votes the Democratic ticket, attends the Baptist or Methodist church, goes home to midday dinner, relies greatly
on high cotton prices and is so good a family *man* that *he* flings wide
his doors to even the most distant of *his* wife's cousins' cousins. . . .
However cool *he* may be toward the cause of Negro education, the
Georgian is usually kind to *his* own servants and not a little apprehensive of hurting their feelings." [italics mine]

Save perhaps for their religious preferences, Georgians have changed
a great deal. Typically, more of them than not vote Republican (in
presidential elections at least). Not many of them go home to a midday
meal, and if they do, they are likely to call it lunch rather than dinner.
Likewise, relatively few Georgians exhibit much curiosity at all about
cotton prices anymore. Finally, and most important, Georgians now
come in more than one color and sex.

In the wake of more than half a century of dramatic changes, even
the most reckless essayist would know better than to refer to the
"average" Georgian, let alone discuss his or her lifestyle or values.
Yet whether we are lifelong residents, homesick expatriates, or fast-
assimilating newcomers, a great many of us persist in identifying ourselves as Georgians, believing that we know what this means even if
that meaning is clearly not the same for all of us. Our differences notwithstanding, however, what all self-designated Georgians share either by birthright or adoption is a common past. Not all of it is pretty
or pleasant to recall (whose is?), but any attempt to understand the
character and personality of contemporary Georgia must take into account its sometimes disturbing, sometimes appealing, but always rich
and eventful historical odyssey.

GEORGIA AS A COLONY

As we shall soon see, having absorbed their fair share of critical scru-
tiny, plus a good bit of plain old abuse over the years, Georgians are a

mite sensitive about the way they and their state are perceived. As a result, we may as well deal with it right now, at the beginning. Contrary to what you may have heard, read, or been taught, Georgia was not settled by convicts of any sort. Even otherwise amiable Georgians are downright touchy on this point. (As a native Georgian teaching United States history to northern college freshmen, I used to inform my students that when I heard anyone repeat the outrageous falsehood that Georgians are descended from thieves and murderers, it made me so mad that I wanted to shoot him or at least take his wallet.)

Those familiar with Georgia's history as a European outpost know that it actually began not with English convicts but with Spanish explorers and missionaries whose first contact with the area came nearly two centuries before Georgia was chartered in 1732. Georgia's founder, James Edward Oglethorpe (and the twenty other trustees to whom Georgia's royal charter was granted), did hope, initially at least, to promote penal reform and the relocation of the homeless and downtrodden to an idyllic New World wilderness offering "fertile lands sufficient to subsist all the useless poor in England." Like most proponents of noble experiments, Oglethorpe was given to exaggeration. He described Georgia as "always serene, pleasant, and temperate, never subject to excessive heat or cold, nor to sudden changes; the winter is regular and short, and the summer cool'd with refreshing breezes." Georgia was, in short, "a lush, Edenic paradise, capable of producing almost every thing in wonderful quantities." Charged with overseeing Georgia's settlement and ensuring its growth, the trustees reasoned that because it occupied roughly the same latitude as China, Persia, and the Madeira Islands, the new colony could supply the silks and wines that England was currently forced to purchase from producers outside the British Empire. Georgia, then, seemed to offer that most rare and wonderful of coincidences, an opportunity to do what was morally good, serve the national interest, and make a buck in the bargain. Moreover, populated by sturdy and sober yeomen and tradesmen—lawyers were banned as were slavery, Catholicism, and hard liquor—Georgia would provide an excellent defense perimeter for the prosperous colony of South Carolina, which was attracting altogether too much attention from the Spanish in Florida.

It was small wonder that many investors and proponents found the Georgia experiment irresistible; nor was it surprising that this seemingly ideal combination of philanthropy, capitalism, and national interest went awry. There was no shortage of people wanting to go to Georgia, and because those chosen as the colony's initial settlers would receive a host of benefits, including free passage, fifty acres of land, and supplies and foodstuffs for a year, they were screened carefully—so carefully, in fact, that the first Georgians were perhaps the most selectively chosen group of colonists to come to British North America.

They came from the ranks of small businessmen, tradesmen, and unemployed laborers, representing a "London in microcosm" with the "large debtor element" notably underrepresented and nearly absent altogether.

Georgia's economic future hardly went as planned either. The mulberry trees that grew wild throughout Georgia were not suitable for silk production, but even when colonists secured the proper variety of trees, silkworms found the colony's cold snaps a bit too nippy for their tastes. Meanwhile, those who have sampled the fruits of such modern vineyards as are compatible with the local climate and soils will have little difficulty understanding why Georgia never became the colonial equivalent of the Napa Valley.

Colonial Georgia suffered an unfavorable balance of trade because its production of goods for export (hampered to some extent by the trustees' regulations) was too feeble to finance the importation of goods from abroad. Restrictions on rum and landholding were eventually relaxed, but the young colony languished, remaining the smallest and poorest British royal possession in North America. In later generations, Georgians would balk at admitting their state had begun as a buffer for South Carolina. Likewise, they would not rush to concede that Georgia ultimately survived by becoming more like South Carolina. Yet, early on, discontented Georgians began to cast envious eyes on the wealth and lifestyles of the Carolina rice planters whose crops provided a major export commodity that supported a much more lively commerce than Georgia enjoyed.

Georgia's trustees had warned steadfastly against slavery and single-crop plantation farming, but their moralistic arguments were no match for the avarice and ambition of their critics, especially the prominent members of Savannah's business community, not to speak of George Whitefield, the colony's leading minister of the gospel. The arguments of the proslavery faction were ably summarized by Thomas Stephens, whose father was actually secretary to the trustees and their chief agent in Georgia:

> And indeed the extraordinary Heats here, the extraordinary Expences in maintaining, hiring and procuring White Servants, the extraordinary Difficulty and Danger there is in clearing the Lands, attending and Manufacturing the Crops, working in the Fields in Summer, and the poor Returns of Indian Corn, Pease and Potatoes, which are as yet the only chief Produces of the Land there, make it indisputably impossible for White Men alone to carry on Planting to any good Purpose. . . . The poor People of Georgia, may as well think of becoming Negroes themselves (from whose Condition at present they seem not to be far removed) as of hoping to be ever able to live without them; and

they ought best to know, and most to be believed, who have made the Experiment.

Ignoring protests that "those folk who wanted to bring in Negroes, . . . would put an end to Men's Work," the proslavery advocates pushed their case until they got their way in 1750. Two years later, the trustees returned their charter to the crown, and the ill-fated efforts to maintain Georgia as a morally pristine backwoods utopia came to an end.

By 1760 more than one-third of Georgia's population were slaves, and by the eve of the American Revolution, the figure was nearly one-half. James Wright, who became the royal governor in 1760, had held a variety of positions in the South Carolina bureaucracy, and hence he led the way in the Carolina-ization of Georgia. Georgia's population increased almost tenfold in the 1750s and 1760s, and expanded production of rice and indigo spurred the colony's economic upturn. Governor Wright played a key role in Georgia's physical growth as well, negotiating treaties with nearby Indians that increased the colony's land area approximately fivefold.

Although the trustees had been specifically forbidden from owning land, holding office, or profiting from the colony in any way, their successors in the royal government chafed under no such restraints. Indeed, Governor Wright and his cohorts were soon among the colony's most affluent landowners and slaveholders. By 1773, sixty people owned at least twenty-five hundred acres, and together they held more than 50 percent of the colony's slaves. Colonial policies encouraging land speculation facilitated this consolidation of wealth while ambitious yeomen faced major financial obstacles in becoming rice or indigo planters. As time passed, the small farmers of Georgia saw themselves steadily losing ground relative to the affluent planter minority, and they blamed their difficulties on the royal government that seemed so acutely attuned to planter interests. Colonial officials responded with open contempt; Colonial Council president James Habersham described their critics to Governor Wright as the people who were "really what you and I understand as Crackers."

As this reference suggests, Georgians can assert a long-standing claim on, as one writer described it, "one of the oldest pejoratives in America." In recent years, "Cracker" has enjoyed widespread usage as a derogatory reference to whites—usually poor whites—employed primarily by blacks. Historically, however, Crackers suffered the abuse and slights of a number of socially superior whites, both northern and southern in origin. Ethnically, the original, prototypical Crackers were probably of Scots-Irish descent. Dr. Samuel Johnson had defined a Cracker in 1755 as a "noisy, boasting fellow." Backcountry Crackers enjoyed a reciprocally disdainful relationship with their

Anglican, low-country detractors. In 1775 the Rev. Charles Woodmason, an English-born Anglican missionary, quickly became disgusted with the uncouth "Crackers" who disrupted his sermons and seemed inclined to "bluster and make a Noise about a Turd." Crackers, Woodmason believed, behaved so believing "they have a Right because they are Americans—born to do as they please . . . to any Body." As time passed, the stereotype of Cracker as backwoods boaster was augmented by the practice of "cracking" corn to produce the meal for corn bread, which was the staple of the Cracker diet. A somewhat less opprobrious derivation came from "whip-crackers," herdsmen who used long whips tapered to a cracker to drive their cattle in the unfenced forests and free ranges of antebellum Georgia and Florida. Cracker herdsmen were often people of considerably better economic circumstances than appearances might have suggested, but the term remained a derogatory one, especially as time passed, among blacks, who often ridiculed the white trash who occupied the scrub lands around the plantation and after emancipation proved to be their major antagonists.

The Cracker/planter schism grew more pronounced as Georgia drifted into the American Revolution. "Drifted" is an appropriate term because Georgia played a relatively minor role in the conflict. Georgia was the only colony to comply with the Stamp Act, and it sent no official delegation to the First Continental Congress. Georgia's emergent political leaders reached no firm consensus on the question of independence, and within the colony, matters of faction and ingroup/out-group squabbling remained paramount. Defenders of the Crown faced opposition from a Cracker coalition largely drawn from out-of-power planters and their representatives and the "country" faction drawn from non-Anglican upcountry planters and farmers and artisans from the towns. Again, this coalition was loose at best, as exemplified by the fatal shooting in a duel of Button Gwinnett, a country faction leader, at the hands of Lachlan McIntosh, a member of the more conservative out-of-power planter faction. Naturally, when the British showed up and occupied Savannah in 1778, matters became even messier.

"War" may be a misleading term for the American Revolution as it played out in Georgia, for it implies a degree of organization and structure seldom observed in the thirteenth colony during the conflict. While it may not have been war, it was certainly bloody. With Tories in control of Savannah and the low-country plantation areas, fighting raged in the backwoods, where guerrilla activity amounted less to pitched battles and sieges than to skirmishes, ambushes, lynchings, and cold-blooded murder.

From this context emerged one of Georgia's most heroic and mythologized historical figures, Nancy Morgan Hart, a backcountry patriot of the first order, who at the time of the Revolution lived in the Broad River wilderness of present-day Elbert County with her husband, Benjamin Hart. Legend and lore have it that Nancy was anything but the stereotypical southern belle. In 1825 a Milledgeville newspaper offered this description:

> In altitude, Mrs. Hart was almost Patagonian, remarkably well-limbed and muscular, and marked by nature with prominent features. She possessed none of those graces of motion which a poetical eye might see in the heave of the ocean wave or in the change of the summer cloud; nor did her cheeks—I will not speak of her nose—exhibit the rosy tints which dwell on the brow of the evening or play on the gilded bow. No one claims for her throat that it was lined with fiddle strings. That dreadful scourge of beauty, the small-pox had set its seal upon her face. She was called a hard swearer, was cross-eyed and coarse-grained, but was nevertheless a sharp-shooter.

Legend has it that local Indians stood so in awe of Nancy that they named a stream near her cabin "War Woman Creek." In Nancy's case, the truth may indeed be stranger than fiction and thus all the harder to verify, but her most documentable exploit went something like this:

Disdaining flight in the face of the British advance into the hinterlands from Augusta and Savannah, Nancy had made her cabin a refuge for patriots who sought to harass the local Tory populations. When six Tories descended upon her cabin and accosted her about this, she feigned submission and appeared to comply with their demands to prepare a meal for them. As she did so, she dispatched her daughter, Sukey, to the spring ostensibly for water but actually to blow the conch shell kept there to summon help when it was needed.

Meanwhile, as the smell of turkey, venison, and hoecake filled the cabin, the Tories broke out a jug of whiskey and began to pass it around, even asking an all-too-amenable Nancy to enjoy a swig or two. As the mood grew mellower, the men failed to notice that Nancy was pushing their muskets out through cracks in her cabin wall. When they finally realized what she was doing, she immediately shouldered a musket and demanded that they "surrender their damned Tory carcasses to a Whig woman." Nancy's crossed eyes presented her Tory captors-turned-captives with a dilemma. It was difficult to tell where her gaze actually fell, as one of them learned when he sought to make a furtive move for his musket and paid for his mistake with his life. A quick-thinking Sukey quickly passed her mama another musket, and after a second Tory fell, the remainder thought better of such foolhardiness. Eventually Benjamin Hart arrived and quite possibly earned his lasting reputation as a wimp by suggesting that the Tories be shot. The fiery Nancy objected vociferously, insisting on hanging the men on the spot.

Though most of Nancy's exploits are totally unsubstantiated, on December 12, 1912, a gang of workers grading a railroad discovered six skeletons in shallow graves about a half mile from the apparent site of Nancy's cabin. This discovery may or may not have substantiated Nancy Hart's most famous escapade, but in this case, as in not a few others where Georgians are concerned, image and symbolism count far more than reality. Nancy Hart was a fitting symbol of the white population of upcountry Georgia in the Revolutionary Era. Crude, illiterate, no strangers to hardship or conflict, they were survivors, and the longer they survived, the more social and political momentum they gained.

OPPORTUNITY AND SLAVERY IN ANTEBELLUM GEORGIA

Because royal forces remained in control of the more established population centers for much of the Revolutionary conflict, the backcountry naturally gained independence and influence during this period. With political power redistributed, men like Elijah Clark, the hero of many a backcountry skirmish, rose to prominence. Although the impact of the confiscation of Tory property is easily exaggerated, it helped to reshuffle Georgia's economic hierarchy, as did the disruption of agriculture and commerce brought on by nearly seven years of armed conflict. British bounties on the production of indigo were gone forever, and rice production remained below prewar levels for nearly twenty years.

As the once-mighty fell, the once-lowly rose. Public land policy was a boon to the ambitions of an upwardly mobile yeomanry. Fees were minimal, and heads of household could claim as much as two hundred acres for themselves with additional allowances for their dependents and up to ten slaves. A desperate Revolutionary government had offered generous land bounties to any white man who had fought for the patriot cause in Georgia, including not only non-Georgians but even British deserters. As a result, few white males failed to qualify for free land.

So-called treaties with various Indian tribes made more land available and helped to unleash a veritable orgy of speculation and corruption culminating in the 1795 Yazoo Land Fraud, in which four land companies bribed legislators to approve their acquisition of 35 million acres (nearly 60 percent of the land area that now constitutes Alabama and Mississippi) at the cost of only $500,000. In the wake of this scandal, the legislature quickly shifted to a lottery system that made land available at about seven cents per acre. Under this new plan, more than one hundred thousand individuals and families laid claim to approximately three-fourths of Georgia's land.

After the Yazoo fraud, Gov. James Jackson opened the negotiations that led in 1802 to the ceding of the western lands beyond the Chattahoochee to the federal government. This action allowed Alabama and Mississippi to escape the fate of being part of Georgia, and in the bargain, Georgia acquired two neighbors for whom its residents would in years to come thank God again and again. As part of the cession agreement, Georgia's leaders secured a promise that all remaining Indian land claims in Georgia would be erased as soon as was feasible. Andrew Jackson's victory over the Creeks in the War of 1812 helped to facilitate this process, and under pressure from land-hungry Georgians, the state's officials mounted and maintained a relentless campaign of harassment and legal and political coercion until 1838 when the last sizable contingent of Cherokees, Georgia's only remaining native people, was marched along the Trail of Tears to Oklahoma.

The removal of the Cherokee was one of the most shameful chapters in the state's history, one that revealed the rapacity and brutality that lay behind the emerging economic and social order in antebellum Georgia. John G. Burnett, a soldier who served as an interpreter, was a sad witness to what he called "the execution of the most brutal order in the History of American Warfare." Burnett remembered seeing helpless Cherokees arrested and dragged from their homes and driven at the bayonet point into the stockades. "And in the chill of a drizzling rain on an October morning, I saw them loaded like cattle or sheep into six hundred and forty-five wagons and started toward the West. . . . Many of these helpless people did not have blankets, and many of them had been driven from home barefooted. . . . The sufferings of the Cherokees were awful. The trail of the exiles was a trail of death."

In the half century following the Revolution, Georgia emerged as a social, economic, and political paradox as its leaders gave both rhetorical and legal sanction to the promotion and extension of liberty, democracy, and opportunity, even as they increasingly acknowledged the state's growing dependence on slavery. By 1789, all taxpayers (including women, in theory, but not in practice) were entitled to vote. The state had a popularly elected two-house legislature, and opinion leaned ever more heavily toward popular election of all public officials. The new Constitution of 1798, however, acknowledged federal precedent by calculating a county's representation in the legislature according to a formula whereby five slaves were deemed the equivalent of three white constituents. This move reflected not only the resurgence of the old plantation counties, but the spread of slavery into the upcountry as well.

The pivotal event in this trend was, of course, the appearance of a viable "cotton gin," a machine that separated cotton fiber from the seeds and, thereby, made it feasible to grow hardier varieties of the plant in hitherto unsuitable upland areas and in larger quantities than was possible when the fiber and seeds had to be separated by hand. The impact of the cotton gin may be measured by comparing Georgia's cotton production in 1791 (a thousand bales) with its output in 1801 (twenty thousand bales). Within a short time, Georgia led the world in cotton production. As a result, the decline in its slave population was reversed dramatically, and by 1820, slaves accounted for 44 percent of the state's population.

The cotton boom not only revitalized slavery, but also democratized slave ownership, at least for a time, as yeomen farmers managed to acquire both land and slaves. As Numan Bartley observed, "After almost a century of frequent strife and social conflict, white Georgians seemed to have arrived at a consensus that rested on the production of the white staple with black labor on land that had been taken from red people."

In the late nineteenth and early twentieth centuries, white Georgians would include in their reminiscences of the slavery era recollections of the happy, contented retainers who seemingly toiled without fatigue, sang rather than sweated, and generally bore their enslavement without frustration or resentment. This imagery was of great psychological value to whites. It assuaged their guilt over slavery and ultimately reaffirmed the wisdom of the Jim Crow system. It even proved valuable to the would-be architects of the New South who, in their search for popular acceptance, seemed at every turn to invoke the glories of the Old South. That this mythology was patently implausible seemed to make little difference. Certainly, ample evidence abounds in interviews with former slaves conducted by WPA workers during the New Deal. Born in Georgia in 1844, William Colbert recalled the story of his brother January, who slipped away to see a woman on another plantation. When he was caught, January's owner tied him to a pine tree and announced:

"Now, nigger, I'm goin' to teach you some sense."
Wid dat he started layin' on de lashes. January was a big fine lookin' nigger, de finest I ever seed. He wuz jus four years older dan me, an' when de massa begin a beatin' him, January never said a word. De massa got madder and madder kaze he couldn't make January holla.
"What's de matter wid you, nigger?" he say. "Don't it hurt?"
January, he never said nothin', and de massa keep a beatin' till little streams of blood started flowin' down January's chest, but he never holler. His lips was a quiverin' and his body wuz a shakin', but his mouff it neber open; and all de while I sat on my mammy's and pappy's steps a cryin'. De niggers wuz all gathered about and some uv 'em couldn't stand it; dey hadda go inside

dere cabins. Atter while, January, he couldn't stand it no longer hisself, and he say in a hoarse, loud whisper: "Massa, Massa, Have Mercy on Dis Poor Nigger!"

Not all slaveholders were as cruel as January's, but the potential for such brutality was always there in the slaveholding society of early nineteenth-century Georgia. Though many of Georgia's slaveholders were quick to take on the airs and trappings of aristocracy, most of them sprang from humble or, at best, modest origins. Margaret Mitchell captured quite well the origins and rapid rise of many a Georgia planter in her *Gone with the Wind* depiction of the short but swaggering, "loud mouthed and bull headed" Gerald O'Hara. "With the deep hunger of an Irishman who has been a tenant on the lands his people once had owned and hunted," Gerald longed with "a ruthless singleness of purpose" to have "his own house, his own plantation, his own horse and his own slaves. And here in this new country . . . he intended to have them."

Chafing in the employ of his brothers in Savannah, Gerald capitalized on two of his prime assets, his facility at poker and his "steady head for whiskey," to become the owner of a gone-to-seed plantation. With what he could borrow from his brothers and secure from mortgaging the land, he bought a few hands and moved into the old overseer's place while he dreamed of a great white house to replace the one that had burned down a few years earlier. Clearing fields and planting cotton and borrowing more money and buying more slaves and land, "little, hard-headed blustering Gerald" soon had his dream house and even won social acceptance when the lordly Mrs. Wilkes conceded that despite his "rough tongue . . . he is a gentleman." And what was the educational and cultural pedigree of the newly anointed gentleman? He could read, write, and cipher, but "there his book knowledge stopped. The only Latin he knew was the responses of the Mass and the only history, the manifold wrongs of Ireland. . . . After all, what need had he of these things in a new country where the most ignorant of bogtrotters had made great fortunes? in this country which asked only that a man be strong and unafraid of work?"

New Hampshire native Emily Pillsbury was one of many critical and condescending northern visitors who seized on the educational deficiencies of the so-called planter aristocracy in antebellum Georgia. "To those educated in New England, the ignorance that is seen in many portions of the northern part of Georgia is truly astonishing; many cannot read a word, or write their own name. I have had merchants say, that in transacting business with many men of great wealth, they have found them obliged to use a mark for their signature."

Like so many northern observers, Pillsbury often confused poor whites with the South's sizable body of independent yeoman farmers.

She gave little credit to Georgia's nonslaveholding whites for their independence and self-sufficiency, noting with disapproval that "besides coffee they seldom use any thing that is not the product of their own industry."

In addition to their victimization at the hands of the planters and their inherited inclinations to poverty, Pillsbury traced the plight of Georgia's lower-class whites to the absence of a system of common schools. It was here that she drew the sharpest and perhaps most ironic distinction between Georgia with its "deplorable state of ignorance" and her native New England: "At that age when the youth of the North are confined at hard lessons for six hours a day from one season to another, these [Georgia] children are wasting the spring of their lives, in the fields and woods, climbing trees, robbing birds' nests, or breaking up the haunts of squirrels, and engaged in every such kind of mischief, enough of which is always to be found for idle hands to do."

"Mischief" was hardly confined to children in antebellum Georgia. In "The Fight," humorist Augustus Baldwin Longstreet described a violent encounter between Billy Stallings and Bob Durham, who were believed by their Georgia peers to be "the very best men in the country" which, as Longstreet explained, "means they could flog any other two men in the county." Each man had his own following, and though there was much agitated speculation as to which of these two "best" men was actually the better, the fisticuffs-loving locals were much frustrated because the two actually got along quite well, despite the best efforts of one Ransy Sniffle, who, in Longstreet's words, "never seemed fairly alive, except when he was witnessing, fomenting, or talking about a fight." Whereas Billy and Bob were physical specimens of the first rank, Ransy's appearance reflected a childhood in which he had "fed copiously upon red clay and blackberries," the result being a "complexion that a corpse would have disdained to own." In height, Ransy stood "just five feet nothing, while his average weight in blackberry season [was] ninety five."

Ransy finally succeeded in bringing Billy and Bob to blows by reporting to Bob on Billy's disrespectful conduct toward Bob's wife. The ensuing combat, "a fair fight," led to incredible carnage. At its end, Billy "presented a hideous spectacle. About a third of his nose at the lower extremity was bitten off, and his face was so swelled and bruised, that it was difficult to discover in it anything of the human visage." Meanwhile, the "victor," Bob, was missing his entire left ear as well as a large chunk of cheek and the middle finger of his left hand, which he had opted to abandon between the clenched teeth of the determined Billy.

Longstreet's account was more caricature than pure fiction. In *The Mind of the South*, W. J. Cash neatly summarized the aims and aspirations of many a frontier-bred Georgian when he wrote, "To stand on his head in a bar, to toss down a pint of raw whiskey at a gulp, to fiddle and dance all night, to bite off the nose or gouge out the eye of a favorite enemy, to fight hard and love harder than the next man, to be known eventually far and wide as a hell of a fellow—such would be his focus." Not surprisingly, such behavior made a less-than-favorable impression on visitors to antebellum Georgia. A staid New Englander complained of being "greatly annoyed in the middle of the night by the swearing and vociferation of a number of young men who had been drinking. I do not think I have heard so much swearing, indicating habits of the grossest profaneness at any public house where I have stopped within the last 20 years. There is great reason to fear that Georgia is preeminent in this vice."

Lest such uncouth behavior be attributed solely to the crude country folk, Cash observed that "what is true of the poor white was true in a fashion of the planter and yeoman farmer as well." Anyone who doubts Cash's sweeping generalization need only take note of the rambunctiousness of the sons of Georgia's planters as manifested in the disciplinary records of the University of Georgia. Drunkenness, gambling, and reckless discharging of firearms were constant occurrences, and fighting and armed conflict were alarmingly common. In 1831 an argument reportedly developed between two students, one of whom announced to the other that "If you will go down into the woods, I'll whip you like hell." When the other replied, "This is as good a place as any other," the former accommodated him by stabbing him. (Both students were expelled, then subsequently reinstated.)

Clearly, the propensity for violence had little to do with social standing or intellectual ability. Eventually dismissed from the university, the quick-witted Robert Toombs was a notorious rule breaker and mayhem maker. Pursuing a long-standing feud with two fellow students, Toombs attacked them at various times, wielding a knife, a hatchet, and a pistol. A fiery orator who went on to serve as a United States senator and a Confederate general, Toombs became one of Georgia's earliest and most ardent advocates of secession.

Although it pains descendants of Confederate soldiers, myself included, to admit it (and, hence, many still refuse to), the central issue that ultimately drove a deeply divided Georgia from the Union and propelled it into the bloody and economically ruinous conflict, known locally as the War between the States, was the future of slavery. Orators like Toombs may have invoked the principles of states' rights and an overheated sense of individual, state, and regional honor, but by 1860 slaveholding had long since become the key to fulfilling the white Georgian's version of the American Dream.

For many, this fantasy was well worth fighting for. With an average per capita value of $900 in 1860, slaves represented a source of wealth far more important than the cotton they cultivated or the land on which that cotton grew. The average slaveholder in Georgia was five times wealthier than the average northerner, and a white Georgian who owned but two slaves and nothing else was as well off financially as the average northerner. Georgia's largest slaveholders were some of the richest people not only in the nation but in the world. At the time of his death in 1859, Joseph Bond owned eight plantations (six in Dougherty County and two in Lee County) and five hundred slaves, and his estimated net worth exceeded a million dollars. In 1858 his plantations had yielded a cotton crop worth $100,000.

Slaveholding meant both wealth and status, and hence, lawyers, doctors, merchants, and anyone else who could do so moved quickly to purchase slaves, acquire land, and thereby assume a primary identity as a "planter." Not surprisingly, the mania for slaveholding resulted in as much as half of Georgia's total wealth being invested in slaves. At approximately $416 million, the estimated aggregate value of slave property in 1860 was nearly forty times that of the state's total investment in manufacturing.

Scarlett O'Hara spoke with lighthearted disdain when she observed that "she'd never seen a factory or known anyone who had seen a factory," but the consequences of Georgians' zeal for slaveowning were serious indeed. In a real sense, slaves were highly mobile capital, and their owners were also highly mobile capitalists. The image of the O'Haras' unshakable ties to Tara may have made for excellent melodrama, but as history, it was generally unrepresentative. By the late antebellum period, continuous cotton cultivation had largely exhausted the soil in many of the old cotton counties to the north and west of Augusta, and many of the area's largest slaveholders had relocated to the still "wild" and frontierlike counties around Columbus. The profitability of slavery and the mobility of slaveholders combined to stunt the expansion and diversification of urban or small-town economies. Slaveholders had little incentive to transfer lucrative investments in slaves to fledgling businesses and industrial enterprises when they had no tangible stake in the local community per se. As a northern visitor observed, when a planter was asked about his investments, "he will point in reply, not to dwellings, libraries, churches, school-houses, mills, railroads, or anything of the kind; he will point to his Negroes—to almost nothing else."

We should keep in mind that however shortsighted it may seem in retrospect, the overwhelming concentration of Georgia capital in slaves was not at all irrational, in the purely economic sense. In 1860, the 6 percent of white families who owned at least twenty slaves held over half of the state's property value. Meanwhile, roughly half of the thirty thousand Georgia farmers who owned fewer than a hundred acres were slaveholders with fewer than five slaves. Though not rich compared to their planter neighbors, these yeomen maintained a relatively secure and independent existence by concentrating first on subsistence crops and then growing smaller amounts of cotton for domestic use and the market as well. In good years, members of this sturdy yeomanry had managed to climb to higher rungs in the slave-holding hierarchy, although as slave prices rose dramatically during the 1850s, this feat was increasingly hard to accomplish.

GEORGIA GOES TO WAR, AND WAR COMES TO GEORGIA

The widening gap in wealth and opportunity between slaveholders and nonslaveholders only heightened tensions as the debate over secession grew more heated. Because Georgia was centrally located within the South, its decision was absolutely crucial to the success of the disunionist movement. Not only was Georgia the second-largest state east of the Mississippi (before West Virginia became a separate state, Virginia was the largest), but it had the most population, the most slaves, and the most slaveholders of any Deep South state. On the other hand, two-thirds of Georgia's white population were non-slaveholders. Consequently, the stakes were high and the atmosphere tense as the legislature met in the capital city of Milledgeville in mid-November 1860. If Georgia failed to secede, hopes for the creation of a separate, unified southern nation would be dimmed considerably or even extinguished altogether.

As the Milledgeville debates unfolded, the likelihood that Georgia would remain in the Union seemed real indeed, given the prominence of Unionist leaders such as Alexander Stephens (later vice president of the Confederate States of America) and a friend of the newly elected Abraham Lincoln. The secessionists had some able spokesmen as well, including Henry L. Benning, who took to the podium near the end of the debate. A lawyer and judge, Benning was acting in part as a stand-in for his old college friend and longtime rival Howell Cobb. Benning considered himself intellectually superior to Cobb, and while he lan-guished in relative obscurity, he had grown increasingly frustrated as the more politically astute Cobb rose to prominence in state and na-tional affairs.

Although he became the namesake of Georgia's Fort Benning, as a general (nicknamed Old Rock), Benning fell well short of winning the recognition he desperately sought. Still, he had his one shining hour as he stood before the legislature on November 18, 1860, and made his impassioned case for secession. He raised certain legal and consti-tutional issues, but Benning's real focus was the future of slavery, and his "first proposition" was "that the election of Mr. Lincoln to the Presidency of the United States means the abolition of slavery as soon as the party which elected him shall acquire the power to do the deed." Benning foresaw abolition as "one of the direst evils of which the mind can conceive." He predicted that soon after any abolition decree "a war between the whites and the blacks will spontaneously break out everywhere . . . in every town, in every village, in every neighborhood, in every road . . . a war of man with man—a war of extermination." In Benning's mind, the only way to escape the "horrors of abolition" was to leave the Union: "Men of Georgia! It is our business to save ourselves. . . . And if nothing else will save us but going out of the Union, we must go out of the Union, however much we may deplore it."

The legislature ultimately approved a bill authorizing a convention to be elected by a statewide vote on January 2, 1861. This vote yielded a bare 51 percent majority vote for delegates favoring secession, and seventeen days later, the convention produced a similarly narrow vote, 166–130, in favor of secession.

Considering the slim margin by which the ordinance of secession was ratified, Georgia's "fire-eaters" exhibited remarkable bravado. A widely circulated, certainly apocryphal, story about fiery disunionist Robert Toombs illustrates the differences in the attitudes of white Georgians as they entered and emerged from the Civil War. With war imminent, General Toombs (Toombs was one of the Confederacy's many disastrous "political" military appointments) supposedly strode down the street in his hometown of Washington. He encountered a coquettish southern belle who twirled her parasol, blinked her eyes, and demanded to know, "General Toombs, do you really think we can whip them Yankees?" The supremely confident Toombs reassured her immediately: "Why, my dear, don't you worry yo' pretty little head. We can whip them Yankees with cornstalks."

Four years later, Toombs, looking considerably less confident, had the misfortune to encounter the same female, looking not so young and feeling not so coquettish. When she spied Toombs, she accosted him straightway, reminding him, "General Toombs, you said we could whip them Yankees with cornstalks!" "Yes, my dear, I did," the quick-witted Toombs gloomily conceded, "but the sons-a-bitches wouldn't *fight* with cornstalks!"

The war had not long progressed before most Georgians realized it was no laughing matter. Early thoughts of a quick victory dissolved into waves of tragedy and despair as young men by the thousands lost their lives on distant, then not-so-distant, battlefields, while deprivation and a growing anxiety about survival became a way of life on the homefront. In October 1862, Mrs. A. E. Moore of Fort Valley wrote Georgia's governor Joseph E. Brown, complaining that salt was $125 per sack and flour $40 per barrel. "How in the world are poor people to live?" Mrs. Moore asked. A widow with three small children who was also supporting her mother, Mrs. Moore demanded, "Must poor widows and helpless orphans be brought to suffering even for bread?"

Since Georgia's men in gray were hearing much the same thing from their loved ones, desertion soon became a major problem. Indeed, it is surprising that desertion rates were not higher. Confederate troops suffered horribly from even more severe shortages of their own, and they compounded matters as they began to strip the countryside of food, livestock, and other necessities. From Whitfield County in September 1863, John W. Cain complained that the Confederate cavalry was taking horses, killing sheep and hogs, stealing chickens, and even digging potatoes out of the ground. "All manner of depredation is committed," Cain reported to Governor Brown. When Georgia's home guard was pressed into service in defense of the state, members complained of having to leave families and crops and expressed fears of a Negro uprising. On Christmas Eve 1864, one Chattooga County citizen-soldier informed Governor Brown that his colleagues were "in no condition for fighting, for they are distressed so much on account of their families and property that they seem to care for nothing else."

If any Georgians yet had cause to doubt it, Gen. William Tecumseh Sherman's 1864 conquest of Atlanta and subsequent march to the sea clearly taught them that war was indeed hell. Shocked that he had begun "to regard death and mangling of a couple of thousand men as a small affair," Sherman himself reported to his wife that "we have devoured the land. All the people retire before us and desolation is behind. To realize what war is, one should follow our tracks." On the road to Atlanta, a member of Sherman's party saw a young mother skinning a cow while her little daughter, obviously starving, tore at the raw carcass with her hands.

As Sherman's troops approached Atlanta, a Mariettan, Minerva McClatchey, bemoaned their uncivilized behavior: "They took everything, tore the green grapes from the vines, tramped over the garden, and destroyed everything. If this is the way they do in the daytime, what may we expect tonight?" Those in Sherman's path saw not just the destruction of property but of the social and moral fabric as well. Nancy Jett complained that several of her friends had turned to "whoring," sometimes going into the Union camps to "fetch their beaus home at night."

As the battle for Atlanta raged, B. W. Froebel described "shells . . . screaming across the sky like blazing comets" and shells raining down "like sulfurous hail." Even Sherman's adjutant, Henry Hitchcock, was shocked by what he described as "the grandest and most awful scene" of Atlanta as it was consumed by "huge waves of fire, roaring, blazing, furious flames."

When Sherman's columns left much of Atlanta in ashes and rubble and moved south toward Macon before turning toward Savannah, Dolly Lunt Burge recorded in her diary a visit from Yankee "demons": "To my smoke-house, my dairy, pantry, kitchen and cellar, like famished wolves they come." Beset for a month by blue-clad invaders, Mary Jones of Liberty County saw in her desperate plight the wrath of Jehovah as well as that of Sherman: "Clouds and darkness are around us. The hand of the Almighty is laid in sore judgment upon us. . . . We are a desolate and smitten people."

After reaching Savannah, Rufus Mead, a Union soldier from Connecticut, was nothing short of exultant: "We had a glorious old tramp right through the heart of the state, rioted and feasted on the country, destroyed all the RR, in short found a rich and overflowing country filled with cattle, hogs, sheep and fowls, corn, sweet potatoes, and syrup, but left a barren waste for miles on either side of the road, burnt millions of dollars of property, wasted and destroyed all the eatables we couldn't carry off and brought the war to the doors of the Georgians so effectively, I guess they will long remember the Yankees."

Mead clearly had a gift for understatement. On December 16, 1864, as Sherman prepared to make the city of Savannah a Christmas present to Pres. Abraham Lincoln, a disconsolate F. M. Hawkins pleaded with Governor Brown to do what he could to "stop the effusion of innocent blood, stay the hand of the destroying angel, open the way to negotiation and expedite peace." Blaming the conflict on the politicians who "continue to grovel in human blood for place, power and wealth," Hawkins warned that if "this fratricidal conflict" was not brought to a speedy end, "ruin, fearful ruin, to our whole people will be the inevitable result."

Peace brought no immediate relief, however. In May 1865 Eliza Frances Andrews noted in her journal that "our own disbanded armies, ragged, starving, hopeless, reckless, are roaming about without order or leaders, making their way to their far off homes as best they can. Everything is in a state of disorganization and tumult. We have no currency, no law save the primitive code that might makes right. We are in a transition state from war to subjugation. The suspense and anxiety in which we live are terrible."

Eliza Frances Andrews no doubt reflected the gloomy outlook of the majority of white Georgians as military hostilities ceased. Black Georgians enjoyed an entirely different perspective, however. Theirs was a transition from subjugation toward what they hoped would be a far better life, one in which they would enjoy the benefits of personal freedom, political legitimacy, and economic opportunity. Even with the war in its early stages, slaveowners had noted a pattern of independence and insolence among their slaves that grew only more pro-

Kennesaw Mountain National Battlefield Park

nounced as the conflict progressed. When Union troops drew near, escapes became more common, especially after Sherman's troops began making their way to Atlanta. Escaping slaves made their way to Union lines, many of them to enlist in the fight for freedom. More than thirty-five hundred Georgia bondsmen served the Union cause. Incredible as it seems in hindsight, most white Georgians expressed great surprise and dismay that their slaves would desert them and flee to the Yankees.

The reaction of Mrs. H. J. Wayne, recorded as Sherman approached Savannah, was fairly typical: "We left Savannah in a very great hurry as the Yankees had cut every road and were in force only three miles from the city. . . . Every one of my negroes left me the morning I left which was a great shock as they did not even appear unwilling to come with me but they are so artful and have such an idea of freedom. [O]nly three or four families left before me and all of their servants ran away but mine have always appeared so faithful that I had too much confidence in them."

Upon claiming their freedom, black Georgians set out immediately to reunite their families and settle down in a stable home environment. A Georgia planter conceded that it "was commonly thought that the Negroes, when freed, would care very little for their children, and would let them die for want of attention, but experience has proved this surmise unfounded."

Meanwhile, for the cruel master who had so brutally whipped William Colbert's brother January, there was no family left to reunite: "De massa had three boys to go to war, but dere wuzn't one to come home. All the chillun he had wuz killed. Massa, he los' all his money and de house soon begin droppin' away to nothin'. Us niggers one by one lef' de ole place and de las' time I seed de home plantation I wuz a standin' on a hill. I looked back on it for de las' time through a patch of scrub pines and it look' so lonely. Dere warn't but one person in sight, de massa. He was a-settin' in a wicker chair in de yard lookin' out ober a small field of cotton and cawn. Dere wuz fo' crosses in de graveyard in de side lawn where he wuz a-settin'. De fo'th one wuz his wife."

RECONSTRUCTION: ADVANCE AND RETREAT

While black Georgians had set about even before the war's end to build a new world for themselves, white Georgians undertook, insofar as possible, to recreate the old world that had been destroyed by the war they fought to save it. Under the leadership of provisional governor James Johnson, white politicians forged a postwar constitution acknowledging the supremacy of the United States Constitution and the abolition of slavery. It also repealed the ordinance of secession and repudiated the state's war debt (in excess of $18 million). The new constitution extended the vote to only "free white male citizens," however, and the legislature soon passed a number of vagrancy and antienticement statutes designed to restore white control of black labor. The legislature authorized public schools for whites without mentioning blacks, who were also excluded from service on juries. Both houses of the legislature rejected the Fourteenth Amendment, which aimed to extend the rights of citizenship and due process to blacks. The legislators also elected former Confederate vice president Alexander H. Stephens and former Confederate senator Herschel V. Johnson to the United States Senate.

These actions, along with the more extreme measures taken by some of Georgia's southern neighbors, helped to strengthen the hand of the radical Republicans in Congress and, in turn, to bring on Military Reconstruction in the spring of 1867. After federal troops oversaw the registration of black voters, a new constitutional convention accorded blacks the rights of citizenship, the vote, and the ostensible guarantee of equal protection of the law. Republican strength in Georgia drew primarily on a tenuous coalition of former unionist whites, who were not in the main particularly enamored of the notion of black equality, and the newly enfranchised freedmen. Hence the convention, in a move that proved to be significant indeed, shied away from a straightforward guarantee of the right of blacks to hold office after Democratic delegates threatened to bolt the convention if such a provision were approved. The delegates elected as well to retain the highly exclusionary poll tax as a prerequisite for voting.

The ensuing elections, held in 1868, foretold the brief and turbulent future of Congressional Reconstruction in Georgia. White Republicans courted white votes with assurances that blacks could not hold office in Georgia even as fifty black Republicans sought legislative seats Meanwhile, Georgia Democrats pursued a strategy that was part politics and part guerrilla warfare. Former Confederate general John B. Gordon, a Yankee-inflicted scar adorning his cheek, was the Democratic nominee for governor and the acknowledged head of the Ku Klux Klan in the state. With the Klan functioning as the terrorist arm of the Democratic Party and Democratic leaders insisting that whites who voted Republican "should be driven from the white race, as Lucifer was driven from heaven into a social Hell," the Democrats put up a strong late effort, but Republican Rufus Bullock nonetheless captured the governorship, thanks in no small measure to the support of black voters.

The early days of Bullock's administration seemed full of promise. The legislature ratified the Fourteenth Amendment, and the governor dismissed the issue of white supremacy with the observation that "all civilized men are citizens." (It would be more than a hundred years before a Georgia governor again took such a moderate position on race.) Bullock promised "peace and plenty," but the Republicans in the legislature were divided and undisciplined. The Democrats succeeded in ousting all but four of the thirty-two blacks elected to the legislature on the grounds that the state's constitution did not provide for black officeholding. (The favored four were mulattos and were accorded the curious status of "honorary whites.")

The ensuing general election of 1868 featured all manner of violence and intimidation, and although blacks sometimes gave as good as they got, in the wake of the sweeping Democratic victory, Republican officeholders were at severe personal risk of injury or death whenever they appeared in public. With lawlessness and disorder continuing, Georgia was again placed under Military Reconstruction. Black legislators returned to claim their seats in December 1869, and twenty-two conservative Democrats were disqualified by a military board. The legislature again ratified the Fourteenth Amendment and the Fifteenth Amendment as well and also authorized the creation of a segregated but ostensibly "equal" system of common schools. Unfortunately, however, this renewed effort at Reconstruction was over shortly after it began. Democrats claimed control of the legislature in another violence- and intimidation-marred election in December 1870. With the election of Democrat James M. Smith as governor in 1871, Georgia was effectively "redeemed" from Radical Reconstruction. The poll tax subsequently kept blacks away from the polls in large numbers as did the continuing threat of violence.

The ups and downs of Reconstruction for black Georgians manifested themselves with particular clarity in coastal McIntosh County. A New Jersey native who had served as a leader in the so-called "Sea Island experiment" in black self-sufficiency ordained by General Sherman during the war, Tunis G. Campbell represented McIntosh County as a state senator and served as a justice of the peace. Campbell insisted on equal representation of blacks on juries and otherwise championed their rights to the point of making himself a source of "constant annoyance" to local whites. In 1873 the legislature ousted Campbell from his seat in that body and appointed a board of commissioners to take over local government in McIntosh County. At age sixty-three, Campbell was sentenced, on trumped-up charges of improper conduct, to a year at hard labor, a year which he served, ironically enough, as a leased laborer on a plantation.

Meanwhile, Governor Smith urged blacks to "get down to honest hard work," and the legislature set about to see that this admonition was followed, passing a host of statutes designed to restrict the mobility and economic rights and opportunities of the freedmen. Historian Eric Foner cited Georgia's example as "the most comprehensive effort to undo Reconstruction," and Smith offered a suitable benediction for this effort when he remarked that with Reconstruction out of the way, whites could "hold inviolate every law of the United States and still so legislate upon our labor system as to retain our old plantation system."

LIFE AND LABOR IN POSTBELLUM GEORGIA

It was one thing to retain the old system but quite another to make it profitable again. In 1860 the average white male Georgian was worth about $4,000, approximately twice as much as the average nonsouthern male. By 1870 this figure had plummeted to about $1,400 (in 1860 dollars), far less than half the earlier figure and now less than three-fourths of the nonsouthern average. Economic problems of all sorts abounded. The loss of the slave labor force dealt a severe blow to productivity. Cotton production remained below 1859–60 levels for two decades. The loss of approximately $416 million in slave capital and, just as important, collateral left Georgia agriculture in dire financial circumstances.

While the South was out of the Union, the national banking system had been reorganized without input from the representatives of southern agriculture. As a result, banks were, to say the least, scarce in the land of cotton. In 1894 fully 123 of Georgia's counties had no banks of any sort. With such banks as there were refusing to make loans when land was the only available collateral, all but the most affluent of Georgia's farmers turned to merchants and large planters for credit. They secured this credit by mortgaging not their land but their crops. (Lenders believed quite rightly that cotton could be converted to cash more readily than could land.) Hence, under the so-called "crop-lien" system, farmers found themselves mortgaging an unplanted crop at an unspecified rate of interest for a loan of undetermined value. The deficiencies of such a credit scheme were obvious enough. For a typical farmer, the question was not whether he built up a substantial debt at a huge rate of interest but simply to whom (planter or merchant) he ultimately owed that debt. The general decline in world cotton demand throughout the late nineteenth century suggested that cotton growers should diversify their operations, but the crop-lien system required the cultivation of a cash crop to secure the lien. As a result, Georgia farmers were induced to grow more and more of a crop for which they could expect to be compensated less and less. Since the size of the lien often exceeded the market value of the crop, recurrent, mounting, crippling, and ultimately destructive debt was a way of life among Georgia farmers. Through forced sales and foreclosures, anyone who supplied credit soon acquired land in sizable quantities. Meanwhile, on the other side of the ledger, many families who had owned their land for generations found themselves either turned off it or farming it as tenants and still subject to the onerous lien system.

Meanwhile, having refused to work for their former masters in closely supervised gangs (an arrangement they found all too reminiscent of slavery), large numbers of Georgia's landless freedpeople actually chose tenancy as their best available option. Initially, at least, many blacks managed to make some progress by contracting to work for a portion of the crop in exchange for varying kinds of support, ranging from housing, food, clothing, and other necessities to seed, fertilizer, and the use of mules and implements. Yet where blacks had initially entered into sharecropping arrangements as more or less autonomous "partners in the crop," as time passed whites succeeded in reshaping the sharecropping system to their own advantage. Through a combination of coercion, custom, and law, they gradually gained more and more control over the sharecroppers' lives, destroying their cherished autonomy and replacing it with close supervision of every phase of cotton production. At the same time, through a series of laws and questionable legal rulings, these planters also succeeded in gaining control over the marketing of the crop so that the cropper generally had little or no say about where and when the cotton would be sold or at what price. On "settlement" day, croppers lined up at the plantation commissaries or the farmers' porches to learn how they had fared (or more accurately how the landlord said they had fared). Even if the croppers received an honest settlement, the odds against them were bad enough, since the effective interest rate charged by merchants during the 1880s hovered around the 60 percent mark. All too often, however, the black cropper had to contend with being "counted out" by the white man. Not surprisingly, Georgia blacks often repeated a folk saying common throughout the South:

Weighing cotton, Milledgeville, 1934

> An ought's an ought
> And a figger's a figger.
> All for the white man
> And none for the nigger.

Not all blacks accepted this somber reality, but when they did not, they usually found that the price of demanding fair treatment was high indeed. Martin Luther King Sr. recounted an incident from his childhood that occurred in 1911 but might have taken place at almost any point during the last years of the nineteenth century or the first half of the twentieth. As a twelve-year-old boy, "Daddy" King had gone along when his own father went to "settle" with the landlord. King's father warned him repeatedly to keep his mouth shut, but when the landlord ignored the money due his father for his cotton seed, the young man was unable to contain himself, and he blurted out, "But, Poppa . . . ain't nothin' been said about the cotton seed."

The landlord turned "beet red," and threatened to kick young Martin's "little butt."

The elder King's response astonished not only the landlord, but the crowd of white onlookers as well: "Don't nobody touch my boy, Mr. Graves. Anything need to be done to him, I'll take care of it."

The furious landlord moved nearer to his tenant, demanding to know, "Who the hell you think you're talking to, Nigger?"

A loose circle formed around the two men, but the tension was broken when young King again spoke up, reminding his father, "Ain't nothin' been said yet 'bout the cotton seed!"

The tension erupted into laughter as the white men howled about the temerity of the young black boy, and they were soon urging the landlord to pay Martin's father what he owed him.

The elder King received his money, far more than his son believed even existed, but he also received a chilling assurance from the landlord: "Boy, . . . I'm gon' see from now on that you get everything you got comin'. I'm gon' see to it personally. . . ."

Young Martin failed to grasp the significance of these remarks, and he was hurt and confused by his father's anger at him as the two rode home. At sunrise the next morning, he began to understand. The landlord and some of his men had come and taken the mule and some of the implements upon which his father had been paying and ordered him to be off the place by sundown. The family packed their belongings into the wagon, but since the landlord had taken the mule, they had to push the wagon toward town. Years later, King recalled that experience: "The look on Papa's face told me we were in trouble. He was in pain. For getting only what was right, what was due him, he now had to get off the shares he'd been working. His family was without a home. What did being 'right' mean, I wondered, if you had to suffer so much for it?"

In some ways, Georgia's white tenants fared little better. Though they were less vulnerable to physical violence and coercion and could therefore demand "fairness" from their landlords with less risk, they found themselves in a system and a situation that seemed to them intrinsically unfair. In the antebellum era, Georgia's white yeomen had been able to enjoy a relatively independent existence on their own land, practicing what economists later called "safety-first" agriculture by growing their own foodstuffs (any surplus of which might be bartered for items not produced by the farmer) and then devoting whatever time or acreage that remained to cotton, the proceeds of which might be accumulated to purchase slaves and more land. The end of slavery and the rise of the crop-lien system brought about the demise of safety-first agriculture as merchants offered credit for cash crops only, forcing yeomen to grow more cotton and, increasingly, to become purchasers of some of the foodstuffs they had formerly produced. Efforts to fence in the open range further threatened their self-sufficiency by restricting their ability to raise livestock and allow it to graze in the open, uncultivated woodlands and fields. The long-term result, readily discernible even in the short term, was that small-scale white farmers found themselves drawn in ever-increasing numbers into a destructive downward spiral of dependency, debt, and tenancy with little hope of reversing their own fortunes or holding out the hope of a better life for their children. If Georgia's white farmers had ever approximated Thomas Jefferson's heroic ideal of the sturdy, independent, salt-of-the-earth agrarian, by the late nineteenth century any such resemblance was scant indeed.

Census statistics reflected a disturbing trend. In 1880 more than half of Georgia's farms were tilled by their owners; by 1920 two-thirds were worked by tenants. In the latter year, the average size of a Georgia farm was less than 20 percent of what it had been in 1860. Finally, whereas in the early postbellum years, most of the state's tenants were black, by 1900 nearly half of them were white.

Having little to lose but their misery, Georgia's farmers rose in political revolt at the end of the nineteenth century. The most dynamic figure in the agrarian uprising in Georgia was Thomas E. Watson. Born into a once-prosperous plantation family fallen on hard times, Watson worked first as a teacher, then became a successful attorney, and ultimately reclaimed his family's plantation holdings in McDuffie County, near Thomson. He won a legislative seat in 1882 and went to Congress in 1890. Watson became an eloquent spokesman for the Populist Party, which had grown primarily out of the Farmers' Alliance, an organization that spread from Texas into Georgia. The Alliance movement stressed cooperative action, and its Georgia branch was notably successful in establishing a state cooperative farm exchange in Atlanta that bought fertilizer and other supplies in high volume and made them available at lower prices than would otherwise have been possible. The Alliance also sought the assistance of Washington, however, championing the "subtreasury plan" whereby farmers would store their crops at strategically located warehouses and receive loans of up to 80 percent of their value. Hoping to relieve the credit shortage that had proven so disadvantageous to most farmers, the Alliance spokesmen also called on the federal government to expand the money supply by printing new currency to fund the loans issued through the subtreasury plan. Not surprisingly, most conservatives and even many moderates considered the subtreasury plan unspeakably radical.

To many white Georgians, the most radical aspect of the Farmers' Alliance–Populist threat was not economic but racial, for the agrarian insurgency reached out to blacks and called on them to join in a counterattack on the forces that seemed bent on impoverishing and humiliating all but the wealthiest and most powerful farmers of both races. Since the end of Reconstruction, conservative and relatively affluent white Democrats had managed to maintain their political dominance by bombarding lower-class whites with the threat of the "negro domination" that was certain to result if whites did not remain politically unified. Recasting the issue in terms of simple self-interest, Watson argued that "the accident of color can make no difference in the interest of farmers, croppers, and laborers."

His efforts won Watson all manner of vituperation as well as threats of physical abuse and even death. He and his followers also faced the reality of economic intimidation by planters, merchants, and bankers. Though they made no grassroots appeals to black voters, white conservatives worked with key black leaders to claim a large share of the black vote. Beyond that, there was the simple matter of fraud. Watson lost his bid for reelection to Congress in 1892, primarily because of his poor showing in Richmond County, where ten thousand voters somehow managed to cast more than twelve thousand ballots. Watson went on, however, to achieve national status as a Populist leader, gaining the party's nomination for vice president in 1896.

Even as Watson received this recognition, however, at the national level the Populists were signing their own death warrant. After the Democrats had reached out to them by writing into their platform the Populists' call for the free and unlimited coinage of silver and nominating free-silver advocate William Jennings Bryan for president, Populists took the bait and endorsed Bryan before naming Watson as their vice-presidential choice. Watson and the Populists were quickly lost in the shuffle as conservative Democrats left the party in droves, and Bryan went down to a predictably devastating defeat.

The demise of the Populists at the national level said much about the American political system, but their ill-fated assault on the status quo was perhaps even more revealing about the intertwined social and political realities of life in turn-of-the-century Georgia. Certainly, the Populist debacle underscored the strength of the Democratic Party in the state, but, more important, it demonstrated that the color line was still the bottom line in Georgia politics. A frustrated Watson complained, "You might beseech a Southern white tenant to listen to you upon questions of finance, taxation, and transportation; you might demonstrate with mathematical precision that herein lay his way out of poverty into comfort; you might have him 'almost persuaded' to the truth, but if the merchant who furnished his farm supplies (at tremendous usury) or the town politician (who never spoke to him excepting at election times) came along and cried 'Negro rule!' the entire fabric of reason and common sense which you had patiently constructed would fall, and the poor tenant would joyously hug the chains of an actual wretchedness rather than do any experimenting on a question of mere sentiment."

The defeat of the Populist insurgents not only shut the door on prospects for a color-blind political alliance but also paved the way for a comprehensive effort to provide long-term solutions for the state's racial and economic problems once and for all. Led by Henry Woodfin Grady, the "New South" crusade sought to promote prosperity through economic diversification, especially the rapid expansion of industry. Grady, who was born to comfortable circumstances in Athens, went on to become the editor of the *Atlanta Constitution* and Atlanta's biggest booster. He insisted that the only hope for Georgia and the South at large to throw off the long-term economic subjection that was even more insidious than the unpleasant interim of Reconstruction lay in industrial development: "The farmers may farm as wisely as they please, but as long as we manufacture nothing and rely on the shops and mills and factories of other sections for everything we use, our section must remain dependent and poor."

To illustrate his point, Grady recounted on numerous occasions an apocryphal account of a funeral he claimed to have attended in Pickens County, Georgia: "They buried him in the midst of a marble quarry: they cut through solid marble to make his grave; and yet a little tombstone they put above him was from Vermont. They buried him in the heart of a pine forest, and yet the pine coffin was imported from Cincinnati. They buried him within touch of an iron mine, and yet the nails in his coffin and the iron in the shovel that dug his grave were imported from Pittsburg [*sic*]. They buried him by the side of the best sheep-grazing country on earth, and yet the wool in the coffin bands and the coffin bands themselves were brought from the North. The South didn't furnish a thing on earth for that funeral but the corpse and the hole in the ground."

To remedy this deplorable situation, Grady urged his fellow Georgians to stop feeling sorry for themselves and get about the business of rebuilding their state. Grady realized, however, that, given the scarcity of capital in the state and region, this rebuilding process would go nowhere without the financial assistance of northern investors. Hence, he preached the gospel of sectional reconciliation: "Every dollar of Northern money reinvested in the South gives us a new friend in that section."

The clean-living, baby-faced Grady quickly established himself as the South's most eloquent spokesman for economic change. Being too young to have taken up arms against the Union in 1861 made Grady even more respectable in northern eyes, and when the New England Society of New York decided to seek a southerner to speak at its 1886 banquet at Delmonico's in New York City, he was a logical choice. Still in his mid-thirties at the time, Grady did not disappoint, despite having to share the platform with one William Tecumseh Sherman in whose honor the band played "Marching through Georgia," which was, to say the least, hardly one of Grady's favorite tunes.

As the audience, 360 primarily conservative businessmen seeking assurances that their investment capital would be safe in the South, leaned forward, Grady showcased his renowned talent for oratory—and hyperbole: "There was a South of slavery and secession—that South is dead. There is a South of union and freedom—that South, thank God, is living, breathing, growing every hour." To put his audience at ease, Grady paid tribute to Abraham Lincoln, and though he chided him for being slightly careless with fire, Grady all but thanked Sherman for burning Atlanta, from whose ashes had risen a "brave and beautiful city" where "somehow or other we have caught the sunshine in the bricks and mortar of our homes, and have builded therein not one ignoble prejudice or memory."

To say that Grady "laid it on thick" would be to do him a grave injustice. His portrait of the homecoming of a "typical" Confederate veteran "ragged, half-starved, heavy hearted, enfeebled by want and wounds" is but one example: "What does he find when he reaches the home he left so prosperous and beautiful? He finds his house in ruins, his farm devastated, his slaves free, his stock killed, his barns empty, his trade destroyed, his money worthless, his social system swept away, his people without law or legal status, his comrades slain and the burdens of others heavy on his shoulders. Crushed by defeat, his very traditions are gone."

To illustrate the courage and resourcefulness of such ex-Confederates, Grady turned to the example of his "business partner," who found himself not only without home or money but, if Grady is to be believed, without pants as well. After his wife cut up an old woolen dress to make him some britches, Grady's partner went out and made himself rich, parlaying a $5 gold piece given him by his father into a net wealth of $250,000.

With his audience by now alternately cheering and weeping, Grady made his move on their pocketbooks, urging well-heeled investors to "come on down" [quotes mine]: "We have learned that one Northern immigrant is worth fifty foreigners and have smoothed the path to southward, wiped out the place where Mason and Dixon's line used to be. We have fallen in love with work! We know that we have achieved in peace a fuller independence for the South than that which our fathers sought to win by their swords."

JIM CROW'S GEORGIA

The picture of harmony, unity, stability, and progress painted by Grady was more than slightly at odds with the facts. Although Grady insisted that "the relations of the Southern people with the Negro are close and cordial," Georgia led the nation in lynchings between 1899 and 1918, and over the half century between 1880 and 1930, at least 439 blacks were lynched in Georgia. Of this number, 372 of the lynchings occurred in the Cotton Belt and South Georgia, the areas where the black population was heaviest. These regions were also home to the state's largest plantations, whose owners were acutely sensitive to the need to retain control of their black labor supply and often nervous well past the point of paranoia about their safety as they surveyed the masses of blacks swirling around the town square on Saturday afternoons. For whites in these areas, a lynching represented an explosive release of hatred and fear. In the long run, it mattered little to the mob whether the victim was guilty as accused. A hanging or a burning, with all the mutilations and horrors that might accompany it, served notice to local blacks that the consequences of violating the delicate etiquette of white supremacy were severe indeed.

Rather than spontaneous explosions of mob violence, lynchings were more like rituals aimed at reaffirming white supremacy and reminding blacks that any wrong move might bring swift and horrible retribution. In 1899 a crowd of two thousand celebrated a Sabbath afternoon by witnessing the torture, burning, and mutilation of a black victim in Newnan. Accommodating railroad officials had provided special excursion trains for Atlantans, who made the trip down into a full-blown and almost festive outing.

Coupled with what surely seemed at times like nothing less than a reign of lawlessness and terror against blacks came a move to legalize and institutionalize a rigid system of racial separation in Georgia. (In Georgia, as elsewhere, these statutes were soon known as "Jim Crow" laws, drawing their identity from a popular blackface minstrel character.) When segregation finally came under fire in the mid-1950s, its assailants identified it with the intense racism associated with the plantation and the southern countryside in general. In reality, however, segregation was an urban phenomenon, one rendered necessary in the eyes of whites by the destruction of slavery and the increased movement of the black population into the city.

In the years surrounding the turn of the century, Georgia municipalities produced a plethora of ordinances mandating separate seating, facilities, and accommodations in a host of settings from street cars to prison camps to taverns. In settings such as libraries or swimming pools, where segregation was unfeasible, blacks were simply excluded. The color line ran everywhere. Stories about separate Bibles for swearing in witnesses of both races are not exaggerations.

In many cases, these laws merely codified well-established practices, but even so, the emergence of segregation by law rather than custom made the general inclination to discriminate considerably stronger and more respectable. In some cities, blacks protested the new ordinances and tried to initiate boycotts of Jim Crow street cars, but the racial climate in turn-of-the-century Georgia was so hostile that such an aggressive posture was nothing short of suicidal. Georgia blacks had little choice but to accede, for the time being, at least, to the new order by retreating from any sort of social contact with whites and establishing and strengthening their own economic, social, civic, and religious institutions. This network of churches, clubs, lodges, and businesses provided a strong sense of community that sustained black Georgians through three-quarters of a century of life under Jim Crow, and it remains a vital part of their cultural identity even today.

As Georgia whites took steps to institutionalize their control over social interaction with blacks, they moved simultaneously to neutralize them politically. The Constitution of 1877 required the payment of a poll tax in order to cast a ballot in Georgia. In 1900 the Georgia Democratic Party established a statewide primary system as a means of nominating its candidates for office. The primary was supposed to be more democratic than the old system of selecting candidates at conventions, but the new statewide primary was open only to Georgians with white skin. Since the Democrats were firmly established as the dominant political party in the state, winning the Democratic primary was tantamount to election and, therefore, exclusion from the white primary meant exclusion from the only election in Georgia that mattered.

Although the poll tax and white primary seemed to provide formidable barriers to black political participation, Georgia's Democratic leadership was still not satisfied. Consequently, disfranchisement became the central issue in a 1906 gubernatorial campaign that unleashed the horrible potential of white racial passions. With the Atlanta papers bombarding readers with stories of atrocities committed by blacks, lynchings and other abuses were rampant, and a few days after the election a bloody four-day race riot swept across Atlanta.

In 1908 Democratic leaders pushed through a constitutional amendment requiring potential registrants to pass a literacy test. Ostensibly to provide loopholes for whites who could not meet the literacy requirement, the amendment offered exemptions to veterans or descendants of veterans, to those who owned property of a certain value, or to those who were of "good character." These exemptions were available, however, only to those who had paid their poll taxes. To be sure, registrars judged literacy on a sliding scale according to color, and a black physician or teacher who showed the temerity to attempt to register was likely to be found illiterate by a registrar who might well have only a few years of formal schooling himself, while a truly illiterate white might "pass" the test with ease. For many whites, however, the very act of taking the test amounted to exposing their illiteracy even if their skin color largely guaranteed that they would be allowed to vote. By the same token, although whites seemed to have a variety of routes by which to circumvent the literacy requirement, to choose any of them was to admit to illiteracy, and such an act was singularly unappealing to the masses of poor but proud white Georgians. Hence, despite their ostensible purpose of disfranchising only black Georgians, by the second decade of the twentieth century, the cumulative effect of the poll tax, white primary, and literacy test was that almost no blacks and few lower-class whites were casting ballots in Georgia.

Although the advocates of disfranchisement identified it in terms of the general goal of strengthening white supremacy, its specific result was to determine as well, for decades to come, which whites would in fact reign supreme. More specifically, disfranchisement was a movement by, of, and for the Democratic Party. The removal of the bottom one-third of the potential electorate provided powerful insurance against a renewal of the Populist or Republican challenge. In the wake of disfranchisement, Georgia became and remained for more than half a century a solidly Democratic state, its political system functioning overwhelmingly to the benefit of a limited segment of the population and effectively insulated from any challenge by those whose interests it excluded.

The tripartite system of political neutralization, legalized discrimination, and extralegal coercion and terrorism amounted to white Georgia's "final solution" to the "race question." As early as 1885, Henry Grady had been telling all who would listen that "nowhere on earth is there kindlier feeling, closer sympathy, or less friction between two classes of society than between the whites and the blacks of the South today."

Ten years later, with racial tensions running high and the outlook for black progress as dim as it had been since the Reconstruction era, black educator and spokesman Booker T. Washington was invited to speak at the opening session of the Cotton States Exposition in Atlanta. Intended to showcase the South's progress, the exposition had a target audience consisting primarily of the investors and entrepreneurs that Grady and his disciples had been wooing so ardently. Ironically, exposition organizers drew criticism from local whites, both for their decision to have a special building for exhibits featuring black accomplishments and for their decision to allow Washington to speak, while many Atlanta blacks boycotted the extravaganza in protest of the strict policies of segregation that governed the affair.

Introduced as "a great Southern educator" and a "representative of Negro enterprise and Negro civilization," Washington began his speech under the glare of a broiling late afternoon sun. Putting his white audience at ease, Washington assured them that "the wisest among my race understand that the agitation of questions of social equality is the extremest folly." In the most famous passage from the speech, he reasoned that "in all things that are purely social, we can be as separate as the fingers, yet one as the hand in all things essential to mutual progress." Washington asked only for fairness and cooperation from whites, assuring them that by providing reasonable economic and educational opportunities for blacks, whites "can be sure in the future, as in the past, that you and your families will be surrounded by the most patient, faithful, law-abiding, and unresentful people that the world has seen."

One reporter insisted that no event since Henry Grady's speech at Delmonico's in 1886 had demonstrated "so profoundly the spirit of the New South." The comparison between Washington and Grady was apt enough. Not only were the language and tone used by each man almost eerily similar, but both presented what historian Paul Gaston called "the strange mixture of wishful thinking and calculated opportunism that gave to the myth of the New South its singular force." Like Grady, Washington sought the assistance of northern financiers— "Christlike philanthropists," as he liked to call them, and also like Grady, he felt the need to assure southern whites that his efforts posed no threat to the "southern way of life."

GEORGIA: WHERE TWO WORLDS COLLIDE

It was fitting that Washington gave his famous speech in Georgia, for in no other southern state did the symbols of progress and primitivism appear in such startling juxtaposition. As the outspoken black leader W. E. B. Du Bois put it, "Georgia connotes to most men national supremacy in cotton and lynching, southern supremacy in finance and industry and the Ku Klux Klan." Attending a picnic in 1896, a Georgia youth paid a nickel to hear his very first phonograph recording. At first, an excited Mell Barrett thought he was hearing a convention or some other meeting. Then young Barrett heard a voice say, "All right, men, bring them out. Let's hear what they have to say," and he listened with growing horror as two men confessed to a rape and began to beg for mercy. Barrett then heard, "the sounds of shuffling feet, swearing men, rattle of chains, falling wood, brush, and fagots, then a voice—shrill, strident, angry, called out, 'Who will apply the torch?' 'I will,' came a chorus of high-pitched, angry voices." Barrett heard the "crackle of flames" and then the victims asking God to forgive those who were putting them to death. Finally, only the sounds of the flames remained.

Barrett described his reaction: "My eyes and mouth were dry. I tried to wet my lips, but my tongue, too, was parched. Perspiration dripped from my hands. I stood immobile, unable to move."

When the man next in line asked Barrett, "What's the matter, Son—sick?" the man in charge of the concession—"sensing what my trouble was"—hastily surmised, "Too much cake, too much lemonade. You know how boys are at a picnic."

No prominent figure better personified the contradictions that abounded in turn-of-the-century Georgia than Rebecca Lattimer Felton, the state's foremost feminist and leading reform advocate. Born into a well-to-do plantation family and married to a wealthy planter-politician, Felton attached herself to a host of causes. She condemned the convict-lease system because it exposed female convicts to sexual abuse by guards and fellow prisoners. On the matter of prohibition, Felton was as dry as they came, pointing out that "if it is morally wrong to kill one's neighbor by the bullet, it is morally wrong to kill him by the grogshop." Like many of her cohorts, Felton moved from crusading against the saloon to championing women's suffrage. In fact, she joined the two causes, pointing out that an all-male electorate had failed to support candidates who favored prohibition. Felton was not much for pulling punches. Some of her statements seemed to anticipate the most aggressive of today's feminist rhetoric: "The marriage business is a lottery. You can draw a prize, but you are more apt to draw a blank." She also told a no-doubt-shocked group of state senators that many married women in Georgia "are only permitted to live, wait on their masters, bear children, and . . . are really serfs, or common treadmill slaves in the homes where they exist until they die." When some Georgia women prominent in the United Daughters of the Confederacy spoke out in defense of "the manhood of the South," she retorted that "if they prefer to *hug their chains,* I have no sort of objection."

Despite Felton's strong stand, Georgia was the first state to reject the Nineteenth Amendment. Still, she spoke out for equal pay for women who performed the same jobs as men and compulsory education for rural white women. Felton wrote books, articles, and newspaper columns and spoke at numerous public gatherings. In 1922, at age eighty-seven, she became the first woman to serve in the United States Senate when she was appointed to fill the seat vacated by the death of Tom Watson.

As a feminist, Felton seemed well ahead of her time, and, in many ways, she was. In others, however, she was clearly a product of the established order in Georgia. This was most obvious in her advocacy of lynching. As with her condemnation of the convict-lease system, Felton's views on lynching derived from what she viewed as a threat to white women, in this case the supposed danger of rape by black men. When it came to conjuring up lurid visions of lustful black males assaulting virginal white maidens, Felton could easily equal any of the South's most virulently racist demagogues: "If it requires lynching to protect women's dearest possession from raving, drunken human beasts, then I say lynch a thousand negroes a week if necessary." Felton was so adamant on this point that it became almost suicidal to cross her. When a prominent Nashville clergyman challenged her views as unrepresentative, Felton denounced him as a "slick-haired, slick-tongued Pecksniffing blatherskite" and proceeded to taunt and malign him thereafter in her columns and other communications. In 1902 when Andrew Sledd, a young professor at Emory College, wrote an article in the *Atlantic Monthly* calling for an end to lynching and a calmer approach to discussing race relations, Felton led a campaign of

Prison labor, Gwinnett County, 1920

harassment and intimidation that encouraged the young professor to resign from Emory and leave the state.

Felton's rabid support of lynching was more disappointing because she seemed very "progressive" in many of her views on women's rights. In reality, however, Felton's pronouncements on lynching almost paled beside those of Tom Watson, the bitterly disillusioned former Populist, who once had not only condemned the practice of lynching but preached a gospel of racial unity. By the turn of the century, however, a vituperative Watson was explaining that "in the South, we have to lynch him [the Negro] occasionally, and flog him, now and then, to keep him from blaspheming the Almighty by his conduct, on account of his smell and his color." As far as Watson was concerned, "Lynch law is a good sign: it shows that a sense of justice yet lives among the people."

Watson's hatred did not stop with the blacks whose votes he had once courted but whose disfranchisement he now endorsed. In his newspaper and magazine writings, Watson called the attention of his betrayed and disillusioned Populist brethren to all sorts of Catholic and Jewish conspiracies. Dismissing the pope as a "fat old dago" who consorted with "voluptuous women," he treated his readers to accounts of "What Happens in Convents" and other such revelations.

Watson's bigotry brought out the worst in many of his fellow Georgians. On a summer night in 1915, the Ku Klux Klan was reborn atop Georgia's Stone Mountain. Watson did not attend, but his spirit was clearly there. Watson also played a key role in one of the most tragic episodes in Georgia's history, the lynching of Leo Frank. Frank, a Jew and a northern one at that, was the superintendent at an Atlanta pencil factory. One of his employees, fourteen-year-old Mary Phagan, was found murdered in the basement of the factory on April 27, 1913.

Frank admitted to having been at the factory and paying the girl her wages (on a holiday, when the factory was shut down), and he was immediately taken into custody. Though there was a black suspect—later implicated by evidence much stronger than any associated with Frank—public opinion, fanned yet again by the Atlanta press, seized on Frank as the killer, especially after the newspapers ran several examples of Frank's alleged sexual perversion. The police seemed equally committed to the idea of Frank's guilt, and the trial, which lasted thirty days, was conducted in an atmosphere of mob hysteria. Officials feared an acquittal might produce a riot, and court officials received messages such as "Hang the Jew or we will hang you." Not surprisingly, Frank was convicted and sentenced to die.

Every court that reviewed the case expressed doubt as to Frank's guilt, and the verdict was condemned not only in the North and in other parts of the world, but, surprisingly enough, even in southern states such as Tennessee and Texas. Many Georgians quickly grew resentful of this criticism and outside interference in their affairs. The *Atlanta Journal* had called for a new trial, only to back down quickly when its circulation plunged. At this point, Watson plunged into the fray, asserting that "Frank belonged to the Jewish aristocracy, and it was determined by the rich Jews that no aristocrat of their race should die for the death of a working class Gentile." As time passed and Frank's execution was postponed several times, Watson demanded to know, "How much longer is the innocent blood of little Mary Phagan to cry in vain to heaven for vengeance?"

When rumors mounted that outgoing governor John M. Slaton would commute Frank's sentence, Watson headlined his weekly *Jeffersonian* with "RISE! PEOPLE OF GEORGIA." When Slaton did indeed commute the sentence on the day before his term ended, a mob wounded and disabled sixteen of the troopers who had to be called in to protect him, and the ex-governor had no choice but to flee the state. "Our Grand Old Empire State Has Been Raped!" insisted an outraged Watson, who continued to flog the case, warning that "the next Jew who does what Frank did, is going to get exactly the same thing that we give to Negro rapists."

Finally, on August 16, 1915, a mob of twenty-five men entered the state penitentiary in Milledgeville, took Frank out, and drove 175 miles to Marietta, where they hanged him from a tree. Clearly well planned, the lynching came off without a hitch. "For audacity and efficiency," wrote historian C. Vann Woodward, "it was unparalleled in southern history." Like countless lynchings of blacks, the grisly affair became both ritual and festival. An estimated fifteen thousand men, women, and children filed past Frank's casket in an Atlanta morgue after officials had been compelled by numerous threats to display it. On the day of the lynching, soon-to-be hillbilly recording star Fiddlin' John

Carson stood on the courthouse steps in Marietta all day, playing again and again the "Ballad of Little Mary Phagan":

> Little Mary Phagan
> She went to town one day;
> She went to the pencil factory
> To get her little pay.
>
> Leo Frank met her
> With a brutely heart we know.
> He smiled and said, "Little Mary,
> Now you go home no more. . . ."
>
> Come all of you good people,
> Wherever you may be,
> Supposing little Mary
> Belonged to you or me?

The disturbing image of Georgia embodied in the Leo Frank affair was reinforced by the account of Robert E. Burns, whose 1932 book *I Am a Fugitive from a Georgia Chain Gang* (and the subsequent film version) only added to the widespread perception of Georgia's benightedness. Given the conditions that prevailed in the state at the time when H. L. Mencken set out in 1931 to identify the "worst American state," many Georgians understandably grew apprehensive. According to Mencken's criteria, of the forty-eight states Georgia ranked forty-fifth in wealth, forty-sixth in education, and forty-third in health. In the "culture" category, Mencken deemed only Arkansas, Alabama, and Mississippi more deficient than Georgia. Meanwhile, in the "public order" category, the tendency of white Georgians to lynch black Georgians put the state in the forty-sixth rank, indicating that only Mississippi and Wyoming were more violent and disorderly. Not surprisingly, Mississippi won Mencken's designation as the "worst" state, but Georgia's boosters could take little comfort in their state's overall ranking of forty-fifth.

At this sad point in its history, Georgia might well have been the focal point of W. J. Cash's 1941 classic book, *The Mind of the South*, a brilliantly executed argument for the existence of a unified and uniquely southern set of values and beliefs that had emerged in the antebellum era, matured and hardened in the crucible of the Civil War and Reconstruction, and persisted without fundamental alteration throughout the first four decades of the twentieth century.

Some readers objected to the title of Cash's book because *The Mind of the South* presented an intellectually stagnant, emotionally dysfunctional white South as essentially mindless. As used by Cash, however, "mind" actually referred to an aggregate regional temperament, an indelible historically and culturally imprinted code of conduct that produced the distinctive and often bizarre behavior that gave the South its peculiar identity. Certainly, Cash's portrait was anything but flattering. His South was one of schizophrenia and excess marked by startling juxtapositions of hedonism and piety and hospitality and violence. More troubling still was Cash's focus on the "savage ideal," a peculiarly southern strain of anti-intellectualism and hostility to criticism or innovation forged during Reconstruction and still the dominant feature of the southern mind more than fifty years later.

Anyone who doubted that Cash's "savage ideal" applied to the "mind" of Georgia's white leadership need only consider the sentiments of the state legislator who spoke out in opposition to a bill allowing local governments to fund public libraries. Acknowledging the need for only three books, Rep. Hal Kimberly admonished his constituents to "Read the Bible. It teaches you how to act. Read the hymn-book. It contains the finest poetry ever written. Read the Almanac. It shows you how to figure out what the weather will be. There isn't another book that is necessary for anyone to read, and therefore, I am opposed to all libraries."

THE TALMADGE ERA

Although there were clear deficiencies in the state's social and political systems and its cultural institutions, its most serious deficiencies were economic. Plummeting cotton prices and the general malaise of the Great Depression combined to make Georgia a state whose agriculture showcased the evils of the old plantation system at its pernicious, exploitive worst. Studying Greene and Macon counties, Arthur F. Raper found "depleted soil, shoddy livestock, inadequate farm equipment, crude agricultural practices, crippled institutions, a defeated and impoverished people." Having grown up as one of these people in Bacon County, Georgia, Harry Crews explained their existence in more graphic terms: "Whether on shares or on standing rent, they were still tenant farmers, and survival was a day-to-day crisis as real as the rickets in the bones of their children or the worms that would sometimes rise out of their children's stomachs and nest in their throats so that they had to be pulled out by hand to keep the children from choking."

No writer provided more devastating depictions of southern poor-white life than Georgia's Erskine Caldwell. The son of a socially committed Presbyterian minister, Caldwell grew to share the concerns of his father, who once observed that sharecroppers were "as bad off as a toad in a post hole. It's a disgrace that human beings have to live like that."

Years later, Caldwell described his own observations of the rural poor in depression-era Georgia: "I could not become accustomed to the sight of children's stomachs bloated from hunger and seeing the ill and aged too weak to walk to the fields to search for something to eat. In the evenings I wrote about what I had seen during the day, but nothing I put down on paper succeeded in conveying the full meaning of poverty and hopelessness and degradation as I had observed it." Perhaps not, but Caldwell's *Tobacco Road,* published in 1932, became a symbol of the evils of the sharecropping system and the ills and suffering endured by a worn-out people trying to live on worn-out soil.

Not everyone in rural and small-town Georgia suffered under the status quo. The pivotal person in the prevailing order in Georgia was described to Ralph McGill as "a certain type, small town rich man." Profiling this figure, McGill explained, "Usually, he lived in the best house, on the best hill in the town, or at the shadiest corner, a block or so off the main street—and always his home sought to sustain the legend of the South as a place of many mansions."

Depending on where he lived, the "small town rich man" owned "the gin, the turpentine works, the cotton warehouses," and "the tobacco warehouses." Wherever he lived, he was invariably "a director in the bank" and the owner of the town's largest store from which he sold "fertilizer, plows, machinery, food, fencing, seeds, patent medicines, poultry and livestock." Beyond that, he or one of his relatives also owned the local automobile dealership.

Financially and politically, he was perfectly positioned: "He controlled credit. He knew the financial predicament of every man in his section of the county. He knew the United States senators, and the congressman from his district was always a 'friend.' He could write to Washington about a job for someone in his community. He could do the same with the governor. . . . He made a contribution at campaign time, always to the right man, and if in doubt, to both candidates. He had a hand in the political patronage in his county. He 'advised,' or selected, the men who ran for the legislature."

The key to the long-standing political preeminence of the small-town rich man was Georgia's county-unit system. Mandated by the legislature in 1917 for use in state primary elections, the county-unit system had traditionally been employed at state Democratic nominating conventions, where delegates voted by counties, each county casting two votes for each representative it elected to the state legislature. Since each county sent at least one representative and no county sent more than three, this system was severely biased against urban counties, and as they grew, the discrimination against them increased proportionately. By way of illustration, in the 1946 gubernatorial primary the county-unit system gave 264 voters in sparsely populated Chattahoochee County the same clout as 28,184 voters in fast-growing Fulton County.

When it came to manipulating the county-unit system and in the process personifying the overwhelming rusticity of Georgia politics,

Eugene Talmadge at a campaign rally, 1942

no one ever came close to Eugene Talmadge. Born on the family plantation near Forsyth, Talmadge earned a law degree from the University of Georgia and eventually purchased a farm on Sugar Creek in Telfair County. Claiming to be "a real dirt farmer" and quickly becoming known as "the Wild Man from Sugar Creek," Talmadge upset a powerful incumbent to become commissioner of agriculture in 1926. As commissioner, he proved both flamboyant and reckless. Promising to raise hog prices in Georgia, Talmadge used state funds to purchase hogs for slightly more than the eight-cent-per-pound market price in Georgia with an eye toward shipping them to Chicago, where they could be sold for eleven cents per pound. At his behest, the state dispatched eighty-two carloads of them northward to be offered for sale in Chicago at nine cents per pound. Contrary to Talmadge's claims about the superiority of Georgia swine, however, the poorly fed hogs lost so much weight during the trip that the state suffered a net loss on this venture in excess of ten thousand dollars.

This incident stayed with Talmadge his entire political career, and, ironically, he managed to turn it into more of an asset than a liability. In 1931 the great hog caper resurfaced alongside charges that Talmadge had placed several relatives on his departmental payroll and the disclosure that he had traveled to the Kentucky Derby at state expense. By this time, however, Talmadge had managed so successfully to portray himself as the champion of the little man that his "Shore, I stole, but I stole for you!" explanation was more than sufficient for the majority of his constituents, and the following year when Gov. Richard B. Russell sought and won a seat in the United States Senate, Talmadge moved into the governor's mansion.

Talmadge would win the governorship four times, primarily because of his genius for manipulating the emotions of Georgia's rural white electorate and capitalizing on its rurally skewed county-unit system. (Talmadge reportedly bragged that he had never campaigned in a county with a streetcar in it and urged his "country" supporters to come visit him at the governor's mansion and "we'll piss over the rail on those city bastards.") On one level, Talmadge seems an almost comical character. Certainly his rallies appeared to present a caricature of the redneck "wool hat" mentality that prevailed among the white residents of the Georgia countryside in the 1930s and 1940s. "Old Gene" was likely to arrive driving a team of mules or even oxen. Wearing red suspenders, he would mount the platform and work the crowd masterfully. Shunning anything resembling a prepared text, he took his cues from supporters, often "plants" who shouted from the front ranks of the crowd or sometimes from nearby trees: "Tell 'em about them lyin' Atlanta newspapers, Gene." Or "What about them hogs you stole, Gene?" At the conclusion of Talmadge's performance, a hillbilly band would strike up, and with the corn liquor flowing and the green flies swarming, his supporters would feast on barbecue or fried fish under the broiling Georgia sun.

As a politician and a political leader, Gene Talmadge was always entertaining and often amusing. He was, however, far from harmless. His wooing of the wool hat boys by cutting the price of an automobile license plate in Georgia to three dollars created a tremendous stir, drawing tag purchasers from as far away as Brooklyn and inspiring Fiddlin' John Carson to compose "The Three-Dollar Tag Song" and sing, with the accompaniment of his daughter, "Moonshine Kate":

> I gotta Eugene Dog, I gotta Eugene Cat.
> I'm a Talmadge man from my shoes to my hat.
> Farmer in the corn field hollerin' whoa, gee, haw.
> Kain't put no thirty-dollar tag on a three-dollar car.

Talmadge's goal was to embellish his credentials with the dirt farmers, but the real beneficiaries of his action were the corporations with large fleets of vehicles, while the losers were the local governments in rural areas (which also suffered by Talmadge's efforts to reduce the ad valorem tax rate), because the decrease in tag revenues cut sharply into the state's school fund, forcing hikes in local taxes in order to keep the schools open. Elsewhere, though a self-proclaimed friend of the "working man," Talmadge accepted a twenty thousand dollar contribution from textile industry leaders during his 1934 reelection campaign, and on the day after his election, he declared martial law, using the National Guard to break the 1934 textile strike in Georgia and incarcerate the strikers in a hastily constructed camp near Atlanta. In this case, as in many others, Talmadge did not shrink from acting dictatorially or from using troops to back up his actions. When Talmadge's opposition to the New Deal led legislative opponents to block passage of a state appropriations bill in 1936, he declared martial law and summoned National Guardsmen to oust forcibly both the state treasurer and comptroller general. At his order, a welder's torch was brought in to open treasury vaults and remove money.

As the dominant force in Georgia politics for nearly twenty years, Talmadge sometimes seemed invincible. Yet he did operate within limitations, and the setbacks he suffered demonstrated that, contrary to appearances perhaps, Talmadge-era Georgia was undergoing some important changes. For all his popularity within the state, Talmadge got little encouragement when he sought to become a national political figure. A 1936 "grassroots convention" to choose an anti-Roosevelt candidate for the Democratic presidential nomination was supposed to be a political springboard for keynote speaker Talmadge, but despite his first-rate, intensely demagogic performance, support for his candidacy failed to materialize, even in Georgia counties he was considered to have "in his pocket." Talmadge was soundly beaten in his effort to oust Richard B. Russell from the Senate in 1936, and in 1938 when he made a similar run against Georgia's senior senator, Walter F. George, voters largely ignored his campaign, focusing on the battle between George and President Roosevelt's anointed candidate, U.S. district attorney Lawrence Camp. Talmadge's condemnation of the New Deal as a combination of "wet-nursin' frenzied finance and plain damn foolishness" hurt him with voters who viewed both FDR and his program as "a godsend."

Talmadge's indiscretions also cost him politically during his third term as governor. Shortly after his election in 1940, he launched a campaign to purge the state's institutions of higher learning of all "foreign professors trying to destroy the sacred traditions of the South." Talmadge sought to oust the president of the state teachers college at Statesboro and the dean of the College of Education at the University of Georgia. At one point, Talmadge entertained thoughts of ridding the university of all pernicious "furrin" (i.e., non-Georgia) personnel, but when he discovered that this group numbered more than seven hundred, he gave up on the idea. Meanwhile, however, at his behest, various committees searched the state's textbook lists and university libraries for "subversive" publications. In response to these high jinks, the Southern Association of Colleges and Secondary Schools dropped the state's ten white colleges from its accredited list.

In the 1942 gubernatorial election, the first for a four-year term, the *Atlanta Journal* declared Talmadge's reelection candidacy "an insult to Georgia's intelligence" and helped to rally the state's theretofore dormant "better element" against him in his race against Attorney General Ellis G. Arnall. Despite his indulgence in such unfamiliar rhetoric as "academic freedom," Arnall managed to outdistance a disgusted Talmadge, who remarked that for all of his opponent's talk about education, "It ain't never taught a man to plant cotton."

GEORGIA TURNS A CORNER

Indications that times were changing in Georgia grew more pronounced throughout the World War II years. In 1944 the U.S. Supreme Court invalidated the white primary, thereby clearing the way for blacks to vote in the 1946 elections. Meanwhile, the CIO launched its "Operation Dixie" organizing campaign, challenging Georgia and the South's reputation as a bastion of cheap, docile labor. Within this superheated context, Eugene Talmadge made his final bid for the governor's office. Running against "better element" candidate and successful businessman James V. Carmichael, Talmadge and his forces made no secret of their intention to ground their campaign in the defense of white supremacy and the other virtues of the "southern way of life" and to concentrate their efforts on enough rural counties to make the county-unit system work its malapportioned magic one more time. As for the newly enfranchised black voters, Talmadge openly encouraged his supporters to intimidate them, advising that "if the good white people will explain it to the negroes around over the state just right, I don't think they will want to vote." Although he gave lip service to white supremacy and defended the county-unit system, Carmichael was clearly the choice of the state's more affluent urban voters. Predictably, the "lying Atlanta newspapers" cut loose at Talmadge with both barrels, labeling him a "blatant demagogue," a "panderer to the passions of the ignorant and to the fears of the timid, . . . a blatherskite, a cheap fraud and a menace to the security and the welfare of us all."

When it was all over, Carmichael had garnered a plurality of the popular vote, but true to fashion yet again, Talmadge had made the county-unit system work for him, and on the basis of the unit vote, he won the election. The outcome of the 1946 gubernatorial primary reflected the stalemate that prevailed in a state with one foot in the future and one in the past.

More progressive Georgians had long been concerned about the embarrassment that Gene Talmadge often caused, but little that Talmadge had done in life could compare with the chaos that ensued in the wake of his death in December 1946. Because Talmadge died before taking office, the task of selecting a governor fell by constitutional mandate to the legislature, which was charged with counting the ballots and naming the official winner. If no candidate received a majority, the legislature was to choose between the two receiving the most votes. Anticipating Gene's impending demise, a number of his supporters had organized a general election write-in campaign for his son, Herman, already known throughout the state (whether with affection or disdain) as "Hummon." Hummon's supporters argued that he would be the logical choice, but outgoing governor Ellis G. Arnall insisted that the constitution required him to remain in office "until his successor be chosen and qualified." In Arnall's view, that successor was and should be only the duly elected incoming lieutenant governor, Melvin E. Thompson.

Meanwhile, much to the consternation of the Talmadge camp, the initial vote count showed that 669 hard-core Talmadge haters had written in Carmichael on their general-election ballots. Behind Carmichael came not the younger Talmadge but perennial Republican write-in candidate D. Talmadge Bowers with 637 votes. Herman had apparently received only 619 write-in votes, and because the legislature was to choose from only the top two candidates, the son of Gene Talmadge was apparently denied the opportunity to succeed his father. As "luck" would have it, however, officials in Talmadge's home county of Telfair made a startling last-second discovery. Some 56 write-ins for Herman had been misplaced among the returns for the lieutenant governor's race. Subsequent examination of these newly discovered ballots brought further and even more startling revelations. All of the "misplaced" votes for Talmadge had been cast by dead people, many of whom displayed a remarkably similar handwriting style. As one journalist reported, "They rose from the dead in Telfair County, marched in alphabetical order to the polls, cast their votes for Herman Talmadge, and went back to their last repose."

However extraordinary the circumstances may have seemed to external observers, Herman Talmadge now had 675 votes, and the legislature lost little time in declaring him governor. Arnall refused to vacate the office, and the Talmadge forces kept alive a family tradition by seizing both the governor's office and the mansion itself. Shortly thereafter Arnall passed on his claim to the governorship to Thompson, who set up shop in an office downtown, a sort of ruler-in-exile who had never left the state. Finally, on the order of the state supreme court, Thompson became governor in March 1947, but he served only briefly and ineffectively. Herman Talmadge won a special election in 1948 and sought to assume his father's mantle as the champion of the racial and political status quo in Georgia.

Although it made Georgia the butt of numerous jokes in the national media, the "three governors" controversy marked the beginning of a significantly different if not altogether new era in Georgia politics. Herman Talmadge would go on to be a staunch defender of the "southern way of life" and even claim authorship of a pamphlet entitled *You and Segregation* in which he insisted "GOD ADVOCATES SEGREGATION," but he also sponsored a 3 percent sales tax that increased dramatically the funding available for the public schools in Georgia and became a tireless champion of industrial development as well.

Efforts to bring industry to Georgia had actually begun to intensify during the years after World War I. Although the boll weevil had arrived in Georgia several years earlier, it became a major problem only in the early 1920s. As a reflection of the boll weevil's impact, cotton production fell from 2,122,000 bales in 1918 to 588,000 in 1923. In Greene County, a crop of 21,500 bales in 1919 dwindled to an astonishing 326 bales in 1922. The boll weevil plague shook Georgia's agricultural order to its very foundations. Nearly two of ten Georgians (almost a half million in all) left the state during the 1920s. The majority of those who fled were black. Meanwhile, by 1930 more than half the state's labor force had undertaken nonagricultural pursuits. With Georgia's farm economy seemingly headed toward collapse, voters had already approved a constitutional amendment allowing local tax exemptions for new factories.

At the same time, manufacturing employment and population growth undergirded an urban boom that seemed wholly incompatible with the economic deterioration of the countryside. A "Forward Atlanta" campaign spotlighted the ascendance of urban Georgia, where three of ten Georgians had taken up residence by 1930. The exodus from the farm continued throughout the 1930s. The New Deal's Agricultural Adjustment Administration (AAA) introduced a program of subsidized acreage reduction, triggering what one historian called "a vast enclosure movement" that swept thousands of Georgians from the land toward an uncertain future either in one of the state's larger towns or cities or, ultimately, in a city north of the Mason-Dixon line. In AAA's first seven years, Georgia lost 40 percent of its sharecroppers. AAA payments helped to finance the large-scale purchase of tractors that signaled the beginning of the end of the mule's reign as the flesh and blood symbol of southern agriculture.

For many years after they ceased to rely on mules to plant and plow cotton, Georgia farmers hung on to at least one mule to work their gardens until the garden tractor finally completed the process that its larger ancestor had begun. Bemoaning the mule's disappearance from the Georgia landscape, Harry Crews recalled that when he was a boy in South Georgia, "horses were playthings that few people could afford; mules put grits on the table and bought the baby's shoes. From a farmer's point of view, though, one of the best things about a mule is the care he takes about where he puts his feet. He will walk all day long beside cotton that is eight inches high and never step on a hill of

Sawmill scene, Swainsboro, 1935

it. A horse will step all over it. A horse just doesn't give a damn. If a mule steps on your foot, you can be sure he meant to do it."

The emerging revolution in Georgia agriculture contributed as well to the beginnings of a transformation in the economies of hundreds of small towns across the state. Few of these communities, if any, had an industrial base sufficient, especially in the midst of the depression, to absorb the swelling surplus of farm labor. In these areas the displaced farm workers promised to contribute little more than names to the relief rolls, and they certainly were incapable of consuming the goods and services that merchants, lawyers, bankers, and insurance agents had to offer. Facing a threat to their own survival, the state's small-town middle class followed in the footsteps of their Atlanta brethren in the hopes of rejuvenating their faltering local economies.

Despite New Deal recovery efforts and the expanded crusade for new industry, World War II was the pivotal event in Georgia's economic transformation. Defense expenditures supplied the capital necessary to fuel the more rapid industrialization required to free the state completely from the grips of plantation agriculture and modify a manufacturing sector dominated by cruder, labor- and resource-exploitive "plantation industries." The war brought massive federal spending to Georgia, which was second only to Texas in attracting military training facilities. Fort Benning was the largest infantry training post in the world; Warner Robins Air Force Base employed as many as fifteen thousand civilians at one point. Every major city sported some kind of military installation. Defense-related industry also made a major contribution to the state's economy. Bell Aircraft in Marietta employed twenty thousand workers, shipyards flourished in Savannah and Brunswick, and ordnance plants opened in Macon and Milledgeville. The impact of this capital transfusion quickly revealed itself in per capita income, which climbed from less than $350 in 1940 to over $1,000 by 1950. The mechanization and consolidation of agriculture also accelerated during and after the war. In 1940, six of ten Georgia farms were tenant operated, but by the mid-1950s, only one-third were farmed by nonowners. In the same period, the number of farm tractors rose from fewer than ten thousand to approximately eighty-five thousand, while the total number of farms declined precipitously and the average farm acreage rose just as dramatically.

At war's end, Georgia stood on the brink of an era of economic, political, and social modernization. Low-wage industries like textiles, apparel, and lumber and wood products continued to dominate, but the income growth of the war years began to attract the attention of market-oriented industries. Per capita income reached nearly 70 percent of the national average in 1950 with much of the state's growth centering in Atlanta, where income already surpassed the national figure. The Georgia capital became a center for companies seeking access to Georgia's and the Southeast's burgeoning consumer markets. The automobile industry found the city a prime location, and the list of its other new firms soon amounted to little less than a recitation of the Fortune 500.

If the preservation of white supremacy was the primary responsibility of Georgia's governor during the 1950s and early 1960s, the recruitment of new industry was by no means an inconsequential obligation. Hence Georgia's governors during the period were both super-segregationists and super-salesmen. As Gov. S. Ernest Vandiver explained, "If you send an industrial representative to these places, he talks to his counterpart in the business, but a governor—any governor—gets to the president and chairman of the board where the final decisions are made."

As the likelihood of civil rights conflict grew, the efforts of Georgia's governors to recruit new industry took on definite sectional overtones. In 1952 when the governor of Rhode Island complained of "raiding" by southern governors, Gov. Herman Talmadge escalated the rhetorical combat, vowing, "If he wants war, we'll give him war." Back home in Georgia, the newspapers reported on the governor's industry-seeking forays to the North much as if he were a latter-day J. E. B. Stuart conducting a daring raid behind enemy lines.

The desire of Georgia's political leaders to promote economic change while preserving the racial status quo was not so contradictory as it seemed. Like the rest of the southern states, Georgia found its primary appeal to industrial investors was its presumably inexhaustible supply of "100 percent Anglo Saxon" workers so desperate for work of any sort that they would be grateful for even the meagerest of wages. The phrase "100 percent Anglo Saxon" not only implied white—most plants coming to Georgia during this period hired blacks only for the most menial and distasteful jobs—but native-born workers, presumably more resistant than their northern immigrant counterparts to the entreaties of union organizers. Indeed, Georgia was (and, to a surprising extent, remains) a bastion of antiunionism. Not only did Gene Talmadge use the state militia to break strikes, but the state legislature passed a rigid right-to-work law. At the local level, towns such as Sandersville, Baxley, and others required unions to pay a two-thousand-dollar license fee plus five hundred dollars for each local resident they recruited. When challenging the constitutionality of such a statute in Cuthbert, CIO representative Lucy Randolph Mason reportedly asked the city court judge (who was also the mayor) whether he believed in the Bill of Rights. When he asked her, "What is the Bill of Rights?" Mason directed his attention to the United States Constitution and its guarantee of the freedom of peaceable assembly. "We don't need any of that in Cuthbert," the mayor/judge responded. "The only laws we know are local laws."

Across most of the state, it was always open season on union workers as law-enforcement officials either looked the other way or joined in when would-be organizers were harassed, beaten, or run out of town. Blatant antiunionism was an altogether respectable bias, even among the state's more respectable businessmen and development promoters. In 1965 the state chamber of commerce published a flier entitled "Take a Tip from the Beaver, Mr. Businessman," urging employers to band together to resist unionization efforts in their area. When industrialists looked at a potential site, the pamphlet warned, their first question was often "How many unions are nearby?"

Persistent resistance to unionization went hand-in-hand with the progressively intensifying and expanding effort to create new industrial jobs. For many years, Georgia communities had been courting industries through the use of all sorts of favors and financial incentives. A 1937 survey revealed that Douglasville had not only provided a free building for a garment factory, but paid the employees while they learned their jobs and gave the company a five-year exemption from local taxes as well. Meanwhile, Washington, Georgia, had won a shirt factory by collecting twenty thousand dollars through public subscription and promising to match this with funds amassed by wage deductions from the plant's workers, who had signed promissory notes in order to get jobs that would pay them, on average, about five dollars a week.

Although development experts frowned on such reckless and unregulated activities, by the 1960s the state of Georgia had a full arsenal of development incentives including tax-free bond financing for new industrial buildings and a host of other provisions deemed likely to lure more manufacturing jobs to a Georgia location. Throughout the state, communities large and small had organized various development groups aimed at facilitating their transformation from farm market and processing centers into full-fledged industrial behemoths. There were notable successes in this area; manufacturing employment rose by 27 percent between 1950 and 1960 alone. Yet for most of Georgia's towns and some of its cities, the primary selling point remained a large pool of cheap, unskilled labor, a reality reflected in the state's industrial base. As of the mid-1960s, more than 75 percent of the work forces in 76 of the state's 159 counties were still employed in the textile, apparel, and lumber and wood-products industries.

While Georgia at large remained in the grip of a low-wage economy, the Atlanta area surged ahead. As novelist Anne Rivers Siddons wrote, in the "headlong, heart-spinning, gold-bitten, high-bouncing decade" of the 1960s, "there was no place on earth like Atlanta." By 1970 the five-county metropolitan area accounted for 33 percent of the state's people, 38 percent of its jobs, and 42 percent of its personal income. This pattern of concentrated, uneven growth played a key role in bringing sweeping social and political changes to Georgia. Urban-rural tensions had begun to simmer well before Gene Talmadge had emerged as the dominant figure on Georgia's political scene. By the 1960s even the most casual observer could discern that the interests, aims, and ambitions of Atlanta's political and economic leaders were dramatically different in many ways from those that prevailed in the state at large.

GEORGIA AND THE "SECOND RECONSTRUCTION"

In the wake of the 1954 *Brown v. Board of Education* decision, the majority of white Georgians and their representatives in the legislature vowed to close the public schools rather than accept integration. Elected governor in 1954 to succeed Herman Talmadge (although he seemed more reminiscent of Gene), S. Marvin Griffin assailed the "meddling demagogues, race-baiters, and Communists" who were "determined to destroy every vestige of state's rights," and swore to defend "Georgia's two greatest traditions—segregation and the county-unit system." In 1958 Griffin's successor, Ernest Vandiver, seemed equally defiant when he promised that "no not one!" black would be educated with whites during his term as governor. The following year, when a federal court ordered desegregation of the Atlanta public schools, the likelihood of school closings loomed large. Rather than opt for this course immediately, however, the legislature created a special committee to study the matter and report back to them in 1961. Although the majority of white Georgians seemed ready to close the schools, many leaders of Atlanta's business community believed such action would be disastrous for their city's economic future. It was particularly significant, therefore, that the special legislative committee was chaired by influential Atlanta banker John A. Sibley. The committee held hearings in each of the state's ten congressional districts, listening to some eighteen hundred witnesses, all but two hundred of whom were white. Despite claims that 55 percent of those interviewed had favored school closings, Sibley and a majority of the committee recommended local option on the matter of choosing between closing the schools or operating them on an integrated basis.

Meanwhile, even as the Sibley Commission prepared its report, the state faced its first real confrontation on integration, not in Atlanta but in Athens, when a federal court ordered the immediate admission of black applicants Charlayne Hunter and Hamilton Holmes. There was talk of closing the university, but despite a nasty campus riot, the crisis gradually eased. The sacred principle of Jim Crow had been breached, and yet the university still functioned, and the sun still rose over one end of Sanford Stadium and set over the other.

Both the Sibley Report and the decision to keep the University of Georgia open reflected the long reach and deep pockets of the Atlanta business and financial community. Indeed, the integration of Atlanta's public schools in the fall proved anticlimactic and uneventful. Plans for just such an outcome had been painstakingly laid by longtime mayor William B. Hartsfield, who had already been telling all who would listen that his beloved dynamic Atlanta was simply "too busy to hate." The city was deluged with reporters as the schools opened, but there was, in fact, little to report, and the irrepressible Hartsfield arranged for these journalists to take a bus tour in order to see, among other things, the city's "fine Negro homes." Afterward, he hosted a cocktail party for the visiting press, including Charlayne Hunter, who had recently broken the color barrier at the University of Georgia.

The well-publicized events in Atlanta and Athens notwithstanding, as the 1960s began, whites and blacks in rural Georgia continued to interact with each other in much the same fashion as they had been for nearly a century. Georgia novelist and social critic Lillian Smith believed that most southern white children were taught "to love God, to love one's white skin, and to believe in the sanctity of both." Smith's 1944 novel, *Strange Fruit,* was a searing story of miscegenation and murder that concluded with the lynching of an innocent young black man. Reflecting on the lynching, an elderly white woman is obsessed with the smell of the young man's burning flesh, while a poor white who lost both his legs in a sawmill accident finds his sexual potency restored by this grisly reassertion of white supremacy. No segment of the book has greater force, however, than Smith's treatment of the relationship between Tracy Deen, a young white boy, and Henry McIntosh, the son of Tracy's family's housekeeper, who will eventually be lynched for Tracy's murder.

Black or white, every child who grew up in the Jim Crow South recalls vividly the first time he or she discovered that, despite their physical proximity, playmates of different colors lived by different rules. Smith captured the trauma of this discovery in an incident that occurs when Henry is eight and Tracy seven and they are playing on the sidewalk. When Henry refuses to yield to a young white girl on a tricycle, a collision results. Both Henry and Tracy laugh, but Mamie, Henry's mother, does not:

> Mamie whipped her boy. She whipped him, saying, "I got to learn it to you, you heah! I got to. You can't look at a white gal like dat, you can't tech one, you can't speak to one cep to say yes mam and thanky mam. Say it atter me. Say it!" And Henry, squalling and catching his breath in strangling gasps, said it after her, word for word, three times, as she urged him on, tapping his legs with the tip of the switch as he said it. Then black legs whitened by the lash of his lesson, snuffling and dazed, he ran into the cabin and like a shamed dog crawled under the bed.
>
> Mamie's big brown hands took the switch and slowly broke it to pieces. . . . She stood there staring across the roof of the big yellow house in front of her. Stared so long that the small white boy watching her thought she must not be able to find what she looked for. . . . "Mamie," Tracy had said the word with no idea behind it, "Mamie."
>
> She looked up, brown face wet with her crying, and twisted. "Go!" she said, "go to your own folks!" she said. And he turned and ran quickly, cut to the bone by the new strange words.

Like Tracy, I grew up in a segregated, race-dominated South, living in the midst of blacks but often wholly apart from them. The entirety of my twelve years of education in Hart County, Georgia, was spent in all-white public schools. I recall vividly the cold rainy mornings during my early school years when I boarded the bus for Nancy Hart Elementary School (a brand new building as of my third-grade year), while the black children who lived around me trooped up the road on foot to get their education at Colored Zion School, a two-room ramshackle building in what had once been a cotton field. The threat of integration brought consolidation and the construction of the new Hart County Training School for blacks, but my alma mater, Hart County High School, was not integrated until the fall of 1965, the year I went on to the University of Georgia.

As I reflect on all the racial inequities that I observed as a youth, I cannot escape a feeling of shame that I raised no objections and relatively few questions about the way things were. While neither of my parents was a racial egalitarian by any stretch of the imagination, both seemed, from my perspective, at least, to treat black people as decently as the prevailing codes of caste etiquette would allow. My father regularly lent money to blacks who came seeking it. Though he charged no interest, he expected them to pay him back eventually and to be available to help him or my mother when they called them. On such occasions, I observed that my parents often "paid" their black helpers with old clothes or shoes rather than cash. I noticed that the response to this form of payment was often less than enthusiastic, but when I asked my parents about it, they assured me that their black neighbors much preferred having a good warm (if old) coat to receiving a few dollars (which they would probably only "throw away" in any event). Somehow, even then, I doubted this priority, but I also knew that a black couple down the road had named one of their sons for my father and one of their daughters for my mother. I also observed that every summer, when the now-adult offspring of many local black families returned from their homes "up North," they always stopped by to see my folks, and there seemed to be genuine pleasure taken in these visits by all those involved. Even on these occasions there were inconsistencies and contradictions. While our black visitors always called my father "Mr. Joel" and my mother "Miss Modena," I had never heard my parents or any other whites use these titles when addressing or referring to blacks.

It was impossible to overlook the general impoverishment of our black neighbors, but I often heard whites attribute this to "sorriness" or irresponsibility. Beyond that, I was hardly wallowing in affluence myself, living in a small frame house with no underpinning or even indoor plumbing. (The latter came when I was twelve. I rejoiced at no longer having to bathe in a washtub on the back porch or brave the black widows and snakes in our old outhouse, but more than that, in my own juvenile way, I felt a vague satisfaction in having finally joined the middle class.)

Only when I was a few years older did I begin to understand the economic implications of race. My father had given a friend of his the hay off our pasture in order to get the pasture mowed. When the friend asked me if I would like to work a half day, helping him and his hired hand, a middle-aged black man named Boston Gaines, to get the hay up, I eagerly agreed, since I had planned a big trip to a nearby county fair that evening. We began around noon and worked until six P.M. or even after. Though a robust country lad, I was unaccustomed to such labor and was totally exhausted by "quittin' time" when my father's friend approached me and, nodding toward his black helper, asked, "Be all right if I pay you same as Boston?" "Yessir," I blurted out, thinking this only fair, after all. With that, he handed me the princely sum of $2.50, exactly half of what he paid his black employee for a twelve-hour day. Somehow, I managed to thank him, though I was totally stunned. I had gotten myself through the punishing afternoon only by thinking of all the money I would have to spend at the fair. I did go to the fair, where I quickly spent my hard-earned $2.50. (I forget on just

what, but I do remember thinking, "Well, there goes a half day's pay.")
Later, when I complained to my father about his friend's lack of generosity, he only shook his head and pointed out that I had agreed to accept the same pay as Boston. Clearly, this incident stuck with me, although it was some time before I actually grasped the lesson it should have taught me on the spot.

Change did not come easily or rapidly to the society in which I grew up, yet in 1946 (the year before I was born), a truly remarkable Georgian, Katharine Du Pre Lumpkin, saw in the contemporary scene "the old life continuing, yet a rising tide against it." The self-described "daughter of an eloquent father, reared in a home where the Confederacy is revered as a cause, holy and imperishable," Lumpkin graduated from Brenau College in Gainesville and went on to earn a Ph.D. in economics from the University of Wisconsin. Her family's move to the sand hills of South Carolina afforded her the chance to observe the poverty and struggle of poor whites. Later, her collegiate involvement with the interracial activities of the YWCA led her to realize that race "was nonexistent, only a fiction, a myth, which white minds had created for reasons of their own" and that "wage-earning whites and Negroes were, functionally speaking, not so unlike after all." As she surveyed the South of 1946, Lumpkin noted that the cumulative impact of depression, war, agricultural mechanization, and industrial development was weakening the region's resistance to racial change. As she looked back from the perspective of 1980, however, Lumpkin realized that black southerners had played the key role in the South's transformation: "The protest movement furnished incontrovertible evidence to any and all who had failed to comprehend, that black people were asserting that the time was now for an end to their burden of discrimination and segregation."

In Georgia, the sit-in movement began in Atlanta in 1960 and spread across the state, affecting almost all of the state's cities of any size. The most widely publicized white-black confrontation in the state during the civil rights era came in and around Albany in Southwest Georgia. Student Nonviolent Coordinating Committee (SNCC) volunteers arrived in the fall of 1961 to begin a voter registration drive, and Albany was soon the scene of the largest black protest effort since the Montgomery bus boycott. In retrospect, the "Albany Movement" represented a turning point in the civil rights crusade as large numbers of working-class blacks joined student organizers and activists in what would become the prototype for later protests in Birmingham and other cities. The Albany campaign led to mass arrests, and as local jails bulged, the overflow of the prisons spilled out to lockups in outlying counties. Inside the jails, demonstrators were often subjected to all kinds of abuse.

SNCC workers who fanned out from Albany faced an even more hostile reception in Terrell County, where beatings, bombings, and drive-by shootings were commonplace. Such terrorism, reminiscent of the Reconstruction era, no longer sufficed to maintain the status quo. A pivotal figure in the Albany Movement, Charles Sherrod endured numerous beatings and threats, but he reported back to SNCC headquarters in Atlanta that "the structure is being shaken to the very foundations. . . . It is no longer a matter-of-fact procedure for a Negro to respond in 'yes, sirs' and 'no, sirs.' The people are thinking. They are becoming. In a deep Southwest Georgia area, where it is generally conceded that the Negro has no rights that a white man is bound to respect, at last, they sing, 'We Shall Overcome.' There is hope!"

Across the state, the sit-in movement attracted large numbers of blacks and a few whites. In Augusta, a white power structure, fearful of the prospect of demonstrations during the Masters golf tournament, acquiesced to peaceful desegregation of lunch counters and theaters in the spring of 1962. In Augusta, as in Atlanta, the desire for economic growth played a key role in the initial desegregation of public facilities. When asked why he and his cohorts had capitulated so readily to integration demands, a white political leader explained, "We were afraid they'd bring in Martin Luther King."

Such comments were echoed again and again across Georgia and throughout the South. Though he went on to study at Crozer Theological Seminary and Boston University, Martin Luther King Jr. was more than anything else, perhaps, a product of his Georgia heritage. His father had made his way to Atlanta and worked his way through Morehouse to become pastor of Ebenezer Baptist Church. The young King grew up in relatively comfortable middle-class circumstances, secure in his parents' love and insulated to some extent from the injuries that the Jim Crow system could so easily inflict. King's father set a stern but courageous example, correcting whites who called him "boy," refusing to allow his children to use segregated public transportation or attend segregated theaters, and encouraging other blacks to register to vote.

His father's dignity as well as the strength of his family's ties to the black religious community (his maternal grandfather was a minister as well) and the strength of the King family itself left young Martin secure in his own racial identity. That security was not allowed to go entirely untested in Jim Crow Georgia, however. As a high-school student, King participated in an oratorical contest in Dublin. Returning that evening to Atlanta on the bus, King and his chaperon were ordered to surrender their seats to white passengers, and when they failed to move quickly enough, the driver began cursing, calling them "black sons of bitches." Forced to stand for the remainder of the ninety-mile

Martin Luther King Jr., Vine City rent demonstration, Atlanta, 1966

ride back to Atlanta, King later wrote, "That night will never leave my memory."

Ironically, it was segregation on public buses that would vault King, then a young minister in Montgomery, into the national spotlight. King understood that segregation warped southerners of both races, and he showed a remarkable genius for making his efforts to bring it to an end seem beneficial to whites as well. Drawing on the teachings of Mohandas Gandhi, King cited the moral responsibility of disobeying unjust laws. He praised student demonstrators, noting that "when these disinherited children of God sat down at lunch counters, they were in reality standing up for what is best in the American dream and for the sacred values in our Judeo-Christian heritage."

As headquarters for King's Southern Christian Leadership Conference, Atlanta served as King's base of operations, and even as he became a national and global figure, he remained a Georgian. He invoked the "red clay hills of Georgia" in his famous "I Have a Dream" speech during the march on Washington. King is probably best remembered for his eloquence on this occasion, but his most impressive composition was his "Letter from a Birmingham Jail," written with a stub pencil on the margins of a newspaper that contained a statement from a group of white ministers in Birmingham who had accused King of being an outside agitator, and an impatient one at that. King's reply was passionate and, to a great many previously uncommitted readers, highly persuasive as well:

> . . . Perhaps it is easy for those who have never felt the stinging darts of segregation to say, "Wait." But when you have seen vicious mobs lynch your mothers and fathers at will and drown your sisters and brothers at whim; when you have seen hate-filled policemen curse, kick, brutalize and even kill your black brothers and sisters with impunity; when you see the vast majority of your twenty million Negro brothers smothering in an airtight cage of poverty in the midst of an affluent society; when you suddenly find your tongue twisted and your speech stammering as you seek to explain to your six-year-old daughter why she can't go to the public amusement park . . . and see tears welling up in her little eyes . . . ; when you take a cross-country drive and find it necessary to sleep night after night in the uncomfortable corners of your automobile because no motel will accept you; . . . when your first name becomes "nigger," and your middle name becomes "boy" . . . and your last name becomes "John," and when your wife and mother are never given the respected title "Mrs."; . . . when you are forever fighting a degenerating sense of "nobodiness"; then you will understand why we find it difficult to wait.

Although he had his share of detractors, King is the most widely admired Georgian who ever lived. Several years after his assassination, another Georgian, novelist Alice Walker, praised King for making it possible for her and millions of other southern blacks to feel at home in the land of their birth: "He was the One, The Hero, The one fearless Person for whom we had waited. . . . He gave us back our heritage. He gave us back our homeland; the bones and dust of our ancestors, who may now sleep within our caring and our hearing. . . . He . . . restored our memories to those of us who were forced to run away, as realities we might each day enjoy and leave for our children. He gave us continuity of place, without which community is ephemeral. He gave us home."

The civil rights revolution allowed Georgia blacks to reclaim not only their homeland but their political rights as well. As of 1964 scarcely more than one-fourth of Georgia's voting-age blacks were registered to vote. Blacks represented 34 percent of the voting-age population, but in the entire state there were only three black elected officials, all of them elected during the preceding three years. The Voting Rights Act of 1965 brought sweeping changes to the state's political landscape. By 1990 the state boasted 495 black elected officials, and black registration had increased by 80 percent since 1964. These changes had not come without considerable resistance and defensive maneuvering by white politicians who engineered shifts to at-large elections, majority-vote requirements, and other ruses likely to dilute the black vote. Various litigation efforts and pressures from the U.S. Justice Department gradually brought relief in these areas. The federally coerced creation of black-majority voting districts contributed significantly to an increase in black officeholding, although critics charged, with some justification, that this tactic simply created predominantly white districts elsewhere, districts likely to elect representatives hostile to black progress. Statewide, black voters played a key role in ousting Herman Talmadge from the United States Senate in 1980, but black candidates consistently fared poorly with white voters. In 1981 former ambassador to the United Nations Andrew Young got less than 9 percent of the white vote in winning the mayoral election in Atlanta. In the 1990 gubernatorial runoff primary, Young received less than 26 percent of the white vote. Racially polarized voting remains a barrier to further black political advancement, especially since registration and turnout is usually about 10 percent higher among whites than blacks, but black Georgians nonetheless enjoy a degree of political influence unthinkable only three decades ago.

Social, political, and emotional empowerment often went hand in hand, but they came more rapidly for some black Georgians than for others. When Macon native Melissa Fay Greene arrived as a VISTA Legal Services worker in McIntosh County in 1975, she found that, despite its Reconstruction era history as a black enclave presided over by Tunis G. Campbell, the civil rights movement seemed to have bypassed the area entirely. She also found a coastal backwater where many of the county's four thousand blacks still spoke Gullah, a synthesis of English, Scottish, and African dialects. Ten years after the passage of the Voting Rights Act of 1965, though blacks accounted for half the county's population, they had not elected a single black public official. In *Praying for Sheetrock*, Greene described the changes that came to McIntosh County as the black community finally awakened to its political potential. The story was one of inspiration and disappointment, courage and corruption (especially in the pivotal case of black activist Thurnell Alston), but in her final assessment, Greene concluded, "Of course, it is not enough, but it is a beginning. The descendants of the Scottish settlers start to view the descendants of the African slaves not as aliens in their midst, and not as servants, but as neighbors, colleagues, partners, fellow Americans and increasingly, as leaders, as a rich human community without whom McIntosh County—financially, among the poorest counties in Georgia—would be halved, bereft, and truly poorer than any chart could document."

A NEW ERA

If the Voting Rights Act seemed to revolutionize Georgia politics, it was arguably no more significant than the Supreme Court's 1962 *Gray v. Sanders* decision, which invalidated the county-unit system. The outcome of the University of Georgia's integration crisis and the Sibley Commission report had already symbolized the ascendance of the state's, and especially Atlanta's, urban business elite, and the court's ruling ensured that this ascendance would be more than symbolic. The 1962 gubernatorial primary, the first election to be affected by the decision, proved to be a fitting contest for such a role, for it pitted a proponent of the new, urban, growth-oriented ideology against a bona fide representative of Georgia's Talmadge-haunted old order. Handsome, articulate Augusta lawyer Carl E. Sanders promised growth and harmony and explained, "I am a segregationist but not a damn fool." Sanders's opponent was none other than former governor Marvin Griffin, who again made the defense of segregation at all costs the cornerstone of his campaign. The apparent philosophy of Griffin's ethically lax first administration was aptly summarized by one journalist as "if-you-ain't-for-stealing-you-ain't-for-segregation," and as he surveyed the residue of Griffin's fiscal recklessness, his successor, Ernest Vandiver, complained, "The state of Georgia was buying rowboats that would not float. Some were wisely sent to parks without lakes." The flamboyant Griffin promised to "put Martin Luther King so far back in the jail that you have to pump air to him," but this election was to be decided by popular, not unit, votes, and Sanders's sweep of the metropolitan areas put him in the governor's office. Analysts of all sorts hailed Sanders's triumph as a victory for the urban moderates over the rural traditionalists, but for a supporter of the defeated Griffin, the key to understanding his candidate's demise lay not in demographic analysis but in the simple reality that "somebody ate Marvin's barbecue and then didn't vote for him."

In his inaugural address, Sanders proclaimed, "This is a new Georgia. . . . A Georgia on the threshold of new greatness." Sanders's proclamation may not have been wrong, but it was certainly premature. Sanders recognized the need to upgrade education at all levels in Georgia, and his efforts produced impressive and sweeping improvements in teacher salaries, facilities, and scholarship programs. As governor, Sanders also stressed economic growth, but the 1966 election suggested that the old era was not quite over in Georgia. In the Democratic primary, former Atlanta restaurateur Lester G. Maddox outdistanced former governor Ellis Arnall. Maddox had won the hearts of many of Georgia's nonmetropolitan whites by waving an ax handle in the faces of pickets at his segregated Pickrick restaurant in Atlanta, and for the most part, he was not perceived, for better or worse, as much of an Atlantan. Signs proclaiming "Maddox Country" adorned trees and telephone poles from Hahira to Hiawassee and the entirety of rural and small-town Georgia that lay in between. A high-school dropout, the feisty Maddox was known as "ol' Ax Handle" to many admiring whites who turned out to vote for him in huge numbers.

Maddox's candidacy was by no means the only novelty in the 1966 election. Democratic dominance had been a way of life in Georgia since the late nineteenth century. Outside Atlanta and a few old unionist strongholds in the mountains, Republicans were so rare that they constituted little more than a source of amusement or object of idle curiosity for the great mass of "yellow dog" Democrats who made up the overwhelming majority of the Georgia electorate. In reaction to the civil rights initiatives of the Kennedy and Johnson administrations, however, Georgia whites joined their counterparts elsewhere across the Deep South in deserting the party of their fathers in droves during the presidential election of 1964.

Hence it was hardly surprising that, for the first time since Reconstruction, Georgia Republicans put a serious contender on the 1966 gubernatorial ballot in the person of Congressman Howard "Bo" Callaway, scion of a wealthy textile dynasty near LaGrange. Callaway was clearly the uptown candidate, favored by business interests and suburban whites, but though more discreet than his opponent, he was hardly a crusading integrationist. Illustrative of the similarities and differences between Maddox and Callaway was a story widely circulated during the campaign. It seems that two old South Georgia white men were debating the relative merits of the two candidates. One asserted, "Well, I'm voting for Lester, cause he's ag'in the blacks." "But Bo's ag'in the blacks, too!" the other responded. "Yeah," countered the first, "but Bo thinks ever' body who don't make $20,000 a year is black."

When the votes were counted, the results were predictable. Callaway carried middle- and upper-income white areas, while Maddox swept the blue-collar and rural white votes. As a result of an organized write-in campaign for Arnall, neither candidate received the majority required for election, and twenty years after the infamous three-governors controversy, the legislature once again found itself choosing the governor. Since 230 of the 259 members of the general assembly were Democrats, the choice was never in doubt. Perhaps the most unlikely candidate ever to win the Georgia governorship, Maddox assessed his accomplishment: "It really wasn't too difficult to be elected. All that was necessary was to defeat the Democrats, the Republicans—on the state and national level—159 courthouses, more than 400 city halls, the railroads, the utility companies, major banks and major industry, and all the daily newspapers and TV stations in Georgia."

Most political observers predicted the worst. Rev. Martin Luther King Jr. saw Maddox's triumph as "indicative of a deep corroding cancer in the Georgia body politic. Georgia is a sick state produced by the disease of a sick nation. I must confess that Mr. Maddox's victory causes me to be ashamed to be a Georgian."

Maddox was none too anxious to claim common citizenship with King, either. He referred consistently to King's "communistic" activities, and at King's death, having called in state troopers to protect the capitol, he gave them orders, in the event of violence, to "shoot them down and stack them up." Such statements were all too typical. Thankfully, Maddox was not as bad a governor as most had expected. He appointed more blacks to state posts than had his predecessors, and he also proved generous in his support for education. Yet although he remained popular with less affluent white Georgians, Maddox failed to create anything resembling an effective working relationship with the general assembly. He also insisted on continuing to preach the gospel of segregationism and condemned his opponents and critics as communists and cowards. Maddox hardly left office in disgrace, or certainly in any more disgrace than he had entered it. He was, after all, resoundingly elected to the office of lieutenant governor in 1970 and managed to make considerable trouble for his successor.

As he laid plans to succeed Maddox, former state senator Jimmy Carter of Plains took note of the strength of the governor's support among rural whites. Accordingly, his gubernatorial campaign bore both racial and class overtones as he courted the supporters of Maddox and George Wallace and attacked his principal opponent, former governor Carl E. Sanders, as "Cufflinks Carl," an elitist country-club liberal, out of touch with the concerns of the so-called "common man."

Upon taking office, however, Carter changed his tune and perhaps ushered in the "new era" that his defeated opponent had hailed prematurely some eight years earlier. "I say to you quite frankly," Carter began, "that the time for racial discrimination is over. . . . No poor, rural, weak, or black person should ever have to bear the additional burden of being deprived of the opportunity of an education, a job, or simple justice." Both symbolically and substantively, Carter followed through on his inaugural address, making an impressive number of black appointments and hanging a portrait of Rev. Martin Luther King Jr. in the capitol. Carter also went on to sponsor an extensive agenda of governmental reorganization and judicial and penal reform.

A GEORGIAN IN THE WHITE HOUSE

As of the mid-1970s, Georgians could point with pride to many positive changes that had come to their state in recent years. Yet for all this improvement, a certain inferiority complex lingered. Georgia-born humorist Roy Blount Jr. explained: "Georgia is a place you get sent to or you come from or you march through or you drive through. Convicts settled it. It's got some fine red dirt, hills, vegetables and folks, but I don't believe anybody has ever dreamed of growing up and moving to Georgia." Although not altogether accurate historically, Blount's penetrating observation helped to explain why Georgians were stunned and delighted (initially at least) with the election of one of their own to the presidency in 1976. An engineer-turned-agribusinessman-turned politician, Jimmy Carter stepped into the void of confidence induced by the back-to-back traumas of Vietnam and Watergate to offer Americans a soothing combination of honesty, humility, and quiet confidence. A great many political pundits, northern-bred, by and large, had some difficulty accepting the premise that a drawling Southern Baptist Sunday school teacher could actually run the country, but drawing heavily on the support of black voters, Carter managed to hold off a late surge by Republican opponent Gerald R. Ford and become the first Georgian ever to hold the presidency.

In Georgia and across the South generally, Carter's victory triggered a massive outpouring of what might only be called "redneck euphoria." (According to Blount, the simple realization that "a Southern Baptist, simple-talking, peanut-warehousing, grit-eating 'Eyetalian'-saying Cracker" had somehow managed to win the Democratic presidential nomination led his brother-in-law, Gerald—just returned from teaching English in England—to exclaim, "We ain't trash no more!") Meanwhile, a host of national publications joined the Dixie love feast, seizing on Carter's election to celebrate "the South as New America." For a brief period "redneck chic" was definitely in vogue as reporters descended on Carter's Sumter County home of Plains, lavishing much of their attention on the wit and wisdom of his charming and strong-willed mother, Miss Lillian, and the antics of "first brother" Billy, a wise-cracking, beer-swilling, shoot-from-the-hip small-town character, who distinguished between rednecks and "good ole boys" by noting whether when riding around in their pickups drinking beer they threw their cans out the window or tossed them in the floor of the truck. With Rev. M. L. "Daddy" King Sr. opening the day with a prayer service at the Lincoln Memorial, Carter's inauguration was replete with sweetness and irony, all of it suggesting in one way or another Georgia's emergence as both symbol and substance of a united and ascendant South.

As is usually the case, however, what seemed too good to be true actually was. The fascination with Georgia accents faded quickly as did amusement with Billy's increasingly drunken and boorish antics. Washington insiders complained about a surfeit of Georgians in their midst, though no such laments had seemed to go up when previous administrations had been saturated with White House personnel from Massachusetts or California. The teetotaling and unpretentious Carters were soon under fire for lacking "class," and runaway inflation and soaring interest rates took their toll beyond the beltway as well. When, in true Southern Baptist fashion, Carter lectured the American people about the need to lower their expectations, he breached the fine line between preaching and meddling for a generation steeped in instant gratification and self-indulgence. His inability to deal effectively with the Iranian hostage crisis sealed his bitter fate as he lost the presidency to Ronald Reagan, whose saber rattling and posturing for the religious right made him sound (save for the drawl) more southern than Carter. Many Georgians still express dismay at Carter's performance as president, but since his return to private life, his role as an international negotiator for peace, his profound faith in democracy and human rights, and his commitment to human uplift have won him unequivocal respect across the nation and around the world.

CHANGING TIMES

Though many observers speculated that Jimmy Carter's Georgia roots had been no particular asset to him in dealing with the Washington political establishment, Carter's rise to national leadership symbolized a broad-based, if perhaps somewhat grudging, recognition that the South had indeed changed dramatically. Certainly, as the twentieth century drew to a close, signs of change were everywhere in Carter's native state. In a Georgia that was once nothing less than an impregnable Democratic fortress, save for Carter, no Democratic presidential candidate since 1964 has garnered more than one-third of the white vote. As of 1995 Georgia's eleven-member congressional delegation included eight Republican congressmen and one Republican senator. In the early years of the Republican Revolution, local aspirants often ran as Democrats while sporting bumper stickers and yard signs touting the GOP presidential ticket, but these days, increasing numbers of courthouse offices are occupied by full-fledged, honest-to-goodness Republicans who have brazenly campaigned as such.

Those who worried that the old days of flamboyance and rusticity were gone forever now that the state's politics had become respectably bipartisan could at least take heart from the 1994 race in Georgia's Sixth Congressional District. This contest pitted former congressman and actor Ben Jones, who once played Cooter on the television series *The Dukes of Hazzard,* against incumbent and House minority whip Newt Gingrich. Gingrich went on to become Speaker of the House after winning a free-swinging battle that featured such homespun one-liners as "Newt's got enough money to burn a wet dog" and inspired headlines like "'Cooter' Nips at Newt."

Although Georgia politics did not always reflect it, the state's commitment to education has also grown considerably in recent years. Whereas at the end of the 1920s, Georgia had ranked dead last among the southern states in its support for public education, by the 1990s, expenditures for schools, when measured as a percentage of per capita income, were near the national average. Achievement test scores also approached national norms, although wide disparities in educational achievement levels still separated rural and metropolitan school systems. In higher education, a generously endowed Emory University has emerged as one of the South's most prestigious private institutions, while Georgia Tech and the University of Georgia have achieved national distinction in a variety of fields. Atlanta's Spelman College is the first historically black school to be named the nation's premier liberal arts college by *U.S. News and World Report.*

On the economic front, in 1950 nearly a million Georgians lived on farms, but forty years later, the farm population was barely eighty thousand. The agricultural sector of Georgia's economy had not only shrunk but changed its shape as well. Once the state's dominant cash crop, cotton accounted for only 3.5 percent of farm income. Poultry and peanuts were far more significant, accounting for 28.7 and 11.3 percent, respectively, of farm income. Across the state, much of what had formerly been cropland had been given over to "tree farming." Growing pine trees put the land to sound economic use, although it created relatively few jobs and contributed significantly to rural depopulation.

As employment in agriculture fell, employment in manufacturing had grown at roughly twice the national average. As we have seen, much of the early growth in manufacturing employment came in what were characterized as low-wage industries, including textiles, apparel, food processing, and lumber and wood products. In 1950 low-wage industries accounted for 83 percent of the state's manufacturing jobs. By 1970 this figure was down to 67 percent, although twenty years later it still stood at 60 percent. Manufacturing employment grew at the rate of 4 percent during the 1980s, but many Georgia communities were hit hard by plant closings, especially in the textile and apparel industries, where, across the state, ninety-eight hundred jobs were lost between 1989 and 1992 alone.

Though Georgia's political leaders were often quick to criticize Washington for its intrusion into the state's affairs, there was no denying the beneficial impact of federal spending on the state. Georgia's success in attracting major military installations paid off handsomely. Military payrolls alone accounted for $1.1 billion in earnings in 1989, a figure well in excess of farm earnings and one to which might be added more than $1 billion in military-related civilian earnings. In some areas, military installations were absolutely crucial to local economies. In Macon–Warner Robins (Robins Air Force Base) and Columbus (Fort Benning), they accounted for 20 percent or more of total earnings.

Although economic and political leaders had long insisted that industrial development would be the state's salvation, the damage that it inflicted on the environment of a state whose pristine beauty had captivated scores of visitors seemed to some too high a price to pay, even for "progress." In their efforts to entice industry to Georgia, state and local officials had offered cheap labor and also free and essentially untrammeled access to the state's natural resources. Not surprisingly, this approach led to some serious examples of exploitation and abuse. When the Union Camp Corporation came to Savannah in 1935, local leaders not only promised nominal rents and protection from competition but pledged as well "to secure the necessary action and, if possible, legislation on the part of the governmental bodies concerned, to protect and save you [Union Bag] harmless from any claims, demands or suits for the pollution of air or water caused by the operation of the plant." Furthermore, Savannah's officials agreed that "in case litigation arises or suits are brought against you on account of odors and/or flowage from the proposed plant that the Industrial Committee of Savannah will pay all expenses of defending such suits up to a total amount of $5,000."

A reputation for hospitality to pulp and paper mills explained why several generations of Florida-bound northern tourists instinctively thought of Georgia whenever they smelled rotten eggs. Concentrated in the southern and coastal counties, the pulp and paper industry was releasing more than 35 million pounds of toxic pollutants into the air and water by 1990. Four paper mills along the Savannah dumped more wastewater into the river each day than Atlanta's 2 million people put into the Chattahoochee, a stream with major pollution problems of its own. EPA officials found oxygen levels so low that they concluded that only the "hardiest" fish could survive in the waters of the lower Savannah. Federal agencies and environmental activists occasionally managed to push Georgia's legislature to take corrective action, but to chamber of commerce officials, the stench of the paper mills was "the smell of jobs," and through threats of plant closings and skillful legal maneuverings, the companies managed to avoid the most stringent measures needed to clean up their acts entirely. Georgia's pattern of advance and retreat on environmental issues explained why the state ranked thirty-sixth overall in a national environmental survey released in 1991.

Any student of Georgia's recent history or even a reasonably observant tourist, for that matter, is likely at some point to utter the reminder, "Well, there's Atlanta, and then there's Georgia." By the end of the 1980s, the eighteen counties of the Atlanta metropolitan area accounted for 44 percent of the state's population, 48 percent of its employment, and 52 percent of its personal income. Only the Atlanta-area counties enjoyed a per capita income level above the national average in 1989. Beyond that, no other metropolitan area was even above the state average. In fact, only 15 of Georgia's 159 counties exceeded the state average, while 93 showed income figures less than 75 percent of the national norm, and in 11 of these, per capita incomes were less than even 60 percent of this figure.

In 1994 *Fortune* magazine selected Atlanta as the fourth best city for "global" business operations. "Even in Baghdad they know Atlanta," the writer noted. Such news as well as reports that the Atlanta area led the nation in job creation in 1993 reinforced the impression of thoroughgoing prosperity in and around the Georgia capital. Yet if, as some insisted, there were "two Georgias," then there were also "two Atlantas," one marked by suburban affluence and the other by inner-city poverty. In fact, the state's most startling contrasts in wealth and income could be found within fifteen miles of each other in Fulton County. North of the city in the Dunwoody Country Club area, family incomes typically exceeded $150,000, while downtown in the housing projects around Spelman and Morehouse colleges, 94 of every 100 residents lived below the poverty level. Overall, 27 percent of the residents of the city of Atlanta fell into this category, giving the South's ostensibly most prosperous city the distinction of being the nation's ninth poorest with a poverty rate slightly higher than that of Mississippi, the South's and the nation's poorest state. In fast-growing outlying counties like Cobb and Gwinnett, median family income soared above $48,000, and by 1990 the Atlanta area had become the nation's most popular destination for relocating blacks. Yet nearly half of downtown Atlanta's black neighborhoods actually grew poorer during the 1980s. By 1990 in metro Atlanta blacks were four times as likely as whites to be poor.

Though much of the state's most rapid growth was concentrated in the counties around Atlanta, economic development also brought major changes to the Georgia countryside, where for thousands of Georgians the symbol of instant upward mobility became not the sky-scraper but the satellite dish beside the double-wide mobile home. Modular living and multi-channel viewing seemed to carry revolu-tionary sociological implications, but Georgians quickly clasped these innovations to their cultural bosoms. Those who did not get enough fire and brimstone, pulpit-thumping preaching on Sunday could find it in abundance on any day and at any hour on their satellite receivers. At the same time, those inclined to more hedonistic amusements in-sisted with mock seriousness that they could tell by the angle of a friend's dish whether he was watching the Playboy channel. At the same time, the double-wide quickly entered local legend and musical lore as well. A popular ditty among country music fans celebrated the charms of the "Queen of my double-wide trailer."

Double-wide trailers were readily associated with young couples coping with the potentially destructive stresses of making ends meet. They were also notoriously susceptible to destruction by the fre-quent tornadoes that swept across Georgia. Hence a popular joke went something like this: "What do a tornado and a South Georgia di-vorcee have in common? . . . Sooner or later, they're both gonna get the double-wide."

Across rural and small-town Georgia, the process of change was sometimes rapid and sweeping and other times uneven and slow but always fascinating. As in the rest of the southern states, an industrial economy came late to Georgia, the consequence being that manu-facturing plants could take simultaneous advantage of rural electri-fication and farm mechanization by fanning out across the country-side to employ the cheap labor rendered even more expendable by the transformation of the farm economy. If casual observers were often struck by how "rural" a state Georgia was, closer observers were even more surprised by the number of industrial plants that dotted the rural landscape. Georgia led the nation in carpet production by the 1990s, and most of the carpet-manufacturing facilities were concen-trated in mountainous Northwest Georgia. As a result, Murray County, which was virtually saturated with carpet plants, enjoyed the distinc-tion of being the nation's most industrialized county in terms of the percentage of the labor force employed in manufacturing. Eleven other nonmetropolitan Georgia counties joined Murray on the list of the nation's top seventy-five counties in this category.

Given the concentration of manufacturing employment in apparel and textiles, it was hardly surprising that women made up a sizable percentage of Georgia's industrial workforce. In the early post–World War II years, these women often continued to be farm wives still re-sponsible for all the cooking and chores they had handled before they began to work an eight-hour shift in a cotton mill or garment plant.

Country stores were a focal point for rural folk before fast-food restaurants came to small towns. The man on the far right is James C. Cobb's father; third from the right is his grandfather.

The husbands of these women continued to farm, by choice in some cases, of necessity in others, since there often were no jobs for them in the local "sewing plants." Such men soon became known as "go-getters," because their principal daily responsibility was transporting their bread-winning (and still bread-making) wives to work. As 4:30 P.M. approached each afternoon, many a rural Georgia husband would rise from his seat on a Coca-Cola crate at the crossroads store, check his watch, and say, "Well, boys, I got to go get 'er."

There was considerable sacrifice in dignity involved in becoming a "go-getter," and as the impossibility of making any sort of decent living as a small farmer became inescapably apparent, most farm men were forced to accept whatever industrial employment they could find. Having reached this point in his mid-fifties, my father put our farm in the Soil Bank Program, which paid us more to simply let it lie fallow than anyone could remember making when we had farmed it. When he finally found a job in a local shock-absorber plant, I thought we were rich. For the first time ever, I had an allowance, and we were able to trade in our woefully embarrassing (to me, at least) 1948 Chevrolet for a very respectable 1956 Ford. In the material and financial sense, we were clearly much better off than we had ever been. Yet though my father was doing a good job as a provider, he did so at considerable sacrifice of status, and, I'm afraid, self-respect. He had cherished the independence of farming in a way that all who are born and bred to it seem to, and the idea of submitting to the whistle and the regimen of the factory filled his heart with dread. His morning goodbyes to us were protracted and almost pathetic, as if he was journeying to an alien and hostile place from which he might not return. He lived for the weekends, which he devoted in large measure to tending his garden, the only activity that seemed to give him any satisfaction. As I recall him now, I reel back past the slump-shouldered figure, carrying the unfamiliar lunch pail and shuffling reluctantly toward his job at "the plant," to recall the jaunty pose he always adopted as, Tampa Nugget clenched between his teeth, he steered his John Deere tractor and Allis Chalmers combine across the fields he knew and loved so well.

Georgia novelist Erskine Caldwell captured the passion for the land that gripped Georgians of both races in the person of *Tobacco Road* protagonist Jeeter Lester, who, for all his depravity, sought incessantly to borrow a mule and secure the credit necessary to buy the seed and the guano he needed to plant one more cotton crop. This urge was particularly strong in the spring when others were preparing to plant their crops, because "the smell of newly turned earth, that others were never conscious of, reached Jeeter's nostrils with a more pungent odour than anyone else could ever detect in the air. That made him want to go out right away and burn over the old cotton fields and plant a crop."

Though his efforts to grow one more cotton crop came to naught, Jeeter refused to give up, knowing that his identity—his very manhood—was tied to breaking the land and making it grow cotton. When advised repeatedly to seek work in a nearby cotton mill, Jeeter refused, despite his poverty, to exchange his soul for a steady paycheck: "No! By God and Jesus, no! . . . That's one thing I ain't going to do! The Lord made the land, and He put me here to raise crops on it. . . . The land was where I was put at the start, and it's where I'm going to be at the end."

Having come of age during rural Georgia's transformation from agriculture to industry, I was witness to a number of changes that signaled the waning of a way of life. One of these involved revival meetings that had traditionally been staged in late summer so as to coincide with "laying-by time" (the point when the cotton was too large to cultivate, and therefore farmers could withdraw from their fields and wait for the bolls to mature and open for picking). As industrial employment increased, this schedule was maintained, but most churches gave up on the traditional two-a-day services, since only the older members and children were free to come to church on weekday mornings and fewer women were at home to "feed the preacher" his midday meal. At church suppers and the legendary dinners-on-the-ground (remember that in those days "dinner" meant the midday meal), the onset of industrialization manifested itself in the appearance of various kinds of sandwiches prepared in haste using canned pineapple, processed pimento cheese, and fast-blackening bananas spread on store-bought "loaf bread." Even the traditional staple, the ham biscuit, lost much of its appeal with the appearance of that most abominable of all modern culinary innovations, the canned biscuit.

Changes in foodways mirrored the larger changes in rural and small-town life. In the nearby town of Hartwell, "progress" could be measured in terms of the appearance of fast-food "chain" restaurants. The Dairy Queen arrived first, followed at some length by a Tastee-Freeze. Much later came a Hardee's (which at least fixed decent biscuits), a Pizza Hut, and a Kentucky Fried Chicken. Hartwell's emergence as a place to be reckoned with, however, came only with the ascendance of the golden arches.

Although I was satisfied that the opening of a McDonald's meant my hometown had definitely arrived, even I was surprised that a Wal-Mart opened in Hartwell shortly thereafter. More than any comparable business enterprise, a Wal-Mart store seems to bring dramatic alterations to the shape and pace of life in the community where it is located. Once a center of social as well as economic activity, especially on Saturdays, downtown streets or the courthouse square are noticeably quieter because many shoppers have already made their purchases at Wal-Mart, which not only offers lower prices and wider selections (plus a snack bar) but also stays open late on weeknights. The result is a fundamental alteration in traditional patterns of economic and social interaction at the community level.

Evidence of change abounds throughout contemporary Georgia. Those who look closely, however, can also find that the old ways have not entirely disappeared. Doubtless, many a tourist has been mystified, amused, or aggravated by the persistence of the old custom of pulling off the road and stopping the car while a funeral procession passes by. Whenever I encounter this practice, I am always gratified, for it suggests that the personalism and caring that were fundamental elements of southern life at its best are with us yet, even as expressways, malls, and condominiums threaten to make us strangers in our own land. Proper respect for funeral processions is only part of the appropriate ritual surrounding what a friend of mine calls the "southern way of death." Food plays an even more integral role. Bereaved loved ones are swamped with it as soon as word of their loss begins to spread. Organized by Sunday school classes, the ladies of the church show up without fanfare and prepare meals for the grieving family, offering hugs, condolences, and tender recollections of the departed. Through these acts of compassion and their dishes of potato salad and macaroni and cheese, they not only express sympathy and love but offer the comfort that only a sense of belonging to a community can bring. I have attended many funerals at the Cedar Creek Baptist Church (where I became the Georgia Baptist that I will always be).

Despite the sadness that I feel, I always come away with a better sense of who I am, because, on these occasions at least, the old world in which I grew up is still there, and even after all my wanderings, I still feel a part of it.

Such venerable traditions survive even in suburban Atlanta and other dynamic areas throughout the state where they are often observed amidst the hubbub and swirl of runaway growth. In Forsyth County (where civil rights marchers and Klansmen clashed in 1987 and where fewer than twenty African Americans lived in 1990) the number of households increased by 70 percent between 1980 and 1990. The result was a full-scale boom, which had the landscape sprouting "highbrow" residential developments such as "Dressage" and "Olde Atlanta Club." Meanwhile, as residents of Shakerag and Frogtown watched in both bewilderment and amazement, the princely sport of polo made its debut in an area where possum hunting had not long ago been the principal leisure-time pursuit. Passing through small towns across Georgia, motorists note the arrival of the egg roll and the taco in what had once been the undisputed domain of the "plate lunch." On a recent visit home, I drove through the Reed Creek community whence my mama's people came and observed in what had been the remotest and "roughest" part of the county a new restaurant called Reed Creek Trattoria. This pleasant little establishment shares a crossroads with a gas station and a hardware store, and on its front door a sign offers the following "definition": "Trattoria—A place to eat; restaurant, casual, informal cafe. Fresh, simple food found throughout Italy and Reed Creek!"

A LITERARY AWAKENING

The economic and demographic changes that swept across Georgia in the years after the Great Depression not only manifested themselves in significant changes in lifestyles and popular culture but formed the backdrop for a literary awakening as well. Writing in 1917, a contemptuous H. L. Mencken described Georgia as a literary wasteland where "intellectual stimulation" was "utterly lacking" and insisted that "in thirty years it has not produced a single idea." Georgians were not inclined to suffer such insults in silence. Mencken received repeated floggings on the editorial pages of dozens of Georgia newspapers, and he was also swamped with hate mail from outraged Georgians who were convinced that he surely must have leapt to his critical conclusions without reviewing Georgia's considerable contributions to American culture. They reminded Mencken and his equally condescending colleagues that Newton County, Georgia, was the home of the first Boy's Corn Club in the South and that Mrs. F. R. Goulding of Savannah was the first to suggest setting Heber's "From Greenland's Icy Mountains" to music. Another writer called Mencken's attention to "Georgia's brilliant poet," Frank L. Stanton (whose most famous composition was entitled "Mighty Lak' a Rose").

If these responses seemed only to confirm Mencken's put-downs, the painful truth was that Georgians leapt to the defense of the literary reputation of their beloved state with precious little ammo at their disposal. They might have cited the writings of Sidney Lanier, whose concern for preserving the land and the South as a region where people lived on the land put him at odds with Henry Grady's late-nineteenth-century New South crusade and made him the spiritual ancestor of the Nashville Agrarians, who attacked industrialism in the 1920s. Yet as an essayist and a poet, Lanier never made it to the big time. Critics complained of his sentimentality and his obsession with rhythm and rhyme, and his primary audience became several generations of Georgia school children who were compelled to memorize either his "Song of the Chattahoochee":

> Out of the hills of Habersham,
> Down the valleys of Hall,
> I hurry amain to reach the plain,
> Run the rapid and leap the fall. . . .

or "The Marshes of Glynn":

> As the marsh-hen secretly builds on the watery sod,
> Behold I will build me a nest on the greatness of God. . . .

Otherwise, the would-be defenders of Georgia's literary virtue could turn only to Joel Chandler Harris, respected today as an excellent local colorist who made a major contribution by collecting and preserving black folklore in his "Uncle Remus" tales. To a disdainful Mencken, however, this latter activity made Harris "little more than an amanuensis for the local blacks." Always quick to judge and merciless when he did, Mencken scoffed that when Harris began to write on his own "as a white man . . . he swiftly subsided into the fifth rank."

If Georgians' emotional attacks only gave the hateful Mencken an even bigger chuckle at their state's expense, in just a few years the laugh would be on him, for, save perhaps for Mississippi, no state contributed more richly than Georgia to the post–World War I regional literary awakening that we now know as the Southern Literary Renaissance. In its complexity and diversity, the literature of modern Georgia provided an accurate reflection of the rapidly evolving society from which it flowed. Georgia's new breed of writers often seemed obsessed with debunking the myth of the glorious Old South past and exposing the evils of the status quo, yet—like the citizenry at large—they were also more than a little ambivalent about the changes they could already see and apprehensive about a future they could only imagine.

Best known for his novels *God's Little Acre* and *Tobacco Road,* Erskine Caldwell was Georgia's and the South's best-selling author. In this category, Caldwell bested not only William Faulkner but fellow Georgian Margaret Mitchell. Born in 1900, Margaret Munnerlyn "Peggy" Mitchell spent a year at Smith College before returning home to "keep house" for her widowed father. After a year on the debutante scene in Atlanta, she became a reporter for the *Atlanta Journal.* Mitchell quickly became the talk of polite society as she established a reputation for salty language and fast living. Her credentials in the latter category derived in no small part from an infamous Apache dance routine that she performed at a charity ball in 1921. In 1922 Mitchell married Berrien K. "Red" Upshaw, a former University of Georgia football player. The handsome and flamboyant Upshaw had credentials as a less-than-solid citizen that reportedly included a stint as a bootlegger running illicit alcohol between the Georgia mountains and Atlanta. The Mitchell-Upshaw union lasted but a few tumultuous months, and in 1925 she married the much more sedate John Marsh, an advertising executive for the Georgia Power Company. The victim of several automobile accidents, Mitchell began writing a novel while recuperating from a broken ankle. Dubious of its merit, she did not submit it to an editor for several years.

Mitchell insisted that she never intended that Scarlett O'Hara become the heroine of her novel, but as the dominant character in the book, the nervy and resourceful Scarlett emerged as just that. Mitchell claimed that she deplored Scarlett's selfishness and vulgarity, but there seems to have been more than a little of Peggy in the character of Scarlett. As a young girl, Mitchell had been as flirtatious and manipulative as they came; toying with men, she treaded seductively along a fine line whereon she encouraged their ardor and abruptly spurned their advances. In fact, as she admitted, she harbored a deep-seated fascination with sexually aggressive males: "I used to have an elegant time in my early youth . . . by giving a life like imitation of a modern young woman whose blistering passions were only held in check by an iron control. It frequently succeeded so well that all thoughts of seduction were tabled and rape became more to the point."

As a novel and even more so as a movie, *Gone with the Wind* became the absolute embodiment of the romantic "moonlight-and-magnolias" vision of the Old South. Mitchell found this both ironic and disturbing, for she had seen her book as a frontal assault on the Old South myth. "I certainly had no intention of writing about cavaliers," she wrote, adding, "Since my novel was published, I have been embarrassed on many occasions by finding myself included among writers who pictured the South as a land of white-columned mansions whose wealthy owners had thousands of slaves and drank thousands of juleps. I have been surprised, too, for North Georgia certainly was no such country—if it ever existed anywhere—and I took great pains to describe North Georgia as it was. But people believe what they like to believe and the mythical Old South has too strong a hold on their imaginations to be altered by the mere reading of a 1,037 page book."

Whatever Mitchell's intentions, thanks to her novel and the subsequent film, countless readers and viewers in the United States and all over the world were reinforced in their vision of an Old South where planters ruled benignly over their grateful and happy slaves. If there was considerable irony in Margaret Mitchell's unwitting association with an Old South myth she set out to debunk, there was much deeper irony in the career of another well-known Georgia writer, Augustan Frank Yerby. An African American, Yerby studied at Paine College, Fisk University, and the University of Chicago and during the 1940s wrote several short stories built around racial themes. Critics appreciated this work, but Yerby went on to fame and considerable fortune by largely ignoring such concerns in most of his later work. Published in 1946, Yerby's *The Foxes of Harrow* sold over 2 million copies, and in the two decades that followed, Yerby was the dominant figure in the southern romance genre. Solidly researched and vividly detailed, Yerby's novels were targeted for a white female audience, many of whom apparently never realized that their favorite author was black. And why should they? As Jack T. Kirby observed, "Yerby's South was Margaret Mitchell's without Mammy. There are baronial estates supporting fabulous wealth, decadent aristocrats and frontier swashbucklers on the make, pallid indoor belles and flushed hellions a la Scarlett or Jezebel. . . . Blacks figure as characters hardly at all."

Though not nearly as successful commercially as Caldwell, Mitchell, or Yerby, Flannery O'Connor now ranks as Georgia's most critically acclaimed writer of fiction. Like Lillian Smith and fellow Georgian Carson McCullers, O'Connor often shocked her readers. A Roman Catholic, she viewed with critical detachment the entrenched, obsessive, and, in her portrayals, often hypocritical and hollow devotion of her fellow southerners to fundamentalist Protestantism. Yet if O'Connor was frustrated with most of the inhabitants of her "Christ-haunted" region, she was no more sympathetic to liberal critics and antagonists who indulged their own vanity, preached their own gospel of relativism, and denied the existence of original sin. In *Wise Blood,* O'Connor's Hazel Motes even attempts to establish "the Church without Christ" in a dilapidated automobile that ends up covered with kudzu in a Georgia pasture. In one of her most famous short stories, "A Good Man Is Hard to Find," a daffy old matron leads her entire family to destruction at the hands of "the Misfit," a cold-blooded killer, who blames his troubles on Jesus Christ and defines pleasure solely in terms of the harm he can inflict on others. When, in the course of trying to save her own life, the old lady stops urging him to seek Jesus and tries to embrace him as one of her own children, he shoots her at point-blank range and offers a fitting inscription for her tombstone, observing that "she would of been a good woman, if it had been somebody there to shoot her every minute of her life."

Like her contemporaries, O'Connor was witness to a rapidly accelerating process of change that brought the destabilizing and depersonalizing effects of industrialization and agricultural mechanization to the rural and small-town South. In "The Displaced Person," O'Connor told the story of a Polish immigrant, Mr. Guizac, who finds work as a hired hand on a run-down Georgia farm and revitalizes it through his energy, industriousness, and mechanical expertise. Yet, for all the economic benefits he brings, Guizac is also infected with alien values. His employer, Mrs. McIntyre, is impressed by Guizac's accomplishments and happy with the potential profits his efforts may reap for her, but she also worries that Guizac is a stranger to the society and culture in which he lives. Her fears are confirmed when she learns that he plans to get a female cousin into the United States by betrothing her to a local black man, and in the story's startling conclusion, she looks on silently, offering no warning, as the unsuspecting Guizac is flattened by a runaway tractor.

O'Connor specialized in calling attention to the spiritual shortcomings of her characters, but unlike Lillian Smith, she was no crusader for change. In fact, some of her most appreciative readers were distressed with her coolness toward the civil rights movement and several of its leaders. O'Connor remained dubious of the presumption of northern superiority and made no secret of her suspicion of "all those who come from afar with moral energy that increases in direct proportion to the distance from home." While southern liberals worked assiduously to bring the South into the American mainstream, O'Connor was concerned not by "the fact that the South is alienated from the rest of the country but by the fact that it is not alienated enough, that every day we are getting more and more like the rest of the country, that we are being forced out, not only of our many sins but of our few virtues."

Known for the Gothic settings and grotesque characters she created, Flannery O'Connor had a worthy successor in Harry Crews. Born to a poor white family in Bacon County, "the worst hookworm and rickets part of Georgia," as he called it, Crews set much of his fiction in the scrub pine, sandy-soil areas of South Georgia or North Florida. His first novel, *The Gospel Singer,* was especially evocative of O'Connor's fascination with the hypocrisy of Bible Belt fundamentalism, and Crews explained in the epigraph to his book that "men to whom God is dead worship one another."

Concerned with alienation of southerners from a regional society and culture rapidly losing its identity and meaning, Crews set his 1976 novel, *Feast of Snakes,* in a miserable South Georgia town whose traditional rattlesnake roundup has degenerated into a tourist attraction. Crews's central character, Joe Lon Mackey, is a former high-school gridiron star who always had his way with the cheerleaders but never mastered the fine art of reading and writing. Denied the opportunity to pursue collegiate stardom, he finds himself trapped in a miserable, frustrated existence, living in a mobile home with a wife with rotten teeth and two smelly infants for whom he feels little affection. After a torrid sexual encounter with his old girlfriend, Berenice, who has gone on to fame as a baton twirler at the University of Georgia, Joe Lon eventually goes on a homicidal shooting spree and is thrown by an angry mob into a pit full of writhing reptiles. As the novel closes, he struggles to his feet with snakes hanging from his face.

Like so many contemporary writers, poet and novelist James Dickey dealt with the transformation of southern life in his novel *Deliverance.* When Dickey's four suburbia-softened protagonists seek to reinvigorate themselves through the conquest of a wild North Georgia river, they encounter a group of murderous and perverted mountain men who only make the struggle with the river all the more desperate and terrible. The three who survive emerge feeling neither heroic nor, in any perceptible sense, better for their ordeal.

Historian David R. Goldfield noted that the civil rights movement went a long way toward removing "the public obsession with race," thereby allowing southern "whites to regain contact with other cultural elements such as past, place, and manners." Goldfield might have said the same for southern blacks, especially southern black writers. Whereas Richard Wright and Ralph Ellison struggled with a world dominated by the pervasive and confining realities of color, their successors felt less urgently the need to analyze the effects of white antagonism. Hence they could focus on the strengths and soft spots, complexities and contradictions of African American life.

Born, like Harry Crews, to a sharecropper family, Alice Walker grew up near Eatonton, studied at Spelman and Sarah Lawrence, and worked as a civil rights activist in Mississippi during the 1960s. Yet Walker's fiction was distinguished by her desire to look beyond (though certainly not ignore) white oppression and explore themes of community, identity, and gender in her writing. Walker had journeyed to Africa in search of her proverbial "roots," and in her short story "Everyday Use," a young woman named Dee, who, thanks to having her African consciousness raised, now calls herself Wangero, comes home to visit her impoverished mother. Wangero begs her mother to give her some handmade quilts that are already promised to Maggie, her disfigured and inarticulate sister, who is about to marry an ignorant, mossy-toothed country black man. Having refused the offer of these "old-fashioned" quilts when she went away to college, Wangero now wants them to hang on display. "Maggie can't appreciate those quilts!" she argues with unintended irony. "She'd probably be backward enough to put them to everyday use."

In *The Color Purple,* Walker went on to explore male-female and female-female relationships within the black family and community, stressing the strength and courage of her female characters as they struggled for fulfillment in a world dominated not just by whites but by males as well. More recently, Tina McElroy Ansa offered an irreverent look at the cult of matriarchy in *Ugly Ways,* a novel that reaches a riotous conclusion as the ever-combative Lovejoy sisters fall to scuffling at the funeral home, accidentally dump their mother's corpse on the floor, and proceed to deliver a series of recitations on her shortcomings as a parent.

GEORGIA'S MUSICAL TRADITIONS

The role of Georgians in creating a new regional persona went well beyond the written page. Georgia performers contributed heavily to the creation of new musical traditions that were rich, complex, and ultimately intertwined in a process of cultural interaction and commercialization that produced a number of fascinating and distinctive musical styles. One of Georgia's musical pioneers was Fiddlin' John Carson, a major figure in the formative years of country music. Having gained notoriety for his incessant playing of the incendiary "Ballad of Little Mary Phagan" from the Marietta courthouse steps on the day Leo Frank was lynched, Carson seemed very much rooted in Cash's South. Founded in an indigenous folk and gospel tradition and recorded in 1923, his version of "Little Log Cabin in the Lane" became the first commercially successful "country" recording. Yet Carson's record sales depended ultimately on his ability to create new material, and he became one of country music's first professional composers. Carson's version of "There Ain't No Bugs on Me" commented on the Ku Klux Klan and the evolution controversy and even took an irreverent poke at famous evangelist Billy Sunday, noting that Sunday's church was always full because the people came "from miles around to hear him shoot the bull."

On the other side of the color line, Georgia not only produced blues legends Blind Willie McTell and Gertrude "Ma" Rainey, but Villa Rica's Thomas A. Dorsey, the son of a Baptist minister, who wrote and performed a number of explicitly raunchy blues tunes only to turn away from this sinful life to become a prominent gospel composer. Among his five hundred compositions, Dorsey listed hymns such as "Take my Hand, Precious Lord," and "There Will Be Peace in the Valley," a song

Rosa Lee Carson, "Moonshine Kate," and Fiddlin' John Carson onstage in LaGrange, 1925

made famous by Red Foley and recorded by a host of other white performers as well. The conflicts between the secular and spiritual also manifested themselves in a number of other Georgia performers. Save perhaps for the incomparably outrageous Jerry Lee Lewis, no southern musician seemed more torn between his hedonist impulses and puritan upbringing than Macon's Little Richard Penniman. A rock 'n' roll pioneer, Little Richard began his career in blues clubs and went on to record sexually charged tunes such as "Tutti Frutti" and "Good Golly, Miss Molly" only to turn to preaching and Bible study and then proceed to bounce back and forth between the Lord's work and the Devil's music. Meanwhile, Augusta's James Brown employed a host of gospel-derived techniques as he claimed the title "Godfather of Soul," and Macon's Otis Redding also achieved legendary status in the same genre. Finally, Albany native Ray Charles produced an astounding blend of the sacred and the secular in songs such as "I Got a Woman" and "What I Say" and went on to make himself all but synonymous with Hoagy Carmichael's immortal "Georgia." While early white rock 'n' rollers succeeded in adapting their country and gospel heritage to the heavy beat of rhythm and blues, Charles was one of the few black performers who reciprocated by recording an album of country favorites that sold over 3 million copies. As the blues, gospel, and country stylings moved toward the intersection that would yield the revolutionary musical hybrid known as rock 'n' roll, they reflected a pattern of change, both broad and deep, encompassing urbanization, industrialization, and the emergence of a youth culture distinguished by a considerably less rigid moral code than the one offered them by their parents.

Country music chronicled this process of change with particular candor. For nineteen-year-old Decatur native Bill Anderson, the view from the top of the hotel in then-tiny Commerce sufficed as inspiration for "City Lights," a song in which he imaginatively surveys a beckoning "Great White Way" only to reject the big city's allure when he reaches the conclusion that he "just can't say 'I love you' to a street of city lights." Anderson later offered a nostalgic reconsideration of the good old days when times were bad in his hit song "Po Folks," which told of a family who were such a "hungry bunch" that even a wolf would not approach their front door without "a picnic lunch." Anderson's "po folks" had something money couldn't buy, however, and instead of shivering from the cold or complaining about hunger, they simply "patched the cracks and set the table with love."

Whereas several country tunes have provided inspiration for movies, Anderson's "Po Folks" may have been the only one ever to launch a restaurant chain. Featuring mass-produced "home cooked" vittles washed down by mason jars full of iced tea, Anderson's Po Folks restaurants appealed to those who, now that they no longer had to subsist on an occasional meal of cornbread, beans, and greens, found the restaurants an appealing way to make a brief visit to the simple pleasures of the past without returning to its hardships and trials on a permanent basis.

THE GOOD OLD DAYS

By the mid-1980s, nostalgia was in vogue not just in country music, but in literary and journalistic circles as well. In *The Year the Lights*

Blacksmith's shop near Covington, 1940s

Came On, Terry Kay recalled how the coming of electricity to rural Georgia helped to break down the social barriers between town and country but did so only at the cost of the "intangible security people have always enjoyed in isolation." In Kay's novel, rural electrification begins a process that television and air conditioning would subsequently accelerate, as a people accustomed to constant contact with nature suddenly began to spend more time indoors developing, as Kay put it, "pretensions about the sophistication of having electricity."

In the course of telling his tale, Kay offered many a familiar vignette from small-town Georgia life, especially in his description of Rev. Bartholomew R. Bytheway's "Speaking-In-Tongues Traveling Tent

Tabernacle revival" and the dramatic spiritual transformation of one Laron Crook, whose conversion "made St. Paul's experience on the road to Damascus seem like a migraine headache in comparison."

Elsewhere Olive Ann Burns's *Cold Sassy Tree* told the story of a young man's coming of age in a small Georgia village modeled on the town of Commerce (which, ironically, had been the "big city" model for Bill Anderson's "City Lights"). No writer better captured the spirit and rhythm of rural and small-town life in Georgia than Fayetteville physician and author Ferrol Sams Jr. In *Run with the Horsemen*, Sams displayed his considerable talents as a storyteller. One of his favorite characters was Mr. Lum Thornton, who lived at the poor farm but hung out at the barbershop:

> One spring day Mr. Lum Thornton was rared back in his chair on the sidewalk, leaning against the light pole. His shirt sleeves were rolled halfway up his forearms and his collar unbuttoned at the neck. He had such thick, vibrant body hair that the boy was reminded in amazement of an animal pelt. . . . Up the sidewalk, regally erect and self-assured, on her way to call on Mrs. Babcock, swept the venerable and proud Miss Hess Meriwether. Pausing to acknowledge the nodding heads and respectfully murmured greetings of the group, her eyes fixed on the contented figure seated at the edge of the sidewalk. "My word, Lum," she said, "are you that hairy all over?"
>
> The chair never budged. The eyes of the pauper met the eyes of the aristocrat. "Miss Hess," he drawled, "hit's a damn sight wuss'n that in spots."

By the early 1990s, South Georgia school teacher Bailey White had become National Public Radio's most popular commentator. A master storyteller, White captivates her urbane listeners with a skillful combination of down-home detail and sophisticated wit as she tells of life with her offbeat though spunky and appealing mother and succeeds somehow in making Thomasville seem a somewhat cuddlier and sometimes wackier version of Garrison Keillor's Lake Woebegone slid South.

The propensity for wistful recollection was not peculiar to middle-class whites. Harry Crews's *A Childhood: The Biography of a Place* is perhaps the most touching and realistic memoir of poor-white life a southerner has produced. As a youth in Bacon County, Crews suffered through the loss of his father, a bout with polio, and an almost total immersion in scalding water. The night after his father was buried, all the meat disappeared from the family's smokehouse, stolen according to Crews by one of his father's friends. "It was a hard time in that land, and a lot of men did things for which they were ashamed and suffered for the rest of their lives," Crews explained. "The world that circumscribed the people I come from had so little margin for error, for bad luck, that when something went wrong, it almost always brought something else down with it. It was a world in which survival depended on raw courage born out of desperation and sustained by a lack of alternatives."

For all the hardships he and his people had known there, however, Crews was by no means alienated from his South Georgia roots. He recalled with genuine affection the one-Saturday-a-month pilgrimages his family made to Alma, where around the square

> the dusty air would be heavy with the pleasant smell of mule dung and mule sweat. . . . Farmers were everywhere in small groups, talking and chewing, and bonneted women stood together trading recipes and news of children. . . . Sometimes I would have as much as a dime to spend on penny candy, but better than the taste of the candy was finding a telephone in a store and standing beside it until somebody used it. I never talked on one myself until I was almost grown, but I knew what a phone was, knew that a man's voice could be carried on a wire all the way across town. No film or play I have ever watched since has been as wonderful as the telephones I watched as a boy in Alma, Georgia.

Crews denied that he was "singing a sad song for the bad good old days, wishing he was back barefoot again traveling in wagons and struck dumb by the mystery of telephones. . . . What I am talking about here is a hard time in the shaping of the South, a necessary experience that made us the unique people we are."

If such recollections were surprising coming from a Georgian who had known the hardships Crews had experienced, the same could certainly be said for Alice Walker. Yet Walker actually seemed to express sympathy for her "Northern brothers" who "have never experienced the magnificent quiet of a summer day when the heat is intense and one is so very thirsty, as one moves across the dusty cotton fields, that one learns forever that water is the essence of all life. In the cities, it cannot be so clear to one that he is a creature of the earth, feeling the soil between the toes, smelling the dust thrown up by the rain, loving the earth so much that one longs to taste it and sometimes does."

Walker explained that she was "nostalgic" not for "lost poverty" but for "the solidarity and sharing a modest existence can sometimes bring." Nor did she intend, Walker wrote, "to romanticize the Southern black country life." Yet, as she saw it, "No one could wish for a more advantageous heritage than that bequeathed to the black writer in the South: a compassion for the earth, a trust in humanity beyond our knowledge of evil, and an abiding love of justice."

Not all Georgia authors focused their wistful recollections on rural and small-town life. In *Peachtree Road,* Anne Rivers Siddons captured the heyday and described the demise of "Old Atlanta" society as reflected in the tragic disintegration of one affluent Buckhead family. Other observers saw little to celebrate in Atlanta's emergence as the quintessential symbol of a northernized South, lost for a second and final time to the Yankees—this time, ironically, through success rather than failure. Such was the perspective of Georgia-bred journalist Marshall Frady. Having made a name for himself primarily by showcasing the South's benightedness before the rest of the nation, Frady seemed to have received a massive injection of mellow by the mid-1970s. He recalled longingly a South that once seemed like "America's Corsica— an insular sunglowered latitude of swooning sentiment and sudden guttural violence, always half adaze in the past." That imagery was fading rapidly, however, as Frady surveyed a South teetering on the verge of being rendered "pastless, meaningless, and vague of identity." Below Atlanta, in the "aboriginal landscapes of *Gone with the Wind,"* a horrified Frady encountered "a Santa Barbara gallery of pizza cottages and fish 'n' chips parlors, with a 'Tara Shopping Center' abruptly glaring out of fields of broom sage and jack pine."

Dismayed by this physical transformation, Frady was even more distressed by the "cultural lobotomy" evidenced by the disappearance of the "musky old demagogues" he had once loved to pillory and even the "chigger bitten tabernacle evangelists" whose "fierce tragic theologies" were little in evidence in suburban Atlanta, where bumper stickers read "PEOPLE OF DISTINCTION PREFER JESUS."

BUCKLE OF THE BIBLE BELT

As Frady suggested, many of Georgia's itinerant evangelists have folded their tents, but despite the social, economic, and demographic changes that had swept across the state in the last half century, Georgia remains the buckle of the proverbial Bible Belt. In 1990, 58 percent of Georgia's population belonged to some religious denomination. Indeed, in three counties, Baker, Clay, and Dooly, the aggregate church membership was larger than the population itself. In all likelihood, to meet a Georgia churchgoer was to meet a Baptist. Baptists accounted for 60 percent of all the state's church membership, while the next strongest denominational competitor, the Methodists, could boast only 15 percent of Georgia's religious adherents. By way of contrast, Roman Catholics, who accounted for 39 percent of church membership nationwide, accounted for less than 6 percent in Georgia, with much of that population concentrated in the metropolitan Atlanta area. The dominant religious subgroup in Georgia was the Southern Baptists, whose emphasis on individual salvation had traditionally led them to support far-flung missionary enterprises elsewhere in the world while local congregations paid less attention to social welfare concerns in their own communities. Forty-two percent of Georgia's church members were Southern Baptists in 1990, but this group was hardly monolithic. Philosophical and doctrinal differences abounded and often erupted into open conflict. Such was the case at the Sardis Baptist Church near Hartwell, where in 1994 a heated dispute about pastoral authority led to a schism in the church and a legal battle that divided friends and even husbands and wives and revealed not only some deep-seated differences in belief but the intensity with which these beliefs were held.

Whatever their differences, Georgia's more conservative religious groups maintained a common vigil against certain secular encroachments, mustering their forces wherever and whenever the prospect of liberalized liquor laws or legalized gambling manifested itself. Zell Miller staked his 1990 gubernatorial campaign on a statewide lottery whose proceeds were to be dedicated to supporting education. Following legislative approval, the lottery question went to the voters on November 2, 1993, and attracted nearly as much attention as the presidential clash between Bill Clinton and George Bush. Early polls showed majority support for the lottery, but a grassroots campaign against it gradually gained momentum as election day drew near. Organizers of GAAG (Georgia Alliance Against Gambling) did not rely solely on a religious message and attacked the lottery as a social evil rather than a sin, stressing its potential to accelerate the already alarming deterioration of the entire social fabric. Still, the antilottery campaign drew heavily on the support of Georgia's large church-going population, and many churches sported outdoor signs with antilottery slogans.

Returns showed that the late-developing opposition movement, which narrowly missed defeating the lottery proposal, drew heavily on the support of older, rural, church-going voters. On the other hand, support for the lottery was strongest in the state's urban counties, especially metropolitan Atlanta. The vote also broke along racial and class lines, with blacks supporting the measure by a two-to-one majority, while whites opposed it by a narrow margin. In general, voters earning less than $30,000 per year supported the lottery, while those earning more than $50,000 were more likely to oppose it. (First-year statistics on lottery participation revealed a similar pattern: Ticket purchasers were more likely to be black and less affluent.) Owing to heavy participation by purchasers from neighboring states, the Georgia Lottery set a first-year sales record, generating income equivalent to $160 for every resident of Georgia. This figure was good news for Georgia high-school students, because in addition to a variety of other programs, the lottery-driven HOPE ("Helping Outstanding Pupils

Educationally") program promises a full-tuition, four-year college scholarship to students who have a B average in high school and maintain the same average during their freshman year in college.

OLYMPIC GEORGIA

If many Georgians at large hardly knew what to make of the lottery craze, they were alternately amused, bewildered, and sometimes angered by Atlanta's wholesale, hell-for-leather, heart-on-its-sleeve courtship of the 1996 Olympic Games. Atlanta's Olympic quest apparently began early in 1987 as the inspiration of Atlanta lawyer Billy Payne, who quickly enlisted the cooperation of Mayor Andrew Young and the city's chamber of commerce. There ensued a tedious process and protracted courtship and competition in which Atlanta first bested Minneapolis–St. Paul as the preferred site of the United States Olympic Committee and then went on to confront four other competitors, including Athens (not the one just down the road, where the Bulldogs first played in 1892, but the other one, where the first modern Olympics were held in 1896). Clearly Athens had both sentiment and symbolism going for it, but as the International Olympic Committee (IOC) proceeded through several votes, Atlanta gained increasing support, going over the top when Toronto was eliminated.

In addition to Payne, a key player in the Atlanta effort had been the by-then former mayor Young, whose global connections from his days as United States ambassador to the United Nations stood him in good stead. There was considerable irony in observing a black southerner courting African support for bringing the Olympics to a part of the world once notorious for its treatment of blacks. At any rate, on September 18, 1990, the announcement in Tokyo of Atlanta's selection elicited a riotous response from the 350 Georgians in attendance, while back in Atlanta, where it was six in the morning, approximately two thousand early risers watched the triumph via satellite amidst fluttering confetti, fireworks, and the release of twenty-five hundred balloons. Another huge celebration ensued that evening, followed by another the next morning.

Some more skeptical Georgians quickly grew tired of what became a marathon of self-congratulatory rhetoric and celebration, and those anxious to deflate Atlanta's balloon soon had their chance. Apparently selected without much consultation or market research, the 1996 Olympic mascot "Whatizit" made its debut at the closing ceremonies of the 1992 Olympic Summer Games in Barcelona. To describe the debut as inauspicious would be an understatement of truly Olympic proportions. In fact, only "unmitigated disaster" will suffice. A computer-generated and wholly unendearing blue blob described by one commentator as "a bad marriage of the Pillsbury Doughboy and

Atlanta prepares for the 1996 Summer Olympic Games.

the ugliest California Raisin," "Whatizit" met with "international derision." Among the homefolks, the reception was even less cordial. Stunned members of the Atlanta Committee for the Olympic Games insisted that the unlikely mascot would grow on folks, but, their stiff upper lip notwithstanding, they proceeded with vigorous reassessment of what steps might be taken to improve the mascot's marketability.

The result was a transformed mascot, cuddlier and more expressive, sporting bigger feet, and bearing the nickname "Izzy." None of these changes pacified Izzy/Whatizit's Georgia-based critics who found him objectionable precisely because his regionally neutral nerdiness seemed to stem from a desire to avoid any potential association of the Olympic Games with the South. One Georgian said, "I don't get where he's coming from. I don't really see how it represents anything specific to Atlanta, to the South—to the country, even. It ought to stand for something." Journalist Bert Roughton had other ideas as to why some of the 57 percent of Atlantans polled in September 1993 found even the remodeled mascot objectionable: "Atlanta has been reinventing itself since it was reduced to ashes in the Civil War. . . . Maybe that's why we all recoiled so much when we first laid eyes on Whatizit. Maybe there was an uncomfortable recognition of something too familiar. Maybe it's just the ugly truth: Izzy is us."

The reimaging of Atlanta has long been a favorite local pastime, but for all the efforts in this direction, as the 1990s unfolded, Atlantans found themselves facing yet another identity crisis. Ironically, after selling their city as the site of the 1996 Summer Olympic Games, the city's leadership wound up hiring a consultant (appropriately named Joel Babbit) to select a slogan describing what it was that they had actually sold. The search produced a flood of suggestions from the Henry Gradyesque "Atlanta: From Ashes to Axis" to the more candid but less inspiring "Atlanta: Not Bad for Georgia" to the also accurate but decidedly unpoetic "Watch Atlanta Transmogrify." Some warned that the great search for a slogan was likely to culminate in something along the lines of "Atlanta: A southern city of great hospitality where the weather is generally fair, the business climate is positive, a number of large buildings exist, and you can have fun at Underground." The eventual choice, "Atlanta. Come Celebrate the Dream," was slick, sophisticated, and suitably bland, so much so that cynical observers suggested replacing it with "Atlanta: Where the South Stops" or "Atlanta: It's 'Atnalta' Spelled Backwards."

Outside Atlanta, many Georgians were unwilling to buy into ·the pursuit of Olympic gold—or, in reality, green—especially if it entailed a massive disruption of their lifestyles and traditions. The decision to bring Olympic soccer to Sanford Stadium in Athens left a number of that city's residents less than overjoyed. Tens of millions of dollars and major international attention notwithstanding, some Athenians would just as soon invite William Tecumseh Sherman to visit the Classic City and present him with a blowtorch when he arrives. Certainly, this is the case with one resident, who warned, "What we're in for is 80,000 drunks who don't speak English invading Athens and burning down our town." When Olympic soccer comes to Athens, this gentleman plans to take off on vacation for "somewhere quiet . . . like Bosnia."

One of the major objections to holding the soccer matches in the University of Georgia's Sanford Stadium was that doing so meant widening the field, which in turn meant removing the hallowed hedges that ringed the gridiron. To many Georgians, the only sport that mattered was played in the fall "between the hedges," and they were loath to see that sacred space violated by anything, let alone a game of which they knew little and about which they cared less. Soccer had made some inroads among the younger set in Georgia's metropolitan areas, but even in the midst of the long-awaited ascendance of the Atlanta Braves, football remained an absolute and pervasive passion. From "midget" or "pee-wee" games during the week to high-school encounters on Friday nights to the exertions of the Bulldogs and the Yellow Jackets on Saturdays, football was an ever-present source of entertainment, vicarious achievement, emotional catharsis, and, in many cases, an outlet for the expression of community, state, and regional pride as well.

THE GREAT SYMBOL WAR

Regional pride, especially its sources and symbols, was a matter of keen interest to many Georgians. Of all the cultural ramifications of

Atlanta's Olympic preparation, none provoked more verbal fireworks than the great state flag controversy. Adopted in 1799, Georgia's first state flag consisted of the state's coat of arms on a field of blue. A new post-Reconstruction banner resembled the first flag of the Confederacy and featured a vertical blue strip and horizontal bands of red and white. The state's coat of arms was added to the flag in 1905. This banner flew over Georgia until 1956 when the legislature moved to incorporate the familiar Confederate battle flag into the state flag.

Defenders of this flag insist that this modification was meant to honor Confederate soldiers, but it came at a time of confrontation, when the state's white political leaders were rallying to the cause of massive resistance to the 1954 *Brown v. Board of Education* decision and vowing last-ditch defiance of any and all desegregation efforts. Flag critics also pointed out that the day before the state House of Representatives approved the flag-change bill, it had passed by a vote of 179 to 1 the so-called "Interposition Resolution," which declared the U.S. Supreme Court's school-integration decrees "null, void and of no effect" in Georgia. At the time, state representative Denmark Groover of Macon insisted that the new flag would "show that we in Georgia intend to uphold what we stood for, will stand for, and will fight for." A former member of the legislature who opposed adding the Confederate emblem to the state banner was absolutely convinced that the intent of the bill's supporters was to affirm their support for segregation. He offered an analogy that anyone familiar with Georgia could readily understand: "There was only one reason for putting that flag on there. Like the gun rack in the back of a pickup, it telegraphs a message." (The association of the new state flag with the "southern way of life" was pervasive indeed. As an elementary- and high-school student in the late 1950s and early 1960s and as a high-school teacher in the late 1960s, I recall that all classroom films acquired from the Georgia Department of Education began with a vivid shot of the state flag accompanied by a robust rendition of "Dixie.")

After the passions of the civil rights era had cooled somewhat, several individuals and groups launched assaults on the flag, the most notable coming in 1987 after a widely publicized incident in which white supremacists waving rebel flags attacked civil rights marchers in Forsyth County. Finally, in May 1992 Gov. Zell Miller announced that he would support legislation to restore the pre-1956 flag and called the current flag "the last remaining vestige of days that are not only gone, but also days that we have no right to be proud of." Changing the flag would require "sheer guts," Miller acknowledged, but as the great-grandson of a Confederate soldier wounded at both Chancellorsville and Gettysburg, Miller found the flag a blemish on the state's image, and he added, "Frankly, I do give a damn."

Not surprisingly, with its large population of blacks and nonnative whites and its economic stake in projecting an image of enlightenment and harmony, the Atlanta area provided the strongest support for removing the Confederate battle flag from the state's official banner. Meanwhile, supporters of the flag feared that the next step might be a sandblasting of Stone Mountain, especially after a black clergyman admitted that his dream is that someday folks will look up at the world's largest stone carving and say, "Who are those fellows?" Casual observers saw the flag controversy pitting the "fergit" crowd (composed of black activists and a smattering of white liberals) against the "fergit, hell" crowd (personified by the Sons of Confederate Veterans). In reality, the dispute was hardly that simple. Some polling data from Georgia showed that a majority of black respondents expressed no objection to keeping the state flag as it is. Meanwhile, though pro-flag partisans insisted that white southerners saw it as a memorial to their heroic Confederate forebears, a 1992 survey indicated that fewer than 20 percent of the southern whites polled could even claim such an ancestry. On the other hand, even white southerners of the liberal persuasion were sometimes a bit testy where the flag was concerned. When asked by an argumentative northerner why the South needed a flag when the North doesn't have one, even the affable Roy Blount Jr. wanted to respond, "That's because the North isn't a place. . . . it's just a direction out of the South."

Though it often sparked heated and intemperate rhetoric on both sides, the assault on Confederate icons nonetheless raised intriguing questions about the appropriate symbols for a new southern identity. The same was true of the growing popularity among black tourists of memorials such as the Martin Luther King Jr. Center for Social Change, the Ebenezer Baptist Church, and other civil rights landmarks elsewhere in the South.

Miller's move against the flag required considerable courage, but polls consistently showed as much as 60 percent support for keeping the flag as it was. By January 1994 the governor was facing reelection, and though he was seldom inclined to raise the flag issue, when someone else did, he simply conceded, "I gave it my best shot. I lost. . . . I lost that one big."

Despite Miller's strategic retreat, the flag question simply refused to go away. Following the lead of the Atlanta City Council and the Fulton County Commission, the Atlanta–Fulton County Recreation Authority decided to remove the flag from Atlanta–Fulton County Stadium, the home of the Atlanta Braves. At the Georgia Dome, where the Atlanta Falcons play, the presence of the flag sparked 1994 Super Bowl–day protests from various civil rights groups as well as a group of about fifty reporters who wore black arm bands and declined to enter the press box until after the national anthem had been played. Meanwhile, with the Olympics still two years away, the Hyatt, the Westin Peachtree Plaza, and other major downtown Atlanta hotels stopped flying the state flag, and Holiday Inn Worldwide asked its Georgia franchises to do the same.

THE MULTIPLE PERSONALITIES OF MODERN GEORGIA

Although issues like the flag controversy and the lottery seemed to emphasize the ideological divisions separating metropolitan Georgians from their rural counterparts, some of these differences were easily exaggerated. For years, observers had predicted that in combination with an influx of in-migrants from outside the region, the urbanization of the South's population would undermine the conservative values that seemed deeply rooted in rural and small-town areas. In Georgia, as elsewhere, this prediction went more than slightly awry. Instead of urbanizing according to the classic pattern, Georgia "metropolitanized" or suburbanized, owing primarily to the fact that its economic transformation came well after the advent of the automobile, which allowed workers to live at some distance from their jobs. The subsequent construction of an extensive network of interstate highways (Atlanta was one of only five cities nationwide where three interstate highways intersected) further facilitated this process. Finally, contrary to expectations, immigrants to metropolitan Georgia proved only marginally less conservative on many issues than their neighbors in the countryside.

Indeed, Atlanta's affluent suburban counties often found themselves at odds on many social concerns with the majority black and culturally diverse central city itself. The growth and increasing activism of Atlanta's gay and lesbian community sparked controversy on a variety of fronts. The annual "Hotlanta River Expo" became the centerpiece for one of the largest gay gatherings in the nation and exemplified the increasing openness of the gay lifestyle in and about the city.

Ironically, the Hotlanta River Expo, featuring a giant raft race, was staged on and about the Chattahoochee River, which served as a sort of moat between Atlanta and ultraconservative Cobb County to the north. Fed by in-migration and white flight from Atlanta, Cobb's population (88 percent white in 1990) had soared from less than two hundred thousand in 1970 to more than five hundred thousand in 1990. Approximately one-third of its residents were college graduates in 1990, as compared to less than one-tenth in 1970. In 1990 median household income was more than 30 percent higher than the national average. Cobb County was the site of the Leo Frank lynching in 1915, and it was represented in Congress by former John Birch Society activist Larry McDonald until his death in 1982. The city council of the Cobb County town of Kennesaw made headlines worldwide when it enacted an ordinance in 1982 requiring each head of household to own not just a gun but the ammunition for it as well.

The gay lifestyle came under direct assault in Cobb County in the summer of 1993 as Marietta's Theatre in the Square offered a production of *Lips Together, Teeth Apart,* a play that contained references to AIDS and gay neighbors. Controversy over this production culminated in a county commission resolution declaring that the gay lifestyle was "incompatible with the standards to which this community subscribes" and purporting to send a "message to policy makers of this country such that a previously silent voice will now be heard." As the commission debated, supporters and opponents of the resolution massed outside, with one of the supporters carrying a sign reading "Praise God for AIDS." Commissioners also voted to withhold all public funding for the arts lest some of the funds be spent to promote the homosexual lifestyle.

Gay activists launched a counteroffensive, staging a "Queer Family Picnic" in Marietta and spearheading an effort to divert businesses from Cobb County, which had just constructed a $43-million convention center. As did the controversy over the state flag, the Cobb County brouhaha soon spilled over into preparations for the 1996 Olympic Games. Atlanta gay-rights groups protested vigorously the Olympic Committee's decision to hold the Olympic volleyball competition in Cobb County. "Olympics Out of Cobb" was the theme at the 1994 Lesbian and Gay Pride Festival, which attracted well over a hundred thousand participants.

On the other hand, outside Interstate 285 (Atlanta's equivalent of Washington's beltway) the county commission's action enjoyed considerable support. Although the threat of continued protests and the calls of various organizations for gays and lesbians to flock to Atlanta in 1996 ultimately led Olympic organizing officials to withdraw the volleyball competition from Cobb County, the tensions engendered by the gay rights issue showed little sign of subsiding.

Although many expected that the "bulldozer revolution" accompanying urbanization and industrialization would scrape away the last vestiges of southernness, John Shelton Reed has found, paradoxically enough, that those white southerners most positively affected by the economic and demographic changes that transformed the South seem to be those most interested in clinging to their identity as southerners. In Reed's words, "It is those who are most modern in background and experience . . . who . . . are most likely to think in regional terms, to categorize themselves and others as 'Southerners' and 'non-Southerners' and to believe they know what that means." As if to underscore Reed's argument, across the state thousands of upwardly mobile Georgians dote on the latest issue of *Southern Living* in much the same fashion as their less affluent ancestors once pored dreamily over the pages of the Sears Roebuck catalog.

The concerns of many of these self-assertive contemporary southerners manifested themselves in the humor of the yuppie-good-old-boy humorist Lewis Grizzard. Conservative—and sometimes reactionary—Grizzard epitomized the ambivalence of many white southerners who have embraced the economic and material benefits that have come their way while remaining skeptical and sometimes resentful of some of the social and political changes that have accompanied these gains.

Grizzard became sports editor of the *Athens Daily News* at nineteen and held the same position at the *Atlanta Journal* by the time he was twenty-one. After leaving the *Journal* in 1975 for a brief stint as a freelance writer, he journeyed north to join the sports staff of the *Chicago Sun-Times*, where he became executive sports editor. Miserably homesick and freezing, Grizzard literally begged for the chance to leave Chicago in April 1977 and take a $12,000 pay cut to become a sports columnist for the *Atlanta Constitution*. He detailed his experiences as a newspaperman and his odyssey in the frozen North in *If I Ever Get Back to Georgia, I'm Gonna Nail My Feet to the Ground.*

Grizzard had never worked as a columnist, but his return to Atlanta marked the beginning of a remarkable rise to fame. He went on to see his column syndicated in 450 newspapers and to write twenty books, many based on themes and stories he had introduced in his columns. Grizzard also became a popular entertainer, commanding as much as $20,000 per performance and recording a number of comedy albums. Grizzard's small-town boyhood and adolescence in tiny Moreland, Georgia, provided him with a huge repertoire of stories about local characters (usually caricatures thereof). A master storyteller, he laced his stories with country colloquialisms such as "bad to drink" or "come up a real bad cloud." (The former is self-explanatory; the latter describes the onset of a severe thunderstorm.) His candid country-boy perspective shaped his reaction to all his experiences. In a hilarious story entitled "There Ain't No Toilet Paper in Russia," he described Peter the Great's palace as "fifteen times bigger than Opryland."

An unabashed participant in rat killings and other such rustic amusements as a youth, the well-traveled Grizzard nonetheless confessed to having twice seen Pavoratti live (once in Paris and once in London), to having sat through at least the first act of *The Marriage of Figaro*, and to visiting the Louvre. To compound matters, Grizzard owned two pairs of Gucci loafers, wore Geoffrey Beane cologne, and used the gun rack behind the seat of his truck to hold his golf clubs.

Yet, although he had eaten caviar at Maxim's in Paris, Grizzard insisted that he liked pork barbecue better. He reveled in his "redneck" heritage and did not hesitate to remind "transplanted Yankees" who deliver "long diatribes about the South's shortcomings" that "Delta is ready when you are." Plagued by a congenital heart problem and reluctant to curb his rambunctious lifestyle, Grizzard narrowly escaped death during heart surgery in 1993, and hence his last book proclaimed *I Took a Lickin' and Kept On Tickin' and Now I Believe in Miracles*. Grizzard survived to see his beloved Georgia Bulldogs through one more season and to mourn the passing of his faithful dog Catfish. He ran out of miracles, however, in March 1994 when complications from high-risk heart surgery caused the brain damage that took his life at age forty-seven. Grizzard's last days were as poignant as his stories were funny. Only a few hours before his final surgery, he married (in the hospital) for the fourth time. His death was mourned by readers and fans around the nation, but nowhere as in the South and especially in Georgia.

Perhaps mindful that their readers lived in a society where continuity and change often occupied the same space, the management of the *Atlanta Journal-Constitution* chose to offer its readers a new but no less Georgian perspective when it chose Rheta Grimsley Johnson as the successor to the duly departed Grizzard. If it might have been—and often was—said of Grizzard that "he's bad to drink, but he's a good ol' boy," it was equally appropriate to say of Johnson, "she's a liberal, but she's a good ol' girl." Grizzard once claimed that his grandmother was the only person he knew who believed "the moonshot's fake and wrestling's real," but Johnson's Grandma Lucille also suspected that the moon landing had been staged in the Arizona or Nevada desert. Grizzard certainly would have approved of Johnson's column, written in reflection on her first day at work at her new job in Atlanta, in which she recalled her family's Colquitt, Georgia, roots. Johnson remembered that even after her family had moved to Alabama (which is in the central time zone), her mother insisted on keeping her schedule according to eastern standard "Georgia time" and on maintaining a subscription to the *Miller County Liberal* so that she could keep up with the doings back in Colquitt. Grizzard would have been less than thrilled with Johnson's next column, however, which she devoted to an enthusiastic account of the life and promising career of a gay country singer from Tupelo, Mississippi.

Though more tolerant of diversity and change, like her predecessor, Johnson bristles when others—especially northern "others"—presume to disparage Georgia or its people. As we have seen, sensitivity to criticism has long been common among Georgians, and understandably so, given their state's turbulent past and controversial reputation. Beginning as the noblest of social experiments, it quickly became a haven for profiteering and human exploitation. Though it produced some of the antebellum era's wealthiest and most influential figures, it got (and still gets) a bum rap as a dumping ground for the down and out, and worse yet, the criminal as well. For much of its history, the dubious sobriquet Cracker stuck to Georgians like the state's famous red clay. During the secession crisis, Georgia's decision seemed absolutely crucial to the success of the southern independence effort, but after suffering both the torching of Atlanta and Sherman's March to the Sea, the state could not escape widespread popular association with an entire region's defeat and degradation. Even Henry Grady's ballyhoo about Atlanta's rise from the ashes did little to undermine Georgia's reputation as a pathetic symbol of a beaten-down and backward South.

When the nation plunged into World War II, raw statistical comparisons may have indicated that two or three of its southern neighbors were in sadder shape, but as the land of lynching and the Leo Frank case, the birthplace of the modern Ku Klux Klan, and a state grown infamous for the brutality of its penal system and the depravity of its demagogues, Georgia boasted stellar credentials to represent the southern way of life at its worst. In *The Mind of the South*, W. J. Cash had argued that the South of 1940 still bore a strong resemblance to the South of 1840 and stressed resistance to change as the key to the survival of the southern mind. Certainly the last half century of Georgia's history has seen dramatic alterations in both the state's economy and social structure. Yet historian George B. Tindall has observed that "to change is not necessarily to lose one's identity; to change sometimes is to find it." Georgia's recent experience underscores Tindall's point, for it suggests not an end but a beginning as Georgians embark on a voyage of self-discovery, one that, hopefully, will lead to widespread rejection of what Katharine Du Pre Lumpkin called "the old dogma, that but one way was Southern, and hence there could be but one kind of Southerner."

Certainly, Georgia has come a long way since Eugene Talmadge dismissed as a "furriner" anyone "who attempts to impose ideas that are counter to the established traditions of Georgia." This is not to say that Talmadge's point of view has disappeared entirely. Witness the Savannah lawyer who argued in January 1993 that "when a true Georgian looks at the [state] flag with its Confederate emblem, he sees the beauty of his Southern heritage." These remarks were addressed to *Atlanta Journal-Constitution* columnist Colin Campbell, who had expressed his support for Gov. Zell Miller's campaign to remove the Stars and Bars from the Georgia flag. Though he was not born in the state, Campbell's own Georgia ancestry stretches back to the 1730s and includes both Maj. William S. Grady, who died for the Confederate cause, and his son, a certain Henry Woodfin Grady, whose credentials as a Georgian were fairly difficult to dispute. As Campbell pointed out, to deny the designation "Georgian" to anyone who refused to embrace the current state flag was to exclude (in all likelihood) most of the nearly 2 million blacks, many of them natives, who lived in the state, as well as a sizable number of other residents born and raised elsewhere in the nation and the world.

Anyone who failed to see Campbell's latter point needed only to head out from Atlanta down Buford Highway, described as "Chinatown, Little Moscow, and the Latin Quarter melded into one" and perhaps the only place in the Southeast "where you can listen to a sermon in Korean, get tax advice in Vietnamese, and rent a Cantonese or Spanish video." In Chamblee and Doraville, the Asian population more than doubled during the 1980s, while the Hispanic population more than quadrupled. Even farther out, in the Gainesville area, the number of Hispanic residents swelled by more than 725 percent during the decade, accounting for more than 20 percent of Hall County's population increase over the period.

By the 1990s it was next to impossible to define what it meant to be a "true Georgian" or, for that matter, to identify, in Eugene Talmadge's words, "the established traditions of Georgia" to which "true Georgians" were bound to adhere. Yet despite our inability to reduce ourselves and our values to a handy composite profile, the majority of us continue to see ourselves as southerners in general and Georgians in particular. The state flag controversy made this reality abundantly clear. John Head, who grew up in Jackson, rejected the suggestions of a pro-flag partisan that "black people aren't really Southerners," insisting that "the South is my home. . . . I am a Southerner." Head refused, he explained, "to allow others to say what that means," and he declined as well to "accept the Confederacy as the South at its best" or to "accept the Confederate battle flag as an emblem in which all Georgians can take pride." Head went on, "I criticize the South, not just because I believe it does not do well enough, but because I know it can do better. Love, not hate, is the basis for that criticism."

Black Georgians had been raising critical concerns for generations, but as Head's comments suggest, by the 1990s they were speaking not as disaffected exiles in their own land but as bona fide insiders who felt a genuine sense of involvement in the affairs of state and society. Fearful that Olympic-inspired efforts to accentuate Atlanta's positives might lead to neglect of the plight of the city's poor and homeless, a number of whom might be displaced as a result of the games, novelist Tina McElroy Ansa proclaimed herself "a child of Atlanta" and "a daughter of Georgia," who wanted Atlanta "to look as spiffy to the world as any staunch city booster."

Ansa was also concerned, however, with "Atlanta's well-earned image as a beacon of conscience . . . a place that forged the conscience of Martin Luther King Jr. and W. E. B. Du Bois and *Constitution* editor Ralph McGill." The only way to show the world Atlanta's strength of moral conviction, Ansa believed, "is in how we treat the weak as well

Hamilton Holmes,
Charlayne Hunter-Gault,
and Jesse Jackson at a
press conference
following Jackson's
Holmes-Hunter Lecture
on the University of
Georgia campus,
November 5, 1992

as the strong, the down-at-the-heel as well as the well-heeled, the slow as well as the swift." To Ansa, the big question was, once the games were over and the crowds had gone home, "how will we Georgians, we Atlantans feel about the Olympic image we presented to the world and, more importantly, to ourselves."

Certainly, no Georgian had demonstrated greater courage in challenging what had once been the most sacred of Georgia's "established traditions" than Charlayne Hunter-Gault, who, along with Hamilton Holmes, had broken the color barrier at the University of Georgia in 1961. On her first full evening on campus, Hunter-Gault had drifted off to sleep as white students outside her dormitory chanted:

> Two, four, six, eight,
> We don't want to integrate. . . .
> Eight, six, four, two,
> We don't want no jigaboo.

Twenty-seven years later as she returned to address the graduating class of 1988, Hunter-Gault had not forgotten "the strains of those peculiar Southern lullabies," but her message was neither defiant nor bitter. Instead, she offered her own surprisingly positive assessment of a contemporary southern mind still marked by continuity but also reshaped by change and, most important, retaining a vital and almost inspiring distinctiveness.

"As we shared our destiny," Hunter-Gault admitted, "I believe we came to know each other in new aspects, and I believe we came to acknowledge and respect both each other's abilities and each other's ways of life." She described the South as the nation's only "true melting pot," explaining that "through the events of our toil and our tumultuous history we have become a definable people." None of this was to say that many differences and some considerable bitterness and mistrust did not yet exist between black and white Georgians, but however unequally it may have been shouldered over the years, the shared burden of their history had instilled a common sense of identity.

Born under Jim Crow in Memphis and living in Atlanta after a brief sojourn in the North, Larry Conley agreed that "this connection to the past—even a past that was often brutal and ugly and stupid—in a strange way binds Southerners together. It's our past, good and bad, and we take equal ownership of it." Conley was but one of many African American southerners who made the decision to return and stake their claims on their homeland. Led by Atlanta, Georgia gained eighty thousand blacks by in-migration between 1985 and 1990 alone. Many of these seemed to share the opinion of Savannah native Harold Jackson, who, after living in eight states, had concluded that "I'd rather be in the South than any place else." Part of Georgia's attraction was certainly its economic dynamism, but, as Jackson put it, "It's not just that the opportunities are here. It's that the opportunities to solve the problems that exist are here, too."

Though by no means all of them were as optimistic as Jackson, many black Georgians seemed to take heart in the realization that they lived in a state where, when all the pluses and minuses had been tallied, things had clearly changed for the better in recent years. Still, for all the tangible evidence of progress, this sense of identification with Georgia and the South was rooted no more in empirical reality than in an almost spiritual longing for kinship with both people and place. Many years ago, Richard Weaver insisted that "being a southerner is definitely a spiritual condition, like being a Catholic or a Jew, and members of the group can recognize one another by signs which are eloquent to them, though too small to be noticed by an outsider." At the time of Weaver's observation, "southerner" was a designation reserved for whites only, but although they were not always terribly specific, many contemporary South-watchers insisted that despite their differences southerners of both races could draw on a shared sense of understanding as they interacted with each other. As John Shelton Reed explained, "Shared understandings . . . make communication easier, and these are the kinds of things people tend to mention these days when you ask them what makes the South what it is."

Mary Hood offered this hypothetical illustration of Reed's point when she demonstrated the distinctive way in which southerners approached the question of identity:

Suppose a man is walking across a field. To the question "Who is that?" a Southerner would reply by saying something like "Wasn't his granddaddy the one whose dog and him got struck by lightning on the steel bridge? Mama's third cousin—dead before my time—found his railroad watch in that eight-pound catfish's stomach the next summer just above the dam. I think it was eight pounds. Big as Eunice's arm. The way he married for that new blue Cadillac automobile, reckon how come he's walking like he has on Sunday shoes, if that's who it is, and for sure it is." A Northerner would reply to the same question (only if directly asked, though, never volunteering), "That's Joe Smith." To which the Southerner might think (but be much too polite to say aloud), "They didn't ask his name, they asked who he *is*!"

Finding such impressionistic evidence a rather flimsy premise on which to stake a claim to cultural distinctiveness, a number of external critics and even a few southerners themselves worried that the zealous insistence on the continuing significance of southernness had degenerated into an exercise in mythologizing and self-caricature. Certainly the outlines and features of the contemporary southern (and Georgian) identity were subjective and fuzzy at best, especially compared to the strikingly clear and starkly recognizable portrait drawn by Cash over fifty years ago. On the other hand, however, Cash's sharper imagery resulted in large part from his narrower focus—on the mind of the white male South, a mind clearly circumscribed by racial and sectional antagonism. In a changed Georgia, where the opinions of blacks and women mattered more and the question of race less, one was likely to encounter a more pleasing but also more confusing and, in some ways, no less schizophrenic picture. Along these lines, a recent *Atlanta Journal-Constitution* poll (including both black and white respondents) showed southerners listing both country music and the blues and Robert E. Lee and Martin Luther King Jr. as relevant symbols of their South.

This phenomenon was hardly new. Over the course of their state's history, Georgians have constantly revised and reshaped their identity, often embracing the symbols of both tradition and change as their own. For example, "I'm just an old Georgia Cracker" soon became a disarmingly self-deprecatory reference, and for years, the minor-league Atlanta Crackers were more than a minor passion for the state's baseball fans.

Tourists and newcomers to Georgia often expressed both amazement and dismay at some of the state's dietary mainstays, especially grits. Rather than apologize for this local delicacy, Roy Blount Jr. took the offensive, paying tribute to:

> True grits, more grits, fish, grits and collards,
> Life is good where grits are swallered.

On the other side of the ledger, despite their reputation for conservatism, Georgians were quick to incorporate into their culture any number of the changes that came their way under the general heading of "progress." The long-standing popularity of moonshine notwithstanding, Coca-Cola quickly achieved widespread acceptance as the state's beverage of choice, so much so that even when a thirsty Georgian intended to drink a Pepsi, he or she was nonetheless likely to say, "Let's go get a 'Co-Coler.'" Although tourists often joked about the prodigious patches of kudzu that covered roadsides and utility poles, abandoned automobiles, and vacant houses throughout the state, the fast-growing plant imported from Japan to combat soil erosion quickly took root as the state's unofficial vine. From one end of Georgia to the other, communities with no better premise for celebration or self-promotion sponsored annual kudzu festivals replete with bake sales and beauty pageants culminating in the selection of a kudzu queen. Poet James Dickey even saw fit to immortalize these fast-growing "Far Eastern Vines" in verse, noting that

> In Georgia, the legend says
> That you must close your windows
> At night to keep it out of the house.

First-time sojourners through the Georgia countryside might relate as well to these slightly altered musings of would-be poet Frank Gannon:

> What this is
> I do not know
> There is a hell of a lot of it [though].

Finally, its propensity for altering local economic and social patterns notwithstanding, Wal-Mart had become, for 68 percent of an *Atlanta Journal-Constitution* poll's respondents, "very" or at least "somewhat" important to their definition of "today's South." In 1993 another poll asked the question "When you think about what the city of Atlanta is noted for, nationally and internationally, what is the very first thing that comes to mind?" The most common responses dealt with associations (good and bad) that had been formed relatively recently:

Response	% of all responses
Olympics	28.8
The Braves	10.8
Crime	7.9
Business/Industry/Jobs	5.8

Compare these to the percentage of respondents choosing more "traditional" associations with Atlanta:

Response	% of all responses
Hospitality	3.0
Gone with the Wind	2.2
Southern/South	1.3

More often than not, rather than choose between old and new, Georgians opted to blend or simply juxtapose the two. Thus, an electronic message board at Atlanta's Peachtree Baptist Church recently read, "Being Born Again Means Being Plugged Into A New Power Source." In the mid-1980s, as I attempted to unravel the "enigma of Sunbelt Georgia," I noted the simultaneous popularity of "cracklin's and caviar" in a culturally ambivalent Atlanta where diners scrambled with equal fervor for tables at the ultra-chic Nikolai's Roof (atop the Hilton downtown) and the decidedly downhome Harold's Barbecue (near the federal penitentiary on McDonough Boulevard). A decade later, Nikolai's Roof appears to have lost some of its appeal (though only to a host of even trendier, more yuppie-oriented competitors), but a recent visit to Harold's reveals no such loss of luster. Indeed, the Formica is shinier than ever, and the cracklin' corn bread remains— pun intended—a heavy favorite on the menu.

As the twentieth century draws to a close, the cultural landscape of Georgia is a jumble of contradictions, contrasts, and peculiarities, a delight to observe, but a nightmare to analyze or even describe. John Berendt captured the insularity and eccentricity of Savannah in *Midnight in the Garden of Good and Evil*. Based on an actual murder case, Berendt's tale involved a controversial though socially prominent antiques dealer, a black transvestite known as "the Lady Chablis," a voodoo priestess, and an offbeat inventor who was obsessed with finding a way to make goldfish glow in the dark.

Georgia's musical scene remains both rich and diverse. Augusta is home to not only James Brown, the "Godfather of Soul," but internationally acclaimed mezzo-soprano Jessye Norman. In Athens the phenomenally popular R.E.M. quickly established the Classic City as a magnet for musicians and musical groupies from all over the world. Meanwhile, the Atlanta Symphony Orchestra long ago achieved international prominence under the direction of the renowned former conductor Robert Shaw and continued its reputation under conductor

In April 1995 Nobel Laureates of Literature met at the Carter Center in Atlanta at a gathering sponsored by the Atlanta Committee for the Olympic Games (ACOG) Cultural Olympiad and *The Georgia Review. Left to right, seated:* Claude Simon (France, 1985), U.S. Poet Laureate Rita Dove, Wole Soyinka (Nigeria, 1986). *Left to right, standing:* Octavio Paz (Mexico, 1990), Kenzaburo Oe (Japan, 1994), Derek Walcott (Trinidad, 1992), Jimmy Carter, ACOG President and CEO Billy Payne, Rosalynn Carter, journalist Ted Koppel, Joseph Brodsky (Russia, 1987), Czeslaw Milosz (Poland, 1980)

Yoel Levi. For Atlantans given to "lower brow" or perhaps "lowest brow" musical forms, there is the lively "redneck chic" scene in which young fans of both bohemian and preppy persuasion are drawn to Slim Chance and the Convicts, Redneck Greece Deluxe, and other groups who specialize in raunchy rockabilly interspersed with parodied renditions of country classics and bawdy uptown takeoffs on downhome humor.

Atlanta's commitment to the visual arts gave rise to the High Museum of Art, an imposing structure whose innovative and imposing architectural profile often competed with its exhibits for the attention of its visitors. Georgia produced a goodly share of highly regarded artists, none of them more remarkable than painter Benny Andrews, one of ten children born to a black sharecropper family near Madison (Andrews's father, George, was also a talented artist and his brother, Raymond, a well-known writer). Andrews's most highly regarded works present large-scale portrayals of black and white life in rural Georgia. As of the mid-1990s one of Georgia's most famous artists was the Rev. Howard Finster, whose rustic and eccentric creations reflected the influence of the divine visions Finster regularly received. A painter and sculptor, Finster adorned his work with scriptural admonitions and proverbs. Fittingly enough, in 1994, the High Museum announced the purchase of a sizable amount of Finster's work from his two-acre "Paradise Garden" near Summerville.

"GEORGIAN AS HELL"

As William Faulkner explained, true affection for one's homeland requires that we love not just *because* but *despite*—because of its virtues and despite its faults. Consequently, the two sometimes seem difficult to separate. Although most Georgians express great pride in their state's progress, many who believe that Georgia is leading the rest of the South toward the mainstream of American life also fear that their once-wayward state will emerge from this baptism cleansed not only of many of its sins but of some of its most vital and affirmative traits as well. In other words, they worry that the social and economic changes once thought necessary for Georgia's salvation may, paradoxically enough, actually wind up costing it its soul.

Such an outcome would be unfortunate, but it is not inevitable, and it certainly is not imminent. In fact, despite the almost warp-speed proliferation of strip malls and sushi bars, as well as a number of other similarly dismaying developments, a 1994 poll showed that, by a two-to-one margin over both Alabama and Mississippi, respondents both within the region and without thought Georgia was still the nation's most "southern" state.

Not all of today's Georgians might express themselves quite as unequivocally as the South Georgia tobacco farmer who informed a visiting journalist in 1938 that "we Georgians are Georgian as hell," but, on the other hand, a great many others—native and newcomer, black and white, resident and absent—not only care deeply about our state's identity but consider it integral to our own. With so many individuals and groups trumpeting their particular versions of what it means to be a Georgian and attaching great emotional significance to the symbols that seem to convey that meaning most effectively, spirited disagreement has been inevitable. Still, the fact that Georgians are now squabbling among themselves rather than doing battle with outsiders on this matter only underscores the significance of the changes that have come about in recent years. The current conflicts are likely to subside, however, only when more of us who cherish our identities as Georgians begin to realize that the legitimacy of this distinction depends not so much on our determination to claim it for ourselves as on our willingness to share it with others.

NORTHWEST GEORGIA

Mary Hood

TROPIC OF CONSCIENCE

Encroaching on primal societies, the explorer finds, indeed *brings,* a serpent in every "paradise"—which, always ready, has other serpents waiting there.
—Ihab Hassan

Ever since the angel stood at the east gate of Eden flashing that sword back and forth to speed Adam and Eve on their way, someone somewhere on earth has been grumbling, "There goes the neighborhood." More often than not the remark refers to falling trees, as much as to community values or standards. We no longer know paradise or wilderness except as a myth. Perhaps that is why we yearn for both, and why we raise such holy rows about endangered eagles and the Etowah snail darter. The fallen state of nature is coeval with man's; it has been downhill since the beginning, yet a view of Georgia from the air reassures both the champions of growth and the protectors of wilderness. Georgia is 70 percent forested and 60 percent urban, and most residents like those numbers; they add up, somehow, to 100 percent home.

Nowhere is the balance of "nature" and "man" more clearly defined than in the northwest section of our state. Any color map shows a cheering amount of green (the Chattahoochee National Forest's almost three-quarters of a million acres) and blue—quick brooks and creeks, moody rivers with their highs and lows, lakes and farm ponds, municipal impoundments, and massive reservoirs built for flood control and hydroelectric power generation. Most provide recreation as well. On this side of the state, west of the Blue Ridge Divide, the waters drain west and south toward the Gulf, into tributaries of the Toccoa (flowing into the Tennessee), the Coosa (into the Alabama), and the Chattahoochee (into Appalachicola Bay). The rivers and waters of Northwest Georgia bear witness to the wilderness history of the state in the Muskogean Creek and Iroquois Cherokee names that remain: Toccoa, Chattooga, Coosa, Etowah, Euharlee, Armuchee, Nottely, Conasauga, Tallapoosa, Tinsawattee, Oostanaula, Oockillokee, Coosawattee, Cartecay, Oothcalooga, Salacoa, Chickamauga, Connesena, and Coahulla.

All of these waters rise in Georgia; we receive no waters from other states. Though our streams and rivers flow outward, all rise from within the present boundaries.

In colony times, before there was a state, the lines were quite different. The British crown intended to support its claims all the way west to the Mississippi River. Earliest mapmakers had guessed at much, but managed to get "Georgia's" ridges and valleys in generally the right places, though the rivers were drawn tidily flowing in a north-south direction, so the maps look like a giant's plan for curbside parking, with the Gulf of Mexico as the sidewalk. At this point most of the colonists dug in along the coast. They weren't gazing over their shoulder for elbow room, resources, or markets. They were watching the sea for resupply, looking out for hostile nations, not hostile natives.

Meanwhile, bison—the quintessential "western frontier" beast— moved in great herds through these upland valleys, wallowing at the wallows and licking at the licks, calving in season and making tracks and trails through the gaps. At that time, Georgia was all frontier; true west began a musketshot beyond the tidal pools on the Atlantic coast. When the Europeans sank acquiring fingers into their first buffalo pelts—hospitality gifts of natives—they luxuriated in the "fleeces" with shrewd but ignorant pleasure. If they did not understand what manner of beast they were dealing with, the buffalo did. They left through the gaps, westward, and some of the natives followed them. Others stayed. And others came along to take their place and chances.

Trade developed between the natives and the coastal residents. By the 1740s and 1750s northern pressure from the European colonists pushed the Cherokee further south and west from the Carolinas, causing boundary disputes and battles with the Creek and Choctaw, whose traditional hunting lands and resources had become stressed from years of overhunting for deerskins to trade to the coastal colonists. After the battles, the boundary lines were always settled along watercourses. The white-tailed deer became depleted in the 1700s with the turn of hunting economy from subsistence to profit. The European traders priced everything in so many skins. As these traders saw the deer dwindle, they began to deal in dearer plunder, intriguing with the coastal planters whose labor-intensive crops of rice, cotton, cane, and indigo required more manpower than the colonists had available.

Traders now offered human beings, either using them directly as trade goods along the coast in colonies where slavery was not forbidden (as it was in Georgia in the beginning) or to sell to the Caribbean planters wherever they could bring a price. The Creek, who had had a tradition of warring only for cause and only until one of their men died—when they considered the battle settled—now began to pick fights simply to take prisoners to barter for manufactured items at the trading posts. They swapped hostages for black powder and weapons, food items, European finery, shoes, calico. Cloth was needed, since the supply of deerskins could not be relied on for clothing. They had to purchase food because their agriculture could no longer support them; the lands were disputed, and their farmers either warring or hostage. For the native people, their culture in upheaval and their numbers decimated since the mid-1500s when DeSoto and his men introduced new weapons and diseases, the trading post system gave the death-blow to what had been self-sufficient native communities of hunting and farming with central granaries, social feasting, and distribution that honored the ideal of a common wealth. Stability within the remnant of their Mississippian Culture eroded as the methods of capital-ism—one man's making a surplus and using it for his own private ad-vantage—became generally adopted.

The wars went on for years, with various alliances and confedera-tions among native peoples and the representatives of the crowns of Europe. The groups pitted and vied, promised and forsook. The Chero-kee generally sided with the English; the Creek, whose traditional lands had been under pressure the longest, tried them all—English, Spanish, French—and if they became cynical sooner, who can blame them? In what is now Northwest Georgia, the Creek and the Chero-kee—in matters generally non-European, although expansion pres-sure as the wilderness opened to settlers must be factored in—warred until about 1755. After the Creek Nation lost the Battle of Taliwa to the Cherokee leader Oconostota, and receded south of the Chatta-hoochee, the whole northern portion of Georgia comprised the Chero-kee Nation.

Legend persists that these territorial matters were settled with a ball game. History argues against legend. No one knows. No one knows certainly where the final and decisive battle between the Creek and the Cherokee was fought, but tradition has been strong enough to focus in the Ball Ground area of north Cherokee County, near the Pickens County line. The state has erected a marker directing our gaze eastward toward "the confluence of Long Swamp Creek and the Etowah River."

Despite the fact that the marker is located in a town called Ball Ground, the marker testifies that final battle at Taliwa was fought, not played. Old chiefs in depositions on microfilm in the National and the Georgia Archives from the Office of Indian Affairs and the Cherokee Agency mention the peace, not the war, agreeing that there was a fifty-mile-wide "green belt"—where various bands could inter-act, trade, or hunt without incurring war penalties. Neither group ever claimed to own the land. Ownership was foreign to them; land could not be owned. It was not ownership but freedom of passage that had to be decided. These ideas don't translate well, which may explain why one agent mentions that the Creek "loaned the Cherokees the land after the Revolution and finally let them have it." The fifty-mile belt lies between the Etowah's south bank and the Chattahoochee, the area that is under great pressure even today, being contended and settled as the "outer perimeter."

Although the marker for Taliwa stands in downtown Ball Ground commemorating what would have been terrible hand-to-hand battle, many of the Cherokee boundary (and other) disputes between "towns" within their own nation were settled in a more sensible way—by playing fierce winner-takes-all games of Indian ball ("little brother to war"), a forerunner of lacrosse. Their bottomland "play fields"—some plainly visible today though planted in crops, others overgrown now in trees—were all located along the watercourses. Water was essential to physical life but equally essential in ritual, for healing as well as in preparation for war and for ball play, during which the Cherokee settled matters of honor and romance. When the ethnologist James Mooney studied among the Appalachian Cherokee in the late 1800s, he discovered fourteen verbs for "washing," as well as sacramental respect for running water (all of the streams in the Blue Ridge are quick). Along its course, the Etowah River—in its floodings and deposits—had smoothed fine broad bottomlands, prime for agriculture but also for these ball fields and, later, for horse racing. Dog-sized equine fossils have been found in the state, but these were prehistoric; there were no such animals as we know them today. The first horses passed through these hills and valleys and struggled across the wilderness in the retinue of the Spaniards in 1540 as DeSoto plundered his way toward the Mississippi. It is said.

If historians, archaeologists, town fathers, and the DAR vary and differ, it is not on the fact that DeSoto was here, only on the possibility that DeSoto was *here,* that is, in any one particular spot where a motor court, gift shop, or picnic area with a bronze marker makes its traditional claim, "going for the gold" just as DeSoto did. Recent research and discoveries have redrawn the maps of the Spaniard's route, and like a river changing course, certain towns have been left high and dry.

For instance, on a stone plaque near the front door of the city auditorium in Rome, Georgia, the Daughters of the American Revolution in 1933 commemorated the coming of the "first white men" in June 1540 to the "fertile province of Ichiaha and the town of the same name" located "at the head of the river called Cosa," more than "fifty years" before the settlement of Jamestown, Virginia. In the words of modern authorities, *No way, José.* White men, yes, and black, also, for the Spaniards had soldiers, servants, and slaves of color. But this was *not* the site of Chiaha. Current research, local partisans, and continuing controversy have assigned Chiaha—one of the great towns of the Coosa people—its place as far south as Mobile and as far north as

Knoxville. It is generally believed however that Rome is the site of Ulibahali, a town where DeSoto carried the "detained" Chief of Coosa, took hostages and slaves in collars and chains, and commandeered anything those slaves could haul off from the ransacked granaries in late August and early September, leaving the natives nothing for the winter. This reality is a far cry from the DAR plaque's presentation that mentions that the Spanish were "welcomed by the Indian inhabitants, and where they dwelt . . . enjoying such hospitality, peace and tranquillity as they were not to know again upon this continent."

If "they" refers to "the Indians" instead of the Spanish, the plaque might pass modern muster. The truth is that DeSoto was such poor company that several of his own officers "vanished," and one, Francisco Rodriguez Manzano, a nobleman of Salamanca, went AWOL from Ulibahali on a wild grape chase. It isn't known—will never be known for sure—but it is possible that it is Manzano's sword found at the King Site, several miles west of Rome, in 1982. Perhaps he died of foul play; he well could have been murdered for that steel. Whereas in Mexico the natives had thought the horses of the conquistadors were gods, and had slain them ritually and in awe of the iron shoes which they then laid on their altars, in the Southeast when horses were taken in battle, they were despised as grain-eating resource-squandering prisoners of war and put to death at once, though they could have been used to barter and ransom captives. The Coosa knew from experience what to do with steel besides worship it.

Bone evidence in native burials throughout the South indicates that the encounters between the natives and the Spanish became increasingly inhospitable and violent. The accounts of the secretaries and clerks of the expedition afford wry and unintentional humor. The "gentleman of Elvas" wrote that when DeSoto arrived at Ulibahali (present-day Rome) he found a palisaded village, the first they had encountered. DeSoto advanced inside the walls with twelve cavalry and some infantry "and found all the Indians under arms, and judging from their manner, he thought them evilly disposed."

That idea is, in retrospect, a good but tardy guess, yet even if the Spaniards had been more prompt at interpreting the signs, they could not have had manpower or time to erect the line of boulders atop Fort Mountain that has been attributed to them. In the days before carbon dating it was easier to blame the Spaniards, either DeSoto in 1540 or Juan Pardo in 1567, for the piled stones (a few the size of compact cars) and dugout caves necklacing the mountain for 855 feet. The paths and the tower were built in the 1930s, by the CCC; that is a fact. It is also a fact that the mountain is 2,835 feet above sea level, but this fact, being geologic, will change over time. Mountains rise and erode.

So does fame. As for that, even now, when anthropologists have estimated the mountain's local-stone, unmortared fortification (or whatever it is) to be at least a thousand years earlier than the Spanish expeditions, some lamentable human tendency toward cultural boosterism persists in honoring legends of "moon-eyed peoples." Though the error persists, nothing in modern accounts or in the native remarks on record indicates any reference to blue-eyed or fair-skinned peoples. "Moon-eyed" may have indicated watchers of the night sky, perhaps implying some primitive astronomical use of the mountain's "bastions and pits." Such walls and pits are not unique in the southeast, but they remain everywhere unexplained.

Plaques at the site mention the Welsh Prince Madoc, who is supposed to have done so many things as America's first white man that he would have had to live here over three hundred years. Logic doesn't enter into it. Things are not always what they seem. The bronze historical markers are actually cast aluminum. Some should be cast down. One, installed by the state of Georgia near the stone wall in 1968, mentions that "some historians give a measure of credence" to the Prince Madoc origin of the wall, despite the fact that the historical Madoc came along—or didn't—a thousand years later than the building of the Woodland Era wall! But his eyes were allegedly the right color and shape, and Welsh pride (and the British crown's pride during the Age of Exploration) needed to lay a prior claim to the New World and finesse the Spanish. Welsh pride received its greatest puff in the twentieth century when a woman from Chattanooga published a fictional account of Madoc and the alleged landing at Mobile Bay with (according to a nineteenth-century romance) thirteen shiploads—as John Krich might put it—of tourists with no destination but distance, claiming everything in the wilderness and leaving evidence of nothing. One is reminded of Lord Byron's warning: "A book's a book although there's nothing in't."

We want to belong, and we want to last. One way to do both is to identify with great causes (whether winners or losers—heroes are what we hope for) and grand scenes. Being is only the first of belonging; the majority is longing itself. "We attach the thread of History to the place where the thread of our (personal) memories breaks, and when our own existence escapes us, we live in that of our ancestors," K. P. Moritz has written. Fort Mountain's improbable Welsh sailors, any of North Georgia's traditional "Indian princess" yarns, buried treasures (from the DeSoto era, the time of the Trail of Tears, and from Sherman's March to the Sea) all are great stories, and howevermuch they strain credulity and logic, some want to believe them, want to keep on digging, despite evidence of our senses and science, despite everything. As a bookmobile librarian from one of the area's remote routes said, "We wouldn't want to go back to early times, but they make good memories."

We are all newcomers to this world; it was made of sunstuff billions of years before any of us got here to homestead. We will never prove up. It is so hard to stand before the past and admit: We just don't know. At about the same time that Fort Mountain's historical markers were being cast, an expert, stumped, warned in the body of his report: "It is easier to say what this wall is not than what it is." Still, the legends endure. Despite those regrettable official plaques, there is plenty of room for doubt atop Fort Mountain. In fact, space has been cleared for busloads, for picnickers, for photo opportunity. We stand on the summit, aim and focus, casting our grain of salt to the winds. Every snapshot has to have its caption, and the word for caption comes from the word for grasp. We claim and name what we can never own—just as the Coosa did, and the Spanish, the Creek and the Cherokee. And just as they, we let go, and move on, reluctantly.

Perhaps the hardest thing to accept is that we must move on, that what we struggle to defend is as perishable as our own sweat. These arrayed stones and the empty pits remind us, mock us: Wilderness finds us, even when we do not seek it. Strayed things go wild, seeking the next generation. Gone things might as well never have been. The merest blind mole, tunneling by its inner light, freely trespasses below our strife-worn boundaries. Foxes trip across the dust of our lines fallen in pleasant places. Deer browse hock-deep in grass of our gone homeplaces. And the hawk's cry chills us as it freezes the rabbit in its endless trials. The stones of Fort Mountain, weathered but insoluble, draw their silent line on common ground, defending it past death, past comprehension. Only this much is mine, but mine forever, says the fool, forever.

Sooner or later, we do move on, in space or in time. Someone will come after us, because there is a future. We are not the point, we are part. Such a vantage, such a moment puts us in our place. Humbled, we are exalted; our view becomes a vision. For a moment, we have felt it—kinship with the ones who stood there before us—for whatever reason—and with the ones who will come after, whether they acknowledge us or not. We've come close.

"Though no two centuries are very much like each other," Eudora Welty has written in *The Eye of the Story*, "some hours perhaps, are; moments are; critical moments nearly always are. Emotions are the same. We are the same. The man, not the day, is the lasting phenomenon." The weathered summit of Fort Mountain is worth its legends; we learn that not knowing does not necessarily mean ignorance. Sometimes it means mystery. We go to see what we can see, but also what cannot be seen. We cannot stay, but we want this to last. "Let it be like this for the next ones," we pray. Seeing connections. And we wind back down into the valley that much larger, as though we had surveyed and battened on eternity. That is one of the things that wilderness—the green and blue places on the maps—can do for us.

What we can do for the wilderness is another question entirely. And that brings us, in every sense, back to earth and the mundane—though in no way mere—matter of maps. The hardliners who hold with the notion of nature "where every aspect pleases and only man is vile" find much to criticize in the view from the mountaintop. The valley has its patches and bald spots, its quarries, its subdivisions, neon, billboards, resorts (a kind of gold mine), and the manufactory haze and hum of the here and now. That, after all, is where we really are.

"You are here." X marks the spot on the map in the visitors' center at Etowah Mounds State Park in Cartersville. A relief map of Northwest Georgia in time-honored map colors (blue waters, green forests, and earth-colored fields) shows how the highways and rivers and railroads all took the easy route alongside or around the mountains. Here and there a summit or a cove or a crossroads has no color at all, the pigment and legends worn entirely off the map into its underlayment by the touch of pilgrims. "Here," they explain, pointing out where the old kingdom of Coosa is now drowned under the reservoir of Carter's Dam. And, "There," they say, following the rail line north from Kingston, toward Adairsville where the Great Locomotives chased. Some point out where they live, where they have come from, where they are going. Where the uncle fished up the hundred-year-old plow from Lake Allatoona. Where the car ran off the road after the prom. Where, shivering, they sang the sun up at Easter. Where they roast all night in the mill melting and coiling steel. Where the dog bows its head while the family says grace before meals. Where they're going to move when they win a million. Where they thought they saw the eagle.

Pilgrims have polished that map's mountain knobs like the toe of a statue saint. It looks as though there is a snow cap, or as though these oldest of earth's mountains were still rising, forcing themselves up white as bone through the ocher and pinegreen plastic surface. These hills actually did that once. More than once. Geologic forces and eons of rain have weathered them down from their former incomprehensible heights—miles!—which they surged up to when the continents clashed and broke. It's not over. Every gunite pool, See Rock City birdhouse, concrete curb jockey, eternal flame and VFW flagpole, every lifetime-guaranteed funeral vault, hummingbird windsock, deer stand, Swift Mart, gravel quarry, and burpless cucumber patch is on the move, westward, at the rate of about nine feet in the average lifespan. The Old World is slowly receding, drifting away

Artifacts from Etowah
Indian Mounds State
Historic Site

like Daisy's green dock-light at the end of *Gatsby*. You can't blame a traveler for putting out a fingertip to the relief map to steady up.

Geology texts explain things in cookbook terms, mentioning sinks and cauldrons, breaking and crushing, folding, mixing, dissolving, pounding, rising. They mention layers and crust and crumble. A major fault line extends from Maine down the Blue Ridge and under the floor of the Great Valley, down which, in Georgia, Interstate 75 runs. The fault veers west at Emerson and heads for Alabama. Earthquake activity along this fault line has included (but not in human lifetime) volcanism and folding, as well as various underground leachings and backfillings, subsidences, and surface erosions. In a core sample, then, you would not be looking at a linear history; time would be out of joint, eons shuffled like so many cards. Old rocks lie beneath younger. Under pressure, sediments from "the great shallow warm inland sea" have become stone. Pores and cracks have refilled, like cream puffs, with soft stuff—mineral-rich deposits—which have also hardened. Whole mountains have eroded away into the emptying valleys, all of it washing toward the Gulf of Mexico as the tide went out on that upland shore forever.

It is the oldest recipe in this world. The ancient founding of these valleys and ridges began when time began. There is fossil evidence here of the earliest life-forms on earth. This "new world" is not so new after all. When folks say "old as the hills," these are the hills they mean.

The mountains present the most basic obstacle to human travel; they are in the way. The valleys and their rivers offer passage out, and reason to stay. From the first, Georgia has been a place people and animals wanted to get through because it has the southernmost easy gap through the Appalachians toward the west. The first trails were game trails. Native trails followed the game. War paths took their own direct routes. The paths of peace were then as now generally the high road, two friends wide.

During colony times, the north-south route through the Appalachian backcountry was the Great Philadelphia Wagon Road, connecting Pennsylvania to Roanoke, Virginia; Charlotte, North Carolina; and branching in South Carolina, both prongs reaching toward Augusta, Georgia. There was no other road upon which anything but foot or horseback travelers could move. Nor was there a single accurate line on any map. In 1763 royal surveyors Charles Mason and Jeremiah Dixon accepted a commission, packed their transits, sector, and telescopes in a featherbed, and left England for the American field where they led thirty-nine roustabouts, rod and chain men, cooks and axemen, cutting a corridor thirty feet wide and in 1765 planting their "Post mark'd West"—milestone zero of the famous Mason-Dixon Line. It was the most accurate boundary mark made on the new continent at that time. In reality it was the simple boundary line between the colonies of Pennsylvania and Maryland, but in effect it would be the fault line upon which the nation would break a century later, deciding slave or free. The two men surveyed southward into the Blue Ridge Mountains. On their return, they replaced their wooden markers with stone and turned toward the Ohio. Their axemen had more than once threatened to leave because of rumors and threats of Shawnee war parties. In 1767 their native guides and guards warned them, "You go no further." Mason then recorded his final note on the journey: "233 Miles, 3 Chains and 38 Links from the Post mark'd West."

Just eight years later, in 1775, Daniel Boone led his party of thirty men southwest off the Wagon Road at Roanoke toward the Cumberland Gap, cutting the "high way" over which—by the year 1800—two hundred thousand mostly Scots-Irish pioneers would creak and rumble along at speeds of up to three miles a day. Their journey took months. This was the Wilderness Road, the first useable wagon road through the southern Blue Ridge. One branch of it forked southward to Knoxville. Knoxville and Augusta remained unconnected except by the native Upper Trading Path's numerous pedestrian windings through the Creek and Cherokee nations. It seemed an obvious step to connect the towns through Georgia. Perhaps to the Cherokee it seemed harm-less, or merely inevitable. At any rate, in 1805 they signed the treaty of Tellico, granting the U.S. government the right to build a federal road (today's U.S. 411) through their nation from Knoxville, Tennessee, south toward Ramhurst in Murray County where the road forked, one branch going into Alabama and the other east toward the Chatta-hoochee and thence toward Augusta and the fall line of the Savannah. The federal road followed the old trails, sometimes built upon them. Here and there modern roads (county maintained, state, and even the interstates) pass close enough to the old roads that the keen eye can still pick out the trace of embankment and bed, wagon-wide, where stagecoaches, turkey drovers, circuit riders, and whip-cracking ox-drivers burlyed and churned their way through the backcountry.

Then as now, settlements and towns built up along the highway. People were not only moving through on these roads; they were also settling. And they were unsettling. "This beautiful and beloved coun-try of the Cherokees is now passing into the occupancy of the Geor-gians. Our land is wedged with settlers and droves of land hunters, to which we daily cry, 'Robbers! Robbers!'" grieved the *Cherokee Phoenix*, January 1833.

The Creek had already moved south and west, but their people did not believe in selling land, and so when word of the United States' offer came to their "chief" William McIntosh, he managed to negotiate privately. For cash and other considerations, he sold the Creek lands. They no longer had any right to live in Georgia. After years of ces-sions, the councils became resolute; law among the Creek was well known—death (as justice) to any who sold away any more lands. Mc-Intosh settled his fate as well as his people's. Acting without their con-sent or knowledge, and as much on his as their behalf, he signed pa-pers selling all Creek lands in Georgia, for cash and considerations, the cash to be shared with his people, but the considerations for him-self: that the government of the United States set aside a private earl-dom for him, on the Chattahoochee. He had a plan. He had hoped that U.S. soldiers would protect him, but he managed to enjoy his home only a short time. The justice-dealers of his people found him, on what is called today the McIntosh Reserve, in south Carroll County. The Creek executioners allowed McIntosh's non-Creek family mem-bers and women to leave; the men were killed on the spot, and the fine log home burned. McIntosh's grave, on the site, for years had a plain unpolished boulder marker, but latterly, in recognition of his service to the United States as a soldier in the War of 1812 and in a Florida border skirmish in 1818 (with the rank of brigadier general) he now also has a marker such as any veteran is entitled to. The reserve is today a quiet place, a little eerie at twilight. Old flowers and gnarled trees necklace the homesite. The narcissus called by country women "butter and eggs" dot the meadow in spring. There is a small lake, and a sound of water rushing.

The Creek had followed the streams, had known the woodlands so well they never had to cross wide water. Those old trails had drawn the Cherokee along them, and showed the Europeans the way into the rich country of North Georgia. The European maps had been mostly of the coast, with the interior and native nations unmarked. Every foot on the land made a mark that the next seeker could follow. The land itself was the map. Early explorers' reports and knowledge were both so sketchy that it is not hyperbole to call any either fool or hero who came to investigate. "Some paths were found, but no one knew or was able to guess which to take," Rodrigo Ranjel noted in 1539 as Hernando DeSoto stared at the continent in bewildered surmise. More than two hundred years later George Washington complained to Congress that he was "obliged to make shift, with such sketches as I could trace out from my own observations and that of Gentlemen around me." The explorers and pioneers did what most people do, when lost—they asked directions of people from around there, and managed with what they got, just as Cortes, when exploring Mexico, had to trust a cacique's map made of calico.

Dense forests—the natural cover for the land east of the Mississippi—prevented close mapping. An early surveyor (1775) disclaimed, "every where covered with woods . . . no Churches, Towers, Houses or peaked Mountains to be seen from afar, no means of obtaining the Bearings or Distances of Places, but by the Compass, and actual Mensuration with the Chain." Errors crept in, especially in iron-rich areas that could deflect the compass needle. That, and other surveying errors, for years left the state line in dispute between Georgia and Tennessee. The issue has been settled recently—although decriers of billboard kitsch may not think so—in Georgia's favor. Diehard Tennessee partisans still feel that Rock City (and the locomotive General) belong in Chattanooga. Habitual boundaries and the legal do not yet congrue.

Before there were any cadastral boundaries at all, before a surveyor could demand and receive forty pounds of prime leaf tobacco for pinning down the European colonial claims at the corners, when the "earth-apple" globe still *had* dark corners, "the South already existed," as Alan Gallay points out in his introduction to *Voices of the Old South*. The South may have been "discovered" and mapped and claimed and settled by the Europeans, but it wasn't invented by them. The land and climate of the Northwest Georgia region has tended to shape the people and their choices, from the earliest humans thousands of years ago, enjoying the post-glacial climate that fossil evidence shows to have been cooler in summer and warmer in winter, allowing species that are now found only in South America or in the boreal forests, including the Beautiful Armadillo and the Noblest Chipmunk. Today's current migrant irruptions from the snow and rust belt into the sun are but the latest in a long history of migration and accommodation, from the first people, to the latest with their U-Haul or their Mayflower backing into the drive, so busy planning how to change the South into "home" they don't notice how the South is changing "them" into "us."

"Welcome to Georgia" the sign at the border says. "We're glad you've got Georgia on your mind." That wasn't exactly how the Cherokee phrased it, although their traditional greeting was something like, "You have come, it is good," or just "good." *Asiyu.* From the first, the Cherokee tried to believe that. In their early encounters with Europeans, they had noticed how the white men wrote words. These "talking leaves"—documents and treaties on paper—mystified and seemed magic to the Cherokee. They also noticed how the "talking leaves" sooner or later seemed to speak to the white man's advantage. However civilly they were worded, the event was the same: In the century before Removal, the Cherokee signed thirty-seven treaties. All thirty-seven began with the words, "a tract of land ceded to. . . ." They wanted to be able to do this—to make paper leaves talk—and Sequoyah, one of the great geniuses of language, without being able to read or write English at all, figured out in the early 1800s how to "leaf talk" in Cherokee. This required a new alphabet or syllabary. Sequoyah worked out a syllabary. A syllabary is not precisely an alphabet, but is rather a group of symbols each representing a sound, or syllable, of the spoken language. Once the symbols for the sounds are learned, anyone who can speak the language can read it. Sequoyah decided to print his own newspaper, but he needed readers. He had, of course, to teach them how. His daughter was his first student and had mastered the written language by age six, but Sequoyah's own people did not believe in him, or apprehend the power of his invention till he showed that his own little girl could "hear" the leaves and make them talk.

In the Henderson census of 1835, reports of the Cherokee villages showed that as many as one in four natives were literate in Cherokee. They did not, however, learn to read English. They did not think they needed to; they had their own newspaper and press, their own constitution, and their own courts. They had even won acknowledgment of the right to their own national existence from the Supreme Court of the United States. But within ten years of the watershed moment when Sequoyah's daughter read to the assembled leaders, the Cherokee nation had discovered that leaves and leaders didn't always talk true, and the nation was on its way to Oklahoma over the Trail of Tears, moving westward in winter through hunted-out territory, along the way passing through the camps and villages of some of the Creek who had been driven out only a few years before. They left behind, some would say, everything. Many, who resisted, had been arrested in their own homes, others run down in the fields where they fled. Few had time to settle their affairs or to pack, or even to sweep the cabin and burn the broom for luck. In some instances white settlers moved right in, before the fires went out. In other towns the cabins and orchards went to utter ruin. All over the mountains there remain in sheltered coves "Indian peach" trees, remnant of the diaspora.

Scarcely twenty-five years after Gen. Winfield Scott and his troops "escorted" the Cherokee west to Oklahoma Territory, federal troops again marched into Northwest Georgia. Another war. The nation watched as the troops gathered at the top of the geographic hourglass north of Dalton. The hourglass pinched between Resaca and Allatoona Pass, on the Etowah. Time was running out for the Confederacy. Sherman called the Etowah the "Rubicon of Georgia"; he would cross it. The autumn before he did, South Carolina's Charleston *Daily Courier* in an article headed "The Western Situation" reported—on September 17, 1863—that firing had been heard near Summerville in Chattooga County. Nathan Bedford Forrest could roar, "No, Goddammit, no!" as often as he pleased; he couldn't stop the Northern army, not for long. Neither could General Bragg.

At Chickamauga, which kindly historians refer to as "a bungled Confederate victory," we can see firsthand that the land heals before the people do. In fact, any comparison of geologic versus human cataclysm shows a plain fact: Nature may be catastrophic, inconvenient, or just plain horrible, but nature is never—as man is—inconsiderate and intentional. Perhaps that is why we call natural disasters "acts of God"; and war, hell.

A site interpreter at the Chickamauga National Battlefield Park (America's oldest and largest) explains that the cedar groves and thickets on the day of the battle in 1863 looked like open field, shot up and shot down, adding their pungent new-pencil fragrance to the smoke and blood of the day. The groves and glades have come back, dense and sweet and clean. All over the limestone country of the uplands there are cedars, but these are special. In Georgia, only at Chickamauga do such aboriginal cedar glade ecosystems still exist, preserved accidentally by the park perimeters themselves. If those interested in preserving the battlefield had not persuaded the government to create and set aside the park, the glades would be as gone from Georgia as the Cherokee, buried by progress (a great epitaph for Peace).

In China, maps were sometimes made of silk. One such map from Hunan offers explicit and sad details of a twelve-year war: "35 families [in village] all moved away" and "108 families, none back" and the simple stark desolation of "now nobody." On first reading we may think of the Cherokee villages, plundered and confiscated; that was a

THE TRAIL OF TEARS

When the first European settlers came to Georgia with Oglethorpe, they negotiated a land treaty with the local Native Americans. When Georgians desired more land, they negotiated new treaties, some legal and some not. These treaties forced the natives to keep moving westward. For a hundred years this process of moving the natives west—to the Oconee River, the Ocmulgee, the Chattahoochee—continued. The Creek Indians were completely removed from Georgia in the late 1820s. Only the Cherokees remained. White Georgians desired their productive farmlands, extensive plantations, prosperous businesses, and the gold discovered in Dahlonega. With the support of Pres. Andrew Jackson, Georgia's leadership began to survey Cherokee lands and give them away by lottery in 1832.

Under Principal Chief John Ross, the Cherokees fought for their nation through the proper legal channels—the U.S. legislature and Supreme Court. Yet as the situation grew more difficult and Georgians began to forcibly remove the Cherokees from their homes, a small group of Cherokees decided they would negotiate a removal treaty for their people. Led by Major Ridge, his son John, and his nephew Elias Boudinot, the Treaty Party signed the Treaty of New Echota in December 1835.

Although the treaty was considered fraudulent by Ross, the official Cherokee government, and the majority of the Cherokees, the U.S. Senate ratified it by a one-vote margin in May 1836. For the next two years the Cherokee government tried but failed to legally resist the treaty's implementation.

In the spring of 1838 Gen. Winfield Scott and U.S. troops moved into Cherokee territory to remove the people. Crude stockades temporarily housed the Cherokees with what few belongings they had time to gather. Extreme drought and subsequent low river levels delayed their departure for Indian Territory (west of the Mississippi River) until fall. As a result, at least four thousand of the fourteen to fifteen thousand Cherokees died on the trip from malnutrition, serious illness, or exposure to the cold and early snow. Translated from the Cherokee as "the Trail Where They Cried," the Trail of Tears was a tragic, devastating sacrifice of thousands of lives and a painful memory for the survivors who nonetheless built a new nation in the West.

—Alice Taylor-Colbert
Shorter College

Overleaf: "Guiding Light," by Cherokee artist Donald Vann

Chickamauga National Battlefield Park

war. But the Civil War also left its desolations. The term Reconstruction has a ring of hopeful hammerblows, of quick rebuilding and fresh paint. In fact postbellum Georgia—especially along Sherman's fifty-mile-wide sooty track in the northwest corridor—had all the cheer of a fire sale among bankrupts. Schools and mills and factories had been burned, the field crops and stores depleted from attrition and ransacking. Paper itself was at a premium. Many church minutes and business records were "lost"—either from burning or because the paper was used for other purposes. Some homes and churches were spared burning, to serve as headquarters or hospitals for first one side and then the other as the lines formed and gave way after Chattanooga fell and Gen. Joe Johnston began "one of the great retreats in history," heading for Atlanta and what the markers call "notable instances of heroism and disaster," with Sherman in tow. For about thirty miles on either side of today's Interstate 75, chimneys and foundations and the occasional steeple were all that remained taller than the scorched fields. One can explain the desolation there and then, but how, in the other places where cycles of human boom and bust have run their course in dozens of lost hamlets across Northwest Georgia? The wind blows across sedge-grown fields, and sparrows fly in and out broken windows. Trees grow into the light through sinking shingles. Rust-roofed gins from the 1880s, boarded-up homesteads and tenant quarters from boll weevil days, toppled factory chimneys and mine-heads, blank-glazed thread mills, steps and the collapsed coping of a ruined well, a ring of fine old shade trees and lilies and patent roses lost in brambles remind us that we are not all that is mortal, our life-work and our heritage can be disestablished as well.

What has happened? And who, seeing these evidences of hard times, would believe they signal "good news"? Yet demographic and economic factors indicate "progress" despite the many ghost towns and habitations for owls. After the First World War, there was a popular song, "How You Gonna Keep 'Em Down on the Farm (after they've seen Paree)?" After the depression and Second World War, the tune was the same but a slightly different lyric. "How You Gonna Keep 'Em Down on the Farm (after they've seen the farm)?" The per capita cash income in Georgia in 1940 was $332—57 percent of the national figure—down, believe it or not, $10 from the 1929 figure. In 1990 it was $17,045. Agricultural employment dropped in the 1950s, but per capita income rose to 71 percent of the national average. There's a clue. People have been moving nearer the towns where they could find wage work. Today, in the mid '90s, Georgia's per capita income is in the 91 percent range compared to the national average.

Newcomers and displaced natives who buy into the meretricious myths and southern stereotypes, tucking in to the grits and gravy at country (with a "k") gift and pit stops along the highways, sooner or later notice that the joke is on them, with interest, as the credit card bills arrive for their purchases of yeehaw gewgaw vulgarisms, Tara tureens, Belle Watling Madame Alexanders, postcard replicas of outhouse doors, snuff label coasters, pantyhose "tater" bins, hillbilly flashlights, granny fannies, leaking farmboys, birdbath bluejays, "fergit, hell!" license plates, concrete dwarves, and all those pig, duck, holstein, and Bulldawg mugmats, earrings, nightlights, slippersox, cast-iron Great Locomotive Chase doorstops, and Mayberry calendars. Giftshop corn isn't all it's cracked up to be. And it may be expressing something about the buyers besides their taste or wit. Anthropologists say we joke about what we fear. Perhaps northern transplants who buy (and send back to friends and family) images that are—in the final analysis—neither true nor positive may have a horror of assimilation, of being not merely lost in the "wilderness," but of being devoured. The superficial is a game of sight, not insight. When the newcomers learn where the stumps are, when they build a few bridges and sound the depths, they'll rest easier. And sooner or later they're going to wake up and smell the potpourri (peach and magnolia), and quit feeling superior to the people who were here before they got here and start feeling superb about those who are just arriving on the frontier. A few already have the hang of it. They have invested in some tatting and monogrammed drawnwork, teacups and sterling, Junior League recipes for chicken mull and teacakes and have opened a boutique of their own, selling to natives and newcomers alike genteel and gracious artifacts and calligraphed replicas with kinder, gentler mottoes such as

It's a Southern thing;
You wouldn't understand . . .

courting, in the surge of appreciation and uncaveated gentrification, a return to all the excesses of sentimentality and rank that Mark Twain skewered and roasted as "Absolute South," the lie that keeps on living and the cow that keeps on giving. Thus progress and nostalgia bring the circle full. And what it is full of is what makes the farmer's garden grow. Green.

Harry Crews has written that what the South has been obsessed with and haunted by is not race or place but the dream of neighborhood. "The entire Deep South and all its people were one enormous neighborhood . . . separate and distinct from the experience of other Americans," he says, regretting the loss of our ways, as though the social map had gone blank or been overwritten with alien legends, as well may be. We have the look of roses—or kudzu—that are looked at. "Now our manners are gone and our idiom turns up in the *Journal of Popular Culture*," and the South has been corrupted (by McDonald's and sociology) "all the way to quaint."

Some eroded small towns—and their uneroded "values"—are about to be "put on the map" again. Planned communities, gentrification, a theme park for Gone with the Wind, and the general population shift from north to south and from urban to exurban have given a boost to what may be a southern thing, but which seems to be simply human—the dream of functional families and neighborhood. Modern communications and transportation have made possible as never before city life in rural areas. The myth (of security) is as good as a mile. Not to mention lower taxes. But even in the areas where subdivided suburbia has not yet come, things have changed, our ways with our means. A bookmobile driver in a mountain county says that most of the children along the route do not use the service because both parents have to work and are away from home and children are in day care if not in school. "This is a rural rural area," he explained. Not long ago "rural rural" would have meant that both parents would be home, and the children also, working in the fields or woods; home and work were centralized around the family farm. Today, they work at the paper mill or in the carpet factory or sewing or cleaning houses for the subdivision builders or building the houses themselves. Or they drive a school bus or an EMS unit or commute across counties to work at the defense plants, or power plants, or in hospitals or the convenience store or sewing factory or in the quarries or mines. Or they are—as one country newspaper editor put it—"employed in public works"—governing, or guarding, or cleaning, or clerking, or reading meters, laying pipe, securing and maintaining the general welfare.

Some few—and it doesn't take as many, because of the machines and chemicals that seed, weed, and feed, hoe and mow, and even harvest—still risk pursuing happiness in farming. It's big business now. Plowing and other tractor work can be done from a climate-controlled cab, with tape deck, TV, and phone. More cotton is grown now in these rich bottomlands and valleys than in the days when cotton was king. Machines do the field work, stripping the stalks four rows at a time, hauling it to the compactors that press it into semi-trailer-sized blocks, and other machines haul it to computerized ginning and warehousing, though there is still plenty of back-and-brain trouble to be taken before the seeds rattle through the rusty duct across the lot to the seedhouse like hail and drop onto the two-story heap silent as snow. The gins still run night and day at harvest, and farmers must wait, but now they can pass the time at the Waffle Hut and hear it's their turn by pager-beeper.

Unlike the hunters and gatherers, the conquistadors and pioneers before us, we have not had to migrate to better times; they have found us. Change—like the road—came our way. Our isolation—which has been the Darwinian and chief factor in southern speciation—has ended; we are no longer separated from the rest of the nation. Improved transportation, equitable freight tariffs, radio and television, satellite communications, computer connections, local units of the state university system, and libraries in every county have done a number on Absolute South, and that number—whatever it is—is "parity."

The importance of railroad freight-rate parity must not be slighted, for the ICC's punitive inequities against the South after the Civil War worked always to keep Georgia, by artificial means, "extractive and agricultural," which phrase is the economic equivalent of barefoot and pregnant. It cost more to ship goods made *in* Georgia *of* Georgia's raw materials than it did to ship the raw materials alone. It was, in fact, ridiculously cheap to send raw goods north. It cost more to deliver goods (made of Georgia materials) within the state than it did to import northern goods made of the same materials that first had been shipped by rail north to the factories.

The system of unfair rates lasted almost a century. During that time, Northwest Georgia's human landscape could be characterized by unpaved roads, shoeless children, one-room schools, unpainted homes, privies, cottoned-out and sedged-over fields, and subsistence and tenant farm workers, or cottage industries such as chenille and home sewing. Wage workers not farm-employed had jobs in extractive industries, gathering or harvesting natural resources for northern processing and consumption. Because those items could be shipped at rates lower than other regions could ship theirs, Northwest Georgia's lumber and pulpwood, sand, gravel, coal, phosphate rock, fertilizer, ores of iron, manganese, barium, and ocher, as well as ceramic clay, baled cotton, pig iron, and cottonseed oil were stripped from the state with most of the profits going to the northern manufacturers and railroads. The freight rates for shipping were from 10 to 50 percent higher for cloth than for baled cotton, about the same rate higher for clay made into dishes and plumbing goods, and ingots into steel plates and tools. When the ICC adjusted the schedules—and not without irony on Memorial Day in 1952—the War finally ended, and true reconstruction began. Northwest Georgia's many natural resources—including the citizens—could at last be used to their fullest.

Dalton calls itself the carpet capital of the world, and the interesting story of how the industry grew from the cottage work of individual tufters who put their bright chenille-work on clotheslines in their front yards along U.S. 41 is preserved in the Crown Gardens and Archives in Dalton. In the beginning, the tufters dreamed up their own patterns, competing with each other for sales of their bedspreads and rugs and bathrobes and toys to tourists on their way to and from Florida. The clotheslines are in some instances still in use, but for yard sales and quilts; chenille has long since become automated, moving from the little houses by the road they renamed Peacock Alley because of one particularly common pattern with its rainbow of colors. The solitary crafters merged into guilds and—as technology learned to do what they had invented by hand—into mechanized workers in the massive mills of prefab steel and brick all across the valleys.

Innovations have helped keep the carpet economy steady through several booms and busts. One industry in Summerville recycles plastic soda bottles into polyester fiber, carpet fiber, and Super Bowl souvenir cups. County newspapers across the region all have help wanted ads; many run twice, once in English and once in Spanish with special days

Tufted textiles on Peacock Alley, 1940

when the interviewers *se habla*. There is plenty to do. Technical schools and the HOPE scholarships are helping supply skilled workers. Colleges both private and public offer opportunity for career development and placement. National and international investors have sited plants in the area, some with developing local management as well as workers, and others with imported.

Not all Georgians see technological and population growth as an unadulterated boon. Some regret the passing of the four-way stops—unlit by any blinking cautions—at country crossroads where brim-tipping and smiles and commonest sense and courtesy directed the encounters of friends, or if of strangers, with an acknowledgment that we are *all* strangers and pilgrims. But the four-ways have been widened to four lanes, no-nonsense balk-lines painted, with signals for turn lanes and the lights themselves wearing deep hoods to prevent anxious commuters from peeking, revving on orange to jump the green, eager for a split-second's advantage over other motorists and the clock.

Farms and orchards and landmark woodlands have been subdivided and named for the trees they replace. Where several generations of a single family worked the land for their living, now one generation of several families lives. Before the Second World War families looked forward to biannual court weeks and rare trading days in town, and once a year parents traced around their children's feet with pencil on brown wrapping paper, ordering-off for school shoes the rural mailman would bring in a twine-tied parcel from Sears.

Today's mall-shoppers have their choice—not only of shoes but also of malls with their infinite variety and throngs of others seeking. Yet newcomers and oldtimers alike may go hours in the crowds without meeting anyone they know. They swoop home through the drive-through, scooping up dinner on the run, sideslipping onto sideroads, and darting into their own lodgings like colonial martins each into its particular gourd.

Some companies relocating their workers from the North have filled whole blocks in the new subdivisions with "their" people who lockstep into the new enclaves and haunts like settlers circling the wagons before an attack. A couple of winters in the southern sun—you don't have to shovel rain—and their defensive perimeters blur a bit; they begin to unfurl and flex. They've brought their politics with them, and for the most part this means Republican. Some counties in Northwest Georgia still vote Democrat, but as one Paulding County newspaperman—who has seen it all, from the coming of the boll weevil in the '20s to the '90s remodeling of the cotton gin into a restaurant—says, "It's a matter of time."

There are a goodly number of churches—nondenominational, inter-denominational, congregational, connectional, Pentecostal, holiness, Saturday-sabbath and Sunday morning mainstream, backwater, quick water, stillwater, storefront, backyard, free-for-all, closed, open, brush-arbored, handlettered-on-campertruck, stained-glassed and bell tow-ered, mobile homed, double-sessioned, *en español,* in Korean, in sign language ("Sunday" is the same as "wonderful"), canvas-tabernacled, clapboarded and clear-paned, granite and gargoyled, tar-papered, shin-gled, or carven-stone—dotting the region, a southern phenomenon which in Northwest Georgia is as much a temperamental as political sign—of fierce independence and autonomy and yes, in some cases, crankiness—of the residents, as it is of religious fervor. In a recent census, there were twelve Catholic congregations and two synagogues in the fifteen counties of Northwest Georgia, and hundreds of main-line, slabbed-off sui-generic Protestant congregations. Some might call these evidence of organized religion. Others might call it a wilderness of steeples. All would agree they point toward paradise.

Corra Harris, wife of a circuit-riding hard country minister, be-lieved that the mountains and climate of North Georgia worked on the temper of the citizens. She found the Primitive Baptists of the backwoods coves had "honest, cold-weather spirits," taking religion "as the earth takes a hard frost. They freeze to Almighty God and lift their strong hearts like naked boughs to the inclement weather of this present life . . . and ask no softness of salvation." Records of charter and constitution mention Rules of Decorum, Articles of Faith, and Lists of those "lost" and "saved," "excluded," and—wryly—those "on committees." (Vengeance is mine, saith Nominations.) The congrega-tions chose locations near water, camping like Israel on its way to Zion. Many bear the name of springs and creeks, in whose currents they risked death for baptismal assurance of life in paradise.

"When the point of arrival is settled in advance, it exercises a gen-eral attraction, we desire it, it emits signs," Michel Butor has said, re-ferring to the subtle psychic and emotional allure of journeying. In the Tropic of Conscience called the Bible Belt, the signs are less subtle. In fact they can be billboard bold, actual and concrete. At times they have been actually concrete, although those roadside PREPARE TO MEET THY GOD cast cement crosses have either weathered away, been struck down by the hellbent, kudzued under, or collected by mu-seums. Once they were numerous as Burma Shave pickets. On the back roads, still visible, a few of the corrugated barn-roofing valen-tines holler

GET RIGHT
WITH GOD.

Someone has said that only in the South would there be a market for greeting cards with a picture of camel-skinned, locust-fed John, that voice in the wilderness. Inside, the message: "You vipers! Who told you to flee the wrath to come? Merry Christmas!" One reformed sinner called himself "Johnny Hell." His particular and not-so-peculiar mission was roadside rocks. Everywhere he went he painted the warnings. One, on an irregular stone in a U.S. 41 roadcut near Lake Allatoona, cried out

BE PREP
A RED
TO MEET THY
G O D.

Lorenzo Dow, the Audubon-era itinerant Wesleyan evangelist, passed through Northwest Georgia just after the American Revolution, traveling from Clarke County across the Cherokee Nation, over the Chattahoochee and into Alabama, with the word of God, a map, a pocket compass, and a parchment pass stamped with Georgia's seal. He started with an extra suit, a good cloak, a cased hat, umbrella, luggage, whip, socks and shoes, a watch, cash, and a good horse. He returned barefoot, cloakless, clockless, threadbare, and wrote in his diary that his hatcase and umbrella had been "spoiled by prongs of trees." He accepted no money along the way, fearing accusation of evil. If that was the gentle dove side of Dow, his wily serpent side told him not to disclose—among the predominantly Baptist crowds he drew—that he was Methodist.

"Denominational competition was keen," Alan Gallay has written of that era. If rivalries were keen, so was need. A "friend of religion" returning from a trip to gold rush era Fannin County reported "people not sufficiently interested in temperance." Andrew Jackson, having soldiered through Georgia on several campaigns, would have been glad to find such people. Obviously his unrelieved upland marches stayed in his memory; when he got to the White House he ordered taverns to be built every twenty miles or so along the federal road.

Before removal, Cherokee held the rights—in their territory—to run the lucrative inns and stage stops. James Vann, whose home at Chatsworth remains a marvel of federal culture, gained his wealth from federal road businesses including a tavern and ferry. He was by all accounts a shrewd businessman but a bad customer. He was drunk when shot from cover, killed at Buffington Tavern in Cherokee County, backlit in the door of his own inn. The log structure survives in poor repair in a pasture, but Vann's grave—he was buried near where he fell—is gone, lost in time. No marker remains. His monument is his home itself, and worth a visit in any weather or light.

Justice of the Peace, Dade County, 1940s

In a display case at the Vann House is a ring worn by Joe Vann, James's son, who left Georgia in the Removal, and prospered in the West, losing and gaining fortunes racing, betting, and drinking. His horse, Miss Lucy Walker, and his steamboat of the same name are legendary. One evening, warned his steamboat could not deliver any more speed in a race or it would deliver them to hell, Joe didn't think about it long. The ring survived.

The temperance wars went on for years. In front rooms all over the area, whole families "took the pledge," signing their names to the page in the family Bible, which had a pre-printed certificate for just such an occasion. Womenfolk—who could not vote till 1920 or serve on juries in Georgia till World War II—led the campaign for passage of the Act of Prohibition, and it passed the Georgia legislature in 1907. It put the legal distillers and vintners out of business and accelerated the era of moonshine. In Haralson County near the Paulding line, there is a monument of remarkably unvandalized marble—a thunderball-topped pole—testifying to another alcohol-related ambush and death. The memorial honors Alice Wildie Adams, wife of Rev. Robert Stewart. Born in 1888, Alice was "assassinated by Rum Runners at this Place" on November 13, 1924. There are houses around, some modest, some grand, others boarded up, but the village's stores have gone to ghosts. Twilight afflicts the pilgrim with poignant agoraphobia. One is reminded of the Latin word for wilderness: *solitudo.*

The town itself dwindled not from shame but in one of the general cycles of boom and bust the mining industry has known. When copper and sulfides were discovered near there, the hope was that the area would be "bigger than Ducktown" (the Tennessee Copper Company's mine across the Georgia line at McCaysville), so they named the new (and now fallen) place Draketown, bittersweet consolation to the boosters in their quiet tombs that the rival mines at Copperhill are gone now too.

West of Draketown, Bremen headquarters the Sacred Harp tradition in Georgia. Every week the newspapers across the region advertise conventions where fa-so-la or shape note will be sung. Poet Coleman Barks, a native of Lookout Mountain, calls shape note an Ur language: "The words [of the hymns] are sacred so they sing fa-so-la first to get the tune right." The singers square off, the four "voices" facing each other and the leader in the center. Everyone sooner or later gets to lead; no one hangs back. It is righteous to sing and to lead the singing; it is not "showing off." All the singers keep time, holding their black wider-than-tall hymnals in one hand and pumping the tempo with their other. In a full meeting the effect of the tradition's lydian modes and melody line in the middle, or "below" the other parts, is startling, primordial, thrilling. To the novice all the hymns sound like "Amazing Grace" except "Amazing Grace."

While the music lasts the Sacred Harp singers are Rembrandtian. One has the impression of chiaroscuro, of stopped time, and above all, of the faces of the singers, totally immersed, blending the sound— which hardly seems to come from them, so much larger it is and not of this world. It is a sound track, literally, across the wilderness. Sacred Harp tradition developed in the backcountry revivals of the Great Awakenings of the early nineteenth century where there were open-air meetings and no accompanying instruments. Shape-note singing required no long instruction. The results were so welcome that often people met to sing, even when there was no preaching available. Camp meeting and brush arbor homecoming singings developed in summer when the fields had been "laid by" (the last hoe work done till harvest time when the crops "began to move" in fall, first to barn and then to market).

All over North Georgia the campgrounds still continue the tradition. Not all feature Sacred Harp singing, which has for the most part moved into air-conditioned halls and sanctuaries, but they have still got the wilderness in their voices. As the times have changed, the shape-note family has diverged, one keeping the pure a capella fa-so-la tradition contained in the Sacred Harp hymnal. Sacred Harp singings "go by the book," its ancient songs so familiar that the leaders and singers make requests by number instead of title. The melodies have stalwart old-world place name titles, and the lyrics deal with dreadful hardships,

Sacred Harp singing, Holly Springs

farewells, havoc to wayfarers, loneliness and desolation, and holy manna in the wilderness.

The other branch of the shape-note family tree has gone modern, adopting piano, fiddle, guitar, and drums for accompaniment. This is the driving Appalachian southern gospel sound, more reedy and nasal, upbeat and peppy since the depression era, its pilgrim voices focused on heavenly reward; not just getting there, but getting theirs. The gospel conventions call themselves shape-note singers, but they use songbooks, not hymnals. The glorybound books are paperbound, small and thin, and at each convention old as well as new songs are performed.

There are no solos in Sacred Harp, the concert, the accord being the point, as though marching to Zion takes all there are of them and all they've got. On the other hand, the shape-note gospel singers offer solos, instrumental riffs and virtuosities, and above all, quartets, male, female, or mixed, performing in modern harmonies and modes.

Though integration has changed the complexion of school choirs, churches have for the most part remained ethnically discrete. Black southern gospel has developed its own tradition and conventions, its music with its own character, tempered by spiritual call and response, tempos, and harmonies. The distinctions between the black and white traditions are cultural and not denominational.

Homecoming and singing and dinner "on the grounds" has remained a part of community life at Chubbtown in Floyd County even though the town itself has pretty much gone. The church remains, monument to the dream of "a free black" named Henry Chubb who in 1865 purchased 120 acres of land for $7.50 per, staking claim (with his seven brothers) on a portion of earth as well as heaven. These were hard times, after the war. Henry and his brothers managed. They built and fenced and planted, and made a world.

Others fared worse. Did what they had to. Got by. Records show that a "former slave named Easter" contracted with a white man to hire out her son in exchange for "a fat hog" and some cash, and the boy's board for a year. Whites and blacks did what they could, including boiling the salt from the smokehouse dirt. New meaning to the phrases "salt of the earth" and "dirt poor." How welcome in Allatoona the wagonload of corn and salt from Jonesboro must have been a year after the end of the war!

Is it any wonder then that "paradise"—a garden with a wall, and wilderness beyond—haunts the music, hopes, and the landscape of North Georgia? Marquees-on-wheels remind travelers to "pray for the lost." Like hired hecklers at an emperor's triumph, calling "Look behind and heed that you are mortal!" the signs warn and harry. "Live each day as if it was your last. It may be!"

Howard Finster, the painter mechanic preacher visionary from Pennville, has been warning his neighbors and the world for years. "God Owns Space," his official postcard for Paradise Gardens announces. The motto is written under a stalking cat's neck—lion in the streets seeking whom to devour? Its eye, like the *annuit coeptis* eye in the pyramid on the U.S. dollar, stares wide open, unblinking, confrontational, and sure. That cat means business. So does Finster. His gardens are free, and like the way to Paradise, open with a door, with a maze. He has captioned everything; at his place, there is a lot to read.

Howard Finster in Paradise Gardens, Pennville, 1980

One must read the lot to catch the signs of the times. They are labeled by day month year hour minute and second, as well as the number of their creation, rather like a McDonald's sign:

HOWARD.s 1991 ViSiON. AND. 20.000.267—
WORKS. SINCE. 1976. THE. BiG. BOTTLE.
DONT. GO. WiTH. iT. ASK. ABOUT. THE. PRiCE.—

for example. He calls the gardens his "lifetime collection from two years old, one city block of one hundred thousand things known and unknown." His vision and whimsy peer out from every thicket and cranny, offer wisdom up from the paths underfoot, and in the bicycle-parts bower percolating wrens in its eternal twilight. God bless you all out there, he adds, from every available surface, including his camper truck and his vintage cars. "By Howard Finster, man of vision and God," he has written and signed with his Sharpie, getting the Word out on every smudge and fingerprint, seeing, he says, the faces of angels everywhere.

At the turn to Finster's Paradise, on the opposite side of the street, there is a business selling tuxedoes and tombstones. Early ledgers from Bartow County mention sales of "foodstuffs and coffins." Toward the Tennessee line there is a tanning parlor which also does deer processing. And if you need a lift, how about calling the Fire Baptized Holiness Church and Taxi Stand? Redundancy makes for clarity. At the outskirts to Buchanan an official green highway sign announces at the bridge that you are about to cross,

LITTLE RIVER
RIVER

and in Emerson, there is a remnant of the native trace labeled officially OLD OLD ALABAMA RD. There are also Old Alabama Road and Alabama Road, and if you think they'll get you to Alabama, try. There are as many ways of getting lost as found. Early settlers used to sew a special pieced square to their baby's quilt; it was called the turkey track, and it was meant to charm the child from wandering, getting lost in mountain thickets of rhododendron and "ivy" so dense and disorienting they were called "laurel hells." Not only children got lost in them, and adult survivors of their gloom staggered home changed, not always for the better.

For people who think it couldn't happen today, or happen to them, there is good news and bad news, and it's the same thing: There is wilderness left, enough to go around. Georgia's landscape, resources, and history are like a giant natural and spiritual Home Depot; over the door the legend in Cherokee: *Asiyu. You have come; it is good.* We need to know where we've come from to know where we're going. And we need to keep our eyes open whether we've been here all our life or have only recently arrived. In *Life on the Mississippi* Mark Twain tells of three indispensable survival skills for a river pilot: Pay attention, read beyond the surface, and be ready for change. If, as he says, one loses the romance of a sunset for the truth of its portent, then it is a fair exchange.

The native eye has a sure instinct for what is familiar, and for what is outlandish. A school bus driver plunged her Bluebird to a halt in Haralson County near where a car idled and New Georgia Guide pilgrims studied a marker. She reversed, backed up, and opened her window to call down, "You from Atlanta? I thought you were." And without further call or pause for credentials or explanation, gave directions to the Hungarian cemetery at Budapest. "I live just this side of town," she said gesturing toward Bremen. "Brick house on the right. You stop by and we'll talk sometime," she urged, and as she drew the window shut,—"My husband's people," she said—then drove on. The directions didn't seem so good at first, but then the cemetery miraculously was there, under a canopy of long-leaf pines, their cones big as pineapples wind-tossed down onto the graves and paths.

The white marble crosses stand out very stark against the dark pines and the depth of the woods. This was a people. A whole culture had survived transplant to this red soil to grow and make fine wines. They had come from Hungary to do so, two hundred families on two thousand acres, by the invitation of a local land developer. They named their villages here after their villages there—Tokaj, Niytra, and Budapest. They built good sturdy buildings, and some of their honorable stonework remains. When they died, they were buried here, facing toward their homeland. Buried in this earth they worked so hard to bring to life. All three of their villages are gone now, their enterprise and community ruined, unable to adjust when Georgia passed the prohibition law in 1907. The ones who left went north to work in the Pennsylvania mines.

Georgia maps still show the unlikely place name—Budapest—and there is a historical marker on the highway, since 1988, the centenary of their arrival. There is also a kind of peace, though it is a graveyard sort of peace.

Someone says, "The generations of man lap over like the feathers on a bird leaving no bare spaces." And that feels good to hear, feels right. It seems to be the very truth of the way the land survives and heals itself, from us and for us. The wind has shifted, and there is a chilly breeze blowing in from Alabama; a front is passing through, and the sky darkens. On the wind comes the sound of the traffic on the interstate. At first it seems to be a natural sound, only gradually drawing one's attention, like the wind itself; it seems not a violence but a flurry, just another sigh on the breath of time.

Jane Powers Weldon

TOURING NORTHWEST GEORGIA

The gentle contours of Northwest Georgia, terrain less rugged than the Blue Ridge mountains to the east, offer pleasing vistas of knolls and coves, mountains and lakes, and hiking trails to entice the modern explorer. Traditional travel patterns in the northwestern corner of Georgia are shaped by two topographical features, the ridge and valley section and the Cumberland Plateau, both of which cut diagonally across the state from Tennessee on the northern border to Alabama on the west. The region's distinctive ridges and plateaus provide long vistas from the roads across their heights and close views of rocks and vegetation from the routes that twist from valley to valley to span the mountains. The coves between ridges and peaks form a more intimate ambience of small farms, hamlets, and crossroads stores that have replaced rural post offices as gathering places for neighborly exchanges.

Early dwellers of the area were American Indians, whose melodic river names—Conasauga, Coosawattee, Oostanaula, Oothcalooga—prevail to this day. Wagon roads, then modern pavement followed the Indians' footsteps that shaped primitive trails along the high ridges. Today's visitors can wander those roads to explore mysterious mounds built by early American Indians, the later Cherokees' sophisticated villages, small farms that grew after the land lotteries, routes of Civil War battles and destruction, and twentieth-century monuments to past events or present pleasures. Along the way travelers will discover communities of handcrafters and folk artists, monoliths of modern textile manufacturing, verdant national forests, and evidence of attempts to repair the devastation strip mining and chemical manufacturing have wrought on the environment.

TOUR ONE

From the Kennesaw area take Ga. 92 and Ga. 381 to New Hope and Dallas; Ga. 61 to Villa Rica and Carrollton; U.S. 27 Alt. to Whitesburg; Ga. 5

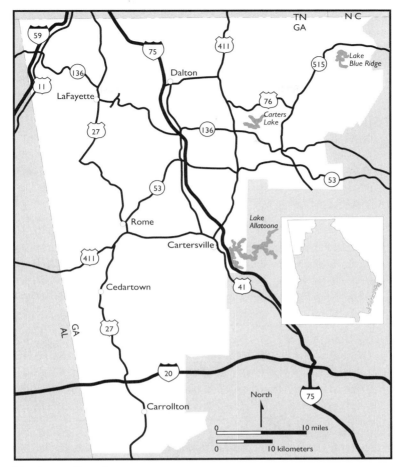

Northwest Georgia

*to Roopville; U.S. 27 to Carrollton and Bremen; U.S. 78 to Tallapoosa; Ga.
120 to Buchanan; U.S. 27 to Cedartown; U.S. 278 to Rockmart; Ga. 113 to
Cartersville; U.S. 411 to Pine Log; Ga. 140 to Adairsville; county road
627 (Hall's Station Road) to Kingston; Ga. 293 to the Cassville vicinity.*

The Northwest Georgia tour originates near Dallas, location of the
Civil War battles of New Hope Church, Pickett's Mill, and Dallas. Ga.
92 and Ga. 138 lead there to the south from U.S. 41 near the Kennesaw Battlefield. Brown highway signs point the way to Pickett's Mill
State Historic Site on Mt. Tabor Road. The Pickett's Mill Site, where
the battle is reenacted each year in late May, is said to be one of the
best-preserved Civil War battlefields in the nation. Interpretive exhibits and directions for hiking the battlefield are available at a visitors'
center. A depression-era Works Progress Administration (WPA) road-

ie park and historic markers at New Hope give an overview of action the vicinity, where, from May 25 until May 28, 1864, Confederate troops held the line against Federals moving toward Atlanta.

In and around **Dallas**, the county seat of Paulding County, are High Shoals Falls, public golf, and the Southeastern International Dragway. South of Dallas, near Villa Rica and I-20, are several overnight accommodations and restaurants.

From Dallas, Ga. 61 leads south to **Villa Rica**, named for the vein of gold discovered before the city and county were established. One of the oldest towns in western Georgia, Villa Rica long had the reputation of being a rough and rowdy mining town but today is a tranquil strip of brick storefronts along the railroad. It was the home of Thomas Dorsey (1899–1993), first a blues writer and performer with Gertrude "Ma" Rainey and later composer of "Peace in the Valley," "Take My Hand, Precious Lord," and other popular gospel songs. A state historical marker commemorates his career, and Mount Prospect Baptist Church, founded by his kin, has a museum room that includes material on Dorsey.

From Villa Rica, Ga. 61 proceeds south to the Carrollton bypass, from which U.S. 27 Alt. continues to **Whitesburg** and Ga. 5W, the road to the McIntosh Reserve. About 2.5 miles west of Whitesburg, a small sign points to the left. On the banks of the Chattahoochee River is the McIntosh Reserve, a Carroll County park with "passive" recreation facilities on land once a plantation owned by Chief William McIntosh. McIntosh's father was a Scot; his mother, a Creek Indian. William McIntosh was chief of the Cowetas, a Creek subtribal group. Outraged Creeks killed him on April 29, 1825, for betraying them when he signed the Treaty of Indian Springs that ceded all Lower Creek lands. He is buried across the road from a two-story dogtrot log house, moved to the park from Centre, Alabama, but believed to be similar to McIntosh's home, which was torched at the time he was killed. Southeastern Indians demonstrate traditional skills at an annual festival in the park the last weekend in October. The park includes hiking trails and weekend primitive camping.

The drive from Carrollton to the McIntosh Reserve and back traverses lands that in the late nineteenth century were cotton farms. Mills grew from the abundance of cotton, and textiles are still a prominent industry in Carroll and neighboring counties. The direct return route to Carrollton is by way of U.S. 27 from **Roopville**. An alternative is to continue westward from Roopville on Ga. 5 and north on a county road to **Bowdon**, once called the Athens of the West because of a small state college that existed there until the depression. On the outskirts of Bowdon, a roadside sign in 1994 read "Welcome to Bowdon, established 1853, population 1853." The Bowdon Area Historical Society has produced a walking tour that includes a few Victorian- or

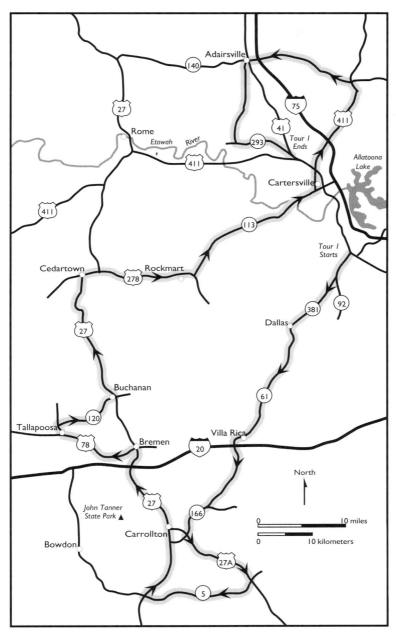

Northwest Georgia, Tour One

Queen Anne–style buildings, one of them a bed and breakfast inn. Most structures were built after a tornado destroyed a large part of the town in 1934. Ga. 166 east returns to **Carrollton**. One approach to John Tanner State Park (see below) leads north from Ga. 166.

Sacred Harp, traditional shape-note congregational singing once widely enjoyed, is enthusiastically and actively preserved in the South. The National Sacred Harp Foundation's headquarters and museum (see appendix) are in Carrollton, and "singings" are held regularly in many towns.

Carrollton is home to West Georgia College and a historic district of well-preserved older residences. The local historical society provides a walking tour of the Intown South Historic District, and the chamber of commerce publishes a visitors' guide listing points of interest. Kennedy Chapel on the West Georgia College campus was named for Pres. John F. Kennedy and dedicated by Attorney General Robert Kennedy, his brother. John Tanner State Park, northwest of the city, has a lake, camping, and other overnight accommodations.

Bremen, in Haralson County on U.S. 27, is a clothing manufacturing center; some plants here and in other area towns offer true factory outlet stores. In **Tallapoosa** (once called Possum Snout), west on U.S. 78, is a cooperative gallery displaying the art of several area residents, including that of Leroy Alman. The West Georgia Museum depicts small-town life at the turn of the century, displays a local taxidermist's craft, and contains artifacts of Creek Indians who lived along the Tallapoosa River. Nearby **Buchanan**, the county seat, boasts a Queen Anne–style former courthouse, built in 1891–92, owned by the local historical society, and listed on the National Register of Historic Places.

U.S. 27 continues north to Cedartown and Rockmart. The Polk County Chamber of Commerce provides a driving tour brochure for the vicinity. In **Cedartown**, the county historical society's building, begun as a children's library in 1921 and now used as a museum, was designed by noted Atlanta architect Neel Reid. Cedartown's Big Spring, covered to protect the municipal water supply, once drew Cherokee and white settlers to the area. The town owes its name to the many cedar trees, indicating limestone deposits, in the surrounding valley. (See Cave Spring, below.)

Cedars and fields of grazing cattle are typical sights on the farms along Morgan Valley–Antioch Road or U.S. 278 to **Rockmart**, where the terrain becomes more hilly. Near Rockmart in earlier days slate was quarried, bricks were made, and iron and gold were mined. Consequently, many structures in Rockmart are built of local slate and brick. The post office houses a New Deal mural, "Kiln Room, Cement Plant," painted in 1941 by Reuben Gambrell for the U.S. Treasury Department Federal Section of Painting and Sculpture.

From Rockmart, Ga. 113 leads to Cartersville. Off that highway to the north is the village of **Euharlee**, where there are a country store and covered bridge (1886). Reputedly the oldest in Georgia, the bridge is clearly visible, but access may be restricted. At **Stilesboro**, where the Stilesboro Academy (1859) is picturesque but not open to the public, Union forces stabled horses in the academy during the Civil War.

Cartersville, the seat of Bartow County, is called a historic crossroads community because of several notable sites in the area. Many are described in a brochure and map distributed by the Cartersville-Bartow Tourism Council; the map is recommended for touring the interesting but sometimes remote sites in this county. South of town the Etowah Indian Mounds, a National Historic Landmark and state historic site with museum interpretation, were the ceremonial center of the largest Indian settlement in the Etowah Valley from A.D. 1000 to 1500. At one time as many as three thousand Mississippian Culture natives lived near the mounds.

More recent mounds and water-filled excavations in the county indicate former strip mining and quarrying for abundant mineral deposits. The slag heaps are being covered by kudzu, a fast-growing vine that is flourishing green in the summer and a mass of gray tentacles in the winter. Beneath the kudzu, Georgia's notorious red clay appears reddest of all in Bartow County.

Civil War sites include the Battle of Allatoona Pass, where trenches and gun-ports are still evident; a monument to an "unknown hero"; Confederate cemeteries at Cassville and Kingston; and a lone chimney evident where Cooper's Furnace iron works in the nineteenth century weekly turned out twenty to thirty tons of pig iron. The iron works

Yarn Dyer, Cartersville

were a part of bustling Etowah, a milling and manufacturing center almost totally destroyed by Sherman's troops during the Civil War. What wasn't ravaged by fire met its end in flood when the Army Corps of Engineers built Allatoona Dam and the rising waters covered the village's remains. A railroad trestle over the Etowah River near the furnace was burned and rebuilt six times during the Civil War. The bridge's pilings are visible in the water near Riverside Park, beside the U.S. 41 bridge.

In Cartersville the Etowah Arts Council holds changing exhibits, and a cooperative gallery sells clay works, baskets, paintings, and other works of local artists and artisans. North Georgia traditionally has nurtured dynasties of potters; one is the Gordy family. Near Cartersville the late William B. Gordy operated a kiln now used by his grandson, Darrell Adams.

The Bartow History Center documents the county's past with exhibits on Cherokee lands, pioneers and plantations, home and farm life, and the Civil War. The first outdoor Coca-Cola sign (1894), carefully preserved, adorns a wall of Young Brothers Pharmacy in downtown Cartersville. Roselawn, open to the public, is the restored home of turn-of-the-century evangelist Sam Jones, who began his ministry preaching as a Methodist circuit rider and ended it with a sophisticated, rousing delivery that modern television evangelists would envy. North of the city, to the west off U.S. 41 at **Cassville**, stands Noble Hill–Wheeler Memorial Center, a black history museum and cultural facility housed in the first Northwest Georgia school built with Rosenwald Foundation funds for the education of black children.

Recreation possibilities abound in the Cartersville-Bartow area. Allatoona Lake offers picnicking, water sports, bird watching, hunting, fishing, and camping at several areas maintained by the U.S. Army Corps of Engineers. Riverside Park, below Allatoona Dam on the Etowah River, has picnic sites and a boat launching ramp. At Red Top Mountain State Park and Lodge, on the lake, are a lodge and restaurant, campsites and cottages, hiking, swimming, picnicking, miniature golf, tennis, fishing, and boating. The park and commercial resorts in the area rent boats. For an overview of the lake and dam, exhibits at the Resource Manager's Office and Visitor Center describe the archaeology, early settlers and development of the area, recreation, and the dam's construction. On weekends a soaring club at Etowah Bend Airport offers demonstration flights for the general public. One of many restaurants in downtown Cartersville is the tiny Four-Way Lunch, a local institution.

On U.S. 411 north, William Weinman Mineral Museum, named in honor of a pioneer in barite mining in Bartow County, educates visitors about earth sciences, rocks, minerals, fossils, and gemstones, especially the rich mineral deposits in the earth around Cartersville.

Barnsley Gardens,
Woodlands

Those interested in minerals, geology, and caves in the vicinity can obtain more information and directions at the museum. Automobile aficionados may want to visit Old Car City U.S.A., also on U.S. 411 north of the Weinman Museum. Farther north on U.S. 411, **Pine Log** United Methodist Church (1842) and campground are just west of the highway, under a rail overpass and near the site of an early Indian trail crossing. In an open-sided tabernacle, descended from leafy shelters called brush arbors, church families and friends have gathered annually for over a century for a week-long religious revival. (See "protracted meetings" in Northeast Georgia tour.) The narrow valley with parallel roadway and rail bed is a reminder that this area's topography was favorable for strategic strikes at the Western & Atlantic Railroad during the Civil War.

From Pine Log, Ga. 140 leads west to **Adairsville** and, close by, Barnsley Gardens. Adairsville includes a 170-acre commercial and residential section listed on the National Register of Historic Places. Its town center, a few blocks from the main highway, remains a bucolic collection of turn-of-the-century shops and a church. At the depot in 1862 the locomotive Texas joined the northward pursuit of the General during Andrews's Raid.

Hall Station Road, left off Ga. 140 west of town, leads south to Barnsley Gardens Road, well marked by signs. Englishman Godfrey Barnsley in the 1840s built a twenty-four-room house for his bride and laid out extensive gardens in a naturalistic English landscape style. Today the main house at Barnsley Gardens is a picturesque ruin, but under the ownership of a Bavarian prince and his wife, the gardens have been extensively renovated and replanted. Several other buildings are being moved to the grounds, which now have, in addition to the gardens and ruins, a museum in the original kitchen and service wing, gift shop with snack bar, restaurant, and garden shop selling heirloom plants and rare books on gardening in Georgia.

Each spring in its Confederate cemetery **Kingston**, to the south, holds a commemoration publicized as the nation's oldest Confederate Memorial Day. The Kingston History Club Museum is open only by appointment (inquire locally). There is another Confederate cemetery east of U.S. 41 in Cassville, a crossroad that was once among the region's largest settlements. U.S. 411 travels west to Cave Spring and the beginning point for tour two.

TOUR TWO

From Cave Spring, take U.S. 411 north to Rome; U.S. 27 to Mount Berry and Summerville; Ga. 48 to Cloudland; Ga. 157 and 136 to Trenton [alternate from Cloudland: Alabama 117 to U.S. 11; U.S. 11 to Trenton]; backtrack on Ga. 136 or 193 to LaFayette; U.S. 27 to Chickamauga, Ft. Oglethorpe, Rossville, and Chattanooga; Ga. 189 to Lookout Mountain; backtrack through Rossville to Ft. Oglethorpe; Ga. 2 to Ringgold (continue to Ga. 71 for Red Clay); U.S. 41 to Tunnel Hill and Dalton.

The second tour begins southwest of Rome in Floyd County at **Cave Spring**, which is easily reached by U.S. 411 from the Cassville vicinity, at the end of tour one, or from Cedartown, about midpoint in tour one.

Cave Spring is a small town that for years has remained basically unchanged. Since the Georgia School for the Deaf, founded in 1846, moved to a rural campus, the school's decaying old buildings have been deserted except for one used by the town government. The school's original administration building functioned as a field hospital for both Confederate and Union troops during the Civil War. In Rolater Park, the buildings of Cave Spring Manual Labor School (1839) and a small Baptist chapel are better preserved, and one, Hearn Academy Inn, is a bed and breakfast inn.

A natural limestone cave in the park is open during the summer. The large spring flowing from the cave feeds a swimming pool and supplies water for the town and a commercial bottler. About ninety Cave Spring historic buildings and sites, many of them craft and antique shops, are listed on the National Register of Historic Places. Because Cave Spring is near Cedartown (see above), trips to the two towns could be combined easily. From Cave Spring, U.S. 411 north toward Rome travels through Vann's Valley, a flourishing farming area

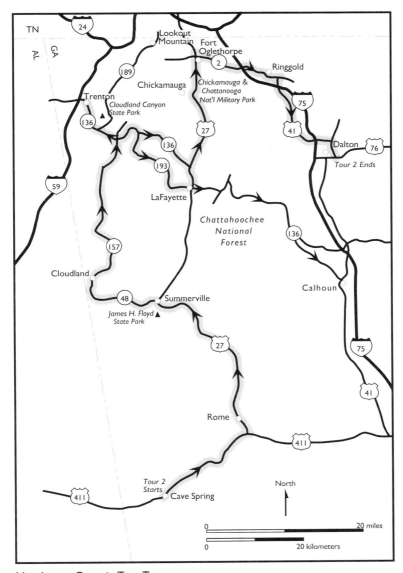

TN

AL GA

24

Lookout
Mountain

Fort
Oglethorpe

2

Ringgold

189

Chickamauga

Chickamauga &
Chattanooga
Nat'l Military Park

75

Trenton

Cloudland Canyon
State Park

27

41

136

136

Dalton

76

59

193

Tour 2 Ends

LaFayette

Chattahoochee
National
Forest

136

157

Cloudland

Calhoun

48

Summerville

James H. Floyd ▲
State Park

27

75

Rome

41

411

North

*Tour 2
Starts*

Cave Spring

411

0 — 20 miles

0 — 20 kilometers

Northwest Georgia, Tour Two

producing crops typical of much of the Georgia countryside. Across Northwest Georgia during the growing season, the traveler will see fields of corn, sorghum, soybeans, and cotton, which, after many years, some farmers are reintroducing as a cash crop.

South of the intersection of U.S. 411 and 27 is Floyd College, a two-year division of the state's university system. An optional side tour from the Floyd College area is a drive to Chubb Chapel United Methodist Church (open on Sunday only for regular services), a simple frame building that is the sole remaining structure of Chubb-town, a free black community established in the 1860s. South of Floyd College on U.S. 27, two right turns on Booger Hollow and Chubb roads lead through sparsely populated farms and woodlands to the chapel.

At a traffic light on U.S. 411/27 at the **Rome** city limits, signs point to the west to Lock and Dam Park, a recreation area where boaters have access to the Coosa River. Farther north, at the Darlington Drive–Old Lindale Road exit of U.S. 411/27, Darlington Drive to the west leads to Darlington Upper School, a private academy on Old Cave Spring Road. Old Lindale Road, to the east, proceeds to **Lindale** village and cotton mills, operating since the late 1890s. Across the street are a picturesque pond and mill, a National Register listing.

The Old Cave Spring Road to the right (north) travels to a light at Main Street/South Broad Street; a left turn leads the traveler directly into Rome. On the left before a bridge is historic Myrtle Hill Cemetery. Among those buried here, high above the city, are Confederate soldiers; Ellen Axson Wilson, Pres. Woodrow Wilson's wife; and Charles Graves, America's World War I "Known Soldier." Though Graves was killed and buried in France in 1918, his body was reinterred in Rome in 1922. Because he was one of the last dead to be returned after World War I, the government designated him its known soldier. The hill affords a view of downtown Rome, where the Etowah and muddy Oostanaula rivers join to form the Coosa, fleetingly half green, half ruddy brown. A marker at the foot of the hill commemorates the Battle of Etowah, fought in 1793 between Gen. John Sevier's troops and a thousand Cherokees.

The best course for exploring Rome from this point is to continue north through town and to turn left onto Turner McCall Boulevard. Shortly thereafter, the Greater Rome Convention and Visitors Bureau will be visible on a hillside just off the boulevard. The bureau, housed in a small depot moved from Reeves Station, Georgia, is open every day and provides printed or tape-recorded walking and driving tours with specific directions to Between the Rivers Historic District, Oak-dene Place Historic District, Heritage Park, Ridge Ferry Park, the Braille Trail in Marshall Forest, and other places of interest.

A machine shop lathe at the visitors' center is all that remains of the Noble Foundry, destroyed, as was much of Rome, by Union troops in November 1864. Farther up the same hill is the site of Fort Norton, where in June 1863 Rome's citizens built three earthen fortifications to protect the city from advancing Union troops.

Downtown attractions include the old Floyd County courthouse (1892), with local artists' work displayed in the lobby; the Capitoline Wolf statue of Romulus and Remus, a gift of Benito Mussolini in 1929; the city clock tower (1871) and museum; older commercial buildings restored for mixed use including artist and craft galleries; and a New Deal mural by Peter Blume, "The Two Rivers," in the post office lobby at the new Federal Building, corner of First Street and Sixth Avenue. Several historic churches are situated through the district.

Educational institutions in Rome include Floyd College (above), Darlington Schools, Shorter College, and Berry College. Darlington Lower School, on Shorter Avenue, is housed in Col. Alfred Shorter's antebellum home, briefly used by Sherman as his base during his invasion of Georgia. Shorter College, on one of Rome's seven hills near Darlington Lower School, has long been noted for its liberal arts and music programs.

Chieftains Museum, a National Historic Landmark, on Riverside Parkway was the home of Major Ridge (1771–1839), a Cherokee assassinated for his part in the Treaty of New Echota that ceded Cherokee lands. The house museum and grounds on the banks of the Oostanaula River contain interpretive exhibits with Indian artifacts, a Civil War collection, a river boat, and an archaeological dig. Elsewhere, excavations have uncovered evidence of prehistoric Indian settlements beside the Coosa River. A Spanish sword and other relics found near the Coosa support the theory that Hernando DeSoto and his troops in 1540 passed through the area that is now Floyd County.

Berry College, north on U.S. 27 at **Mount Berry**, was founded early in this century by Martha Berry, whose family lived on the antebellum plantation that today is a part of the college's twenty-six-thousand-acre campus, the world's largest. A map of the campus may be obtained at the school's main entrance. The many historic or scenic buildings of Berry include Possum Trot, a log cabin where the school began; a large overshot water wheel; House o' Dreams on Lavender Mountain; the Gothic structures of Ford campus, funded by Henry Ford; and an operational dairy farm and beautiful farmland traditionally cultivated by work-study students. Union troops camped during the Civil War in the yard of Miss Berry's family home, Oak Hill (1847), now open as a house museum. The nearby Martha Berry Museum exhibits an art collection given to the college over the years and memorabilia of Miss Berry and the schools.

There are several good public golf courses in Rome. The city has motels, restaurants, and fast food service, but to the north following this tour route, there are few overnight accommodations between Rome and Ft. Oglethorpe at the Tennessee border.

U.S. 27 leads north from Berry College to **Summerville**, in Chattooga County. The traveler passes between Simms Mountain to the west and Johns and Little Sand Mountains to the east, enters the Chattahoochee National Forest, and encounters the topographical region of ridge and valley and Cumberland Plateau. On the southern outskirts of Summerville, James H. Floyd State Park lies in the shadow of Taylor Ridge. Tent, trailer, and pioneer camping; good fishing in two lakes; boating (electric motors only); picnicking; and the proximity of the national forest are attractions.

The Summerville post office displays a New Deal mural, "Georgia Countryside," by artist Doris Lee. Small antique shops and flea markets are relatively recent additions to the town, as is a fine regional library building north of the business district. The chamber of commerce is housed in the old high school, built in 1914. A short side trip to the north leads to Paradise Garden and Trion.

Textile milling began in Chattooga County as early as the middle nineteenth century. **Trion**, west of U.S. 27 north, is the home of Mt. Vernon Mills, world's largest denim mill; adjacent to it is another of the typical mill villages that dot Northwest Georgia. Some mill sections predate the Civil War.

Visionary artist Rev. Howard Finster and his family, some of whom work with him, have a studio about halfway between Trion and Summerville in **Pennville** next to Paradise Garden, a maze of decorated structures and found objects that Finster has fashioned into fanciful sculpture. The garden is at the end of Rina Street, east of U.S. 27.

Other artists' studios, including some chain-saw wood carvers, are in Summerville, Cloudland, Rising Fawn, and Mentone, Alabama. The concentration of artists, artisans, and musicians in these mountains has spawned several popular arts and crafts festivals, among them the Howard Finster Art Festival, held each May in Summerville. A well-known clay studio is at **Rising Fawn**, a settlement named for a Cherokee male—not a princess—who lived on upper Lookout Creek. A popular festival, now defunct, was the clothesline art and craft show given each fall near the state's northern border at Plum Nelly (plum out of Tennessee, and nelly out of Georgia).

There are two viable courses for the journey into the "State of Dade," a county that seceded from the Union before the state of Georgia voted to do so and did not formally reenter the nation until 1945. Ga. 157 follows the Lookout Mountain plateau from Cloudland to Ga. 136, which leads west to Trenton. An alternate route from Cloudland is Ga. 117 into Alabama to Mentone, about nineteen miles from Sum-

Cloudland Canyon

merville. Through a broad valley, U.S. 11 leads from Mentone to Rising Fawn and the Dade County seat, **Trenton**. Roads north through either northwest Georgia or northeast Alabama follow the scenic Cumberland Plateau. The plateau's distinctive topography was critical in battle strategy during the Civil War and earlier, when American Indians fought the colonists on Lookout Mountain in a skirmish reported to be the last of the Revolutionary War.

The plateaus, ridges, and valleys of extreme northwest Georgia were home to American Indians as early as the Paleolithic period. Evidence of early inhabitants includes mounds, artifacts, and skeletal remains, most of them on private property and inaccessible to all but professional archaeologists.

Spectacular natural sites easily reached or viewed include Cloudland Canyon, Sitton's Gulch, Lookout Mountain, Sand Mountain, and Taylor's Ridge. Cloudland Canyon State Park, on Ga. 136 on the western side of Lookout Mountain, is one of the state's most beautiful parks. For visitors who are unable to hike the park's six miles of trails, accessible overlooks afford good views of the deep gorge cut by Sitton's Gulch Creek. The park also has tent and trailer sites, cabins, group camps and shelters, walk-in campsites, tennis courts, and a swimming pool. Cloudland Canyon is such a popular area for observing fall leaf color that the park's cottages are usually booked a year in advance. Class three and four canoeing is an exciting but hazardous sport on the Little River, in a deep gorge on the Alabama side of the Lookout Mountain brow. The East Fork of the Little River flows a tamer, scenic course.

To the east of Cloudland Canyon, off Ga. 136 and 193, Ga. 341 travels through historic McLemore Cove, named for Chief John

McLemore, a Cherokee who lived there before 1826, when he went west. The beautiful mountain valley of farms and modest homes stretches north and south between Lookout and Pigeon Mountains. Ellison's Cave and Rocktown, similar to Rock City (see below) but undeveloped, are on Pigeon Mountain, east of McLemore Cove. Either Ga. 136 or Ga. 193 will lead into **LaFayette**, where at John B. Gordon Hall, Confederate general Braxton Bragg planned his strategy for the Battle of Chickamauga. Built in 1836 as Chattooga Academy, the brick structure is not presently open to the public but is visible from U.S. 27 (business) near the center of the commercial district. The old Walker County courthouse (1917) is now a museum. The Lee and Gordon Mill (1836), operated until 1968, has been restored.

A scenic side trip through the Chattahoochee National Forest passes on Ga. 136 eastward from LaFayette to Calhoun. At the crossroad at **Villanow**, Edwards Country Store (1840), the oldest operating store in the state, is a popular place to stop for a snack or camping provisions. The road is a pleasant alternate route to John's Mountain Wildlife Management Area, Keown Falls, or the Cherokee and Civil War sites around Calhoun. Ga. 136 travels the route of General McPherson's troops through Snake Creek Gap to Resaca and Calhoun (see below). The byway is picturesque at any time, but especially in the autumn.

Just north of LaFayette in **Chickamauga**, the Gordon-Lee Mansion served as U.S. general William Rosecrans's headquarters and as a Union hospital during the Battle of Chickamauga. The house is now a bed and breakfast. Chickamauga was established at Crawfish Springs, location of a Cherokee council house and the county's first courthouse. The railroad depot on Gordon Street, rebuilt in 1891, is now a public museum.

From Chickamauga and LaFayette, U.S. 27 north travels through Chickamauga and Chattanooga National Military Park, eight thousand acres preserved in Walker and Catoosa Counties to commemorate thirty-four thousand casualties of one of the Civil War's bloodiest engagements, the Battle of Chickamauga, September 19–20, 1863. The park visitors' center features a multimedia program, displays, exhibits, and the extensive Fuller Gun Collection. Park wildlife includes deer, wild turkey, fox, raccoon, rabbit, opossum, reptile, amphibian, and residential and migratory birds. Information on other parts of this engagement is found at Point Park on Lookout Mountain, where another visitors' center interprets Orchard Knob, Signal Point, Missionary Ridge, and Lookout Mountain battles. The route to Lookout Mountain is marked by signs in Rossville and Chattanooga. On both sides of the state line, there are also commercial interpretations of the battles.

At **Ft. Oglethorpe**, a closed twentieth-century military installation adjacent to Chickamauga Park's northern border, the Sixth Cavalry

Museum on the fort's parade field exhibits Sixth Cavalry memorabilia, clothing, and equipment and has a small section dedicated to the Women's Army Corps (WACS) headquartered at Ft. Oglethorpe. A drive around the street encircling the parade field provides a good view of the private houses that once comprised officers' row. Travelers to Ft. Oglethorpe and the Chickamauga battle sites should also investigate the Chattanooga Aquarium and several museums and cultural sites in the city.

A short distance south of the Tennessee border in **Rossville**, the family home of Cherokee chief John Ross is open to the public. In 1797 his grandfather, trader John McDonald, built the log house beside Poplar Springs on the Indian trade path to Augusta. Ross, though more Scot than Cherokee, remained loyal to his Native American people, traveled with them on the Trail of Tears, lived with them in the Oklahoma Territory, and served ably as principal chief from 1828 until his death in 1866. The house, spring, and lake are a National Historic Landmark.

From the vicinity of Point Park on Lookout Mountain, Ga. 189 leads south to Covenant College, which had its beginning in the old Lookout Mountain Hotel, or the "Castle in the Clouds." From the mountaintop campus the traveler can see a panorama of the surrounding countryside. South of the college at McCarty Bluff is a launching pad where one may hang glide, watch others sail from the rim of the mountain, or view the broad valley and Sand Mountain to the west. About six miles south of the village of **Lookout Mountain**, Tom's Dulcimer Shop is one of the few instrument-making shops in the state. Tom Hicks and his family make Appalachian dulcimers and autoharps in the building and display their wares at craft fairs.

Before the days of interstate highways and limited highway signs, travelers saw beside federal and state roads old barns with the slogan "See Rock City" painted on their roofs. A few survive, but the words now adorn more birdhouses than barns. The successful advertising ploy drew people from throughout the United States to the huge rock formations at Lookout Mountain, Georgia. (That Rock City's brochure is published in six languages attests to its continuing attraction for diverse visitors.) During the depression, Garnet and Frieda Carter built paths from which the boulders could be viewed, developed underground caverns with lighted fairy-tale scenes, cultivated indigenous plants along the walkways, and named the attraction Rock City; it remains an unusual combination of nature and commerce. Garnet Carter built the world's first miniature golf course on Lookout Mountain in the late 1920s.

Battlefield Parkway (Ga. 2) travels from Ft. Oglethorpe to **Ringgold**, the Catoosa County seat. There the private Whitman House (1858) may be seen at the corner of Mountain and Tennessee streets. From its balcony the family watched the Battle of Ringgold,

Early "billboard" in Northwest Georgia

November 27, 1863, and after the battle Gen. Ulysses Grant made the house his headquarters. Evidence of cannon fire by Joseph Hooker's guns during the Battle of Ringgold is visible on the walls of the Ringgold railroad depot. A WPA roadside relief map on U.S. 41 describes nearby Civil War activity.

A side trip for Cherokee history enthusiasts who plan to travel to the capital at New Echota is the historic site Red Clay, to the northeast, again barely across the Tennessee line. From Ga. 71 north of Dalton, Wilson Caldwell Road (immediately south of the state line) travels west to Red Clay Road, which leads north to the historic area. Red Clay was the last eastern capitol of Cherokee government. When the state of Georgia stripped native people of their sovereignty, the Cherokees moved their capital from New Echota to this site. Although all the buildings are reconstructed, the Indians' clear sacred spring, Blue Hole, flows from a grove at Red Clay into the Conasauga and Coosa river systems. (See New Echota, below.)

Back in the Ringgold vicinity, the community of **Tunnel Hill** owns a railroad tunnel built in 1850 through Chetoogeta Mountain. The oldest railroad tunnel in the South, it played a strategic role in the Civil War, and Andrews's Raiders (Union spies sent to Georgia to destroy the railroad) passed through the tunnel in their attempt to reach Chattanooga. They abandoned the stolen locomotive General, however, near Ringgold. At old Tunnel Hill village, to the east of U.S. 41, historic markers beside the railroad tell the story and the location of the tunnel. South of a one-lane covered bridge on Clisby Austin Road near the tunnel, the Clisby Austin House (private), both a Confederate hospital and Sherman's headquarters, can be seen.

For years tourists and locals alike called U.S. 41 from **Dalton** south to Cartersville "Peacock Alley" because small shops displaying bed-spreads decorated with brilliant peacock-feather and other colorful designs lined the highway. Dalton's huge textile industry began soon after the turn of the century as cottage enterprises of bedspreads tufted by hand and peddled for two or three dollars. Now Dalton is the "Carpet Capital of the World." In the Crown Cotton Mill's antebellum offices, 715 Chattanooga Avenue, the Crown Gardens and Archives exhibits photographs and artifacts of the industry's history and the Civil War. Detailed information on other sites in Whitfield and Murray Counties is available in the same building. The Dalton Development Authority also publishes a walking tour and map of the city's historic downtown.

A wire sent to Chattanooga from the depot (now a restaurant) in Dalton's center warned that Andrews and his raiders approached on the General. Brass nails in the depot floor mark the center from which the town's original circular city limits were surveyed. Modern sites are Dalton College, a commuter school; the Creative Arts Guild, on West Waugh Street, which has visual arts exhibits as well as classes and performances; and the Dalton Regional Library on Cappes Street. Like many town and regional libraries, it is a source of local infor-mation and resources.

Northeast of Dalton, on Ga. 2 just off Ga. 71, is Prater's Mill, a grist mill built by slave labor in 1855. At this historic site, listed on the Na-tional Register, both Union and Confederate troops camped at differ-ent times in 1864. The grounds, with some picnic facilities, are open daily, but the buildings are accessible and the mill is operating only during semiannual country fairs each May and October. West of Dal-ton, off Walnut Avenue (at I-75) on Dug Gap Battle Road, are Civil War breastworks at the Dug Gap Battle Park, maintained by the local Civil War Roundtable. On Walnut Avenue near I-75 are several motels and restaurants.

TOUR THREE

From Resaca, south of Dalton, continue on U.S. 41 to Calhoun; take Ga. 225 to New Echota. From New Echota, take Ga. 225 to Spring Place; Ga. 52 Alt. to Chatsworth; U.S. 411 and local roads to Carter's Dam; Ga. 2 and 52 to Fort Mountain and Ellijay; U.S. 76 to Blue Ridge; Ga. 5 to McCaysville; Ga. 60 to Mineral Bluff; Ga. 2 back to Blue Ridge; U.S. 76 to Ellijay and Talking Rock; Ga. 136 and 136C to Hinton; Ga. 53 to Jasper and Tate.

Travelers taking U.S. 41 from Dalton to Calhoun pass near the site of the Battle of **Resaca**, May 13–15, 1864. Several roadside markers and

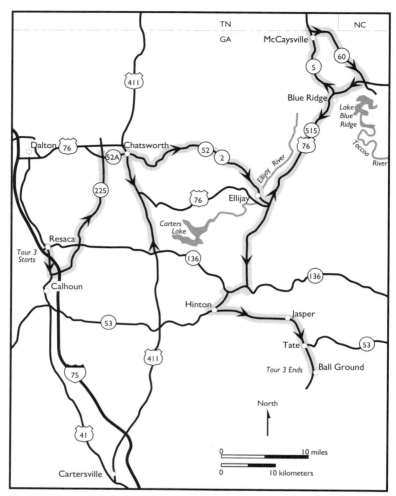

Northwest Georgia, Tour Three

a WPA relief map interpret troop movement in the area. Two miles north of Resaca and a short drive to the east on Confederate Cemetery Road, Confederate soldiers who died in the battle lie buried. Two sisters who lived near the battleground established the cemetery when they began moving bodies from the spots where they fell and burying them in orderly rows. The Battle of Resaca is reenacted each year in May on the site of the struggle.

As General Sherman advanced to Atlanta, on much the same route that today's travelers drive down U.S. 41, he made his Gordon County headquarters in **Calhoun** at the Brown house, now called Oakleigh, the home of the Gordon County Historical Society. The house on South

Wall Street (U.S. 41) contains historical material, and a newer wing holds a large collection of dolls.

The renowned tenor Roland Hayes (1887–1977) was born to former slaves on a farm near Curryville, west of Calhoun. Though his own countrymen were slow to recognize his accomplishment, Hayes was acclaimed across Europe for his performances of art songs and spirituals. In England, he sang in private audience for King George V and Queen Mary. Roland Hayes was posthumously inducted into the Georgia Music Hall of Fame in 1991, and each fall the citizens of Calhoun and Gordon County honor his memory with a music festival.

Recreational facilities include county-owned Salacoa Creek Park, which has camping, swimming, boating, and picnicking facilities; several golf courses, including a fine municipal course, and a national forest. For plane buffs, Mercer Aircraft Museum exhibits vintage airships on Belwood Road, in a field clearly visible from I-75, a few miles south of Calhoun.

To the west of the town, Arrowhead Public Fishing Area, John's Mountain, Hidden Creek Recreation Area, and the Chattahoochee National Forest have opportunities for wilderness hiking, camping, picnicking, and trout fishing. From Ga. 136 west, near Villanow, Ga. 203 (Pocket Road) leads south to Lake Marvin and the Pocket Recreation Area, open April 1–November 13. Site of a Civilian Conservation Corps camp from 1938 to 1942, the area now has campsites, picnic sites, the Keown Falls hiking trail, and John's Mountain Overlook. This side trip intersects at Villanow with one from LaFayette (see above). Between Villanow and Resaca, beside Ga. 136, a historical marker relates the Battle of Snake Creek Gap. Hidden Creek Recreation Area is accessible from Ga. 156 near Rosedale.

Among the most significant sites of the Cherokee Nation is **New Echota**, a few miles east of Calhoun on Ga. 225. In 1825, Cherokees established their capital, New Echota, near the confluence of the Coosawattee and Conasauga Rivers to form the Oostanaula. The Cherokees had a sophisticated government modeled on that of the United States, their own written syllabary, and a newspaper. A minority faction, including Major Ridge and Elias Boudinot, the newspaper editor, in 1835 illegally negotiated the Treaty of New Echota to relinquish Cherokee claims to their eastern lands. Despite the treaty's illegality, Georgians hungry for land continued to pressure the federal government, and the Cherokees were removed by force in 1838. New Echota was a center of the removal activity that led to the Trail of Tears. A state historic site and a National Historic Landmark, the restored village includes the original home of a Moravian missionary, Rev. Samuel Worcester; Cherokee-built structures that have been moved to the grounds; a reconstructed courthouse; and an interpretive center. The newspaper shop prints on a flat-bed press and distributes souvenir

Supreme Court Building, New Echota State Historic Site

replicas of the *Cherokee Phoenix*, written, as was the original, in both English and the Cherokee syllabary devised by Sequoyah.

From the Cherokee Nation's capital at New Echota, this tour flows naturally to another important Cherokee site, the Vann House at **Spring Place**, north of New Echota on Ga. 225. James Vann, a wealthy Cherokee chief, built the impressive brick mansion in 1804. Though a harsh leader, Chief Vann welcomed Moravian missionaries to the territory because he wanted them to educate Cherokees at mission schools. After an unknown rifleman killed him, his youngest son, Joseph ("Rich Joe"), inherited the house and farms and lived there until shortly before the westward removal. Much of the house construction is original, including elaborate hand-carved mantels and wainscoting, hardware, fireplaces, and an ingeniously cantilevered stair. Administered by the state as a historic site, the Vann House is furnished with antiques and reproductions in the style the Vanns enjoyed. Near the house is the old Spring Place Methodist Church (private), which served the white settlers who followed Cherokees into the territory.

From Spring Place, Ga. 52 Alt. leads to **Chatsworth**, the Murray County seat, where the courthouse, on the National Register of Historic Places and open to the public, sits on a rise at the town's center. North of Chatsworth, atop Grassy Mountain, is Lake Conasauga, the highest lake in the state. Tent camping and summertime interpretive nature programs are among its features. Parts of the Cohutta Wilderness Area and the Chattahoochee National Forest border the county's eastern edge. The wilderness area, the southern end of the Appalachian Mountains, is the habitat of rare or uncommon fish and plants and other wildlife. The interior is accessible by footpath.

South of Chatsworth, near Ga. 61 and U.S. 411 at **Ramhurst**, portions of the old Federal Road, used by American Indians and traders, are paved and still in use. Where the new one deviates from the course, the careful eye can see beside it depressions that mark the old road. Farther south, Carter's Dam impounds a beautiful mountain lake over four hundred feet deep in places. Near the small museum and interpretive center in the resource manager's office, scenic overlooks give good views of the lake and surrounding mountains. The lake's development is permanently limited to one marina with rental facilities.

Back to the north, the center of Chatsworth is the departure point for Fort Mountain State Park, which is on Ga. 52 about seven miles to the east. The mountain is named for an ancient 855-foot-long rock wall built at the highest point. Some archaeologists date the wall as early as 2000 B.C., but no one knows who built it or why. Hiking trails approach the wall, though none follow its length, and it can be viewed from a stone tower built by the Civilian Conservation Corps. The state park has other trails, rental cabins and tent camping, and a small lake. Chatsworth, Fort Mountain, and the Zell Miller Mountain Parkway have restaurants and lodging.

Across the mountain to the east is Ellijay, from which U.S. 76 leads north to Blue Ridge, in Fannin County. Three brochures distributed at the visitor center in **Blue Ridge** describe excellent self-guided driving tours at varying levels of difficulty, including a gentle, scenic drive through Dial Valley and along the Toccoa River, where a Cherokee fish trap (a V in the water's flow) is visible in the river near Van Zandt's Store. Information on white-water rafting and tubing is available lo-

Dining room, Vann House, Spring Place

cally. Blue Ridge Lake, in the Chattahoochee National Forest near Morganton, is an unspoiled mountain lake with recreational possibilities that include camping and fishing. Since over 40 percent of the county is national forest, it abounds with outdoor activities and scenic vistas.

The visitor center also displays brochures on and examples of staurolites (St. Andrew's crosses or "fairy crosses"), a silicate mineral formation prized by collectors and found around Blue Ridge and Tate. An 1839 grist mill operates at Skeenah Mill on Ga. 60. The Appalachian Trail begins on Springer Mountain near the southern intersections of Gilmer and Fannin Counties (see Northeast Georgia).

Ga. 5 from Blue Ridge or Ga. 60 from Morganton travel north to **McCaysville** in the Copper Basin, an area of red hills that for many years were left barren by copper smelting's sulfuric acid by-product. Although copper mining has halted and new methods to capture the acid have allowed vegetation to creep slowly back across the hills, a picture of the process and the surreal landscape it created is possible through a visit to the old Burra Burra Mine site and Ducktown Basin Museum in Tennessee. The museum also displays interesting exhibits on the Cherokees who inhabited the area.

Where the Toccoa River crosses the Tennessee state line in McCaysville, it becomes the Ocoee, venue for white-water slalom races during the 1996 Olympic Games. A scenic alternate tour from Ga. 60 goes south through the mountains to Dahlonega (see Northeast Georgia tour).

Fannin and Gilmer Counties are noted for apple production. **Ellijay** holds a fall Apple Festival and Arts and Crafts Fair at which apples and apple products abound. Several orchards operate roadside stands in both counties or allow customers to pick their own fruit. Many acres of Gilmer County are part of the Chattahoochee National Forest, which includes the Rich Mountain Wilderness Area. Hiking, white-water canoeing and kayaking on the Cartecay River, trout fishing, fishing on the Coosawattee River, and water sports at Carter's Lake are popular outdoor activities.

Ga. 515/5, the Zell Miller Mountain Parkway, is a scenic drive through several mountainous counties. From Ellijay it meanders south to areas of Pickens County that are rich in Cherokee history, but few Indian sites are extant or accessible. Stores, houses, missions, and removal stockades have fallen and rotted; traces of the old Federal Road can be seen beside some modern roadways. From Ga. 5 near **Talking Rock**, Ga. 136 west skirts the Talking Rock Wildlife Management Area, a public hunting area (information from the Georgia Department of Natural Resources), and crosses the white-water Talking Rock Creek. Northwest of the southern spur of Ga. 136 at **Hinton** and

THE RESACA CONFEDERATE CEMETERY

After the Battle of Resaca in May 1864, Union troops removed their dead; but the defeated Confederates had no time to do more than hastily cover the bodies of the four hundred dead lying where they fell on the fields and hillsides. Col. John F. Green owned some of the land where the battle occurred. After he and his family returned to their home, his daughters Mary and Pyatt noticed that rains were washing away the thin layers of dirt covering many bodies. The sisters reburied some men in their flower garden and began a campaign to reinter all the fallen dead in a true cemetery. Their father donated over two acres within the battlefield, and a ladies' memorial association gathered donations to establish the first Confederate cemetery in Georgia and one of the first in the South.

Though all Georgia citizens were extremely impoverished following the war, contributions of nickels, dimes, single dollars, and even ten dollars from newspaper columnist Bill Arp came in a steady flow, enough to begin the reinterment effort. Late in the century the memorial association was able to erect a marker:

> We sleep here in obedience to law;
> When duty called, we came;
> When country called, we died.

Although a few bear names, most of the headstones in the cemetery mark the graves of unknown dead. The graves are encircled by
a wall of Stone Mountain granite with a gateway arch erected early
in the twentieth century by noted Calhoun builder and horticulturist W. Laurens Hillhouse.

—Jane Powers Weldon

Overleaf: Entrance to Resaca Confederate Cemetery
Above: Laurens Hillhouse in Harbin Peach Orchard, Calhoun, 1892

Ga. 53, John's Mill on Scarecorn Creek grinds white corn into meal on the weekends.

Ga. 53 (Sam Tate Highway) east leads back into **Jasper**, the Pickens County seat, where the 1906 jail has been restored and listed on the National Register of Historic Places. The jail and several public buildings are faced with marble, the county's major resource. Many otherwise modest homes in Pickens County flaunt marble columns supporting their front porches and marble chips for driveways. From Jasper east, Burnt Mountain Road and Ga. 136 are drives with scenic vistas, especially the view from the top of Burnt Mountain.

South of Jasper in **Tate** are the Georgia Marble Company headquarters, quarries, and still more evidence of the quarrying industry in the county. The company's owner, Col. Sam Tate, built the pink marble Tate House in 1923 to showcase his products. It is now a bed and breakfast inn. The old Federal Road once passed the site, location of the Harnage Tavern and the first court of Cherokee County. The local elementary school is reported to be the country's only marble public school building. Colonel Tate, a philanthropist and eccentric, promoted the use of marble throughout the country, not just on public buildings in his native Georgia. During the Georgia Marble Festival each October, the quarries are open for tours, but the year-round view of the shafts from Ga. 53 between Tate and Marble Hill is interesting and worth a look.

Old Ga. 5 leads south from Tate into Ball Ground, named for the Indian stickball games played there, and the northern area of the Metropolitan Atlanta tour. As an alternate, Ga. 53 leads west from Tate toward Dawsonville and the Northeast Georgia tour.

NORTHEAST GEORGIA

John C. Inscoe **APPALACHIAN OTHERNESS, REAL AND PERCEIVED**

In August 1966 a twenty-four-year-old graduate of Cornell University came to the Rabun Gap–Nacoochee School to teach freshman and sophomore English. Eliot Wigginton had no sense of mission or purpose in coming to this peaceful mountain valley in Georgia's northeasternmost corner. He had entertained thoughts of beginning his teaching career in more exciting locales, such as San Francisco or Boston. What ultimately led him to this remote corner of his home state was nostalgia—boyhood memories of pleasant weekends spent exploring the even more placid valley of Betty Creek nearby. Growing up in Athens, Wigginton had often accompanied his father, a noted landscape architect at the University of Georgia, when he visited the Jay Hambidge Center, a quaint but lively retreat for artists and craftsmen. "I went to the Southern Appalachians to teach," Wigginton later wrote, "because I had always been attracted by their special visual appeal—sometimes warm and human in scale, and sometimes vast and foreboding."

In the midst of a rather disastrous first semester, facing increasingly unruly and uninterested students, Wigginton proposed a number of project ideas to his classes that he hoped might engage them and salvage something from the wreckage before the school year was out. Only one idea struck a chord: a student-produced literary magazine. With teacher and pupils directing their collective energies into it, the first issue appeared early in 1967. The students chose to name their magazine *Foxfire*, the term given a phosphorescent fungus indigenous to the thick, damp undergrowth of southern highland forests. It proved an instant success locally, its six hundred copies selling out within a week.

While the majority of its pages were devoted to poetry and fiction derived from both student writings and outside submissions, the key to the magazine's popularity proved to be a brief section on Rabun County people and places. Local readers found especially lively read-

165

ing in an interview with an elderly former sheriff, who recounted in vivid detail for Wigginton's tape recorder the story of a Clayton bank robbery in 1936 and his own bumbling pursuit of the Zack Springel "gang" through the Georgia mountains and their ultimate capture weeks later in North Carolina. The response to that interview led Wigginton and his students to take more seriously advice given him earlier by novelist Marguerite Stedman, a guest at the Hambidge Center. She reminded Wigginton that the best work of authors like William Faulkner and Mark Twain grew from their intimate knowledge and love of their surroundings and their roots and urged him to let his students do likewise. "Go dig the gemstone out of your own hill," she said. "Make your students curious, then proud, of their homes."

Thus armed with tape recorders, note pads, and lists of questions, students approached their grandparents, their elderly neighbors, and various local raconteurs. In so doing, they tapped into a mother lode of information and wisdom about their own rich mountain heritage and discovered to their delight that the range of topics and people willing to expound on them was almost limitless. One sample listing of subjects covered refers to "hog dressing, log cabin building, mountain crafts and foods, planting by the signs, snake lore, hunting tales, faith healing, moonshining, and other affairs of plain living." Another issue provided coverage of sourwood honey, midwives and granny women, corn shuckings, house raisin's, quiltings, pea thrashings, log rollings, raising sheep and weaving wool, and "how-to" features on making ox yokes, tub wheels, and foot-powered lathes.

The originality of the concept—making local traditions, history, and folklore, and the elderly people who embodied them a source of adolescent enthusiasm and productivity—soon attracted national publicity. The appeal of the final product—its rich, often raw, and constantly varied subject matter—won the magazine a national readership. The *Foxfire* phenomenon was soon underway. Both as a continuing chronicle of Appalachian life and culture and as an innovative educational model of "cultural journalism," it has continued unabated. In 1972 Doubleday published *The Foxfire Book*, a sampling of the best pieces produced in the magazine. It became a best-seller and spawned nine more volumes to date, along with a Broadway play and television movie. Suddenly, Northeast Georgia, often assumed to be a minor appendage to the Southern Appalachians, served as the epitome of the mountain South to a nationwide readership.

By sheer coincidence, just as *Foxfire* was reaching the height of its popularity, American readers and moviegoers were exposed to another, and very different, view not only of Appalachian Georgia, but of Rabun County. In 1970, Atlanta-born poet James Dickey published his first (and until 1993 his only) novel, *Deliverance*. It quickly became one of the year's best-sellers, and Hollywood wasted no time in capitalizing on its success, producing an equally well-received film version in 1972.

Dickey's saga tells of four Atlanta suburbanites who embark on a weekend of whitewater canoeing on the Cahulawasee River, a thinly veiled fictionalization of the Chattooga River. (The linkage was confirmed when the movie was actually filmed in that rugged canyon that forms Rabun County's eastern border with South Carolina.) Once underway, the novice adventurers encounter not only a far more physically challenging and dangerous river than they had expected or were prepared for, but equally threatening local inhabitants as well. Their excursion becomes a horror story as they are forced to wage a life and death struggle against both. The story could just as easily have been set in the West or in Canada if the natural wilderness alone had been the novel's central challenge; it is the human element within that setting that renders this story distinctly southern, and Appalachian.

Dickey provides what must be the most demeaning characterization of southern highlanders in modern literature, and much of the power of his novel—and the film—lies in his descriptions of the alien and hostile world of these North Georgia mountaineers. Lewis Medlock, the group's only outdoorsman who planned the weekend to introduce his citified friends to the grandeur of this rugged wilderness he loves, explains mountain people in terms that Dickey's subsequent plot fully supports. "These are good people," he tells his companions. "But they're awfully clannish, they're set in their ways. . . . Every family I've ever met up here has at least one relative in the penitentiary. Some of them are in for making liquor or running it, but most of them are in for murder. They don't think a whole lot about killing people up here."

Early impressions of local inhabitants suggest ominous character traits that later plague the Atlanta foursome. Ed Gentry, the novel's protagonist and narrator, describes the little town from which they embark on their river journey, the last vestige of civilization, as "sleepy and hookwormy and ugly, and most of all inconsequential." The gas attendant, he claims, "looks like a hillbilly in a badly cast movie." Dickey's subsequent descriptions progress from the merely eccentric and degenerate to the demented and ghoulish. Gentry muses, for example, at the number of missing fingers he's encountered in the rural South, and notes how many mountain folk exhibited "crippling or twisting" illnesses or deformities. Such thoughts make him uneasy and eager to escape, by whitewater, from this "country of nine-fingered people."

The film intensified Dickey's already exaggerated hillbilly stereotypes, and the power of the visual medium made for even more indelible impressions of a deprived and depraved people. Among the most striking images in the movie is that of an anemic, moronic boy on the porch of a dilapidated shanty who holds his own in a rousing banjo duet with another of the Atlantans, as his emaciated, humorless family look on. The crux of both novel and film is an encounter with two demented mountain men who have trailed the canoeists and sexually assault two of them, an act that sets off a chain of murder, self-defense, vengeance, and deception and turns this action-adventure tale into a riveting horror story.

Not surprisingly, Rabun County residents and other North Georgians resented *Deliverance* for its depictions of local characters as wretched, malevolent perverts and for its dredging up of the most base stereotypes of the southern mountaineer. Dickey defended his portrait of the region, noting that it was during an extended stay in Italy that he began to appreciate from a distance America, and particularly North Georgia's "wild country," which he had come to know well through numerous canoe and bow-hunting trips. "Just thinking about that country," he said, "always gives me the same feeling of excitement and fear," a feeling spurred by being in "an unprotected situation where the safeties of law and what we call civilization don't apply. . . . There are men in those remote parts that'd just as soon kill you as look at you." Insistent that much of what took place in the novel was based on actual incidents, Dickey made it clear that it was as much the barbarity of certain fellow Georgians as the challenges of the wilderness they inhabited that he sought to convey to a national readership.

Eliot Wigginton was among those quick to take strong exception to what Dickey and Hollywood had done to his adopted county. The first issue of *Foxfire* to appear after the film's release opened with an editorial entitled "From the Land of Nine-fingered People," in which he denounced this depiction of a region peopled totally by sinister and sub-human beings. "It powerfully reinforces a stereotype we have been fighting with *Foxfire* for eight years," he wrote, "that of the hick with his liquor still, ignorant, depraved, stupid—sometimes laughable—his only concession of the "finer" things begin an occasional crude 'dulcimore' or banjo hanging on the wall of his battered, filthy shack."

Battered and angered by Dickey's depiction of them, Rabun County residents soon came to appreciate the antidote to such abuse embodied in the collective self-portrait that *Foxfire* represented. Buck Carver, a moonshiner and musician who was among Wigginton's favorite subjects and most valuable sources, stated that *Foxfire* "enlightened some people that we're not the dumb sons of bitches . . . they've made us out to be." It was, he declared, "the best thing that's ever happened to Rabun County." After Dickey, he was more appreciative than ever of the fact that Wigginton "has published nothing that's hurt us." George Reynolds, long Wigginton's right-hand man and an accom-

Rafting on the Chattooga River

plished folklorist and musician in his own right, accompanied students to Australia to carry the *Foxfire* message to rural schools there.
Deliverance had recently aired on its network television and Reynolds
found himself constantly having to explain to his Australian hosts:
"No, folks in North Georgia really aren't depraved, dangerous, and
strange-looking."

Both Eliot Wigginton and James Dickey have had much to do with
the way in which modern Americans perceive the mountain South.

It is pure coincidence that they drew on the same county in north-eastern Georgia to do so, and rather ironic that it was this "edge" of the Appalachians, so often ignored or minimized by chroniclers of the southern highlands, that suddenly came to epitomize the whole. Their contrasting portraits of Georgia highlanders range in approach from reverential celebration to utter contempt. As such, they embody both the best and the worst of the southern highland experience and the contradictions inherent in how it has long been perceived by and conveyed to others: its physical grandeur and its primitivism and backwardness; its bounteous natural resources and their often ruthless exploitation; its continual lure for outsiders and yet its inhabitants' alienation and isolation from the outside world; the romanticization of mountain culture as remnants of a simpler, more virtuous rural lifestyle and value system and the contemptuous degradation of the ignorance and degeneracy of its people.

Southern Appalachia has been subject to as much myth, misconception, and stereotyping—positive and negative—as any part of the country, and the mountains of Northeast Georgia have been an integral part of what one recent scholar called "the invention of Appalachia," and others have termed its "otherness." George Reynolds once observed that in examining Appalachia or any other region exploited for its natural wealth, the mainstream culture tends to deride yet romanticize those who live on the land being exploited. This dichotomy has certainly held true for the way in which North Georgians and their world have long been and continue to be perceived and understood.

Georgia's mountains, like the larger chain to which they are linked, are among the world's oldest. While geologists date the underlying base rocks of the Blue Ridge to over a billion years ago, the mountains themselves emerged from 250 to 400 million years ago as continental shifts forced marine sediments together and upward to form this vast and complex range. Its peaks once rose to four or five times their present height, and over the past 100 million years or so, have worn down to their present heights, with less rugged and more rolling and rounded configurations. Georgia's mountains connect to the Appalachian whole in different ways and are both geologically and geographically disconnected. The state's northwestern highlands consist of the Cumberland Plateau, the Unaka range, and an area known simply as the Valley and Ridge. The state's northeastern mountains derive from a very different source: They are part of the eastern Blue Ridge range, an almost unbroken chain that runs through Virginia and North Carolina and extends for nearly a hundred miles into Georgia, a spinal cord in effect of the eastern Appalachians.

The Blue Ridge either rises up or tapers off (depending on one's perspective) in Georgia. Although none of its peaks compare in height

Outing at Tallulah Gorge, circa 1900

with North Carolina's Smokies and Black Mountains, many of which rise to over six thousand feet above sea level, several of the Blue Ridge's more rugged features lie within Georgia's borders. At least eight peaks exceed four thousand feet in elevation, including the state's highest and perhaps not coincidentally, most accessible peak, Brasstown Bald; Springer Mountain, one of its most climbed, given its designation as the starting point (or terminus) for the Appalachian Trail; and Blood and Tray Mountains, the highest peaks crossed by the trail in Georgia. The Appalachian Trail crosses fourteen states along its 2,021 mile course from Georgia to Maine; its 79-mile route in Georgia serves as the most tangible sense of its linkage to the eastern seaboard's highlands. Two of eastern America's most rugged gorges—the Talullah and Chattooga—lie within this corner of Georgia. They, along with several of the South's most scenic waterfalls, those of Amicalola (the state's highest), Toccoa, and Anna Ruby, and at one time Talullah, are (or were) among the most spectacular of the natural attractions that have long drawn visitors to the region.

William Bartram, the Philadelphia Quaker naturalist and wilderness explorer who moved through this region in the course of his well-chronicled southern tour in 1775, was among the many travelers introduced to the Southern Appalachians by way of Georgia. One of the first and most eloquent in articulating his impressions of the area's topography, he was also fascinated by the abundance and variety of the region's flora. He marveled at the versatility of the southern mountain soil and climate and was intrigued to find that they supported the same plant life he knew in Pennsylvania and even

Canada, from rhododendron and flame azalea to red spruce, white pines, birches, and ashes. He took even more delight in new discoveries, such as the Fraser magnolia and ginseng. The latter is a small red-berried plant, the roots of which contain aphrodisiatic qualities so valued by the Chinese that "sang" diggers have long profited from what remains one of the more lucrative exports from Georgia and other Appalachian highlands.

Bartram encountered few white men as he ventured beyond the foothills of South Carolina and into Georgia's highlands. This was still Indian country—referred to as the Cherokee Mountains as often as the Appalachians—and except for an occasional white trader, his only contacts were the Cherokees themselves. The largest tribe in the South, the Cherokee were the mountaineers of Native Americans in part by choice and in part because, from the 1720s on, they had been pushed or negotiated into occupying higher and more remote areas; by the end of the eighteenth century, their world was confined to the highlands of North Carolina, Tennessee, and Georgia, and even that shrinkage remained steady and inevitable until it climaxed with the infamous removal of 1838 and 1839. Bartram wrote extensively and with much admiration of the Cherokee he met on his 1775 trek. He didn't live long enough to recognize the sad irony of his observation that they were intelligent, tenacious of the liberties and natural rights of man, and "ready always to sacrifice every pleasure and gratification, even their blood, and life itself, to defend their territory and defend their rights."

The dangers inherent in this determination of the native populace were well-known; and such knowledge kept the imposing northern wilderness of the youngest of the thirteen American colonies virtually unsettled until after the American Revolution. Even then, settlers rarely moved into the mountains themselves and those settling the adjacent foothills did so at considerable risk.

Like many of the region's first white residents, Maj. Jesse Walton moved onto property in the Tugaloo River valley he had acquired as a land grant to Revolutionary War veterans. It was his misfortune to settle in this most remote outpost of the North Georgia frontier at a time of considerable tension between Cherokees and whites. Fully conscious of his vulnerability, Walton joined his few neighbors in 1786 in urging the new state assembly just established in Augusta of "the present sircumstance [sic] of Our Frontier." "Our people," they petitioned, "is much alarmd at the late hostilitys acted by the Indians on the Ocone and Expect Every moment when it will be our unhapy fate. . . . Our settlement at this time is verry weak not Consisting of more than 45 men." Such concerns were justified. Three years later, Jesse Walton was one of several in the community killed during a particularly brutal Cherokee attack. He had remained behind to defend his farm while his family had sought refuge at a nearby fortress and thus survived.

Such attacks were hardly one-sided; retaliatory strikes were a predictable aftermath. In 1792, Gov. Edward Telfair reported an incident in Franklin County in which fifty-nine men "did, in a lawless manner, go into the Cherokee nation, burn a town, and kill three Indians." He concluded by acknowledging the cyclical nature of such hostilities: "There is reason to apprehend that some serious and early attack is meditated by the Indians against the settlers in that quarter."

Thus in patterns already well-established in the American frontier tradition and that would continue for nearly another century across the continent, Northeast Georgia developed as a frontier environment characterized by hardship, violence, and vulnerability. But while encounters between Native Americans and white settlers took place throughout much of inland Georgia at one time or another, the mountains were part of another pattern as well. What linked the region specifically to the rest of Appalachia was the extent to which that frontier stage of development lingered long after the rest of the state and of eastern America had advanced well beyond it.

Tensions between whites and Native Americans did not long deter white settlement in Northeast Georgia. An inn known as Traveler's Rest was established in the 1830s and still stands, on the site of Walton's homestead, now in Stephens County. Devereaux Jarrett purchased the property in the 1820s and, taking full advantage of its location on the well-traveled post road, built an imposing two-story twelve-room structure that served as inn, trading post, stagecoach stop, and post office. Jarrett soon became known as the "richest man on the Tugaloo Valley," and if British geologist George Featherstonhaugh is to be believed, was an impressive specimen of a frontier entrepreneur. Jarrett, according to his foreign guest after an 1837 stay at Traveler's Rest, was a "quiet, intelligent, well-behaved man," whose hospitality led Featherstonhaugh to muse, "What a charming country this would be to travel in, if one was sure of meeting such nice clean quarters once a day."

But such comforts were far from common in Georgia's upcountry. Its rough-hewn frontier character remained apparent long after more civilized society had overtaken much of the rest of the state. From such distinctions, the fascination and stereotyping of mountaineers began to emerge. During one of his several extensive tours of the southern backcountry in 1790 that included several days in North Georgia, that most well-traveled and self-chronicled of Methodist bishops, Francis Asbury, observed of his highland hosts who were then beleaguered by Native American hostilities, "O, poor creatures; they are but one remove from savages themselves."

As would prove to be the case for much of the Indian displacement across the continent, North Georgia's ultimate showdown between white newcomers and Cherokee natives was triggered by gold. The rough and rowdy opportunists it brought into the hills added considerably to the image of the violent and uncouth backwoodsmen who would later evolve into the southern hillbilly.

Varying accounts place the first discovery of gold in the region in present day Hall, Habersham, White, and Lumpkin Counties between 1826 and 1828. The most popular account credits Benjamin Parks as the man who set off Georgia's gold rush, in part because he spent so much of his later life retelling his tale of discovery. While hunting deer along the Chestatee River in 1828, Parks happened to kick up a bright stone that proved to be a gold nugget. The "twenty-niners" who rushed into the region created a rough and rowdy society consisting, according to one observer, of "thieves, gamblers, and murderers—quarrelsome, drunken and malicious—forming altogether a lawless, ungovernable community." Such a description would have been equally applicable to both the far western boom towns and the clashes with Native Americans a generation later. Yet, with more immediacy, it contributed to the growing perception of Appalachian society as a permanent frontier that proved hard to shake; these untamed frontiersmen became the antecedents in effect of James Dickey's highland degenerates nearly a century and a half later.

The region's first boom town, Auraria, soon gave way to a far more substantial permanent center of activity, Dahlonega, five miles to its north. There is a trace of irony, perhaps, in the fact that a Latin-named town would fall to its Cherokee-labeled rival. (Talonega is the Cherokee word for gold or yellow.) For by the time of its founding, the days of the Indians' continued habitation on the land were already numbered. With complicity from both state and federal governments, and opposition only from the U.S. Supreme Court, Cherokee rights to this gold-laden turf proved but a minor inconvenience for the miners who flooded onto it. By 1830, legislative and judicial wheels were turning to clear the region of its native populace, processes that culminated in 1838 with the forced removal from the state of more than thirteen thousand Cherokees. Escorted during the unusually extreme winter of 1838 and 1839 across half a continent, five thousand died along the infamous route that those who survived labeled the Trail of Tears. A Massachusetts missionary who witnessed the round-up and departure declared, "The state of Georgia—that cruel, that unfeeling, unmerciful, conscience-seared, heart-hardened state—commenced her operations."

David Williams, the most thorough historian of Georgia's "gold fever," has noted the irony in the fact that very soon after the Cherokees were cleared out of the region and the Dahlonega mint began operation, the reason for both began to wane. After a decade of mining that produced a phenomenal $20 million in gold, the Lumpkin County mines began to play out in the 1840s. By the time gold was discovered in California, many of the "twenty-niners" were ready to head west as "forty-niners." The phrase "there's millions in it," corrupted into "there's gold in them thar hills," originated as a ple miners to stay put by state geologist Matthew Stephenson or courthouse steps in Dahlonega in 1849.

Scholars of the Appalachian South have long argued that the degrading stereotypes of mountaineers were largely a post–Civil War phenomenon. Yet as a result of either their primitive living conditions, the remoteness and sparsity of their settlement patterns, or the sheer ruggedness of the wilderness in which they resided, Northeast Georgians—whether victims of gold fever or not—found themselves characterized in such terms almost from the point of initial settlement. William Gilmore Simms, antebellum South Carolina's most distinguished man of letters, wrote one of the more widely read descriptions of the region in his massive 1834 novel, *Guy Rivers*, "a frontier tale of the miners." He set his tale in "the wildest region of the then little-settled state of Georgia—doubly wild as forming the debatable land between the savage and the civilized—partaking of the ferocity of the one, and the skill, cunning, and cupidity of the other."

Others were not as quick to make such distinctions. During the 1840s, Emily Burke, a New Englander who spent a decade teaching in Savannah, recorded what she knew of Georgia's mountain residents based only on hearsay from Savannahians in her *Reminiscences of Georgia*, published after her return to the North. In an entry entitled "Habits, Pursuits, and Ignorance of the People in the Northern Part of the State," she wrote that "when compared with New England, its inhabitants are all of one hundred years behind the times in education, and in all kinds of improvements." Of their antiprogressive ways, she noted, "In building their houses, they change little, if any more, from one generation to another, than the robins do, who build their nests now just as the first robin did that gathered her sticks and moss, and hatched her innocent brood in the garden of Eden."

Others wrote of the crudity of life in the hills. One observer described the mountaineers he encountered in 1835 as "tall, thin, cadaverous-looking animals, as melancholy and lazy as boiled cod-fish"; another noted that the "rudeness of manners among these dwellers in the woods is unpleasant to those accustomed to courtesy and respect," while another described the inhabitants he encountered as "too much given to low and vulgar habits," concluding that "a spirit of enterprise is wanted."

Yet such expressions of contempt for Georgia highlanders were almost always accompanied by rapturous descriptions of the setting in which they eked out so bleak an existence. A particularly ebullient description from the period cited "the grandeur of the lofty Yonah, the magnificence and terrific splendor of Tallulah, the quiet and romantic vale of Nacoochee, and the thousand brilliant landscapes that adorn and beautify the face of Nature" in Georgia's northeastern corner. Tallulah Falls in particular inspired effusive descriptions in both poetry and prose. First discovered by white men in 1819, this spectacular falls dropped over six hundred feet into one of the deepest and most rugged gorges in eastern America.

A pristine wilderness remained a constant lure, despite its distasteful inhabitants. What would become the most vital mainstay of North Georgia life—tourists—followed all too quickly on the heels of miners and frontiersmen. Hotels and summer resorts sprang up throughout the foothills and more accessible mountain communities, and soon catered to Savannahians and other low country planters who sought to escape the summer heat, humidity, and mosquito-induced disease.

As early as 1827, a popular *Gazetteer of Georgia* noted that "It is not necessary that we pack off to the North, to kill the ennui occasioned by our long summers; there are objects of interest enough in our own State . . . among them, the waterfalls and cascades and caves and mountains and valleys, all over Cherokee country." Singling out Toccoa and Tallulah Falls, along with Clarkesville, Cleveland, Gainesville, and other "healthy and pleasant places for visitors," the guide book optimistically assured readers that "should it be said that polite people cannot be entertained at those places—let it be remembered that for fifty years, there was but one old Indian hut at the Saratoga Springs, the most fashionable watering-hole in the world." These communities combined to make the state's highlands "the summer retreat of Georgians from the low country, and help to unite in closer bands, the dweller of the sea-shore, and the inhabitant of the mountain."

The highest praise seems to have been reserved for Clarkesville in Habersham County. "From its exceedingly romantic location, the salubrity of its atmosphere, and the additional charm of courteous hospitality in its inhabitants," extolled an 1839 commentator, "it is a favorite place of resort during the summer months for the denizens of the more southern and less healthful portions of our State." Two years later, another observer concurred, calling it "decidedly the most interesting village in the northern part of Georgia." He went on to describe it as a community of three hundred residents, which served during the summer months as a resort for "forty to fifty of the most wealthy and accomplished families of Georgia and South Carolina, a number of whom have erected and are erecting elegant country seats in its immediate vicinity." The chief attraction for this seasonal influx was quite simply, he wrote, "some of the most romantic scenery in the world."

The Civil War brought into even sharper focus the exceptionalism of the mountain South. Highland Georgia provided a particularly striking example of how both values and lifestyles at odds with those elsewhere in the state and the South led to very different responses to the sectional crisis and the waging of war.

Topography, climate, and soil kept northeastern Georgia marginalized from the plantation economy and slave labor force that defined so much of the lowland South. When more predominant southern interests felt threatened enough by a Republican regime in Washington to leave the Union, highlanders were not nearly as convinced of either the necessity of so drastic a step or the extent to which they would be better served by belonging to a southern Confederacy. The vote by mountain counties in the state referendum on secession in January 1861 revealed a fairly evenly divided electorate, with substantial pockets of Unionist strength in several of the most mountainous areas.

Antisecessionist strength in the highlands had much to do with the region's very limited attachment to slavery. In 1860 slaves made up only 2 to 3 percent of the population in the state's northernmost counties and between 10 and 15 percent of the foothill populace. Across the region, less than 10 percent of white households owned slaves. But opposition to slavery among mountaineers fed more on class resentments than on any moral opposition to the peculiar institution. A North Georgia secessionist reported to Gov. Joseph Brown that "Our people are generally ignorant, honest, unsuspecting, and the idea of a dissolution of the Union at first struck them with horror." Unionist "demagogues" played on those fears by convincing them "that they are not interested in the nigger question, that [secession] was all for the benefit of the wealthy, and that various state and local secessionists ought to be hanged."

Governor Brown, who had grown up in Union County and was an avid secessionist, effectively countered such pleas with race-baiting tactics. Recognizing that racial prejudices were at least as strong as class resentment among his fellow highlanders, he very astutely warned them of the physical threat that marauding liberated slaves would bring to them, adding: "I would call upon the mountain boys as well as the people of the lowlands, and they would come down like an avalanche and swarm around the flag of Georgia with a resolution that would strike terror into the ranks of the abolition cohorts of the North."

Once Georgia's place in the Confederacy was assured and the attack on Fort Sumter meant that its independence would have to be militarily defended, Brown's prophecy seemed to be fulfilled. Many North Georgians revealed just how conditional their initial Unionist sentiments had been as they quickly capitulated to the swelling tide of southern nationalism and cast their lots with the Confederate cause. Unionists became a beleaguered minority in those early, heady months of the new southern nation.

But war weariness combined with increasingly intrusive demands of the Confederate conscription and confiscation policies to add a swelling contingent of disaffected to the ranks of more constant Unionists. The influx of military deserters and civilian refugees further inflamed the volatile and increasingly violent temperaments of Georgia's mountaineers. Within a year of the war's outbreak, a Lumpkin County constituent informed Governor Brown that "these blue mountains of Georgia are being filled with tories and deserters. . . . The Union men are very abusive indeed . . . for there is no law or men to keep them."

Northeast Georgia is the only area of the state in which not a single Civil War–related battlefield, monument, or other significant site has been set aside by either state or national authorities; no region of the state has fewer historical markers related to the war. Yet the lack of any real invasion by enemy forces hardly meant that the area's highlanders experienced the war only at a distance. Internal divisions quickly led to disarray in the form of numerous atrocities in which mountain residents were both perpetrators and victims. Many men sought to avoid military service and hid out in remote wilderness regions for the war's duration, resorting to theft, vandalism, and other forms of lawlessness.

Others vented their frustrations with the Confederacy with firm commitments to its opposition. By the end of the war, the northernmost counties supplied nearly as many men to Union companies (with enlistment opportunities readily accessible in federally occupied East Tennessee) as to Confederate service. Dawson, Pickens, and Union Counties (the latter named in 1832, long before this crisis) managed to create a full Union regiment, the First Georgia State Troop Volunteers, from among their own residents. It stirred enough resentment from local Confederates that a dozen of its enlistees and their civilian supporters were captured by home guard units and executed in Gainesville in November 1864. The same month, another group of restless, anti-Confederate young men from Fannin, Towns, and Union Counties, some of whom had earlier deserted Confederate companies, suffered a similar fate. Just after defecting into Tennessee in an attempt to enlist in federal service there, the six were ambushed and savagely massacred by a ruthless band of Confederate guerrillas.

These internal clashes added to the already well-entrenched image of southern mountain society as primitive and violent. In moving through Georgia's Blue Ridge mountains after an escape from a Confederate prison train in 1864, Union officer John Kellogg was surprised to see "three or four men at work digging sweet potatoes—each man with a musket strapped to his back." He compared the situation with that of the early pioneers, who "were compelled to defend themselves against the North American savages in a war prosecuted without regard to the laws governing civilized nations." Yet these armed farmers, he continued with dismay, were "in the interior of Georgia, one of the older States, in the noon-tide of the nineteenth century. There men were not warring with savages, but with their fellow men of the same race, with their neighbors, their former friends and acquaintances."

Civilized society did indeed seem far removed from wartime North Georgia. Yet the tensions inherent in the sectional conflict soon subsided there after 1865; other than several Republican strongholds in the region, most remnants of its wartime Unionism seemed to evaporate quickly. North Georgia College, established as a land-grant and military institution in Dahlonega six years after the war's end, embraced both the ideology and ritual of the "Lost Cause" with no apparent dissent from within Lumpkin County, one of the region's most contentious during the war. The local newspaper reported in 1877 that local cadets marching before Dahlonega residents "brought vividly to mind the brilliant display made on our streets some years ago by the valiant little band of [Confederate] 'Home Guards,'" with no reference made to the local Unionists whose repression had kept those home guards so busy.

A more extreme manifestation of the clouding of the war's meaning to Georgia's highlanders lies in the recent debate over the state flag. The Confederate battle flag has no stauncher supporters than mountain residents; it flies prominently throughout the region, and appears frequently on T-shirts and bumper stickers. When Gov. Zell Miller, a native of Young Harris in Towns County, proposed that it be eliminated from the state flag, highlander opposition was as vehement as that anywhere in Georgia. Yet in the flurry of petitions, signs, posters, and other protests staged by local Save-Our-Flag committees, no one seemed to acknowledge the irony that such regional support for the Confederacy had not been nearly so strong during its existence as it is now. Nor did they recognize the related paradox: that mountain residents widely regarded the two governors from among their midst, Joe Brown and Zell Miller, as having betrayed them, the first by his support of the very cause of which they now feel the second is insufficiently supportive. When Brown declared in 1861 that Georgia's highlanders would "swarm around the flag of Georgia with a resolution," little could he have known that his words would more accurately describe attitudes 120 years later than they would the war years just ahead.

If the specific ideological differences that split the mountain populace have since become muddled, one explanation for some consistency amid the contradictions here lies in the streak of independence and rugged individualism long recognized as basic to the mountain character. It was opposition to undue government intrusion that fueled resentment of both debilitating Confederate policy then and attempts to change the flag now. "People just don't like minorities or authorities telling them what to do," explained a Blue Ridge store owner in 1992.

That defiance, along with the brutality and lawlessness that characterized the mountains' messy "war within a war," took on new and even more pronounced forms after the war. For north Georgia and other parts of southern Appalachia, such behavior soon came to be seen as endemic, the legacy of a violent and vicious frontier populace that would continue to stigmatize the region until well into the twentieth century.

The stereotypical traditions of defiance, brutality, and lawlessness continued into the twentieth century as a result of moonshine wars. It was as moonshiners, in fact, that North Georgians staked their only claim to national prominence—at least until the era of *Foxfire* and *Deliverance*. While generally ignored or dismissed as tangential to any other discussion of southern Appalachia, Georgia moonshiners' pitched battles to defend their illicit stills against federal revenuers brought them the sort of journalistic coverage they had somehow managed to avoid since the heyday of Dahlonega gold and Cherokee removal.

These clashes coincided with the late-nineteenth-century "discovery" of Appalachia by everyone from social workers and missionaries to local color writers and journalists, and while no other aspect of mountain life seemed to draw these chroniclers to Georgia, moonshine did. Articles in *Harper's Monthly*, *Atlantic Monthly*, *Cosmopolitan*, and *Lippincott's Magazine* kept northern readerships fully informed of how Georgia mountaineers managed to thwart the increasingly aggressive efforts by federal officials to make them law-abiding citizens. Even in the vastly expanding historical scholarship on Appalachia currently underway, the only work in which Georgia's mountains figure in more than fleeting references is Wilbur Miller's *Revenuers & Moonshiners: Enforcing Federal Liquor Law in the Mountain South, 1865–1900*, in which no state rates a longer index entry.

The production of moonshine—a catch-all term applied to corn whiskey, applejack, or peach brandy—had long been as much a part of mountain life as making syrup or slaughtering hogs. It was only during the Civil War that the federal government raised revenue by requiring anyone involved in the manufacture and sale of alcohol to purchase a license and to pay taxes on every gallon produced. These requirements, continued in modified form after the war, imposed a particular hardship on mountain families, for whom this liquified form of harvest was often among the few marketable commodities they had to sell. This was especially true for more remote areas, such as Union County, where one observer noted that farmers "raise a few

Federal agents arrest a moonshiner and destroy his still, 1890s.

hogs, a little wheat, and make the bulk of their crop in corn," which in liquid form generated the only cash many were likely to see.

North Georgia became a particularly active center for "moonshine" production in the decades following the Civil War. The Tallulah district of Rabun County earned a reputation for the fine quality of its mountain dew, though the uninitiated often found it "a vile production, repulsive in taste and smell." In 1885 a New York reporter described the effects of Rabun County's finest brew on a companion: "The instant he has swallowed the stuff he feels as if he were sunburned all over, his head begins to buzz as if a hive of bees had swarmed there, and when he closes his eyes, he sees six hundred million torch-light processions all charging at him, ten abreast." He soon passed out, and took a full forty-eight hours to sober up.

Georgian highlanders also drew attention for the intensity with which they resisted government attempts to stifle the most lucrative of their time-honored traditions. Wilbur Miller estimates that in 1876 four-fifths of all federal law enforcement efforts and court cases in Georgia's mountains involved illegal liquor issues, more than for the highland areas of any other state. As the federal crusade to eliminate, or even control, bootleg activity heated up, so did the resistance of those who felt unduly persecuted. Another scholar reports that North Georgia counties were the most violent in Appalachia, with alleged casualties inflicted on federal agents there nearly twice the number suffered by revenuers in Tennessee, the second most dangerous assignment. In 1886, the U.S. marshall for North Georgia reported to the Justice Department that moonshiners had killed two of his deputies and four guides (much-resented local collaborators), had shot at four other agents, and had stabbed a fifth.

In conveying this activity to an apparently eager national readership, northern correspondents were often sympathetic, if condescending, in their portrayals of the beleaguered mountaineer. An 1897 article in *Cosmopolitan* (no relation to the current women's magazine) on "Moonshining in Georgia" opened with the salutation of "typical moonshiners at work" to federal agents who burst into their log cabin: "Wall, stranger, yo'uns, I reckon, calkelates as how you is powerful smart to trap we uns as is only working up the corn, so as the folks kin have rations to eat and a bed to lay on. But we uns will hev our turn yet, durn your pesky revenues!"

An *Atlantic Monthly* feature in 1902 demonstrated its sensitivity to the impact the moonshine wars had on children. Maintaining that their outlook was "pathetic in the extreme," it described childhoods spent in the midst of constant alarms, and children who never knew when their father would walk out of their cabin never to return alive. "There will come years of work in hidden mountain distilleries, arrests, prison walls, battles, murders, and who can tell what else? Yet through it all they will be following the precepts that came to them in the cradle—living the best life they know."

Despite the heart-rending terms in which journalists portrayed these beleaguered highlanders, they never failed to fall back on the same belittling stereotypes to which mountain people had long been subjected. The *Cosmopolitan* correspondent concluded his account with a devastating, but all too typical, summation of their backwardness. "The comforts of modern civilization are almost entirely unknown to these mountaineers," he proclaimed. "So apart from the rest of the world are these Georgia mountaineers and moonshiners that they remain in almost total ignorance of important current events. It is often asserted that many of them do not yet know that the late civil war is over. . . . Such are the people on whom the revenue officers are forced to wage a constant warfare."

For most mountain residents, whether active participants or not, the moral implications of their whiskey and brandy production was never an issue. Moonshining, one correspondent explained, "is the one illegal act at which nearly all natives, regardless of their financial condition or religious belief, have from time immemorial winked." They claimed never to have understood the government's obsession with locating and destroying their stills, and saw nothing shameful or dishonorable about the jail time served by those taken prisoner-of-war in these encounters. On the other hand, many recognized, and even reveled in, the illicit nature of what they were doing. A Union County resident recalled his father, who made a considerable profit by bottling his corn crop. Yet to the dismay of those with whom he did business, he spearheaded the campaign to make the county dry. "Father was a realist," his son explained. "He knew that whiskey making and whiskey drinking was not going to disappear from Choestoe, but he said it was a good influence on the young people not to have it so evident."

Such warfare continued well into the twentieth century, but the nature of the war changed considerably with modernization. Prohibition greatly increased the profitability of moonshining in the 1920s, and its production, as historian Ray Rensi has phrased it, "went from a craft to an occupation." With new emphasis placed on quantity over quality, new techniques and additives altered the process of production, polluted and even poisoned much of the final product, and intensified the efforts by federal and state officials to stop it.

The new urban demand for mountain-produced brew made "blockade running" a central part of the contest. Attempts to outrun officials as they transported their product to more distant markets led moonshiners to design "tanker cars" (the most effective of which was the 1940 Ford) and to master deft driving maneuvers, both of which they put to use in high-speed chases. Though the end of Prohibition meant a drop in price, their supply routes established during the 1920s and their more mobile battle tactics continued to fuel the trade through midcentury.

Gov. Zell Miller explained in his 1976 memoir, *The Mountains Within Me*, the changes he had observed in the business since those days. "I grew up with moonshiners and understood them," he wrote in a particularly enlightening chapter devoted to the subject. "I had classmates who worked at stills" and some of those who "hauled liquor in their 1940 Fords . . . were among my best friends." But since World War II, fewer mountain families continued to engage in such trafficking, and "those who do, for the most part, are a breed apart from their ancestors for whom making whiskey was a personal, custom-sanctioned activity that was incidental to their total livelihood and not a calculated, law-breaking enterprise." Many, in fact, are no longer even native to the region, but "outsiders who have chosen the mountains as the best place to carry on their illicit operations, and most of the others are bankrolled in their activities by underworld elements in the cities who make all the profits and take few of the risks." Miller concluded that "there is as much difference in their operations and traditional moonshine as between the dark and bright sides of the moon."

Though production has declined drastically since the 1970s, moonshining is not yet a lost art. It seems to have resumed much of its earlier character—family operations geared primarily for their own, or at least local, consumption. There also seems to be more tolerance, and even empathy, by local officials toward these modest personalized

Vegetable peddler with ox-drawn wagon, Gainesville, early twentieth century

operations. As the Dawson County sheriff explained his own laxity to Ray Rensi, "How can I arrest them folks for what I used to do when I was younger?"

Twentieth-century modernization impacted northeastern Georgia in many other ways as well. For its inhabitants, the very concept of progress proved a relative term, taking on a wide variety of meanings as to just what constituted improvement to one's lifestyle, community, or sense of regional development. In *Blood Mountain*, a poignant memoir of early twentieth-century life in Union County's Choestoe community, Edward Shuler recounted what "a new age of progress" meant to its residents. "New conveniences that made our lives easier," he wrote, included riding plows, cribs with mechanized cornshellers, better saddles and more ornate harnesses, which he claimed made their mules seem happier once they began wearing them, and "cake" soap for personal hygiene at least, though lye continued to be used to wash clothes.

For others, progress meant greater access to the outside world. Georgia's more remotely situated highlanders had long been aware of the extent to which their isolation and economic stagnation were integrally linked and that the key to real prosperity lay in providing more ready access to distant markets. An early Rabun County historian made a tongue-in-cheek claim that to reach his area in the mid-nineteenth century meant one had to "go one day by railroad, the next day by horse and buggy, a third day on horseback, a fourth day on foot and then on all fours until you climbed a tree, and when you fell out, you'd be in Rabun County."

Railroads provided the greatest promise of overcoming physical remoteness. Proposals for an interstate Blue Ridge Railroad that would cut across Georgia's northeasternmost corner were in the works as early as 1838. But it was well after the Civil War when iron bands finally made their way into the region. Gainesville was the first beneficiary, with an Atlanta connection completed in 1874. Over the course of the 1880s and 1890s, Athens was gradually linked by track to Cornelia, Clarkesville, Clayton, and other points due north as far as Franklin, North Carolina.

Mountain residents anticipated the transforming effects of such connections well before they became a reality. A mountain woman echoed the sentiments of many when she exclaimed, "We hope ere long to hear the stately tread of the Iron-horse in our midst. Then indeed will open a new era among us!" With the iron horse's arrival, few were disappointed. A simple announcement in a Habersham County newspaper in 1882 suggested just how momentous the impact on mountain life could be: "The first two bales of cotton that were ever brought to Clarkesville arrived last Monday morning. This is some of the good effects of the railroad." A *Foxfire* account of the Tallulah Falls Line's construction provides a more thorough summary of those "good effects," stating that it "gave residents jobs, bought things from them, took them places, brought visitors to see them, shipped out their farm produce, brought in things they couldn't raise or make, provided depots to gather in, kept them company, provided excitement, and even supposedly helped some people forecast the weather by the sound of the whistle."

In parts of the mountains untouched by the railroad, residents expressed the same enthusiasm, even well into the twentieth century, for the transforming effects mere paved roads could have on their economic well-being. In the 1910s and 1920s, Georgia, in cooperation with neighboring states, made great strides in creating a highway system through the mountains. An east-west route linking Spartanburg with Chattanooga ran through Clayton and Hiawassee, and another moving north-south between Atlanta and Asheville linked Gainesville, Cleveland, and Clayton along the way. Both were greeted with genuine excitement by the counties and communities through which so much new traffic would pass.

The preeminence of Gainesville to the region's commercial vitality was very much a function of its railroad connections with the lowlands beyond and to the paved roads that strengthened its linkages to other highland communities. While some mountain merchants and farmers established trade networks with either Atlanta, Athens, or Augusta, the more ready accessibility of Gainesville, nestled at the base of the Blue Ridge, made it the primary destination for market-oriented farmers through much of northeastern Georgia. An elderly

Union County farmer recalled the importance Gainesville had played to his family and others in the late nineteenth century. "Every other week, we would go to Gainesville by wagon," he recalled. "People from Blairsville and Choestoe would try to make it to Cleveland in one day," where they would camp, before moving on to Gainesville as part of an increasingly lengthy wagon train, sometimes consisting of as many as thirty wagons. Once in the Hall County seat, wagoners converged on the town square, where they sold their hams, chickens, eggs, sorghum syrup, buttermilk, yellow root, and apples, and used the cash received to purchase from local merchants flour, sugar, coffee, bolts of cloth, overalls, and other staples, or to pick up from the train depot goods ordered by means of that great innovation of late-nineteenth-century merchandising, the Sears-Roebuck catalog.

In 1940 the WPA guide to Georgia conveyed the extent to which Gainesville continued to serve the region in this capacity, while growing in other ways as well. "On Saturday afternoons," the guide stated, "farmers from the surrounding countryside park their cars or wagons around the public square and market their produce; mill workers stand in groups on the street corners; and fashionably dressed young women and military students in cadet-gray uniforms from the near-by schools fill the shops and drug stores." Gainesville's diversification as the industrial and educational hub of the region is apparent in that succinct description of a Saturday afternoon on the square. Cotton, hosiery, and furniture factories were all a part of the community's economic base by then, and Brenau College and Riverside Military Academy drew students from throughout the northern half of the state and well beyond.

But it was as a poultry center that Gainesville would make its most distinctive mark on the region's economy, and even that other mountaineers claim credit for. Edward Shuler suggested in his memoir that it was Union County wagoners and those like them from neighboring counties who made the city the chicken processing capital of the world. The mountains' finest fowl, he claimed, were raised in the Choestoe district, and wagoners adapted the layout of their wagons to carry nothing but chickens to a Gainesville market given increasingly over to poultry and eggs. (Two Choestoe farmers raised turkeys as well, he noted, but usually sent them to Augusta.)

While the increased interconnectedness of Northeast Georgia has been a major function of twentieth-century modernization, its landscape and economy were to be reshaped by the incursions of far more formidable forces: corporate exploitation and government intervention, both state and federal. New opportunities for tapping into the vast natural wealth of the region coincided with a sudden awareness of the need to guard against, or at least regulate, such encroachments on both its natural resources and its scenic beauty.

Georgia's first major environmental battle was fought over one of its most celebrated and visited sites, Tallulah Falls. The statewide showdown over its survival was not only a dramatic foreshadowing of issues with which businessmen, developers, government officials, and environmentalists would continue to wrestle throughout the rest of the century; it was also the earliest example of the considerable impact tourism could and would have on the region's economic future.

Since the 1880s, when railroad connections brought increasing numbers of visitors from Athens and Atlanta into Northeast Georgia and particularly to the falls, the small settlement perched on the south rim of the vast Tallulah gorge grew into a major tourist resort. No other single site in Georgia's mountains attracted as much attention or as many people until the relatively recent emergence of Helen. By the turn of the century, three large hotels and numerous guest houses and cottages could accommodate nearly a thousand guests at a time. All were situated within easy access to the railroad depot (one of its few buildings still standing) at the town center. Equally accessible were other trappings of the tourist trade, including souvenir shops, an eighty-foot observation tower, and a Museum of Historical Relics and Curiosities. A much promoted tightrope-walking across the gorge in 1886 attracted several thousand spectators brought to the scene by a dozen or so specially chartered excursion trains. (An equally publicized high wire venture across the gorge by Karl Wallenda in 1970 drew even larger crowds.) In 1901 town officials staged a Blue Ridge and Tallulah Falls Exhibition that must have been among the first and more grandiose of the craft fairs now so integral a part of the region's tourism.

This heightened interest in the falls led to a greater awareness of its exploitable economic potential in other ways, and simultaneously, to an equal awareness of the need to safeguard its future against such exploitation. In the midst of a nationally raised consciousness of the dangers "grasping capitalists" posed to New York's Niagara Falls, Georgians recognized how vulnerable Tallulah was as well. An Atlanta newspaper editor in 1905 proposed that "some time, when Georgia is in a cultured and generous mood, . . . the state should buy that magnificent domain of scenery and ozone which takes in Tallulah Falls and make it the most beautiful state park and reservation this side of Yellowstone."

It was electrical power companies that moved first to tap Tallulah's great potential. From 1908 to 1911, the Georgia Power Company (soon thereafter to become the Georgia Railway and Power Company) maneuvered itself into ownership of enough property to launch its grand scheme of using the falls to provide electricity to Atlanta. To do so meant replacing the falls with a dam, a massive project already well underway when the opposition finally mobilized.

The preservationists' campaign was organized and led by the formidable Helen Dortches Longstreet, widow of Robert E. Lee's valued but controversial "old war horse," Gen. James Longstreet. A native of Carnesville, Mrs. Longstreet spent most of her adult life in Gainesville, where she met the elderly general and married him in 1897, six years before his death. Under the auspices of the Tallulah Falls Conservation Association, she worked tirelessly and nearly single-handedly to stop what she called "commercial pirates and buccaneers," who were not only "rapacious, greedy money-worshippers," but—in her mind, much more damning—Northerners as well, of "the class that did the most mischief when the Federal army tried to ruin the South" once before. That they would "forcibly seize the loveliest jewel the State possesses and make it a frightful noisome cess-pool of malaria" she found "the most insulting act that could have been offered the state." Despite her efforts and the support of the state legislature, a court decision in 1913 ruled in favor of the power company. In part, Mrs. Longstreet's failure was one of timing. According to E. Merton Coulter, whose *Georgia Waters* provides the fullest account of this battle, she "stormed the heights with as much or more vim and determination than her husband General had used at Gettysburg to take the Round Tops. Maybe it was delay in both instances which prevented victory."

Construction of the dam and power plant were completed in the fall of 1913, and Tallulah's raging waters were channeled into the production of eighteen thousand horsepowers of electric power, most of it carried by wire directly to Atlanta, where it powered the city's trolley cars. Within several months new generators increased that output more than fourfold, making Tallulah the nation's third most productive hydroelectric facility then in existence. In 1914 Georgia Power began work on Mathis Dam, seven miles upriver from the Tallulah gorge, with the idea of creating a storage reservoir for its Tallulah plant. That reservoir became Lake Rabun. Over the course of the next fifteen years, six dams were constructed along a twenty-eight-mile stretch of the Talullah and Tugalo rivers, with a total drop of nearly two thousand feet from the top of the Burton dam, the uppermost, to the base of the Yonah dam. The stair-step arrangement that allowed for this drop was unique for its time, and upon the system's completion in 1927, Georgia Power (as it had again become) could boast the most fully developed continuous stretch of river in the United States. It was the object of much attention by engineers and developers elsewhere and served as a model of sorts for the Muscle Shoals and Tennessee Valley Authority projects that soon followed it.

While the dam destroyed both the falls and more gradually the resort community nestled along its south rim, the gorge itself remained
as spectacular as ever. Ironically, what had been considered one of the
first sites for state park status as part of the preservation campaign
early in the century became in 1994 the newest addition to Georgia's
state park system, with thirty-one-hundred acres leased from Georgia
Power along the northern rim of the gorge.

In response to charges of their disregard of the natural beauty they
were destroying in building their first dam, Georgia Power officials
argued, with considerable foresight, that the lakes created by this and
other dams would more than compensate in terms of both enhanced
scenic appeal and their ultimate economic contributions to the region.
Georgia Power has taken great satisfaction since in noting that the vast
lake system it created—Tugalo, Rabun, Seed, Burton, and Yonah—has
indeed lived up to both promises. The company was quick to initiate a
progressive program of land management and wildlife protection both
on the shores and in the waters it owns. In ensuring the scenic value
of the lakes, the company has also much enhanced local economic
prosperity. Lakeshore homes have so increased taxable property
values that Rabun and Habersham Counties soon found themselves in
better financial condition than any other two purely rural counties in
Georgia.

Other corporate and government agencies have contributed as well
to transforming Northeast Georgia into a vast lake district where no
natural lakes exist. In the early 1940s, the Tennessee Valley Authority
created five reservoirs in the Upper Hiawassee Valley, two of which fall
into Northeast Georgia: Lake Nottely in Union County was created by
the dam built at the highest elevation in the entire TVA system; and
Lake Chatuge straddles Georgia and North Carolina, with its lower
half in Towns County, almost enveloping its county seat, Hiawassee.
The economic impact of these lakes on local development came far
more slowly than did that from the Georgia Power projects. Nor were
local residents as eager for the sort of potential progress these lakes offered. As late as 1978, an informal history of Union County mentions
Lake Nottely only once, and then only in a photograph caption which
states that the lake's creation destroyed some of the county's best farmland. Only in the past decade and a half have their assets come to be
fully appreciated as lakefront and lakeview property have created substantial and locally profitable retirement communities in both Union
and Towns Counties.

The region's largest lakes, Lake Sidney Lanier and Lake Hartwell,
are more recent creations, both constructed by the U.S. Army Corps of
Engineers in the late 1950s and early 1960s. Their greater accessibility
to large population centers has made them far more popular recreational draws than the more remote TVA reservoirs. Lake Lanier's

thirty-eight thousand acres of water, supplied by the Chattahoochee River, lie primarily in Hall County, but it shares its 607 miles of shoreline with Forsyth and Dawson Counties. With Northeast Georgia's largest community, Gainesville, situated at its northern end and most Atlantans within an hour's drive of its southern end, Lanier attracts an astonishing 16 million visitors annually, making it the most heavily utilized Army Corps of Engineers lake in the United States. It not only justifies its label as metropolitan Atlanta's favorite water wonderland; it also provides Atlantans with much of their drinking water. A major part of its appeal lies in the twelve-hundred-acre state-created Lake Lanier Islands, a resort and amusement complex of golf courses, sandy beaches, water slides, hot tubs, and restaurants and lodging facilities, with plans for additional water rides and a dinosaur theme park currently in the works.

The larger Lake Hartwell, created in 1962, separates Georgia from South Carolina and consists of nearly fifty-six thousand acres of water supplied by the Tugaloo River above and supplying the Savannah River below. The Georgia portion of its 962 miles of shoreline is shared by Toccoa and Stephens and Hart Counties, and provides all three with considerable lakefront property and recreational facilities which account for much of their revenue, just as these other man-made resources do for well over half of the counties in northeastern Georgia.

Lakes make up only a small part of the property in Northeast Georgia that falls under government control. The federal government is the largest single landholder throughout Appalachia by reason of the rich forest resources it owns and manages, and its prominence is particularly conspicuous in Georgia's mountains. As was true throughout southern Appalachia, lumber companies made vast inroads into Northeast Georgia during the 1890s and over the next twenty to thirty years took a heavy toll on much of its virgin wilderness. In a typical scenario, railroad magnate Henry C. Bagley of Cincinnati discovered the vast pine and poplar forests of White County, with many trees over twenty-five feet in diameter. He turned the small adjacent crossroads of Helen and Robertstown into logging camps, where local "wood hicks" were mobilized to cut the giant virgin timber from nearby mountains and transport it to a sawmill in Helen that, at its height in 1910, turned out seventy thousand board feet of lumber daily. Within a couple of decades, wholesale clearcutting had stripped hillsides bare, which in turn led to the disappearance of game and the onset of such serious erosion that the Chattahoochee River ran red with silt.

Only in the 1910s did the national conservation movement, inspired several years earlier by Pres. Theodore Roosevelt among others, begin to focus on forest resources east of the Mississippi. Georgia woodlands first came under government protection with the creation in 1918 of the Nantahala and Cherokee National Forests, each of which spanned adjacent woodlands in North and South Carolina as well. The U.S. Forest Service continued to expand its holdings in the 1920s and 1930s, as it came to focus its acquisitions on those vast areas stripped, clearcut, and then abandoned by lumber companies.

In 1936, the federally controlled wilderness in Georgia's mountains was consolidated into the Chattahoochee National Forest, which then spanned a half million acres; subsequent additions have increased its area to nearly 750,000 acres, about three-fourths of which lie in its northeastern section. No other single national forest in the southern Appalachians is as vast. Combined with the lakes under federal management, the Chattahoochee makes the U.S. government by far the largest landholder in Northeast Georgia. Over 60 percent of Rabun County falls under federal ownership, as do over half of Towns and Union Counties.

While extensive logging operations continue within the Chattahoochee, they are carefully monitored and managed. Since 1964 twelve sections within the forest—half of which fall in northeastern Georgia—have been designated as wilderness areas, which puts them off limits to any timber harvesting, road building, or other construction. Watered by over a thousand miles of rivers and streams, over five hundred species of wildlife now thrive within the Chattahoochee's bounds.

Several individual rangers have taken particular pride in their contributions in this area, and none more so than did Georgia's first U.S. forest ranger, Arthur Woody. Through the 1930s up until his death in 1946, he devoted his energies and resources to restocking bear, trout, and other depleted species. But it was his efforts on behalf of white-tailed deer that earned him almost legendary status among North Georgians. Woody, nicknamed the "barefoot ranger" for his refusal to wear either shoes or a uniform, claimed that it was his father, a hunter, who killed North Georgia's last deer in Fannin County in 1895. In 1926 he traveled with his family to the Pisgah National Game Preserve in North Carolina, where they acquired five fawns. He later adopted three more that had been abandoned by a traveling carnival in Cleveland. He raised and eventually released them all into the forests of north Lumpkin County. Through his efforts and those of the seven young deer and their progeny, an estimated two thousand white-tails roamed the Chattahoochee by 1941, when the first deer-hunting season was reinstituted, a move that pained Woody, who still knew many of the deer by name.

Just as vital as the woodland and wildlife preservation in the Forest Service's management scheme is the utilization of its lands as recreational resources for the region's burgeoning human population. Dozens of campgrounds and picnic areas are scattered throughout the Chattahoochee, and over 430 miles of hiking trails wend their way through it, including 79 miles of the Appalachian Trail. In 1994, with government purchases of scattered acreage between its point of origin on Springer Mountain and the North Carolina border, Georgia became only the third of the fourteen states through which the trail passes in which its length is fully protected as federal forest land. (West Virginia and New Jersey are the other two.)

The state itself has invested a great deal in the conservation and tourism of the region. Georgia boasts one of most extensive and fully developed state park systems in the South, and no part of the state can claim as many of those sites as can its northeastern corner: Twelve of the state's sixty parks and historic sites fall within the region, including the system's oldest, Vogel State Park, and its newest, Tallulah Gorge State Park. Most take advantage of scenic locales and are situated either on lakes, like Hart, Tugaloo, and Moccasin Creek; near waterfalls, like Amicalola Falls and Unicoi; or on mountain tops, such as the state's highest park, the spectacularly situated Black Rock Mountain facility.

The linkage between these facilities and the natural beauty of their settings is of course the key to their popularity and ever increasing usage by campers, lodge and cabin-dwellers, and conventioneers. But more commercialized means of drawing visitors into the mountains have proved at least equally as effective. None is more phenomenal than the creation of Helen, perhaps the region's only site whose popular and commercial success compares to that of Tallulah Falls at the turn of the century. The tiny town's remarkable drawing power might be termed even more phenomenal in that it has managed to appeal to so many without the presence of a major natural feature—falls, gorge, peak, or lake—to add to its allure (though Unicoi and Anna Ruby Falls are fewer than five miles away and the Chattahoochee, still little more than a stream, flows serenely through its center). Helen's transformation was more dramatic because of the depths to which it had sunk. Once the lumber companies abandoned the region in the 1920s, the community's decline was swift. Described in Georgia's original WPA guide in 1940 as "a cool valley town where pleasant cottages contrast with shabby old frame buildings," Helen degenerated further after that; by the late 1960s, its business district consisted of a rundown motel and sixteen concrete buildings, nine of which stood empty.

Only in 1969 did this quiet and remote village take the step that made it the site in Georgia that now hosts more visitors annually than any except Atlanta and Savannah. A meeting of three local businessmen a year earlier set the transformation into motion. Bemoaning the fact that considerable traffic moved straight through their business district en route to the scenic wonders of the peaks and waterfalls beyond, storeowner Pete Hodkinson and his companions wondered what they could do to stop some of those cars long enough for their occupants to spend a little money in Helen. Painting their storefronts was an approach they had heard worked well in boosting business in another small and withering community, Hamilton, Georgia. They approached the area's foremost artist, John Kollock of Clarkesville, for ideas. Kollock recalled that they "really just wanted me to suggest a color scheme to paint the buildings," but having done military service in southern Germany in the 1950s, Kollock thought of remodeling Helen in a far more substantive way, transforming it into a Bavarian village. Hodkinson loved the idea and proved the prime instigator in convincing his fellow Helen storeowners to go along with the scheme. By 1972, Kollock's designs had taken tangible form, and a trickle of curious visitors soon became a flood.

Pete Hodkinson remained a central force in Helen's continued development. He was, according to a colleague, "a good example for us back in the days when Helen was a last refuge of the free spirits. He was a little crazy in a lot of ways. . . ." Hodkinson was a visionary, but an unusually effective one, and his spirit of fun infused the town with as much a sense of activity as of place, a spirit still integral to its distinctiveness. Much of its success lay in the variety of "events" he staged, ranging from the annual Oktoberfest and Helen-to-the-Atlantic Balloon Races to more spontaneous events such as wagon and motorcycle races through Helen's main street and the Great Easter Olive Hunt, in which participants searched a grass field for olives while holding martinis. Like the town he created, Pete Hodkinson was fun-loving, energetic, exaggerated, and obsessive. He was killed in a hot air balloon accident over Toccoa in 1976, and thus did not live to experience fully the extraordinary success of his collaborative scheme for giving passing traffic a reason to stop and spend a little money in Helen, Georgia.

There is a curious irony that for a region in which residents exhibit such pride of place and so staunchly defend their southern and highland identities, the most successful attraction is a community thoroughly disguised as a European village. Such foreign role-playing has proven contagious. Four miles away from Helen, at the juncture of two of the area's most pastoral and celebrated valleys, the Nacoochee and the Sautee, stands the Old Sautee Store. Once a combination of rambling old country store (White County's oldest in continuous operation) and antique museum, the store is now first and foremost a Scandinavian boutique, and it stops more traffic than ever.

Other recent attractions have translated equally inventive make-believe into widespread interest and commercial success. The Chateau Elan in Barrow County has expanded its winery into a resort complex built around an imposing facsimile of a French estate. Cleveland's Babyland General Hospital, the point of origin for a once irresistible fad, Cabbage Patch Kids, operates as a delivery room, maternity ward,

Old Sautee Store

and adoption agency all geared toward the continued procreation and dissemination of the large stuffed dolls.

While such anomalies have proven to be popular—and lucrative—means of luring visitors into the North Georgia foothills and mountains, other communities have tapped into a more genuine sense of their own heritage to generate tourist dollars. Seasonal festivals celebrating mountain life or local history have become a prime means of doing so. Ironically, many have modeled such events on Helen's oldest and richest tradition, the Bavarian celebration of Oktoberfest. Its chief attractions, according to its promotional literature, are "authentic bands from Europe performing polkas, waltzes, sing-a-longs and Helen's famous Chicken Dance" and German cuisine such as "Bavarian wurst, sauerkraut, and imported wines and beers."

German culture or food is hardly necessary to instigate such extended participatory activity, and other North Georgia communities have succeeded in looking much closer to home, and usually in less ambitious ways, for thematic variations on the Oktoberfest concept. Dahlonega's "Gold Rush Days" in October clog its square with as many tourists as the gold fever did prospectors in the 1830s. In addition to added opportunities for panning gold (a year-round option for visitors), the town crowns a Gold Rush king and queen, who preside over a parade, and sponsors contests such as a pig-calling and liars' competition. Blairsville boasts the world's largest sorghum festival. Over several fall weekends, local mills begin "crushing and cooking" in the mornings and demonstrate the full process of sorghum making throughout the day.

The list goes on. Gainesville touts its origins as Mule Camp Springs with its Mule Camp Market, the most distinctive feature of which is its "running of the mules," billed as "similar to the running of the bulls in Pamplona, Spain, but not as dangerous. Starting time depends on the mules." Hiawassee hosts the Georgia Official State Fiddler's Convention at its Georgia Mountain Fairgrounds; Ellijay and Cornelia both celebrate the harvest season with fall apple festivals; Unicoi State Park holds a woodcarvers' "Whittle 'In" in May; Dillard sponsors an October cabbage festival (not likely to be mistaken for the pre-Christmas Cabbage Patch Kids weekend in Cleveland). Homer stages the world's largest Easter egg hunt.

All the best in preindustrial mountain life, it seems—whether real or perceived—is displayed, sold, eaten, or reenacted in these annual rituals of nostalgia and commercialism. The rich heritage of the Appalachian South that *Foxfire* has documented has been rendered in even more quaint, old-fashioned, and wholesome terms. In effect, such festivals commodify mountain life and culture and present them to an eager and easily amused public.

Yet many of these celebrations represent far more than mere tourist gimmicks or culture commercialized. Again, like *Foxfire*, the impetus behind many of these staged gatherings lies in a collective community consciousness of a lost past. They provide a means of instilling age-old skills and values in new generations of mountain youth. In Blairsville, for example, the Sorghum Festival commemorates a dying tradition. Once produced in abundance and a staple of mountain tables applied not just to pancakes and breakfast biscuits but to meats, beans, and corn bread at other meals, sorghum has now become a taste that younger generations raised on Aunt Jemima syrup have not acquired. Twenty-five years ago, there were more than two dozen sorghum mills in operation around Blairsville. Now there are no more than seven or eight and local residents are very much aware not only of the decline in syrup production locally, but also that their community remains as one of its last strongholds. As much as or more than the tourist dollars it brings in, this festival is a concerted effort to keep the tradition alive.

The artisans of Georgia's mountains are equally as sensitized to the past and to their roles in perpetuating otherwise endangered skills that they see as integral parts of their heritage. The tourists who buy the quilts, woven cloth, baskets, candles, woodcarvings, stools and chairs, pottery, or ironwork may or may not make any conscious link between their purchases and the region they're touring; if they do, they often view them as authentic, if quaint, souvenirs of a primitive society, without realizing how essential such skills and the products resulting from those skills were to earlier generations. "A fellow who growed up on a farm in the hills never forgot his raising," a Cherokee County farmer once noted. "Just about everything he had was homemade. It was a homemade life." Or as folklorist John Burrison has termed it, it was "an age of hands," when local craftsmen and women provided the vast majority of the goods, tools, and furnishings needed for the functioning of mountain farms and households.

Folk potters in the region seem particularly conscious of the vital historical tradition from which their work stems. In 1992, more than a thousand people gathered at Mossy Creek, just south of Cleveland, for a centennial celebration of North Georgia's preeminent Meaders family of potters. John Milton Meaders built his White County operation in 1892, an operation his sons, his grandsons, and their wives have maintained ever since. The last of John's six sons, Cheever Meaders, articulated the family's sense of obligation to that legacy in 1967 when he noted: "This handmade pott'ry is going to be gone after a while. You take it plumb outta existence, nobody to make it, and in ten years people'd be wondering how that's made." It was in that year, just before his death, that the Smithsonian Institution assured that neither the technology nor the artistry of the Meaderses would be forgotten. It produced a documentary film of him at work and made Meaders face jugs a prominent part of both Washington's first Festival of American Folklife and its permanent museum displays. That exposure, in addition to close bonds with Eliot Wigginton that led to generous *Foxfire* coverage, dramatically increased the demand for the Meaderses' work and gained them widespread recognition and new-found prosperity.

John Burrison dedicated his 1983 book, *Brothers in Clay,* the definitive treatment of Georgia's folk pottery, to Cheever's son, Lanier Meaders, "without whom all this would just be history." Early in the twentieth century more than nineteen shops operated within "hollering distance" of each other. Such a concentrated community of potters was not unique in the state. Burrison fully chronicles others, including several that lie in its northeastern corner.

But it is the Meaderses who have best articulated the legacy they perpetuate. Burrison quotes Lanier Meaders on the importance of pottery to earlier generations of mountain residents. "Just about everything else at one time in this part of the country depended on it," he said, and later mused that clay jars and jugs "were as important back in the old days as mobile homes are now; poor folks couldn't live without them." His father, Cheever, once recalled the local demands for their product: "What about six or eight wagons a-standing up there, come every day a-wanting pottery to put their stuff in, and us might-near working day and night at it. It was more so in the fall of the year when stuff was getting ripe and ready to put up." Lanier later elaborated on what at least a substantial portion of that "stuff" was. The "only two truly craft people" in the 1930s, he claimed, were the "whiskey maker and the pottery makers. In fact they were the only two occupations going, and they had something in common; they'd make the whiskey and the potter would make the jugs." He recalled that revenue officers viewed with suspicion the fact that four or five hundred jugs gathered in his father's yard one day would be gone the next. Their inquiries of Cheever as to who purchased them and why produced noncommittal responses, though both parties were fully aware of the only enterprise that demanded so many jugs at once.

North Georgia musicians have also long assumed special roles as guardians of their regional heritage. When they began to seek out and record the folk music of the mountains in the late 1970s, Art and Margo Rosenbaum wondered whether "the sounds of these traditions might still be widely heard in mountain cabins, old-fashioned churches, and back-country dance halls," or whether they had been obliterated or irrevocably altered by the intrusions of modern life— interstate highways, suburban and vacation development, and the pervasiveness of pop and country music disseminated by television and radio. The Rosenbaums found, to their relief, that the traditional forms of musical expression they sought were very much alive in Georgia's highlands, preserved and still performed by what they call "extraordinary folk, usually older, individualistic and at times even eccentric, possessed of keen memories, authentic and exemplary performing styles, and a commitment to the 'old-time way.'"

In the book resulting from their research in the region, *Folk Visions and Voices*, the Rosenbaums chronicle the diversity of the musicians they encountered: the multigenerational family string bands of the Ellers of Hiawassee, the Chancey Brothers of Boardtown, and the Childers of Jasper; Jake Staggers, a black banjo-picker in Toccoa; and fiddler Ray Knight, a self-defined "old-timer" from Dahlonega. In discussing their music, all these performers convey a strong sense of place and past—the elaborate kinship ties that bind them to earlier generations of musicians and the distinctive highland heritage that shaped their songs in both form and content. The rich oral tradition, both spoken and sung, that these performers embody and that Art Rosenbaum has so beautifully captured is striking in its historical grounding of their own and their region's past: Ray Knight composed songs of both the antebellum gold rush and his own escape from the Dawsonville jail in the 1950s; the Ellerses sang of their pioneer roots in Towns County and of their Unionist grandfather who hid along Hall Creek from Confederate conscription officials; Jake Staggers recalled playing for white folks' dances up on Panther Creek in the 1930s, where "a big jug of corn liquor" often led to brawls or shootouts; and the Chancey brothers jovially reminisced about their combined moonshine and music making during that same depression decade, with the eldest declaring "'Course I was only drunk one time in my life—got drunk when I was sixteen and stayed drunk till I was

The Eller Brothers, Vaughn and Lawrence, with Ross Brown, Upper Hightower, 1979

thirty." This music and the many messages it conveys remain among the most vital expressions of regional identity to many North Georgians and among the most vivid of the many links between their past and present.

The Georgia Mountain Fair has for nearly four decades provided a rather remarkable venue for the demonstration of the creativity and artistry of both highland craftsmen and musicians. Yet another example of the region's extraordinary commitment to its heritage, this annual production is, like Helen, a success story inspired by a businessman's vision. In 1950, Herbert Tabor, an insurance man in Ellijay, responded to complaints about the area's declining status that he heard at the Towns County Lion's Club in nearby Hiawassee by suggesting that the club sponsor a fair. It began as a moderately successful weeklong crafts fair, attended by over a thousand people from Towns and neighboring counties. But Tabor's commitment to the region and its heritage soon made it much more than that. "The mountains are his main business," Celestine Sibley wrote of Tabor in 1954. "He loves them. He loves mountain people and knows hundreds of stories about them. He never misses a mountain event if he can help it, be it a cemetery working at Young Harris or a vesper service on top of Brasstown Bald."

From that sense of place and culture came a unique fair that provides as comprehensive and varied a representation of mountain life, past and present, as is possible, with scarcely a trace of commercialism. The number of demonstrations, performances, and exhibits, many of them full-scale permanent replicas of pioneer farm and vil-

NORTHEAST GEORGIA POTTERS

THE MEADERS POTTERY

About five miles south of Cleveland on Ga. 75 lies the rural community of Mossy Creek, historically the largest folk-pottery community of nine such centers in Georgia, home to some eighty farmer-potters since the area was settled in the 1820s. The best-known name among those potters is the Meaders family, which established a shop and kiln in 1893 to produce functional stonewares coated with the regionally characteristic woodash- or lime-based alkaline glazes. The original site, until recently operated by Lanier Meaders (famous for his face jugs and awarded a National Heritage Fellowship by the National Endowment for the Arts), is still in use but not open on a regular basis; other members of the family produce ware that can be seen in crafts shops throughout North Georgia.

GILLSVILLE

On Ga. 52 about twelve miles east of Gainesville (at the juncture of Hall and Banks Counties) is another active folk-pottery center, like Mossy Creek in White County. Here, long-standing clay clans like the Hewells, Cravens, and Fergusons produce hand-thrown, unglazed horticultural wares, making Gillsville the garden-pottery center of the Southeast. The pottery tradition there blossomed in the late nineteenth century, as family-trained potters responded to the need for food storage vessels on local farms. At Hewell's Pottery, which is open to the public Mondays through Saturdays, one can see three generations of the family working together, producing ash-glazed stoneware (including face jugs) as a sideline to the horticultural wares that have been the chief stock-in-trade since the 1940s. The stoneware is fired in an old-fashioned, wood-burning "tunnel" kiln, behind which recreations of an old "jug shop" and "mud mill" have been erected. The Hewells celebrate their pottery heritage every fall at a public "Turning and Burning" festival.

—John Burrison
Georgia State University

Overleaf: Pottery shop of Cleator Meaders, Jr.
Above: Three generations of Hewell family potters, Gillsville, 1993

lage life, grew steadily and soon earned for the fair a reputation far beyond the region. By the early 1970s, a local newspaper said of it, "like a huge stone tossed into the economic lake, the ripples are spreading farther and farther. Motels within a seventy-five-mile radius know when the nine-day event is underway. Space becomes scarce and reservations are necessary. Local businessmen directly feel the impact. They can't avoid it when 100,000 visitors pour into this small community." Since then the fair has expanded to a twelve-day run attended by as many as 170,000 people in recent years. It is hard to imagine a venue more appealing or more conducive to creating an awareness and appreciation for the richness of this heritage which, while undoubtedly indigenous to the southern Appalachians, also stirs a sense of the broader pioneer spirit that defines for so many their American heritage as well.

The ongoing success of these various attractions, events, and sites reflects a growing interest in the region, an interest that has translated into economic growth. Other than suburban Atlanta, no area of Georgia is witnessing as much economic expansion as are its Blue Ridge mountains. Real estate and home construction are as central as tourism to the region's economic vitality. The boom in retirement and second home development has accelerated over the past two decades and shows little sign of leveling off. In Rabun County, for example, seasonal or migratory dwellings made up a fourth of all housing units in 1980; by 1990, they accounted for more than half, a trend equally apparent in other counties. Because the construction of these homes is now the region's leading industry, and among its largest employers, the standard of living for many in this traditionally poor corner of the state is significantly higher.

Distinctions can be drawn in terms of who these new homeowners are. In Rabun and the more remote counties to its west, Towns and Union, retirees account for the vast majority of new building. Senior citizens now make up more than a fifth of Union and Rabun's residents, and a fourth of that of Towns, which now boasts the highest median age of any county in Georgia. Lumpkin, Dawson, and Hall Counties, with more ready access to Atlanta and other urban centers, attract more "getaway" home building, with cabins and second homes designed primarily for weekend or summer use. Habersham and White Counties have capitalized on both segments of the housing market. Highway construction also fuels the construction industry, as more four-lane arteries extend into and across the region to accommodate the increasing flow of traffic bound for a variety of highland destinations.

Such growth has remained more suburbanized than urbanized in nature, if only because so many of those moving into the area are temporary visitors, second homeowners, or seasonal residents. Thus in strict demographic terms at least, Northeast Georgia remains as fully rural as it has ever been. Despite its proximity to Lake Lanier and its self-defined role as the gateway to mountain tourism, Gainesville's population growth has been modest, fluctuating between fifteen and seventeen thousand over the past three decades. Yet it still remains more than twice the size of the region's next largest communities, Toccoa and Winder. Over half the county seats in Northeast Georgia still claim fewer than two thousand residents; five have populations of between four and eight hundred.

Yet the "suburbanization" of the region's mountains and lakes has been dramatic in its impact on both, and has become a source of real concern to environmentalists. The pristine wilderness that draws so many newcomers into the area is endangered by their very presence, as overdevelopment brings with it multiple forms of erosion and pollution that threaten its water, its woodlands, and its wildlife in a variety of direct and indirect ways. New homeowners themselves, once they've staked a claim to their own piece of the Blue Ridge, also worry about further growth. As the chairman of Lake Rabun's planning board once observed, "Everybody who builds a house on one of those lakes wants it to be the last house built in the county."

But it is the native populace of the region that most resents the trends that have so radically transformed their communities, lifestyles, and economic status (even if more and better jobs are among the effects). A Rabun County resident's explanation to Jim Kilgo as to why "they ain't near the game in these mountains they used to be," was simply "Too much goddam Atlanta." A familiar saying throughout the area is that the way to flare local tempers is to "Shoot their dog or tell 'em you're from Florida." More serious concerns lie in the extent to which the real estate boom, like the nationalization of forest land two generations earlier, has squeezed many residents off the land. A Dillard resident spoke for many fellow highlanders when he expressed his frustration at the fact that vastly inflated property values and accompanying taxes have either forced many to sell out or much diminished their chances of purchasing property locally. "The damn realtors are a terrible plague," he declared. "They've got land so dang high a native boy can't buy it at all."

More than any other part of Georgia, its northeastern corner has always been and continues to be shaped by its allure to outsiders. The vast and unalterable appeal of its scenic beauty and moderate climate has long drawn explorers and tourists in the region; their ranks have now been joined by campers, hikers, and boaters, along with retirees and second-home vacationers. Opportunities to exploit and/or utilize the region's abundant natural resources have also long provided an irresistible lure to a variety of powerful forces, ranging from gold-digging "twenty-niners" and logging companies in the nineteenth century to Georgia Power, TVA, and the U.S. Forest Service in the twentieth. Other intrusions by governmental authority have left indelible marks on North Georgians in a variety of forms, whether U.S. troops removing Cherokees, Confederates harassing Unionists, or revenuers battling moonshiners and blockade runners. In a very real sense, the current tensions between longtime residents and recent arrivals can be viewed as part of these deeply rooted historical patterns. Viewed from that perspective, James Dickey's *Deliverance* becomes a parable of the clash between natives and outsiders and the extent to which a vast and untamed wilderness has always been central to the conflicts between the two.

Yet the offense taken by many North Georgians to *Deliverance* suggests another trend very much at play—their concern about how they and their region are characterized. Through a variety of means—the *Foxfire* phenomenon, the Georgia Mountain Fair, local museums, exhibitions, and historic sites, and those numerous festivals celebrating everything from gold rush and mule train days to sorghum, woodcarving, and fiddlings—residents have not only worked hard to create an awareness and an appreciation for the rich and distinctive heritage of mountain life; they have also demonstrated the extent to which the region's rich human legacy has become an integral part of its appeal to outsiders. Zell Miller was quite right when, after touting the development of his native region in recent years, he concluded, "But of all the great things that have happened and are planned, all are dwarfed into insignificance by the enduring grandeur of the mountains themselves." It is indeed comforting to know that such natural assets will survive the forces of modernization, suburbanization, and tourism to which the region is being subjected; but it is also gratifying to know that its distinctive historical legacy has remained of equal significance in shaping both the identities of Northeast Georgia residents and the appeal their region continues to hold for so many others.

Steve Gurr

TOURING NORTHEAST GEORGIA

Northeast Georgia is the state's land of mountains and waters, and what the land and climate offer has drawn travelers to the region since the late eighteenth century. Federal and state parks and forests have been major forces in the preservation of Northeast Georgia's beauty and resources. These efforts along with healthy commercial motives have been significant in bringing attention and services to this region since the publication of the original *Georgia: The WPA Guide to Its Towns and Countryside* in 1940.

Local populations in more sheltered areas of the region continue to be bound to the traditions of Appalachia. Here still the visitor has the opportunity to see tradition in the midst of change, nature in the midst of the manmade. The delightful persistence of this combination makes Northeast Georgia among the state's most treasured resources.

The Northeast Georgia under consideration here consists of fifteen counties bounded on the north by North Carolina, on the east by South Carolina, on the south by an imaginary line just north of Athens, and on the west by a line raggedly made of the western shore of Lake Lanier and fanning northwestward in the direction of, but not quite reaching, the Zell Miller Parkway, Ga. 5.

There are no cities proper in this region. Gainesville, in Hall County, is the largest community and the leading service hub. Athens is another important service and educational center just outside the limits of the region, and Atlanta is growing daily toward the north and east.

While Georgia as a whole contains a black population of more than 30 percent, most of the fifteen counties in the northeast region report a black population of less than 5 percent; of these, four have no black population at all, according to the 1990 census. Like so many of the cultural characteristics of the region, the distribution of race in Northeast Georgia is a product of geography and economic history. Slavery was not introduced widely into the area because large-scale cotton farming was impossible for much of the land there.

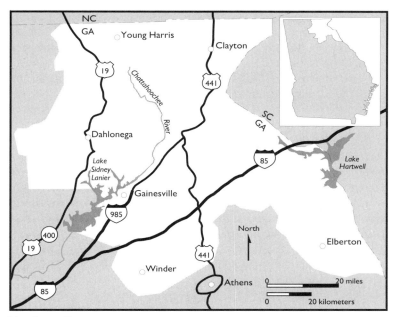

Northeast Georgia

The agriculture and economy of the region have always been on a smaller scale and more diversified than the middle and lower areas of the state. One of the symbols of this region's economic history is the chicken house—the long, low, metal-topped building seen near farm houses throughout the area. Raising chickens for meat, for eggs, and for income is an important factor in the lives of area citizens. Thousands of independent contractors who might be called hyphenated farmers rather than traditional farm folk raise chickens under contract to large corporations. Hyphenated farmers keep chicken houses to supplement incomes from a variety of other jobs, from blue-collar labor to corporate law practice. The industry gives the region more than incomes and a particular architecture. The processing plants have provided abundant labor-intensive, low-skill jobs that have attracted migrant and immigrant populations. Asian and Spanish-speaking newcomers have made a multicultural society that failed to reach the hills via the cotton culture and came instead on the wings of chickens.

Many travelers come to this part of Georgia to see the colorful leaves in the fall. The season starts in the higher elevations in early October and reaches the southern boundary of the region around the first of November. The pleasant fall weather and the bright foliage historically have been a magnet to the region since long before the creation of such man-made wonders as Lake Lanier or Helen. The addition of more travelers, better roads, and recent commercial attractions can make autumn weekends a traffic nightmare. Travel during the workweek is a good idea, and a local contact who knows the back roads is always helpful.

Northeast Georgia ideally should be visited in several seasons, on small roads, slowly, again and again.

HOW THESE TOURS WORK

The following tours examine Northeast Georgia in three units that form a pattern of pie-shaped slices radiating from the southwestern corner of the region, south to north or west to east along major highway corridors. For purposes of the tours it is assumed that many travelers will come to this part of the state via Atlanta. Beginning at other points, however, should not cause any confusion.

Tour one, the westernmost tour (U.S. 19–Ga. 400 stem), includes sites in Dawson, Lumpkin, Union, Towns, White, and Hall Counties. The region includes the beginnings of the Appalachian Trail, Georgia's gold-mining country, the highest peak in the state, and Georgia's largest recreational lake.

Tour two (U.S. 129, U.S. 411/Ga. 365) covers the central portion of the region. Here are rafting rivers, mountain lakes, quaint town squares, Georgia's own Alpine tourist mecca, and some of the most beautiful vistas in the state.

Tour three (I-85 stem) follows a corridor north from Atlanta past vineyards, auto racing venues, the birthplace and resting place of baseball legend Ty Cobb, and Georgia's granite capital. Along the route, at Banks Crossing, is one of Georgia's most popular commercial crossroads.

TOUR ONE: WESTERN NORTHEAST GEORGIA

Less than an hour's drive north of Atlanta on Ga. 400 (U.S. 19), the traveler catches the first glimpses of the North Georgia mountains in the distance. Just before the Dawson County line, Ga. 400 crosses Settendown Road and Jot-em-down Road. Dawson Forest Road (left off Ga. 400, which is not, at that point, controlled access) allows for entering **Dawsonville** via the "old road," by turning right off Dawson Forest Road onto Ga. 9. This route leads to the town square of Dawsonville, past old and newer dwellings, chicken houses, and the other vernacular architecture of the region. The faster but also scenic route follows U.S. 19 and Ga. 400 north, exiting to the west at Ga. 53 toward Dawsonville. Almost immediately Lumpkin Campground Road crosses Ga. 53, and the campground is to the left of the intersection.

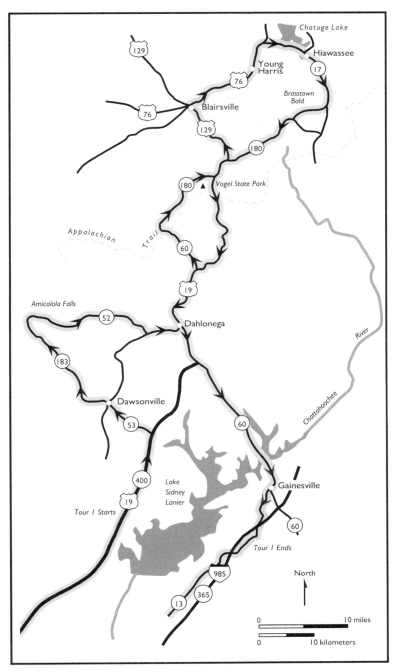

Northeast Georgia, Tour One

The Lumpkin Campground was established around 1830 on what had originally been Cherokee land. The original meeting site for church gatherings was an arbor made from brush (a latticework of native growth layered over a wooden framework). This brush arbor, common to many such campgrounds, was replaced in the 1840s by a wooden structure, and gradually families constructed a number of small wooden cabins, called tents. These families would come to spend several days in "protracted meetings" to participate in services and enjoy the social gatherings of fellow worshippers.

The practice of camp meetings continues more than a century and a half after its beginnings here, and some thirty-five cottages remain for revivals and family reunions. Today a visit to this place evokes a time long ago. From every side orderly rows of weathered wooden tents, reminiscent of old country stores or perhaps the set of a western movie, face the large open meeting place. Large oaks contribute to the feeling of yesteryear. Vehicles are not allowed onto the grounds, but a visitor may park nearby and walk among the structures at any time, any day. Visiting when there is no service in progress may be more moving for some than seeing a service.

Back on Ga. 53 toward Dawsonville, the Etowah River Road is about two-and-one-half miles from Lumpkin Campground. The Etowah River Valley was the site of Cherokee Indian farming before their removal and gold prospecting and mining by settlers in the nineteenth century. It is now dotted with horse farms and weekend retreats. After a few miles the paved portion of the road ends. The traveler may backtrack to Ga. 53 or follow the Etowah River Road to its end, turning left on Ga. 136, left on Ga. 9, and thus to Dawsonville.

At the center of Dawsonville is the vernacular-style Dawson County courthouse (ca. 1858). The county was formed in 1857 and named for William C. Dawson (1798–1856), congressman and U.S. Senator. The flavor of twentieth-century Dawson County may be observed in the Dawsonville Pool Room, which pays tribute to the native stock-car racing heroes of the region, especially Bill Elliot, a NASCAR championship auto racer of the 1980s and 1990s.

Amicalola Falls State Park (sixteen miles northwest of Dawsonville) is reached via Ga. 53 to Ga. 183 to Ga. 52. The park features overnight facilities—basic camping, cabins, and a lodge with restaurant—and the highest waterfall in Georgia. An eight-mile "approach trail" near here leads to the southern terminus of the Appalachian Trail at Springer Mountain. Trail facts are available at the park information center. Fishing and an abundance of wildflowers and beautiful native vegetation are other attractions. The park is administered by the Georgia Department of Natural Resources. (See the appendix for contacts and more information.) Dahlonega is about twenty miles east

Amicalola Falls

from Amicalola Falls along a winding forest road with frequent glimpses of the mountains to the north.

Dahlonega is the seat of Lumpkin County, which was established in 1832 and named for Gov. Wilson Lumpkin. The historic Lumpkin County courthouse on the square was built in 1836 and today houses the Gold Museum. The museum, administered by the Parks, Recreation and Historic Sites Division of the Georgia Department of Natural Resources, depicts the story of the discovery of gold in Georgia in the 1820s, the history of the industry, and its social and cultural consequences. The Dahlonega square itself has a pleasant, small-town atmosphere.

Nature in the form of gold and copper first attracted white settlers to this region of Georgia. Tourists followed, and today Dahlonega is a busy tourism-based community; home of North Georgia College, Georgia's state military college; and site of a number of seasonal festivals and special events. Nearby commercial establishments offer a chance to pan for gold or to go rafting on local waters. There is an especially nice view of the town itself (highlighted by the gold-leaf-covered tower of the North Georgia College administration building) on the south side of the town near the local hospital. Tourism has provided Dahlonega with many antique, gift, and novelty shops and restaurants, including traditional family-style establishments that are always busy feeding tourists.

From Dahlonega U.S. 19 heads north to a left turn on Ga. 60 four miles from the Dahlonega square. The road winds through hardwood trees that make it a spectacular leaf-viewing route in the fall, when color peaks in late October or early November. This road crosses the Appalachian Trail at Woody Gap in the Chattahoochee National Forest at the edge of Union County. The gap is named for the legendary Ranger Woody, also known as the barefoot ranger. William Arthur Woody, area native (1884–1946), worked for the U.S. Forest Service from 1912 until 1942. He was the first ranger in what is now the Chattahoochee National Forest. He was as unorthodox in his methods as a conservationist as he was in his appearance. Weighing over two hundred pounds, barefoot Woody chased poachers, befriended the native population, and personally led the reintroduction of white-tailed deer and brook trout to this region.

At Woody Gap (fourteen miles from Dahlonega) are picnic tables and rudimentary rest facilities. At Suches signs point toward Blairsville on Ga. 180, which passes Lake Winfield Scott and its U.S. Forest Service park facilities (see appendix) twenty miles north of Dahlonega.

As Ga. 180 merges with U.S. 19 and 129, Blairsville is to the left (eleven miles); to the right is Vogel State Park (covered later on this tour). South of Blairsville is a University of Georgia agricultural experiment station with its interesting seasonal offerings visible from the highway.

Blairsville is the seat of Union County, created in 1832 and named for its early unionist political sentiments. The courthouse, erected in 1899, contains a local history museum (open June–October).

This leg of tour one (Dawson County to Blairsville) may be concluded by returning to Atlanta via U.S. 76W to Ga. 5/575 (Zell Miller Parkway) or by continuing tour one to Gainesville via Brasstown Bald, DeSoto Falls, Vogel State Park, Cleveland, or Dahlonega. It may also be continued to the Northwest Georgia tour.

From Blairsville, U.S. 19/129 leads to Nottely Lake, and U.S. 76E leads to **Young Harris**, a college town and home of Gov. Zell Miller. The campus of Young Harris College, founded in 1886, has a number of charming buildings named to honor benefactors and is a major cultural asset to this region. Brasstown Valley Resort, a state recreational facility on the eastern side of Young Harris, includes golf and other leisure opportunities.

From Young Harris U.S. 76 leads to **Hiawassee**, the Towns County seat, along Lake Chatuge. For the traveler there are various accommodations along the lake shore. At Hiawassee the Georgia Mountain Fairground offers a full season of musical programs from the spring through early fall. A special highlight is the Georgia Mountain Fair, held in the first two weeks of August each year. Among the attractions are local crafts and products of regional agriculture as well as a variety of entertainment built around the cultural themes of the region.

East of Hiawassee, U.S. 76, Ga. 17, and Ga. 180 carry the traveler to Brasstown Bald (nine miles; watch for signs pointing to the right), Georgia's highest peak at 4,784 feet above sea level. Four states can be seen, weather permitting, from the observation area at the visitor information center, which offers interpretive programs. For a small fee, visitors may take a shuttle bus up the steep, half-mile trail from the parking lot to the center or they may walk. The Brasstown Bald Visitor Center is operated in cooperation with the Chattahoochee-Oconee Heritage Association and is owned and maintained by the U.S. Forest Service. The road up to the bald (Ga. 180 Sp.) is one of the few places where rhododendron, a pink-blossomed mountain shrub, is still blooming in June.

From Brasstown Bald, Ga. 180 to the right passes through **Choestoe** (cho-es-TOE-ee, "the place of the dancing rabbits") near the home of the poet Byron Herbert Reece (1917–58). At U.S. 19/129, a turn south toward Dahlonega takes the traveler to Vogel State Park (eleven miles south of Blairsville), which is, for camping and cabin accommodations, Georgia's oldest and largest state park and among its most popular. The Walasi-Yi Center on the Appalachian Trail is at the Union–Lumpkin County border. Here are examples of the Civilian Conservation Corps (CCC) New Deal–period architecture that influenced many of the state's park facilities.

South of Vogel along the winding U.S. 19/129 is DeSoto Falls (fourteen miles north of Dahlonega). A 650-acre recreation area features a series of five falls along a three-mile section of the DeSoto Trail, named for the Spanish explorer Hernando DeSoto. According to tradition, he brought his exploration party to this area in 1540. Information on hiking trails and overnight camping is available at the site.

From DeSoto Falls U.S. 19S and Ga. 60 lead back to Dahlonega, and Ga. 60 on to Gainesville. Along this route north of the city of Gainesville are several bridges and adjacent recreation sites across Lake Lanier (more later) and the Chattahoochee River.

Gainesville is the chief commercial center of the region, with abundant amenities including lodging, restaurants, and medical and automotive services. Local restaurants and bed-and-breakfast inns are good places to find out more about the local people.

Green Street on U.S. 29 Bu., the major north-south route through Gainesville, goes past large turn-of-the-century houses that have been converted into commercial establishments. Green Street includes part of the campus of Brenau University (formerly Brenau College for Women). Brenau began in 1879 as Georgia Baptist Seminary and became, by the twentieth century, a private women's college. Pearce Auditorium on the Brenau campus, a fine beaux-arts building, includes a beautifully restored theater and auditorium where community concerts and plays take place amid the decor of an earlier time. Next door is the Brenau Art Museum. A short distance from the campus the "Cottage Victorian" houses an impressive period clothing collection. The Quinlan Art Center (514 Green Street) exhibits nationally noted as well as local and regional artists and provides educational and instructional programs in support of local and regional artists.

The intersection of U.S. 129 Bu. and Ga. 13 is sometimes called the crossroads of Northeast Georgia. It is the civic and commercial center of the Gainesville–Hall County community. Gainesville is the seat of Hall County, established in 1818 and named for Lyman Hall, governor of Georgia and a signer of the Declaration of Independence. The Hall County courthouse was funded by the WPA and constructed in 1937 following the destruction of the earlier building by a devastating tornado in April 1936.

Roosevelt Square, adjoining the Georgia Mountains Center, the city hall, and the county courthouse, is dedicated to Pres. Franklin D. Roosevelt, who visited the city after the tornado. He was instrumental in getting aid for the city and returned in 1937 to help dedicate the new courthouse. The city hall and courthouse are built of white marble in the stripped classical motif. Near this complex at 121 Spring Street is the federal courthouse, with its New Deal mural featuring a Civil War scene, "Morgan's Raiders," painted by Daniel Boza in 1936. The Georgia Mountains Museum, a local cultural facility, is located nearby in what was formerly the Green Street Fire Station. Here are found artifacts of local history; the poultry industry; the late cartoonist and naturalist Ed Dodd, creator of Mark Trail, an early manifestation in American popular culture of the environmental movement; and other revolving educational exhibits. The Georgia Mountains Historical Cultural Trust, parent organization of the museum and also sponsor of the Railroad Museum located at Academy Street and Jesse Jewell Parkway, in the summer of 1994 began the process of joining Brenau University in a long-range plan to build a new musuem facility on the Brenau campus.

Ga. 13S passes by the Elachee Nature Science Center, a public nature preserve and educational center that includes a nature museum and participatory exhibits, wildflower garden, nature trails, and special programs designed to foster an understanding of and appreciation for the natural world. Thousands of acres of watershed were given to a local public authority as Chicopee Woods and today include not only Elachee but also a golf course, an agricultural center, and exhibit/event area.

Chicopee, a mill village built in the 1920s, is adjacent to the entrance to Elachee. The village is a charming, planned community of neat red-brick houses once owned by the mill and housing only mill employees. Individual private ownership since the 1960s and the decline and eventual closing of the mill have led to a refocusing of the community as a popular area for modest housing in an attractive setting. On Ga. 13 west beyond Elachee and Chicopee is Oakwood, a growing community and commercial center also approached by I-985 at exit 4. Oakwood is the location of Gainesville College, a two-year unit of the University System of Georgia, and Lanier Area Technical Institute (one mile north of exit 4 on Ga. 53–Mundy Mill Road). The campus of Gainesville College is a favorite local recreational area with tennis courts, running track, walking trail, and a broad expanse of green where soccer and kite flying are popular. A college theater and art gallery are part of the Continuing Education/Performing Arts complex on the campus.

Lake Sidney Lanier, one of Georgia's most popular recreational sites, is found at the conclusion of this tour of the western portion of Northeast Georgia. Though this route assumes an approach from Gainesville and Oakwood, for those travelers coming from Atlanta on I-985 (Lanier Parkway), exit 2 provides an approach to Lake Lanier via Ga. 347 (also from Atlanta via Ga. 13 and Peachtree Industrial Boulevard, which becomes McEver Road). The lake may be approached from the west from Ga. 400. Lake Lanier is a thirty-eight-thousand-acre, man-made impoundment created in the 1950s by damming the Chattahoochee River. Nature conspires with human labor to create this leading recreational feature of Northeast Georgia.

Fishing, boating (sail as well as all sizes of power), camping, picnicking, and simply enjoying the beauty of the mountain horizons across the lake are the chief activities associated with Lake Lanier.

Lake Lanier Islands, a state authority, is a major recreational development. Activities and facilities there include two golf courses, a water park, shops, restaurants, resort-level lodging, camping facilities, stables, bike riding, and special seasonal events such as festive holiday lighting tours. Boats of all kinds may be rented, and launch ramps are available for those who bring their own boats. There are entrance fees as well as specific activity fees.

Around the shores of Lake Lanier, which touches Gwinnett, Forsyth, Dawson, and Hall Counties, are numerous federal- and state-managed public picnic, camping, and boating parks. Many offer splendid lake and mountain views. While swimming areas are designated, many inviting-looking places to wade are treacherous, and there are no lifeguards at these areas. Life preservers are recommended for children playing *anywhere* near the water and for *anyone* entering the water. Users should exercise caution in regard to swimming, wading, or boating.

Seasonal fishing tournaments and sailing contests offer exciting competition, and sunny weather, regardless of the season, brings thousands of boats of all descriptions up and down the lake from near the dam at Buford to the Chattahoochee River north of Gainesville. The dam at Buford may be reached from McEver Road west from Oakwood and Gainesville past Buford and on toward Sugar Hill (Gwinnett County). There is a Buford Dam Road to the right off McEver (later Peachtree Industrial). A number of picnic and dam and river viewing sites are near the dam. The sight of the Chattahoochee emerging from Lake Lanier and heading for Atlanta is impressive and well worth a detour. The resource manager's office near the dam has exhibits on the area's natural history and early inhabitants. The bridges crossing the lake on Ga. 60, 11, 284, 53, and 369 offer nice views of the lake or the Chattahoochee. Public boat ramps are located near many of these bridges.

Travelers may return to Atlanta via I-985/85 or return to Gainesville and the beginning of tour two.

TOUR TWO: CENTRAL NORTHEAST GEORGIA

Between Gainesville and Cleveland on U.S. 129N are breathtaking views of the mountains in the distance. The ruined rock chimneys of old home places mark the path northward, as do numerous churches, chiefly Baptist and Methodist, small neat houses, and, in the distance, newer mountain-view retreats. Hot boiled peanuts, fruit, jellies, and honey are sold along the roadway during the tourist season. Fall has

MOONSHINERS AND AUTO RACING

The history of American stock-car racing is intertwined at least to some degree with the making, and especially the transporting, of illegal, non-tax-paid spirits (moonshine). The Dawson and Lumpkin County area of Georgia was an active region of this industry in the mid-twentieth century. Much 'shine hauling was done from the hills of Northeast Georgia southward into the urban market around Atlanta. Fast, "souped-up" autos, especially Fords, were modified not only for speed but also for load capacity. It was in part from the native engineering genius of local shade tree mechanics that a transition was made from runnin' liquor to runnin' stock cars on dusty oval dirt tracks around the southeastern United States. While NASCAR racing has grown well beyond these geographic limitations, there is still the traditional link with an earlier pastime, one that was a product as much of the bitter poverty and economic necessity of the region as it was of the imagined romance of the moonshine business.

—Steve Gurr

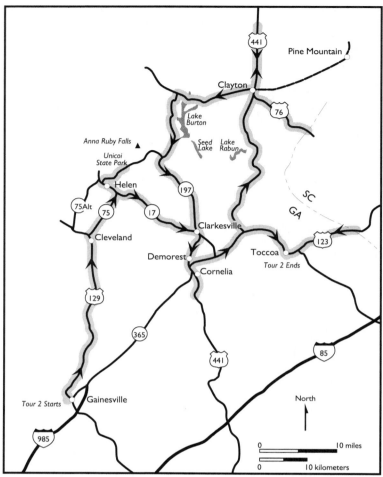

Northeast Georgia, Tour Two

an extended leaf-viewing season in October and November; spring and summer offer escape from the heat of the flatlands to the south.

Just before the center of **Cleveland** (eighteen miles north of Gainesville) is Babyland General Hospital on the left. At this popular tourist stop fanciful dolls called Cabbage Patch Kids are "adopted" in mock solemnity. Cleveland has at its center the old White County courthouse (ca. 1859–60). Restored in 1994 by the local community, it houses local history exhibits. The state legislature named White County (1857) for David T. White, a friend of one of the county's founders.

Around the central square of the courthouse are antique shops as well as ordinary commercial establishments. Of special interest as late as the spring of 1994 was the "World's Largest Collection of Afghans," a gallery shop that seemed a bit incongruous in Northeast Georgia. Truett-McConnell College, a Baptist institution, is a mile or so to the east of the square.

From Cleveland the traveler may follow Ga. 75 or 75 Alt. north to Helen and Unicoi State Park. The nine miles from Cleveland to Helen pass through pleasant countryside with a number of commercial establishments appealing to the tourist. Here, as elsewhere in Northeast Georgia, there is a mix of the new, the old, the odd, and the interesting: Blackriver Bar-B-Q, ersatz Alpine architectural trim, beautiful mountain views, streams, and houses of longtime natives and more recent summer dwellers.

The Nacoochee Valley Historic District along Ga. 75 south of Helen is one of the most beautiful regions in Georgia. A state historical marker notes the discovery of gold on Duke's Creek in 1828, an event that precipitated the white settlement of the area. The Sautee-Nacoochee Valley is the site of a distinctive Indian burial mound. Atop the mound is a delicate gazebo. The view of this mound up the valley is one of the most photographed in the state. Approaching **Helen** from Sautee-Nacoochee, one sees the miracle of tourism that has risen there since the late 1960s, converting what was once a sleepy village beside the Chattahoochee River into a man-made Alpine fantasy where even chain restaurants conform to the adopted style. All manner of eating, sleeping, buying, and viewing are available in Helen, as are horse-drawn rides and entertainment for children in the form of a small amusement park. Throughout the autumn, Helen celebrates Oktoberfest with special events.

Unicoi State Park and Anna Ruby Falls are on the outskirts of Helen via Ga. 75 north and Ga. 356 to the right. Unicoi is a popular location not only for weekend travelers but also for family reunions, meetings, and conferences. In addition to camping and picnicking, the park offers boating, fishing, and cabin and lodge accommodations. The gift shop in the lodge carries beautiful handmade quilts and other local crafts. A large restaurant serves the complex.

Anna Ruby Falls (entrance adjacent to Unicoi State Park) is a double falls fed by two creeks, Curtis and York, coming off Tray Mountain. A .4-mile path from the visitor center leads through a delightful assortment of native flora and fauna. The brevity of the path should not mislead; the steep incline of parts of this walk justifies the benches along the way. Returning from Unicoi toward Helen, the traveler may take the Russell Scenic Highway (Ga. 348 off Ga. 75 S) into the region of tour one or continue tour two via Ga. 17 to Clarkesville.

Clarkesville is the county seat of Habersham County, which also includes Baldwin, Cornelia, and Demorest. The county was created in 1818 and is named for Georgia revolutionary-period leader Maj.

Sautee-Nacoochee Mound

Joseph Habersham (1751–1815). Early in the nineteenth century the Clarkesville area was a summer retreat for coastal Georgians attracted by the temperate weather. The home of Richard W. Habersham (1786–1842; congressman; nephew of Joseph Habersham), a stone house on U.S. 441 north of Clarkesville, was traditionally considered eighteenth century but of late has been proved to be early- to mid-nineteenth century in origin (private). Many outstanding examples of nineteenth-century architecture are hidden away in the surrounding countryside, most closed to the public except for occasional special benefit tours. Among the excellent public buildings in Clarkesville is the Grace Episcopal Church, built between 1839 and 1842.

Demorest is located south of Clarkesville on U.S. 441. The small, picturesque town in Habersham County was established in 1889 as a temperance settlement and planned community. (The Demorest Home, Mining, and Improvement Company was the sponsoring body). The people who came here were New Englanders and Midwesterners, and the look of the community today bespeaks an influence unlike those typical of Northeast Georgia. The community attracted an active Chautauqua series, and there was a high level of civic-mindedness and care for the public areas of the community. The Methodist-Congregational Church is one of the vestiges of the town's interesting history. It was instrumental in the support of what is now Piedmont College, which had its beginnings in 1897 as J. S. Green Collegiate Institute.

The residential streets off U.S. 441 have a number of charming residences dating from the beginnings of Demorest. There are seasonal house and walking tours. Baseball Hall of Fame member Johnny Mize, a native of Demorest, retired here. Mize was a power-hitting first baseman who played for the St. Louis Cardinals and the New York Giants and Yankees.

U.S. 441 south from Demorest leads quickly to several interesting sites that are close to Ga. 365—Cornelia, Baldwin, and Lake Russell. **Cornelia** is home of the Big Red Apple. This monument to apple farming in the region is located in the center of Cornelia next to the rail line and the former depot, which now serves as an information center. "North Georgia," by Charles Trumbo Henry, a New Deal–period mural depicting the apple orchards, has been moved from its original location in a 1930s post office to the new post office in a shopping strip on U.S. 441.

Baldwin, adjacent to Cornelia, is headquarters for Fieldale Farms, one of the giants of the poultry industry in North Georgia. From here there are important ties to much of the investment and work that is represented by those thousands and thousands of chicken houses seen throughout Northeast Georgia.

Two miles northeast of Cornelia on Ga. 13/U.S. 123 is the Lake Russell Recreation Complex, part of the Chattahoochee National Forest. It provides camping, picnicking, swimming, boating, and fishing. There are no cabins, and campsites offer neither individual electric nor water hookups. Special programs in the recreation area are planned for each weekend of the season, which runs from Memorial Day to Labor Day.

Back at the intersection of Ga. 365 and U.S. 441 near Cornelia, the traveler may follow either of two continuations of tour two: Ga. 365/U.S. 123 to Toccoa and on toward South Carolina or U.S. 441 northward toward North Carolina. At Cornelia, "old" or historic 441 returns to Demorest, while the new U.S. 441 route is part of Ga. 365 for several miles before dividing, Toccoa and Ga. 365 to the right and U.S. 441 north toward Clayton to the left. The U.S. 441 north option is first here.

Near the Hollywood exit from U.S. 441 are magnificent views of the mountains to the north. The drive from Hardman Road to the left off U.S. 441 and back to the right on old 441, then left on Orchard Road, leads toward Glen-Ella Springs Inn and Conference Center. Glen-Ella, a century-old inn listed on the National Register of Historic Places, has been restored to comfort levels far beyond those of its beginnings but retains the natural charms of the turn of the century.

Both U.S. 441 and old 441 lead north toward Clayton, Mountain City, and Dillard. **Tallulah Falls** is at the county line between Habersham and Rabun Counties and is best seen by taking the old 441 loop. The Tallulah Falls Railroad was extended to Tallulah Falls in 1882, beginning the history of the town. It was the site for summer homes from Athens-area residents, and several fine hotels were built to accommodate other tourists. The waterfall, prior to the damming of the Tallulah River in 1913, was one of the most spectacular in the United States. Tallulah Gorge is three miles long and six hundred feet deep, having been cut through hard quartzite by the river. Remnants of its heyday as a tourist attraction from the 1930s to the 1950s can still be seen, especially at the historic 441 loop. Nearby Tallulah Falls School was established by the Georgia Federation of Women's Clubs in 1909 to provide an education for poor, isolated mountain children. A short drive off old 441 to the west leads through the campus, which includes a small museum and some good examples of local stonework in older buildings.

North from Tallulah Falls, U.S. 441 enters Rabun County. A number of commercial campgrounds are near this route of rivers and lakes. Honey, cider, apples, seasonal fruits, and boiled peanuts are roadside staples, as are antiques and now even fast-food establishments. Along U.S. 441, entrances to recreational facilities that are part of the Chattahoochee National Forest lead to the power company lakes, which will be covered later in this tour.

Clayton is the seat of Rabun County, established in 1819 and named for Gov. William Rabun. Clayton has long been the commercial center of the area, serving tourists as well as town folk with a sizable town center and services. The old Clayton Hotel and the Clayton Cafe, both main-street establishments, offer a good mix of tradition and the new. As with all driving in Georgia, it is essential to make an effort to see the heart of the communities near state and federal highways that increasingly bypass what was once the center of local commerce and society. **Mountain City** is a small community along U.S. 441 north of Clayton. Just at the town entrance, signs point to Black Rock Mountain State Park, the highest in elevation of all Georgia state parks. A great view to the south is available, as are camping and cabin accommodations in this facility. During the winter months Black Rock is often the first place to have snow in Georgia, and it enjoys a temperate climate even during the hottest months of the summer. Mountain laurel and rhododendron are abundant on the mountain in the spring and early summer.

Between Mountain City and Dillard, side roads offer picturesque scenes from an earlier, simpler time. Old hotels, some still in operation, are reminders of years gone by, and rustic houses, their stacked rock chimneys like monuments to tradition, reveal the lifestyles of the hardy souls who have inhabited this region for generations. In the community of **Dillard**, just north of Mountain City, the Dillard House is a dining tradition in North Georgia. There is a beautiful valley view back south toward Black Rock Mountain from the Dillard House. Dillard's little commercial strip offers antique stores as well as traditional tourist services and farm produce in season.

In Dillard, Betty Creek Road to the west is one of the great little unheralded roads in Georgia. It travels along an undisturbed and beautiful valley close to the rush of civilization and the stream of tourism.

On this road is the Hambidge Center, established in 1934 to encourage local crafts, especially weavers who in the thirties became famous for their fine products and were known as the Weavers of Rabun. Mary Hambidge established the center as a place of inspiration and creativity where individuals might enjoy the serenity of the area as they pursued their crafts. Almost half a century after its founding, the Hambidge Center provides residential fellowships in arts, education, science, and business. One of Georgia's most picturesque public views is that of Rabun Gap–Nacoochee School to the left of U.S. 441 just south of Dillard. Like the Berry Schools near Rome and Tallulah Falls School, this school was another institute established for isolated mountain children early in the twentieth century.

It was at Rabun Gap that the first seeds of what became the internationally famous Foxfire Project began. In the mid-1960s Eliot Wigginton, an English teacher at Rabun Gap–Nacoochee School, stirred the interests of his students by involving them in local history, culture, and the folkways and life of the people of Northeast Georgia. Soon the students were producing a magazine that came to be called *Foxfire* and was based on interviews and photographs of the people of the area. *The Foxfire Book*, built on articles from the magazine, was published in 1972 by Doubleday. More than ten volumes have since been printed. The project gave rise to widespread emulation of Wigginton's efforts among educators and to a number of Foxfire courses for teachers. The Foxfire Collections on U.S. 441 in Mountain City encompass a museum with artifacts of Appalachian living, a bookstore carrying Foxfire publications, and a gift shop.

Four miles north of Dillard on Ga. 246E, with several quick nips in and out of North Carolina, is Sky Valley, a private resort community with golf and the only commercial snow-skiing in Georgia. Back in Clayton U.S. 76E leads to the South Carolina state line on the Chattooga River, which has been designated a national "wild and scenic river." Rafters can be seen from the river bridge. Those interested in rafting this river should consult the appropriate authorities as to levels of difficulty.

Another road east from Clayton, the Warwoman Dell Road north of U.S. 76, crosses the Bartram Trail about three miles from town. This is approximately midpoint of the forty miles of the National Recreational Trail marked by yellow and black signs. The beginning point is to be found about two miles from Dillard on Ga. 246 at the summit of Rabun Bald, Georgia's second-highest peak at nearly forty-seven hundred feet above sea level.

West and south of Clayton, Lakes Burton, Seed, and Rabun are major attractions to this corner of Georgia. West of Clayton on U.S. 76, one approaches the lakes (Burton first) by turning left onto Charlie Mountain Road, proceeding past Lake Seed, and returning to

U.S. 441 south of Clayton at Lake Rabun Road. Georgia's "power company lakes" are a source of great pleasure for a wide variety of people: those lucky enough to hold one of the long-term leases allowing "cabins" along the lakes' shores; those almost as lucky who have friends with leases or who are able to rent one of the cabins for a spell during the summer; boaters who keep sleek, mahogany Chris-Craft power boats in local commercial slips; or those who simply ride the shores of these lakes, taking in the beauty of blue skies, white clouds, green forest, and blue-green waters.

Ga. 197 takes the traveler down the western side of Lake Burton and beside the Soque River. The scenic route goes by Moccasin Creek State Park and a state fish hatchery where trout are raised to stock the streams of Northeast Georgia. Visitors are welcome at the hatchery.

One of the great traditions of Lake Burton is LaPrade's Restaurant, cabins, and marina. Family-style dining has been a specialty since the beginnings of this establishment, first operated to feed the workmen who came to the area for the building of the Tallulah River Dam in 1913. South of Batesville, the drive passes the Mark of the Potter, a commercial establishment specializing in the work of local artists and artisans. Ga. 197 leads back to Clarkesville where the traveler may take Ga. 365 back toward Gainesville or head for Toccoa on Ga. 17.

Toccoa is the seat of Stephens County, which was created in 1905 and is named for Alexander H. Stephens, governor of Georgia, U.S. senator, and vice president of the Confederacy (see East Central tour). The town itself was founded in the 1870s when it was part of Franklin County. Toccoa may be reached from the south via Ga. 17 north off I-85 (twelve miles), from Clarkesville (tour two) via U.S. 441N and Ga. 17 (sixteen miles), or from Gainesville via Ga. 365 (forty miles).

The Stephens County Historical Society maintains a local museum in Toccoa off Ga. 123 near the center of the town. Here are found exhibits of local interest, including items related to the late Olympic medalist Paul Anderson, native son who held world weight-lifting titles in the mid-twentieth century. The 1940 Georgia Guide described Toccoa in part as a place where "a tribe of Indians . . . lived peaceably . . . and used this locality as a trading center. Older residents tell of plowing up many Indian artifacts, including pottery, beads, pipes, and weapons." The town, long removed in time from its native origins and from the mid-century America of the old guide, today remains a commercial center for the area and the site of significant small manufacture, especially in wood products, chiefly burial caskets. One of Georgia's most beautiful waterfalls is found on the campus of Toccoa Falls College near Ga. 17 north of the center of town. To the east of Toccoa off U.S. 123, the Georgia Baptist Assembly maintains an impressive recreational and conference center for its members.

The Georgia Department of Natural Resources operates Traveler's Rest, a historic stagecoach inn six miles east of Toccoa off U.S. 123

Traveler's Rest

near the South Carolina state line. Traveler's Rest is a National Historic Landmark. The antebellum (circa 1830s) structure was host to travelers both famous and common during much of the latter half of the nineteenth century and features paneling and other items of structural interest including a ninety-foot-long porch.

The Stephens County countryside contains some interesting natural phenomena in addition to Toccoa Falls. Currahee Mountain, an imposing rock outcropping, is off U.S. 123 south toward Gainesville. There are a number of local parks and recreational facilities. A comprehensive listing of local attractions and facilities can be found at the Toccoa Welcome Center. From Toccoa, Ga. 17 south to Lavonia in Franklin County joins tour three.

TOUR THREE: THE I-85 CORRIDOR

I-85 north of Atlanta toward Greenville, South Carolina, provides a mere glimpse of or a closer look at one of northern Georgia's revived industries, wine making. Chateau Elan at exit 48 is less than an hour north of Atlanta, but it is a world away in its luxury and charm. Near the vineyards is a French-chateau-style visitors' center with a restaurant, gallery, shops, and winery tour. Since its beginnings in 1981, the Chateau Elan complex has grown to include golf courses, spa, tennis center, inn, and residential community. The chateau is site of special seasonal events ranging from "British Car Day" to a summer music festival and gourmet food shows. For a less elaborate North Georgia winery experience, a visit to Chestnut Mountain Winery is in order. It is to the south of I-85 at exit 48 and also maintains a wine-tasting room at Banks Crossing (see below).

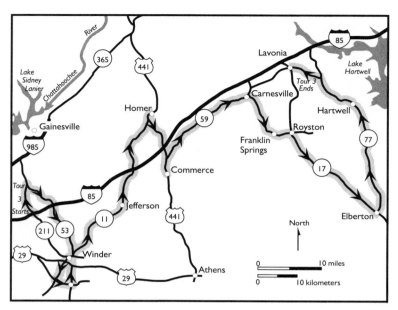

Northeast Georgia, Tour Three

Ga. 211 to the left out of the gates of Chateau Elan leads to Ga. 53. Road Atlanta is to the right (south) on Ga. 53. (The traveler wanting a faster trip by a few minutes at the loss of some more countryside travel may turn right from Chateau Elan to I-85 and take the next exit, 49, toward Gainesville.) Road Atlanta is a 2.52-mile scenic road-racing course sanctioned by the Sports Car Club of America (SCCA). Here a full season of racing events includes motorcycle and vintage auto racing as well as world championship SCCA and several recognized sanctioned events. In addition to racing, special events include music festivals and car club gatherings. Camping is also available during March to November activities.

From Road Atlanta, exits 48 and 49 off I-85N take the traveler to Barrow County's seat of local government, **Winder**. Barrow County is one of Georgia's youngest counties, created in 1914 and named for David Barrow, chancellor of the University of Georgia (1906–25). There is a local history museum in the old Barrow County Jail (circa 1915), a Gothic Revival building near the town's center. The Barrow County Historical Society sponsors the facility containing an interesting collection, primarily photographic, of displays around the themes of communities, schools, business, health, and the social and economic history of the area. In addition to the photographs there are a number of tools and other effects of life in an earlier time and a special collection related to the Russell Family (see below). Housed and displayed in this museum is a striking example of the public art of the New Deal in the form of a relief that was originally in the Winder post office. Of all the New Deal public art in the northeastern part of Georgia, Marion Sanford's "Weighing Cotton" is one of the most dramatic, and it is thoroughly documented. This one piece justifies the museum and a visit to it. The Barrow County courthouse was built around 1920 in the neoclassical style and has the usual Georgia historical marker giving a brief official history of the county.

One mile south of Winder on Ga. 81 are Fort Yargo and Will-A-Way Recreation Center emphasizing special services for the disabled. The original fort was constructed in the late eighteenth century for defense against the local Indians. Camping, picnic, and group meeting sites are available as are boating and water sports. The community of **Bethlehem** is five miles southeast of Winder on Ga. 11. A surprising number of nonresidents take advantage of the special Christmas season postmark used at the town post office.

About a mile west of Winder on U.S. 29 is **Russell**, a community founded and inhabited by a distinguished family of that name. Russell's founder, Judge Richard Brevard Russell, and his wife, Ina Dillard, reared here a large family of accomplished Georgians, notably Richard B. Russell Jr., U.S. senator from 1933 until 1971. The Russell Memorial Cemetery is located off a dirt road near the Russell home on U.S. 29.

The next point on the tour, **Jefferson**, may be reached by returning to I-85N and taking U.S. 129S or by following Ga. 11 from Winder. (The latter is preferred for the countryside crops and local color.) Jefferson is the county seat of Jackson County, founded in 1796 and named for Gov. James Jackson (1757–1806). The Jackson County courthouse was built in 1879 and occupies a handsome lot high above the town itself. It was in Jefferson that Dr. Crawford W. Long in 1842 removed a tumor from the neck of a patient using sulfuric ether as an anesthetic. While there remain disputes as to the primacy of his procedure, Dr. Long is generally recognized as the pioneer in this area of medical science. A museum in Jefferson is devoted to Dr. Long, the story of his accomplishment, and local history in general, with artifacts and photographs related to those subjects. There are a number of beautiful older residences and commercial properties in the town. The side streets in the neighborhood of the Long Museum offer especially good examples of private homes that have retained or had refurbished their nineteenth-century charm and fine details. Jefferson is the home of an exceptional outdoor athletic facility, a high school track and field complex that has been one of Georgia's premier locations for state-level competition in track and field events. Jefferson is fortunate in having had substantial private support for that facility and many other aspects of public education, thanks especially to the generosity of the Bryan family of that community. Jackson County's three public school systems—Jefferson, Commerce, and Jackson County—are testimony to the persistence of tradition and the importance of local community identification in Northeast Georgia.

On the north side of Jefferson, Ga. 82 takes the traveler toward Maysville. Hurricane Shoals Park is 7.5 miles from Jefferson along this route (north side of I-85, exit 51 or 52). This is one of the relatively unsung natural attractions of Northeast Georgia. The Creek and Cherokee considered these shoals on the North Oconee River to be a sacred place of peace where blood was not to be shed. A small white settlement was made there in the 1780s. Today the shoals serve as a place for picnics and family gatherings. A nonprofit organization, the Tumbling Waters Society, is devoted to the improvement and promotion of the shoals (open weekends only April–May, daily June–September).

From Hurricane Shoals Ga. 82 Sp. continues to **Maysville**, a small community alongside the railroad track and once the center of a bustling cotton commerce. With its Victorian cottages spotted around the village, it retains a sense of being frozen in time. Antique shops occupy several of the original brick stores facing the railroad tracks along Ga. 52.

From Maysville, Ga. 98 leads north to **Homer**, the county seat of Banks County, formed in 1858 and named for Dr. Richard E. Banks. The fine antebellum courthouse in the Greek Revival style was saved from demolition and restored in the early 1990s. From the grounds of this building a view of the village of Homer seems, and is, ages away from the hubbub a few miles down the road at Banks Crossing. As late as 1994 there remained north of Homer on U.S. 441 a nice example of a 1940s tourist court with small neat cabins strung out along a section appropriately named "Shady Grove." Long since fallen from use for its original purpose, Shady Grove Tourist Court no doubt once provided a restful stop along the way for many tourists of half a century or more ago. According to a sign at the city limits, Homer hosts the "world's largest Easter egg hunt," which takes place each spring.

Traveling back south on U.S. 441, the traveler passes the entrance to the Atlanta Dragway, site of regional and national competition among drag racers of motorcycles and automobiles of various classes as sanctioned by the National Hot Rod Association. (The use of the name Atlanta in this case is a seventy-plus-mile stretch.) Traveling south from Homer on U.S. 441 or leaving I-85N at exit 53, one arrives at the exceptionally busy intersection of I-85 and U.S. 441. Here a late twentieth-century phenomenon called Banks Crossing, a busy shopping complex of dozens of factory outlets, has risen on the landscape. Thousands of travelers and shoppers bound especially for this location take advantage of bargains real or imagined in what is for some a fascinating collection of American commerce, eateries, and gasoline stations. One of the distinguishing features of the crossing is an especially large establishment that had its origins in the pottery-making tradition of the area but is now a bazaar of "yard art," birdbaths, a sizable plant nursery complex, and gewgaws and gimcracks from around the world. All this makes an interesting contrast to Homer.

South on U.S. 441 across I-85 is the Jackson County community of **Commerce**. Commerce retains much of the charm of a late-nineteenth-century railside bustling commercial center that served the local farm community. The novel *Cold Sassy Tree* (1975), by Olive Anne Burns, is set in Commerce, known originally and in the novel as Harmony Grove. As with many Georgia communities near interstate highways and blessed with a town-center-avoiding bypass, downtown Commerce seems almost a ghost town. Its many vacant storefronts stretch alongside the rail line, which bisects what was once a busy Northeast Georgia community, fed first by cotton and later by the tourists on U.S. 441. In the 1950s the traveler headed to the Georgia mountains passed through the middle of Commerce and past the Uncle Remus Motel, which featured as its chief decor an enormous Br'er Rabbit astride the motel office. While the world-famous characters of Georgia writer Joel Chandler Harris are appropriate to the state, a more logical location would have been near Eatonton (home of Harris) in Putnam County, many miles to the south. Perhaps the edifice was simply Commerce's way of saying "welcome to Georgia," 1950s style.

From Commerce the last leg of the I-85 tour may begin on Ga. 59 (Commerce to Carnesville) or at I-85. **Carnesville**, just off I-85 north and west of Royston, is the seat of Franklin County, established in 1784, the oldest and most diminished (by the creation of new counties from its lands) of all the counties in northeastern Georgia. The Franklin County courthouse was built in 1906 in the Neoclassical Revival style with a Greek cross floor plan with entrances on each side of the town square.

The town of **Franklin Springs** is just off I-85 south of Carnesville. Victoria Bryant State Park is located off U.S. 29 four miles west of Royston. There is an interesting covered bridge crossing Nail's Creek on Ga. 16 in Franklin County. **Royston**, known as the hometown of Ty Cobb (although Cobb was actually born in rural Banks County), honors the memory of that controversial baseball great with several facilities named for Cobb. A marble likeness of Cobb is located at the city hall–community center, and pilgrims are known to visit the family mausoleum in the local cemetery just south of town on Ga. 17. The memorial at city hall includes a stone marker with relevant statistics about Cobb's baseball career. In the office area of the building are a few notices of Cobb including a small bronze plaque and a visitor registry. The mausoleum is a stark white rectangular marble stone marked simply "Cobb." Cobb, the "Georgia Peach," was known for his mean-spirited ball-playing, racism, and violent temper.

Ga. 17 south leads from Royston to **Elberton**, the "Granite Capital of the World." On Ga. 17 shortly before entering Elberton on the left, just behind the railroad track, is a series of fifteen granite whimsies: automobiles, trucks, motorcycles, a teddy bear, and such that have no inscription save the handwritten note on a paper sign: "No rubbing or decorating."

Elberton is the county seat of Elbert County, formed in 1790 and named for Revolutionary War figure and Georgia governor (1785–86) Samuel Elbert. The courthouse, built in 1893 in the Romanesque Revival style, includes important granite elements befitting its location. The granite industry has dominated this area from its beginnings in the late 1880s to its present-day role as the nation's largest quarrying and monument manufacturing district. Visitors may explore the Elberton Granite Museum with its artifacts and exhibits (limited hours). The tourist may see first-hand by merely driving about the community the material that has done so much for the community: as it comes from the earth, is processed, and finally is hewn and polished into monuments of all descriptions. It is especially interesting to note how common fine polished granite signs seem to be in the area. Just off Ga. 77 north of Elberton are the Georgia Guide Stones, a series of granite tablets rising on a hill and inscribed with prescriptions for world peace and harmony in a number of ancient and modern languages. This curiosity, which was erected in 1980 and sponsored by a "small group of Americans who seek the age of reason," is worth the short trip out of Elberton. Ga. 72W leads to Athens (East Central Georgia tour) by way of Bobby Brown State Park.

Ga. 77 north from Elberton leads to **Hartwell**, county seat of Hart County and adjacent to Lake Hartwell on the Savannah River, the Georgia–South Carolina line. Hart County is the only Georgia county named for a woman. Nancy Hart was a folk heroine of backcountry fighting during the American Revolution in Georgia. It was at her cabin in the area that became Elbert County that Nancy fended off a half-dozen Tories who set upon her. Hart State Park, three miles north of Hartwell off U.S. 29, is another tribute in the form of a boating and camping recreational facility. The local historical society has renovated a cottage for its headquarters.

From Hartwell, Ga. 77 and 77C lead back to I-85, the connector to **Lavonia**, after Royston the second-largest community in Franklin County. The historic residential structures in Lavonia represent the stages of settlement and development of the area. Among the residential styles found there are Georgian Revival, Victorian Eclectic, Neoclassical, Queen Anne, Gothic Revival, Renaissance Revival, Craftsman, and the regionally familiar Greek Revival.

Golfer Bobby Jones with baseball great Ty Cobb

Six miles northeast of Lavonia on Ga. 328 is Tugaloo State Park on Lake Hartwell. Here are found camping sites, cottages, boating, fishing, and picnic facilities as well as hiking and nature trails.

From the northern limits of I-85 in Georgia, the traveler may easily return to the Atlanta area via the interstate, explore the mountains and lakes of the central portion of the Northeast Georgia tour by heading for the Toccoa area, or head south toward Athens and the tour of East Central Georgia.

METROPOLITAN ATLANTA

Timothy J. Crimmins and Dana F. White

LOOKING FOR ATLANTA

Atlanta Braves pitcher Pascual Perez was lost. As he sped along Interstate 285 for over three hours in the heat of late afternoon August 20, 1982, he looked in vain for a sign directing him to Atlanta–Fulton County Stadium, where he was to be the starter that evening. He twice circumnavigated Atlanta's 62.5-mile ring road, stopping three times for directions. Perez—a dark-skinned, Spanish-speaking immigrant—was on a quest for his place in Atlanta. For Perez it was simple: A pitcher's mound and a win would do it. Lost in Atlanta, Perez missed his starting assignment. The Braves won despite his absence, on the strong arm of baseball legend Phil Niekro. "Perimeter" Perez became a short-lived legend himself, representing the many who have struggled to find their way through and around Atlanta.

The city owes its location—at the juncture of the upper and lower Piedmont Plateau and about fifty miles south of the foothills of the southern Appalachian Mountains—to civil engineer Stephen H. Long, who was looking for a terminus for the Western & Atlantic Railroad. In 1836 the state of Georgia chartered a railroad to be constructed through the mountains of the northwest part of the state. Long's quest was to find a suitable place east of the Chattahoochee River where the state-built Western & Atlantic could link with privately owned railroads coming from Augusta and Savannah.

In September 1837, Long drove a surveyor's stake into the red-clay earth along the present-day Marietta Street, a mile or so east of Underground Atlanta. Since this marked a location and the beginning point for a major construction project, Atlanta, a city under construction ever since, had its birth.

Stephen Long had no idea he was bringing a metropolis into the world. It has taken the perspective of history to give a heroic dimension to the unrecorded event of hammering a surveyor's stake. Long himself left town after railroad construction was completed, still believing the conventional wisdom that great cities would grow only on coastal harbors and navigable rivers. Its surveyor thought the location would be good enough "for one tavern, a blacksmith shop, a grocery store, and nothing else."

"Shortsighted" and "goal-oriented" are easy descriptives for the founding father who abandoned his city, but civil engineer Long lacked more than an urban vision; he lacked the boosterism and hyperbole that have come to characterize the inhabitants of this metropolis. Not so for Samuel Mitchell, Henry Grady, Billy Payne, and a host of urban hucksters who have propelled Atlanta from little more than a railroad crossroad in the 1840s into one of the ten largest metropolitan areas in the United States in the 1990s. They have, literally and figuratively, invented Atlanta.

Samuel Mitchell had an urban vision. He was no relation to Margaret, who a century later gave a fictional dimension to Civil War Atlanta as exaggerated as that of any city booster. In the 1830s the earlier of the Atlanta Mitchells owned 202 acres of woodland a mile southeast of the spot where Stephen Long drove his surveyor's stake. Because he saw promise in the railroad, Mitchell cut a deal with the state: In exchange for the relocation to his property of what would become a railroad junction, he provided, free of charge, a right-of-way through his acreage, a place to build a passenger station, and land for a public plaza in front of the terminal. After the state relocated the end of its line to his property, Mitchell promptly subdivided it into streets and blocks, offering for sale what he promoted as prime real estate for commercial and residential purposes.

What followed Mitchell's invention and promotion was urban growth: the construction of the first of three Union Stations, a number of freight depots, and two-, three-, and four-story brick buildings. By the late 1850s commercial rows lined Whitehall, Decatur, and Marietta streets; church spires established a skyline; a combination city hall/ county courthouse occupied the highest ground in Samuel Mitchell's land lot, and fine residences along Washington and Peachtree streets housed the families of a prospering commercial elite. Along the railroad tracks fledgling factories emerged, with working-class housing in their shadows.

Samuel Mitchell saw a future in railroad-generated commerce, but he was not alone. Because of the geography of the region, nineteenth-century Atlanta became the nexus of a rail network linking a growing city with the industrializing Northeast and Midwest. Today metropolitan Atlanta is dotted with communities founded along an emerging railroad network. East Point, College Park, Marietta, Norcross, Chamblee, Lithonia, and Jonesboro were towns that entrepreneurs established along the web of rails coming into Atlanta. Railroad junctions and freight and passenger depots offered the promise of commerce and industry. Local promoters like Samuel Mitchell subdivided land parallel to the rail right-of-way and sought speculators to buy while the price was low, following the real estate maxim "Buy by the acre, sell by the lot." One town, for instance, was invented twice, first as

Manchester in the hopes of attracting factories; later, after industrialists failed to respond, College Park, an idyllic place to establish boarding schools.

Until the mid-twentieth century, these towns were linked by rail to Atlanta but separated by farm and woodland. They are now part and parcel of a metropolis, linked by the automotive lifeline of a rim-and-spoke expressway system and the late-twentieth-century suburban environment of shopping malls, ranch-style houses on cul-de-sacs, and four lanes lined with flashing neon signs announcing McDonald's, Exxon, Big B, and Kroger.

This is the scenery that befuddled Pascual Perez in his search for Atlanta Stadium. As he whizzed around the perimeter highway and across the landscape of the modern city, looking desperately for a recognizable landmark, he saw exit signs that directed him to Northlake Mall, Southlake Mall, Cumberland Mall, Perimeter Mall, and Greenbriar Mall. As he surveyed the horizon at these exits, he could see high-rise buildings that might indicate a downtown. They did not indicate the downtown he was looking for—the location of the stadium—and they were not mirages. Fin de siècle Atlanta is ringed with the "new" downtowns of what Joel Garreau calls "Edge City."

American edge cities are the creation of the last generation of city growth. Garreau points out that two-thirds of all American office facilities are now located on the peripheries of cities. In Atlanta, they

Decatur Street railroad station, 1893

Interstates 85 and 285 cross at the Tom Moreland Interchange, also known as "Spaghetti Junction"

ring Interstate 285 but are clustered primarily on the northern perimeter between I-85 and I-75, and the majority of Atlantans commute from a home outside the perimeter to a place of work outside the perimeter. Most Atlantans have just as much trouble locating Atlanta Stadium as did Pascual Perez, because the city they know is that of the ring, not the center.

During rush hour, morning and evening, Atlanta commuters tune in radio traffic reports: "A jack-knifed trailer on the northbound connector," . . . "Rubber-neckers slowing traffic southbound on Georgia 400," . . . "Spaghetti Junction tied up in knots," . . . "No serious delays beyond the Marietta Loop." The sounds of the city morning and evening are the warnings being issued on automotive radios by hovering eyes in the skies, the commuter advice guiding Atlantans along and around the expressways that unite their metropolis. A half century ago, Atlantans downed a cup of morning coffee and walked to the garage for their cars or to the trolley stop for the next arrival. Once out of their houses, they joined other commuters who were, for the most part, heading downtown. Office workers and store clerks, bank presidents and janitors, lawyers and government bureaucrats, barbers and beauticians were united in a common commute.

Today Atlanta is a less unified city. Half of Atlantans live *and work* beyond the limits of the perimeter highway. They travel, not to the common "downtown" of the Petula Clark song, but along the interstate highways that give the rim-and-spoke pattern to the city. Atlanta spreads amoeba-like along these expressways, creating a metropolitan area expanding into eighteen counties.

Since most Atlantans do not regularly venture inside the perimeter, they have to consult a map to discover that the stadium is immediately south of the historic downtown, at the nexus of Interstates 75/85 and 20. Atlantans are likely to have the same impression of the stadium as most Americans who watched the baseball playoffs from 1991 to 1993 and the 1991 and 1992 World Series. They see it in their minds' eyes through a camera lens on color television.

Atlanta Stadium has a baseball diamond that is familiar as well to viewers of Ted Turner's Super Station—locally, channel 17—where the Braves have been part of the regular summer programming for over a decade. Built in the mid-1960s, the stadium, which brought National League baseball and professional football to Atlanta, was the product of a campaign of urban promotion that pushed the city to national prominence. Having done its work and played a role in the ultimate in sports promotion, helping to attract the 1996 Olympics, the stadium is slated for demolition in 1997. It will become another piece of lost Atlanta, the litany of demolished buildings that includes the minor-league stadium on Ponce de Leon Avenue, the passenger and freight depots in the heart of downtown, nineteenth- and early-twentieth-century luxury hotels, avenues of Victorian residences, textile mills, pencil factories, and the earliest skyscrapers.

The stadium provides what passes for a center for metropolitan Atlanta. There is nothing like a winning team to unify a city. In a self-consciously multicultural society, however, the national attention of a winning baseball team also brought controversy.

The tomahawk chop and the Indian chant produced headlines highlighting a dispute between American Indian (red) and majority (white) cultures. Coming as late as 1991, the controversy surprised many, but it should have surprised few that the conflict was less territorial than it was symbolic. In Atlanta, image always counts and is a factor in almost any equation.

The chop and chant controversy developed during the Braves' "from worst to first" Miracle Season, gathered force during the National League championship playoffs, and erupted during the World Series. The controversy centered not on the field, but in the stands. At issue, for American Indian Movement spokespersons, were dress (faux Indian regalia), behavior (mass imitations of weapons descending— the so-called tomahawk "chop"), and especially voice (a rhythmic chant meant to inspire the home team and dispirit the foe). While the regalia was time tested, if not time honored, the chant and chop had recently been imported to Atlanta from Florida.

One individual sometimes identified with transforming the ballpark's ambiance from funereal to fun-loving—the stadium is now recognized, if not always celebrated, nationally as the "Chop Shop"— was Deion Sanders, an alumnus of Florida State University, where chop and chant have been vetted by Seminole leaders. The icon of the Indian Brave, however, long antedated the flamboyant "Neon Deion" (the two-professional-sports superstar, who himself followed the trail of dollars from Atlanta's Baseball Braves and Football Falcons to the Cincinnati Reds and the San Francisco Forty-Niners).

Chief Nocahoma, the real-life Eli Walker, was uncontestably the all-time favorite of Atlanta fans. Preceding every Braves' home game in the 1970s and 1980s, the chief, attired in full tribal regalia, performed a victory dance on the pitcher's mound to call upon spirits to inspire the team. (For results, check the 1966–90 won/lost records.) At the end of the dance, the chief would race from the mound to left field—often in pursuit of a leggy, mini-skirted, blonde "Indian Princess," whom he would swoop into his arms at the warning track. During games, Nocahoma inhabited a raised tin teepee, cantilevered from the left-field stands, where he entertained children and from which he would emerge to lead an occasional cheer. Fans regarded the temporary removal of the teepee in the final weeks of the 1982 season, so as to provide seats for the divisional race, as an ill omen. With the teepee gone, the home team lost fifteen of seventeen games; with its reintroduction, the Braves clinched the divisional championship. Cause and effect, pure and simple.

Late in his tenure, the chief was joined by the "Bleacher Creature," a fuzzy co-mascot. Both were replaced, shortly before the Miracle Season of 1991, by new mascots: "Rally," a cuddly fuzzy; and Homer the Brave, a performer in baseball uniform sporting an oversized plaster head, sculpted along the lines of the team logo, that was dominated by a death's-head rictus. New management, seemingly cognizant of the inverse ratio between the number of mascots in view and success on the field, banished all such creatures from the playing area. Subsequently, if not consequently, the Braves experienced three consecutive championship seasons and promised a fourth in the ill-fated Strike Season of 1994.

The 1996 Olympics gave Atlantans the opportunity to revive the mascot debate. Olympic marketeers met the challenge of producing an "official" mascot for the Atlanta Olympic games with "Whatizit?" or "Izzy," another fuzzy cuddly creature with the twofold purpose of entertainment and profit. Izzy was not received well by the pre-Olympic public in the city, primarily because it had no association with Atlanta, but then, again, neither did Coca-Cola when it was introduced in 1886.

Izzy and Coca-Cola are local creations; the "Braves" were an import, by way of Milwaukee, which had held title to both term and team for thirteen seasons. Originally, the franchise called Boston home. There the team was, at various points, called the Bees and the Bean-eaters, monikers more likely to invoke laughter than controversy. But

The Atlanta Braves

the name Braves, while an import, does speak to a Native American past, joining a legacy of words left by the original settlers of the region: Allatoona, Cherokee, Chattahoochee, Kennesaw, even Peachtree—names permanently attached to the Georgia terrain.

ATLANTA: A STATE OF MIND

"Atlanta" now dominates and defines a region, harboring layers of a past that can be read in its landscape. First there is the geography. Through the heart of the city—from east to southwest—runs a ridge of land a thousand feet above sea level. The hilly terrain rises to the Appalachian Mountains to the north and west and descends to the fall line and Coastal Plain to the south and east. The original "braves" subsisted in a forested region, migrating along ridge-line trails that later became wagon roads for Europeans and African Americans. The railroads, in turn, followed the trails, bringing a new layer of development and a new identity to the region.

The name Atlanta is also an original creation, invented by railroad-builder J. Edgar Thompson in 1845 to replace its first official designation, Marthasville, a name selected by local boosters to curry favor with the governor of the time, whose daughter's name was Martha. Thompson, who later became president of the Pennsylvania Railroad, left a name whose image could be shaped and reshaped by generations of promoters. Marthasville, provincial sounding at best, certainly did not have the malleability of Atlanta.

In carving a city out of the forested wilderness, Atlantans sought to fashion a place that looked to the future. Its captains of commerce sought to emulate the growth and prosperity of Chicago and New York, where marshals of merchandising and manufacture created retail and industrial empires. But for all of its hankering after the glitter of northern growth, Atlanta remains a city of the South, rooted, for better and for worse, in the economy, culture, and history of the region.

Traditionally, the Civil War has been cited as the key transition point in southern history: "antebellum" describing the first period; "postbellum" everything after. Offering an alternative perspective, one based upon continuity rather than disjunction, historian Bennett H. Wall has contended that "no major changes occurred in the planting, cultivating, and harvesting of the staples—tobacco, cotton, corn, rice, and sugarcane—between 1612 and 1933." "Antebellum" and "post-bellum," according to this periodization, fail to describe the basic stages of southern history; "traditional" and "modern" more accurately mark their progression. The transformation of Wall's agricultural South, and hence his periodization, has its equivalent in the urban South.

In *The Urban South* (1954), the first comprehensive overview of urbanization in the region, sociologist Rudolph Heberle described the section as "one of the frontier provinces of the Euro-American system," with its role "resembling that of the Balkan and eastern European region in the other hemisphere. The similarities are striking," he continued, "agricultural surplus production concentrated on large estates or plantations; crop specialization export in vast areas (as in Roumania or Hungary); late development of secondary industries." These Eastern European correspondences, Heberle concluded, demonstrated "that the so-called 'colonial' character of the South's economy has retarded the urbanization of the region." Ironically, as this unflattering, but once-apt, description appeared in print, the urban South, in conjunction with the agricultural South, was well under way in its transformation from a traditional to a modern society. Southern cities, once termed "colonial," would soon be categorized as "Sun Belt."

When demographer C. A. McMahan set out in *The People of Atlanta* (1950) to examine the prewar decade of 1930–40, his "research universe" encompassed a central city with a population of about 300,000 within a "Metropolitan District" that included "satellite incorporated cities and suburban unincorporated areas" comprising "a large portion of Fulton and DeKalb Counties and small portions of Cobb and Clayton Counties." Since the combined totals of the three last-named counties, taken together, barely approached the 200,000 person mark, McMahan's Metro Atlanta numbered, generously, about a half-million people. Today, the "Metropolitan District" has been replaced, in the terminology of the Bureau of the Census, by the "Standard Metropolitan Area" (SMA) and/or the "Daily Urban System" (DUS). Today, in 1995, by these definitions, Metro Atlanta is made up of eighteen counties, which number over three million inhabitants; comparatively speaking, then, the population of the metropolitan region of Atlanta approximates the size of the entire state of Georgia during the immediate pre–World War II decade.

What has occurred in the heart of the Georgia Piedmont over the past half century has been nothing less than the urbanization of the region, or, more accurately, the urbanization of the state. In a single lifetime, Georgia has been transformed from a rural to an urban society. Of the three million Georgians who inhabited the state during the prewar decade, about a third lived in urban areas; of the seven million residents in the mid-1990s, more than four million live in metropolitan areas; and of those four million metropolitan inhabitants, as indicated earlier, about three million are Atlantans. Essentially then, almost one-half of the population of the state of Georgia resides in the single sprawling metropolitan agglomeration called Atlanta. The other half looks to Atlanta with pride, interest, fascination, concern, suspicion, outright hostility—or some combination of the above.

Atlanta is as much a mind-set as it is a place. For much of the present century, Atlantans have evoked the "Atlanta spirit" to define their city's unique character. Sloganeering has given varied expression to said spirit: from Atlanta, "the city too busy to hate," to "Atlanta, the new international city," on down to "Atlanta, the world's next great city." Still, it is the currently chic expression "Atlanta, a city without limits" that best captures the dynamics of its civic spirit, the force geographer Peirce Lewis has called the "stain of Atlanta," which is working its way across the Georgia landscape.

The incorporated city of Atlanta is no longer, as it was a half century ago, a city dominating a "metropolitan district." Today, the central city's population of some 400,000 people is but a fraction of the metropolitan total of about three million. Today, compared to half a century ago, Metro Atlanta no longer encompasses just "a large portion of Fulton and DeKalb Counties and small portions of Cobb and Clayton Counties." By 1990, Greater Atlanta embraced eighteen counties: seven of them classified as "core"—Clayton, Cobb, DeKalb, Douglas, Fulton, Gwinnett, and Rockdale; and the other eleven as "hinterland"—Bartow, Cherokee, Coweta, Fayette, Forsyth, Hall, Henry, Newton, Paulding, Spalding, and Walton. Tomorrow, seven of the Metro Eighteen are projected to be the fastest growing of all the state's 159 counties: Fayette, Gwinnett, Cherokee, Cobb, Clayton, DeKalb, and Fulton Counties, in that order. Modern Atlanta is fast becoming what geographers call a "primate city"—that is, an urban area that dominates its region. It resembles that reversal of the accepted order of things that, in common parlance, is often described as the tail wagging the dog.

The only problem with the Atlanta region is that, in the waggish words of Gertrude Stein, there is no there there. If Atlanta is a state of mind, many who live in Metro Atlanta identify themselves as Atlanta residents only when they are out of the region or the country. Otherwise, they claim the constituent, unmelded parts of subdivisions associated with towns and counties. They may root for the Atlanta Braves, watch local (Atlanta) news, and fly in and out of the Atlanta airport, but they think of themselves as urbanites and suburbanites, from Cascade and Dunwoody, Fayette and Lithonia, Snellville and Lilburn, Norcross and East Cobb. The chamber of commerce can toot the horn of Atlanta population statistics, but being counted among the population of the tenth-largest metropolitan area in the United States does not create self-proclaimed Atlantans.

For many, Atlanta is a state of mind created, in part, by writers whose provenance has been the city. Most famous, of course, is Margaret Mitchell, whose *GWTW* legacy has been a money machine for the past half century. A blue-chip investment, it is neither a stock nor real estate. It is, instead, that uniquely Atlantan phenomenon, the *Gone with the Wind* fixation.

GWTW is a historical novel, a blockbuster motion picture, and a business enterprise. Most recently, it has become the latest version of what historian James C. Cobb christened "the selling of the South." In Cobb's terms, the "selling" of the region once meant "industrial development." In *GWTW* terms, the sales center on something far less tangible: specifically, the history—or one version thereof—of the Old South.

In Midtown Atlanta, the historical effort constitutes enshrinement: the rehabilitation of Margaret Mitchell's apartment house, which she dubbed "The Dump," at Fourteenth and Peachtree streets, where she wrote what "Windies" call her "epic." Mercedes/Daimler plans to go for the Olympic gold by restoring the Mitchell house and using it for marketing and entertaining during the summer of 1996. Thereafter, plans are for a surround of museum and support structures, transforming the site into a veritable *GWTW* superblock.

In suburban Atlanta, historical vision has transcended reality: "The first time around, history is a drag," observes poet and National Public Radio commentator Andrei Codrescu. "The next time around," he concludes, "it's entertainment." And large-scale entertainment, since Disneyland opened in 1955, translates into "theme park."

The vision of a *GWTW* World bedazzled any number of metropolitan Atlanta counties during the early 1990s. Clayton, since it is "the county" in Mitchell's novel, was the early favorite, while Henry County came on as a challenger in the stretch; still, Douglas County galloped ahead toward the finish line. In the race, the stakes were high: the promise of jobs and millions in tourist dollars, deutsche

Movie premiere of *Gone with the Wind*, December 1939

marks, and Japanese yen. Not only would its "history" be entertaining, but it would even be defined by entertainment—namely, that of the motion picture industry. Not the Civil War South of the fictional Scarlett O'Hara, but the depression-era sets and stages of the larger-than-life David O. Selznick would define this theme park. History could not afford to be "a drag" this time around.

The attraction of *Gone with the Wind,* fiction and/or film, defies logical explanation. Less historical novel than costume drama, *GWTW* is a work of limited imagination and artistry, its sole "epic" quality being its length—a thousand plus pages, five hours of screening time. Still, even its harshest critics hesitate to describe *GWTW* as "elephantine." "Gargantuan"—that is, of enormous appetites—better describes the book, film, and phenomenon. Since disproportionate appetites seem also singularly Atlantan, *GWTW* and the city of its birth appear an ideal match.

Any account of the 1936 novel, the 1939 motion picture, the 1991 sequel novel, the 1994 sequel television mini-series, or the 1995 theme park leads almost immediately into an accounting of the millions of copies sold, multi-millions of tickets purchased, and more millions for television rights auctioned off, as well as theme park acreage assembled, purchased, and developed. From the outset, the dollar sign has marked the days of *GWTW*: from Margaret Mitchell's initial bickering over the book contract, to her legal struggles over foreign copyright violations, to the Mitchell estate's litigiousness in safeguarding The Property, the bottom line has remained the bottom line—money. *GWTW* was, and remains, a hot property; hence its unique place in the mythology of the city.

The monetary lessons of *GWTW* have not been lost on another Atlanta family with an interest in protecting a legacy: the King estate. Having fashioned the Martin Luther King Jr. Center for Nonviolent Social Change to perpetuate the work of the Atlantan who won the Nobel Peace Prize for his leadership of the Civil Rights Movement, members of the King estate have begun to follow in the footsteps of the Mitchell estate. They treat the words that Martin Luther King Jr. used to forge a movement to end segregation as "intellectual property," requiring the payment of royalties for use in newspapers and publications.

Moreover, in 1994 the estate locked horns with the National Park Service, which planned to open a museum on Auburn Avenue in the neighborhood where King was born and is buried. The Park Service intended to design a facility to honor King and to interpret his life and work for the public. The estate believed that the free museum would compete with one that it planned, one that would use the technology of a theme park, one that would charge for entry, and one that would pay the estate for the right to market Martin Luther King Jr.'s legacy. This effort sparked critical reaction from Cynthia Tucker, editor of the editorial pages of the *Atlanta Constitution* and heir to the mantle of both Henry Grady and Ralph McGill, who noted the irony of a money-making museum: "King taught the nation to live up to its stated ideals of freedom, justice and equality. But the center that bears his name, ironically, could come to represent an abiding American principle little noted in the history books but nevertheless somehow passed on to every succeeding generation—veneration of profit. King's heirs want to turn his dream into a money-making scheme."

It seems that the King estate studied the history of the city's most famous soft drink. The Coca-Cola Company has gone to great lengths to protect its copyrighted trademarks: Coke and Coca-Cola. The company has made legal fortunes in the city by paying lawyers to sue those who dared to misuse the Coke name or substitute an inferior product. The company has also concocted its own Disneyesque creation: the World of Coca-Cola in Underground Atlanta, a high-tech, feel-good account of the history of Coke and its promotions.

If Stephen Long and Samuel Mitchell have not acquired mythic proportions for their roles in founding a city at this location, *GWTW*, Coca-Cola, and now, Martin Luther King Jr. are part of the Atlanta iconography. As such, they merge history and myth. They are used to represent idealized versions of the Old South and several iterations of the New South. The mythic aspect of *GWTW*, Coke, and King is the American story of the struggle for success; all have a special resonance in the city of Henry W. Grady, the premier and ultimate mythmaker who popularized the notion of a New South in the 1880s.

In modern Atlanta, Grady's writings are less likely to be read than spotted. His 1886 boast that "from the ashes . . . we have raised a brave and beautiful city," for example, periodically graces bumper stickers, shopping bags, and T-shirts. (Since Grady's estate was not as careful about the intellectual property that he left behind, hucksters use his words without the need of royalties.) Remarkably, Grady's uncritical promotion of the city escaped serious artistic challenge for more than a century. Not until the publication of Anne Rivers Siddons's *Peachtree Road* (1988) did Atlanta's prosperity-at-any-price philosophy experience sustained critical review. This best-selling novel featured the "set," as they called themselves, whom poet James Dickey, who was one of them himself, immortalized as the "Buckhead Boys." Siddons delved into what sociologist Floyd Hunter had termed the "power structure," the world of the commercial-civic elite that within the decade transformed Hunter's "regional city" into a "new international city." With all this undeniable physical improvement, Siddons asks, what had been lost to progress? Her questioning of Gradyesque mythmaking has been echoed in such subsequent "serious fiction" as Marilyn Staats's *Looking for Atlanta* (1992) and Warren Leamon's *Unheard Melodies* (1990), as well as in the "detective fiction" of Celestine Sibley, Patricia Houck Sprinkle, and especially Kathy Hogan Trocheck, whose *Every Crooked Nanny* (1992) features developers as stereotypical arch-villains.

Other voices from other traditions, both late and early, also challenged the "brave and beautiful city" myth. Playwright Alfred Uhry portrayed "other" Atlantas, those of a Jewish elite and an African American servant class, during two lifetimes of racial transformation in the urban South in his award-winning play, and later film, *Driving Miss Daisy* (1986–87). Earlier still, in *The Souls of Black Folk* (1903), W. E. B. Du Bois offered his own unique vision of this city "south of North, yet north of the South, . . . the City of a Hundred Hills, peering out from the shadows of the past into the promise of the future"—a future that had to transcend any "dream of material prosperity as the touchstone of all success" to include artistic, intellectual, and spiritual development in its unfolding. "We must have ideals," Du Bois wrote, "broad, pure, and inspiring ends of living,—not sordid money-getting, not apples of gold."

Du Bois, a founder of the National Association for the Advancement of Colored People (NAACP) and editor of its journal, *The Crisis,* came to Atlanta in 1897 to teach at Atlanta University. While here he articulated his vision of a "New South" where by "every civilized and peaceful method we must strive for the rights which the world accords to men, clinging unwaveringly to those great words which the sons of the Fathers would fain forget: 'We hold these truths to be self-evident: That all men are created equal. . . .'" *Souls of Black Folk* was written in the new light of the twentieth century by a fiercely proud and intellectually commanding African American. It has taken most of the century to bring home the meaning of at least some of those words.

With its challenge to Atlanta's civic spirit, Du Bois's "City of a Hundred Hills" recalled an earlier vision, that of Gov. John Winthrop of the Massachusetts Bay Colony who prophesied to his people in 1630 that "Wee shall be as a Citty upon a Hill, the eies of all people are uppon us." Now, a century later, as "the eies of all people" are focusing ever more on the Olympic City, the gulf between Grady's claims and Du Bois's challenge takes on increasingly momentous meaning.

The legalized segregation of Grady's New South has given way to a movement for integration, fashioned in part in Atlanta by Du Bois and Martin Luther King Jr. Du Bois tried to warn Atlantans off from "sordid money making" and to inspire them to loftier goals of the human mind and spirit. King preached to civil rights followers of the role of suffering in the redemption of all people, not just African Americans. From a Georgia prison where he was being held for resisting the color line, King wrote to his wife: "I have the faith to believe that this excessive suffering that is now coming to our family will in some little way serve to make Atlanta a better city, Georgia a better state, and America a better country." The long-term effect of the advice of Du Bois and King is not clear. On the eve of the 1996 Olympics, the inspiration for many is the green of the cash register, not the gold of athletic achievement.

REGIONAL CITY

Floyd Hunter called it "Regional City." His 1953 monograph, *Community Power Structure: A Study in Decision Makers,* was typical of the social-scientific case studies of the 1940s and 1950s, which attempted to comprehend the general by elaborating on the specific: Thus, according to such a conceptual scheme, Chicago embodied "Midwest

Metropolis"; Newburyport, Rhode Island, "Yankee City"; Muncie, Indiana, "Middletown"; and Atlanta, "Regional City." Yet Hunter's Atlanta case study defied typicality, in that it was defined not so much by its region—the South—as it was by the close-knit leadership cadre that governed it, the select few whom he labeled a "power structure." Four decades later, journalist Otis White would describe them and their successors as "perhaps the most dominant business leadership in the country, ruling everything from city hall to the state capitol to the arts to the civic sectors. And it's no accident. Atlanta's business leaders are successful because they are singleminded. They know what they want and how to get it, and their successes build on one another."

This same group has also been called a "civic-commercial elite," but probably its best characterization is the personal sketch drawn by one of its key players, business leader and two-term mayor Ivan Allen Jr.:

When I looked around me to see who was with me in the new group of leaders, I found my lifelong friends. Almost all of us had been born and raised within a mile or two of each other in Atlanta. We had gone to the same churches, to the same golf courses, to the same summer camps. We had played within our group, worked within our group. . . . We were white, Anglo-Saxon, Protestant, Atlantan, business-oriented, nonpolitical, moderate, well-bred, well-educated, pragmatic, and dedicated to the betterment of Atlanta as much as a Boy Scout troop is dedicated to fresh milk and clean air.

Whether, in fact, so narrow and tight-knit a group exercised so much control has been questioned. Without question, however, is the reality that many Atlantans have accepted portrayals of an operative power structure as gospel, have found comfort in the thought that benevolent paternalists were really "in charge," and have longed for a return to these Good Old Days. The Power Structure Era in Atlanta, from the end of World War II through the late 1960s, survives as the city's Golden Day—a kind of Cracker Camelot.

Once the war was over, the city's leadership quickly grasped the contours of national and, especially, regional change. As the population of the United States shifted during the early postwar years into a saucer-shaped configuration that stretched down the southeastern coast, and then followed the northern borders of the Gulf of Mexico into the southwestern deserts, on up along the Pacific Coast as far north as the Canadian border, a new "mega-region" was taking shape—a "Sun Belt." The processes of regional change seemed all but inevitable; still, not every Sun Belt city would profit equally. In scriptural terms, many might be called, but few would be chosen. Atlanta's power structure dedicated itself early on to securing for their city a place among the elect.

The beginning point that transformed the city into a metropolis was the "Plan of Improvement." Proposed initially in 1949 and enacted in 1951, the plan went into effect on January 1, 1952, when large tracts of land and considerable numbers of people were annexed to the municipality proper: The city's physical area tripled from 37 to 118 square miles, and its population swelled with an additional hundred thousand suburbanites baptized overnight as "Atlantan." Earlier, plans were under way to move these new citizens, and many others too, when in 1946 the city commissioned a traffic plan to accommodate automotive Atlanta. The Lochner Report set a pattern for the complex rim-and-spoke freeway system that would connect major national highways running north and south (I-75 and I-85), as well as east and west (I-20), with metropolitan street patterns by means of a circumferential or "perimeter" or loop road (I-285). Earlier still, in 1929, with the purchase of Candler Field (a former automotive race course on the southside) to serve as the city's airport, Atlanta's leadership anticipated the potential of air traffic for future economic development. Expanded and renamed Atlanta Municipal Airport, the facility eventually mushroomed into Hartsfield International Airport, itself twice reconfigured, one of the busiest transportation nodes in the nation and the world. Thus, as the age of steam gave way to that of internal combustion and jet engines, did the highway and airway networks build upon the city's historic role as transportation hub. In the process, modern Atlanta extended its reach beyond the region to encompass the nation and the world.

In reaching for the golden ring of Sun Belt growth, the all-white Atlanta power elite of the 1960s fashioned a metropolis remarkably changed from that of their childhood. They created a metropolitan region, but they were forced to confront, first and foremost, the issue of race, the great divide that subjugated the needs and interests of African Americans to those of the European American majority. By 1960, while white businessmen and elected officials remained in the driver's seat, African American leaders were wresting the steering wheel from their control.

The ballot box was the ticket to African American ascendency. The NAACP led the charge in the courts against the Jim Crow apparatus that kept blacks from voting, believing correctly that the ballot box was the means to force an end to the color line. Yet the struggle captured in the minds of Americans for this era was not that of the voting booth. All over the South in the 1960s, African Americans staged protests against legalized segregation, at lunch counters, in rest rooms, at movie theaters, in "public" parks and swimming pools. Images from photojournalists and television cameras captured the drama of interracial confrontation. Atlanta's white civic-commercial elite sought in every way possible to avoid the images of confrontation. They did this because they thought pictures of milling white mobs would be bad for business. Behind the scenes was the Atlanta way, and this is the way that its leaders dealt with negotiations to crack the color line. Even before the sit-ins of the 1960s, Atlanta's white power structure had begun a slow process of racial accommodation, and, in the process, laid the foundation for an integrated civic elite.

Mayor William B. Hartsfield, who held office in the 1940s and 1950s, was the first to make a move. He did this not because of advanced "liberal" views, but rather from pressure brought from across the color line. As the story goes, when black leaders asked Hartsfield to hire Negro policemen, he told them to come back when they had ten thousand registered voters. They did.

In 1949, with the consolidation of several groups into the Atlanta Negro Voters League, a power base began to take shape as the numbers (and proportions) of black registered voters rose from three thousand (or 4 percent of the total registration citywide) in 1946, to forty-one thousand (about 29 percent of the total) in 1961, to ninety-three thousand (about 45 percent) in 1969. Voting power translated into coalition building. In his 1965 study, *Big City Politics*, political scientist Edward C. Banfield described in his chapter "Atlanta: Strange Bedfellows" what he called a "three-legged stool" comprising the established power elite, their northside white liberal allies, and the newly organized African American voting bloc.

In his earlier analysis of Regional City's power structure, Floyd Hunter had identified an Atlantan "sub-community" or "Negro community," in which "the pattern of power leadership . . . follows rather closely the pattern of the larger community." That the leadership of this "sub-community" would exert increasing pressure on its allies within the "larger community" soon became increasingly apparent.

Pragmatism persuaded the former segregationist Hartsfield to accept a new political world after the Primus King Case in Georgia doomed the white Democratic primary, the linchpin of black disfranchisement. With African Americans registering to vote in the Democratic primaries, Hartsfield concluded that to survive in politics, he had to make accommodations. His first was the hiring of black policemen in 1948.

The increase of African American voting strength motivated white business and political leaders to dismantle the system of legal segregation. There was, of course, the inevitable vocal white minority, led by the flamboyant Lester Maddox, who, while he failed to attain elective office in the city, was elected governor of the state in 1966. Such was his strength in Atlanta that in the 1961 mayoral elections, segregationist candidate Maddox polled over 50 percent of the white vote, which meant that the black vote provided Ivan Allen Jr. his margin of victory. The power of the ballot, and the race of those casting it, became ever more apparent to those seeking elective office in the city as the 1960s progressed.

African American votes succeeded first in electing progressive white candidates, but in 1973 they were sufficient to elect the city's first African American mayor. Maynard Jackson brought a new era to the city in that year, when he was inaugurated mayor, elected by votes from African Americans who a generation before had been disfranchised. The youthful, dynamic Jackson also represented a new generation of black leadership because he leapfrogged to elective office ahead of those among the black establishment who had been fighting civil rights battles of the 1950s and 1960s and who had been meeting behind the scenes with the white power structure.

Mayor Jackson may have been an Atlantan who was "moderate, well-bred, well-educated, pragmatic, and dedicated to the betterment of Atlanta as much as a Boy Scout troop is dedicated to fresh milk and clean air," as Ivan Allen Jr. had described the power elite of a decade earlier, but he was not "white, Anglo-Saxon," and "business-oriented." Not only was he outside the power structure, but he also determined to confront it over such issues as "minority set-asides" in city contracts, neighborhood protection, and interstate highway construction. During his first eight years in office, Jackson battled, rather than joined, the white power elite.

His successor, Andrew Young, who built his reputation as one of Dr. King's abler lieutenants, soon established his place as "one of the crowd" by adopting a probusiness stance, favoring megaprojects like the Georgia Dome and mega-events like the 1988 Democratic National Convention and, especially, the 1996 Olympics. Billy Payne is the architect and construction chief of the Atlanta Olympics, but the selection of Atlanta as the 1996 site resulted from a "joint venture" promotional campaign led by Payne and Mayor Andrew Young. The head of the U.S. delegation to the United Nations during the early years of the Carter Administration, Young had international contacts, especially among the countries of the developing world. Simultaneously mayor and globe-trotting promoter, Young helped to bring home the gold and in the process became a player within the city's civic-commercial elite.

Mayor Young also strove mightily to shore up a downtown sorely depleted by the competition from commercial and office complexes in the suburbs. Young helped package the support to revive and reconfigure a moribund Underground, and he labored to keep an even balance in the tug of war between two nodes in the downtown: Five Points, the center of banking, and Peachtree Center, John Portman's commercial and office complex that had revived the upper downtown a generation earlier.

What had been a regional city in the early 1960s had become in the 1990s a city of national importance, with aspirations for an international role. Atlanta, a city whose power structure had been divided along racial lines, advanced through the crucible of the civil rights movement toward a stable biracial governing coalition. But at the same time, the centrifugal forces of urban growth were creating a sprawling metropolis where no one was "in charge."

TWO ATLANTAS

The challenge for late-twentieth-century Atlanta is one of making a whole of its parts. Since the end of World War II, the city has been struggling to reinvigorate its downtown and to nurture its expanding suburbs, a process which has civic and governmental leaders at cross purposes, for their interests now lie with the parts of a metropolis rather than its whole. There had been a dramatic change in Atlanta since the revitalization of its downtown in the 1960s became the metaphor for a vibrant Sun Belt city. And the crown jewel of urban redevelopment was architect-developer John Portman's Peachtree Center.

In postwar urban America, the city-within-the-city commercial complex was widely ballyhooed as the first step along what historian Jon C. Teaford has described as the rough road to renaissance, in his book of the same name. Its most dramatic and influential manifestation in Atlanta was the work of architect-builder Portman. While his Peachtree Center property had its counterparts in other contemporary developments—Pittsburgh's Gateway Center (1952–53), Philadelphia's Penn Center (1953), Boston's Prudential Center (1957), and Baltimore's Charles Center (1960), among others—it was Rockefeller Center in New York City that provided the model and demonstrated the growth potential for such ambitious, multiuse commercial campuses.

Started in 1932, during the depths of the Great Depression, Rockefeller Center was not officially dedicated until 1939. Initially planned to include a four-block area fronting on Fifth Avenue, it jumped, during the decades after its dedication, west across Sixth Avenue, to occupy large chunks of an additional half-dozen blocks, thereby fulfilling the developer's dictum that nothing exceeds like success. The example of Rockefeller Center proved to be significant in developmental terms because its history demonstrated that a commercial project of such magnitude was capable not only of securing stability for an area, but also of providing it an internal energy for further expansion.

Such centers, then, have been more than mere passive containers of urban activity; they have also generated new urban energies. The trouble is, the same can be said for large suburban malls on Atlanta's northside, where developers have built adjoining office complexes like Perimeter Center and Cobb Galleria that compete with downtown centers. Portman's Peachtree Center tells an important story, but it is just one of many in Atlanta's postwar boom.

In the three decades before the opening of Peachtree Center's first structure, the Merchandise Mart, only three major highrise structures had been started downtown—all of them in the historic Five Points area. With the construction of two major highrise buildings north of that historic downtown in 1962—the Mart and the Georgia Power Building—it was obvious not only that the central city would undergo revitalization, but also that its downtown would gravitate uptown. Indeed, over its first three decades, Peachtree Center served to draw and anchor such commercial neighbors as the Atlanta Center Limited (the Georgia Pacific Building), the Peachtree Summit complex, One-Ninety-One Peachtree Tower, the Ritz-Carleton Hotel, a rejuvenated Macy's Department Store, and the Georgia Power Corporate Headquarters.

With the office-tower construction of the mid and late 1980s around Peachtree Center and in Midtown and with banking acquisitions and consolidations, the shape of Five Points, the historic center of the downtown and the city, changed dramatically. The power center disintegrated. The First National Bank, C&S Bank, and the National Bank of Georgia all merged into larger and newly renamed banks and relocated their corporate headquarters uptown. The silk-stocking law firms also moved northward, leaving to government the task of revitalizing Five Points.

Government responded. The city of Atlanta invested heavily in the refurbishment of Underground. The state of Georgia expanded its offices into Two Peachtree Street, the former First National Bank Tower, while the College of Business Administration of Georgia State University occupied the old C&S Building. The federal government projected the new Federal Center around the restoration of the 1924 Rich's Department Store. All of these projects were building blocks along Teaford's "rough road" to renaissance, but government was almost the lone agent responsible for reviving the downtown—almost.

Efforts at downtown revitalization are also exercised by the long arm of Robert W. Woodruff, who continues to shape the city in death, just as he did in life, through his Woodruff Foundation. Probably no individual in recent history has had an impact on a single American city comparable to that exerted by "Mr. Woodruff," as he is known locally, on coming-of-age Atlanta. The Mellons have long been a force in Pittsburgh, the Dukes in Durham, and—at various points—the Astors, Vanderbilts, and Rockefellers in New York City; nevertheless, it is unlikely that in recent times, at least, any other person had shaped his city as dynamically and thoroughly as did Woodruff his Atlanta.

Years after his death in 1985, he remains "Mr. Woodruff"—the dominant, larger-than-life power broker, Atlanta's secular patron saint. Such mythic status attached to him because of both his public actions and his personal influence. In the public realm, he personified the aggressive, expansive Coca-Cola Company, which he took over in 1923, and in which he was "officially" active until 1981. Under his leadership, Coke catapulted from national to international significance on the world market, with Atlanta its virtual "company town." In the private sphere, he was "Mr. Anonymous," a mysterious—albeit benevolent—"presence" behind the scenes.

In Floyd Hunter's classic *Community Power Structure,* Woodruff was assigned the pseudonym "Charles Homer" and described by a fellow power player as "the biggest man in our crowd. He gets an idea. When he gets an idea, others will get the idea." Typically, he'd call the "others" in. "He did not talk much. We do not engage in loose talk about the 'ideas' of the situation and all that other stuff. We get right down to the problem." End result: Problem defined; tasks allocated; problem solved. All in private, all behind the scenes.

In Anne Rivers Siddons's novel *Peachtree Road,* a junior functionary of Atlanta's civic-commercial elite described "Mr. Woodruff at the nerve center, with his lines out everywhere, like a . . . spider in the center of a gigantic web. Awful analogy, but he's in touch with literally everything and everybody; nobody makes a move in town without his okay. You'll never hear about it, but it's true. The best thing we've got going for us," this fictional inside-dopester concluded, "is that there's enough money in the power structure to finance the growth" of the city. And Mr. Woodruff held power of attorney over signing the checks.

Until 1974, Robert Woodruff remained behind the scenes. After that, however, he permitted others to attach his name to the many gifts he bestowed upon his city and its citizenry, such as its downtown park, its arts center, various medical facilities, educational institutions, and ongoing benevolent foundations. Initially, "anonymous donor"; transitionally, "Mr. Anonymous"; eventually, "Mr. Woodruff."

As a historical personage, Robert W. Woodruff is still being reckoned with; as a figure from the city's mythic past, he seems omnipresent. For Atlantans of a certain age, "Mr. Woodruff" represents an era when someone was "in charge," when problems were "solved," when things "got done." Such evocative sentiments, oversimplified as they are, can induce public apathy, promote a search for a civic savior, and even justify a "let the other fellow [Woodruff!] do it" escapism unworthy of the man and the myth.

All around Atlanta are memorials to the Woodruff name. In the court of the Arts Center, there is even a statue molded in his image, complete with his signature cigar. Arguably, the likeness is misplaced, for its subject, although an unquestioned patron of the arts, was no aficionado of the muses. He was, instead, an acolyte of power. As the statue of Henry W. Grady graces the street in front of the *Atlanta Constitution*, which he edited and advanced, so too the likeness of Robert W. Woodruff might be more suitably sited nearer the state capitol, near those corridors of power that he knew so well and engineered so masterfully.

The state capitol stands on a high point of the land lot where Samuel Mitchell first sold store-front property in the city. Six blocks west is the Federal Center, built around the remains of an Atlanta institution, Rich's Department Store. Seldom in the annals of American urban history will one find a book-length love letter to a department store, but such is Celestine Sibley's centennial account, *Dear Store: An Affectionate Portrait of Rich's*.

From the middle of the last century to the very recent past, department stores—those great "bazaars" or "mammoth emporiums," as early admirers described them—dominated the commercial centers of major American cities: in Chicago, Marshall Field's; in Philadelphia, John Wanamaker's; in Boston, Jordan Marsh; and in New York City, Macy's. While Rich's was not alone in winning the affection of its clientele, the special love affair between Sibley's "store of legend" and its customers did evince an intensity uniquely its own.

The legends are many—many of them true. There are stories of "brush stroke" reproductions of masterpieces that were "customized" for purchasers: Van Gogh's *Sunflowers* "colorized" to match various decors; or Salzman's *Head of Christ* rendered blue-eyed to confirm the spiritual vision of a valued customer. Then, too, there are the tales concerning Rich's exchange policy. As Celestine Sibley described the downtown store during its heyday, "It's hard to find any family necessity that Rich's won't sell you, and nearly on your own terms, or take back and exchange at your slightest whim—even if, as sometimes happens, you bought it from a competitor." An exception, she related, was the little boy who attempted to trade his baby sister for a "space helmet." Rich's declined the swap but nonetheless sent the boy a complimentary helmet, together with a note extolling the virtues of baby sisters. "'Is this a store or a philanthropic institution?' hardheaded observers have been known to ask," echoes Sibley.

Perhaps not philanthropy, but certainly service—community service, boldly envisioned—developed as a defining characteristic of Rich's. In response to a sequence of municipal disasters, Rich's always stepped forward to offer emergency aid: to neighbors burned out by a fire in 1917 that leveled seventy-three city blocks; to Georgia farmers during an agricultural recession in the 1920s when cotton prices fell drastically, and from whom Rich's purchased five thousand bales at above-market rates; to the municipality's schoolteachers during the Great Depression of the 1930s, from whom the store accepted city-issued scrip and cashed it at face value, with no stipulation that any of that money be spent at Rich's; to the victorious United States Army, over the Labor Day weekend of 1945 when the banks were closed, as a cash advance to pay recently discharged GIs at Fort McPherson; and to survivors, as well as relatives of the 119 victims, of the 1946 Wine-coff Hotel fire. In each instance, Rich's took its stand for Atlanta.

Rich's not only functioned as a place of business but also served as a gathering place for Atlantans and outlying countrymen. In season, it ran an "Easter farm," with an early version of a petting zoo; an out-door harvest sale that drew farmers statewide to exhibit and sell their crops and wares; and, from 1948 until the downtown store closed its doors July 13, 1991, a Christmas pageant that was highlighted by the lighting of a "Great Tree" set atop the "Crystal Bridge" connecting its two buildings that spanned Forsyth Street. To celebrate its eightieth anniversary in 1947, Rich's held a birthday party to which it invited local octogenarians. This immediately became an annual event and regularly drew thank-you letters along the lines set down by the woman who provided Celestine Sibley with the title of her book: "Dear Store," the lady wrote, "Yesterday was my first time to be invited to come to your famous eighty-year birthday party." Such was her de-light with the occasion, she concluded, that "We do not wonder that Atlanta's own Rich's is the store with the heart."

What made every "Rich's fan of any standing," as Sibley described the attachment, remarkably loyal to "Atlanta's own" Dear Store was family, one specific family. Long before cant concerning "family val-ues" became another convenient refuge for scoundrels, Atlantans rec-ognized and valued the role of the Rich family in the store's service to the city and its citizens. For over a century—from Morris Rich (born Reich), the prime mover in establishing the firm here in 1867, to Richard Rich (born Rosenheim), who transformed the firm from a municipal into a regional economic presence—the designation of *Rich's* was more than a mere trade name: It signified trust, commitment, continuity, and, most of all, the personal touch.

In 1959, as the firm approached its centennial decade, its first branch store was opened at Lenox Square. It was followed, later in that same year, by another in the Belevedere Shopping Center, and then, in rapid succession, by branches at Cobb Place in 1963 and in both North DeKalb shopping center and Greenbriar Mall in 1965. The malling of Atlanta was under way: What the railroad had joined together in the nineteenth-century city, the freeway was tearing asun-der in the twentieth-century metropolis. And yet, for most Atlantans, even during the expansive decades following the opening of the "an-chor" store at Lenox Square, the designation "Rich's" continued to mean "downtown"—that familiar sprawl of buildings south of Mari-etta, flanking Forsyth Street, where they lit the "Great Tree" and you rode the Pink Pig.

Rich's "Pink Pig," a childhood memory for many Atlantans

Meanwhile, as the sun shone brightly on the Sun Belt, decay afflicted the Rust Belt. In Detroit, J. L. Hudson's store closed in 1982. "For me," a customer of forty years lamented, "Hudson's WAS Detroit and when it is gone, there will be nothing left." In Cincinnati, the Elder-Beerman store closed in 1985, and Ayres in 1988. In the Big Apple itself, the "battle on 34th Street" was over: Gimbel's closed; Macy's hung on; no winner would claim victory. For many Atlantans, for whom Rich's WAS Atlanta, would there be anything left, if it too were gone? if there was no Mr. Rich at Rich's? Richard Rich died in 1975, and late in the following year, Federated Department Stores of Cincinnati took over the chain, ending the era of the family-owned department store in Atlanta.

In the years following the closing of the downtown Rich's in 1991, the abandoned complex loomed threateningly south of the Five Points MARTA station. The city's power structure was not going to let it molder for long. Mayor Maynard Jackson and Congressman John Lewis worked on legislation to authorize the General Services Administration to construct a new federal center in Atlanta at the Rich's site. The 1924 Store for Fashion, designed by Atlanta classicist Philip Trammell Shutze and the original building on the two-block expanse, is the heart of the new development. But the history that is being told of Rich's at this site is not entirely the one found in Celestine Sibley's adoring book.

The other story of Rich's, and the story of Atlanta's downtown, is that here was the location of the drama and the battle of the color line. The drama of the color line had physical dimensions: "white" and "colored" drinking fountains and rest rooms, "Negro" sections of movie theaters, separate waiting rooms in train and bus stations, and signs in buses telling "colored" folk to sit in the back. For the most part, the downtown was a preserve for whites, with specific signs directing blacks to "their place." There was also an etiquette of race relations, requiring African Americans and European Americans to respond to each other in prescribed ways. Blacks were expected to act deferentially; whites were given the license to be demanding.

There was a color line at Rich's. Black customers had to use rest rooms in the subbasement, next to a snack bar designated for their use. Black employees had a separate cafeteria, rest room, and changing room. The management of Rich's tried to walk its own version of the color line, satisfying both white and black customers. Many African American customers were impressed by the high caliber of service accorded by the sales personnel. But when it came to facilities, two mothers wrote in 1958 saying, "Quite frankly, unless an emergency arises, we do not use the rest room or eating facilities because we feel that for reasons of comfort, sanitation, and self-respect, the token facilities which you provide for us do not reflect the spirit of 'welcome' accorded us in other areas." The experience of the color line for African Americans was summed up poignantly in the same letter: "As mothers, we have found it depressing and embarrassing to take our children across the [Crystal] [B]ridge enroute to the Children's Department, amidst the smell of food and to have to answer their question, 'Where can we eat?' Before beginning a shopping trip we always have to caution our young ones to 'go to the bathroom because you won't have another chance until we come back home.'" Rich's 1958 response to this letter was to construct a new rest room "for colored ladies" on the fifth floor next to the Crystal Bridge, redrawing the color line, but, still, a line.

The 1960s brought to the South and to the city a generational shift. African American college students substituted direct action for letter-writing. They targeted white businesses that denied blacks the full use of their facilities. The action began February 1, 1960, at the Woolworth's in Greensboro, North Carolina. One month later, on March 3, the sit-in movement arrived in Atlanta.

Richard Rich, who knew discrimination because of his German-Jewish ancestry, was caught by the color line: If he eliminated segregation in his store, he would lose his white customers; but if he maintained the color line, he would lose his black customers. By September

1960, he was receiving "cherished" Rich's charge plates in the mail from African American patrons, including John Wesley Dobbs, the grandfather of Maynard Jackson, who, as mayor, would save the structure—if not the store—for the Federal Center.

The moment of direct confrontation at Rich's came on October 19, 1960. In *Parting the Waters: America in the King Years 1954–1963*, historian Taylor Branch recounted why student demonstrators chose Rich's as their primary target of direct action and why they enlisted Martin Luther King Jr. in their demonstration: "Rich's was a symbol of Atlanta, which was a symbol of the hopes of the South, and King was a symbol of the hopes of the Negro people." At eleven in the morning King met with students on the Crystal Bridge. They were refused service at the snack bar but were not arrested for sitting at the counters. Setting their sights higher, King and the students marched, attired in suits and ties or dresses and high heels, to the Magnolia Room, the decorous dining room in the complex. Here King and fifty students were arrested for trespass. They refused bail and spent the night in jail.

The aftermath of this demonstration was profound for the city and the nation. Atlanta was a potential flash point where African American supporters marched in support of King and the jailed students and the KKK counter-marched in support of segregation. Mayor Hartsfield huddled with downtown businessmen and negotiated with African American leaders over the release of the student prisoners, who stuck to their slogan "jail, no bail." At stake was the end of segregation in public facilities. The business community knew that desegregation would have to be enacted by all, lest such a change destroy their white customer base.

Representing business interests, Hartsfield looked for a way to release King and the students and to set up a negotiation that would end segregation in public facilities in the city. The wily mayor used the presidential campaign, which pitted Democrat John F. Kennedy against Republican Richard Nixon, as his out. After cursory discussion with a Kennedy aide, Hartsfield announced that he was releasing the protesters at the request of the Democratic candidate. In explaining it afterward, Hartsfield said that this would "help him [Kennedy] with this doubtful Negro vote all over the nation." He was right.

The demonstrations against segregation in the city's stores continued until March 1961, when the leading merchants signed a joint agreement to desegregate public accommodations. Hartsfield and his white business allies avoided violence; King and African American leaders forced an end to segregation. Rich's, "the symbol of Atlanta," removed its signs of segregated rest rooms and opened its lunch counters and Magnolia Room to African American patrons.

As cities throughout the South—Birmingham, Montgomery, Selma, Oxford, New Orleans, and a list running to embarrassing lengths—

disgraced themselves with their violent, sometimes murderous reactions to the extension of civil rights to African Americans, Atlanta seemed a model of racial harmony. On August 31, 1961, Pres. John F. Kennedy opened his news conference by noting "the responsible law-abiding manner" in which the city had integrated its schools and counseled "all communities which face this difficult transition . . . to look closely at what Atlanta has done." In 1963, Ivan Allen was the only mayor from the region to testify before Congress in behalf of the pending Civil Rights Bill. In 1968, Herbert Jenkins became the sole police chief to serve on the so-called Kerner Commission, the National Advisory Commission on Civil Disorders. This "city too busy to hate," *Atlanta Magazine* proudly declared in 1967, stood as "sort of the national hero of the sixties."

While the city's image mavens were ready to declare victory over segregation, African Americans were not as rosy in their outlook. In 1966, an African American contributor to *Atlanta Magazine* argued that "Atlanta's image only looks good when compared to Mississippi." And in 1968, the black-owned *Atlanta Inquirer,* while confirming its pride in the city, cautioned: "Blacks enjoy Atlanta, but they don't like it as it is."

One of the things that the newer generation of black Atlantans did not like in particular was the paternalism of its white leadership. The white power elite credited and congratulated itself for the relatively smooth transition from legal segregation while largely overlooking the day-to-day efforts of their black counterparts in maintaining civic order. The applause and kudos, it seemed, were reserved for white moderates—*Constitution* editor Ralph McGill and Mayor Ivan Allen. Significantly, the most honored Atlantan, Martin Luther King Jr., received his award from neither a grateful nation nor a proud city but, instead, from an international committee that conferred upon him the Nobel Peace Prize. Even then, Atlanta's leadership debated whether or not to acknowledge Dr. King's achievement publicly. To their credit, they did.

The meaning of Atlanta's moderation has, subsequently, been called into question. In *The Selling of the South,* for example, historian James Cobb characterized Mayor Hartsfield's much ballyhooed success at "integrating" the city's schools by admitting nine black children as "ostentatious moderation." Cobb also criticized "as self-seeking and hollow the moderation of boosters and civic officials in Atlanta," and a handful of other southern cities as well, when their motivation was based on profit, not justice. At the same time, he acknowledged that their moderate stance was "preferable to the tragic silence of the economic elite in Birmingham or New Orleans."

Essentially, for all their self-interested good will, Atlanta's Great White Fathers anticipated remaining in control of a white-majority city. Their Atlanta was a White Atlanta, and their vision of a Black Atlanta would remain that of a "sub-community." The announced closing of the downtown Rich's and the partial demolition for the construction of the new Federal Center produced a flood of memories that were divided along racial lines. For whites there were the memories of Celestine Sibley's Dear Store; while for African Americans, Rich's was the site of both the humiliations of a color line and the triumph of a campaign to end it. Atlanta history, it seems, divides along the color line.

THE OLD IN NEW ATLANTA

Civilizations should be judged, philosopher-longshoreman Eric Hoffer suggested, not according to incidences of invention or innovation but, instead, by levels of maintenance. On the Hoffer scale of civilization, Atlanta would rank exceedingly low. Not the old, but the new has been its focus.

Even measured against a national culture that has all but sanctified the throwaway, Atlanta still seems singularly spendthrift. Perhaps the root cause for its profligate ways is its relative youth and a pioneering spirit that expresses itself in the conviction that Atlanta will somehow always expand the borders of the urban frontier. Perhaps fire, the city's identifying element among the ancient four, is a cause: "Like the Phoenix, from the ashes," which became Atlanta's motto in the wake of Sherman's incendiary efforts of 1864, seemed applicable, as well, to a great conflagration in 1917 and a deadly inferno at the Winecoff Hotel in 1946. Perhaps the Atlanta spirit, as an expression of the New South creed, provides the readiest answer: The New is almost always preferable to the Old; what goes up must come down; to build is better than to maintain. It is also likely to be more visible, more newsworthy, more imageable, and more fun.

Maintenance deferred, preservation delayed: Such is the story of the Old in New Atlanta. Sewers overflowing; landfills filling; water mains bursting; air quality worsening; viaducts and bridges deteriorating and trembling; sinkholes opening, widening, engorging. As the countdown to the millennium ticks away, Atlanta confronts a formidable accounts-payable bill for delayed maintenance on its infrastructure—an estimated $1 billion (past due).

Atlanta is also spending to keep up its status and image of a big-league city, a competition that pits city against city and city against suburb. Sports owners, seeing lower profit margins in older facilities, are demanding and receiving offers for new complexes by threatening or offering to move their teams. In this world, the "new" sports facilities of the 1960s and 1970s are now old. Accordingly, in the early 1990s city fathers determined that Atlanta–Fulton County Stadium was no longer adequate for big-league sports. The state, Fulton County, and the city of Atlanta, in response to threats by the football Falcons to remove to Florida, combined to build a state-of-the-art domed stadium to keep the weather (usually mild) out and the team (predictably bad) in. The Olympic Stadium (reduced in size after the summer of 1996) would keep the Braves (championship caliber) inside the perimeter, rather than risk their venturing to suburban Gwinnett County. The challenge of maintaining the image of big-league city is now a battle to keep the sports venues in the downtown.

A struggle in Atlanta has been joined between the city and its suburbs: The supporters of Congressional Minority Whip John Lewis versus those of House Speaker Newt Gingrich; a Democratic, predominantly African American center versus a Republican, mostly white encirclement; and downtown survival versus edge-city developments. In 1966, there was no doubt the stadium would be built downtown; but in 1994 and 1995, there was a struggle between the city and north Fulton County for a larger basketball facility. For the past three decades, the battle has intensified as the city's office complexes shifted ever outward toward its northern frontier; farther out still, shopping malls, as well as office and industrial parks, proliferated. Initially magnets for office complexes and hotels, these nodes in the suburbs now compete for professional sports complexes.

In the past there have been two Atlantas, one white, the other black. While race remains an important divide in the region today, the two Atlantas could easily be termed "inside" and "outside," with the perimeter highway being the divide. This convenient classification provides a ready measure for physical distance, accessibility, lifestyle, class, and race. It defines the boundaries and expresses the challenges of today's and for tomorrow's Atlanta.

"Outside" the perimeter, particularly beyond its northern borders, there developed a new community form and lifestyle—namely, the exurban. In contrast with older, closer in, more traditional suburbs that were extensions of the city proper, these new exurbs exist within their own spatial and social universes. Often corporate "transferees" from another metropolitan region, on their way up the corporate ladder, simply "exchange" their family domiciles from an exurb of Detroit/Kansas City/Philadelphia for their mirror images in Dunwoody/Peachtree City/Alpharetta. On any particular rung of the corporate ladder, the transferred household might remain for a few years until the next and inevitable move. For many exurbanites, then, mobility is a way of life: on an everyday basis, along the perimeter and its connecting freeways, tollways, and roadways; in career terms, up and out. For many such transient households, then, Atlanta is more a point of reference than a vital place.

Much has changed in the historic center of Atlanta since the early 1960s. Much has been gained: A series of dramatic building booms

Atlanta in the mid 1990s

has transformed the old downtown and shaped a new Midtown (with its breathtaking nighttime skyline); a comprehensive rapid-rail system, with connecting bus routes, has been completed; and the effort to complete the major metro highway system—"freeing the freeways"—is finished. In looking to the twenty-first century, highway planners have designed an "outer" perimeter, at a forty-mile radius, twenty miles beyond the "inner" loop and over two hundred miles in length. (If it is ever completed, Pascual Perez's counterpart will have to stop for overnight lodging while circumnavigating the city.)

Will a second perimeter highway create yet another Atlanta? Atlanta has had a number of incarnations in its 150 years. It will, literally and figuratively, reinvent itself yet again. Samuel Mitchell first envisioned a city at this location, while J. Edgar Thompson gave it the name it carries today. Henry Grady and a host of boosters have highlighted the city's assets and downplayed its shortcomings, creating the Atlanta image. But is it image or mirage? Atlanta is today, in many ways, "a city without limits" (in the words of its modern sloganeers). Yet it is also a city without a center, a city divided by its history, and a city partitioned by its beltway. It has had temporary periods of unity—the 1996 Summer Olympics and a winning sports team, for example. It also has icons of a common culture: Coke, King, and *GWTW*. But, in the end, "Atlanta," an incorporated city and a metropolitan region, remains a state of mind, an artificial creation of diverse promoters, past and present.

Dana F. White # LOOKING FOR AN ATLANTA TOUR

With the mounting of the Cotton States and International Exposition of 1895, Atlanta advertised itself to the world as being in the business of civic celebration and self-promotion. By hosting the Centennial Olympic Games 101 years later, Atlanta automatically took on an international network of partners in its century-long tradition of presenting itself to all comers. As the eyes of the world focused on Atlanta, anticipation (as well as a touch of anxiety) mounted: City Hall issued such euphoric projections as the memorable proclamation that the 1996 Games should prove to be the largest international gathering since World War II; city desks published both glowing projections of the Coming City of the Twenty-first Century and dystopian visions of the downtown of the future, applying terms such as "urbicide" to an anticipated "Olympic Aftermath." The "Olympic Countdown," in sum, initiated an avalanche of words and images that could well sweep over the unprepared visitor to the area.

Guidebooks, guided tours, magazine features, entire issues of magazines, news articles, historical accounts, localized biographies, coffee-table books, and videos arrived in Atlanta well in advance of the Olympic Torch. The purpose of the *New Georgia Guide* is not to compete with the huge array of general and specialized guides to the city. Because the *Guide* covers the entire state, giving other areas equal space with Metropolitan Atlanta, to write an in-depth tour of the metropolitan area would be an impossible task. Instead this introduction will steer visitors to three organizations that give excellent views of Atlanta and recommend a guide to the city's physical composition. The tour will lead travelers farther afield to the lovely small towns ringing Atlanta and discuss a few notable sites within that ring. Many, many other locations are worthy of the wanderer's attention. For identifying those locations and appreciating Atlanta, these gatekeepers of the city's history and culture are good places to begin.

The Atlanta History Center (AHC) is a logical starting point. The AHC displays two major exhibitions on the city's development—one uptown, the other downtown. *Metropolitan Frontiers: Atlanta, 1835–2000,* the more ambitious of the two, is located on the center's Buckhead grounds; the other, *Atlanta Heritage Row*, is situated in

265

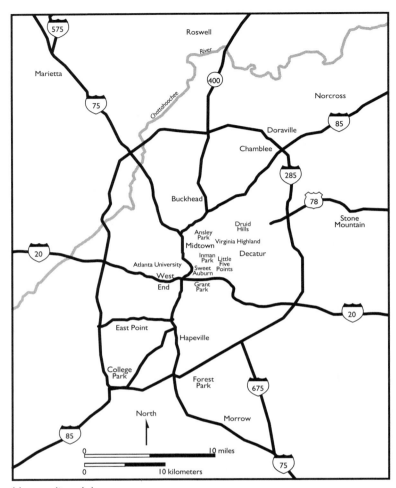

Metropolitan Atlanta

Underground Atlanta in the heart of downtown. As its special contribution to the Olympic Games, the AHC planned exhibitions of regional significance and interest as well as a special reference map keyed to the city's history. The AHC is the place initial inquiries about Atlanta's history should be directed.

The Atlanta Preservation Center (APC) offers a variety of guided tours of both general and special interest. The Martin Luther King Jr. National Historic Site conducts tours of the civil rights leader's birthplace, church, and neighborhood. Between the two of them, the APC and King Site provide distinctive perspectives on the city—about, respectively, its physical fabric and its spiritual vision.

Well before leaving home, the discerning traveler should also consider acquiring three additional tools as preparation for exploring Atlanta: an authoritative guide to the city's structure, the *AIA Guide to the Architecture of Atlanta* (see bibliography); a map of the city to supplement the aforementioned guide—one of a size and substance to serve as a bookmark for that guidebook, such as the plastic-encased Streetwise or Fastmap series; and perhaps a pocket holster of colored pens for highlighting sites to be seen and, later, for recording those actually visited and routes taken. To establish mood and to set the scene, the ambitious traveler should consider delving into a work or two of fiction—whether a full-fledged novel or just a down-and-dirty mystery. (Examples of both are mentioned in the "Looking for Atlanta" essay.) The armchair traveler is likely to be an informed visitor—literally, as well as literarily, prepared to appreciate that "new" city.

The visitor to the Olympic City need not worry about missing some of its newest elements. They are omnipresent. The monumental Olympic Stadium, the spacious Olympic Village, the sculpted Centennial Park (with interior Centennial Plaza), and other "venues"—the in word among Atlantans during the 1990s—are all situated within the confines of the Olympic Ring. The stamp of the Centennial Games on Atlanta is inescapable.

1996: THE YEAR OF THE GUIDEBOOK, ATLANTA STYLE

The avalanche of words and images about Atlanta includes guides to popular tourist attractions and traps, select neighborhoods and urban districts, Civil War battlefields, and such specialized themes as religious groups in the area, its civil rights heritage, Olympic venues, activities for children, and Atlanta's most famous book/film/phenomenon—*Gone with the Wind*. The possibilities seem virtually limitless.

Information about accommodations, dining, transportation, entertainment, local customs, projections of seasonal weather conditions, and the like is the business of commercially produced guidebooks. A visitor's decision about which (if any) commercial guidebook to acquire is likely to depend upon personal taste and budget considerations.

VENTURING FORTH

Choosing sites to visit is the ultimate challenge for the time-bound visitor—especially in Atlanta. Although metropolitan Atlanta is far-flung, sprawling, and somewhat baffling, its in-town neighborhoods often tend to be distinctive, interesting, and sometimes delightful. The *AIA Guide,* which is organized according to neighborhoods and districts, offers a ready entry into the everyday city, the city where Atlantans live and work. For each district or neighborhood, the *AIA Guide* provides a succinct introduction, key map, and a structure-by-structure survey. A quick scanning of its pages should suggest areas that recommend themselves for further exploration. Some are also briefly discussed below.

Exploring the hinterland—that vast area beyond the walls of the central city, the "historic" city—is seldom the work of guidebooks. For a refreshing, different view, Betsy and John Braden's touring suggestions, which follow, breach the walls of the old city and reach out into the new—the metropolitan region that defines modern Atlanta.

Betsy Braden and
John Braden
TOURING METROPOLITAN ATLANTA

Years before Atlanta was mapped in 1837, north-central Georgia was dotted with established communities. When various factors caused Atlanta to grow into the region's predominant city, those other towns survived. Although engulfed or threatened by Atlanta's development, or suffering the "fringe blight" of neon and fast-food eateries, they beckon with small-town friendliness and ambience.

An essential element for touring the small towns circling Atlanta, and many of the sites within that ring, is the automobile. Like most other Americans, Atlantans are almost addicted to driving themselves everywhere they go. Consequently, rapid transit has developed slowly and still does not reach many outskirts of the city. No street maps are included with this tour. Travelers are advised to refer to the locator maps published here, acquire a good area map, and study both before hitting the road.

DECATUR

In this town, founded in 1823, the central square is roomy enough for both the imposing granite Old DeKalb County courthouse (1898), containing DeKalb Historical Society exhibits, and the contemporary MARTA rapid-rail station with its glassed entry. Within a few blocks are several antebellum houses. Across the railroad tracks, the magnolia-framed buildings of Agnes Scott College (1899) form a historic campus and vibrant cultural niche. The college's galleries, performing arts, and other activities are enjoyed by many townspeople.

In Adair Park on Decatur's western fringe stands the DeKalb Historical Complex of two early log cabins and the 1820s Swanton House, a Union command post during the Battle of Atlanta. They can be toured through arrangement with the DeKalb Historical Society. The 1820 Mary Gay House next door is open three mornings a week and by appointment through the Junior League of DeKalb County.

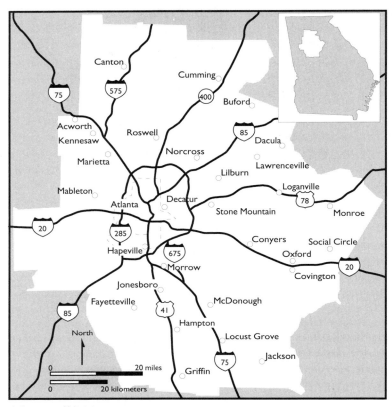

Atlanta and Vicinity

Decatur lies six miles due east of Atlanta, by way of Ponce de Leon Avenue (U.S. 78/278). The DeKalb Welcome Center in the courthouse stocks city and courthouse grounds walking tour brochures and Decatur and DeKalb County driving tour brochures.

STONE MOUNTAIN VILLAGE

Spanish explorers may have been the first tourists to see Stone Mountain. Since then, the huge granite bulk has awed an increasing number of visitors, but only in 1839 was a settlement begun in its western shadow. The town grew, moved alongside the Georgia Railroad tracks in 1845, and suffered damage during the Civil War. (The cemetery holds a number of Confederate graves.) Afterwards, quarrying operations employed stonecutters whose output went into Panama Canal locks and the U.S. Capitol, among other projects. Today's retail district, its three blocks brimming with sundry foods, goods, and services, caters to tourists. The commercialism is tempered by friendly proprietors, a dedicated community spirit, an active arts program, and a local clientele that make Stone Mountain a true working town.

Stone Mountain is fifteen miles east of Atlanta. The Village of Stone Mountain Visitor Center contains brochures of shops and businesses and information on Stone Mountain Park.

MARIETTA

The town clusters around lushly planted Glover Park, the year-round scene of concerts and art exhibits. Marietta was created in 1834, and some of the buildings that line the square date to resort days in the 1850s. Kennesaw House (1855) sheltered Andrews's Raiders before they hijacked the General in 1864. Dozens of showy nineteenth-century houses, including bed-and-breakfast inns, line streets leading into the square. The Zion Baptist Church (1888) is a key African American institution; the 1910 post office now houses an ambitious art museum; and popular restaurants operate in an old hardware store, in an antebellum mansion, and under the Big Chicken, a local landmark on U.S. 41 that must be seen to be believed.

Guarding Marietta's northern approach, Big and Little Kennesaw Mountains are cornerstones of a huge park established where Union and Confederate forces struggled for two weeks in June 1864 (see Civil War section).

Marietta lies twenty miles northwest of Atlanta. The Marietta Welcome Center in the former Western & Atlantic railroad passenger depot (1898) has films, a Historic Marietta walking and driving tour brochure, and a Cannonball Trail driving tour brochure of Civil War sites. These include Kennesaw Mountain National Battlefield Park, General Sherman's headquarters, the Marietta National Cemetery where ten thousand Union dead are buried, and the Confederate Cemetery with three thousand graves. The center sponsors a city walking tour every Thursday except holidays.

ROSWELL

A good stream encouraged Roswell King to establish cotton and woolen mills here in 1839, and his original plan for the related village survives. An open park with a fountain and gazebo is ringed by 1850s buildings filled with shops and restaurants.

A Wednesday morning walking tour surveys the gentry's houses. Chief among them is Bulloch Hall (1839), the childhood home of Mittie Bulloch Roosevelt, mother of a president (Theodore Roosevelt) and grandmother of a first lady (Eleanor Roosevelt). A Saturday morning tour circles the modest dwellings and factory-turned-shopping mall in the old mill district, burned by Sherman's troops in July 1864. The nearby Archibald Smith Plantation Home provides an example of a well-to-do southern farm family dwelling between 1840 and 1880. Roswell's other nerve center lies half a mile north of the square, at Canton and Magnolia Streets where Victorian-era commercial structures form another shopping district.

The Teaching Museum North of the Fulton County school system gives youngsters hands-on experience in a re-created farmhouse, a toy attic, a turn-of-the-century courtroom, and other exhibits. A phone call will ensure that visits don't conflict with large school groups.

Roswell, now a busy commercial center, lies twenty miles north of Atlanta, across the Chattahoochee River. The Historic Roswell Convention and Visitors Bureau, open seven days a week, shows a film and offers literature including a self-guided walking tour. To the north of Roswell on Ga. 372 is Crabapple, a crossroads community of antiques stores.

LAWRENCEVILLE

The massive red-brick historic Gwinnett County courthouse (1885) presides over a business district founded in 1821. A walking tour brochure gives the layout of the meticulously renovated but governmentally inactive structure and explains the monuments and markers on the landscaped grounds. Among them are plaques commemorating two natives: Ezzard Charles, who reigned as world heavyweight boxing champion from 1949 to 1951, and Charles Henry Smith, who in the mid-1800s signed his popular newspaper columns and essays "Bill Arp." A block away, the 1850s building that was home to the Lawrenceville Female Seminary has become the Gwinnett History Museum. Civil War reenactments take place quarterly.

A driving tour brochure points out other county sites, one of the most significant of which is the 1813 Elisha Winn House near Dacula. Restored and open by appointment through the Gwinnett Historical Society, the two-story frame house shares the grounds with four other early structures.

Gwinnett ranks as one of America's fastest-growing counties, and urban sprawl has all but swallowed some of its quainter communities. A little searching, however, reveals nineteenth-century charm juxtaposed with the ubiquitous rail lines. The depot in Norcross, now a restaurant and mini-mall, was built in 1870. Antiques markets pervade most of Old Town Lilburn, and Buford has become an arts enclave. Each town is about ten miles from Lawrenceville, which is thirty-five miles northeast of Atlanta.

MONROE AND SOCIAL CIRCLE

Eight Georgia governors came from the Monroe area, and one left a rich legacy in the 1887 McDaniel-Tichenor House, open daily under the auspices of the Georgia Trust for Historic Preservation. Walton County native Moina Michael started the "poppies for veterans" movement following World War I, and now surrounding highways are planted with the vivid red blossoms. The "poppy lady" is also remembered with a marble bust in the State Capitol.

The renovated Walton County courthouse (1883) anchors Monroe's commercial district. Within walking distance at 205 South Broad Street, the Monroe Art Guild sponsors an art and information center and mounts exhibits in a 1931 post office building. The Davis-Edwards House, open by appointment through the Walton County Historical Society, is an 1845 Greek Revival house with period furnishings and a separate brick kitchen. Monroe is forty miles east of Atlanta.

In nearby Social Circle, the hungry hordes head for Billie's Blue Willow Inn Restaurant to sample the all-you-can-eat buffet. The early-twentieth-century house is one of more than sixty-five built between 1838 and 1916 in this National Register community. A couple of picturesque blocks constitute the business district; at its center stands a replica of the well around which early settlers gathered to drink and swap tales. It's said that their sociability was immortalized in the name selected upon the community's incorporation in 1832.

Social Circle is eleven miles south of Monroe on Ga. 11 or three miles north of I-20E (exit 47). Fox Vineyards & Winery, a mile south of exit 47, offers tours and wine tastings. A full day's loop tour might combine Monroe, Social Circle, Covington, Oxford, and Conyers.

COVINGTON AND OXFORD

Aficionados of television's *In the Heat of the Night* are familiar with the stately Newton County courthouse and other structures that served as backdrop for the fictional town of Sparta, Mississippi. Hollywood ended the series in 1994, but the show was neither Covington's first nor its last, for the picturesque town and its environs are a favorite for location filming.

The 1822 Old Brick Store, open by appointment and furnished by the Newton County Historical Society to acknowledge its various uses as a stagecoach inn, country store, and courthouse, marks the county's first settlement. In July 1864, Union troops destroyed the railroad but spared the town's beautiful houses. Some thirty-four are pictured in a self-guided tour brochure available at the Covington–Newton County Chamber of Commerce. The magnolia-shaded courthouse square holds seasonal lunchtime concerts and an annual Easter egg hunt. Theatrical productions and other arts-related events take place year-round.

Oxford College of Emory University occupies the original Emory campus in the nearby town of Oxford, listed on the National Register of Historic Places. Driving and walking tour brochures point out early nineteenth-century buildings, including those where wounded Civil War troops convalesced, and Soldiers Cemetery. Hearn Nature Trail and geology garden are open to the public.

Covington is thirty-four miles east of Atlanta on I-20 (exit 46). A visit there can conveniently be combined with one to Conyers or Monroe and Social Circle.

CONYERS

There is Conyers, and then there is Olde Town Conyers, well worth seeking. Begun as a railroad watering station prior to 1845, old Conyers still parallels the tracks. Near the restored 1898 passenger depot resides the Dinky, one of only three 1905 Rogers steam locomotives in the world. Behind the courthouse, the Rockdale County Historical Society has amassed four rooms of memorabilia in the old jail. Gingerbread suburbs spread out from turn-of-the-century storefronts; a pavilion and a quarter-acre botanical garden serve as a gathering place for July Fourth fireworks and other festivals. The Georgia International Horse Park, built for the 1996 Summer Olympic Games, is three miles northeast of Conyers. A 1940 New Deal mural, "The Ploughman," by Elizabeth Terrell, adorns the old depot at the corner of Railroad and Center Streets.

Rockdale County has long been a beacon for people with a spiritual bent. In the mid 1990s, as many as twenty-five thousand souls gathered on the thirteenth day of each month at "the Farm," whose owner claimed to receive apparitions of the Virgin Mary. Elsewhere, at the Monastery of the Holy Ghost, Trappist monks sell freshly baked bread and bonsai trees and implements. The church and grounds are open daily. Also near Conyers, traditional Protestants gather each summer for the century-old Salem and Smyrna camp meetings.

Conyers lies twenty-four miles east of Atlanta on I-20 (exit 41).

JONESBORO

Clayton County is the setting for *Gone with the Wind*. Margaret Mitchell's great-grandparents immigrated here from Ireland, and she modeled the novel's Tara on their unpretentious two-story house—a far cry from Hollywood's white-columned version. In reality, there never was a Tara, and even the old Fitzgerald house where Mitchell's ancestors lived is secluded on private property. But there is Jonesboro, then as now the county seat and hub. For five blocks a turn-of-the-century commercial district parallels the railroad tracks over which displaced Atlantans and retreating Confederate soldiers fled following the fall of Atlanta in September 1864. The stone depot (1867) replaced the one Union troops burned, and the quaint little brick jail (1869) on a side street has become the Clayton County History Center.

Historical Jonesboro's Stately Oaks complex depicts country life circa 1839 with a Greek Revival house, outbuildings, and one-room schoolhouse. The urban side is Ashley Oaks (1879) and its luncheon tours. A thirty-two-site driving tour brochure includes the Confederate Cemetery and the 1860 Warren House used by both Confederate and Union forces as a field hospital and command center. A glass-paned museum at the rear of the local funeral home gives a glimpse of early embalming instruments along with the hearse that in 1883 carried Alexander H. Stephens, vice president of the Confederacy and governor of Georgia, from the governor's mansion in Atlanta to his burial site in Crawfordville (see East Central Georgia).

Near Jonesboro, on the campus of Clayton State College, is Spivey Hall, an intimate concert hall known by musicians and music lovers around the world for its superior acoustics. At the 120-acre Reynolds Memorial Nature Preserve in Morrow, the exterior of the nineteenth-century Huie-Reynolds House has been restored, and an adjacent barn is being turned into a walk-through museum. The Atlanta Beach recreation complex, white sand imported to the middle of suburbia, was named the site of Olympic beach volleyball competition.

Jonesboro is fifteen miles south of Atlanta via I-75 (exit 76). The Clayton County Convention and Visitors Bureau has driving tour brochures of the town and county.

JACKSON

Fanning out from the Butts County courthouse (1898) are several blocks of vintage houses. One is the magnificent Carmichael House (1898), a bed-and-breakfast inn with an unusual two-story rotunda. It is open for tours the last Saturday of each month to coincide with downtown merchants' sidewalk sales.

Nearby Indian Springs State Park commemorates an 1821 treaty between the Creek nation and the U.S. government. The New Deal's Civilian Conservation Corps erected the stone buildings, including one over the therapeutic spring that attracted American Indians and later vacationers taking "the cure." Only vestiges remain of the nine hotels that served this once-thriving resort area. At the Indian Springs Hotel, in 1825, Chief William McIntosh signed a second treaty ceding all remaining Creek lands to the state of Georgia. Now undergoing restoration, the building is the site of periodic festivals and is opened at other times by the Butts County Historical Society. For recreation, Butts County offers Lake Jackson and the Dauset Trails Nature Center. South of Jackson on the way to Indian Springs is Fresh Air Barbecue, which has prepared simple but delicious fare since 1929.

Jackson lies forty-three miles southeast of Atlanta via U.S. 23 or I-75S (exit 67).

MCDONOUGH AND LOCUST GROVE

McDonough has one of the metropolitan area's prettiest courthouse squares—a public park with shade trees, benches, a Confederate monument, a flame of freedom, and myriad seasonal flowers to celebrate the annual Geranium Festival. The Henry County courthouse (1897), its Romanesque Revival facade restored to a pristine state, is solid, grand, and listed on the National Register. So is the 1889 jail in the rear. Prosperous, well-kept shops line the square.

McDonough was settled in 1823, and some fine houses linger from that era. Among them, the 1826 Brown House is used by the Genealogical Society of Henry and Clayton Counties and is open to the public during limited hours.

McDonough is twenty-five miles southeast of Atlanta via U.S 23 or I-75S (exit 70). The Henry County Welcome Center/Convention and Visitors Bureau, just west of exit 70, has a city walking tour brochure.

In nearby Locust Grove, a pretty little trackside town, the hardware store is a hundred years old, and the old Locust Grove Institute (1894–1929) building houses the municipal complex.

A few other communities merit a visit. Fayetteville, a small town twenty-five miles south of Atlanta, claims the area's oldest active courthouse, an 1825 gem that now functions as a juvenile court building. Leading to it is the "world's longest courthouse bench"—fifty-eight feet of handhewn heart pine that was once an interior center beam.

Just twenty miles away is Griffin, a city that lies thirty-five miles south of Atlanta. Textile discount outlets are the object of most tourist trips, although a driving tour brochure covers twenty-nine historic points. The 1859 Bailey-Tebault House serves as headquarters of the Griffin Historical & Preservation Society and can be toured by appointment.

IN SEARCH OF . . .

Every city boasts its own distinctive "must-see" sites and attractions. In this section, some of Atlanta's proudest and most memorable are grouped thematically, whether they are situated inside or outside the perimeter highway.

ATLANTA NATURALLY: THE GREAT OUTDOORS

Georgia's temperate climate means its parks and green spaces are heavily used throughout the year. Within metropolitan Atlanta, Stone Mountain Park and Kennesaw Mountain National Battlefield Park are the largest and most accessible open spaces. At Kennesaw Mountain, north of Marietta, exhibits and park rangers interpret the heavy Civil War fighting there, and walking trails honeycomb the large park.

For its variety of attractions, Georgia's Stone Mountain Park in DeKalb County defies easy classification. A Confederate memorial carving embellishes the world's largest exposed granite mountain, upon which laser shows are beamed on summer evenings. Hikers who climb the mountain can look west to view the Atlanta skyline and developing sprawl. The antebellum plantation in the park has nineteen authentic buildings moved from other sites and assembled here. Other features are the Stone Mountain Railroad, a paddlewheel riverboat, an antique auto and music museum, wildlife trails, tennis, golf, fishing, an inn, a conference center, and a family campground.

Closer in, Piedmont Park, bordered by the Atlanta Botanical Garden, and, a few miles to the south, Grant Park, with the bonus of Zoo Atlanta, are favorite outdoor recreation spots. Many smaller public neighborhood parks metro-wide are equipped with playgrounds, playing fields, picnic shelters, and trails. At Vines Botanical Garden in Loganville, a lake and manor house complement the plantings. Loganville is east of Atlanta on U.S. 78. DeKalb College Botanical Garden contains rare and endangered plants, among other species, and the cultivated gardens and woodlands surrounding the Atlanta History Center represent native flora and the history of gardening in Atlanta.

Public golf courses, both municipal and state operated, number more than three dozen; several of them, such as North Fulton, Sugar Creek, and Stone Mountain Park, are top-rated. The area also has many excellent private clubs.

For less managed nature scapes, Fernbank Forest near Decatur, Dauset Trails Nature Center near Jackson, Reynolds Nature Preserve in Morrow, and the Outdoor Activity Center in southwest Atlanta are available. The banks of the Chattahoochee River are threaded with trails, as are the state parks at High Falls, Indian Springs, Panola Mountain, and Sweetwater Creek. In addition to pools and lakes at state parks, public neighborhood swimming pools are plentiful throughout the area, and Atlanta operates at least two indoor facilities.

Lake Lanier Islands, forty-five minutes northeast of Atlanta, is a self-contained, water-based recreation complex that includes a beach, golf, camping, and two resort hotels. The lake offers sailing, power boating, houseboating, and fishing (see Northeast Georgia). Lake Jackson, on the boundary of Butts, Newton, and Jasper Counties, also affords water recreation.

As you'd expect in a city with the nation's largest lawn tennis association (ALTA, with seventy-five thousand members), public tennis courts are everywhere, and many private health clubs with tennis, squash, racquetball, and other facilities offer day rates to nonmembers. The same is true of hotels with health and jogging facilities. The fifty thousand runners in the annual July Fourth Peachtree Road Race make it the world's largest 10 kilometer race. The Atlanta Track Club has information on this and other running events.

Anglers with licenses may cast their lines in the Chattahoochee River and in lakes and state parks, which are also good places to camp. The Wolf Creek Trap & Skeet Range in south Fulton County received a $17-million facelift for the 1996 Summer Olympic Games shooting competitions. Another range, the Cherokee Rose Shooting Resort, is outside Griffin. Hunting season means trips to Starrsville Plantation near Covington for deer, dove, quail, and turkey; or Dogwood Plantation near McDonough, where participants ride mule-drawn wagons to hunt quail and pheasant November through March. A state hunting license is required.

Fruit and vegetables can be harvested at pick-your-own farms in more rural areas. Many farmers sell their produce at the Atlanta State Farmers' Market in Forest Park, where fresh seasonal produce, flowers, shrubs, trees, and gift items may be found.

THE CHATTAHOOCHEE RIVER

The five-hundred-mile-long Chattahoochee River springs from the ground near Helen and flows to the west of Atlanta before turning south on its run to Apalachicola Bay and the Gulf of Mexico. The river supplies Atlanta's drinking water and is one of its greatest recreational resources. North of the city, the river can be fished for trout, bass, bream, and catfish. It can be rafted, rowed, canoed, and kayaked. Its banks can be hiked and played on. Because of its abundant animal and plant life, it is used as an open-air classroom.

The Chattahoochee River National Recreation Area (CRNRA), administered by the National Park Service, stretches along forty-eight miles of the river's banks and extends away from the river bed to as much as one-third mile. Thirteen parks, or "units," punctuate the course, each with marked walking trails, open meadows, picnic tables, and grills. One has a children's playground, another a three-mile jogging and fitness trail with twenty-two exercise stations. Several contain historic house sites, antebellum mill ruins, and other structures. The topography of each unit varies, encompassing forests, beaches, ravines, hills, or marshes. The CRNRA provides a brochure with detailed maps and fishing regulations.

Watercraft rentals are available May through Labor Day at Chattahoochee Outdoor Center (COC), the park concessionaire, which maintains two outlets. COC also provides a shuttle to and from take-out points.

Along the river, Gwinnett County maintains the Jones Bridge and Pinckneyville Arts Center parks. Fulton County's Chattahoochee River Park near Roswell is equipped with a colorful children's playground and a picnicking area with grills. Adjacent is another canoe and raft rental concern.

The private, nonprofit Chattahoochee Nature Center sponsors a broad range of programs for children by age group, summer evening raft rides, special Sunday activities, field trips, and the like. Its grounds contain wetland and woodland trails, a duck pond, marsh boardwalk, and bald eagles.

HISTORY MUSEUMS

Among the city's many repositories of historical artifacts are the Atlanta Cyclorama painting, narration, and museum of the Battle of Atlanta. The African American Panoramic Experience (APEX) covers black cultural contributions to Atlanta and America. Atlanta Heritage Row at Underground Atlanta and the Atlanta History Center are described in the introduction to this section.

Atlanta Museum, in the old Rose mansion on Peachtree Street, is one man's huge and idiosyncratic collection with irregular hours to match. The Jimmy Carter Library and Museum at the Carter Presidential Center details the life and presidency (1977–81) of the nation's thirty-ninth president (see Southwest Georgia). The World of Coca-Cola chronicles the growth of the Atlanta-based soft drink, with lively early promotional materials and free samples.

The Hapeville Depot Museum near Hartsfield Atlanta International Airport contains local and aviation- and railroad-related exhibits. The Gwinnett History Museum and the DeKalb Historical Society Museum feature memorabilia pertinent to those communities (see Lawrenceville and Decatur in the Small Town section). The Buford History Museum houses local mementos. Others are Big Shanty and the Road to Tara museums. In addition, many local communities have their own museums with artifacts or mementos.

HOUSE MUSEUMS

Many historic dwellings, along with the homes of famous Atlantans, are open to the public. The Callanwolde Fine Arts Center, housed in the 1920 Tudor-style mansion of Charles Howard Candler of the Coca-

From the Atlanta History Center exhibition *Metropolitan Frontiers: Atlanta 1835–2000*

Cola family, is listed on the National Register. The Georgia Governor's Mansion (1968) contains one of the country's finest collections of Federal-period furnishings. The 1894 house where Martin Luther King Jr. was born has been restored to represent the time of his birth in 1929. Rhodes Memorial Hall (1905) is modeled after Germany's Rhine River castles. Stained- and painted-glass windows depicting the rise and fall of the Confederacy line the house's staircase. The Wren's Nest, in West End, has been faithfully restored to the days when author Joel Chandler Harris lived there with his large, lively family. The imposing Alonzo F. Herndon Home, also in West End near Clark Atlanta University, reflects the wide-ranging interests of the founder of the Atlanta Life Insurance Company and his family. The Williams-Payne House Museum in Sandy Springs is a restored 1870s farmhouse.

"Small-Town Atlanta" covers the Archibald Smith Plantation (Roswell), Bulloch Hall (Roswell), the Elisha Winn House (Lawrenceville), and other interesting structures.

OTHER HISTORIC HOUSES AND BUILDINGS

Concord Covered Bridge in Cobb County and Pool's Mill Covered Bridge in Forsyth County are two of the last covered bridges in the area. Fort Buffington, marked by a stone monument six miles east of Canton in Cherokee County, was a detention camp for Georgia's Cherokee Indians prior to their removal to Oklahoma on the infamous Trail of Tears. The 1878 Hampton railroad depot has been refurbished as city offices. Starr's Mill (1907) is a Fayette County landmark. The 1832 Mable

House in Mableton is a gallery for the South Cobb Arts Alliance (see Visual Arts section). The circa-1868 Gilbert House in southwest Atlanta serves as a city of Atlanta community arts and cultural center (see Visual Arts). The Mansion Restaurant on Ponce de Leon Avenue fills the Peters House, a rambling 1883 Queen Anne style–edifice, and Anthony's is quartered in a 1797 plantation house moved to Buckhead from east Georgia.

SCIENCE AND TECHNOLOGY

At the Fernbank Museum of Natural History, the chief exhibit depicts the earth's evolution by paralleling it to that of Georgia. Nearby Fernbank Science Center contains varied exhibits, a five-hundred-seat planetarium, observatory, gardens, and Fernbank Forest, with paved walking trails. At SciTrek, the Science and Technology Museum of Atlanta, otherwise incomprehensible test-tube and esoteric physics theory is finally fun, thanks to a plethora of hands-on, interactive displays. It is definitely not for kids only. CNN Center, headquarters of Cable News Network, Headline News, and other facets of Ted Turner's media empire, offers behind-the-scenes tours of its nerve center.

Specialty museums include the outdoor Southeastern Railway Museum with actual engines and rolling stock, the Telephone Museum in the Southern Bell Center, the Center for Puppetry Arts Museum, the lobby displays at Crawford Long Hospital on Georgia's Dr. Long who in 1842 pioneered the use of ether as an anesthetic (see Northeast Georgia), Georgia State University's Johnny Mercer Museum (in Pullen Library) on the life and career of the lyricist who wrote "Moon River"

Herndon Home

Atlantic Center and the High Museum of Art

and 639 other songs, the Federal Reserve Bank Monetary Museum, Georgia State Capitol Museum of Science and Industry, and the small Lanier Museum of Natural History in Buford.

The American Museum of Papermaking at the Institute of Paper Science and Technology, near Georgia Tech, follows papermaking from its earliest forms (about 2000 B.C.) to today's high-tech manufacturing. It includes exhibits on writing surfaces before paper, early recycling experiments, watermarks, and computer-run mills. The Teaching Museum South in Hapeville is a learning experience for school groups, but visitors can tour the recreated one-room schoolhouse, courtroom, and other areas. The Teaching Museum North is in Roswell (see above).

THE VISUAL ARTS

Atlanta's museums and galleries range from traditional to avant garde. They encompass historic houses, commercial galleries, and public ateliers. The works include one of the world's largest circular paintings and the world's largest bas-relief sculpture. "Phoenix Rising from the Ashes," a sculpture recently moved to Woodruff Park, symbolizes Atlanta's own resurrection.

Travelers find art the moment they arrive in the city—in the escalator wells and baggage claim areas at Hartsfield Atlanta International Airport, in the MARTA rapid-rail stations, and on the walls of buildings in the downtown business district. Even tiny Brookwood Station, the city's only Amtrak station, has an imposing statue by Daniel Chester French. Some of Atlanta's art is good, some is bad, but it's all around. Paintings, murals, collages, and photographs hang in government

ONE PERSON'S CHOICE

Colin Campbell, columnist for the Atlanta Journal-Constitution, *in December 1994 wrote his personal year-end list of Atlanta's ten best places to visit. He modified the column for inclusion in the* New Georgia Guide:

TEN BEST ATLANTA SIGHTS
(plus a few more)

Here's a list of ten things in Atlanta I suggest newcomers try to see. (Of course, if the visitors are children, they might want to head instead for the Fernbank Museum of Natural History, SciTrek, or the Center for Puppetry Arts.)

1. Martin Luther King Jr.'s Neighborhood. The once-bustling black district where Atlanta's most honored citizen grew up has disappointed hordes of visitors. And yet King and his legacy remain so important that places like the house where he was born and the MLK Center and Ebenezer Baptist Church really must be seen.

2. The Carlos Museum. Even now, after the museum's expansion, too few locals realize what a gift to Atlanta this treasure chest on the Emory campus is. Less than a tenth of its collections are on display, so you can return to see pre-Columbian art, Africana, beautiful objects from the ancient Mediterranean—plus special exhibits from around the world.

3. The Capitol. Odd, colorful, and relentlessly southern, the State Capitol has developed into a kind of attic-museum of paintings, stuffed animals, flags, scale models, weapons, and much more. Visit early in the year, and you get the added pleasure of watching Georgia's lawmakers at work. The Capitol is also close to touristic standbys like the World of Coca-Cola.

4. Stone Mountain. As weird as the Capitol, only bigger. You should walk, if possible, to the summit of this spectacular knob of granite. And at the foot of the mountain, don't miss the excellent collection of old southern homes.

5. The Atlanta History Center. This isn't a bad place for a tourist to start, considering the sophisticated background it provides. Add the handsome Swan House and the center's other attractions, and you get a quick sense of where Atlanta has come from.

6. The Cyclorama. Another local attraction you can't see anyplace else. Some visitors miss it, thinking it's pro-Confederate or mainly for

kids. But in fact it's a vast painting (whose artists still haven't received the credit they deserve) of the deadly and liberating Battle of Atlanta—high tragedy and triumph on a national scale. (The zoo next door is also worth visiting.)

7. Buckhead. Malls, restaurants, expensive cars. And if the developers ever figure out how to make the area around Lenox fun for people on foot, Lenox could actually become the new "downtown" its boosters claim it is. Till then, try it by car—which offers the added pleasure of cruising along those opulent northside residential streets with their magnificent trees and gardens.

8. The Carter Center. Just getting there and back, along the Freedom Parkway, gives you a splendid view of Atlanta's skyline. The center (offices, gardens, historical exhibits) is dedicated partly to world peace as envisioned by former president Jimmy Carter. It's a short walk from other attractions such as the Virginia-Highland neighborhood.

9. The High Museum. People expecting an art museum on the scale of New York will be disappointed. But the High, in its sleek white shell, is always worth a visit. It's also next door to the symphony, the theater, and one of Atlanta's pleasantest residential neighborhoods, Ansley Park.

10. The Chattahoochee River, plus. I haven't included Piedmont Park because it has strayed too far from its original vision of a green haven of tranquillity. But I must include the parks and trails along the Chattahoochee River.

Visitors with more time or more specialized interests should try the Botanical Gardens, CNN, the Herndon Home, the Wren's Nest, Oakland Cemetery, the Fox Theatre, Peachtree Street from Underground to the Arts Center, and the antebellum mansions of Roswell.

buildings, office tower lobbies, retail stores, community centers, and consulates. Sculpture stands in traffic triangles, shopping malls, hotels, public parks, outdoor plazas, and sports arenas.

At Atlanta's premier museum, the High Museum of Art, named to honor Mrs. Joseph M. High, an early patron, architect Richard Meier's building rivals the collections. Its offspring, the High Museum of Art Folk Art and Photography Galleries, is downtown in the Georgia-Pacific Building. The Atlanta International Museum of Art and Design, also downtown, sponsors ethnic, folk, and design exhibits. The Michael C. Carlos Museum at Emory University, reconfigured and extended by architect Michael Graves, concentrates on pre-Columbian, African, and eastern Mediterranean artifacts and mounts changing exhibitions from its large print and painting collection.

Among the city's nonprofit art centers and galleries are Block Candy Company Gallery, Callanwolde Fine Arts Center, the Chastain Gallery of the City of Atlanta Bureau of Cultural Affairs, Georgia Council for the Arts' Carriage Works Gallery, Hammonds House Galleries and Resource Center of African-American Art, King Plow Arts Center, and Nexus Contemporary Arts Center. Nexus features thought-provoking exhibits and sponsors an innovative press.

Suburban museums and arts centers include the A.R.T. Station in Stone Mountain Village, the City of Atlanta's Gilbert House, the Gwinnett Fine Arts Center in Duluth, the Marietta-Cobb Museum of Art in Marietta's former 1910 post office building, the North Arts Center Gallery at South Terraces in northern DeKalb County, Soapstone Center for the Arts in southern DeKalb County, South Cobb Arts Alliance in the 1832 Mable House in Mableton, and the Spruill Center Gallery and Historic Home (1867 and 1905) near Perimeter Center. TULA in Midtown/Buckhead and Beacon Hill Artists Studios in Decatur feature galleries coupled with artists' work spaces. Calling ahead to determine galleries' specialties and current exhibits is always advisable.

Almost all Atlanta's colleges sponsor arts programs and galleries. Among them are Agnes Scott College's Dalton Gallery, the Atlanta College of Art, Clark Atlanta University's Waddell Collection, Emory University's Schatten Gallery, Georgia Institute of Technology (Georgia Tech) Center for the Arts, Georgia State University Art Gallery, Kennesaw State College's Sturgis Library Art Gallery and the Kennesaw Fine Arts Gallery in the Performing Arts Center, Morehouse College's gallery in the lobby of the Martin Luther King Jr. Chapel, Oglethorpe University Museum, and Spelman College's Camille Hanks Cosby Media Center.

In the governor's office in the State Capitol, the Georgia Council for the Arts rotates exhibits of the work of artists from around the state. The Capitol also houses the State Museum of Science and Industry, an eclectic collection of artifacts, stuffed animals, and dioramas that especially interests children. The museum recently added an exhibit, "Georgia on My Mind," to showcase the state's current attractions. Visitors find art in many other public buildings and businesses, including Atlanta City Hall and Atlanta City Hall East, the Atlanta Life Insurance Company lobby, Georgia Pacific Building, One Peachtree Center office building, Paces West office building, Richard B. Russell Federal Building, Ritz-Carlton hotels in downtown Atlanta and Buckhead, Shrine of the Black Madonna, and West End Medical Center satellite at Bowen Homes. Baseball greats Ty Cobb, Hank Aaron, and Phil Niekro are poised in eternal play near the baseball stadium.

The relief carving on Stone Mountain is the largest in the world, and the Atlanta Cyclorama is one of the largest paintings in the world. Both are discussed elsewhere in this tour.

CIVIL WAR SITES

A major resource for Civil War history is the Atlanta History Center, where a permanent, ten-thousand-square-foot exhibition (scheduled to open in summer 1996) focuses on the Atlanta campaign and how the Civil War transformed the nation. It features hundreds of weapons, uniforms, accoutrements, personal gear, and memorabilia from Union and Confederate soldiers and the country's largest collection of Civil War artillery projectiles.

A few major Civil War sites have been preserved, but unplanned development has long since obscured most of them. Anyone wishing to relive Atlanta's wartime history in depth should buy one of several excellent books and driving tours of the Atlanta Campaign of 1864.

Marietta, Roswell, and Jonesboro played prominent roles in the conflict and have historic walking and driving tours of pertinent sites (see Small Town tour). The 2,880-acre Kennesaw Mountain National Battlefield Park outside Marietta preserves original earthen breastworks and offers hiking and picnicking. In the same vicinity, Kennesaw's Big Shanty Museum houses the General, the steam engine in a Civil War hijacking that inspired a Walt Disney movie. The Texas, the locomotive that pursuers raced *backward* to catch the raiders in the General, is on view at the Atlanta Cyclorama.

The Battle of Atlanta began a few miles east of Oakland Cemetery, where General Hood directed Confederate deployments. Buried at Oakland are five Confederate generals, thousands of Confederate soldiers, and sixteen Union fighters.

General Sherman had his headquarters at a site now occupied by the Carter Presidential Center on Copenhill Avenue. The complex, at the edge of the present-day Inman Park neighborhood, commands a panoramic view of downtown Atlanta.

Confederate breastworks at Fort Walker, in the southeast corner of Grant Park (Boulevard and Delmar Avenue) are vestiges of the war

Stone Mountain Memorial Carving

near downtown Atlanta. The park also contains the Atlanta Cyclorama, a huge painting of the battle. After German artists began it in Milwaukee in the mid-1880s, the painting was moved to Atlanta, where a diorama, narration, and introductory film were added.

After conquering Atlanta, Federal troops camped on the grounds of the present-day Georgia State Capitol. The landscaped lawns contain historical statues, markers, and cannons used in the conflict. Portraits and original battle flags are displayed inside. Diagonally across the street, where Atlanta's City Hall now stands, Sherman set up occupational headquarters.

The Battle of Ezra Church took place on land that is now Mozley Park, at 1565 Martin Luther King Jr. Drive NW. The Battle of Peachtree Creek was concentrated in the area around present-day Tanyard Creek Park on Collier Road NW. Sweetwater Creek State Conservation Park in Douglas County preserves the ruins of cotton and woolen mills destroyed by Federal troops.

For other Civil War locations near the metropolitan area, see the Northwest Georgia tour.

IN A NUTSHELL

In-town sites covered more thoroughly by entire guidebooks include the Downtown/Underground area, sections especially significant in African American heritage, and older neighborhoods.

Early Atlanta flourished around Five Points, the intersection of Decatur, Edgewood, Marietta, Peachtree, and then-Whitehall Streets now marked by Woodruff Park. A short walk to the south, Underground Atlanta is a festival-type shopping mall centering around the original locations of city shops beneath the railroad viaducts. As activity and major streets bridged the tracks, the early buildings were abandoned until a recent commercial venture revived them. Near Five Points and Underground are many structures covered in detail in the *AIA Guide* or Atlanta Preservation Center walking tours.

During the first half of the twentieth century, "Sweet Auburn," running east from Five Points, was the most affluent black neighborhood in Atlanta. The National Park Service headquarters, 522 Auburn Avenue, and the King Center are starting points for tours of the Martin Luther King Jr. Historic District. The district includes the house in which King was born in 1929; the Ebenezer Baptist Church where he, his father, and his grandfather preached; and the Martin Luther King Jr. Center for Non-Violent Social Change with Dr. King's tomb.

Other historic buildings include Big Bethel AME Church (1891); Fire Station Number 6 (1894); Rucker Building (1904); the building that houses the *Atlanta Daily World*, Atlanta's oldest extant black-owned newspaper (founded 1928); Odd Fellows Building (1912); and Prince Hall Masonic Building (1914), where in the 1950s Dr. King organized the Southern Christian Leadership Conference.

Notable also are the Atlanta Life Insurance Company Building; the John Wesley Dobbs Building (circa 1910) containing the African American Panoramic Experience Museum (APEX); Wheat Street Baptist Church (1920); and Sweet Auburn Curb Market (1923).

Near Auburn Avenue are Georgia Hall (1892), the original building of the huge Grady Memorial Hospital complex, listed on the National Register; and the Butler Street YMCA (1918), a longtime meeting place for Atlanta's black leaders.

FARTHER AFIELD

Park-like Oakland Cemetery, founded in 1850, today encompasses eighty-eight acres and a priceless collection of Victorian art and funerary architecture. Historic Oakland conducts weekend guided tours and provides self-guiding walking brochures. Newer, also scenic, Westview Cemetery is the burial site of other eminent Atlantans.

Visits to metropolitan Atlanta's colleges and universities introduce a variety of striking buildings and landscapes, old and new. Nearest downtown Atlanta are Georgia State University, the Atlanta University Center complex, and the Georgia Institute of Technology (Georgia Tech). GSU's urban campus is almost indistinguishable from the commercial buildings around it. At Atlanta University in West End are Spelman College's collection of historic buildings and the Knowles Industrial Building, among others. Georgia Tech, at midtown, is symbolized by its landmark administration building (1888) and the modern, functional structures of the engineering school.

ARTS INFO

The Saturday *Atlanta Journal-Constitution* Leisure Guide, the Wednesday *Creative Loafing* "Happenings" section, and the bimonthly *Atlanta Now*, published by the Atlanta Convention and Visitors Bureau, are sources of information on cultural events. The city of Atlanta provides a telephone "Arts Hotline," listed in the government section of the telephone directory.

Ponce de Leon Avenue leading east borders a chain of parklands planned early in the twentieth century by Frederick Law Olmsted to be the heart of the suburb of Druid Hills (also planned by the Olmsted firm), and the Emory University campus, designed by architects from Henry Hornbostel to John Portman and Michael Graves.

The winding streets of Atlanta's early suburbs are bordered by dogwoods and azaleas that are breathtaking in the spring. At any time of year the neighborhoods are a leafy respite from the city's busier thoroughfares. Among the early developments are Ansley Park, Buckhead, West End, Grant Park, Morningside, Virginia-Highland, Inman Park, and Druid Hills. The houses lining the streets vary from mansion to cottage. In many cases they have been rescued from neglect by young families who are striving to revive aging communities. Cabbagetown, a mill village for workers at Fulton Bag and Cotton Mills, fell upon hard times when the mill closed, but some of its shotgun-style houses are undergoing restoration.

SPECTATOR SPORTS: NOT JUST BIG LEAGUE

Four professional teams call Atlanta home. Football's Atlanta Falcons play in the Georgia Dome, and preseason spectators can visit the Falcon's training camp in Suwanee, to the northeast on I-85. Baseball's Braves play in Atlanta–Fulton County Stadium, but after the 1996 Centennial Summer Olympic Games, they will move to the new Olympic Stadium. Basketball's Hawks and hockey's Knights are also Atlanta teams. A fifth professional team, the Thunder, plays World Team Tennis in July.

Two or three times a year professional golfers invade Atlanta. Early April brings the PGA BellSouth Classic (with tickets available at the gate), and later in the month the LPGA version is scheduled. The Seniors play in June.

The sands of Atlanta Beach, within Clayton County International Park near Jonesboro, improved for Olympic competition, have hosted up to four professional volleyball tournaments a year, May through August.

On Sunday afternoons, May through October, the Polo Club of Atlanta plays matches in Forsyth County, twenty-five miles north of Atlanta off Ga. 400 (exit 12).

More than eighteen thousand people visit the Atlanta Steeplechase each April to watch thoroughbreds race an oval course dotted with brush jumps and to picnic on champagne and caviar. The course, on U.S. 411 between Cartersville and Rome, is an hour's drive from Atlanta. Tickets should be reserved well ahead.

Track fans of a different kind gather each November and March for NASCAR racing at Atlanta Motor Speedway in Hampton, thirty miles south of Atlanta. They can challenge the high-speed track as part of daily sightseeing tours of the facility. Sports car racing (SCCA and IMSA) takes place at Road Atlanta in Hall County (see Northeast Georgia tour).

Emory, Georgia State, Georgia Tech, Oglethorpe, and the schools that constitute the Atlanta University Center are among the colleges that compete in intercollegiate sports. Games and meets are usually open to the public.

Atlanta occupies a unique niche in Georgia—in size, diversity, international flavor, and variety of opportunities for activity. It is important, however, to remember that it, too, is Georgia, influenced by generations of south Georgians, coastal Georgians, and Georgians from the mountains who made the city their home. It is touched as well by those who maintain their regional homes but enjoy directly or indirectly the benefits only an Atlanta can provide. The traveler to Atlanta comes as often from Pavo or Ty Ty as from Denver or Paris. Atlanta holds a feast for the visitor, no matter the point of origin or the distance of the journey. Welcome to the Gate City of the South!

EAST
CENTRAL
GEORGIA

Philip Lee Williams # EAST GEORGIA JANUS

For many people, the history of Georgia seems to begin with James Edward Oglethorpe. And they think the story of East Central Georgia began when colonists from Savannah came up the river to establish on a bluff the city that became Augusta. Little could be farther from the truth.

In fact, the piece of ground we now call Georgia was the home of men and women for thousands of years—from the valleys of the northwest to the sea islands. Because the story of these people has been overlooked or underreported, few native Georgians or visitors know about them. People cannot imagine that there are more than twenty-four thousand recorded archaeological sites in Georgia, or that the Oconee River valley, which slices through this part of the state, was once the site of large and intricate chiefdoms.

The location of villages and campsites built by American Indians has been found in every county in this section of the *New Georgia Guide*. More, the intensive occupation along the Oconee River left a historical legacy that forever affected such counties as Oconee, Oglethorpe, Morgan, Greene, and Putnam.

From Paleo-Indian sites, which reach as far back as 9500 B.C., to historic Indians in the early nineteenth century, people lived, fought, and raised their children in the fertile river valleys and along the creeks. Who were they? How did they live? Archaeologists have made dramatic strides in understanding these disparate peoples, but the knowledge comes slowly.

The Paleo-Indians here during the final centuries of the Ice Age followed and killed animals that became extinct when the climate warmed: mammoth, saber-tooth cat, giant ground sloth. But the idea that these people were strictly hunters is probably wrong. Plants clearly formed a vast majority of their diets, if only because growing them was easier than chasing mammoths with pointed sticks.

By 8000 B.C. the Early Archaic period had begun here, but gatherings of people remained on the band level as they had in Paleo-Indian times—meaning a single family, with a single adult male in charge. There were rarely more than thirty or so in the band, and they moved throughout the year, hunting and gathering. By the Archaic period, all the Ice Age creatures like mammoths and ground sloths were gone as the climate quickly warmed.

The problem with band societies is that it is forbidden to marry someone of your own band because of incest taboos, so bands would probably come together once a year at regular places to find mates. These new mates would then form their own bands.

In the Middle Archaic, probably around 5000 B.C., the projectile points made for hunting were simple, often crude knives and spear heads. This lack of elaboration has led to a novel theory by Dr. Mark Williams of the University of Georgia and the LAMAR Institute. He believes, in a nutshell, that the more boring the archaeological period, the better the quality of life. He equally asserts that in the more fascinating archaeological periods, the more deadly the quality of life.

At any rate, the Middle Archaic was somewhat warmer than our climate today, and game and food plants must have been abundant. Williams imagines the people of the period spending perhaps an hour a day gathering food and the rest of it telling stories, singing and dancing, and generally cooling their heels. By the late Archaic, around 1000 B.C., the population in East Central Georgia was increasing slowly, and for the first time, the people began to eat shellfish such as river clams and mussels. They began to build their first houses—only small oval huts, to be sure—but homes nonetheless. They also began to experiment with agriculture.

An ancient notion that agriculture led to a better way of life is now being questioned by archaeologists. There is evidence that after the introduction of corn and beans into North America, the people did not live as long and were not as healthy. The regular diet of the same foods was clearly not as good as the mixture of varied native plants and meat.

The earliest agriculture in this area ushered in the Woodland period, which would last for a thousand years. These were tribal societies, not bands, meaning the groups could contain several hundred people from a number of families, and for the first time there was need for a chief. However, the chiefs were generally those best suited to lead, and the title was not inherited. There seemed to be agreement about who a chief would be.

The Woodland culture started agriculture in what is now Georgia, but it wasn't growing corn and beans. They grew sunflowers, and also marsh elder, and goosefoot—plants we now consider weeds. They also began to build small mounds for both burials and ceremonies, particularly along the fertile river valleys like the Oconee. Rock Eagle, a stone effigy in Putnam County, was probably not unlike a Woodland funeral home, some scientists speculate. When someone died, the person was brought to the mound and cremated.

The Mississippian period began about A.D. 1000—a time in which the Oconee River valley was the province of kings. Societies by then had become chiefdoms, with social groups ranging from a few thousand individuals to more than ten thousand. With so many people to rule, the chief was no longer merely the best leader, as he was in Woodland societies—he was a god.

The belief that the ruler was descended from the sun and was all powerful placed a vast barrier between the common man and the chief, thereby insuring obedience. These titles were inherited, and during their lives, the chiefs lived on flat-top mounds to elevate them above everybody else physically as well as spiritually. When chiefs died, they were given elaborate burials, often accompanied by items of value to the chief or to the community.

By this time what we call agriculture had first come to this area of the current state of Georgia. Corn and then, a few hundred years later, beans made up the staple crops, though neither was native to the area, having been brought from Mexico. It is unclear why the people switched from native crops to corn, although some researchers speculate there was a religious element in the growing of corn.

Along with agriculture, there was another component of Mississippian life: warfare. Many towns built palisade walls around the chief's mound and lodging as a safe place of retreat during raids. This strategy was obvious, because if your god was killed, the very fabric of life could be destroyed.

The most important Mississippian site in Georgia is not in East Central Georgia, though it held sway over it: Etowah. This fantastic mound site, which is on the tour of northwestern Georgia, appears to have been the political center of everything for miles around, including all the Mississippian people as far as the Savannah River. Just as Atlanta is now the hub of business, industry, and government in Georgia, Etowah for a time was the hub of Mississippian culture.

At its height, the Mississippian culture of the area was powerful, well developed, and culturally rich. Then, about 1350, the entire system began to collapse under its own weight. Local chiefdoms apparently began efforts to extend their power and rule, and the whole system, so precariously balanced for several hundred years, came apart at the seams. Some small local chiefdoms might hold power for a few years and then collapse. Towns with poor chiefs suffered miserably, and so people began to move to places that had stronger or more effective rulers.

By about 1450, the entire Savannah River valley had been abandoned. This desertion seems particularly strange, since the land is fertile and the river powerful; however, there is speculation that it became a kind of no-man's-land between the rising chiefdoms in the

Oconee River valley to the west and groups in central South Carolina to the east. Whatever the reason, it was entirely abandoned when Hernando DeSoto and his army came through in 1540.

For about a century, from 1450 until 1575, the chiefdoms in the Oconee River valley flourished. Archaeological evidence has shown that series of villages and mound sites were major population centers—a world about which school children presently living in the area are as yet almost completely ignorant because of the glacial slowness of educational materials development.

Some time around 1580, the chiefdoms in the Oconee River valley collapsed entirely, though many people continued to live in the area until perhaps 1650. English settlers at Jamestown, however, began to give or trade guns to Indians in the interior, and these Indians traveled through the entire Southeast, taking other Indians for slaves.

The sudden changes radically realigned Indian settlement patterns. Many Indians fled south to the Spanish settlements in Florida, which could offer some protection. Some moved to the Chattahoochee River in the western part of the state, joining others to form what came to be known as the Creek Nation. Still others may have gone to the mountains where they joined the people known as the Cherokees. Because of the movement, the land in East Central Georgia was left unoccupied, and so groups of Indians, such as the Shawnee and Yuchi, came in and settled, forming alliances with the English settlers at Charles Town (later Charleston) and beginning the trade in deerskins. After the Yamassee War in 1715, these Indians moved away, and by the 1770s, there were no American Indians on the Georgia side of the Savannah River. Except for a few stragglers, the original inhabitants of East Central Georgia had left the area forever.

EAST CENTRAL GEORGIA'S DEVELOPMENT

Perhaps the single best sentence about the history of East Central Georgia comes from Numan V. Bartley's book *The Creation of Modern Georgia:* "Cotton and slavery brought great wealth to Georgia, and Georgia paid dearly for it."

Almost from the time white men came up the Savannah in 1736 to found Augusta, the engines of trade and agriculture began to gain a torque that was only finally slowed by the Civil War and then, a half century after it, the boll weevil. When Eli Whitney's cotton gin came along in the 1790s, the landscape and the society of humans on it were changed forever.

The land was reasonably good for cotton agriculture in the interior of the area, spectacular for it nearer the Savannah River. Though the Piedmont's hills from Athens northward made cotton farming difficult, the lower part of the area, from what is now Morgan County east to Augusta, was perfect. It was a land that had been home to thousands of years of human habitation before settlers began to move west from Augusta. By the latter part of the eighteenth century, all of it had white towns and settlements. (It is ironic that in understanding the history of the area, most people know a reasonable amount about the last two hundred years and nothing about the first ten thousand.)

Society flourished as it grew. Augusta's success in what had been the no-man's land between the English, Spanish, Creeks, and Cherokees was the anchor of business and life in an often hostile time. In the 1760s, the French and Indian War brought defeat to the Cherokees in what is now northwestern South Carolina. They moved west to today's Northwest Georgia, from where they were finally removed in Andrew Jackson's genocidal decree of 1838 that brought about the Trail of Tears.

With a minimal threat from Indians, settlers moved quickly up the river valleys and formed new towns, such as Athens, which was destined to be a great seat of learning when the University of Georgia was chartered in 1785.

In a brief essay there is no way to describe the history and growth of eighteen separate counties. But among the forces that shaped East Central Georgia were its initial remoteness from the rest of the settled South; its topography, especially the Savannah and Oconee Rivers; cotton and slavery; the Civil War; the University of Georgia; and the boll weevil. These forces helped to make the towns of Washington and Madison wealthy showplaces of majestic mansions—structures that exist to this day. They made Athens the state's center of learning and thus the cradle of many intellectuals of great stature, from politicians to artists. It gave counties like Hancock and Taliaferro a rich African American culture that struggled against domination by a white minority for two centuries before the races agreed that majority rule worked there.

These forces brought about the great agricultural heritage of counties like Burke, Jefferson, and Washington, which had flatter and richer land for cotton than areas to the north. They made Augusta the focus for business and industry and thus the only large city for more than a hundred miles in any direction. And they finally gave rise to the great forests of Jasper and Putnam Counties.

By 1810, the entire area had towns, stagecoach routes, and a growing sense of what this world was like. It ultimately held the smallest county in the state, Clarke, and one of the largest, Burke. There was a kind of grandeur in the aspirations of the wealthy planters, who ruled the towns and counties and never composed more than a fraction of the population. Yet if the planters sowed the seeds of prosperity, they also sowed the seeds of destruction. From the beginning, slavery was a moral issue that plantation owners could hardly ignore. Small voices may have been raised against it, but the tide was as inescapable as it was pervasive. There was a quality of Greek tragedy that hung about it all, a quality that led equally to a century of national derision and defensiveness before the civil rights struggles of the 1950s and 1960s brought the issue into the open. The truth is that few southerners ever owned slaves but that the cotton barons who did ran that world with an iron hand. They wrapped the economy in such a smothering blanket of aristocracy and noblesse oblige that the rest of society had no choice but to be swept along in the flow. They rushed headlong toward tragedy, seemingly unable or unwilling to see the ultimate indefensibility of their moral position.

The Civil War didn't bring civil rights any more than World War I made "the world safe for democracy." Still, the struggle for a good life in East Central Georgia included far more than the tragedy of slavery. Life is not history.

Following the departure of Indians from the area, it was largely uninhabited for perhaps half a century until Augusta was founded in 1736 on the Savannah River and named in honor of the future mother of King George III. It was at first a military post, but because of its location, it soon prospered as a trading town, and in 1740 Oglethorpe ordered that a road be built between Augusta and Savannah.

The area rapidly drew white settlers. Indeed, the area around Augusta was settled before land farther inland but closer to Savannah. North of the Ogeechee River, men felled timber and planted their first crops in upper Georgia. Louisville was born, benefiting from the closeness of the Ogeechee. The settlers then went north along the Savannah and spread somewhat west toward the site of modern Washington.

The first Provincial Congress for Georgia replaced the original parishes. Three of these first eight counties were in East Central Georgia— Burke, Richmond, and Wilkes. Though the state played a minor role in the French and Indian War of the 1760s, it was deeply involved in the American Revolution. After the fall of Savannah to the British, many back-country patriots gathered at the Burke County jail and in Wilkes County to make plans for a counterattack. When Lt. Col. Archibald Campbell, the British conqueror of Savannah, arrived at Augusta looking for loyalty to the Crown, he was startled to find a force of twelve hundred North Carolina troops across the river spoiling for a fight, as well as a few citizens ready to embrace the Crown. He fled with his troops on February 14, 1779—the same day that patriot militia under the command of colonels Elijah Clark, Andrew Pickens, and John Dooly attacked a force of about seven hundred Tories at Kettle Creek in Wilkes County.

Kettle Creek was, so to speak, a watershed in the Revolution, for it halted the efforts of the British to extend their influence farther inland. Though the victory was a signal one, the British were far from done. They once again rose to take Augusta, though Wilkes County remained free. The revolutionary government of the state was in disarray, and legend says it operated in secret from Wilkes County. By April 1781, the Americans had put the British in Augusta under siege. On June 5, the Crown capitulated, and Augusta was liberated. By the summer of the following year, the British evacuated Savannah.

Elijah Clark, one of the heroes of the war, had a county named after him. There was a great irony in having the University of Georgia grow in Clarke County, however: Elijah Clark, a brave but poor North Carolina frontiersman, could neither read nor write.

By 1804, all the land comprising this section had been carved from the woods and hills, and counties and towns began to form. Indeed, less than a century passed between the landing of colonists at Savannah and the beginning of towns as far west as the Chattahoochee River.

In the eight decades between the end of the American Revolution and the Civil War, East Central Georgia grew at a pace unimaginable to the earliest settlers. The construction of railroads began. For some years, the terminus of the Georgia Railroad from Augusta was in Madison, and that accident of history turned Madison into a haven for wealthy planters, a legacy still visible in the town's mansions.

Though the land was nowhere as good for agriculture as the coastal plain of southwest Georgia, it was settled earlier and thus had time on its side. It also developed a rail network that made shipping cotton inland to Augusta and thence downriver to Savannah relatively easy. Towns began to grow in the southern part of the area from east to west: Waynesboro, Sandersville, Sparta, Madison, Eatonton, Monticello. They also rose in the north: Lincolnton, Washington, Lexington, Danielsville, Athens, and Watkinsville. And in the middle were Greensboro, Warrenton, Gibson, Thomson, and Harlem.

There were also dozens of small towns that would flourish and then disappear. Some rose and disappeared only to rise again. If the towns and the topography were often unalike, however, the reason they grew was not: cotton. This was the land of plantations and slavery, of rising wealth and insufferable poverty, of ambition and failure. And yet its rush toward prosperity was part and parcel of the question of slavery. Without slaves, the entire economy of the area might collapse. With them, economic prosperity seemed assured. It was no wonder that when the war came, East Central Georgia dug in. And though it was spared any major battles during the Civil War, it was changed forever.

THE MAKING OF A MODERN WORLD

In the summer of 1864, a man named Joseph Bearden lived in the college town of Athens. The campus was largely deserted because of the

Civil War, which was raging around Atlanta, some sixty-five miles to the west. Joseph Bearden was a gunsmith and only twenty-six years old at the time. He worked at Cook's Armory making Enfield rifles for the Confederacy, an effort that was clearly failing to stem the flow of Union troops into the state.

Joseph had been born in 1838, when both northern Georgia and South Carolina were just beginning to understand the cotton boom that would lead them deeper into slavery and then into a cataclysmic war. Joseph was from far northwestern South Carolina, and no one is sure how or why he came to Athens to make rifles instead of enlisting to fight. By that summer, however, the situation was so alarming that the Home Guard in Athens was mobilized and sent south to Macon when Gen. William Tecumseh Sherman's troops took Atlanta and began their March to the Sea.

Joseph Bearden must have done his duty reluctantly, but he took a rifle and headed south out of Athens and Clarke County, through Watkinsville, on to Morgan County and Madison. Finally arriving at Macon, he and the guard were promptly involved in a skirmish, and Joseph Bearden took a Yankee bullet in the leg. Hurt, perhaps wanting to see his family, he decided to walk home to South Carolina.

For the rest of his life, family stories have it, Joseph Bearden would not speak of the war or his wound. His focus was only on what was before him. When he died in the spring of 1914, another war was about to break out.

He was my great-great grandfather, and I wish I'd had the chance to meet him.

The effects of that war on Georgia families lasted in the general public for a century and linger today. It was after the Civil War that families in East Georgia *really* took their stand. Some acted as if the defeat of the Confederacy had never taken place and passed that astounding historical lapse down to their children and beyond. Others spent the rest of their lives after the war consumed in hatred. That anger was the sole inheritance of many men and women, some of whom keep it alive even now. For the thousands of slaves, it was the dawn of many generations of unfulfilled dreams and broken promises. Their servitude did not end after the Civil War. The consciousness of the South wasn't entirely changed until the 1960s when a great southern hero named Martin Luther King Jr. emerged to lead a movement that changed everything.

Over that century, however, the world of the South had become so codified that few knew who made the rules or why. Grown men acted as if the antebellum South were the apex of western civilization. And East Georgia, once a sprawling land of dairy farms and cotton land, struggled to find its own identity as Atlanta began its great population explosion. People by the late 1960s had begun to leave their farms for work in the hundreds of towns that are strung on the highways of East Georgia like beads on a string. Some towns, in fact, faded into dust and memory as the farms, one by one, went out of production. The change was profound, and the wrenching of the people from agriculture still echoes in most small towns here.

The antebellum South *was* the land. That world is gone forever, and what remains is a piece of Georgia that is in places progressive and in others poor and simply hanging on. East Georgia is no different.

And yet it is a land of vast and magnificent natural beauties, of friendly small towns and men and women who live out their days in the peaceful splendor of close friends and quiet lives. By and large, they go to church, preserve the order, grieve when they must, and gather around them their own histories with pride. The world beyond is no longer a distant and exotic place, and with television always present, regional dialects are slowly fading.

Joseph Bearden would be too bewildered by it all to speak.

The years after the Civil War were difficult for the area, but the twin anchors of Augusta and Athens kept commerce and scholarship alive. Both cities would help bring East Central Georgia through Reconstruction, but in truth, it was every town for itself. Those situated on the railroads survived. Many only a few miles off them did not.

The area had recovered somewhat when the boll weevil started making its way up from the Southwest after the turn of the century. When it arrived, and when it devastated the cotton crop, the South was changed forever. Small towns like Apalachee in Morgan County had been built by cotton. The bank loaned money each spring, and planters repaid it when the crop came in. This cotton standard was far more fragile than any of them knew. When the boll weevil came, the crops failed, and so did the banks. Apalachee, like many other towns, shuddered. The bank failed, and many people lost everything they had.

The boll weevil, however, was merely the catalyst for an inevitable change. The land, after a century of cotton cropping, was exhausted. What little topsoil had covered the red clay was long gone. Still, agriculture was the basis for the entire region, so when the boll weevil was finally brought under control, the wealthy farmers survived, and the poorer ones moved to town. Throughout the twentieth century, the number of farms fell and the size of farms grew. By the period after World War II, the irony was complete. The time of yeoman farmers had essentially passed, and agriculture had become big business. Though small farms hung on throughout the area, wealthy, faux-aristocratic families once again ran what were essentially pale imitations of the plantations of the 1840s.

Though the area was shaken to its core by all these events, the inevitable crisis of civil rights was also a major force in shaping it. Hidden in such phrases as "states' rights," the issue was no secret. The moral power of the civil rights movement was a powerful tonic to blacks and whites alike in this part of the state. It finally, once and for all, broke down the society that had given control to a few wealthy whites.

Nearing the end of the twentieth century, this part of Georgia is a land more like it had been in 1700 than it was during all the intervening years: vast tracts of forests, abundant game, and miles of road without evidence of human habitation.

THE WORLD OF TODAY

Now only scattered evidence exists of the Paleo-Indians and Mississippians. But the world of even a century ago is an unimaginable and alien landscape as well. So let's leap forward to the present—after all, you're here, not there.

Spread out a map before you and take a look at this area. In the north is Madison County (not to be confused with Madison, Georgia, which is in Morgan County). In the far southeast are Washington, Jefferson, and Burke Counties. In the southwest corner is Jasper County, whose large town is Monticello (with a soft "c," please, not with a "ch" like Thomas Jefferson's home).

In some ways, the towns of East Georgia resemble each other, but the differences are greater than you might expect. Burke County seems so topographically unlike Oconee County, for example, that they might be from different countries. Athens and Augusta are the only two major cities in East Georgia, but the university town straddles broadly curving hills while Augusta is lowland, hard by the Savannah River, which separates Georgia from South Carolina.

There are perhaps two disparate sections of East Georgia. The counties of Madison, Oglethorpe, Wilkes, Clarke, Oconee, Morgan, Putnam, and Jasper form a unit. Some people have called this area stretching from lower Northeast Georgia nearly to the central part of the state the "antebellum trail."

Madison County is one of the rare counties in Georgia with two towns of roughly equal size, Comer and Danielsville. In one stretch on Georgia highway 72, you pass through Colbert, Comer, and Carlton, names people routinely confuse. The tiny town of Neese on Ga. 106 is the site of a National Weather Service antenna. On more than one occasion the signal broadcast from Neese has saved lives when tornado warnings are announced.

Southeast is Clarke County, home of the University of Georgia and the smallest county in the state. It is also one of the most politically liberal and has a low unemployment rate. In the spring, the Bradford pear trees along Broad Street across from the university's campus are glorious. In the summer, Athens is quiet, but the rest of the year uni-

R.E.M.

versity students liven the place up. Many people know Athens from its
music scene in the late 1970s and early 1980s, when bands like R.E.M.
and the B-52's became famous.

Many of you will probably begin your tour of East Central Georgia
from Athens, but don't be in too much of a hurry to leave. Check out
the tour guide for the highlights of Athens, for it is an extraordinary
place, with a rich history stretching back before the year 1800. The
University of Georgia, in fact, is the nation's first state-chartered university, having been put on the books in 1785 (though it didn't start
operating until 1802).

Clarke County and Oconee County originally were melded together,
and the first superior court of the larger Clarke County was held in
March 1802. Only four decades later, the town was booming. By the
end of the Civil War, business was in trouble, the farms were barely
cultivated, and the University of Georgia was closed. Only by great effort was that world brought back to life.

Athens has reason now to face the future with pride. The University of Georgia's magnificent campus and the brilliance of its scholar-

teachers have made it a place of honor and pride. By the mid-1990s, the strong, consistent leadership of the school's president, Dr. Charles Knapp, was paying off in massive new construction. Though beset with the kind of growing pains common to the nineties, Athens was poised for even more greatness.

In his pharmacy in the town of Crawford in Oglethorpe County, Mr. "Boots" Hurt once made the best homemade lemonade in North Georgia. Not two hundred yards from the depot, Marion Montgomery, one of the America's finest literary critics and a novelist and poet, lives. Today, Mr. Hurt is dead and his drugstore is gone, and the railroad tracks, which no longer have agricultural products to take out, have been removed. Oglethorpe County, like Oconee, is becoming home to many people who work at the University of Georgia.

Farther east on U.S. 78 from Lexington are Wilkes County and its county seat, Washington, which is well worth visiting to see its old homes and quiet, tree-lined streets. There are Victorian mansions as well. Don't make the mistake of taking the bypass around Washington, because you would miss one of Georgia's loveliest cities, a quiet and stately place that embodies the history of the South in many positive and progressive ways.

If you drive south on U.S. 441 from Athens, you get to Watkinsville and Oconee County. Oconee (mostly in its southern half) maintains an agricultural heritage. It has a large number of artists and craftsmen, one of the finest public school systems in the state, and a marvelous fall festival that's held each October.

The road forks at a convenience store in Watkinsville. Heading south, you can continue on U.S 441 to Madison or take Ga. 15 toward Greensboro. Either way you'll find pine forests, a few peach orchards, and the gently rolling hills of the Piedmont. This land is beautiful and peaceful, with an element of the English pastoral about it, hearkening perhaps to Wordsworth or Vaughan Williams. It is particularly lovely in the fall and spring. In the summer, due to thunderstorms and heat, it sometimes takes on a tropical cast, and when one of the violet and gray towers of cumulus breaks apart from the wind shear, the countryside turns a brilliant, dripping green.

Morgan County is just south of Oconee. In the northern part, you will pass signs for a town called Apalachee, mentioned earlier. It was once a thriving village, with its own bank, shops, and traditions. Like so many other towns its size in Georgia, its fabric unraveled when the boll weevil appeared between 1910 and 1920. Its culture was cotton, and its lifeblood pumped with every ginned bale of that white gold. When the weevils devastated the crops, the banks failed, and the towns, many of them, dwindled until the last people died or moved away. Houses fell in, the brick was hauled off for other buildings, and the towns survived with nothing but their names. Some, like Apalachee or like Deepstep in Washington County, refused to pass entirely into history and remain, small stops whose residents love them despite their dusty obscurity.

Madison, the seat of Morgan County, is simply one of the finest towns in the state. According to tradition, Joshua Hill, a Union sympathizer and former U.S. senator from Georgia who lived in Madison, went to the edge of town, spoke with Gen. Henry Slocum of Sherman's army, and begged him not to burn the town. Something akin to that event apparently did happen, because the town has numerous antebellum mansions of surpassing majesty and wealth. Evidence uncovered in the past few years, however, suggests that some of the rest of Madison was indeed burned. Union soldiers stole the silver communion service from the Presbyterian Church, but it was returned after the war by a contrite Union officer. The service is now in the Madison-Morgan Cultural Center.

In the past decade, many new residents have moved to Madison, enlivening it and bringing a more cosmopolitan feel to Madison's gorgeous, tree-lined streets. The town was lucky for some four decades to have Adelaide and Graham Ponder as owners and publishers of the *Madisonian*, a progressive and award-winning newspaper that helped guide the town through many difficult years. The Ponders during those years were a major force in helping make Madison one of the great southern towns.

Morgan County (of which Madison is the county seat) was also the birthplace of two great African American artists, the brothers Benny and Raymond Andrews, much-loved and noted painter and novelist respectively. Their father, George Andrews, also came to fame late in his life as an artist.

Putnam County is next driving down U.S. 441. It is one of the most heavily wooded and loveliest counties in the area, with deep forests, many dairy farms, and a huge Indian effigy called Rock Eagle, which is the centerpiece of the State 4-H club center. One of the few stone effigies of its kind extant, Rock Eagle may, in fact, be a buzzard or hawk, but the name certainly suits. The single large town is Eatonton, the birth site of two famous Georgia writers, Alice Walker and Joel Chandler Harris. Walker moved away years ago, and Harris spent most of his working career in Atlanta, but neither is forgotten, and the town is proud to be associated with them. Putnam County also has Lake Sinclair, a large hydroelectric impoundment that delights fishers and boaters year round.

The lines in this guide are a bit arbitrary, but you'll have to leave U.S. 441 and go west on Ga. 16 to reach Jasper County and Monticello. Jasper has virtually no other large town, but Monticello itself is lovely enough to make up for it. The county, like Putnam, is heavily wooded and a haven for deer hunters. The Oconee National Forest stretches along its southern half.

Look at your map and leap back east to Greene County. Greene changed remarkably with the impoundment of Lake Oconee in the mid-1970s, drawing new residents to the shores of what had once been the Oconee River. The arrival of I-20 in the 1960s also sped development in Greene County. Greensboro, the county seat, is a pleasant and lively town, with many fine old houses and numerous churches.

Drive down Ga. 15, and you come to Hancock County and Sparta, with a magnificent courthouse and tree-lined main street. Hancock County is unusual in the area because its population is 80 percent African American. Sparta is the only town of any size in Hancock, which was once a cotton farming area but whose fields have now been turned into forests.

The woodsy nature of the area extends for the twenty-five miles south to Sandersville in Washington County. The southernmost part of our East Central Georgia area begins to show subtle geographic changes. The hills of the northern counties give way to a flatter, sandier area, and vast tracts of pine forests sweep across Washington, Jefferson, and Burke Counties.

The three county seats that make up the southernmost part of the area—Sandersville, Louisville, and Waynesboro—all have a strong sense of history and an even stronger vision for the future. Hancock and Taliaferro Counties had large African American populations and have benefited from their spirit of unity and shared culture. Columbia and Lincoln Counties are hard on the Savannah River and in many ways affected by the river and associated lakes.

Augusta deserves a separate book to itself. James Edward Oglethorpe lauded the settlement of Augusta, saying its settlement was a "great service," and the "key to all the Indian countrey [sic]." Begun in 1736, Augusta grew into the only major city on the state's eastern boundary besides Savannah. Most people today know Augusta as the site of the Augusta National Golf Course and the Masters—the world's most prestigious tournament. But the city is far more than that.

It has its own orchestra. It has many examples of architecture dating back two hundred years. It has, in fact, everything you'd expect from a thriving city and has worked hard to make life better for its citizens. The tour section of Augusta is extensive, and there is no need to recount it all here. Worth another mention, however, is the Riverwalk, a marvelous esplanade on the river, anchored by the Morris Museum of Art.

Visitors to East Central Georgia could easily spend all their time in the peripheral towns of Athens, Madison, Augusta, and Washington.

Each has history and time on its side. And in fact, you should go to all these places and stay as long as you can. A greater sense of what the area is like, however, can only be gained by digging deeper—by heading to the country.

THE INTERIOR: A PERSONAL VIEW

It's a Friday morning in September, and I'm batting it down Ga. 15 in southern Oconee County, trying to balance a cup of coffee in my right hand, drive with my left, and kick an errant golf ball from under the accelerator. The floor of my old Ford pickup truck is filled with straws, notes, napkins, books, and a suspicious-looking pair of pancake-flat sneakers. The radio is so loud it sounds like Travis Tritt is leaning against my eardrum while he sings.

I've been on the road a hundred times, have watched the minor yearly changes of fence lines and tree lines. I know how the smell of a chicken house comes at you from a distance, chokes you for a few hundred yards, and then lingers. I love how the expanse of pastures and grazing cattle connects with the hazy blue of a summer sky. I am intoxicated by the shades of green.

Except for six wayward months in 1972, I have lived in East Central Georgia for all my life, forty-five years and counting now in 1995. I grew up loving the country roads and the plumes of red dust that rise as you drive. I was born to the fields and the woods, and though I came from Morgan County, the life was virtually the same all through this area, except for the two counties with large cities—Richmond and Clarke. The towns were well-ordered, as was the life, revolving around churches and cemeteries, shops and school, the field and the house. Atlanta was no more than a dream, a city rising and growing to the west.

Agriculture was the overwhelmingly dominant force, and virtually all the wealthy and influential families were connected in some way to farming. In summer, the fields of cotton stretched in many places from the road to the horizon, and the stench of pesticides from crop dusters hung like an acrid mist over the red soil and the straight green rows.

You could drive east from Monticello to Eatonton, then up to Madison, over to Greensboro, and south to Sparta without seeing much change in the land or the people who lived on it. And yet the people just across county lines sensed that in some very fundamental way they were different from their neighbors. Maybe a famous person had been born there. Joel Chandler Harris came from Eatonton. Or perhaps the vast wealth of cotton barons had left a legacy of magnificent houses built before the Civil War, as in Madison or Washington. There might be a scenic natural area, or a state park such as the one

Eatonton, birthplace of Joel Chandler Harris

in Crawfordville, which was the home of Alexander Stephens, vice president of the Confederate States of America.

The chance of history saw that one county, Hancock, would become, and remain, a place for African Americans. While most counties in the area have at most a 50 percent black population, Hancock is 80 percent black.

Clarke County has been the home of the University of Georgia since 1802, and the university was actually chartered seventeen years before that. How can you compare a college town in the hills of North Central Georgia to a two-stop-light village huddled between acres of pine forest? You can't, of course, and that may be one of the most salient points about this part of Georgia. Although history has shaped all the eighteen counties here in many of the same ways, circumstance has given them many differences.

Because of the Savannah River on the eastern border, the first white settlers came up to the area that is now Augusta from Savannah in the eighteenth century, long before any whites lived permanently in counties such as Morgan. The Oconee, Ogeechee, and Broad Rivers slice through parts of the area, and the sinuous trail of Briar Creek extends for many miles, going through Warren, Glascock, Jefferson, and Burke Counties. Lakes Sinclair, Oconee, and Thurmond lend a blue filigree to many of the counties.

Rivalries in high school football have lasted for decades. From the mid-1950s to the early 1960s, Morgan County High School in Madison was almost unbeatable. The same was true for Athens High School (later Clarke Central) and for Lincoln County, which is hard on Lake Thurmond and has a population of less than seventy-five hundred.

And yet the area has one thing in common: an intense and long-lasting habitation that began long before white men even knew the New World existed. But you don't think of all that trying to keep a pickup truck in the road as you pass into northern Greene County on Ga. 15. You think of the monster's head rising above a field of dead corn, on a hill not far from the Oconee River. What the heck *is* that? It's actually a massive stylized iron sculpture of a horse that once resided on the University of Georgia campus. Students with nothing better to do egged the poor creature and generally used it as an excuse to have a party. The equine folly was moved to this field, where it has for decades stoically presided over the crops in summer and the fallow land in winter. In the hot months, only its head usually peeks above the cornstalks. I love the damn thing.

A peculiar thing about rivers is the mist that hovers early in the morning, like a fluffy cotton snake-coat. Now it hovers over the irrigation equipment that is turned off but drips white vapor.

The fog begins to break as I steer south across the Oconee River into Greene County, dodging road kill and staring at the thickly crowded clusters of pine in the Oconee National Forest. The road here was moved over a few dozen yards several years back to straighten a bad curve, and all across this part of Georgia, you can see the faint remains of abandoned roads or parts of them. Many of the roads follow the same stage routes and horse paths that existed as far back as the late eighteenth century. This has been the road between Watkinsville and Greensboro for well over 150 years.

There's no other traffic on the road but an ambulance, which comes past me, lights on and siren screaming, to ward off cars that aren't here. When it passes, I finally get the golf ball from beneath my feet and try to look hard at what is before me.

When you grow up in an area, you often stop looking at it in a novel way. Once many years ago, a tourist wearing knee-length shorts, black socks, and black shoes burst into the newspaper office where I was working.

"What is the name of this beautiful vine that you have growing all over the roadsides here?" he asked, breathless with admiration. "A fellow at the gas station said it was something like cashew."

"*Kudzu?*" I said, trying and failing to choke back my astonishment.

"That's it!" he said. "That's it! Do you think anyone would mind if I took a cutting?"

I told him to help himself. I've often wondered if the kudzu ate his house and car or if he found a way to kill it first.

Passing over Harris Creek, I try to put myself in your shoes—to be seeing this land and these towns for the first time, and somehow it seems remote and distant to me. And quiet. And yet that near-adoration for the pastoral life that is part of us who live here is inescapable, somewhat melancholy, and essential to our well-being. No matter what town you visit in this area—including Athens and Augusta—you're never far from the country. Here, it's sometimes hard to believe in the real world of hunger, overpopulation, and war.

As I get closer to Greensboro, the pickup trucks pick up. Most truck drivers drive with one hand and lift their index finger to wave. I do. It's considered bad manners in the country for a truck driver not to wave at another truck driver. I can't remember the last time I saw a truck driver with both hands on the wheel. They're probably trying to change the radio station, grab a sausage biscuit, or get a golf ball from under the accelerator.

Just south of the Mt. Zion Baptist Church—one of hundreds of such structures in the area—the power poles veer east for no good reason and go through a grove of oaks. The power company has cut a perfect cave through the trees for the lines. Look for it.

Closer to town, you see brick, ranch-style houses, neatly trimmed lawns, and hundreds of holstein cattle, closely cropping the fescue. This is dairy country, beautiful land crisscrossed by dirt roads. I pass the Cold Springs Road. It's amazing how many roads are named after springs, but those clear founts, mostly now forgotten, were crucial to early settlers.

When you see farmhouses in Georgia, you have the strong, and usually correct, impression that old people live there. The average age of a farmer in Georgia is in the fifties and has risen steadily since 1950. Farming is fading in the Piedmont, and within the next twenty-five years it may disappear entirely except for tree farming.

A sign says "Welcome to Historic Greensboro, Georgia," and it's true. Almost every county in East Central Georgia has an often colorful past, intertwined with the guilt of slavery and an enduring pride of place. The elevation of Greensboro is a hundred feet less than Athens twenty-five miles north, and the slow slope toward the fall line and the Coastal Plain has already begun.

About twelve thousand people live in Greene County, and population grew about 15.5 percent between 1970 and 1990, a healthy increase. The county is half black and half white, and though it was once an agricultural county, its rural farm population in 1990 was less than 3 percent.

The main drag in Greensboro is a pleasant and busy cluster of shops and stores. The First United Methodist Church is right across the street from McCommons Home for Funerals. A bookstore is on the main corner downtown.

I pass a yard where a child's lavender bicycle is lying on the ground under an oak tree, like a dog curled up asleep for the day. A young man stands idly on a porch wearing his baseball cap backwards. The

Davis House, a magnificent antebellum estate on the right, reminds the tourist of the time upon which the history of this area is centered.

I get out and wander around town for a while and stop to talk to a rail-thin old white man with a gray stubble, freshly laundered overalls, and a Red Man hat. I tell him good morning and ask if he's from Greensboro, and he is.

"You like it here?" I ask.

"I reckon," he says.

"What's good about Greensboro?"

"Hit's home."

"So you wouldn't live anywhere else?"

"No."

"So there's enough to do here?"

"Yes."

"What do you do for a living?"

"I'm retired."

"Well, have a good day."

"Same to you."

I didn't have to ask. He had spent his life as a farmer. It's said the stone cutters, the *scalpellini*, in parts of Italy spoke only between chisel blows and developed a shortened, staccato way of talking. The same is true of farmers, though not their wives. My wife had an uncle like that who used to visit us, stay for an hour, and sometimes not say three sentences.

Farmers are still honored in places like Greene County, where most of the people have been raised on television, travel often, and are no more distant from the world than someone in New Jersey. These towns are full of intelligent, articulate people who are well read and accomplished.

Through town and still Ga. 15, the road is abruptly back in the country, with Sparta twenty-nine miles away. I pass the Minnie G. Boswell Memorial Hospital, which today is crammed with cars. I've heard this is a fine facility, but hospitals in some towns are sad places. People sometimes go to a hospital in Augusta, Athens, or Atlanta to get the bad news, then wind up back in their own small hospitals to spend their last few months close to relatives.

The road between Greensboro and Sparta holds only two very small towns, Siloam and White Plains. The latter was ripped apart by a tornado a few years back, and the scars linger, with snapped trees and a desolate, shattered path where the storm came down. Siloam is a biblical name, of course, and many place-names here are from the Bible, though most come from prominent settlers, admired patriots, or places in the Old World (Athens, Sparta, Aonia). There are also dozens of descriptive place-names like Flat Rock, Deepstep, New Hope, Midville, Sandy Cross, and Shell Bluff. Also common are Indian place-names: Oconee, Ogeechee, Apalachee, and Ohoopee. And please note, weary traveler, that the geographical confusion common in other states is sometimes even worse in a state with 159 counties. Crawfordville is in Taliaferro County, while Crawford is in nearby Oglethorpe County. Madison is in Morgan County, while Danielsville is the seat of Madison County. Washington is the seat of Wilkes County, while Washington County's seat is Sandersville. Don't confuse New Hope in Lincoln County with Good Hope in Morgan County.

I stop in White Plains to get a Coke. An old black man is sitting on a crate in front of the store, a dust-colored dog asleep at his feet.

"Your dog's got the right idea," I say.

"He ain't worth nothing," the man says with a grin. "He used to be a coon dog, but now he couldn't track his own tail."

"I'm getting kind of like that myself."

"Go on now," he says, laughing out loud. "You and me both. I couldn't go huntin' noways. Where you headed?"

"Just down the road a piece."

"Well, it goes on."

When I come back out with my Coke, the dog's tail flaps twice in the dust, but he doesn't raise his head. The man nods his head once and says nothing as I climb back into the truck and head south through the country toward Sparta.

A few miles back I passed under Interstate 20, and the changes it has brought to this area over the past twenty years are important in understanding East Central Georgia. It brought new people to Madison. When I was a boy in the 1950s, it would have been unthinkable to commute from Madison to Atlanta, but it's routine now because of I-20.

(One warning: watch out for pulpwood trucks. They are endemic on Georgia roads but worse in heavily wooded areas like East Central Georgia. As I drive, I'm behind one of the things, which sheds thick blue diesel smoke and wood chips like a horticultural dragon.)

I pass an extraordinarily run-down house with a sparkling new Buick out front. When I was a boy, everyone made fun of the people who lived poorly but always had a nice car. I now find the sight poignant and am reminded how much we value appearance in this life. In fact, many of the houses here between Greensboro and Sparta are in poor condition yet highly decorated with yard art. One house has a pair of pottery swans overflowing with greenery.

The land once used for cotton and row crops now grows hay, and every so often the combines come along and cut the hay for baling, like giving the land another summer crewcut. The round bales that have largely replaced the small, rectangular ones are pleasant to see and remind me of childhood storybook pictures of European haycocks.

There's a ruined concrete silo here at the busy Double S Dairy (established more than half a century ago), with the top gone and the missing blocks resembling dentil molding or the parapet of a castle tower. The land here is gorgeous, and I believe that no farmers care for the land or their animals more than dairy farmers. My admiration for them is genuine and lifelong.

The land is now suddenly enshrouded with fog. Enormous elbows of stone thrust out of the fields in this part of the region, as if some giant were below, sleeping and biding his time. The traveler needs to understand one thing about East Central Georgia: This is the true nature of the area—not Athens or Augusta, which are anomalies. Miles of forest and fields, roadside barbecue stands, pleasant people, thousands of churches, poverty and riches.

Except for a delay for road construction, not much is happening between White Plains and Sparta. As you drive down Ga. 15, you come into town, and for a moment it seems as if you will drive directly into the Sparta courthouse, a magnificent edifice that towers incongruously over the rest of town. I park and wander around the courthouse, noticing the steady drip-drip-drip of water from the window-unit air conditioners. The old hotel here was once a stagecoach stop on the Augusta to Macon line and was the scene of a ball given for the Marquis de Lafayette in 1825.

Hancock County's been around since 1793 and was named, obviously, for the guy with the big signature on the Declaration of Independence. Ironically, in a county that's majority black, there's a marble monument just across the street from the courthouse "For Our Confederate Dead."

I'm staring at the monument when a friend of mine from Watkinsville, Rev. Dick Hoard, pulls up to the curb. We look at each other and break out laughing. Each of us wonders what the other is doing here. Turns out Dick's going to perform a funeral service—his third of the week. We chat for a minute, talking about his new book called *Alone among the Living,* which has just been published. The book is his personal story about how his father, who was a Georgia solicitor, was killed by bootleggers many years before.

I walk down the street, past Caldwell Laundry building, which is some ninety years old. Sparta was once just another dusty little East Georgia town, but the people here planted trees on the sidewalks, painted the place, and now it's a lovely stop, well worth seeing for the architecture and the charm. I walk around town for half an hour and see only one white face. Everyone is friendly to me.

(One thing to note: Small towns in Georgia are places of awnings. Sparta's stores are shaded with all kinds of awnings.)

And it no longer seems odd to see the Mr. Hong Kong Chinese Restaurant in a town like Sparta. (Although it does come as a mild surprise to see a department store where all the window manikins are white.)

Unfortunately, Hancock County isn't growing—in fact lost 6 percent of its population between 1980 and 1990. According to federal

Hancock County courthouse, Sparta

statistics, 33 percent of the black population lives in poverty, while less than half that percentage of whites does. Still, the county has worked hard in the past two decades, and majority rule came hard after many well-publicized battles with the old white power structure. Those years are fading into history now.

As I drive out of Sparta, I keep thinking it's much flatter than Clarke County, and I'm right. Figures show that it's some three hundred feet lower in elevation. I pass through town and head east on Ga. 16, which swings north into Warren County and its county seat, Warrenton, which is twenty-four miles away.

The country suddenly reappears. The only evidence a town is near are the few lumber yards, farm supply houses, and the like.

I pass a historical marker for a school named Rock-by, which had a revolutionary educational method in its day. You'll see historical markers all along Georgia roads, and virtually all of them are worth stopping to read. If you want to get a feeling for the history of the state, get used to pulling over for the green signs with the gold lettering. The honor system at Rock-by expected students to "report their own misdemeanors." Right. Hope springs eternal.

I pass the St. Lewis AME Church.

Just outside Culverton, where there's a lovely and spreading pecan grove, a pulpwood truck, the menace of all secondary roads, comes roaring around me. I'm irritated until I inhale the strong aroma of pine resin, which is so strong it smells like turpentine. Culverton has a Baptist Church, a Methodist Church, and a beer store.

I'm getting passed again, this time by a UPS truck, which is now another omnipresent feature of rural Georgia. No matter where you are or on what road, sooner or later one of those brown UPS trucks will come along. Another golf ball suddenly appears from beneath my seat and rolls under the accelerator, and I'm all over the road trying to get the thing out.

The B&D Ranch is on Ga. 16 between Sparta and Warrenton, and the traveler might not quite believe Georgia has ranches, but it does. They aren't like western ranches in size or prosperity, but the idea's the same, and the cattle graze beneath a solid blue sky.

I pass through the tiny burg of Jewell's Mill and then cross the Ogeechee River and find myself in Warren County. There's something weird about the light this day in September—everything looks like a Technicolor postcard from the 1950s, with the colors bright and saturated but not quite right, either. The sun throws shadows on the sign for Long Creek Baptist Church, which was founded in 1786. It reminds me that the closer you get to Augusta, the older the time of white settlements.

Gunn's dairy here is the kind I love best—lots of outbuildings, silos, open grazing fields, and the omnipresent but pleasantly rich aroma of cow manure. I see dozens of holsteins standing in a farm pond and enjoying the cool water, along with a sign that says, "Welcome to Warrenton."

Warren County's smaller in size and population than Hancock County and Sparta, and it lost almost 9 percent of its population from 1970 to 1990. Its population is 60 percent black, and of that, more than 43 percent lives in poverty. More than half of the Warren County work force is employed out of the county. Shockingly, some 72 percent of black births are to unwed girls and women, a figure not unusual in the area. Still, the town is well kept, and the people have never given up working hard to make it home for themselves and their children.

I take U.S. 278 out of Warrenton heading for Thomson, a twenty-mile jaunt that seems to go by in a blink. The outskirts of Thomson show a busy and growing town, with pizza places, tire warehouses, gunsmiths, car dealerships, decorating centers. There's a gorgeous white brick church at the corner of Hill and Jackson Streets—the First Baptist Church.

I park at the depot: Atlanta 134 miles, Augusta 37 miles. It's now the home of the Thomson-McDuffie Chamber of Commerce Tourism Bureau. There's a monument here to the "Women of the Sixties." That's the 1860s. I'm startled and touched by the monument, which is surmounted by a white marble carving of a woman holding a flag.

Across the street there's something unusual for many small towns in Georgia: a motion picture theater. They're showing *Forrest Gump*. There's a real estate office, the Trust Company Bank Building. Most of the buildings in small-town Georgia look as if they were built at about the same time. The Hughes Building looks different. It has a facade with two large Greek columns and a snarling lion or gargoyle in the top middle.

Thomson calls itself the Camellia City of the South, and I'll have to say it's a pretty place, though the streets are so quiet this morning it could be a quaint movie set before filming begins.

I'm standing on the rails of the CSX Railroad goofing around when I hear, coming around the bend, the dot-dash, dot-dash of a train whistle. Soon the bells of the crossing arms begin to ring, and traffic comes to a halt as the red-and-white arms descend. My foot slips as I try to scramble away, and I get out of the way just in time to avoid being a statistic. The freight train comes lumbering through town, and one of the drivers stopped at the crossing yawns and waits.

On the way out of town, I pass the Thomson School of Dance, the lovely Thomson Middle School, the high school, and a leathery woman driving a Sunbird with a cigarette hanging out of her mouth. There's the National Guard armory, and the vehicles here are painted OD, unlike ones I saw back down the road, which were still sand-colored from Operation Desert Storm.

And here's the standard Hardee's, and there are your standard UPS trucks. It's odd but true that most counties work hard to get rid of their distinctiveness and to make themselves like everyone else. Travelers who take comfort in yet another fast-food restaurant or CNN will find them in most every Georgia town. Those who want the unusual will have to work a little harder. Thomson's a busy place.

A Bonneville that's falling to pieces passes me, with two people inside frozen in their seats, staring ahead like statues.

I head past I-20, which is crammed with restaurants, gas stations, and past Savannah Valley Memorial Gardens and a vast and spreading container nursery. Good Lord, Dudley Nurseries Incorporated just goes on and on, perfectly kept and ordered. I've never seen a nursery quite this large. Then there's the State Patrol barracks, and across from it, Milliken Industries. The Belle Meade looks like a place I've played before—when I was on the golf team at Morgan County High School in the mid-to-late 1960s.

An old fire tower stands in a field of bitterweed, unused for years. They don't use these things much anymore.

The land is starting to change here from what it was around Sparta. It's nothing striking, but there's a subtle increase in hills and in development. I can tell the Piedmont is not far away as I head into northern McDuffie County. There's a vast difference, however, between this and southern Burke County, which is pine flatlands as it nears the Savannah River.

Like horses? I'm passing several horse farms, and I think I've never seen land quite as pretty around here. Then suddenly I'm back in an area of clear-cutting, which has a look of devastation and indifference.

THE GEORGIA WILDFLOWER PROGRAM

Inspired by Lady Bird Johnson's wildflower program in Texas, Rosalynn Carter and the Garden Club of Georgia approached the Georgia Department of Transportation about beautifying rights-of-way along Georgia's highways. In 1973 the DOT began planting wildflowers in highway medians. The project affords relief to pavement-weary eyes and reveals to motorists the many types of wildflowers growing in Georgia. The DOT establishes and maintains the wildflower projects, and the Garden Club gives annual awards to highway personnel who care for them.

—Jane Powers Weldon

This is worse than the lingering tornado damage around White Plains because this was done intentionally.

There's a sign: "boiled peanuts." You probably can't drive twenty miles in any direction in Georgia without seeing one. If you've never tried boiled peanuts, you should know that some people think they're a bit slimy and even clammy. I don't care for them.

Russell's Hunting and Fishing and Grocery pops up. A few cars are parked out front, like horses at a trough. In the country here, these small stores are the center of life, where people still gather to tell the news and cheerful lies. I must have passed twenty of them already this morning, and it's rare when cars aren't around. I could go into any one of them and be treated like I lived next door to it.

Churches, churches. Brinkley Chapel Baptist. Planted pine trees about ready for the harvest. A wildlife management area. Signs: "Break now for peanuts"; "Honey." They're nailed to trees. Just past them, there's a toothless old man sitting at a roadside stand selling— flags? Yep. There's the rebel flag, and also flapping in the slight breeze is California's. Maybe it's not such a bad idea to sell state flags. I hope he's making money, but from the look of his bib overalls, it's probably not much. He may not need much. He's just watching the traffic. He nods at me as I pass, and I nod back.

I'm crossing the Little River and heading into Wilkes County. There's probably no other county in East Central Georgia as much like Morgan County, where I grew up. Its county seat, Washington, is a beautiful town that you cannot miss. I insist that you go to Washington, get out of the car, and take a walk. I'm getting ahead of things here, though.

Wilkes is 474 square miles—almost exactly the same size as Hancock County. Oddly, the average elevation of Wilkes County is a few feet lower than Hancock, which makes no sense at all, except that the eastern part of Wilkes swings toward the Savannah River valley.

If you like cedar trees, you'll love what the map calls Aonia, the first tiny town on U.S. 78 in Wilkes County. When I was a boy, I'd go looking in the woods for cedar trees because they seemed somehow magical in a Grimm's-Fairy-Tale kind of way among the stands of pines and hardwoods. But if there's an Aonia here, I don't see it. Maybe "Aonia" means invisible city.

I'm now a hundred miles on this trip to the interior of East Central Georgia, at the junction of Ga. 80, which from here wanders back south across the Little River to the community of Cadley, where the road forks. Both forks run smack into I-20. But 80 goes back through Warrenton, on south into Glascock County, and then to Waynesboro, where it appears to end.

If you're the kind of traveler who loves adventure, these small roads are often the byways to Americana—places where you might find hand-forged tools for sale or a scene little changed from the nineteenth century.

Here's the Washington golf course, on which I played a number of times in high school. We always had the Class B regional championships here. But while I'm thinking of years past, the country club is suddenly gone, and I'm by the Gibson Grove Baptist Church, a small church with its neat rows of headstones. It's easy to see and think of the present, but there's an enduring sense of the past as living around here. It takes a long, long time to fade completely from living memory after death, which is one reason people put down roots, I think. There is a kind of grand permanence that is understood and which is the job of the living to perpetuate. These people don't have eternal flames burning over their small plots, but they remain in oral history sometimes for generations after they die. There is a comfort in knowing that your town is small enough so that you will be remembered as more than a mossy stone beside yet another white frame church.

I get to Washington and see . . . a Chinese restaurant? Yep. There's also the Hardee's, the Family Store, and the Pizza Hut. But Washington is far more than that. It's a town of mansions and strong civic pride. You don't have to hang out here long before you feel it.

Washington also has a National Guard armory. One gets the feeling that if the enemy ever gets this far, there are plenty of soldiers around to protect us. There's Hopkins Funeral Home in a lovely building, and a funeral's just about to take place. A few men are hanging around outside smoking. You might want to stop at the Washington Historical Museum, which is operated by the city. As you reach here, you'll want to get out and simply walk around. If your idea of the South is "more stately mansions," you'll love it here.

One architectural note. Many people come looking for Greek Revival mansions, and they're here, all right, just as they are in Madison, Athens, and a few other places. But these small towns also have a large number of Victorian houses, which have been lovingly tended for the past century, homes with turrets, broad front porches, and ornate trim. Often, as in Washington, the styles are side by side, and somehow they seem to blend rather than clash. Both are monuments to wealth and order and stability. They are the anchors of many towns.

Still, life goes on, and just past the wonderful Presbyterian Church is the Big Chick and a closed and abandoned Gulf Station covered in Christmas tree lights. I decide I'll hang out here for a while.

I park at the small strip of greenery that juts out from the courthouse. An old black man is sitting on a bench eating chicken from a small cardboard container. He doesn't mind when I sit down at the other end of the bench and look around. Washington has one quite unusual feature: a T-shape instead of a city square. The courthouse is at the bottom of the T and the main street at the top.

"Pretty day," the man says. I look up and see the drifting cotton clouds.

"It sure is that," I say. "You from here?"

"Yessir, all my life," he says. "My daddy and before him, too. Where you from?"

"Over in Oconee County," I say. "I'm just out driving around today."

"You want a chicken leg?"

"I don't think I do, but thanks for asking."

"No need to thank me, there's plenty here," he says.

"Has Washington changed much over the years?"

"It's changed a lot but then it ain't," he says. "Kind of like that, you know?"

I do know. Memory is a fragile gift at times, and southerners in particular hold tight to their childhoods, because generations of men and women, black and white, found reality so difficult that childhood was a constant companion and source of retreat. Southerners watch change with suspicion, and most don't do it for the reasons others in America think. They do it because their great-grandparents did—because in a hard life close to the land, any consolation was better than none at all.

I leave the man to his lunch and wander around. There's another Georgia historical marker here for an inn site on the old stagecoach route. My hometown of Madison also boasts of being a popular place on the stagecoach route. It's good to remind the young ones of history, but I doubt many even know what a stagecoach is. They ran here until 1870, twenty full years after the railroad arrived.

The Wilkes County courthouse was built in 1890, of the ubiquitous yellow brick so popular in those days. It sports a turret on the front, and the architecture looks almost neo-Egyptian in places. But the monument here isn't neo anything. It's for the Civil War dead, of course, and the inscription says: "Lord God of hosts, be with us yet, lest we forget, lest we forget." Then it says, "Know through all time they fought to maintain a just union. . . ."

It's hard to be angry with a hunk of granite and the simple and sincere emotions of the people who put these monuments in every town in Georgia. But I've always felt uncomfortable about them, for much of the state, and particularly the cotton land of East Central Georgia, was built on the shoulders of black people, a fact that somehow was always lost in the overreaching for a little pride after the war ended. It's almost odd now to find someone overtly racist in Georgia; it's really no different from any other state on that score. But the fight over the state flag, which includes a part of the Confederate battle emblem, continues to this day. Long after reality has faded, symbols persist, it seems.

Somehow appropriately, there's another marker commemorating the fact that on May 4, 1865, Confederate president Jefferson Davis, then in full flight from Richmond, held what proved to be his last official duties during a meeting here. Davis was the South's Designated Scapegoat for the war, so the marker was probably erected with a mixture of pride and disgust. (The marker was placed in 1957.)

Still, Washington also has markers for its Vietnam veterans and World War I vets, and knowing the town, I'm sure it enjoys its magnificent architecture without remembering much about the bad old days of the 1950s.

There are other markers, including one for Ben W. Fortson, a native of Wilkes County and Georgia's secretary of state for many years. But if the markers at the courthouse here are not unusual, the Fitzpatrick Building nearby truly is.

It was built in 1898, and its turrets reflect the period quite handsomely. Right now, a huge flock of pigeons is enjoying the early autumn sunshine atop the building. The place isn't in particularly good shape, but it has some stained glass and once must have been an amazing sight in a small town like Washington. The Lindsey store came along in 1919, and there's a barbershop whose lintel notes it was built in 1895.

I'm back on the road. The main drag here is Robert Toombs Avenue, and the home of this Confederate firebrand is astonishingly beautiful (see tour). Here's the Tupper House, there the First Baptist Church, and just past them a mad and wonderful Victorian mansion which is now being restored. Don't miss Washington.

I'm back in the country on U.S. 78 heading toward Lexington in Oglethorpe County, and I pass the Callaway Plantation. It's a grand site, but I always wonder what people feel when they see such a place. Does it remind them of a quiet and courtly life or of slavery? Symbols are important to southerners, but the remaining mansions over the years were more islands of pride in a sea of poverty than anything else. The house is red brick, with columns, and is open to the public.

The country calls. Suddenly, the highway is slicing through deep heavy woods and then open fields that gently angle their burden of cattle up toward the sun. I pass yet another Beaverdam Road. Does every county in America have one?

I'm in Rayle, and there's the Country Video and Bait store, a combination that I suppose makes sense. This small town in eastern Wilkes County has survived only because it's on the highway. Hundreds of small towns across the state no bigger than Rayle vanished in the early twentieth century for one reason or another. Often it was the boll weevil that shut down the bank and thus all the businesses. Sometimes, though, the young people simply moved away, the old people passed

Robert Toombs House, Washington

on, and the town became nothing more than a name. In Morgan County, Drexel was a busy place in the 1920s, but now even the name is forgotten.

I'm in Oglethorpe County now, and there's no doubt I'm back in the Piedmont. The land is full of vast swells and turns, as if the mountains were an ocean and the Piedmont, waves breaking on a shore. The University of Georgia has a beef cattle research farm here, and so the land is wide-open pastures, with lakes and expanses of green. A cattle egret comes over one of the ponds, wings out, and settles lightly on the ground nearby. This is one sight that would have baffled early Georgia ornithologists. These birds aren't supposed to be here at all—they should be enjoying the land in North Africa. Somehow flocks made their way to the New World several decades ago, and now their fleet white shapes can be seen sailing over the fields and pastures. Sometimes they walk awkwardly around the cattle in the fields, like gawky junior partners in the business of grazing.

I'm about 125 miles into the interior of East Central Georgia now, and I'm crossing Buffalo Creek. You wonder how something could be named such a thing. Buffalo might have been around here in small numbers in the early nineteenth century but surely not since then. There's a pleasant elegance in place names. They can carry the freight of deep emotion, or a place can simply take up the name a person called it for years as a convenience.

I pass over Long Creek, and I'm reminded how very little there is on many roads in Georgia but forests and farm land. Here's Oglethorpe County. Next door to Clarke County and the University of Georgia,

Oglethorpe has started to become a bedroom community. Its population grew by nearly 10 percent between 1980 and 1990.

Oglethorpe, like Madison County, is relatively unusual because it has two small towns of roughly equal size—Lexington and Crawford. Because of the way small towns developed in the early nineteenth century in Georgia, most counties have only one large town—the county seat. There is also some kind of unstated rule about the distance between county seats. I figure it to be twenty-five to thirty miles from any town in any direction. Was that a day's ride? I'm not sure, but the regularity of distances in Georgia is intriguing.

Lexington's a lovely little town, into which you're ushered heading west by Bud Alewine's auto salvage. The wrecked cars are lined up in neat rows, like soldiers or obedient schoolchildren. Perhaps it's genetic, but most southern men love these junkyards, even men who don't tinker with cars themselves. There's something alluring about hundreds of taillights, bumpers, carburetors, and timing chains all huddled and waiting. There's an aura of bucolic archaeology about the whole thing. You gotta love Alewine's.

At 130 miles into my East Georgia odyssey, I'm in Lexington, where I stop to wander around a bit. The town is small and pleasant, with yet another marvelous courthouse. The county (I'm reading from the ubiquitous historical marker) was created by an act of the legislature in 1793 and named for Gen. James Edward Oglethorpe. This courthouse, though, is a trip. They're remodeling and restoring it, and for good reason: This must be one of the most unusual courthouses in the state of Georgia. Make sure you stop and take a look.

Nearby is the home of George Rockingham Gilmer, governor of Georgia who "served with distinction in the Creek Indian war." It's silly and pointless to blame historical figures for current interpretations of history, but that phrase is a reminder, nonetheless, of how fragile our views of our own times are. Now we can say that Mr. Gilmer was involved in the attempted genocide of the Creek Indians, who had the temerity to live on land that white people wanted. He saw the world in a different light, and I'm sure he couldn't quite imagine it was wrong. The South has seemed at times to learn the lessons of history slowly, but the rest of the country wrongs us to say we never learn at all.

The standard Confederate marker here was put up in 1916, and it is granite, surmounted by a white, marble Confederate veteran. I've seen such markers all along my journey to the interior, and though I recognize slavery as morally reprehensible, and indeed the loss of the South in the Civil War as a godsend to America, there is a quiet poignancy to these memorials. If the terms of surrender at Appomattox had been as harsh as the Versailles Treaty that ended World War I, these markers might still be hallowed ground. Instead, they weather, they fade slowly, and within another generation or so, the children won't have the least clue what it was all about.

Most of the men listed on the monument died in the Echols Artillery, and many were clearly from the same families, with names repeated over and over.

Back to reality: Right across the street is a sign that says, "The Enforcer, it kills roaches." I'm glad. Another says, "Antiques, Collectibles, Tax Service." Sounds like a useful combination.

I'm back on the road now, heading for the last leg of my trip, and there's this wild plantation plain–style house right here in town, which has been added on to for decades and is now falling to pieces. It's impossible to figure a context for this strange interloper in the peaceful late morning.

I wish I were heading south toward Shaking Rock Park or north toward Watson Mill Bridge State Park, both lovely and interesting sites. But I'm on a mission today. The land here is starting to rise, and looking south and west, you can see the lowlands. The average elevation for Oglethorpe County is seventy-two feet higher than Wilkes, not much of a rise, but you notice it if you pay attention.

Crawford is only three miles up the road, and along the way you see Granny's Kitchen, a flea market, and Truss Plus, which is not a medical store but a house-building supply place. Crawford's changed a lot recently. The railroad that once bisected town is gone, and the depot now sits next to a hump of land that holds only the memory of rails. Hurt's Drug Store is gone, along with Boots Hurt. The building burned some years back. I recall Hurt's Pharmacy with great pleasure. In the mid-1970s it still looked like it did in the thirties, with a framed picture of Franklin Roosevelt behind the counter.

I'm out of town again, heading on toward Athens. All of the area I've seen today is pretty much alike: small towns nearly equidistant, forests, farm land. But if you enjoy the subtleties of town and country and really want to see the history of East Central Georgia, take the time to drive these roads. In its own quiet way, there is a magnificence to it all. The greatest differences in the area belong, of course, to Athens and Augusta, the largest towns, and perhaps to Madison and Washington, which were more prosperous in the early days and thus have an order and elegance that is truly magnificent.

At 140 miles, I'm into Athens–Clarke County.

Athens and Augusta are self-evident as places to visit in this area, and the accompanying tour gives you the places to see and go. But the smaller places, even the roads not taken by prosperity, are well worth the journey. This lazy trip took me just more than half a day, and I've discovered a considerable amount I did not know about an area in which I have lived my entire life.

HITTING THE ROAD

Ultimately, you are the guide, and your route will be determined by your pleasures. If you love architecture, head for Madison or Washington. If you want a thriving, busy place with a young population and live music, try Athens. And if you want to see how a larger city has made something of itself, go spend a couple of days in Augusta.

Remember, though, that this part of Georgia is largely about the land—about the people who have lived here for more than ten thousand years. In the great course of history, our obsession with the last two hundred years is almost laughable in its myopia.

Remember to use all your senses as you travel. You will see the bright blue skies arching above a verdant pasture dotted with holstein cattle. You can inhale the rich aroma of flowering plants in Augusta in the spring. You can hear everything from the heavy thud of rock bands in Athens to the high-pitched call of hawks in the fields near Sandersville. In Madison you can touch banisters that have been rubbed by hands for 170 years. And you can taste the rich tang of barbecue pit-cooked at a roadside stand.

I hope that you fare well.

Jane Cassady

TOURING EAST CENTRAL GEORGIA

Touring this area can be accomplished from two vantage points: Athens or Augusta. Athens, the starting point for these tours, offers variety with the University of Georgia, Georgia Museum of Art, State Botanical Garden, revitalized downtown, music, and sports. Georgia's natural beauty is highlighted in the many lakes and parks in this region. The visitor can participate in pioneer days at Elijah Clark State Park, explore the Broad River at Watson Mill Bridge State Park, go to the observatory at Hard Labor Creek State Park, or play golf at Lake Oconee. The region has a tremendous variety of options for anyone. The Augusta area is markedly different, both topographically and culturally. With their proximity to the Savannah River, Augusta's historic sites are deeply interwoven with the colonial period of Georgia history and the plantation economy that followed. The surrounding counties are predominantly agricultural, although Augusta's growth has spread to these rural areas, creating bedroom communities. Augusta is a good base for touring the surrounding areas, and the city itself deserves a few days of exploration for a feeling of time and place. Maps of Athens and Augusta are available at area visitor facilities.

A word of caution about parts of the tour: Some of the tour routes are long, with few conveniences between towns. A full gas tank is highly recommended for the more rural areas where no gasoline service is available on some deserted roads. Many small towns close their shops, including the gas station, at five in the afternoon. Some stores are closed on Wednesday afternoon, many stores are closed on Sunday, and all state parks and some museums are closed on Monday. A call placed ahead will determine a destination's hours of operation.

TOUR ONE

From Athens, take U.S. 78 to Lexington and Washington; Ga. 44 and Ga. 79 to Lincolnton; Ga. 47 to Pollards Corner; U.S. 221 to Appling, Harlem, Wrens, and Louisville.

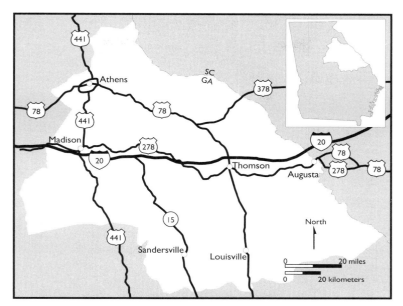

East Central Georgia

In 1785 the General Assembly of Georgia chartered a state university, the nation's first. John Milledge, a member of the university's governing body, selected the site, a location high above the shoals of the Oconee River and far from the distractions and temptations of town life. The community on the edge of the university's campus became **Athens**, a name common to several American communities settled for purposes of higher education. From their beginnings the university and the town have maintained a beneficial relationship. A noted historian of higher education has pointed out that this campus, open, literally, to the town, illustrates the American university's break with the old-world tradition of walled and separated towns and universities.

The commercial center of Athens owes its continued vitality, in the face of regional mall development, to the good neighbors who are the students, faculty, and staff of a thriving center of higher education that in the mid-1990s enrolled almost thirty thousand students. Sidewalk cafes and book shops enhance the ambiance of Broad Street, which borders the main entrance to Old North Campus.

The late-twentieth-century University of Georgia is a sprawling and ever-growing giant with major buildings rising miles from the Georgia Arch (1858), a delicate cast-iron architectural symbol that marks the original entrance to the campus at Broad Street. All the various schools of the university once were clustered around the quad, the oldest portion of the university, now known as North Campus. Today the nineteenth-century architectural reminders of a simpler yet classically inspired learning environment remain the favorites of generations of

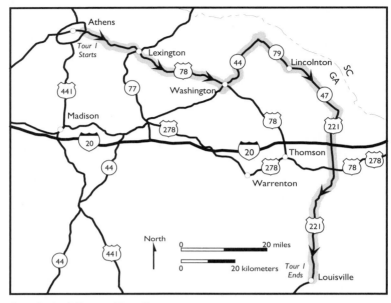

East Central Georgia, Tour One

Georgia graduates and friends. Among those buildings is Old College (1806), the oldest building on the campus and in the city of Athens. Old College was designed on Yale models that were familiar to the several Yale-educated early faculty of the university. Here from a log cabin and a few students in 1801 grew the university of today.

Other important reminders of its nineteenth-century buildings are New College (1823), variously a dormitory, library, and classroom building; Demosthenian Hall (1824), which housed the first literary society on the campus; the Chapel (1832), where the earliest commencement ceremonies were conducted; Phi Kappa Hall (1836), which housed a literary society and served as the library; and the Academic Building (1906), which is, in fact, a combination of two antebellum buildings.

Between the arch and the main library (1953) at the south end of the original campus are more than two dozen nineteenth- and early-twentieth-century buildings, all situated in a beautiful setting of ancient and more modern trees and plantings, fountains and pools, flower beds, and benches where students and visitors may enjoy the traditional surroundings. Behind the law school on the west side of Old Campus is the relatively secluded Founders' Memorial Garden. Just a few steps away from a busy campus on one side and a busy street (Lumpkin) on the other, this place is a favorite for quiet meditation.

The Arch, University of Georgia, Athens

The Georgia Museum of Art, in its new building on the east campus, is an integral component of the new Performing and Visual Arts Center, dedicated to the study of dance, drama, music, and the visual arts. Designated the state's official art repository, the museum houses a permanent collection of nineteenth- and twentieth-century American paintings; the Kress collection of Italian Renaissance paintings; and European, American, and Oriental prints and drawings.

Between the south and north campuses are the connecting tissues of the university: Sanford Stadium (1929), Tate Student Center (1983), and various classroom and related buildings of vintages ranging from the early to the late twentieth century. Prof. F. N. Boney's *A Walking Tour of the University of Georgia* is available locally and is a detailed and well-illustrated guide to a place that can't be given its due in a few lines or pages.

For those touring downtown or North Campus, parking can be a problem, but there is a public parking garage on Jackson Street near the campus. The city blocks around College Square are sometimes described as reminiscent of a bohemian community with busy sidewalk cafes, espresso bars, and lively conversation. More than thirty restaurants and bars are located in the downtown area.

A visit to Athens would be incomplete without sampling rock music, the heart of the city's nightlife, from which grew the early fame of such bands as the B-52's and R.E.M. The Georgia Theater and 40 Watt Club are great places to hear new bands and sample the local music.

An unusual Athens landmark is the double-barreled cannon situated in front of City Hall at Hancock and College Avenues. This gun is prominently displayed to remind passersby of the city's role in weapons production during the Civil War. The cannon was developed in 1863 to protect Athens from Sherman's approaching army, but after it killed nothing more than a cow during field trials, it was retired. It is reputed to be the only mounted gun of its kind.

An early Athens residence, the Church-Waddell-Brumby house, is at Dougherty and Thomas Streets. The house was built in 1820 for the first president of the university and now serves as a house museum and welcome center. In 1967 urban renewal plans included the demolition of this last remnant of early Athens, but the newly formed Athens-Clarke Heritage Foundation rallied to save the house. City and federal officials arranged to move the house to its present site at the Thomas Street corner.

The Morton Theater at the corner of Washington and Hull Streets, believed to be the only remaining black-built vaudeville theater in America, has been rehabilitated and reopened as a cultural and performing arts center. Pink Morton, who built this theater in 1911, was instrumental in the commercial development of Athens. Jazz figures like Louis Armstrong, Duke Ellington, Cab Calloway, and Bessie Smith stopped en route to other venues to play in this well-known music hall. Recently restored to its original splendor, the Morton's weekly performances cover the spectrum from gospel singing to operetta.

On Pulaski Street not far from the Morton is the Ross Crane House, otherwise known as the home of the Sigma Alpha Epsilon fraternity. Ross Crane was a master builder and the architect of some of the city's most significant structures (the Chapel, First Presbyterian Church, the

The Morton Theater, Athens

Hamilton House/Alpha Delta Pi sorority, and the Hunnicutt House). Prince Avenue, originally lined with mansions, retains several Greek Revival structures: the university president's home, Taylor-Grady House (a National Historic Landmark), and the Upson House (SunTrust Bank). Both Taylor-Grady and the Upson House are open and have been carefully restored. The president's home is private.

The university's reputation and enthusiasm for athletics are displayed in Butts-Mehre Heritage Hall, which opened in 1987. Dedicated to the achievements of Georgia's athletes and also headquarters for the Georgia Bulldogs, the hall is named for two of the university's football coaches, Wally Butts and Harry Mehre. Heritage Museum of athletic history, open daily to the public, occupies the third and fourth floors of the facility on Lumpkin Street.

In 1954 the Navy Supply Corps School moved to Athens into the Prince Avenue campus of the old State Normal School when the teachers' college was incorporated into the university. The 1910 Carnegie Library on the Navy Supply Corps campus houses the corps' museum and exhibits a collection of uniforms, model ships, and artifacts of officers beginning with the War of 1812. A tour to these points and others is distributed at the Athens Welcome Center in the Brumby House.

Leaving Athens, U.S. 78 leads east to Cherokee Corner, Crawford, Lexington, and Washington. A DAR marker on the left shortly past the Clarke-Oglethorpe county line commemorates the boundary between the Cherokee and Creek lands that was used to measure distances for a 1773 treaty and survey that ceded much Indian land to the whites. (The marker's location requires a short walk along the right-of-way, since it cannot be safely read from the highway.)

One-half mile west of Crawford off U.S. 78, and indicated by a Georgia historical marker at the highway, are the grave and site of the home of William Harris Crawford (1772–1834), United States representative and senator, president pro tempore of the senate, minister to France in 1813, secretary of war in the cabinet of President Madison, secretary of the treasury under Presidents Madison and Monroe, and unsuccessful presidential candidate. Shaking Rock Park, on the outskirts of Lexington, features huge granite boulders and outcroppings in unusual natural shapes, including the balanced Shaking Rock, Saddle Rock, Table Rock, and Shelter Rock. Shade trees, picnic tables, and an active beaver pond make this a popular picnic site.

Most of the town of **Lexington**, named for the Massachusetts village, is on the National Register, so the walking tour (available at the courthouse) published by the local historic preservation commission is recommended. With its diverse collection of architectural styles, Church Street is reminiscent of a New England village. The oldest documented house is the Joseph Henry Lumpkin House (ca. 1790), residence of the first chief justice of the Georgia Supreme Court. Many classical houses front Church Street, as does the Lexington Presbyterian Cemetery, which contains the graves of three prominent Georgia politicians: George Rockingham Gilmer (1790–1858), governor of Georgia; Wilson Lumpkin (1783–1870), also a governor; and Joseph Henry Lumpkin (1799–1867), a founder of the Lumpkin School of Law at the University of Georgia. The Oglethorpe County courthouse, on U.S. 78, built in 1887 in the sturdy Romanesque Revival style, was recently restored. The first Presbyterian seminary in the South had its beginnings at the Lexington Presbyterian manse (private) where Dr. Thomas Goulding established a school for five students in 1828. The school, later named Columbia Theological Seminary, moved to Columbia, South Carolina, and is now in Decatur, Georgia.

The drive on U.S. 78 into Wilkes County illustrates the contrast of old and new. On one side of the highway, small planes land at the Wilkes County airport. On the other side, the Callaway Plantation historic restoration occupies fifty-six of the plantation's original three thousand acres. This working farm museum, owned by the city of Washington, epitomizes the settlement of the Georgia frontier. As the Callaway family moved in 1785 into the new territory, they built a rough-hewn log cabin with a single room, served by a fireplace for heating and cooking and a loft for sleeping quarters. After five years of hard work, they were able to build a larger frame house with two rooms over two, known as a Piedmont plantation–plain or I-house. The log house became the out-kitchen, set apart from the main residence because of the heat and fear of fire, and other outbuildings, such as the smokehouse, pigeon house, and barn, were added. Most Piedmont and frontier farmers began their settlement in this manner, with simple houses serving as the first residences while fields were cleared and crops planted.

Like many of his peers, Parker Callaway was able to build a more elaborate house, although, unlike them, his prosperity came after the Civil War, when most other landowners lived in poverty. Before the war, the rise of cotton as the major cash crop changed farming practices and the economic conditions of many farmers. Callaway supposedly owned one of the last shipments of cotton to leave Savannah for England before war broke out. Until the end of the war, his profit earned handsome interest in the Bank of England, enabling him to build his Greek Revival mansion in 1869, long after the popularity of the style had waned. Today, Callaway Plantation has fields planted in nineteenth-century traditional crops to illustrate the homestead's self-sufficiency.

During the American Revolution the Battle of Kettle Creek took place in 1779 eight miles from Callaway Plantation. Elijah Clark and John Dooly defeated British Loyalists there. Directions to the battle marker may be obtained from the Washington–Wilkes County Chamber of Commerce (see below).

The town of **Washington**, authorized in 1780, grew rapidly after the American Revolution and became the Wilkes County seat. Its steady growth accelerated when the Washington Railroad was chartered in 1857. A combination of high cotton prices and commerce benefited many residents and probably accounts for the town's large number of fine antebellum homes. U. S. 78 follows Robert Toombs Avenue, where most of the older houses are located. The town's driving tour brochure points out the many historic districts and individual National Register sites. The Washington-Wilkes Historical Museum is a good starting point for touring Washington and obtaining literature. The museum has a notable Civil War collection including letters, diaries, weapons, and the camp chest of Confederate president Jefferson Davis. It was here in Washington that Davis held his last cabinet meeting and signed the papers that dissolved the Confederacy. The city hall annex and chamber of commerce, 104 East Liberty Street, also provides information for tourists.

One of Washington's most notable citizens was Robert Toombs, a member of Congress who briefly was secretary of state of the Confederacy. After Toombs resigned from the cabinet to serve in the army, he was wounded at the Battle of Antietam (1862) but returned to the front later in the war. Eluding capture at the close of the war, Toombs lived in exile in Paris for two years. When offered a political pardon in 1880, Toombs boasted, "I am not loyal to the existing government of the United States & do not wish to be suspected of loyalty." His house, a National Historic Landmark and state historic site, is open and well worth a visit.

In 1888 Dr. Francis T. Willis built the Mary Willis Library (Liberty at Jefferson Streets), an early free public library, in memory of his daughter. Its collection of rare books and genealogical records is housed in a magnificent high Victorian and Queen Anne red-brick building with stained-glass windows. The Wilkes County courthouse was built in 1904 in the Richardson Romanesque style with a multi-gabled roof and clock tower that was destroyed by fire in 1958 and reconstructed in 1989.

To the northeast on Ga. 44, a historical marker west of Sandtown indicates the former location of Heard's Fort, an early, temporary state capital (1780–81) when Augusta was threatened by British forces. The Chennault House, on Ga. 44 near the intersection with Ga. 79, is a two-story, late Greek Revival weatherboard house (ca. 1850). Tradition has it that gold from the Confederate treasury lies hidden somewhere on the plantation grounds. To the south on Ga. 79 is the Matthews House (private), another Greek Revival frame house built in the late 1850s with a full two-story portico.

Recreation and historic preservation define Lincoln County. The entire county, including the three communities of Lincolnton, Double Branches, and Woodlawn, is listed on the National Register of Historic Places. The courthouse at **Lincolnton** was designed in 1915 by G. Lloyd Preacher. The historic town offers a range of commercial and residential buildings, including a house on Humphrey Street ordered in 1911 by mail from Sears-Roebuck and Company.

Clarks Hill Lake is one of the largest inland bodies of water in the South. Many recreation areas around the lake have boat ramps, fish cleaning stations, piers, beaches, playgrounds, and picnic areas, and the Lake Springs area has hiking trails. On the western shores of Clarks Hill is the 447-acre Elijah Clark State Park (entrance on U.S. 378/Ga. 43 northeast of Lincolnton, just before bridge to South Carolina), created to honor a Georgia Revolutionary War hero and frontiersman who led pioneers against the British. A replica of his log cabin home is furnished with artifacts from the 1780s. The Fall Pioneer Rendezvous celebration in October features cooking, Indian dancing, musket loading, and primitive weapon exhibits. On the first Saturday in December a Log Cabin Christmas includes an enactment of the first Clark family Christmas.

Price's Store, south of Lincolnton in the **Double Branches** community, is reached by following signs from Ga. 47S to Ashmore-Barden Road and Double Branches Road. It is one of the state's oldest continuously operating country stores. Attractions are a well-stocked penny candy case, potbellied stove, and homemade country ham biscuits. Mistletoe State Park is reached from Lincolnton by way of Ga. 47 south to Phinizy or Pollards Corner, Ga. 150 west, and a turn north at Winfield. The park provides recreation of another sort—bass fishing, swimming, boating, biking, and hiking. Rental cottages are available.

Appling is reached from Price's Store by way of Ga. 47 and U.S. 221 across Clarks Hill Lake. The road goes near Kiokee Church, founded by Rev. Daniel Marshall in 1772. Once housing the state's first Baptist congregation, it is the oldest Baptist church building in the state and has been called the mother church of Georgia Baptists. The present church, to the northeast of Appling on U.S. 221 and north on Tubman Road near Greenbrier Creek, was built in 1808. The Columbia County courthouse was built in the vernacular Greek Revival style with Italianate influences in an 1856 addition and is one of the state's few antebellum courthouses in continuous use.

Botanist William Bartram traveled along the Savannah River between 1773 and 1777, identifying plants in their native habitats. Markers identify some parts of his trail along Stephens Creek Road (U.S. 221) at Clarks Hill Dam, Thurmond Lake, Lake Spring Picnic Area, Petersburg Campground, Ga. 104, Wildwood Park, Keg Creek, and across Little River Bridge into Lincoln County.

Harlem, south of I-20, birthplace of comedian Oliver Hardy, has an annual festival on the first Saturday in October to honor the memory of Hardy and his partner, Stan Laurel. The festival features a Laurel and Hardy movie marathon, Laurel and Hardy impersonators, races, children's games, and arts and crafts displays.

From Harlem, Ga. 221 leads south to **Wrens**, which was incorporated in 1884 when the Augusta Southern Railroad was laid. One of the town's most famous residents, novelist Erskine Caldwell, grew up there as the son of an Associate Reformed Presbyterian minister. In the tenant farmers the young Caldwell observed when traveling with his father, the mature writer found material for his novels and short stories. The name *Tobacco Road* came from a dirt road used for hauling tobacco in mule-drawn hogsheads to a port on the Savannah River. (For the Erskine Caldwell museum, see the West Central tour.)

Many historians believe that Hernando DeSoto visited Indian villages along the Ogeechee, Oconee, and Savannah Rivers in 1540, passing near present-day **Louisville**. In the next century, a Yuchi village known as Ogeechee Old Town became a trade center and remained so intermittently until unfriendly Indians and their British allies burned it in 1779. The vicinity regained significance in 1786 when the state general assembly decided to establish the new town of Louisville a few miles from Old Town and to designate it the state capital. The Georgia Legislature held its first session there in 1796.

Louisville was laid out along the Washington (Georgia) town plan with a courthouse square and cross streets at each corner of the central square. A state house was completed late in 1795 and remained in use until the legislature, fearing that Louisville's location near Rocky Comfort Creek and the Ogeechee River might be unhealthy, in 1803 commissioned a permanent state house for Milledgeville. The only remaining eighteenth-century structure is the Market House in the center of Broad Street. The market was the commercial center of Louisville and the surrounding area.

Louisville's architecture is representative of late-nineteenth-century styles, especially Gothic Revival. Willis Denny, a Louisville native recognized nationally and perhaps best known in Georgia as the architect of Rhodes Hall (see Metropolitan Atlanta), designed several residential and commercial buildings, including the Neoclassical Jefferson County courthouse. Jefferson County's topography of Piedmont and Coastal Plain was prime land for cultivation of cotton and tobacco, and large plantations flourished there from 1806 to 1864 when the Civil War interrupted shipments of supplies. The Ogeechee River offers fish and game opportunities.

The traveler may choose to pick up tour three at Louisville or to travel north to join tour two near Crawfordville, taking Ga. 171 through Glascock County. The scenery in this rural county, one of the state's smallest in area, is characterized by small farmhouses and sandstone and limestone outcroppings. Kaolin mining is a major industry. In

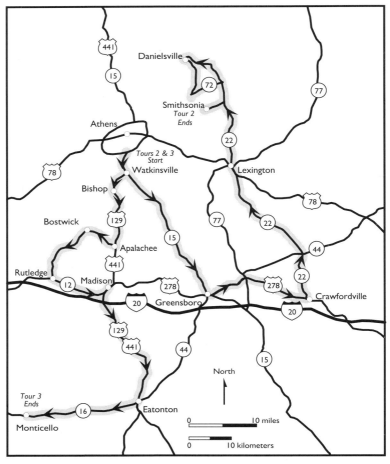

East Central Georgia, Tours Two and Three

Gibson and Mitchell, some older dwellings and brick commercial buildings are preserved, and the courthouse in Gibson is listed on the National Register. From Louisville, U.S. 1/221 leads south to Swainsboro and the Central Georgia tour area.

TOUR TWO

From the Athens loop, take U.S. 441 south to Watkinsville; Ga. 15 to Greensboro; U.S. 278 to Crawfordville; Ga. 22 and 98 north to Lexington and Danielsville; Ga. 22 and county roads to Smithonia.

An early Oconee River bridge, south of Athens on U.S. 441 at the Oconee County line, was a key element in the defense against Stoneman's Raid, a Union attempt to destroy the armory and other government works in Athens during Sherman's raid through Georgia.

Watkinsville was the seat of government for Clarke County until the county seat was moved to the larger Athens. Resenting the move, however, irate businessmen and residents petitioned the General Assembly, which created Oconee County in 1875. Watkinsville's Eagle Tavern, the county welcome center, displays furnishings typical of life on the frontier. Built circa 1790, this plantation plain–style house was a hotel and tavern for travelers from Madison and Greensboro. Artists and craftsmen abound in the county, and Watkinsville's Main Street shops offer a sample of local and regional art. The Eagle Tavern welcome center stocks a directory of artists and a walking tour written as a Girl Scout project. At Happy Valley Pottery, jewelry, pottery, and assorted regional works of art are crafted and sold. A map at the Eagle Tavern gives good directions to the remote pottery, which is off Colham Ferry Road between U.S. 441 and Ga. 15.

A drive south from Watkinsville on Ga. 15 leads to the turn to Elder's Mill Covered Bridge, one of only a few covered bridges left in the state. A brown sign on the right, about 4.5 miles from town, marks the turn. The bridge was constructed in the 1880s on Calls Creek, but the growth of commerce on U.S. 441 between Athens and Watkinsville necessitated a wider road; the covered bridge was numbered, dismantled, and relocated in 1924 to its current location on Rose Creek. The bridge, once a sheltered crossing for carriages, horses, and lovers, now

Elder's Mill Covered Bridge, photographed circa 1975

sits next to Elder's Mill (private), which operated as a grist, flour, and wheat mill until the 1950s.

Along Ga. 15, vistas of pale pink peach blossoms delight the eye in spring, but a visit in summer offers the opportunity to sample freshly picked fruit. Thomas Orchards proffers peaches, barbecue, and cotton ginning, all in one stop. At produce stands one may find pork rinds, tomatoes, peaches, Vidalia onions, jams, jellies, and sometimes AKC puppies!

Agribusiness, whether by direct farming or farm-related industry, has always been important to Oconee and Greene Counties. The green belt of farms produces many crops including hay and corn used mostly for feed. One spot sprouts a most unusual sight—an iron horse. Sculpted by artist Abbot Pattison and placed on the University of Georgia campus in 1954, the one-ton horse was the target of several student pranks. After only two days, the sculpture was lent to a professor of agriculture, who placed it on his Greene County farm. At a curve on Ga. 15, the Iron Horse can be glimpsed watching over a corn field on the left.

When cotton was king in the decades before the Civil War, Greene County and Greensboro prospered. As railroads brought access to markets, several mills were constructed in the 1830s and 1840s. One of the earliest to use water power was built at Scull Shoals, once one of Greene County's largest communities but now abandoned. Ruins of the town and mill are on a forest service road 2.5 miles off Macedonia Road, to the east of Ga. 15, within the Oconee National Forest. The forest also has marked trails for hiking or tranquil walks along the Oconee River.

From Ga. 15 south of Scull Shoals, Boswell Road (unpaved) leads east to **Penfield**, a small National Register district significant as the site of the founding of Mercer Institute, later Mercer University. At the end of Boswell, a turn right onto Callaway and then a left turn lead to the village. The Georgia Baptist Association in 1833 established the institute as a manual labor school to provide training for ministerial students. Structures dating from the 1830s and 1840s, including the chapel, still stand in Penfield. The university was moved to Macon in 1871. A paved county road leads south from the village, past Boxwood (1836) on the right and a Presbyterian church (1876) on the left, to Greensboro and the continuation of the tour.

Greensboro, the seat of Greene County, was founded in 1786 on land the Creeks and Cherokees had ceded to the state of Georgia. A cotton-picking scene and an Indian attack that resulted in the burning of Greensboro in 1787 are depicted in Carson Davenport's New Deal murals in the post office. A fine example of Greek Revival architecture is the Greene County courthouse, the third oldest in the state, built in 1848. The Masons still meet in a third story they added to the structure in 1849.

Old Greene County Gaol (behind the courthouse on Greene Street) was built in 1807 and is among the oldest penal structures in Georgia. Its granite block construction and castellated battlements give it the appearance of a fortress; the cells have little light or ventilation. It can be visited by arrangement with the sheriff's office.

The Virginia E. Evans/Greene County Historical Society Museum, located at Greene and North East Streets, is a repository for historical records and artifacts. Open on Sundays, the museum has an interesting collection of contemporary paintings of local residents. The Chamber of Commerce, located in a restored country doctor's office, has information for walking and driving tours of Greene County and the five historic districts and sites of Greensboro. Two historic houses, Early Hill and the Davis House, have been converted to bed-and-breakfast inns.

Lake Oconee, on Ga. 44 south, has good fishing, swimming, water skiing, and sailing as well as prize golf courses. The Victorian Gothic Jackson house, endangered by the proposed project, was dismantled, moved to a higher knoll, and reassembled on Lake Oconee near Greensboro. It is open as both house museum and the sales office for a golf community, Reynolds Plantation, named for the family land used for the lake project.

Union Point, on 278E, was originally called Thornton's Cross-roads for Redman Thornton, who in 1770 built a house there. The Thornton house was moved to and may be toured at Stone Mountain Park (see Metropolitan Atlanta). Union Manufacturing Company (Chipman-Union) is the industrial center of Union Point. The mill is a complex of twenty historic buildings dating from 1897 to 1900. Much of Union Point's history is tied to the hosiery mill. Tours of the mill may be arranged by calling the mill office, and an informal drive through the town's pleasant residential area is recommended. Along U.S. 278, there are several points of interest, including historic markers for Memorial Park, commemorating the first regimental reunion of the Confederate veterans of the Third Georgia Division, and for the great Buffalo Lick where William Bartram saw deer and buffalo licking a white-colored clay (probably kaolin).

Alexander H. Stephens (1812–83), orator, U.S. congressman, vice president of the Confederacy, and briefly governor, lived at Liberty Hall in **Crawfordville**. The house, a National Historic Landmark; Stephens's library and many of his furnishings; several outbuildings; and the Confederate Museum are near A. H. Stephens State Historic Park, which has tent and trailer sites, picnic shelters, a nature trail, two fishing lakes, and rustic rental cabins. The Civilian Conservation Corps constructed much of the park, beginning in 1933.

Crawfordville's historic commercial district contains buildings from the antebellum period to the early 1900s. The only restaurant in town, Bonner's Cafe, has been open since 1923. The Taliaferro County Historical Society is located in the antebellum post office building on Broad Street and has a museum next door. The courthouse is listed on the national register. The main house of Colonsay Plantation (private), east-northeast of Crawfordville off Ga. 908, was constructed by Marmaduke Mendenhall, first cousin of William Bartram.

Philomath Historic District, north of Crawfordville on Ga. 22, is listed on the National Register. Philomath, "a place for learning," is a small community that in the nineteenth century was the site of a boys' boarding school. Parts of Bartram's Trail are marked near the town, including another buffalo lick described by William Bartram in the late eighteenth century. (For Lexington, see East Central tour one.) Located near Ga. 22 north of Lexington, between Lexington and Smithonia, Big Cloud's Creek Covered Bridge was constructed of heart pine in 1904 in the town lattice design.

Located on the South Fork of the Broad River in northern Oglethorpe County, Watson Mill Bridge State Park is one of Georgia's most picturesque state parks. Its centerpiece is a three-span covered bridge, 236 feet long, built in 1885 in the town lattice pattern. Watson Mill opened in 1798 and for a hundred years operated continuously as a grist, flour, or corn mill. The mill, open as part of the park, originally served as the focal point for community life. Fishing, camping, pioneer camping, and picnicking are now provided.

Madison County's gently rolling hills, verdant forests, and rocky streams enhance its small towns with tree-shaded streets. After **Danielsville** became the county seat in 1817, the town grew around the courthouse, which was built in the Romanesque Revival style in 1901. A statue of Dr. Crawford W. Long, the father of anesthesia, is on the courthouse square, and a short distance out Crawford Long Road is his childhood home (private; see Northeast Georgia tour three). The chamber of commerce has recently restored for its offices the Henry Strickland House, where the first courts of Madison County were held (ca. 1790), on Ga. 98 north of Danielsville. The chamber provides area tour information during business hours. South of the Danielsville courthouse square, Madison Street and Danielsville-Colbert Road lead to Colbert. At Colbert, Ga. 72 goes to Comer, and Ga. 22 goes south from Comer to the sign for Watson Mill Bridge State Park on the left. For Smithonia, a road leads east (to the right) from Ga. 22.

Smithonia was the home of James Monroe Smith (1839–1915), an entrepreneur who began modestly and built a hugh farming empire. His farm was a self-contained agricultural community that included a cotton-seed mill, fertilizer factory, sawmill, gin, oil refinery, corn and wheat mills, a blacksmith shop, general store, hotel, and gas lighting plant. Smith even built two narrow-gauge railroads on his estate. He was elected to both the state general assembly and the state senate. The farm has since been divided, but the house (private) and brick barns remain visible from the road.

From Smithonia the traveler may return to Athens to begin tour one or tour three.

TOUR THREE

Take U.S. 129/441 South to Bishop and Apalachee; local roads to Bostwick and Rutledge; Ga. 12 to Madison; U.S. 441/129 to Rock Eagle and Eatonton; and Ga. 16 to Monticello.

The Georgia State Botanical Gardens are south of Athens on Milledge Extension, near Whitehall. The garden's 313 acres depict ecological regions of the Georgia Piedmont. Trails wind through specialty gardens that include native azaleas, shade and ornamental plants, roses, dahlias, daffodils, rhododendron, herbs, perennials, annuals, and a wetland tract. The glass and steel visitors center and conservatory contains tropical and semitropical gardens, a cafe, and a gift shop. The Garden Club of Georgia recently built new headquarters at the gardens.

White Hall, former home of local financier, banker, and manufacturer John Richards White, was built in 1891 for his residence. Located on Phoenix Road at the intersection of Whitehall Road and Milledge Avenue, the house is near the site of the old Whitehall Mill and village, Georgia's first textile mill complex, established in the late 1830s. The Victorian Romanesque style house was deeded to the University of Georgia in 1936 and restored by its School of Forest Resources in 1978. The private building is open for special tours arranged through the forestry school. Simonton Bridge Road travels on to Watkinsville (see East Central tour two), where U.S. 441 continues tour three.

Bishop, situated on the Central of Georgia Railroad, was established in 1890 as an agricultural community. Today it remains a small rural settlement with antique shops, potters, fruit stands, and some pick-your-own orchards.

Farmington began in 1837 as a retail and trading center for local farms and plantations. From Farmington, U.S. 129 leads south to Apalachee, where Apalachee Road turns west to **Bostwick,** an early planned community. In 1902 John Bostwick, much as did Jim Smith (see Smithonia, above), decided to create his own town and agricultural center. The cotton gin and general store are still operating. The railroad, once located behind the store and Susie Agnes Hotel, has since been removed. Bostwick holds a cotton gin festival in the fall.

A side trip from Bostwick on Fairplay Road travels through Fairplay to Hard Labor Creek State Park, which offers camping, cottages, fishing, canoeing, swimming, golf, and the largest observatory in the southeastern United States. Public viewing nights are usually the second Saturdays of the months from April to October. At the picturesque village of Rutledge, south of the park, U. S. 78/Ga. 12 leads to Madison, as does the quieter, more scenic Dixie Highway, paralleling the railroad tracks.

South from Bostwick on Ga. 83 are Nolan's Store and crossroad. The Nolan plantation covered over two thousand acres from 1856 until the 1970s. A road at the house and commissary bisects Ga. 83 and leads to tenant houses. The two-story Classical Revival house (private) across the street from the commissary was built in 1910. Shortly south on Ga. 83, on the left, stands the older family house, a plantation plain I-form.

Madison, the county seat of Morgan County, is a National Register District known for its well-preserved antebellum homes. The Madison-Morgan Chamber of Commerce building (1887), centrally located on East Jefferson Street, was originally the city hall and fire station. The first fire bell has been returned to the cupola, and the fire-fighters' pole is still intact. Downtown shops display merchandise from antiques to quilts, and Baldwin's Pharmacy is a good place to stop for a cherry soda or milk shake. Housed in an 1895 Romanesque Revival former schoolhouse, the Madison-Morgan Cultural Center is a center for the visual, decorative, and performing arts. The Morgan County African-American Museum, on Academy Street, preserves artifacts of Morgan County black heritage, African paintings and exhibits, and reference material. The 1842 Greek Revival Heritage Hall, headquarters for the Morgan County Historical Society, was the home of physician Dr. Elijah Evans, who moved the house from an in-town farm lot to its present location. Madison merits a leisurely walking tour or at least a slow drive through its neighborhoods. Guides for each are available at Heritage Hall.

The drive from Madison south to **Eatonton** on U. S. 441 has vistas of large dairy and beef cattle farms and fields with huge bales of hay, rolled and stacked. Though the modern rolled bales may be left in open fields, across the South hay is also being stored in historic barns that are too small for large new tractors. Most Piedmont farms are too hilly to support large-scale crop programs, such as those found in Southwest Georgia, and are usually devoted to livestock or timber, Georgia's number-one crop.

At the Rock Eagle archaeological site in Putnam County, an effigy mound of stones piled in the shape of a giant prone bird may have been built by an early stone-mound culture. Believed to date from the Woodland Period (1000 B.C.–A.D. 900), the quartz rock mound can be seen from an observation tower that allows a good view of the bird's shape, 120-foot wing span, and 102-foot length. It is on the grounds of Rock Eagle 4-H Center, operated by the Cooperative Extension

Rock Eagle, Putnam County

Service of the University of Georgia and named for the bird-shaped effigy mound. A lake at the youth center has public picnic areas, boats, and fishing facilities.

On the grounds of the Putnam County courthouse in **Eatonton** is a monument honoring a rabbit and its popularizer. Joel Chandler Harris, author of stories about Br'er Rabbit and Uncle Remus, was one of the earliest people to record black folk tales. The Putnam County native is honored with the Uncle Remus Museum, three blocks south of the courthouse on U.S. 441. In the museum the public may see Harris memorabilia and a facsimile of the fictional Uncle Remus's cabin. (Also see Wren's Nest, Metropolitan Atlanta tour.) When Harris was an apprentice printer to J. A. Turner, editor and publisher of the *Countryman*, he lived at Turnwold Plantation, on New Phoenix Road, off Ga. 16 to the left (north), about seven miles east of Eatonton. The original house there was demolished several years ago.

A modern Putnam County author, Alice Walker, was born in this area in 1944 and grew up in the neighborhood of Ward Chapel, to the north of Turnwold on Ward Chapel Road. She was awarded the Pulitzer Prize for her widely acclaimed novel, *The Color Purple*. The attendant at the Uncle Remus Museum can provide directions to some sites associated with Alice Walker.

From Eatonton Ga. 16 leads through part of the Oconee National Forest to Monticello, seat of government for Jasper County. Much of the surrounding county is characterized by the recreation opportunities of the national forest, Jackson Lake, and the Ocmulgee River at the county's western border. The local chamber of commerce publishes a brochure of brief walking and driving tours that feature landmarks including several examples of antebellum Italianate, Victorian, and Greek "re-revival" houses, as well as interesting church buildings. From Monticello or nearby Sparta, other East Central and Central Georgia tours are convenient.

TOUR FOUR

From Augusta, take I-520 to Ga. 56 to Waynesboro; Ga. 24 to Sandersville; Ga. 15 to Sparta; Ga. 16 east to Warrenton; and U.S. 278 to Thomson.

From its beginnings as an Indian fort under Gen. James Edward Oglethorpe, **Augusta** grew and prospered as a city of grace and culture. The skyline is pierced with church steeples, crenellated roof lines, and modern offices. Boulevards and highways curve around large historic and commercial areas, leading up to "the Hill," once a lively resort and now a thriving community within Augusta. With rapid expansion after World War II, many Augusta residents moved out to new suburbs, creating a widely dispersed population and new commercial areas. Augusta is the hub of a metropolitan area of over 450,000 population.

General Oglethorpe, realizing Augusta's potential for trade and commerce, utilized the trade the Indians had established as a centerpiece for economic development for Georgia before it became a colony. Oglethorpe's idea was to follow the Savannah plan of forty one-acre lots with a square in the center. The town is rich in history (cotton manufacture, industry, commerce, culture, and transportation) and is fun to explore. Several days touring the city would be well spent. If, however, time is limited, the following sites are especially worthwhile.

The Cotton Exchange, at Eighth Street, Reynolds, and Riverwalk, serves as a welcome center and dispenses tour information about Augusta and Richmond County. The building, constructed in 1886 in the Queen Anne/Second Empire style, originally was the city's center for cotton trading. At the height of the activity, over two hundred members brokered cotton on the big trading floor. The Cotton Exchange also operated as a men's club with checkers and card playing and even an occasional cock fight. During restoration in 1990, the original forty-five-foot blackboard was uncovered and is now displayed showing original notations of cotton transactions. The Cotton Museum tells the story of cotton by montage as well as by exhibits about the boll weevil and lien system.

A recent revitalization project for Augusta is the Riverwalk, an esplanade on the levee that links shops, the Morris Museum of Art, an amphitheater, a playground, hotel, and dining facilities. The Morris Museum contains an impressive collection of early to contemporary

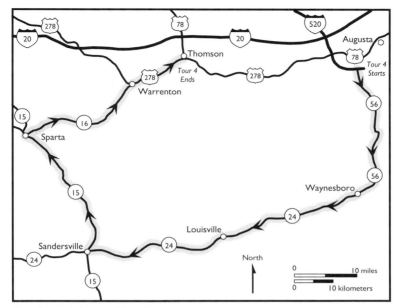

East Central Georgia, Tour Four

southern art. The National Science Center's exhibit hall, a hands-on science education center, is scheduled to open in 1996. Riverwalk is a good spot for viewing several well-known annual boating events, including one of the International Outboard Grand Prix series, an international rowing regatta, and a world-class drag boat race.

The Ezekiel Harris House (1840 Broad Street) is the city's second-oldest structure, built by Ezekiel Harris in 1797 on a hill overlooking Augusta. It is an outstanding example of post–Revolutionary War architecture with its massive gambrel roof, vaulted hallway, and tiered piazzas. It is open to the public.

Saint Paul's Episcopal Church (1918), 605 Reynolds Street, occupies the site of the original fort that General Oglethorpe ordered built to protect the new colonists. With its elliptically vaulted ceiling, the sanctuary is a fine example of a Neoclassical interior. Several notable Georgians are buried in the cemetery next to the church.

Augusta's culturally diverse heritage includes significant contributions from African Americans who were important in the town's culture, cotton industry, and transportation development. The city's location on the fall line enabled it to use water power for industrial development, and with the construction of the Augusta Canal, the textile industry's growth accelerated. Roads and railroads connected the city to other markets. Blacks played an important role in this transportation development, from river dredging and canal excavation to railroad construction.

Riverwalk along the Savannah River, Augusta

Springfield Baptist Church, 114 Twelfth Street, founded in 1787, is a historic independent African American congregation. The original wooden sanctuary, built in 1801 and restored in 1990, is now an education building and small museum telling the history of the church. The present brick sanctuary was constructed in 1897.

The Springfield Community around Springfield Baptist Church is an African American settlement dating from 1783. Lots were laid out for sale by 1789. Development continued until the 1870s, but in 1929 a flood devastated the area. In 1989 the city of Augusta, in the midst of constructing a convention center and office park along the Savannah Riverfront, began archaeological investigation of Springfield. Excavations uncovered evidence of houses from the antebellum and late-nineteenth-century periods and tenement housing associated with a nearby cotton mill and woodworking factory. African architectural traditions link with building traditions in the Springfield area.

Augusta's Laney-Walker North Historic District is bounded by D'Antignac Street and Walton Way, Seventh and Twiggs Streets, Laney-Walker Boulevard, and Phillips and Harrison Streets. Many of the city's early minority populations lived and worked in this district, encompassing a multiethnic working-class community of Irish-American, Chinese-American, and African American residents. By the early twentieth century, the Laney-Walker District was a self-sufficient black community. The 1922 Penny Savings Bank is recognized as one of the most important black commercial buildings in the state. The Lucy Craft Laney Museum of Black History and Conference Center, 1116 Phillips Street, is a local history museum in the home of Lucy Laney, a revered pioneer in education for blacks. Her portrait hangs in the state capitol. A guide to black historic sites is available at the Cotton Exchange.

The Pinch Gut Historic District is bounded north by Reynolds and Bay Streets, west by Gordon Highway, south by Magnolia and Cedar Grove Cemeteries, south by May Park, and east by East Boundary. This is the largest and most intact historic residential area in Augusta. Architectural styles range from early-nineteenth-century Federal to Victorian to early-twentieth-century bungalow. House sizes include large two-story town houses and tiny, one-story, three-room shotgun cottages. The Houghton School represents an innovative local effort toward free public education.

Paine College, at Laney-Walker Boulevard and Fifteenth Street, was founded in 1882. Historically black in enrollment, it was the first educational institution for African Americans to be sponsored in the South by southern churches of both races. The residential, coeducational school became a four-year college in 1890.

Sacred Heart Cultural Center (Greene and Thirteenth Streets; open to the public), once a Catholic church, is a magnificent example of Victorian architecture and detail. The Romanesque and Byzantine elements are exemplified in fifteen distinctive styles of brickwork and brilliant jewel-toned German stained glass. The Old Medical College of Georgia (598 Telfair Street; open afternoons), built in 1835 in the massive Greek Revival style with a Doric colonnade, housed the first medical school in the state and started the tradition of medical education and research in Augusta. With the growth of the medical school, the building was used for other purposes. The Medical College Foundation in 1991 employed architect Norman Davenport Askins to restore the building to its original grandeur. The Romanesque old Richmond Academy Building (1801; 540 Telfair Street) housed the Augusta–Richmond County Museum until the museum moved to its new location on the corner of Reynolds and Sixth Streets. The Gertrude Herbert Institute of Art is housed in the Ware-Sibley-Clarke House, circa 1818. Delicate details of Adamesque architecture are evident in its bow-front porch and bays. Commonly known as Ware's Folly, the house was built by mayor (and later U.S. senator) Nicholas Ware. The public galleries feature regional and southeastern art.

The house museum Meadow Garden (Independence Drive near the intersection of Walton Way and Thirteenth Street), the oldest documented structure in Augusta, was built in 1791 by George Walton, one of the signers of the Declaration of Independence and governor of Georgia when Augusta was the state capital. Originally built as a hall and parlor, it was expanded in 1835 to a one-and-half-story sand hills cottage. The Daughters of the American Revolution own and operate the house.

Only the chimney stands to mark the Confederate States Powder Works, built in 1861. Sibley Mill, constructed in 1880, is immediately behind the historic chimney with the John P. King Mill (1881) adjacent. From the River Watch Expressway entrance to the city, the sight of Sibley Mill is reminiscent of the appearance of old Augusta.

Built in 1845 to connect various areas of downtown with the Savannah River and provide water power to Augusta, the Augusta Canal joined the town and the river and powered four mills that were built beside it. Chinese contract laborers helped enlarge the canal in 1875. Many remained in Augusta; as a result, the city has the oldest Chinese community in Georgia. An incidental use of the canal was recreational, for excursion boating and picnicking on the banks were a popular pastime.

The entire Historic Augusta Canal and Industrial District is a National Historic Landmark. Although the canal has fallen into disrepair, an ambitious restoration project should bring back most of it and make it available for recreation. The city of Augusta, Augusta Canal Authority, and National Park Service publish a brochure for those who want to explore the area. It covers recreational possibilities, new and historic structures, and wildlife from the Riverwalk and Cotton Exchange to the Savannah Rapids Pavilion. The canal begins on the Savannah River in Columbia County at the eastern end of Evans to Locks Road. At the lock and dam, Columbia County has constructed the Savannah Rapids Pavilion, a community resource for recreation and public functions. The old locks and pavilion are about twelve miles from downtown Augusta, by way of River Watch Parkway, Ga. 104, Stevens Creek Road to the right, and Evans to Locks Road to the right at a small sign reading "Savannah Rapids Pavilion."

Walton Way leads to the Hill section of Augusta, a former resort village still known as Summerville. For respite from the heat of town, residents sought the sand hills. By the late nineteenth century, Summerville was so popular that many Augustans settled there, making it Augusta's first suburb. Incorporating an early-nineteenth-century house, the Partridge Inn (2110 Walton Way) was built in the early twentieth century and is still an elegant dining spot and inn. In the heart of Summerville is one of the finest architectural treasures in Augusta. The Church of the Good Shepherd, 2230 Walton Way, was built by John Nesbit in the style of John Ruskin, who advocated that color and decoration should not be artificially applied to buildings but should arise naturally from the patterns, textures, and colors of the masonry, roofing, and woodwork.

The campus of Augusta College reveals layers of history. The property originally belonged to U.S. senator Freeman Walker. His plantation house, Bellevue (circa 1815), is now the college's counseling center. Capt. Matthew Payne, commandant of the U.S. Arsenal, after recuperating from a near-fatal bout of fever at Bellevue, persuaded Secretary of War John C. Calhoun to purchase the Walker estate and remove the arsenal from its unhealthy riverbank location in 1822. The

The Masters Golf Tournament, Augusta

relocated arsenal buildings now house the college's administrative offices. Gen. William T. Sherman served briefly at the arsenal as a young officer, a fact that gave rise to the myth that he later spared Augusta because he had a lady friend there.

The Civil War might have begun at the arsenal except that Capt. Arnold Elzey had the good sense to surrender as a thousand Georgia militia marched up Walton Way. The arsenal produced munitions during the Civil War and during both world wars. In 1957 the United States deeded the property to the Richmond County Board of Education. Military buildings were adapted to educational purposes as the Junior College of Augusta occupied the site. With new buildings, Augusta College grew into its present status as a senior unit of the University System of Georgia.

Golf has become synonymous with Augusta, especially in the spring during the playing of the Masters Golf Tournament at the Augusta National Golf Club, which has as its clubhouse the historic Fruitlands Manor (1854). Much of the beauty of the course comes from its beginning as an indigo plantation and then as Fruitlands Nursery, the first commercial nursery in the South.

Augusta's affiliation with golf began in 1897 with the Bon Air Golf Club, now the Augusta Country Club. By the 1920s Augusta's reputation as a golfing destination attracted all-time great player Bobby Jones, who became the first person to win in a single year golf's "grand slam" championship series—the American Amateur, American Open, British Amateur, and British Open. He hoped to build the perfect golf course, and when he visited Fruitlands Nursery, he exclaimed that the grounds were "perfect . . . and to think this ground has been lying here all these years waiting for someone to come along and lay a golf course on it."

Jones invited Scottish architect Dr. Alistair McKenzie to help him plan the course, employing an entirely original design. The idea was to have the course follow the topography of the nursery. In 1934 Jones hosted the Augusta Invitational Tournament, which the press quickly renamed the Masters. The club is privately owned, and tickets to the tournament are prized; however, practice round tickets are occasionally available.

After exploring Augusta, the traveler may take U.S. 78 or U.S. 1 to Fort Gordon Military Reservation, which was founded as Camp Gordon early in World War II. At the fort, the U.S. Army Signal Museum tells the story of military communications, including Morse code, wig-wag, Native American "code talkers," and communications in space.

East of Fort Gordon via I-520, Ga. 56 leads south to one of the eight original counties in Georgia, Burke County, with a history rich in agriculture and the plantation system. A few of the large plantations still exist, though they are privately owned, usually set back from the highway, and visible only from a distance. They are well worth the drive if one is willing to venture on a less-traveled road.

For a different side trip, from McBean, Ga. 56 Sp. leads southeast to Plant Vogtle Nuclear Power Plant, which has a public exhibit on nuclear power. When William Bartram visited this area in 1773 he noted on a bluff a large bed of giant oyster shells, now on private property.

The Georgia legislature authorized the laying out of **Waynesboro** in 1783 along the same town plan as Augusta, with the courthouse square surrounded by two hundred one-acre lots. The present Burke County courthouse was built in 1857 in a vernacular style with Italianate elements and Victorian clock tower, expanded in 1899, and complemented with a Neoclassical Revival annex in 1940. In the historic business district, a six-block area surrounding the courthouse, are several good examples of late-nineteenth- to early-twentieth-century commercial architecture.

The Burke County Museum, near the courthouse, offers information on Burke County's history. It displays a cotton and bird dog exhibit and an extensive collection of tools and equipment for cotton production. African American heritage is a significant part of Burke County's history. That heritage is celebrated in Waynesboro in the recent rehabilitation of the Waynesboro High and Industrial School, the oldest African American public school in Burke County. The building, now the Economic Opportunity Administration Building, houses several social service agencies. Built in 1920 in the Craftsman style, the school was created to offer an elementary and junior high education for Burke County black students. Haven Church in Waynesboro, an elaborate and impressive African American house of worship, became an architectural model for nineteenth-century African American churches. The Museum of Rural Folkways interprets another aspect of the county's history.

The Burke County Museum can provide directions to these sites and for a side trip to Bellevue Plantation, private and remote but historically significant. Located twelve miles south of Waynesboro on Porter Carswell Road, Bellevue Plantation was part of a royal grant from King George III to Samuel Eastlake in 1767. Bellevue's massive chimneys were constructed with handmade bricks, and its timbers were hand-hewn and joined with wooden pegs.

Burke County is called the Bird Dog Capital of the World. During January and February, the Georgia Field Trials, hunting dog competitions with a long tradition, are held at Boll Weevil Plantation outside Waynesboro. The plantation is a 5,371-acre hunting and fishing preserve, excellent for quail, deer, wild hog, and dove hunting, which can be arranged through the local chamber of commerce.

The drive west to **Sandersville** crosses East Central tour one at Louisville. Sandersville grew around a courthouse square on the old stagecoach road from Louisville to Milledgeville and on the Dixie and Nancy Hart highways. The present Washington County courthouse was built in 1868–69 in the high Victorian Eclectic style after Sherman and his Left Wing burned the earlier courthouse on their march to the sea. Sherman used the Brown House for his headquarters when he marched through town with the Fourteenth and Twentieth Companies. The Washington County Historical Society is restoring the Brown House for its headquarters, now shared with the Washington County Museum in the old sheriff's residence and jail on the courthouse square. The surrounding residential districts display a fine collection of architectural styles from Greek Revival to Tudor. The architect Charles Choate designed many of these residences. The local historical society and chamber of commerce have produced a historic guide to Sandersville. Washington County is known as the kaolin capital of the world, for it is located on the Tuscaloosa fall line where nature deposited a pure, white alumina-silicate clay used for products ranging from pottery to Kaopectate. The annual Kaolin Festival in October celebrates the clay's importance to the city and county.

Warthen, on Ga. 15 nine miles north of Sandersville, was one of the earliest settlements in Washington County. The hewn log jail, built about 1786, confined Aaron Burr in 1807 as he was escorted to Richmond for his trial for treason. Six miles north of Warthen, on the road to Jewell, Hamburg State Park provides camping, boating, fishing, a grist mill, country store, and museum displaying old agricultural tools of rural Georgia.

Ga. 15 continues north from Warthen to Sparta, but a side trip between Sandersville and Sparta is the village of **Linton**, hardly changed in appearance since the mid-nineteenth century when it formed around the Washington Institute, a boarding school established in 1858. Linton contains fine examples of mid-nineteenth-century architecture, among them the Duggan-Evans-Warwick House (private), built for a Washington Institute professor who boarded students. The unusual plan has a raised main entry flanked by travelers' rooms at either end of the wide, plastered porch and also a ground floor of locally made brick.

After a drive down Linton's one road, the traveler heading toward Sparta will see, north of Linton, Glen Mary Plantation on the left. Commanding a knoll, Glen Mary (private) stands in Greek Revival splendor with cranberry etched-glass transom and sidelights and matching ornamental plaster ceilings and medallions. It was restored by a modern Georgia architect, the late Edward Vason Jones, who played a prominent part in the restoration of the White House and the State Department Diplomatic Reception Rooms.

Strategically located on the fall line, the topographical region where the Piedmont meets the Coastal Plain, Hancock County was once important as a crossroads for commerce and culture. Ga. 16, which crosses Ga. 15 at Sparta, follows a part of the Creek Indians' Upper Trading Path (otherwise known as Oakfuskee). The Creeks and the state of Georgia in 1786 signed the Treaty of Shoulderbone Creek at the fork of the creek and the Oconee River. Millmore (circa 1800), at Ga. 16W and Ga. 77 on Shoulderbone Creek, was built of pegged hand-hewn timbers as a water-powered, stone-ground grist mill. The adjacent Vinson house (private; 1820) was moved from Baldwin County.

The Hancock County courthouse (1881–83) is an imposing sight as one approaches historic **Sparta**. An early Indian trading post, Sparta was named to honor her courageous pioneer citizens. The Drummer's Home, located on the site of Old Eagle Tavern, was built as the Edwards House in 1840 and renamed in 1897 because of its popular reputation among salesmen. Now the hotel has been restored as a retirement home. Sparta has a superb array of nineteenth-century structures that are easily viewed on a walk or drive around the village. If a map or tourism information is not available, even an unguided tour by Sparta's older residences is rewarding.

Two progressive African American schools began in Hancock County through the persistence of local blacks. Sparta Agricultural and Industrial Institute, founded early in the century by Linton Stephens Ingraham and eventually added to the county school system, gave teacher Jean Toomer experience on which he based his novel *Cane*. The efforts of farmers Zack and Camilla Hubert to see that their twelve children were educated led to a school at Springfield that is now part of the Camilla-Zack Community Center, a National Register District.

East of Sparta, an interesting stop along Ga. 16 is **Jewell**, or Jewell's

Rock House

Mill. Earlier called Rock Factory, the village was a thriving textile mill community on the Ogeechee River from the 1840s until the mill burned in 1927. A few interesting Victorian houses, churches, mill housing, and a school remain. The Ogeechee River Mill, begun in 1847 in Warren County, was reconstructed in 1949 on the other side of the river in Hancock County. The dam has also been reconstructed. The village green is to the right before the highway crosses the river. Through traffic on Ga. 16 seldom slows when passing Jewell, so caution is advised.

Warren County is noted for areas of natural beauty, from the large pine forests to the banks of the lazily flowing Ogeechee River. **Warrenton**, chartered in 1810 as the county seat, grew around the courthouse square. After the first two courthouses were destroyed by fire, the present one was constructed in 1910 in the neoclassical revival style. Warrenton contains several architecturally interesting buildings, especially along Main Street, which is lined with graceful pecan trees. Fountain Campground, in the northern end of Warren County on Ga. 80, is a United Methodist facility in use since 1800. An annual revival takes place in August in a large open tabernacle surrounded by cabins, or "tents," of individual members.

U.S. 278 between Warrenton and **Thomson** follows the path of the famous Upper Trading Path, an Indian trail that led from Augusta to Indian settlements as far west as the Mississippi River. The main branch of the trail, the Oakfuskee Path, ran past Warrenton, Eatonton, Griffin, and Greenville to Oakfuskee Town, on the Tallapoosa River in Alabama.

For a good overview of McDuffie County, a visitor should begin at the restored Thomson Depot, the headquarters for the Thomson-McDuffie Tourism, Convention, and Visitors' Bureau. A group of ten may reserve an Upcountry Plantation Tour, which follows the developmental history of McDuffie County since its settlement as a Quaker Community in **Wrightsborough** in 1768. (The visitors bureau also provides a map for a self-guided driving tour.) McDuffie County includes most of the original colonial Wrightsborough Township. The county lies across the fall line with the Piedmont's red hills to the north and the sandy Coastal Plain to the south.

Seven miles west of Thomson, **Historic Wrightsboro** (a stop on the Upcountry Plantation Tour) was settled by Quakers from North Carolina. The present Methodist church building, erected in 1810, is believed to be located on the site of early Quaker meeting houses. Revolutionary and Civil War veterans are buried in its graveyard; the oldest tombstone is dated 1800. Although Wrightsborough began as a planned community, today only a few ruins, Wrightsborough Church, and the cemetery are readily visible. Wrightsborough is mentioned in William Bartram's *Travels*.

Between 1782 and 1785 Thomas Ansley built the Rock House, also a stop on the tour, of fieldstone two feet thick. It is the oldest intact house in the state. Ansley patterned his house after those he had seen in his home state of New Jersey with a basement room for cooking meals and a main floor for his parlor and bedrooms. The upper story was finished later into two loft rooms, probably children's rooms. The structure was home to ancestors of former president Jimmy Carter.

Country blues singer Blind Willie McTell is buried in his native Thomson. The town has established an annual music festival in his memory.

Thomson is home to the Belle Meade Hunt, one of the most respected fox-hunting clubs in America. From November to March on Wednesdays and Saturdays, Belle Meade takes to the hounds. The hunt begins with the official blessing of the hounds on the first Saturday in November. Those wishing to view the ritual or the hunt can obtain information at the Thomson Convention and Visitors' Bureau.

From the Thomson exit on I-20, the traveler may return to Atlanta or Augusta or travel U.S. 1 south to Swainsboro and the Central Georgia tour.

WEST
CENTRAL
GEORGIA

William W. Winn # THE VIEW FROM DOWDELL'S KNOB

From 1924 until his death in 1945, Franklin Delano Roosevelt, the thirty-second president of the United States and a native New Yorker, came frequently to Warm Springs, Georgia, to try to regain some strength in his polio-withered legs in the nearly ninety-degree waters that bubble from the slopes of Pine Mountain, one of several high quartzite ridges running roughly southwest to northeast almost in the center of the region we now call West Central Georgia. Legend has it that sick or injured Muskogulgi or Creek Indians, who inhabited this part of Georgia from ancient times until they were driven into Alabama in the 1820s, had used the springs in much the same way.

So had generations of well-to-do antebellum southerners from as far away as Charleston and Savannah and from the surrounding plantations and towns of Columbus, Newnan, LaGrange, Talbotton, Barnesville, and Thomaston. In the years before the Civil War, a spa developed around the springs, whose crystalline waters were then said to possess magical curative powers for everything from skin diseases to rheumatism. Early visitors to the area, including such luminaries as Henry Clay and John C. Calhoun, flocked there in the summer to escape the appalling heat and the mosquito-borne fevers of the lowlands. In those days, the little hamlet of Warm Springs was known as Bullochville, having been named, in a strange coincidence, for Eleanor Roosevelt's grandmother, a Georgian who married Theodore Roosevelt Sr. in Roswell, Georgia. Two decades after the Civil War, so many people were drawn to the ridges that a huge, rambling, three-story Victorian-style hotel, the Meriwether Inn, was erected on the slopes overlooking the springs. The inn's owner, Charles Davis, built two enclosed therapeutic pools for his guests and a large swimming pool, the latter 50 by 150 feet, at the bottom of the hill at the springs. The Meriwether Inn, so outrageously ornate in the Victorian nervousness of its architecture that country folk would travel many miles over dusty roads in mule-drawn wagons just to gawk at it, became a favorite watering hole for what was left of the southern aristocracy and the textile mill owners and their families and the rising business class spawned by the industrialization of Henry Grady's New

South. Some of them liked the spa so much they built rustic cottages on the side of the mountain amid groves of towering oaks and hickories and fragrant pines.

By the time a dispirited Franklin Roosevelt heard about the marvelous restorative powers of the springs and paid his first visit there, the Meriwether Inn had fallen on hard times. The boll weevil had decimated the region's cotton crop, greatly reducing the number of southerners who could afford to patronize the inn. At the same time the expansion of the South's rail system, plus the development of the automobile and an improved network of roads, made it possible for those who still had money to travel hundreds of miles in search of more luxurious retreats. They found them in the grander highlands of the Blue Ridge Mountains in North Carolina and Tennessee and down in Florida where men like Henry Flagler were transforming mangrove swamps and salt marshes into palatial resorts and rococo palaces for the rich. Thus, by Roosevelt's day, many of the cabins around the old Meriwether Inn, never lavish and still without most modern conveniences, had fallen into disrepair. So had the inn, whose weathered exterior appeared to be in rapid retrograde from Victorian to Gothic to Byzantine. Some years earlier, the property had passed into the hands of Davis's niece, Georgia Wilkins of Columbus, who had sold it to George Foster Peabody, the New York banker and railroad magnate who had been born in Columbus. Peabody had largely lost interest in the spa as a tourist attraction, yet it was he who got word to Franklin Roosevelt, stricken with polio in 1921, of the alleged curative powers of the springs. Roosevelt, whose leg muscles were almost completely atrophied and had showed no improvement despite three years of therapy, was desperate for help from any quarter. He arrived on October 3, 1924, stayed until October 20, and fell under the spell of the place. Two years later he bought the inn and the rest of the property around the old spa from Peabody for $200,000.

Over the course of the next twenty years, Roosevelt's incredible energy was to transform the largely forgotten, dilapidated, backwater little mountain spa into an internationally renowned foundation for the treatment of infantile paralysis. And Warm Springs, Georgia, whose name was changed from Bullochville the year Roosevelt arrived, became known around the world as the site of the Little White House, FDR's own rustic retreat where, say those who knew him well, he spent many of his happiest and most productive days and where he was to suffer a cerebral hemorrhage and breathe his last on April 12, 1945.

In his early years at Warm Springs, particularly before he was elected president in 1932, Roosevelt spent much of his time exercising in the spring-fed pool and developing his plans for turning the site of the old Meriwether Inn into an institute for the treatment of polio. For

Franklin Delano Roosevelt at Warm Springs

recreation, he liked nothing better than to go dashing about the rough mountain roads in a Ford roadster, especially equipped with hand controls, flashing his famous smile and bawling out "Hi ya, neighbor!" to total strangers, stopping to speak with any farmer, field hand, or townsman he encountered on the way, swapping jokes and stories and, whenever he found himself in an area known as "The Cove," indulging in a sip or two of the excellent, locally twisted moonshine. To this day, he is remembered fondly, even reverently, by locals, to whom he was part friend, part father figure, and, because of the role he played in pulling the South out of the depression, part savior as well. The affection is particularly strong among older farming people and retired textile workers, who, while Roosevelt was president, wrote him thousands of personal letters and showered him with gifts, including hams and fowl, homemade pies, cakes and jams, curious folk objects of every description and, especially, handmade walking canes. The late Ruth Stevens, who operated the old Warm Springs Hotel during the town's heyday, wrote in her reminiscences of the period that when Roosevelt was elected president in 1932, a poor dirt farmer walked barefoot all the way from Gadsden, Alabama, to Warm Springs, a distance of more than a hundred miles, to bring him a country ham.

"You know, he (FDR) admired people that wore blue jeans," recalls eighty-six-year-old Reuben Bridges, a Cove resident and guitar picker who often accompanied fiddler Bun Wright, a Roosevelt favorite, when he played for the president. "Roosevelt was the poor man's friend. He would stop on the side of the road and talk to people who were plowing if they was wearing overalls. . . . He had time for everybody. He took people off starvation wages and long hours. . . . This country was in a helluva fix when he come along!"

On autumn afternoons, Roosevelt particularly liked to take a shaker of martinis and a few agreeable companions to picnic at a favorite spot on the south side of Pine Mountain known as Dowdell's Knob. From an elevation of thirteen hundred feet, Dowdell's Knob overlooks Pine Mountain Valley, originally known as Valley Plains or the Valley of Hope. The future president of the United States favored the place so much he had a barbecue pit built there so he and his guests could enjoy the view while their steaks or hamburgers were sizzling over hot coals. On any halfway decent day Oak Mountain was visible across the valley, and on dark nights, the lights of the mill town of Manchester glowed in the east, as did, with less certainty, the lights of the little crossroads community of Shiloh, gathered around a cotton gin and Slaughter's Country Store to the south, and the kerosene lanterns in the dwellings of the black tenant farmers and sharecroppers scattered across the valley below.

Under the influence of the martinis, Roosevelt often grew expansive. Sometimes he wondered aloud why there were not more farmers homesteading in the valley. Often, when his companions were male, he told risque jokes and stories. Less frequently, he talked politics: His famous 1932 Oglethorpe University commencement speech calling for "bold persistent experimentation" to solve the nation's economic and social problems had its germination on Dowdell's Knob. On other occasions he would show off his knowledge of local history by telling his guests about old man Lewis Dowdell, the cotton planter who, along with his brother, James, used to own much of Pine Mountain Valley in the days before the Civil War.

"You see that flat rock right over there on the edge?" he asked a guest on one such occasion. "That's where old man Dowdell used to stand on a Sunday morning, whip in one hand and a Bible in the other, preaching the gospel to his slaves and making sure that their attention didn't wander. The congregation were in position on the slope there, to look up at Mr. Dowdell and beyond him at the Lord Himself—though Mr. Dowdell might have been somewhat in the way!"

FDR is long gone now, of course, as are planter Dowdell and all his chattel. Bun Wright died several years ago, and Reuben Bridges says arthritis has so crippled his hands he can't really play anymore. And, in truth, there are fewer and fewer people left in the surrounding countryside who really knew Roosevelt at Warm Springs. Yet Dowdell's Knob still is a beautiful spot for a picnic—it can be downright magical on a moonlit summer's night—and an excellent vantage point from which first-time visitors to West Central Georgia can orient themselves to the region.

For the completely uninitiated, West Central Georgia in this essay consists of twenty mostly rural counties, bisected by the fall line and about evenly divided between Piedmont and Coastal Plain, bounded on the north and south by the upper and lower limits of the old Black Belt, on the west by the Chattahoochee River, and on the east by the Flint River and its watershed. From Dowdell's Knob, the viewer looks down on the land between the two rivers toward the fall line on the extreme limits of the southern horizon. Although much of the region is flat, there are rolling hills both above and below the fall line, in addition to a number of high ridges—none exceeding fifteen hundred feet in height—such as Pine and Oak Mountains. The soil tends to be clay-based above the fall line and sandy below except in the river and creek bottoms where it is customarily dark and rich, with humus a foot or more thick. The dominant trees are pines, oaks, hickories (including pecans), sweetgums, sycamores, and poplars. River birches and cottonwoods line the banks of many of the larger streams. Gums and cypress are the most prevalent trees in the swamps. Pine and saw palmettoes dot the more open areas of the Coastal Plain. It is not a spectacularly beautiful area of the state. There are no Marshes of Glynn or Okefenokee Swamp, no body of water to compare with the Atlantic Ocean or Sapelo Sound, no scenic drive providing vistas quite so stunning as North Georgia's Richard Russell Highway. Yet West Central Georgia has a subtle, perhaps more subjective beauty composed of many individual elements—the dogwood's burst of white amid the greening foliage of the spring forest, the pleasing proportions of the gently rolling landscape, the stark silhouette of a crumbling chimney marking an old cabin site, the way the West Georgia sun can burnish a field of broomsedge until it appears to be on fire, the keening of a cicada on a hot summer day, the sharp, unmistakable smell of pine smoke in the winter air—that tend to accumulate in the memory and gather in the heart where they form a mosaic of genuine beauty. But beware: This is the Deep South, and the sun is a palpable reality most of the year. Spring comes in March; by June it is full summer; and in late July and early August, when the temperature reaches a hundred degrees, the sun burns in the sky with the intensity of a cardinal sin. Winters, however, are usually mild, and there can be long, lovely springs and autumns. Rainfall is moderate, coming mainly in the winter and during the dog day afternoons of summer. Consequently, it is an ideal environment in which to grow peanuts, peaches and, of course, cotton. It is not a particularly forgiving land, as many a farmer has found out, and, God knows, it has extracted more than its share of revenge from those who presumed to make a living off it. Yet there is a local saying that if you stay on the land long enough, it sticks in the mind; if you stay too long, it sticks in the heart.

It is really a land of riverine and creek bottom cultures, initially organized around the Chattahoochee and Flint Rivers and the rich

Peach blossoms

bottomlands of the floodplains. It is also a region of two states, not one, since for most of its western part the Chattahoochee River is the boundary between Georgia and Alabama. In fact, in many ways east Alabama has more in common with those west Georgia counties that line the Chattahoochee—in history, folklore, manners, lifestyle, economy, and language—than the latter have with the rest of West Central Georgia, particularly with those counties drained by the Flint River and its tributaries. Both river basins were extremely isolated throughout much of their history, and although too much can be made of their differences, each has—or had prior to the Age of Television and the Los Angelization of America—a distinct culture of its own.

The rivers themselves are markedly different in appearance and feel. Although the Chattahoochee has its origins in the mountains of North Georgia, in West Central Georgia it appears to be a child of the Lower Piedmont and the Coastal Plain. Its waters are usually deep, sluggish, and stained red by the clay found along its banks. Catfish abound in its depths, and alligators sun on its shores below the fall line at Columbus. Somehow it seems almost natural for its waters to be dammed into a series of impoundments, the largest of which in West Central Georgia is West Point Lake, 25,900 acres of submerged woodlands and old creek beds whose waters beckon to sailors and water skiers and are prime habitat for lunker largemouth bass. The Flint, on the other hand, is shallow and filled with rapids throughout much of its passage through the region, a wild, free river that is a favorite of whitewater canoeists. Although it has its origins in the upper Piedmont, it seems the more transmountain of the two rivers, perhaps because of its passage through the area known as the Cove and the high granite ridges of the eastern extensions of Pine and Oak Mountains. Despite the fact that West Central Georgia has a rich frontier history that lasted for at least 250 years and an archaeological record of Indian occupation that goes back 12,000 years, it was the presence of the rich, virgin bottomland soils of the Chattahoochee and Flint basins, plus the sudden availability of the land consequent upon the removal of the Creek Indians from the area following two treaties signed at Indian Springs in 1821 and 1826, that drew the first real wave of English-speaking settlers into the region. These settlers and their descendants gave West Central Georgia much of the character it bears today.

In the old days, residents of the area were quite proud of the democratic way in which the land was distributed, and there probably is something to the contention, once popular in these parts, that West Central Georgia was initially peopled by the common man, ordinary frontier folk who acquired their property in 202 1/2-acre lots in the state land lotteries of 1821 and 1827. Almost any white person who had lived in Georgia for three years was eligible for at least one draw in these lotteries. A family man with children got two draws, as did a family of three or more minor orphans and a widow whose husband was killed or died in the Revolutionary War, the War of 1812, or an Indian war. An orphan whose father died in the same way also got two draws. In the lottery of 1827, veterans of the Revolutionary War got two draws as did wounded or disabled veterans of the War of 1812 or an Indian war. Most of these early nineteenth-century settlers were Anglo-American whose immediate origin was the Carolinas or Virginia and whose ancestors hailed from southern England. But there were also many Scots and Irish and a few Germans among the hardy folk who followed the old Indian trails and trading paths westward out of Augusta into the wilderness of the Georgia frontier. Most of the settlers had names like Gray, Walker, Nichol, Robinson, Wellborn, Webster, Calhoun, and Fleming, but there was an occasional Duncan or McKnight or McDades or McCoy, as well as Urquhart or Zaigler or Amos. Four of the counties they helped populate were formed by the Georgia legislature after the 1821 treaty, including Monroe (1821), Crawford and Pike (1822), and Upson (1824). Seven were formed after the second Treaty of Indian Springs in 1825, as Coweta, Muscogee, and Troup (1826); and Harris, Marion, Meriwether, and Talbot (1827). Others were formed later from existing counties, as Chattahoochee (from Muscogee and Randolph Counties in 1854), Heard (from Carroll, Troup, and Coweta in 1830), Macon (from Dooly, Houston, Lee, and Muscogee in 1837), Schley (from Macon, Marion, and Sumter in 1857), Stewart (from Randolph in 1830), Sumter (from Lee in 1831), Taylor (from Crawford, Talbot, Macon, Marion, and Monroe in 1852), and Webster (from Randolph in 1856). One, Lamar, was not formed until 1920. Some of the counties—Chattahoochee, Coweta, Muscogee—were given American Indian names, but most were named for well-known Georgians, Indian fighters, or heroes of the American Revolution.

Most of the early settlers brought with them one dream, independence on their own land; one idea, cotton; and one book, the Bible, which, although many of them could not read, still formed the bedrock of all their beliefs about both this world and the hereafter. They wasted no time clearing the wilderness and putting the land to the plow. Ever since Eli Whitney had invented the cotton gin in 1793, making short staple cotton a practical commercial crop, there had existed among the frontier people of the Carolinas and Georgia a perfect mania to acquire the farm lands of West Central Georgia. Cotton and Christ, the dual divinities of the Deep South, contended from the first for the ultimate allegiance of the people. Churches were often formed even before the ground was cleared for the simple huts the people were to live in. They gave them names born of their dreams, as Prosperity and Pilgrim's Rest and Hopewell and Sweet Home and Welcome; and then, as the wilderness was gradually pushed back, New Hope, New Free Run, New Harmony, New Fellowship, New Friendship, New Macedonia, New Providence, New Salem, New Philip, New St. Mathis, New Lebanon, New Corinth, and even New Kovent.

Although it is arguable whether cotton followed Christ or Christ followed cotton into the region, there are accounts of creek bottoms being cleared and cotton seed going into the ground even before the Creek Indians had abandoned the land or the settlers themselves had paused long enough in their frenzy to erect a roof over their heads. The counties formed after the 1821 lottery would have produced the first cotton crops, but those on the Chattahoochee were not far behind. The first cotton was sold in Columbus in November 1828, the year the city was founded, and that same year four hundred bales of cotton were shipped by steamer downriver from Columbus to Apalachicola on the Gulf of Mexico. If it was Christ who animated the people's spiritual life and ruled their Sundays, cotton occupied their dreams and drove them the rest of the week.

Initially the settlers brought only a few slaves with them, but in no time at all there were almost as many African Americans in the region as whites. By 1840, every county in West Central Georgia had more than 1,000 slaves and some had many more. Troup County, for example, had 7,051 slaves in that year; Harris had 6,451; Muscogee, 4,760; Stewart, 4,759; Talbot, 6,766; and Meriwether, 5,407. By 1860, thirty-five years after the Indian lands were opened to settlement, the population of every county in the region was at least half slave. Farm production kept pace. By 1850, every county in the region was producing more than 5,000 bales of cotton annually. Some—Stewart,

Harris, Troup, Meriwether, Talbot, and Monroe—produced in excess of 10,000 bales. Stewart County, formerly one of the wilder and more remote areas of the state—Creek Indians attacked and burned the town of Roanoke there in 1836—produced 19,165 bales of ginned cotton in 1850, second only to Burke County in all of Georgia.

Towns, many of them located on rivers and streams so as to take advantage of the potential water power and for ease of transportation, followed rapidly in the wake of the first settlers. The dates the major towns were founded show how quickly the area was settled after Indian removal: Forsyth, 1823; Thomaston, 1825; Columbus, Newnan, and LaGrange, 1828; West Point, 1829; Lumpkin, 1830; Americus, 1832. With the towns came banks, mercantile establishments, warehouses, and textile factories.

Although there was some resistance in other parts of Georgia and throughout the South to the "odious system" of cotton manufacturing, as the editor of the *Charlestown Mercury* described it in 1829, this was not the case in West Central Georgia. Thomaston got its first two textile mills, Franklin Factory and New Providence Factory, in 1834. Others followed in the Thomaston area, including, in 1841, George P. Swift's Waynmanville Cotton Mill, well known in the antebellum South for the quality of its manufactures. In Troup County, the first textile mill was Robertson Woolen Mill, built in 1847 on Turkey Creek in the Oak Grove Community. The Troup Factory on Flat Shoals Creek went into the textile business in 1848. Columbus, located at the falls of the Chattahoochee and destined to become one of the largest textile centers in the South, got its first mill, the Columbus Factory, in 1838. In 1844 came the Coweta Falls Factory, and two years later, Variety Mills. In 1848, the Howard Factory began operation in Columbus. Two years later, William H. Young, a native New Yorker, began the Eagle Mill, which was to absorb the Howard Factory in 1860 and become one of the largest textile mills in the South. By the time of the Civil War, Columbus was second only to Richmond in textile manufacturing in the South.

Because it was located at the head of navigation on the Chattahoochee, Columbus also quickly became the major inland shipping port and commercial center for west Georgia and east Alabama. Planters and farmers from all over the region brought their cotton to Columbus to sell, and while they were in town, they took the opportunity to resupply their farming operations with groceries, bagging, tools, harness, mules, and slaves. Cotton brokers and commission merchants made Columbus their home base, and by 1845 the city was regularly receiving well in excess of fifty thousand bales of cotton a year (after 1850, this figure jumped to eighty thousand or more bales annually). The bulk of this cotton that was not consumed by the local mills was shipped by paddlewheel steamboat downriver to Apalachicola, from whence it was shipped to New York, Boston, Liverpool, Le Havre, and many other domestic and foreign ports. Throughout the antebellum era, more than a dozen steamboats called regularly at Columbus's old steamboat wharf, which is still in existence.

It would be difficult indeed to exaggerate the hold cotton once had on the lives and imaginations of the people of the region. The profits to be made from a successful cotton plantation were immense for the time and would be substantial today. Textile mills, once established, were even more profitable and, with an infusion of northern capital and know-how, had begun to create an industrial elite in West Central Georgia long before the Civil War. The availability of good cotton land, especially in the upper Coastal Plain and across the river in Alabama, the location of the mills so close to the fields, and a ready mode of transportation via the Chattahoochee River to domestic and foreign markets fixed upon the region an economy and a way of life based largely on cotton. In antebellum times, cotton culture— meaning the planting, cultivation, harvesting, weighing, marketing, warehousing, insuring, brokering, spinning, weaving, and shipping of cotton—was less a way of earning a living than it was a way of life, less a profession or a series of interdependent professions than a disease that infected almost everyone who came into contact with it. And in West Central Georgia, sooner or later, everyone came into contact with it.

The cause of the disease was greed, or, if you prefer, the desire for greater profits. Otherwise moral and upright men and women, pillars in the church and well-beloved of their children and neighbors, thought nothing of enslaving thousands of other human beings, including women and children, on the chance that this year's cotton crop would turn a profit. It wasn't just enslaved Africans and their descendants, however, who were bound to cotton. Ordinary farm folk organized their entire lives around cotton. They went to school in the colder months when they were not needed in the fields to plant, hoe, or pick cotton. They got married in winter or quickly in late July or early August during laying-by time when everything that could be done for the crop had been done. They wore cotton on their backs and next to their bodies. If they died anytime except when the crop had been laid by or after it was picked, their body might be committed to the earth, local wags liked to say, but a proper funeral for their souls would have to wait. Throughout the day and half the night they talked cotton, dreamed cotton, breathed cotton (literally, since cotton lint floated in the air anytime after picking began until the first hard winter rain), and assumed everyone else did the same. They raised a civilization based on cotton and cheap labor, whether slave or free, that existed for the benefit of the lucky, privileged few, but that had the singular advantage—and disadvantage—of affording everyone, white or black, slave or free, male or female, a fixed, well-defined role to play in society. However menial and unremunerative that role, cotton imposed an order on the lives of men that was, for most of them, the only order they had ever known.

The structure of that well-ordered society was patriarchal and paternalistic in the extreme, beginning in the fields with the planter at the top and descending through the small but successful independent cotton farmers to overseers, white artisans, freedmen, and slaves. Mill owners and planters were rough social equals, although planters far outnumbered mill owners in antebellum days. The pecking order was rigidly immobile. Those at the top, planters, were accorded a degree of deference, respect, envy, and resentment such as the English usually reserve for lords of the realm, and they functioned similarly in southern society. According to the October 19, 1841, edition of the *Columbus Enquirer,* planters possessed "magic influence" and could "convert the dullness and solitude of a half-deserted city" into a "bustling, lively, animated" place. "The planter," rhapsodized the paper's editor, "is decidedly the greatest personage in all creation. But for him, the world would positively go into stagnation."

If the planters were the greatest personages in all creation, then slaves were the lowliest. Trapped in a social system that dismissed them as subhuman and an economic system that viewed them as beasts of burden or brood mares for the propagation of more chattel, slaves toiled from can to can't, from first light to dark, with virtually no hope of bettering their station in life. They did almost all the actual work on the plantations and farms, from planting, hoeing, and picking cotton to building wagons and shoeing horses and mules. Many of them became highly skilled artisans periodically rented out by their owners to other cotton farmers or to businesses and families in the towns. A very few, through raw talent, sheer will, and luck, even managed to escape the slave system. Bridge-builder Horace King and the musician Blind Tom Wiggins were two such individuals from this area. But most slaves saw only the underside of the Cotton Kingdom, and it is no surprise that their memory of the experience is the mirror reverse of that propagated by southern romanticists and apologists for slavery.

Yet it is a fact that many residents of West Central Georgia are still proud of the role the region played in the Civil War. Virtually every major city or town of any size sent hordes of young men off to fight. And fight they did, from Manassas to Appomattox. Today, you may see their graves scattered throughout the countryside and in the towns. But West Central Georgia supplied more than men to the Confederate war effort. Small industrialists in Forsyth made shoes, harnesses, tin cups, and even whiskey for the Confederate cause. West Point was an important warehouse and railroad shipping point. Thomaston was a textile manufacturing center for the Confederacy. So was Columbus, whose population doubled during the war because of the numerous war industries located in the city.

By 1860 Columbus was the largest manufacturing—not just textile—center south of Richmond. It boasted a paper mill, cotton gin manufacturer, furniture factory, and several iron factories. During the war, many of these industries turned to the manufacture of material for the Confederate war effort. Some converted to an entirely different type of product. The textile mills turned out cotton duck for tents, gray tweed for uniforms, even Indian rubber cloth and rope for the military. Other wartime entrepreneurs in Columbus produced tents, military caps, gun carriages, shoes, tailored uniforms, weapons, and ammunition. Former tinsmiths Louis Haiman and Brothers became the largest manufacturer of swords in the Confederacy, and they also issued serviceable copies of the Colt Navy pistol. J. P. Murray and John Grey produced excellent rifles. The Columbus Iron Works turned out heavy ordnance, including cannons and mortars, and after it had been leased by the Confederate government, produced steam engines for gunboats, iron fittings, boilers, and other heavy machinery. By the middle of 1862, the Confederate Ordnance Department established the Columbus Arsenal, which fabricated knapsacks and harnesses and eventually took over the manufacture of cannons and ammunition within the city. Columbus even had a Confederate Navy Yard, which built and equipped the gunboat *Chattahoochee* and the ram *Muscogee*, both of which were destroyed by federal troops in 1865. Columbus, with Richmond and Augusta, supplied a huge amount of war goods to the Confederacy.

Because of its isolation, most of West Central Georgia went almost untouched by actual combat in the Civil War until the very last days. For this same reason, Forsyth, Barnesville, Newnan, LaGrange, and Columbus were all major Confederate hospital and convalescence centers where wounded and ill men in both armies received compassionate medical treatment and long-term care. Each of these towns has a hoary tradition connected with some wounded soldier or sainted nurse in the hospitals, but none is better known or more revered in the lore from that war than the young man portrayed in a poem written by Dr. Francis Orray Ticknor, chief surgeon in the largest of the Confederate convalescent centers in Columbus. "Little Giffen of Tennessee," Ticknor's sentimental tribute to a wounded Confederate youth, was once a popular feature of memorial observances across the South, and at one point in the not-too-distant-past, many a southern school child—many a *white* southern school child, that is—could recite it from memory. It began:

> Out of the focal and foremost fire,
> Out of the hospital walls as dire,

Smitten of grape-shot and gangrene,
(Eighteenth battle, and he sixteen!)
Specter! such as you seldom see,
Little Giffen, of Tennessee!

Although there were occasional raids into West Central Georgia by Union cavalry during the war, the only significant fighting took place at the war's end—actually, after the war was over. On April 16, 1865, fully a week after Appomattox, Maj. Gen. James H. Wilson led thirteen thousand cavalry troopers in an assault on Columbus and West Point. Columbus fell with only moderate losses on both sides, but seventy-six men died defending or assaulting Fort Tyler in West Point. The Union troops put all the war industries in Columbus and West Point—the textile mills, warehouses, and foundries, plus thousands of bales of cotton—to the torch. Word of Lee's surrender still had not reached Wilson on April 19 when some of his forces engaged Confederates in Monroe County at the Battle of Culloden, the last fighting in West Central Georgia.

Although the formal hostilities were ended, the war continued to be fought, in spirit, for many years thereafter. Members of the Soldiers' Aid Society in Columbus first observed Confederate Memorial Day on April 26, 1866, and in 1868 there occurred in Columbus one of the more celebrated incidents of the Reconstruction era. George W. Ashburn, a former overseer turned radical reformer after the war, was murdered by members of a masked mob of white men who burst into his sleeping quarters on the night of March 30 and shot him thirteen times. Georgia was still under U.S. military rule after the war, and the murder caused a sensation. It was widely covered by the northern press, including the *New York Times* and Horace Greeley's *New York Tribune*.

Greeley was incensed by the crime, which he interpreted as a political murder intended to show that Georgia in general and the people of Columbus in particular refused to admit defeat or conform to the requirements of the Reconstruction Acts of 1867. Those acts had cut the South up into five military districts and made the district commanders responsible for establishing new state constitutions that would meet the requirements of Congress for full readmission of the southern states into the Union. The heart of the requirements was contained in the Fourteenth Amendment, which guaranteed the civil rights of African Americans and gave them the ballot. Its adoption by state legislatures was mandatory before the southern states could send representatives to Congress and gain full readmission.

Georgia, with her other sister southern states, had just rejected the amendment. Moreover, only a year earlier Georgia had gone through a bitterly contested election, ordered by the U.S. military, to name delegates to a convention to draw up a new state constitution. For the first time, freedmen had registered in great numbers and cast their ballots in support of the delegates of the Radical Party, mainly Republican in character, sympathetic toward the North and opposed to the old leaders who had ruled Georgia prior to the war. The old leaders aligned themselves with the Conservative Party and were, almost without exception, Democrats. The Radical Party swept the elections, and their delegates dominated the constitutional convention that followed. Ashburn had been one of these delegates, which made him the target of widespread animosity from whites throughout the state. He was despised by the white population of Columbus and considered the lowest form of humanity imaginable—a scalawag, that is, a native white southerner who claimed sympathy with the Yankee cause for his own personal aggrandizement.

On April 6, U.S. military authorities in Columbus arrested thirteen well-known citizens of the town, released them on bond a few days later, and then arrested twenty-two persons. Nine men were finally accused of the murder and tried before a military court in Atlanta at Fort McPherson. Among those accused of Ashburn's murder were the county physician, a wharf manager, a prominent merchant, two policemen, a deputy marshal, and three men very active in the Democratic Party. The substance of the government's case was that Ashburn's murder was planned and carried out by the accused, all Democrats and Conservatives, to rid the city of Ashburn, whom they considered a pestilential influence among the black people of the city. The defense, led by Alexander Stephens, former vice president of the Confederacy, attacked the credibility of the witnesses and claimed subornation and intimidation of several key witnesses.

The trial began on June 29, but before a verdict had been reached, it was abruptly terminated on July 24 on order of Gen. George Meade, commander of the U.S. Third Military District, which included Georgia. Three days earlier, the Georgia legislature had voted to adopt the Fourteenth Amendment, which, in effect, returned Georgia to civilian rule. The nine accused men were released and returned to heroes' welcomes in Columbus. Many people have speculated that there was some sort of secret agreement between federal authorities and the state's leaders to drop the prosecution in exchange for passage of the amendment, but such a theory has never been proved.

Feelings about the Civil War run high in Columbus and throughout West Central Georgia even today. Sons of Confederate Veterans, Civil War roundtables, and reenactors abound. Monuments to the Confederacy stand in almost every courthouse square in the region. Many of the monuments are granite or marble columns, some topped by a soldier facing north—toward the enemy. Their inscriptions, often composed or commissioned by members of the United Daughters of the Confederacy, are customarily unreconstructed and as defiant as a rebel yell. They still have the power to shock the uninitiated: "'Sons Of The Choicest Strain Of American Blood, Scions Of Revolutionary Stock, Citizens Of The Purest Section Of This Union' They Lived True To Every Honorable Tradition That Illuminates The Pages Of Our History And At The Call Of Duty They Laid Down Their Lives A Noble Sacrifice On The Altar Of Their Country." So says a monument, in Ellaville in Schley County, erected in 1910 by the Sarah E. Hornady chapter of the UDC.

The one in the historic district of Columbus is scarcely less defiant: "Erected By The Ladies Of The Memorial Association, May, 1879, To Honor The Confederate Soldiers Who Died To Repel Unconstitutional Invasion To Protect The Rights Reserved To The People And To Perpetuate Forever The Sovereignty Of The States."

The granddaddy of them all, however, is undoubtedly the monument in tiny Andersonville, practically in sight of the infamous prison where forty-five thousand Union soldiers were imprisoned and thirteen thousand died. Dedicated to the memory of Capt. Henry Wirz, who was executed by the United States for inhumanity and extreme cruelty (the actual charge was "murder") as keeper of the prison during the Civil War, the granite obelisk was unveiled in May 1909. Its inscriptions read, in part:

> In memory of Captain Henry Wirz, C.S.A. Born Zurich, Switzerland, 1822. Sentenced to death and executed at Washington, D.C., Nov. 10, 1865.
> 'To rescue his name from the stigma attached to it by embittered prejudice, this shaft is erected by the Georgia Division, United Daughters of the Confederacy.'
> Discharging his duty with such humanity as the harsh circumstances of the times, and the policy of the foe permitted, Captain Wirz became at last the victim of a misdirected popular clamor.
> He was arrested in time of peace, while under the protection of a parole, tried by a military commission of a service to which he did not belong and condemned to ignominious death on charges of excessive cruelty to Federal prisoners. He indignantly spurned a pardon, proffered on condition that he would incriminate President Davis and thus exonerate himself from charges of which both were innocent.

Then comes a quote from Ulysses S. Grant, meant to show that it was the Union's decision not to exchange prisoners that caused the inhumane conditions at Andersonville, followed by a quote from Jefferson Davis: "When time shall have softened passion and prejudice,

Andersonville National Cemetery's Georgia Monument, dedicated in 1976. Jimmy Carter headed the commission that obtained the memorial to all prisoners of war.

when reason shall have stripped the mask of misrepresentation, then justice, holding even her scales, will require much of past censure and praise to change places."

The reader is invited to visit the site of Andersonville Prison across the way, with its row on row of white headstones in the green grass and great gaping space where the prison was located, before deciding how much of history will require "past censure and praise to change places." Andersonville is one of a handful of special places in America—Independence Hall, Mount Vernon, Gettysburg, the Lincoln Memorial—that seem to reach out and arrest even the most jaundiced traveler. The best time to go is in the spring when life is renewing itself all around and the dogwoods look like gigantic cotton bolls in the surrounding woods. The worst time, for those travelers sensitive to the voices of the past, is the fall, particularly on a clear, cold day in November when acorns crunch underfoot and the wind makes a melancholy soughing through the crowns of the trees, scaling dry leaves like rain over the grass to tick against the gravestones of the only soldiers who ever longed for reveille—dead ones.

Many people mistakenly think the Cotton Kingdom died with the Civil War and the end of slavery or during Reconstruction. On the contrary, if anything cotton became even more fixed on the South after the war. Reconstruction, which was officially over in Georgia in 1871, really had little effect on the cotton system. The Panic of 1873, however, forced many smaller industries in West Georgia to go out of business. This failure was especially true in Columbus, where a promising and diversified industrial base, including many industries spawned by the war, collapsed for lack of capital. As a result, the textile industry, which was relatively recession proof and had the capital to survive hard times, emerged as practically the only manufacturing industry, other than metalworking, of any size. New and imposing textile operations, some of them many times larger than the largest of the antebellum cotton mills, went up in Columbus, West Point, Thomaston, LaGrange, Hogansville, Newnan, and elsewhere around the region.

The cotton industry was established in Coweta County at Lodi in 1866 with the opening of the Willcoxen Manufacturing Company. The Newnan Cotton Mill was organized in 1888, and the Grantville Mill in 1896. The huge Thomaston Mills, which now operates seven divisions, went into business in 1899, and Martha Mills in 1927. Columbus boomed after the war, beginning with George P. Swift's Muscogee Manufacturing Company, which went into business in 1867 and added new mills in 1882, 1887, 1904, and 1926. In 1869, the old Eagle Mill, burned by Wilson's Raiders, was refinanced, rebuilt, and reopened as the Eagle & Phenix [sic] Mills, one of the largest textile mills in the South. It expanded in 1869 and again in 1876. Then came Swift Manufacturing Company in 1887, Paragon Mills in 1888, and Columbus Manufacturing Company in 1899. In 1912 this latter concern expanded and, in 1920, built its own mill village. Bibb Manufacturing Company opened in north Columbus in 1900 and shortly became an enormous operation, with more spindles under one roof— and more roof—than any other mill in the United States. In 1937 Bibb incorporated its own town, Bibb City, which today remains a separate governmental entity within the city limits of Columbus. Swift Spinning Mills went into business in 1906, followed by Georgia Webbing & Tape in 1927 and Perkins Hosiery Mills ten years later. By the 1940s, there were nine major textile mills in Columbus, and at least a quarter of the city's workers were employed in textile manufacturing.

LaGrange also experienced an explosion in textile manufacturing following the war, especially in the 1880s and at the turn of the century. In 1888, LaGrange Mills was organized, followed by Dixie Mills in 1895, Unity Cotton Mills in 1900, Elm City Cotton Mills in 1905, Dunson Mills in 1910, and Hillside Mills in 1915. The Callaway family's first involvement in the textile industry in LaGrange began in 1900 when Fuller Callaway invested ten thousand dollars in the new Unity plant. Within two decades, he was to become heavily involved in building, managing, and financing numerous mills, and Callaway Mills became a mammoth operation that was continued and expanded by his sons after his death.

The story was much the same in West Point, where the Alabama and Georgia Manufacturing Company was established in 1869, becoming in 1880 the West Point Manufacturing Company, one of the really massive textile operations in the Chattahoochee River Valley. Eventually, West Point Manufacturing included two plants in LaGrange and an operation in the Alabama towns of Lanett, Valley, River-dale, Langdale, Shawmut, and Fairfax. In 1965, West Point Manufacturing merged with Pepperell Mills to become West Point–Pepperell. Tiny Forsyth got into the act when the Trio Manufacturing Company was established in 1899, followed by the Forsyth Cotton Mill in 1915. In 1958, the Bibb Company consolidated several Monroe County textile operations and continues in operation today.

These mills produced—and continue to produce—an amazing variety of products, including yarn, osnaburg cloth, duck, raw sheeting and fine sheets, thread, rope, apparel fabrics, tire cord, seat covers, towels, and denim, as well as providing such services as bleaching, dyeing, sanforizing, and hemming. Over the years, while the mills have changed ownership many times, they have provided employment to tens of thousands of West Georgians and contributed hundreds of millions of dollars annually to the region's economy.

The process was different out in the country, but the result was the same. Through a series of Black Codes and other legislative acts, the rural elite gradually reestablished control over the freedmen who remained in the farming areas. Control of the state legislature also enabled large landowners, including many of the same families that had operated plantations prior to the war, to gain sway of the region's poor white farmers. Both poor whites and the theoretically emancipated blacks soon became mired in a system of tenantry and sharecropping, enforced by a crop-lien system (highly favorable to landlords and supply merchant-bankers) that reduced farm labor to little more than peonage. Ordinary farmers became trapped in a system that demanded they plant the one crop, cotton, for which the landlord and the supply merchant, who often functioned as a sort of farm bank, could expect a ready market. Thus was the hegemony of cotton on the region's farms reaffirmed in short order. As a result, both the acreage devoted to the staple and the number of bales produced annually steadily increased in West Central Georgia from 1870 onward. In 1911, only two years before the boll weevil made its way into the state's western counties, a record crop of 2.8 million bales of cotton was produced in Georgia, much of it in the western counties of the Upper Coastal Plain and the Lower Piedmont.

It was during this period, and during the Great Depression that followed, that the rural landscape in West Central Georgia took on the appearance it has today. From around 1875 until 1925, by which time the boll weevil had wreaked its devastation on the region's cotton crop, virtually every acre of cleared and arable land in West Central Georgia was devoted to the cultivation of cotton, save for that space absolutely necessary for human and animal sustenance (a roof to sleep under, a hog pen, a patch of turnips or collards, a few rows of corn, maybe some oats) and the largely useless sand or rock ridges occupied by the towns. Interspersed between field and town were nu-

MILL VILLAGES

A Georgia historian describes the state's textile mill villages, owned by the mill and rented through withheld wages, as evidence of "industrial paternalism." The villages, often ascending hillsides in hierarchical order, progress from brick tenements to duplexes to single-family cottages to the homes of the foreman and superintendent near the peak of the hill. Built before the automobile was the transportation of the common man, all the dwellings were within walking distance of the mill and within hearing range of the whistle that summoned the workers at shift change. Few village homes were built after the 1920s, and by the 1940s mill owners were beginning to sell the houses to the workers, who did what they could to make the interiors more modern and the exteriors less uniform. Today, some mill villages in larger towns are an eclectic mixture of retired mill workers, their descendants, and young professional families seeking relatively economical, in-town housing.

—Jane Powers Weldon

merous crossroad communities, some of them with colorful names—
Possum Trot, Buzzard's Roost, Roosterville, Pobiddy Crossroad, Lick
Skillet, Devil's Half Acre, Bumphead, Hogcrawl Creek, Frog Bottom,
Dog Crossing, and Logtown—usually consisting of a railroad siding, a
gin house or two for cleaning and baling the cotton, a country store
(province of the merchant-banker who supplied and sometimes bankrolled the farmers), and perhaps a church, ordinarily Baptist but occasionally Methodist. For most of the farmers, home was usually a
plain, unpainted pine house, often no more than a shack, with cotton
planted right up to the door, but it might also be, for the more fortunate, a more substantial, two-story, four-room pine house, universally
called a cotton house in these parts, organized around a central open
breezeway in dog-trot fashion. Some of the well-to-do planters in the
region still owned white-columned mansions, just as their predecessors had in antebellum days, but more often than not, they retreated
to more palatial residences located in the larger towns and let a rural
agent farm out their land to tenants and sharecroppers.

The Civil War is long over now, of course, and traces of the Cotton
Kingdom in West Central Georgia have all but vanished. So, too,
have the people vanished from the farms. The boll weevil, the collapse of the cotton market (cotton fell from thirty-six cents a pound
in 1919 to sixteen cents a pound in 1920), and mechanization on the
farms, especially since World War II, have seen to that. One sees no
graves (Confederate or otherwise), no monuments, no gin houses or
cotton plantations, and no cotton mills from Dowdell's Knob today.
Manchester still glows on a dark night, just as it did in Roosevelt's
day, and Slaughter's Country Store still stands in Shiloh, although the
gin that used to be there and most of the other shops have long since
vanished. Except for a few houses and pastures for beef cattle, the
rest appears to be wilderness. For most of the year, Pine Mountain
Valley is a carpet of green, broken only here and there by the glimmer
of a man-made lake or a farmstead lost in the pines. Across the way,
Oak Mountain forms the last outpost of the Appalachians, its head
crossing the horizon toward the northeast, its southernmost reaches
dwindling, like the tail of some prehistoric beast, down through the
Piedmont toward the Fall Line and the Coastal Plain beyond.

For the first-time visitor to Dowdell's Knob, especially in summer,
the overwhelming impression is apt to be one of forest and unoccupied space. Humankind's hundred-year effort to create a cotton kingdom here, an elaborate and sophisticated enterprise involving thousands of enslaved men, women, and children, plus assorted overseers,
business managers, clerks, brokers, warehousemen, factors, bankers,
ginners, carpenters, blacksmiths, tenants, hoe help, sharecroppers,
shippers, common farmers, and planters, to say nothing of oxen and
mules and horses and machinery, has vanished almost without a

trace. It has weathered to a jumble of rotting boards and rusting iron and been swallowed by a fecund covering of slash pine and broomsedge and kudzu so that it would require a rural archaeologist, if there is any such creature, to locate and identify the remains. From Dowdell's Knob, West Central Georgia is forest.

To a great extent the impression is an illusion, of course. The region's primeval forest has long since disappeared, cut initially to make room for cotton and then replaced by pines grown for pulpwood or by suburban real estate developments, golf courses, and shopping malls where, today, the descendants of slaves and slaveowners, sharecroppers and hoe help, shop side by side in air conditioned comfort for lacy unmentionables in Victoria's Secret, buy designer jeans (the cotton for which was grown in India or China, the material sewn or "assembled" in Mexico, Korea, Taiwan, and Jamaica) at KMart and Wal-Mart, and consume kegs of imported beer in ersatz British pubs and German rathskellers. More than half a million people, 35 percent of whom are black and sizable numbers of whom are Hispanic or Asian, live in West Central Georgia. While most of these people are average folk who enjoy their anonymity and lead ordinary lives involving family, friends, job, and church, some are not. To name a few of the latter:

James Earl Carter, thirty-ninth president of the United States, just back (as of this writing) from successfully negotiating separate agreements between the United States and the governments of North Korea and Haiti, still lives in tiny Plains in Sumter County, where he is at work on his tenth book. Brig. Gen. Jay Hendrix, commandant at Fort Benning, one of the largest military installations in the world (basically for infantry training, Benning also includes the School of the Americas), is in daily contact with the Pentagon and maintains troops in instant readiness for assignment to trouble spots all over the world. Recently, these spots have included Haiti, Somalia, and the Persian Gulf. Michael W. Patrick, president and CEO of Carmike Cinemas in Columbus, oversees the second-largest motion picture theater chain in the United States, with more than nineteen hundred screens in thirty-one states. Millard Fuller, founder of Habitat for Humanity International in Americus, heads a nonprofit, ecumenical housing ministry with 1,092 affiliates in forty-four countries. Habitat has built more than thirty thousand homes in partnership with people in need.

Columbus's Dr. Jack Hughston, founder and leading light of Hughston Sports Medicine Hospital, is probably the best-known knee surgeon in the world, teacher, guru, and ringmaster to a team of orthopedic surgeons whose clients have included some of the world's most famous athletes, among them golfer Jack Nicklaus, Dominique Wilkins of the NBA, international tennis star Steffie Graff, and baseball's Roger Clemens. Howard "Bo" Callaway, former U.S. Secretary of the Army under Richard Nixon and one of the behind-the-scenes architects of the 1994 Republican takeover of Congress, has returned to Callaway Gardens Resort to assume control of the magnificent fourteen-thousand-acre recreation and entertainment complex on Pine Mountain that bears his family's name. Second District representative Sanford Bishop, a young African American lawyer, is the first member of his race to represent the city of Columbus and southwest Georgia in Congress.

The region also can boast of its share of business tycoons, past and present, among them LaGrange's Callaway family, textile magnates whose descendants have enriched the entire region through their efforts to improve the quality of life available to all; the late Robert W. Woodruff, architect of the Coca-Cola empire, who was born in Columbus (where the famous soft drink was actually developed by a local druggist named John Pemberton); the aforementioned George Foster Peabody, also a Columbus native; the Straus family, founders of Macy's, who hailed from Talbotton; and, in the present day, William B. Turner, who heads a family empire in Columbus that includes the W. C. Bradley Company and Synovus, this latter a huge banking and financial services concern with thirty-two banks in three states and assets of more than $6 billion. West Central Georgia has its share also of home-grown corporate giants—Columbus's AFLAC, founded by the late John Amos, is the second-largest writer of non-standard insurance in the world—and successful entrepreneurs who spend almost as much time in Charlotte and Chicago and New York and London as they do in their hometowns.

A list of nationally known artists, novelists, playwrights, journalists, movie producers, and musicians who have roots in West Central Georgia—Erskine Caldwell, Carson McCullers, Gertrude "Ma" Rainey, Lewis Grizzard, Alma Thomas, Chet Atkins, Alan Jackson, John Henrick Clarke, Nunnally Johnson, to name a few—would become tedious because of its length, as would a list of famous athletes—we must list baseball greats Frank Thomas, two-time American League most valuable player, a native of Columbus; Dale Murphy, two-time National league MVP, who lives in or near Grantville; and the immortal Josh Gibson, star of the old Negro Leagues and baseball's best catcher, who was born in Buena Vista. And there are enough well-known politicians, generals, evangelists, faith healers, horse thieves, and murderers with roots in West Central Georgia to staff a fair-sized banana republic.

In culinary matters, the area may be best known for its grits, barbecue joints, catfish houses, and down-home cooking, but it also has its French, Italian, German, and Asian restaurants, its sushi bars, and nouvelle cuisine emporiums. The region also has its symphonic orchestras, art galleries, opera houses, and legitimate theaters, including the beautiful old Springer Opera House, Georgia's State Theater, located in Columbus. Columbus College's Schwob School of Music is considered one of the best educational institutions for serious musicians in the South.

There are a surprising number of first-rate museums: the Columbus Museum, LaGrange's Chattahoochee Valley Art Museum, the National Prisoner of War Museum in Andersonville, the National Infantry Museum at Fort Benning (a gem), the Little White House in Warm Springs, and Jimmy Carter National Historic Site in Plains. Other collections include Columbus's Confederate Naval Museum, two hundred miles from the nearest salt water, and Lumpkin's Westville, a recreated but fiercely authentic 1850s Georgia village. Pasaquan in Marion County is the phantasmagorical compound of the late artist Eddie Owens Martin, who styled himself St EOM and converted his family farmhouse, as some critic has observed, into the world's greatest outdoor advertisement for Sherwin-Williams paint.

Stock-car racing and football are the top spectator sports in the region, but Callaway Gardens Resort also hosts an international steeplechase every November that draws crowds of horse lovers whose enthusiasm and stylish attire would not be out of place at Epsom Downs or Longchamps. Horses are celebrated, too, along with the traditions of the chase, at Ben Hurt Hardaway's Midland Hunt and at several hunt clubs in Coweta County. And, as befits a region that is home to Masters champion Larry Mize and many another top-flight golfer, there are hundreds of holes of golf throughout the area, including four championship courses at Callaway, site of the Buick Southern Open, a regular PGA tour event in the fall.

West Central Georgia is not all abandoned farm land, either. One of the cities of the region, Columbus, is one of the largest in Georgia, with an in-town population of 180,000, a metro population of more than 350,000, and ambitions characteristic of towns three or four times its size. Columbus is undergoing a sort of civic renaissance in its uptown area, with more than $200 million in capital building projects underway, among them a magnificent new Chattahoochee Riverwalk, civic center–coliseum, performing arts center, Challenger Center, Oxbow Meadows Nature Center complex, and downtown science and history museum. Once—despite its huge textile mill complex—one of Georgia's most isolated communities (it was not even on the interstate highway system until 1979), Columbus is also the venue of the 1996 Olympic Games women's fast-pitch softball competition, at the city's just-completed, state-of-the-art softball complex on the South Commons. Other cities in the region—Americus, LaGrange, Newnan, and Thomaston among them—have undergone a rebirth of civic spirit, often kindled by historic preservation projects, such as the magnificent restoration of the turn-of-the-century Windsor Hotel in Americus or Lumpkin's 1836 Bedingfield Inn.

Finally, for all its apparent bucolic isolation when seen from Dowdell's Knob, Pine Mountain Valley must be one of the most carefully scrutinized, endlessly blueprinted, frequently analyzed, photographed, mapped, and publicized pieces of real estate in North America. From 1935 to 1945 it was the scene of one of the New Deal's most heralded rural resettlement projects, Pine Mountain Valley Community, a twelve-thousand-acre pilot relief project of Harry Hopkins's Federal Emergency Relief Administration. As such, it was dear to Franklin Roosevelt's heart and to the hearts and dreams of a host of idealistic New Deal reformers and architects, who planned this rural Utopia in the piney woods of Georgia down to the last detail, including the race, age, sex, and character of the settlers. All of the latter were to be selected from grateful and enthusiastic unemployed Georgia industrial workers displaced by urban technology and eager to rebuild their lives in a rural environment.

The original plan called for three hundred homestead units of four to six rooms each arranged around a town square. Half these units were for subsistence only, and the other half consisted of enough acreage to make commercial farming practical (in theory, anyway). There were to be five decentralized work centers connected by a modern system of roads and quite a bit of other land reserved for recreation, forest, public use, and, particularly, large cooperative farms. The economic plan, which was so detailed it included projected family budgets, was based on both cooperative and specialized agriculture, with two principal staples, poultry and grapes. The poultry industry was to produce both eggs and broilers, and the grapes were to be scuppernongs, from which it was hoped a good, cheap wine could be made. And there were to be row crops and orchard crops and large cooperative dairies. The plan called for some of the row crops to be sold in a large roadside market strategically located at the entrance to the valley. A community center was designed to contain many shops, including a craft shop, and detailed plans were drawn up for a warehouse, garage, cannery, grist mill, and slaughterhouse. The school system was practically cradle to grave and promised progressive education at every level. Finally, a great deal of emphasis was placed on health. There were to be a community infirmary and regular visits from an altruistic physician who would put the welfare and health of the community above considerations of personal income.

All this grand design was committed to paper only after painfully detailed research in the valley. Indeed, there must not be a square inch in Pine Mountain Valley that has not been trod by the shiny shoes of some idealistic, dreamy-eyed, Washington-based New Deal bureaucrat, eager to build that city upon a hill that has been the fan-

Hog killing, a cold-weather ritual on the farm

tasy of American social reformers ever since the *Mayflower* touched these shores. The idea was to provide each carefully selected inhabitant of the community with "a full, free, happy social existence."

Alas, the reality, as so often happens, failed to live up to the fantasy. Many of the projected buildings, including the open-air market, the five decentralized work centers, and about ninety of the homestead units, were never built. The cooperative economy proved to be a failure. Many of the community's colonists felt themselves to be not living, breathing human beings but cogs in the wheels of a grand social design not much different from the industrial machinery that had allegedly driven them to relief. When quite a few colonists turned out to be embittered textile workers, some of whom had been locked out by the mills in which they once worked, constitutionally ill-suited for cooperative living and unfit for farm labor, there was trouble in paradise. It began with mass meetings and proceeded to angry confrontations with community officials, then escalated into threats of violence, pistol waving, barn burnings, and finally midnight lease jumping and forced evictions, all gleefully broadcast by Republican enemies of the New Deal and extensively reported in the press.

Ultimately, the community collapsed of its own weight and as a result of a congressional mandate ordering the Farm Security Administration, which had become responsible for its operation, to sell off all its experiments in cooperative farming. In the middle 1940s the homesteads and farms of Pine Mountain Valley Community passed into private ownership, where they remain today. Fifty years after the termination of the drama, little evidence of the planned community and its original occupants remains in the valley. In fact, today it is difficult to locate anyone who claims to remember much about it. The colonists' beautiful little church, designed by Roosevelt's architect, Henry Toombs, and dedicated to the president, survives, as do some of the original homes and streets—the latter bearing their wonderfully bureaucratic names, as A, B, C, D, etc.—but they are about all. Somehow it seems a sad and inadequate residue of so many lofty dreams. On the other hand, Pine Mountain Valley Community is a reminder that the colony of Georgia was at one time intended to be a utopian experiment, a colony composed of carefully selected "worthy poor" who were given a town lot, a nearby five-acre garden, and a forty-five-acre farm and told to plant mulberry trees and produce silk, wine, olive oil, dyes, and drugs for export to England.

But Pine Mountain Valley is not the only area in the vicinity of Dowdell's Knob that has known the glare of national publicity and the fine hand of social architects. Far from it. Franklin Roosevelt himself once owned twenty-seven hundred acres of farmland in Harris and Meriwether Counties, much of it located just behind the knob on the top of Pine Mountain. The Pine Mountain acreage became known as the Roosevelt Farm. Over the years, because its owner happened to be president of the United States, it received almost as much publicity as the resettlement community in the valley. It was largely an experimental enterprise, although some of its produce and beef went to help feed the patients and staff at the Warm Springs Foundation. Roosevelt was something of an agricultural dreamer himself, having been a member of the Grange in New York as a young man, and he sought to convince area farmers to diversify their crops and abandon their dependence on cotton. He urged them to plant pine trees on waste land and to try their hand at raising cattle, even making his own bull available to them to improve their stock. Many did follow his advice, although there is no documentation to show that their economic condition improved significantly as a result.

Roosevelt spent considerable time, money, and effort trying to make his own farm a profitable investment, but records indicate it never was. In fact, Roosevelt had to subsidize its operation throughout its existence, and he finally gave all of his Georgia land, including the farm, to the Warm Springs Foundation. Today, his old property is almost all grown up in pine trees.

Most of what was once the Roosevelt farm is now part of F. D. Roosevelt State Park on Pine Mountain, a beautiful, ten-thousand-acre public recreational area largely built by the Civilian Conservation Corps—another New Deal relief organization. A modern highway and a twenty-three-mile footpath, the Pine Mountain Trail, run the entire length of the park and offer visitors a chance to see and experience firsthand some of the sights that charmed FDR when he first visited the area.

Surprisingly, however, neither Pine Mountain Valley Community nor the Roosevelt Farm and State Park were the most extensively or successfully planned projects in the area. That laurel goes to Callaway Gardens Resort, located on the western end of the mountain in what used to be known as Mountain Creek Valley. The dream of textile magnate Cason J. Callaway and his wife, Virginia, Callaway Gardens is a horticulturist's and flower-lover's delight, fourteen thousand acres of woodlands, lakes, and wildlife cleverly landscaped to conceal the hand of the developer. In many ways, it is everything the owners of the old Meriwether Inn at Warm Springs dreamed their resort might have been. Callaway's John A. Sibley Horticultural Center features an incredible variety of plants, trees, and flowering shrubs in a man-made environment of great charm and beauty. It is a stunning place to visit in the spring and throughout most of the summer. Many people come back again and again just to breathe in the delightful perfume of the flowers or simply to enjoy the variety of vegetation. The Cecil B. Day Butterfly Center, the largest free-flight butterfly conservatory in North America, with more than a thousand species, draws visitors back repeatedly. The southern location for the PBS series *The Victory Garden*, Mr. Cason's Vegetable Garden, which has more than four hundred varieties of flowers, vegetables, herbs, and fruits, seems to mock Roosevelt's ambitions of a home demonstration farm. If so, the effect is not intentional: Cason Callaway and FDR were very good friends. And there are championship golf courses, lakes, hiking and biking trails, tennis courts, restaurants, and accommodations for the most discriminating traveler.

Despite all these man-made attractions in the area, the impression of isolation and wilderness one gets in the view from Dowdell's Knob sticks in the mind. It persists, too, as one drives through the countryside of much of West Central Georgia, down secluded highways and back roads lined on both sides with towering pines or dense stands of sweetgums, oaks, and sycamores, past fallow fields that once were white with cotton in the fall and are now far advanced in the slow return to their primeval state. This impression is especially strong in the creek beds and river bottoms where trees and vines crowd so closely together the afternoon sun is only a filigree of light through the vegetation, speckling the forest floor and dancing on the waters of the many creeks that wind their way through the area. It is basically correct, because the visitor is looking out on what once was, for at least half its historical life, the southern Indian frontier, last refuge of the Creek Indians in Georgia, and for hundreds of years prior to the Indians' removal to Alabama and then to the west, a vast melting pot of cultures—Native American, Spanish, English, African, and French.

Even today, much of the land has returned to wilderness, and eight of the twenty counties that make up West Central Georgia have populations of less than ten thousand each (six—Marion, Schley, Stewart, Talbot, Taylor, and Webster, whose combined square miles of 1,985 make them larger than Rhode Island—have a total population of just over thirty thousand). There are spots—Yellow Jacket Shoals on the Flint, the falls of Mulberry Creek, a stretch of the Chattahoochee that flows past the old Yuchi Indian village on the Alabama shore, the view to the west across the widest expanse of West Point Lake, portions of Pine Mountain Trail, Patsiliga Creek near Benjamin Hawkins's old Indian agency on the Flint, to name a few—that have the look and feel of another Georgia, another South, another America.

Even the most casual observer would have to notice that the names of the creeks and rivers in this part of Georgia are resonant of another time and another people: Upatoi, Weracoba, Ossahatchie, Hannahatchee, Bustahatchee, Pataula, Hodchodkee, Hillabahatchee, Kinchafonee, Choctahatchee, Lanahassee, Muckalee, Patsiliga, Hackasofkee, Echeconnee, Tobesofkee, Towaliga, Chattahoochee.

The people who left these names on the land were mainly the Muskogulgi or Creeks, although a few of the names are Choctaw, and some probably date back to a slightly earlier people, the Hitchitee. But it was the Creeks who occupied West Central Georgia (and most of the rest of the southern part of the state) when the Europeans first reached the southeastern United States in the early sixteenth century. The Spanish were the first Europeans to set foot in Muskogeeland following Ponce de Leon's exploration of Florida in 1513. Among the early expeditions or *entrada* that penetrated some distance into the

In the hope that the birds will help control mosquitoes and other insects, rural folk fashion hollow gourds into houses for purple martins.

back country were those of Alonzo Alvarez Pineda in 1519; Pamfilio deNarvaez, 1528–35; Hernando DeSoto, 1539–43; Tristan de Luna, 1559–61; Juan Pardo, 1566 and 1568; and Gaspar de Salas, 1596. So far as we know none of these expeditions actually passed directly through West Central Georgia, although the massive DeSoto expedition skirted its eastern edge. The first documented evidence of the Spanish in the area places them at the falls of the Chattahoochee River in 1639. In 1679, Spanish soldiers and priests from the Florida missions came upriver and planted a cross at a Creek village on the Alabama side of the river about twenty-five miles below present-day Columbus. The English, led by Henry Woodward, a British ship's surgeon turned trader, finally reached the Indian towns on the Chattahoochee in 1685. Thereafter the Creeks knew little peace.

Both Spanish and English sought exclusive trade with the Creeks, who lived in numerous villages on both banks of the Chattahoochee from present-day Franklin south all the way to the confluence of the Chattahoochee and Flint Rivers. American Indians also had many towns on the Tallapoosa and Coosa Rivers in today's Alabama, and there were smaller villages on the Flint River in Georgia and scattered up and down the larger creeks. When asked, the Indians said that although their ancestors had originally come from the West, the land of the setting sun, their people had lived in this area for many moons. They pointed out huge platform mound complexes in the underbrush and deep in the forests, saying the earthen heaps had been left by "the ancient people." Modern scholarship has established that the mounds were built by the Mississippian people who flourished throughout the South and Midwest from around A.D. 700 to the time of DeSoto. Smaller burial mounds, built during the earlier Woodland Period, 1000 B.C. to A.D. 700, also dotted the region, as did strange piles of stones, sometimes arranged in circular fashion, that white settlers were later to term "forts." The ground itself seemed to sprout projectile points and remains of clay pots that appeared to be of ancient manufacture. We know now that these points were shaped by the hands of people who inhabited the region during the Archaic Period, 8000 to 1000 B.C., or even earlier, during Paleo times, 10,000 to 1000 B.C.

Each Indian town or *tulwa* was lightly governed by a *miko* or headman and a council of elders. The people appeared to worship, or at least to revere, a supreme being, whom they called *Hisagita immisee*, "Master of Breath" or "Breath Holder." The art of writing seemed to be unknown to them, but perhaps as result, they were magnificent speakers. Around crackling night fires of pine and oak they told long tales about the origin of their people in the West, and sometimes they regaled the English traders and Spanish soldiers with animal stories and tall tales involving strange creatures of the forest and waters.

Friendly and open at first, they became increasingly apprehensive as more and more of their land was gobbled up in a series of treaties by the strange white-skinned people from across the ocean. Early on, they began to refer to the English colonists at Savannah as *Ecunnaunuxulgee*, "People greedily grasping after the lands of the red people." They signed treaty after treaty with the colonists, thinking each one the last, but nothing seemed to hold the tidal wave of foreigners back. From their capitals at Cusseta and Coweta on the Chattahoochee, the Creek headmen tried every stratagem to defeat the foreigners and play them off against each other. It worked for a time, but then the white-tailed deer, upon which the Indians were dependent for sustenance and for practically every article of clothing, began to disappear as a result of their own people overhunting to supply the traders with hides. More quickly than seems possible, the Indians became dependent upon the traders for basic supplies, including food, clothing, and even weapons with which to hunt the disappearing deer. That dependency was their doom. After the American Revolution, their descent was rapid. They fought a brave but futile war against the new American nation in 1813–14, but Andrew Jackson crushed them at Horseshoe Bend. They tried politics and subterfuge to resist giving up any more of their land, but their own leaders betrayed them in the treaties of Indian Springs in 1821 and 1825. By the mid-1830s they were not only gone from West Central Georgia, they were gone from the Deep South, officially "removed" to lands in Oklahoma.

Such, in capsule, is the sad history of a people who lived in this region longer than any other and who may have known it better and loved it more. Their footprints were light upon the land, but they influenced the European settlers in the region in ways we have largely forgotten. Because we have also forgotten much of what we did to them, here is one of their stories as a reminder:

Seven persons went apart, fasted, and took medicine for four days in order to prophesy. Then they came in and reported to the people what they had found out. Then the people said, "We will select seven persons and find out more."

So they sent out seven persons who fasted and took medicine for seven days. At the end of this time they wondered if they should continue their fast for seven months. They fasted and took medicine until the seven months were completed. Then they asked one another if they could not observe their regulations for a whole year. They accomplished it, but when the time was completed they had become wild and feared to go near the rest of the people, so they went into the woods and stayed there.

They asked one another what they should do and finally said, "Let us turn ourselves into pine trees." At that time there were no iron axes but tools made of flint with which little wood could be cut. But when the white men came and they saw them cutting down pine trees with their axes they said to one another, "That has cut us down."

When the whites went on destroying pine trees they said, "Let us turn ourselves into rock. A rock lies undisturbed on top of the ground." But after they had turned themselves into rocks they saw the white people turn to the rocks and begin to use them in various ways.

Then they made up their minds to go above, saying, "We cannot escape in any manner." So they rose and went up into the air, where they became a constellation.

If you are lucky enough to be on Dowdell's Knob on a dark night at the right time of year, you can see the seven wise Indians—we call them the Pleiades—sparkling overhead, brighter than the brightest lights in the valley below. Franklin Delano Roosevelt, who was especially fond of coming to the knob at night, would have seen them often.

Fred C. Fussell

TOURING WEST CENTRAL GEORGIA

Mountain to lakeside, city to farm, canyon to swamp, the West Central Georgia landscape is as diverse as it is beautiful. Columbus, on the extreme western edge of Georgia, is the largest city in the region. Stewart County, in the south, lies in the coastal plain on sandy, eroded lands that were laid down millions of years ago by the repeated advance and retreat of the ancient sea. Meriwether County, north of Stewart by fewer than fifty miles, is the location of the southernmost element of the Appalachian Mountains, the eroded remnants of a mountain chain that was once as massive as the Alps. The Flint and Chattahoochee Rivers, the two major waterways within the region, both flow southward from urban Atlanta, diverge to the eastern and western edges of the region, and then eventually rejoin at the Florida border to empty into the Gulf of Mexico at Apalachicola. The Ocmulgee River, which borders the extreme northeastern corner of the region, courses not to the Gulf but instead runs southeasterly, joins the Oconee, and becomes the Altamaha, which flows into the Atlantic.

West Central Georgia is abundant with historical sites. It was on the lands that lie between the Flint and Chattahoochee Rivers that, following the European invasion of the Americas, the native tribespeople endured their long and tragic effort to maintain their ancient lands and customs. They built their capital city of Cusseta on the Chattahoochee and from there, for a time, held sway over the entire territory of the southern Atlantic seaboard. In the late eighteenth century on the Flint River, near the present-day town of Roberta, Benjamin Hawkins, the United States envoy to all tribal people south of the Ohio River, established his agency and futilely attempted to keep the peace between the Southeastern Indians and the encroaching Americans. By the mid-nineteenth century, the region was second only to the counties of the Georgia coast in agricultural production. It also be-

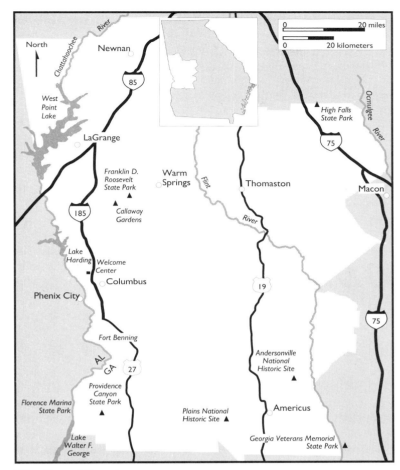

West Central Georgia

came second only to that region in the enslavement of human beings. In 1860 Stewart County alone produced in excess of twenty thousand bales of cotton—with a slave population that approached ten thousand. Cotton, "Georgia wool," has been the watchword in West Central Georgia since the 1830s when the rushing waters at the falls of the Chattahoochee were first harnessed to turn huge shafts to drive the looms and spinning frames of the region's first textile mills.

The major military action of the Civil War skirted West Central Georgia. It was extremely late in the years of the conflict before the region witnessed firsthand any combat at all. But the war was as great a tragedy within the West Central Georgia region as it was in the rest of the nation. Andersonville prison, in Macon County, is certainly one of the best-known Civil War sites in the country. Less well known is the Confederate Naval Works in Columbus.

Searching for relief from the effects of polio, Franklin Delano Roosevelt came here seeking the therapeutic value of the natural springwater baths at Warm Springs, and until his death in 1945 his was a familiar face around the West Georgia countryside. Later in the century, another president would be known to West Georgians, but this time one who was native to the region—James Earl Carter of Plains.

Once the isolated western frontier of Georgia, the West Central region has become conscious of its rightful place in the history of the state and the nation and is ready to share its rich cultural heritage and its bountiful natural assets with all those who will take time to search them out.

TOUR ONE

From Forsyth travel west via U.S. 41 to Barnesville; from Barnesville go west via Ga. 18 to Zebulon and Woodbury (or, alternately, from Barnesville go southwest via Ga. 36 to Thomaston and from Thomaston northwest via Ga. 74 to connect with Ga. 18 to Woodbury); from Woodbury travel south via Ga. 85E to Manchester; then from Manchester west via U.S. 27 Alt. to Warm Springs; from Warm Springs north via U.S. 27 Alt. to Greenville; from Greenville west via Ga. 109 to LaGrange; from LaGrange northwest via Ga. 219 to Texas; from Texas northeast via Ga. 34 to Franklin and Newnan; from Newnan southeast via Ga. 16 to Senoia.

Railroading has a long tradition in **Forsyth**. The first completed passenger railroad in Georgia, the Monroe Railroad and Banking Company, opened there in 1838. Its tracks ran the short distance from Macon to Forsyth. The Monroe County Museum & Store is located in a Victorian-style depot that was constructed at Forsyth in 1899. The nearby freight depot building was built in 1849. Included in the museum collections, which range from prehistoric to recent, is a typesetter's desk that was used by Georgia writer Joel Chandler Harris when he was an apprentice for the *Monroe Advertiser.* The museum is located a few blocks east of downtown Forsyth, on Tift College Drive. The commercial and retail district of Forsyth consists of an eight-block area surrounding the Monroe County courthouse square. Within that area are forty structures dating from the mid to late nineteenth century. The chamber of commerce publishes a walking and driving tour of the town.

In this vicinity are three trips off the beaten path: Culloden, Juliette, and High Falls State Park. A Confederate museum is at the community of **Culloden**, in extreme southwest Monroe County, where, on April 19, 1865, there occurred a battle in which two hundred men of

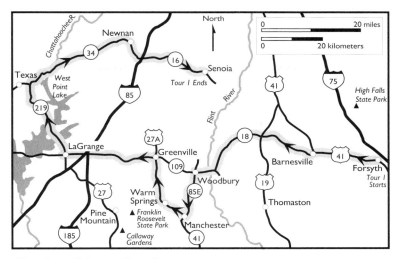

West Central Georgia, Tour One

Worrill's Grays held off an approaching contingent of Union troops. The museum, on Main Street, contains a variety of Confederate memorabilia.

The town of **Juliette** is located northeast of Forsyth via the Juliette Road. This little town has gained recent fame for having been the location for the filming of the popular motion picture *Fried Green Tomatoes*. The Whistle Stop Cafe in Juliette actually serves fried green tomatoes. Visitors may also take a look at the old Juliette Mill building, once said to have been the world's largest water-powered grist mill. The mill ceased operations in 1957. The Rum Creek Wildlife Management Area and Lake Juliette are nearby, as is Jarrell Plantation, described in the Central Georgia tour.

High Falls State Park, north of Forsyth, is located in the very northwest corner of Monroe County via exit 65 on I-75. Facilities available there include sites for tents and recreational vehicle campers, a swimming pool, group shelters and picnic grounds, hiking trails, and a scenic waterfall on the nearby Towaliga River. Visible at the park are the foundations of an early grist mill.

Barnesville is an attractive, busy little community that appears to be somewhat less self-conscious than other, more tourist-oriented towns in the region. While others have made ambitious efforts to revitalize or to make themselves over into somewhat romanticized images of their former selves, Barnesville has managed to develop simply in a way that appears to be natural and unforced. The Barnesville Hardware Store, at 116 Main Street, is just that—a small-town retail hardware store that caters to a rural, agriculture-based clientele. The thousands of items that are offered for sale are housed within an 1878 Gothic Revival style storefront. The oldest business in town, it was formerly the showroom of the Smith Buggy Works, one of four such companies that once operated in Barnesville. In addition, Main Street has several open-front grocery stores and produce markets that feature daily sidewalk displays of fresh vegetables, and there are one or two nice cafes that serve such regional fare as country-fried steak, cornbread, and collard greens. Under restoration by the Barnesville–Lamar County Historical Society is the Barnesville Railroad Depot at Plaza Way. This 1913 structure was the site from which Pres. Franklin Roosevelt, in 1938, turned the switch that first brought electricity to the surrounding rural area.

The old Carnegie Library building, a 1910 structure appropriately located on Library Street in Barnesville, was purchased by an artist who has restored the building inside and out to create living, studio, and gallery spaces. The galleries and studio are open to the public the first week of each month. In September, Barnesville produces a festival called Buggy Days to celebrate its tradition and history in the manufacturing of carriages, surreys, and buggies. A well-planned self-guided walking tour of historic sites in downtown Barnesville is available from the Barnesville–Lamar Chamber of Commerce, located at 109 Forsyth Street.

West of Barnesville a mile or two, on a hilltop on the north side of Ga. 18, is a fine Federal period plantation plain–style structure, the Gachet House. In the early nineteenth century, Gachet, a wealthy Frenchman who was forced to flee revolutionaries at his home on Hispaniola, established this home and a plantation in Lamar County. It was there, in March of 1825, that Gachet hosted his fellow countryman, the American Revolutionary War hero the Marquis de Lafayette, who was touring the United States.

Zebulon is the seat of Pike County. Both the town and the county are named for Zebulon Pike, explorer of the American West. The county was created in 1822, and Zebulon has been the county seat since 1824; the courthouse was built in 1895. The town, which has a pleasant downtown historic area, has a population of about a thousand people.

Concord is a railroad town that has changed little, at least in form, since the turn of the century. There are a half-dozen or more old commercial buildings standing in the town, which has an active cafe, a small grocery store, a couple of shops featuring vintage and other objects for sale, and several beautiful old shade trees along the main street. The trees provide a comfortable shady place on which to stand or sit and simply look around at the town. Twice a year, in May and again in October, a community group stages the Concord Country Jubilee, a festival featuring local crafts, music, dance, and food.

An alternate route southwest from Barnesville is Ga. 36 to **Thomaston**, founded in 1825 and the seat of government for Upson County.

The textile industry has a long history in Thomaston. The first cotton mill to be erected there was Franklin Factory, in 1833. In recent years Thomaston has added other manufacturing interests, including a major piano factory. The Thomaston-Upson Arts Council (TUAC) maintains a gallery space in downtown Thomaston. It also sponsors a community theater. The TUAC Gallery is located just off the southeast corner of the town square at 201 South Center Street, on the ground level of the 1873 Fincher Building, the oldest downtown structure. The space is the site for about ten exhibits a year of the work of local and regional artists and is a good place to pick up a brochure and begin a walking tour of Thomaston.

The major cultural event of the year in Thomaston is the Emancipation Celebration, which occurs annually in late May. This traditional celebration is reported to have begun in Thomaston as early as 1863. According to local organizers, it is the oldest celebration of its kind in the nation. A period writer described an occasion there in 1865 in which "freedmen had a brilliant celebration at this place." Traditionally, the festivities include a parade, public speaking, feasting, and a celebration at the nearby community Lincoln Park.

Early in the nineteenth century, the native clays in the area attracted the establishment of family-operated pottery shops. Viable folk potteries in the West Central Georgia region during the nineteenth and early twentieth centuries operated in Pike, Lamar, Upson, Talbot, Troup, and Coweta Counties. A sizable community of potters, known locally as Jugtown, was established about ten miles north of Thomaston on the Upson and Pike County border.

The picturesque town of **Manchester** is nestled on the north face of Pine Mountain, the southernmost extension of the Appalachian chain. Named for the industrial town of Manchester, England, this is the largest and newest town in Meriwether County. Located only five miles southeast of Warm Springs, Manchester was once the site of a major textile manufacturing company. A relief sculpture created in 1941 by Erwin Frederick Springweiler and titled "Game Bird Hunt" can be seen at the U.S. Post Office on West Main Street. (For Warm Springs, see tour two.)

The little Meriwether County village of **Gay** is the site for one of the region's longest-running and most popular annual celebrations, the Cotton Pickin' Country Fair, held twice yearly—in May and in October. The traditional basketry of the Reeves Family, local African American white-oak basket makers, has been collected widely and is often featured in exhibitions of folk craft.

The county seat of **Greenville** is located near the geographic center of Meriwether County. The Meriwether County courthouse was built in 1903 and burned in 1976. However, the restored building continues to house the offices of government for the county. Just off the town square, northeast of the courthouse, is the old county jail, which now is used as offices for the county tax assessor. The headquarters for the Meriwether County Historical Society are in a nineteenth-century law office building located on the east side of the town square. The Red Oak Creek Bridge, one of the longest wooden bridges in the state, was built by the African American bridge-builder Horace King in the 1840s, possibly after his manumission (see Columbus). The bridge is located between Woodbury and Gay, east of Ga. 74 on Flat Shoals Road.

The town of **LaGrange** was named for the Chateau de LaGrange, the French estate of the Marquis de Lafayette. While traveling through the nearby west Georgia countryside in 1825, Lafayette remarked upon the similarity of the local landscape to that of his own estate in France, thus inspiring the founders of Troup County to select that name for their principal town and county seat. The initial stop for the visitor to LaGrange and Troup County should be the Troup County Archives. The archives, located at 136 Main Street, in addition to its considerable holdings of historical papers and records, is a center for the interpretation of community history. The archives building was constructed in 1917 by industrialist Fuller E. Callaway to house the LaGrange National Bank and the LaGrange Savings Bank. The building was renovated in 1981 for use by the Troup County Historical Society. In the foyer is an exhibit replicating Mr. Callaway's 1905 office, which was originally located in the nearby Loyd Building. Callaway controlled several textile mills, department stores, and a bank in LaGrange.

Walking and driving self-guided tours of LaGrange are available at the Troup County Archives, the Troup County Chamber of Commerce, 224 Main Street, and at several other locations. The Chattahoochee Valley Art Museum, 112 Hines Street, is housed in the beautifully restored 1892 Troup County jail. The museum has transformed the jail's interior into extraordinarily viable gallery, office, and studio classroom spaces. The museum features a permanent collection of art as well as an ambitious schedule of changing exhibitions. LaFayette Square, in the center of town, is the setting for a fountain and a bronze likeness of the Marquis de Lafayette. Bellevue, at Broad and Ben Hill Streets, was the home of U.S. senator Benjamin Hill. This Greek Revival style house, a National Historic Landmark, was built in the mid-1850s and is open for tours. LaGrange College, opened in 1831 as the LaGrange Female Academy, is the home of the Lamar Dodd Art Center, an expansive gallery space devoted to the exhibition of innovative artistic works. The center is named for LaGrange native Lamar Dodd, founder and longtime head of the Department of Art at the University of Georgia. The Dodd Art Center, in collaboration with the Chattahoochee Valley Art Museum, hosts the biannual LaGrange National Exhibition, a highly regarded showing of the new work of contemporary artists from across the nation. A Lamar Dodd painting adorns the cover of the 1990 reprint of the original WPA guide to Georgia. The Troup County courthouse was built in 1938 in the Stripped Classical style.

Late in 1863, in anticipation of approaching Union forces, the Confederate defenders at **West Point** constructed an earthen fort to protect the nearby Chattahoochee River bridges and railroad junction. On Easter Sunday 1865, civilian volunteers, assisted by convalescent soldiers from local hospitals, defended Fort Tyler against Union attackers. At day's end, the outnumbered civilian forces stood down. The earthen ruins of Fort Tyler are accessible, and a marked walking trail at the site is furnished with interpretive signs.

West Point Lake is a U.S. Army Corps of Engineers impoundment of the Chattahoochee River. The dam that creates the lake is located a little over three miles north of the town of West Point. Though the dam's primary purpose is flood control, on the theory that the Chattahoochee River could eventually be made navigable from the Gulf of Mexico to Atlanta, the construction provided for the eventual addition of locks, which would allow vessels to pass upstream. No solution has been offered, however, for the problem of their passage from the head of navigation at Columbus northward through a series of natural falls plus six other man-made impoundments lacking the potential for adding locks. At the concrete and earthen dam for West Point Lake, a monumental stairway leads to a fishing pier at the tailrace and to a pathway and scenic footbridge. The lake extends upstream to the town of Franklin, in Heard County.

A self-guided tour of historic buildings in the town of **Hogansville**, fifteen miles northeast of LaGrange, is available from the Troup County Chamber of Commerce. The town has several dozen private homes and downtown commercial buildings that are of late-nineteenth- and early-twentieth-century vintage.

Although **Franklin** was not incorporated until 1831, it is fairly certain that an eighteenth-century Creek Indian town called Chattahoochee Tallauhassee was situated overlooking the river where the present town now stands. In the literature of the period, the settlement is sometimes referred to as Chattahoochee Old Town, and some community historians believe that the origin for the name of the river itself is derived from that. The Heard County Historical Center and Museum is located just off the northwest corner of the town square in the old Heard County jail, built in 1912 to replace an 1880s structure that was declared "unfit" for prisoners. The jail was abandoned in 1964 upon completion of a new facility on the opposite side of the square. Exhibits in the museum focus on Heard County family history and domestic architecture of the nineteenth century.

West of Franklin, via Ga. 34, is the Flat Rock Camp Meeting Tabernacle, constructed in 1878. This gigantic, open-sided, hewn log structure is one of many such buildings that once dotted the rural Georgia countryside. This particular tabernacle, or arbor, is still used for a week or two each August for congregational retreats, or so-called protracted meeting, at which the participating members spend as much time as possible at the site. There they conduct services several times daily, cook and take meals, and even sleep there inside small frame dwellings called tents. Some scholars believe that the physical form of the camp meeting grounds and the services that occur there may derive in part from that of the Southeastern Indian Green Corn Ceremonial, which is traditionally observed in July or August. Beyond the camp meeting arbor is the unincorporated community of **Texas**.

Twelve miles southwest of Newnan via Ga. 34 is the small community of **Powers' Crossroads**, location on Labor Day weekend of the Annual Powers' Crossroads Country Fair and Arts Festival, one of the longest running and most successful community festivals in the state. Activities at the fair include regional foods and food preparation, grist milling, a collection of horse-drawn vehicles, sorghum syrup milling, and over three hundred artisans and artists plying their handiwork.

Newnan is the county seat of Coweta County. There are many fine county courthouses in Georgia, but the Coweta County Courthouse is one that should be seen inside and out. Built in 1904, this Neoclassical Revival structure is adorned with diverse decorative motifs fashioned from and executed with a variety of materials and techniques. The courtroom is open for visitors during regular business hours. One of the primary points of interest in Newnan is the Male Academy Museum, at 30 Temple Avenue. The museum is housed in a restored seminary building constructed in 1840. Among the museum's holdings are Civil War artifacts and memorabilia, early hand-crafted textiles, and other decorative arts from the nineteenth century. In a changing exhibition area topics of local and southern history are interpreted. The Manget Brannon Alliance for the Arts is both an art gallery and a theater company. The gallery exhibits the work of a different artist each month of the year. Artists' exhibitions open on the first Sunday each month and remain on view through the last Sunday. The Newnan-Coweta Community Theatre Company presents its annual series of performances in the Hatchet Theatre, which is an integral part of the Manget Brannon Alliance for the Arts facilities located at First Avenue and Long Place in Newnan. Newnan is host for several annual festivals. An informative printed tour guide to downtown Newnan is available from the Main Street office on the town square.

Erskine Caldwell, the author of *Tobacco Road* (see East Central tour), was born in Coweta County in 1903. In **Moreland**, south of Newnan on U.S. 27 Alt., the house where he was born is open for touring on weekends or by appointment. Included in the house, along with personal and family memorabilia, is an interpretive display on Caldwell's life and the significance of his contribution to American litera-

Produce stand, Senoia

ture. Caldwell's writing has been extremely popular over the years. His *God's Little Acre* has outsold even Margaret Mitchell's *Gone with the Wind.*

Moreland was also the childhood home of nationally syndicated Atlanta newspaper columnist and humorist Lewis Grizzard (d. 1994), who was born at Fort Benning, Georgia, in 1946. A volunteer group of Grizzard fans in Moreland has established an interpretive center and museum of artifacts to memorialize their town's favorite literary son. Agricultural implements and the accessories of an early-twentieth-century farm household are exhibited at the Moreland Mill Museum in the former W. A. Brannon store building, the site of the Moreland Knitting Mill of the 1920s.

The town of **Senoia** is named for a Creek Indian woman who was the wife of William McIntosh, a leader in the Creek Nation during the early nineteenth century. The Senoia Historical Society provides a printed guide to the historic houses of the town. The 1905 Baggarly Buggy Shop, a large structure next door to the post office, was at one time the local Coca-Cola bottling plant. It houses a collection of vintage automobiles, farm tools and equipment, and other late-nineteenth- and early-twentieth-century materials.

TOUR TWO: UP AND ALONG THE FALL LINE

From Columbus travel north via U.S. 27 to Hamilton and Pine Mountain; from Pine Mountain via Ga. 190 to U.S. 85W; then north via U.S. 85W to Warm Springs; from Warm Springs south via Ga. 41 to Talbotton; from Talbotton east via U.S. 80 to Knoxville.

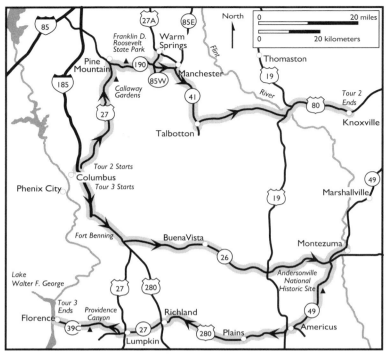

West Central Georgia, Tours Two and Three

The city of **Columbus**, in Muscogee County, was chartered in 1827 by the State of Georgia as "a trading town." The new town was located on the eastern side of the extensive falls of the Chattahoochee River, at a point beside the river where the southern Piedmont meets the Coastal Plain. For many centuries that location had been occupied by the American Indians of the Southeast. However, a series of treaties negotiated between the Indians and the United States in the 1820s forced them to relocate from Georgia to the western side of the river, in Alabama. Thus the way was opened for the establishment and settlement of Columbus. Before the town was a decade old, textile mills were built and operating there. The energy of the swiftly falling waters of the Chattahoochee River was harnessed to power looms and spinning machines and to turn locally grown cotton into cloth for the new community, the South, and the nation.

During the Civil War, Columbus was second only to Richmond in supplying the Confederacy with manufactured goods. Near the close of the war, in the spring of 1865, some of the riverfront textile mills, the cotton warehouses, and a number of other industrial facilities in

Columbus were torched by the occupying Union forces. By August of the following year, the Columbus Iron Works had resumed its activities, and the other industries of the town were close behind. By 1880, Columbus textile mills were running again and producing more cloth than those of any other city in the South. Since then, despite a continuous struggle to escape from a position of relative isolation from the rest of the nation—Columbus was the last city of its size in the U.S. to be connected to the interstate highway system (1979)—Columbus has come into its own as an urban center that is host to all the amenities, as well as some of the problems, that a city of its size acquires over time. The population of the extended Columbus area, including Fort Benning, Phenix City, Alabama, and a selection of nearby suburbs and communities, exceeds half a million people, a statistic that seems to surprise everyone, even those who live there. Columbus is truly *the* city in the West Central Region of Georgia.

In downtown Columbus, alongside Front Avenue between Twelfth and Sixth Streets, is the northernmost and primary section of the Chattahoochee Riverwalk, one of the newest outdoor facilities in the city. It offers outdoor recreational, scenic, and cultural opportunities for resident and visitor alike. The riverwalk is a beautifully designed and executed broad brick-paved pathway that meanders from the edge of the old city southward all the way to Fort Benning. Strangely enough, the project resulted from the need to improve the city's combined overflow sewer system. Adjacent to the upper section and first leg of the Chattahoochee Riverwalk, the Columbus Iron Works Trade and Convention Center occupies the brick buildings of the old Columbus Iron Works, a foundry that operated from 1853 until the 1970s. During the Civil War, this Columbus foundry was a manufacturer of cannons for the Confederacy, and at a nearby related site, ironclad gunboats were built (see Confederate Naval Museum, below). Following the war, the iron works went literally from sword to plowshare as it turned from weaponry to the manufacturing of agricultural and home-use implements and equipment. Later, from the 1880s to the 1920s, the company grew in significance in the production of commercial ice-making machinery. The entire riverfront industrial district has National Historic Landmark status.

The Columbus Chamber of Commerce is located at 901 Front Avenue, just across the railroad tracks, a few steps north of the Columbus Iron Works. The chamber offices are in the building of the old Southern Plow Company, a part of the iron works that is now known as One Arsenal Place. A few blocks farther north on Front Avenue (between Tenth and Twelfth Streets) are the offices of the W. C. Bradley Company, historically a mainstay in the business, agricultural, and industrial life of Columbus and the region. The company's original cotton warehouses were burned after Union forces captured Columbus in April 1865. Several of the buildings now occupied by the company date as early as the late 1860s and represent some of the first postwar construction to occur in the city. The Bradley Museum, located in one of these buildings at 1017 Front Avenue, is an extensive corporate art collection that is open to visitors at no charge during regular business hours, Monday through Friday. The collection consists primarily of contemporary American realist paintings of subjects related to the company's activites in agriculture and industry. Included are examples of the work of the African American painter Thomas Jefferson Flanagan. At 1229 Front Avenue are the Eagle and Phenix Cotton Mills, established in 1851 as the Eagle Mill but burned by the Union Army in 1865. The company was reorganized afterward as the Eagle and Phenix Manufacturing Company. Immediately to the south of the Columbus Iron Works complex is the Chattahoochee Promenade, a public park that borders the banks of the Chattahoochee River between Fifth and Eighth streets. On the promenade a series of interpretive markers delineates events and people of note in the history of the city. An amphitheater on the riverside provides the scene for numerous musical performances and is a popular location for outdoor weddings.

About a block from the Chattahoochee Promenade, at 700 Broadway, are the offices for the Historic Columbus Foundation, the locus for historic tours and the significant historic preservation movement in the city of Columbus. From here, at Heritage Corner, tours of the primary historic sites in the old city are available daily. The Walker-Peters-Langdon House (1828), at 716 Broadway, is a Federal-style cottage believed to be the oldest surviving house in the city. Nearby is the Pemberton House and the adjacent kitchen/apothecary shop. This house was occupied by John Pemberton from 1855 to 1860. Pemberton was the originator of the formula for Coca-Cola, and there is a notion that the drink may have been brewed first in Columbus and not in Atlanta, as is generally thought. The shop building houses a collection of pharmacy paraphernalia and Coke memorabilia. At 708 Broadway is the Woodruff Farm House, a mid-nineteenth-century house that was moved to its present location from a site outside the city. It now houses the foundation's gift shop. Behind it is a "trader's log cabin" that symbolizes the kind of houses built by American and European traders who came into the region during the late eighteenth and early nineteenth centuries. Other significant historic buildings in the immediate area of the Columbus Historic District include the Pemberton Country Home (712 Broadway), the Wells-Bagley House (22 East Sixth Street), the Goetchius House (405 Broadway), and the rectory for the Church of Saints Philip and James (442 Broadway). The

PIT BARBECUE

The area around Columbus has been called the world's center for the southern pit barbecue (also spelled barbeque and bar-b-q) tradition, a cooking method in which pork meats—usually Boston butts or ribs, but sometimes whole hogs—are lovingly roasted over logs of green blackjack oak and hickory. The logs, set to smolder slowly beneath the meat, are placed down deep within a brick or an earthen pit. Pit barbecue, or as far as that goes, any other style of southern barbecue, has nothing to do with those portable gas or charcoal grills that clutter the side porches and backyard decks of countless suburban houses around the United States. To cook on one of those is *not* to barbecue, but to *grill!*

A check of the Columbus telephone directory will lead the curious to any of over thirty locally owned and operated barbecue places in the area. There the delicious and savory regional fare is slowly cooked in sweet smoke, then prepared and served in as many varieties as there are cooking establishments (and don't bother looking in the Yellow Pages under "restaurants"—go directly to "barbecue" for a complete listing).

DO THIS: From barbecue places listed in the Yellow Pages, select one whose name you like, or better yet simply stop at one you happen to pass on the street. Go in and check out the menu. It's probably posted on the wall above the serving area.

Be prepared to answer the following questions when ordering your barbecue:

Here or "to go"? If you want to eat in the restaurant (and you do), say "here."

Sandwich or plate? For dinner, the noon meal, most people prefer a single barbecue sandwich, which is a hamburger bun filled with barbecue, coleslaw (sometimes served on the side), pickles, and sauce, customarily accompanied by a Coke and a small bag of potato chips. They usually reserve the more ample barbecue plate for supper—the traditional leisurely evening meal. A plate consists of meat, slaw, pickles, Brunswick stew, bread, onions, a variety of sauces, and possibly baked beans, French fries, and dessert.

Chipped or sliced? If you want your meat finely chopped, then say "chipped." Sliced means slabs of meat cut about one-quarter-inch thick or wedge-shaped, bite-sized, chunks.

Inside or outside? This question refers not to where you would like to be seated while dining, but to the dark-toasted, crusty *outside* portions of meat—as opposed to the juicy, pink, tender *inside* cuts.

Hot or mild? There are as many varieties of barbecue sauce as there are barbecue cooks. Some sauces are very spicy, so if you're a beginner start with caution and work your way up. You may also be asked to choose between red and yellow. Red sauce is usually slightly sweeter than yellow and is tomato based. Yellow sauce is generally very spicy (hot with cayenne pepper) and is mustard flavored. Both are delicious, and either perfectly complements the smoky flavor of the tender meat.

Those choices are the basics. Others might concern the various side dishes and beverages traditionally served with pit barbecue. Those may include coleslaw—plain or barbecue (barbecue slaw is coleslaw with, believe it or not, barbecue sauce mixed in); breads (corn bread, light bread, or French bread); beer, Coke, or tea (sweet or unsweet—always iced); French-fried potatoes or potato salad; chips; various styles of Brunswick stew (another topic for another time); pickles; onions; and, of course, such traditional southern desserts as pecan, coconut, or buttermilk pie, ice box custard, and banana pudding.

Try it all—you'll love it!

—Fred C. Fussell

Folly, 527 First Avenue, is the only known double octagon house in the United States and has been designated a National Historic Landmark. It is believed to be an antebellum structure that was converted into its present form around 1861. The original dwelling on this site was home for Julia Forsyth, daughter of Georgia governor John Forsyth.

Within an area dubbed High Uptown is another grouping of domestic structures of historical interest in Columbus. The Robert W. Woodruff birthplace at 1414 Second Avenue is where life began for the Atlanta industrialist responsible for making Coca-Cola into one of the first truly global consumer products. The circa 1870 Rankin House at 1440 Second Avenue is the home of the Junior League of Columbus and is open for touring several days each week. Rankin Square occupies the 1000 block of Tenth Street between Broadway and First Avenue. This building, once the Rankin Hotel, is now home to a variety of offices, shops, and restaurants. Among them is the Institute for the Study of American Cultures (ISAC), a nonprofit group devoted to researching the theory of pre-Columbian contact between prehistoric American and certain old-world cultures. The group plans to install a permanent exhibition interpreting ancient graphic and writing systems that have been reported from American archaeological sites. The Three Arts Theatre, 1029 Talbotton Road, is the home of the Columbus Symphony Orchestra.

Among the historic sites in Columbus that are significant to African American history and culture is the William H. Spencer House, Fourth Avenue and Eighth Street. It was the home of the first superintendent of Columbus's black schools. The Liberty Theatre (1925), 821 Eighth Street, was once a movie house as well as a performance hall. It was the most important entertainment center for the black citizens of Columbus during the period preceding racial integration. Notables who appeared there include Gertrude "Ma" Rainey, Marian Anderson, Ella Fitzgerald, Ethel Waters, Lena Horne, Duke Ellington, Cab Calloway, and Fletcher Henderson. The St. James AME Church (1875), 1002 Sixth Avenue, is noted for its lofty steeple and massive, elaborately carved front doors. The First African Baptist Church, 901 Fifth Avenue, was founded in 1830 and is the oldest black church in Columbus. Claflin School, 1532 Fifth Avenue, was the first public school in Columbus for black students. The Isaac Maund House, 1608 Third Avenue, was built in 1890 by a black textile worker. A two-story frame cottage at 805 Fifth Avenue was the last home of the "mother of the blues," Ma Rainey, who was born in Columbus in 1886 and died there in 1939. During her lifetime, she achieved only a limited measure of fame and popularity, but her robust vocal style and personal strength opened the way for other black performers who were struggling to break into the fledgling recording industry. She is buried in Porterdale Cemetery on Tenth Avenue. Her house will ultimately be a blues museum.

Crossing the Chattahoochee River from Columbus to Phenix City, Alabama, is the Dillingham Street Bridge. The original bridge at this site, the first ever to span the Chattahoochee, was built in 1832 by South Carolinian John Godwin, who was assisted by Horace King, his enslaved foreman. King was apparently a genius in construction engineering. At times of low water, remnants of the piers King designed and built are visible beneath the Dillingham Bridge.

The Springer Opera House, 103 Tenth Street, was built in 1871 by Francis J. Springer. In 1965, a group of preservationists was able to acquire the building and restore it to its current appearance. The Springer is a National Historic Landmark and was designated the official theater of the state of Georgia by Jimmy Carter when he was governor. Such diverse famous persons as Edwin Booth, John Philip Sousa, Will Rogers, William Jennings Bryan, Franklin Roosevelt, and Oscar Wilde have appeared on its stage. Today, the Springer Theater Company, led by a staff of professional artists and administrators, presents a full annual series of performances on the main stage. The opera house museum and archives, open to researchers, hold items of national significance in the history of the theater.

The James W. Woodruff Confederate Naval Museum, 201 Fourth Street, exhibits the remains of two Confederate naval warships—the gunboat CSS *Chattahoochee* and the ironclad ram CSS *Jackson*. Huge portions of the ruins of the two vessels were salvaged from the waters of the Chattahoochee River by a group of volunteers in the early 1960s. Exhibited with the boats are weapons, hardware, tools and implements, and additional materials related to Confederate naval history.

The Columbus Museum, 1251 Wynnton Road, is one of the newest stars in Columbus's crown. This eighty-six-thousand-square-foot art and history center, reopened in April 1989 and incorporating a museum dating from 1954, is the largest in Georgia outside Atlanta. American art and regional culture are the primary emphases of the collection. Within a dozen gallery spaces dedicated to the exhibition of fine and decorative arts are the museum's remarkable collections of American painting and sculpture; regional folk art and traditional craft; American, European, and Asian decorative arts; and an impressive series of major traveling and temporary exhibitions. Other highlights are Chattahoochee Legacy, a long-term installation; an award-winning film that introduces it; and Transformations, for children.

Columbus, like many other southern towns, has produced its share of outstanding literary artists. Carson McCullers (1917–67) and Nunnally Johnson (1897–1977) are two natives whose contributions to literature have received critical recognition. The work of the two is quite different. Johnson is actually best known as the screenwriter who produced, among many others, the script for John Ford's film of Erskine Caldwell's *Tobacco Road*. McCullers published her first novel, *The Heart Is a Lonely Hunter*, when she was only twenty-three years old. This and other works, including *Reflections in a Golden Eye* and *The Member of the Wedding*, reflect the experience of her growing-up years in the southern cotton mill town of Columbus.

The campus of Columbus College, a senior unit of the University System of Georgia, is located in the northeastern quadrant of the city. Columbus College's Fine Arts Hall is the frequent location for exhibitions of the work of students and of guest artists from around the nation. The college's music and drama departments each offer full seasons of performances there. The annual Festival of Southeastern Indian Cultures at Columbus College is an effort led by the Department of History to present and interpret the traditional cultures of the American Indian tribal groups of the Southeastern United States, particularly those that consider the Lower Chattahoochee River Valley region to be their ancestral homeland. The festival is presented on campus each year during Columbus Day weekend.

In Harris County lies the western side of the ending segment of the Southern Appalachian Mountains—the Pine Mountain Ridge. Within this region—where the mountains, the Piedmont, and the Coastal Plain converge—are some of the most celebrated, some of the strangest, and some of the most beautiful natural areas to be found in Georgia.

Hamilton is located about ten miles south of Callaway Gardens via U.S. 27 and is the seat of government for Harris County. During the latter part of the nineteenth century, Hamilton was the home of B. F. White, who was important in the development and popularization of Sacred Harp singing. Sacred Harp singing is a traditional form of Christian congregational music in which the human voice, the "sacred harp," furnishes the entire and only source of instrumentation. Sections of western Georgia and eastern Alabama remain today among the primary regions within the southern United States for the continuation of the tradition. (See Northwest Georgia tour one.)

Callaway Gardens is one of the most visited resorts in Georgia. It was conceived and created by textile magnate Cason J. Callaway and his wife, Virginia Hand Callaway. Callaway Gardens is an educational, charitable organization owned and operated by a nonprofit organization, the Ida Cason Callaway Foundation. (Ida Cason Callaway was Cason Callaway's mother.) The gardens consist of over fourteen thousand acres of woodlands containing native and exotic flora, a series of spring-fed ponds and lakes, native wildlife, and a full array of facilities for the accommodation, entertainment, and education of tourists and vacationers. Callaway Gardens includes the John A. Sibley Horticultural Center, which features a remarkable changing exhibit of floral displays, including an annual summertime topiary series. The adjacent Cecil B. Day Butterfly Center, among the largest glass-enclosed butterfly conservatories in North America, has a collection of over a thousand tropical butterflies in free flight. Mr. Cason's Vegetable Garden is planted annually with up to four hundred varieties of flowers, vegetables, herbs, and fruit trees. Robin Lake Beach (summer season only) is the largest man-made inland beach in existence and, in season, features daily performances by Florida State University's "Flying High" Circus, swimming and sunbathing, paddle boating, and other sun and water activities. There are a number of annual special events. Callaway Gardens has a fine golf course, and a five-mile biking and hiking trail winds through the grounds.

In addition to that which is available within the gardens, food and lodging can be found just north at the little village of **Pine Mountain**, which is the site of a variety of crafts galleries, artists' studios, and shops featuring vintage furniture, books, and oddities.

Franklin D. Roosevelt State Park is located on Pine Mountain. The west entrance is only a mile or so south of Callaway Gardens. This state park contains ten thousand acres of Southern Appalachian woodlands. It includes thirty miles of hiking trails, two lakes, horseback riding, family and group camping and picnicking facilities, rental cabins overlooking Pine Mountain Valley, and a series of scenic vistas strung along Ga. 190, a narrow two-lane roadway that twists through the center of the park and winds along the ridge of the mountain. Each year in September, former members of the Civilian Conservation Corps who worked to create the park in the 1930s gather there for an annual reunion. Within the park, paralleling and sometimes criss-crossing Ga. 190, is the thirty-mile-long Pine Mountain Trail, which offers the hiker a great year-round look at the local terrain. Dowdell's Knob, a lofty hilltop located near the east end of the park and trail, affords a spectacular view of the adjacent valley and hills to the south. Dowdell's Knob was a favorite spot for Pres. Franklin Delano Roosevelt, who frequently visited the site from his Little White House at Warm Springs. He enjoyed going there to picnic and relax in the shade of the surrounding pines and oaks. A small barbecue pit, constructed from local stone and used frequently by Roosevelt and his guests, remains in place. A marker commemorates its use by the late president.

Roosevelt's Little White House is less than one mile south of Warm Springs. The state park complex includes the Little White House, the cottage where President Roosevelt lived while being treated at the Warm Springs center and where he suffered a fatal stroke in 1945 while sitting for a portrait. The unfinished portrait is on view there. A museum on the park grounds exhibits Roosevelt memorabilia, in-

Roosevelt's Little White House

cluding a remarkable collection of handmade crafts and folk art given by their makers to the president. An informative orientation film interprets the importance to FDR of the treatment center, the town of Warm Springs, and the surrounding rural countryside. The entire village area including the Little White House is designated a National Historic Landmark.

The National Fish Hatchery and Aquarium, located just southeast of Warm Springs on Ga. 41, displays a variety of local species of fish, birds, reptiles, and other wildlife in a series of indoor exhibit installations that incorporate both live animals and mounted specimens.

The little town of **Warm Springs** is an active tourist-oriented community. The close proximity of Roosevelt's Little White House, the Warm Springs Foundation, Callaway Gardens, the National Fish Hatchery, and Roosevelt State Park has influenced the character of what might otherwise have been a fairly typical Georgia town. The business district in Warm Springs includes over fifty shops and restaurants. Most of the downtown buildings are of late-nineteenth- or early-twentieth-century vintage and have been maintained or restored to reflect the period during which they were constructed.

Dominating the central square of the town of **Talbotton** (TALL-ba-tun) is the Talbot County courthouse, built in 1892. The very first session of the Georgia Supreme Court met at Talbotton in 1846. Talbotton was the first American home for Lazarus Straus, a Jewish merchant who came from Europe in 1854. His sons, Oscar, Nathan, and Isador, developed Macy's Department Store in New York City and distinguished themselves as major philanthropists in the early years of the twentieth century.

The Zion Episcopal Church in Talbotton is among the most appealing historic structures in West Georgia. This wooden Gothic-style building was completed in 1848. The interior of the church is made from finely crafted unpainted native woods. The communion rail and lectern are black walnut, and the box pews, walls, and ceiling are native longleaf pine. The hand-pumped organ, installed in 1850, is still used for services. The church interior features an upstairs balcony, or gallery, which was the designated seating in antebellum times for slaves. Straus-LeVert Memorial Hall is a well-crafted Greek Revival building dating to 1830. It was built to house the LeVert Female College, which was named in honor of Octavia Walton LeVert, a granddaughter of George Walton, signer of the Declaration of Independence from Georgia and an early governor of the state. The building now serves as the Talbotton Community House.

Talbot County, particularly the area south of Talbotton along Ga. 41, is a principal region for growing Georgia peaches. In the early spring the rolling hillsides between Talbotton and Geneva virtually glow with the blossoming orchards of peach trees. A few months later, in June and July, the highway is dotted with roadside stands from which the delicious fruit is peddled to passersby. The Big Lazar Creek Wildlife Management Area is seven miles north of Talbotton near U.S. 80. There is a public fishing lake with a picnic area, primitive camping, a boat ramp, and a fishing pier. U.S. 80 to Knoxville passes tiny Prattsburg and rolling farmland in northern Taylor County.

In the center of the main street at **Roberta** is a massive stone monument to Benjamin Hawkins, principal agent to the Southeastern Indians during the late eighteenth and early nineteenth centuries. Hawkins, as a demonstration to the Indians of the superior results of using such modern agricultural methods as plowing, established a model farm at his agency on the nearby Flint River. The site of Hawkins's farm and agency is six miles southwest of Roberta at the Crawford County community of **Francisville**, near where Ga. 128 crosses the Flint River. Hawkins's grave, marked with a stone and bronze monument, is located at the agency site, where he died in 1816.

Knoxville, the county seat of Crawford County, was the birthplace of John Pemberton, the originator of Coca-Cola. Knoxville is an unincorporated community that lies only one mile east of Roberta, the largest town in the county. The Crawford County courthouse, built in 1832, is among the oldest in the state. (The Fayette County courthouse was finished in 1825.) On the courthouse square is a monument to Joanna Troutman, a young woman who was living nearby when, in 1835, Georgia volunteers were mustered to assist in the struggle to liberate Texas. As the soldiers passed through Knoxville, Miss Troutman presented them with a flag that she had sewn, to be carried as a symbol of their cause. The flag was a simple rectangular field emblazoned at its center with a contrasting single star. In 1913, the body of Joanna Troutman was removed from its grave in Crawford

County and transported west to be reburied in the Texas State Cemetery at Austin. There, a bronze statue was erected above the grave of Crawford County's Joanna Troutman, the designer of the original flag of the "Lone Star" state of Texas.

A side trip for travelers interested in the location of historic potteries is a visit to Middle Georgia Pottery. The factory was first established in the nineteenth century by a potter named Elbert Merritt, who in the 1860 census is listed as a jug maker in Crawford County. His kiln and clay mixer from the original pottery works still exist at the site now operated by Bill Merritt. To reach the pottery, one should go three or four miles east of Roberta on U.S. 80, turn right at Sandy Point Road, go to a dead end (on the left will be the Southeastern Holiness Campground), turn right on Knoxville Road, and follow the signs to the pottery, about two miles on the left.

TOUR THREE: AROUND THE COASTAL PLAIN

From Columbus travel south via I-185 to Fort Benning; from Fort Benning travel south via U.S. 27 to Cusseta; from Cusseta travel east via Ga. 26 to Buena Vista, Ellaville, Oglethorpe, and Montezuma; from Oglethorpe travel south via Ga. 49 to Andersonville and Americus; from Americus travel west via U.S. 280 to Plains and Richland; from Richland travel west via Ga. 27 to Lumpkin; from Lumpkin travel west via Ga. 39C to Florence.

Of the 160,000 total acres in Chattahoochee County, 129,000 acres are within the boundaries of the **Fort Benning Military Reservation**. Additional land belonging to Fort Benning is in Muscogee County, and still more acres are on the west bank of the Chattahoochee River in Russell County, Alabama. Fort Benning is huge, yet it is one of the few "open" military installations in the country. Visitors are admitted freely. There is a visitor welcome and orientation center located at the entrance to Main Post, south of Columbus. The National Infantry Museum is one of the finest collections of military memorabilia and artifacts in the world. Its exhibits trace American infantrymen from colonial times to the present. Its collection includes over fifteen hundred firearms ranging from a sixteenth-century Spanish cannon to contemporary American and other weaponry. Special exhibits within the museum include the Hall of the U.S. Infantry, the Axis Powers Exhibit, and the Hall of Flags, showing military band instruments, silver presentation pieces, and military art and documents. Cannons and other artillery pieces from various historical periods are exhibited outdoors in front of the museum. The museum is in Building 396, on Baltzell Avenue, Fort Benning. Admission is free.

Riverside, built in 1909 as a summer residence of the Bussey family of Columbus, was purchased by the army to become a part of Fort

Fort Benning

Benning in 1918. The Bussey family home now serves as the residence of Fort Benning's commanding general. The Airborne Jump Training Towers were constructed at the fort in 1942 as a part of the first American military parachute training program. These red and white, 250-foot-tall towers are used to indoctrinate airborne trainees into the sensation of descending from above.

Doughboy Stadium, a football field, was built in the 1920s by soldiers at Fort Benning as a memorial to those who lost their lives in World War I. Lawson Army Airfield, the airport for Fort Benning, was built on the site of Cusseta Town, capital of the Lower Creek Nation until treaties between the Indians and the United States forced their removal to the Alabama side of the Chattahoochee River. Near there, on both sides of the river, traces are visible of the old crossing of the Federal Road, which during the late eighteenth and early nineteenth centuries was the principal route from Charleston to New Orleans. Despite the Creeks' vigorous protests, the road was constructed across their lands in Georgia and Alabama. An outcrop of the Ripley Formation, a geological deposit consisting of marine fossil beds, is located near the Upatoi Creek bridge on U.S. 27 at Fort Benning. Local authorities must be consulted about collecting geological specimens from federally owned lands.

Cusseta is the county seat and the only incorporated town in Chattahoochee County. The Chattahoochee County jail, built in 1902, now houses the county archives and library. The county's original courthouse, built in 1854, was moved to the living history museum of Westville, near Lumpkin. A mile or so north of Cusseta, a transmission tower, completed in 1960, is visible day and night from many miles distant. For more than ten years it was the tallest man-made object on the planet, holding that distinction until the mid-1970s when it was surpassed by the Sears Tower in Chicago. River Bend Park is a U.S. Army Corps of Engineers access point on Lake Eufaula, adjacent to the southern edge of Fort Benning, a few miles south of Cusseta. The park has a boat ramp, picnic and primitive camping areas, and a grand panoramic view of the upper reaches of Lake Walter F. George on the Chattahoochee River.

The hilltop town of **Buena Vista** is the county seat of Marion County. The county has two historic courthouses. The newest, in Buena Vista, was built in 1850 and is still in use. The older one is located seven miles north of Buena Vista at **Tazewell**, which was the county seat from 1838 until 1850. Buena Vista (BEW-na VIS-ta) was originally called Pea Ridge. It was renamed to commemorate a famous battle of the Mexican War in which a number of Georgians participated.

When Eddie Owens Martin (a.k.a. St EOM) heeded the call of a personal visionary experience to return to his rural Marion County home from a life in New York City, he began one of the strangest extended sagas in the history of American artistic expression. Born in 1908, Martin began work on his masterpiece of environmental visionary art near Buena Vista in the late 1950s. His work continued there until a few years before his death in 1986. The result of the years of creative effort by St EOM can be seen west of Buena Vista, a few yards off the Eddie Martin Road, at Pasaquan, a four-acre complex of brightly painted walls, pagodas, walkways, buildings, and sculptures depicting the artist's vision of the future. Anyone in Buena Vista can give specific directions; it's about three miles west of town via county roads.

Pasaquan

The Schley County courthouse at **Ellaville**, built in 1899, replaced one that was constructed in 1858, the year following the creation of the county from sections of adjoining Marion and Sumter Counties. During the Christmas holidays the courthouse is outlined in thousands of small white lights.

Macon County is almost equally divided into two parts by the Flint River, and the two halves of the county belong to two distinct geographical provinces. The half west of the Flint River lies in the rolling fall line hills province, and the eastern half lies in the relatively flat Fort Valley plateau. Macon County is home to a community of Mennonites, whose farmlands lie to the east of **Montezuma**. Six miles east of Montezuma is a locally famous restaurant that specializes in traditional Mennonite cuisine—with southern overtones! Oglethorpe has been the county seat for Macon County since 1854, when the government was moved there from the now-extinct town of Lanier. A Macon countian named Sam Rumph was the developer of the Elberta peach, the mother strain of Georgia's peach industry. There is a historic marker commemorating Rumph's accomplishments in Marshallville, fourteen miles north of Montezuma on Ga. 49. Marshallville, founded in 1849, contains several fine examples of antebellum architecture in the relatively undisturbed context of a small agricultural community. The west main street historic district is of special note.

Its official name was Fort Sumter, but the name **Andersonville** is the one that will be forever etched into the chronicles of the United States of America. Andersonville prison was the largest Confederate military prison constructed during the Civil War. During the fourteen months of its existence, over forty-five thousand Union prisoners of war were held within its twenty-six acres, and thirteen thousand died there. By authorization of the United States Congress, Andersonville Historic Site serves as a memorial to all Americans who have been held as prisoners of war. Exhibits effectively interpret the suffering experienced by those who were incarcerated there. In 1994 the U.S. Congress authorized a new National Prisoner of War Museum and interpretive center for the prison site. Andersonville, also an active national military cemetery, is nine miles northeast of Americus via Ga. 49.

Americus was founded in 1832 on the site of the old Creek Indian Agency granary, which was still in use in the late nineteenth century. Americus became the county seat the year after Sumter County was created in 1831. The city's past can be found in its vintage architecture. The business district is dominated by the Windsor Hotel, 125 West Lamar Street, a massive brick structure that occupies a full city block. It was built in 1892 as a winter retreat for wealthy northerners seeking to escape the cold. The notable residential architecture of the town is clustered along Rees Park, Taylor, College, South Lee, and

Church Streets. A printed guide to the architecture of Americus is available from the Americus–Sumter County Chamber of Commerce or the Sumter Historic Preservation Society. Georgia Southwestern College in Americus began in 1908 as a high school. By 1932, it had become a part of the University System of Georgia. Southwestern and its students and faculty have been a major factor over the years in cultural and historic preservation efforts in Americus. Koinonia Farm, a Christian commune, was founded in 1942 in rural Sumter County with only four people and 440 acres of land. Today, the community has increased its land holdings to about 1,500 acres and supports a population of approximately eighty people. The founders of the commune, Clarence and Florence Jordan and Martin and Mabel England, established a set of social precepts that flew in the face of the southern social code of the time. The communal lifestyle of its members, along with concerted efforts to empower the poor, an open attitude of racial reconciliation, and a philosophy of nonviolence, has made Koinonia and its members the target of racial violence since the middle decades of this century. Today Koinonia is probably best known for its role in the organization of Habitat for Humanity, which is headquartered in nearby Americus. Koinonia is located on Ga. 49, south of Americus. Tours of its facilities and farming operation are available.

The national attention Koinonia attracted in the 1960s was pale in comparison to that given nearby **Plains** a decade later. A much more promising Sumter County was personified in Jimmy Carter. People everywhere came to know Plains through the eye of the camera that seemed to record every moment in the presidential campaign of 1976. Plains was, and is, a small town born of turn-of-the-century agriculture. The railroad tracks string out along the town facing a single block of commercial brick buildings: hardware, grocery, antique, farm supply stores, and the like. A wooden railroad depot, saved from destruction by becoming famous as Carter's "campaign headquarters," is a notable feature remaining from the prepresidential Plains days. Now the entire town is a historic site administered by the National Park Service.

Several buildings associated with President Carter attract visitors: the depot, the school the president and First Lady Rosalynn attended, Carter's boyhood home, brother Billy's service station, and the present Carter residence. On the eastern side of town out U.S. 280 is a state welcome center where visitors may find extensive information about Plains and the region. For the original excitement of a small southern town caught up in a presidental campaign—well, you had to be there.

Upon Georgia's secession from the Union, the town of **Preston**, county seat of Webster, was the first to fly the Confederate flag. The county's original name was Kinchafoonee, a Creek Indian word that is also the name of a local stream, a major tributary of the Flint River.

Plains

The county is almost entirely agricultural. Peanuts, pecans, and pine trees are the principal products of the land.

The red brick Stewart County courthouse at **Lumpkin** was built in 1906 and, following a fire, was rebuilt in 1923. It is the fifth such structure to occupy the town square since the founding of the town in 1832. The Lumpkin public square lies atop one of the highest hills in Stewart County. During the middle of the last century, when the surrounding farmlands were free of trees and were blanketed in fields of cotton, the former two-story, hewn-log courthouse could be seen atop its high hilltop perch from more than ten miles away. Surrounding the courthouse square in Lumpkin is an array of vintage commercial buildings, most of which were constructed during the early years of the twentieth century. Beyond those, on a marked driving route called the Stagecoach Trail, can be seen more than a dozen finely designed and maintained antebellum houses, some of which are occupied by descendants of their original nineteenth-century builders. Facing the courthouse, on the northwest corner of the town square, is the beautifully restored Bedingfield Inn, built in 1836 and now operated by the Stewart County Historical Commission as a house museum. Behind the detached kitchen of the Bedingfield Inn sits the Lynch House, an excellent example of a hewn-log, dogtrot house, typical of the small farmstead households that abounded in Georgia until the 1930s.

A little over a mile southeast of the Lumpkin town square, on the Troutman Road, is the village of Westville, an outdoor living history museum that attempts to portray a rural southwest Georgia town during the middle of the last century. The strength of the exhibits at Westville is the remarkable collection of mid-nineteenth century buildings, most notably the Grimes-Feagin House (Stewart County, 1840), the Old Damascus Methodist Church (Early County, 1879), the Bryan House (Stewart County, 1831), a wood screw cotton baling press (Floyd County, 1851), the Chattahoochee County Courthouse (1854), and the Merritt House (Knox Bridge, South Carolina, 1845). Some of Westville's structures were moved there from Col. John Word West's original collection at Jonesboro; his "Fair of 1850" provided the core of the present village. The remaining buildings came from nearby towns and farms in Southwest Georgia or were replicated to represent those styles for which no period example could be acquired.

Located approximately seven miles south of Lumpkin is a major archaeological center, the Singer-Moye Site. It is owned, maintained, and protected by the Columbus Museum. Unusual for its distant location from a major watercourse, this complex of prehistoric earth mounds was a center for commercial and religious activity among the Native Americans who lived in the region about seven hundred years ago. The pyramidal Mound A at the Singer-Moye site is the fourth-largest prehistoric earthwork in Georgia. It rises over forty-five feet above the surrounding wooded terrain. The archaeological staff at the Columbus Museum is planning for the future installation of an interpretive center at the site.

A part of Providence Canyon State Conservation Park, the impressive Providence Canyon was once popularly known as "Georgia's Little Grand Canyon." The official name for these spectacular canyons, locally known as gullies, derives from a nearby church. The canyons are particularly beautiful during July and early August, when the bright natural colors of the sand and clay walls are augmented by the

Westville

Providence Canyon

brilliant red blooms of the plum-leafed azalea (*Rhododendron prunifo-lium*), a rare and protected native shrub that thrives in the cool, moist, shaded depths of its natural habitat near the canyon's floor. Providence Canyon presents an extreme example of the kind of rampant soil erosion that plagued many of Georgia's farmlands for decades during the early twentieth century. The configuration of the canyon walls continues to change from the force of wind and water upon the exposed, brilliantly colored, loosely bound earth. An interpretive center at the park entrance houses exhibits of photographs, fossils, and artifacts related to the natural and human history of the area. The park is located on Ga. 39C, about seven miles west of Lumpkin.

Florence Marina State Park, one of the newest in the state park system, features boating, camping, fishing, tennis, and swimming. The Kirbo Interpretive Center near the park entrance displays historic, prehistoric, and other local history and natural history materials. Tours are available on Saturday mornings of the nearby Rood Creek Archeological Site, the second of two major Mississippian period earth mound complexes in Stewart County. Florence Marina State Park is located on the site of the abandoned nineteenth-century town of Florence, near the shores of Lake Walter F. George, sixteen miles west of Lumpkin. The Bluffton Formation, the only geological zone in Georgia in which dinosaur fossils are found, outcrops in several locations in Stewart County near the town of **Omaha**. A concrete marker commemorating the site of a locally famous skirmish between early Georgia settlers and the native Creek Indians at Shepherd's Plantation is located about a half mile north of the entrance to Florence Marina State Park.

At the village of **Louvale**, ten miles north of Lumpkin on U.S. 27, a roadside row of neat wood frame church buildings dates variously from the late nineteenth to the mid-twentieth centuries. Louvale was once the westernmost point of a rail line that ran across Georgia and as a result was the scene of a bustling commercial district that included boarding houses, cafes, and stores. Today fewer than a hundred people remain there, but the frontier spirit survives in their animated conversations and stories, their delicious pork barbecue, and in the friendly "never met a stranger" hospitality. Stewart County abuts the Southwest Georgia region and is a good place to join that tour.

CENTRAL GEORGIA

William Hedgepeth # THE HEART OF GEORGIA

It is a cloudless autumn day in Peach County, a few miles beyond the Blue Bird Body plant, and, bearing a hot bagful of barbecued ribs and Brunswick stew, I have turned up a tiny dirt road off state highway 96 just outside Fort Valley and come to a resting spot beneath a pecan tree.

This pecan grove stands alongside a five-hundred-acre field of fully bloomed cotton, bordered at the far edges by tall pines. There are no houses or human structures in sight. And so, in the quiet privacy of this setting, I get out, idly pick up a few pecans that lie on the ground, and climb onto the hood of my car to sit on the roof and gaze out over the cotton field as I prepare to eat my ribs and stew.

In moments I notice a quick stirring in the center of the field, and suddenly, pouring upward from the cotton and leveling off on a flat plane parallel to the blanket of whiteness, hundreds upon hundreds of birds—blackbirds, I think—take flight in a tight, flat, rectangular formation that looks for all the world like a carpet, a magic flying carpet made of birds. And this silent carpet rises, then swoops low, nearly brushing the bright cotton, and finally rises again to flow on out over the field in perfect form, making a slight undulating billow as it passes over the pine trees at the distant edge, and then grows small as it fades out of sight against the giant blue middle Georgia sky, flying due southeast.

If you were here—or if anyone else were—we would marvel over this sight and assure each other that we had actually witnessed the same thing. And we might realize, with a glimmer of a chill, that there's nothing whatsoever in this setting to define this particular time; it could be any time at all: these birds and this cotton—a crop that almost seems like some strangely resurrected emblem of a nearly forgotten age. This special field, in fact, is part of Georgia's biggest crop of cotton since the mid-1930s.

We might see ourselves soaring along the route with that magic carpet of birds out there, flowing over the landscape, dipping low over many another such cotton field, winging their way into that vast bulge of Georgia that stretches south of the ever-defining fall line: the mildly rolling but mostly flat sandy soil laid down as recently as the time of the earliest man, and the piney woods and the tilled fields and overgrown hulks of dilapidation left by those generations of immigrants who still considered themselves frontiersmen and yeomen in these parts.

Those blackbirds might be flying right now along the course of the sluggish Ocmulgee River, past places like Kathleen and Hawkinsville, Abbeville, Rhine, and swooping in a sharp loop along the southern boundary of Telfair County; and all they'll ever have to do for food as they fly along is open their beaks and scoop in their fill of all the gnats that harry the air by the millions in these parts.

We are talking about the very center section of our esteemed state, the *fillet* of Georgia, you might say—specifically these twenty-six sub–fall line counties that, if they constituted a separate state of the Union, would rank just under Vermont in size and would be the forty-fourth largest state in our nation—larger than such other states as New Hampshire, Massachusetts, New Jersey, Hawaii, Connecticut, Delaware, and Rhode Island. (Hell, Laurens County alone—whose county seat is Dublin—is more than two-thirds the size of Rhode Island!)

We are talking about a segment of this earth with a very distinctive spirit, the kind of landscape that has molded some mighty souls. If all the rest of Georgia were somehow to shrink more or less equally on all sides by about, say, 30-or-so percent, what would remain would be exactly this very essential piece of our heartland.

And what, you may ask, lies within that heart?

We drop down through a ruffle of clouds, and all at once we see the paved highway down there, and it is filled right now with traffic moving in just one direction. And all those flat sandy roads twining out of the countryside from all around, and all the trenched and seamed wagon routes and rustic bypaths that lead toward McRae are practically bumper-to-bumper with country people in their old cars—black jalopies from the Laurel and Hardy era—and their old trucks and two-horse wagons and buggies and oxcarts. And there are still other people, families, walking along the roadsides. The license plates on the cars read: Georgia 1934.

The citizens on the roads are predominantly of Celtic ancestry or of Anglo-Saxon stock, and they feel as if they've been living in these parts nigh onto forever, trying to make a go of things. Their own ancestors were farmers or frontier pushers who originally came into these middle Georgia latitudes in the early nineteenth century with the availability of former Creek Indian lands and the birth stirrings of the cotton culture. They are sharecroppers and tenants and small-scale single-family farmers on their last legs, and small town merchants whose livelihood depends on the farmers: men mostly in overalls and their best white shirts and simple farm women in bonnets and print dresses, and their tow-head children, wearing shoes for once. And there are babes in arms, many of the boy babies named Eugene.

These people who work the land were in desperate shape long before the Crash of 1929. Thanks to the drastic drop in cotton prices after World War I and thanks to overproduction and thanks most of all to the boll weevil that struck Georgia in the early twenties and ate up all the profits for all of those common-sense farmers who'd cast their entire lot with the single crop they believed was as good as "white gold." In 1934 Georgia's farmers make up half the state's population and a majority of the voters. They are good, honest, God-loving, hardworking folk with sun-seared faces and knotted hands who are groping en masse for anything that might offer a sliver of hope or help them out of their cascading despair. They are as poor as rural poverty can take them.

But today they are moving along with heads held high, eyes widened with anticipation. The men wear their battered wool fedoras with new pride. They are headed for one of the most exciting and soul-stirring high water marks of their lives: not just a political rally, but something that's sure to be an all-out, rip-tail roaring, spirit-soaring showcase of verbal pyrotechnics by Georgia's number-one political ringmaster, the one man with both the power and the desire to make things happen for them: Gov. Eugene Talmadge, Old Gene, Our Gene, the Wild Man from Sugar Creek. Running for reelection.

In his first term as governor, Gene delivered on every promise, no matter what extremes he took to do it. In 1933 he ousted every anti-Talmadge department head or state official, proclaimed martial law, and flanked the state buildings with armed militia. Beyond that, he took on banks, corporations, railroads, utilities, and the federal government. The upshot was that he lowered taxes, lowered power rates, lowered freight rates, lowered railroad passenger rates, lowered telephone rates, and fulfilled his pledge to give the people $3 tags for their autos—all while getting the state out of debt. He's a ruthless, "no frills" guy, and his strength is in his directness and honesty.

To these "wool-hat boys," Gene is a godsend. "Till Gene Talmadge was elected, they had no one to speak for them," his widow, "Miss Mitt," said decades later. "He knew their problems. He could talk exactly like they did." As his son, former U.S. senator Herman E. Talmadge, recalled: "He could be eloquent, and at times was. But most of the time he could just speak the language of the ordinary Georgian, and he could simplify a complex issue where an idiot could understand it. There wasn't any doubt about what he meant or what he was saying. So many speakers, you know, are so obtuse. You listen to 'em you don't know what in the hell they're saying. My daddy wasn't that way. Every word was like a bullet with a razor edge."

At the site of the speaking, preparations have been going on for days: Here's a speakers' platform of fresh-cut, paintless pine standing beneath the shade of an outstretched oak, and there are long tables heaped with barbecued beef, pork, and chicken—the cows, hogs, and hens having been contributed to Gene by local admirers. All in the most festive of settings: flags, circus bunting, posters, fireworks, a high school band.

And here are the crowds: upwards of twenty thousand Georgians, nearly all white, in their cleanest clothes, eating, rubbing shoulders, and listening to "Fiddling John" Carson and his daughter, "Moonshine Kate," who travel with Gene and always spark up his rallies with their famous cornpone ditty, "The Three-Dollar Tag Song":

> I gotta Eugene dog, gotta Eugene cat,
> I'm a Talmadge man from ma shoes to ma hat.
> Farmer in the cawnfield hollerin' whoa, gee, haw,
> Kain't put no thutty-dollar tag on a three-dollar car.

Amid the shift and jostle of the crowd, Old Gene himself, resplendent in a white linen suit, makes his entrance on an oxcart, and everyone shrieks with glee. He climbs from the cart, slapping backs, shaking hands, and clambers up to the podium. His appearance is electric. No one has ever seen anyone else quite like him: of medium height, lean and sure-footed, with dark hair, an unruly lock of which falls over his forehead like Napoleon's. He has a wide mouth with thin lips that cut straight across his face, giving him a resolute appearance. But his most startling feature is his eyes, which crackle with intensity as they peer from behind horn-rimmed Harold Loyd spectacles. "He had a greyish blue eye," says Herman Talmadge. "Most people thought he had brown eyes, or even black. He had the most penetrating eye I've ever seen in my life. Almost hypnotize you when he looked at you." It all adds up to a wildly magnetic charisma that raises goosebumps of the spirit.

"My fellow countrymen," he begins, to the cheers of the crowd, and then launches into a revival-style oration about the virtues of rural life and hard work and the demonic big interests who try to keep their foot on the windpipe of the common man. On cue, one of his plants, a young lad perched in a tree, calls out, "Tell us about them officials you ran out of office, Gene." Gene says, "I'm a-comin' to that, son." He points his finger straight out over the lectern and says, with a grim ferocity, "A lot of people say they like what I did, but don't like the way I did it. I don't either, but if a bunch of hogs get into your fields or your garden or your flowers and won't come out when you say 'sooey, sooey, sooey,' then you have to use language and methods that hogs and pigs understand."

The thousands gathered roar their approval—and out in the deeper boondocks the scores of farmers gathered around battery radios in scattered tiny country stores cheer too. And someone in the crowd yells, "Pour it on, Gene," and another yells, "Take off your coat, Gene," and the governor strips off his coat to reveal bright red galluses, the sight of which whips the crowd into a near frenzy, and he offers a rare grin. But in moments he's a-weavin' and a-wavin' up and down the platform, mopping his brow with a red bandanna, which evokes another roar, then rolling up his shirtsleeves—"lay it on 'em, Gene, lay it on 'em"—and launching into an arm-waving spellbinder, with every word and gesture at his command. Baying like a hound, crying, howling, laughing, defying the outer world in words of thunder. To emphasize a telling point he'll give a snap of a gallus strap with his thumb, and they are mesmerized.

He makes the audience see rivers in the sky. He lightens their souls, lifts them up, wherever they want to go, which is home—the farm. The farm means home to Georgians in the 1930s. And that's what Talmadge talks about. "The value of this land and a day's work in the sun has got to come back," he reminds them, and then offers the assurance that if he, Gene Talmadge, has anything to say about it, "We are going back to the sanctity and the common-sense and honesty of the old horse and buggy days."

Gene Talmadge was overwhelmingly reelected that year, 1934, and won the governorship a third time in 1940. In 1946—after a stupendous personal effort, in a blatantly racist campaign—he won the governorship a fourth time at age sixty-one but died from illness and ex-

Gene Talmadge campaigning, 1940s

ertion before being sworn in, leading to Georgia's famous "Three Governor Controversy."

The point is, he was "the Solid South at its solidest." He was a rhetorical superstar who usually got what he wanted, but he stands in history as the last compellingly effective defender of the Old Way and all it entailed, of the kind of Georgia that existed before the rest of the world intruded. In the face of industrialization, the New Deal, and social changes sliding from every direction, Talmadge dug in his heels and preached defiance and denial. He wasn't the sort of leader who could guide people into an unfamiliar age, but because he was so good at voicing the baser racist instincts that abounded at the time, he became an unfortunate role model for far too many of the southern political leaders who succeeded him.

As to the people, the farmers who responded with their votes to Gene Talmadge, starting in 1926, and then later to Herman Talmadge—who was governor from 1949 to 1955 and U.S. senator from 1957 to 1980—they have continued to dwindle as a percentage of Georgia's population. In 1910, 61 percent of all Georgians were rural farm dwellers; in 1920 it was 58 percent, dropping by 1930 to 49 percent and then 44 percent by 1940. As of 1990, only 1.2 percent still lived on the farm.

But here, in middle Georgia, where Talmadgeism first took root, defenders of the farm faith still hold fast. Even if their sons and daughters or their grandchildren have taken on careers in the towns of Georgia's heartland, their own hearts, and those of their offspring, are still forever tied to the land, this particular land; and they all still retain an unquenchable fondness in their genes for that same ideal picture of self-sufficient, totally ungoverned rurality that Talmadge once dangled before the hope-filled eyes of their grandparents.

People in these parts still talk high words about Old Gene. The more senior of these are of the World War II generation—those now in their seventies and eighties who endured the depression and then the war and who begat the baby boomers, and who are now passing from the scene in growing numbers. They triumphed over more momentous events than any other generation since the Civil War. They are the last remaining among us to have lived through those years on our behalf. To them, the people they knew and things they went through meant a lot. And since we are all, after all, just stories telling stories, somebody's got to take note of these things before history rolls over us, for surely the opposite of learning is forgetting.

The Alcovy River rises at the end of an intricate and vastly webbed network of creeks, streams, rills, and springs bubbling out of obscure sites in the forested mountains of north Georgia. It tumbles out of the red hills and comes into its own as a bona fide river in Gwinnett County,

Herman Talmadge (third from left) at a campaign barbecue, 1950s

between Lawrenceville and Dacula, then runs down through Walton and Newton Counties and empties into Jackson Lake in Butts County.

The Yellow River emerges some twenty miles west of the Alcovy from the same labyrinthine tangle of mountain springs and sources and begins its formal course out of DeKalb County near Stone Mountain, then pours down through Rockdale and Newton Counties and thence into Jackson Lake.

Meanwhile, the easygoing South River trickles out of south Fulton County, near Lakewood, then twines through DeKalb, past Panola Mountain, meandering onward to form the border between Henry and Rockdale, and finally, like the other two, spills its contents into Jackson Lake. And here is where the main event starts:

The mighty Ocmulgee, a tribal word for "bubbling water," begins its seaward rush out of this same lake, aiming straight south toward Bibb County. About halfway there, it picks up the added volume and velocity of the Towaliga River, which joins forces with the stronger river just above Juliette. Now the Ocmulgee moves on to mold the western contours of Jones County, then plunges down into Bibb and straight through the heart of Macon. Macon, Georgia's fourth-largest city, owes its birth, life, and present happiness to the Ocmulgee.

From Macon, the big river rolls on southward, spilling down over the fall line—woo—picking up speed. It rallies further support first from Tobesofkee Creek in Bibb, next from Echeconnee Creek out of Houston County, and then Mossy Creek and Big Indian Creek farther on down. With all these resources under its belt the Ocmulgee, now fatter than ever, swirls down the western border of Bleckley County, past Hawkinsville in Pulaski, through Wilcox and then eastward and up along the southern boundary of Telfair, adding Horse Creek and Turnpike Creek before reaching Lumber City, where it picks up the contents of the Little Ocmulgee.

About eight miles east of this point, at the juncture of Telfair, Montgomery, and Jeff Davis Counties, the Ocmulgee finally convenes with middle Georgia's other main river, the Oconee, to form the mighty Altamaha River, which roars forward in a southeasterly swooping arc into McIntosh County, past the port of Darien, and out into that great Atlantic Ocean, which brought everyone here to begin with.

Transportation, communication, accessibility: These were the determining features that made development of the frontier possible, and the Ocmulgee's whirling current to the sea offered the pioneering soul all three. And so it was, with the gradual ceding of Indian land between the Ocmulgee and the Oconee, that the hardiest frontiersmen made their way up this river and ensconced themselves around Fort Hawkins, built in 1806 on the Ocmulgee's east bank in the area that was to become Macon.

These pioneers were joined by a steady stream of settlers, mostly from North Carolina, who, when the Indians withdrew farther west in 1821, renamed the village Newtown. When Bibb County was formed the following year, taking most of its land from the northern part of Houston County, the legislature decreed, first, that a fresh town should be laid out on the west bank of the Ocmulgee and, second, that it be named after Nathaniel Macon, a North Carolina politician who retained a popular following at that time among many of the new immigrants. Macon, as originally laid out in 1823, was supposedly modeled after ancient Babylon. For luck.

Macon became a cotton market and trading center for Bibb and the sixteen surrounding counties and ferried its wares to the seaport of Darien by flatboats that plied the Ocmulgee, and later by steamboats. The steamboats carried on a brisk traffic until the riverbanks became so denuded of the trees, whose wood stoked the hungry steam boilers, that silt and eroded topsoil finally clogged the waters, altered the channels, and eventually made commercial riverboating impossible. The last steamboat foundered and sank around the turn of the century. After this, the city cast its lot entirely with railroads, which eventually branched out to connect the city with every place of commercial importance. Ironically, the first steam locomotive to set wheel in Macon was brought upriver in a steamboat in October of 1838 and was named the Ocmulgee.

Today, the big thick city of Macon—which lies astride the fall line roughly a dozen miles above the geographic dead center of the state—seems forever suspended between historical eras. In terms of the "feel" of the place, it appears to occupy some unique status between a serious industrial center and a spacious, unhurried small town. Actually, speaking as one reasonably acquainted with Macon over the years, I'd say it's a little big for a town and a little slow for a city. In any case, it has been bustling along at a leisurely pace since the days of its founding and was at the peak of its relative prestige when cotton was the be-all and end-all of Georgia's economy.

The Baptist-run Mercer University and the Methodists' Wesleyan College, the oldest chartered college in the world to grant degrees to women; plus Fort Valley State, an early land-grant college; Macon College, a two-year institution; and Middle Georgia College in Cochran, another two-year school just down the road in Bleckley County, add up to educational opportunities unimaginable in earlier times.

Within the city proper, large columned mansions line the broad, palmetto-strewn parkways in the Intown Historic District, and hidden birds twitter in the magnolias. Having been spared the direct ravagements of the Civil War, a la General Sherman—who veered east on his southward march to the sea and pounced on hapless Milledgeville—Macon is able to lay claim to a wide variety of intact edifices representing many architectural styles.

Here the early Federal-style symmetrical structures stand across the cherry-tree-lined avenues from massive, columned Greek Revival buildings such as the city hall and the Cannonball House (the only house in town actually struck by a Union cannonball). Here the Gothic Revival's steeply gabled, lacilly detailed cottages, such as the birthplace

Downtown Macon

of Sidney Lanier, share the same city blocks with lavishly ornate Italianate showcase places with their cast-iron balconies and columns and cupolas. Perhaps the most numerous dwelling places are of the Victorian era's especially popular Queen Anne style, with their wraparound porches, turrets, towers, and big chimneys. They're all here: Second Empire, Colonial Revival, Classical Revival, plus shotgun and Craftsman. Then the depression, for obvious reasons, put a certain damper on the city's further architectural experimentation.

Today, all these looming reminders of old-time cotton prosperity stand quietly cheek-by-jowl with one another, punctuated by church spires and microwave relay towers and new office buildings that loom above the level of the trees. In the Historic District many trees bear posters reading "Notice: Drug Free Zone."

To the outer world, the only connection between Macon and drugs harks back to the city's brief heyday as a center of the rock 'n' roll culture. Macon's contribution to the music world includes Lena Horne and Little Richard, who used to sing for pennies in the local juke joints, and Otis Redding, who sat on the dock of the bay in San Francisco and moaned, "I left my home in Jaw-juh."

Phil Walden's Capricorn Records made Macon a powerhouse in the recording industry and most notably gave the Allman Brothers to the world. Then Duane Allman crashed his motorcycle on a Macon street and was killed in 1971, and the band's bass player, Barry Oakley, died in another cycle crash at nearly the same spot exactly a year later, and things slid downhill from there.

Nowadays these once-disreputable musical rowdies from Macon's past are to be officially immortalized in the Georgia Music Hall of Fame, currently under construction, and in the ongoing refurbishment of the Douglass Theater, a music hall, and later a movie house, where Little Richard and Otis and Ray Charles, Howlin' Wolf, Bo Didley, James Brown, and all the rest of the best of the black rhythm and bluesmen regularly performed back in the old days of hard-core segregation.

In the white, Neoclassical Washington Memorial Library, which houses the local archives, a marble bust of Sidney Lanier gazes over the unhurried comings and goings of scholars. The historical feature of the month is an account of Amelia Earhart's landing here in an autogyro in November 1931. As the *Macon Telegraph* reported: "While some 800 Macon men and women watched, an autogyro like a big yellow butterfly, buzzed over Miller Field yesterday morning, swooped close to the ground, paused and lit. From it stepped Amelia Earhart, most famous of women fliers, smiling and smaller than most people expected."

Well, needless to say, Amelia never made it back. But not very long after her visit, in 1936, the city fathers and civic heads of Macon became airplane enthusiasts themselves. At least they got their eyes off the ground.

What prompted their interest was the devastating effect of the Great Depression on Macon and Bibb County, whose entire economy had hitherto been almost totally entangled—in all of its multifarious commercial and cultural ramifications—with agriculture. In the face of ruin, their first plan had been to expand livestock production and diversify the local crops. But then, lo, an answer appeared in the skies—in the form of the war clouds over Europe.

Because Macon had earlier secured a naval ordnance plant, Maconites had established a good political relationship with Rep. Carl Vinson, then-chairman of the House Naval Affairs Committee, who let them in on the government's plans to locate one of five major air depots—places to maintain military aircraft and train aircraft repair teams—in the Southeast. Through Vinson they requested that consideration be given to their area. They offered the government, as a gift, any suitable tract of land in the vicinity. Now all the Macon promoters needed to do was find several thousand available acres nearby.

At about this time a certain Charles B. "Boss" Watson, postmaster of Wellston in the northern part of Houston County, began buying up parcels of local land. Wellston, a village of forty-seven purely rural souls, offered all the highlights of a one-horse town: a grocery store, a sawmill, a stop on the railroad line. In time, Watson gathered enough land so that Macon was able, in the spring of 1941, to offer the government immediate access to eighteen hundred acres, with seven hundred more available on demand.

Other cities were also vying for the depot, including Atlanta, Dublin, Albany, Milledgeville, Cordele, and Vienna. Finally the race was narrowed to Atlanta and Macon, and when the army engineers took account of Wellston's rock-free level land and virtually virgin terrain, and when the Maconites further secured promises from local contractors to build three thousand new homes, Representative Vinson was able to wire the local chamber of commerce in June of 1941 that the deal was done. Macon had won by offering, for "one dollar and other good and valuable considerations," the total of 3,108 acres—of land that lay in another county, Houston. It may seem odd that Representative Vinson, from Milledgeville, represented the Sixth Congressional District, which included neither Bibb nor Houston County.

By January of 1942 the first buildings were occupied of what was first called the Wellston Air Depot, then Robins Field, in honor of General Augustus Warner Robins, and finally, by October of that year, Warner Robins Army Air Depot.

Meanwhile, thousands of people were pouring into the area, and little Wellston was virtually consumed. In March 1943, the village gave up its name and the city of Warner Robins was incorporated. "Boss" Watson, the farsighted postmaster, was its first mayor. Warner Robins became a genuine wartime and then Cold War boomtown. With the depot here, the once-bucolic people of Bibb, Houston, and the surrounding counties finally began doing things of actual global significance. As it presently stands, the complex including Robins Air Force Base and Warner Robins Air Logistics Center (as it is now called) covers 8,790 acres and employs over four thousand military and sixteen thousand civilian personnel, making it Georgia's largest single industry. Its total annual economic impact on middle Georgia as of 1990—and on Macon, the city that literally gave Warner Robbins its wing—was $1.8 billion.

Following a map, I find myself on Ga. 247 into Warner Robins, and soon notice that this is the Gen. Robert L. Scott Highway. I sure know who Scott is. As a fighter pilot with the famous Flying Tigers in China, then-Colonel Scott was not only one of America's first "aces" of World War II, but he wrote the 1943 bestseller—later made into a popular movie—*God Is My Co-pilot*. I remember he hailed from Macon and wonder if he's still alive.

The Museum of Aviation, located on the edge of the Air Base, is a treasure trove for people intrigued with warbirds of yesteryear. There are, in fact, enough such people that nearly 2 million have come here since its opening in 1984, making it one of middle Georgia's largest tourist attractions.

Positioned around the main three-story blue building are some eighty of the most famous planes in the world. Inside are exhibits depicting, among other things, a WWII British airfield with a P-51 Mustang and a rotunda featuring America's current top-of-the-line fighter, the F-15 Eagle. There are also photos of American fliers in Burma and a large oil portrait of then-Colonel Scott in his Army Air Corps uniform. On inquiring, I am told that not only is Scott still alive, but he has an office on the third floor and is probably up there now.

No sooner have I run upstairs than Brig. Gen. Robert L. Scott Jr. himself emerges from his office with outstretched hand. He has just returned from a speaking engagement in North Georgia, telling the audience, he says, "about my sordid life, how I've lied and cheated and stolen to do things I wanted to do."

Since 1986 he has been a volunteer here at the museum, which provides him with a fine office with big windows. "I do anything I can help the museum by doing," he says. "People call here asking me to make speeches, and Peggy will say, 'He doesn't take honoraria, but if you give a little check to the museum, he'll come make it.' So that's the way I handle it."

Scott speaks at a fairly rapid pace with a mild southern accent in a baritone voice barely frayed with age. He is, in fact, a few months shy

Museum of Aviation, Warner Robins

of eighty-seven, yet every bit as trim and fit as his fifty-year-old portrait downstairs. His hair, once dark, has receded across the top of his head, and what remains gives the impression of a snow white wreath. His eyes are a clear sky-blue.

He says he grew up in Macon from the time he was two and that his first flight was off a building in Macon—and into a thorn bush sixty-seven feet below, at the age of twelve. His most recent flight was a few days ago in an F-15, and if the weather looks good he's going to do it again tomorrow.

"I've been very fortunate," he says. "And God knows, I had the one girl in the world who would stand for her husband doing things like that. They blew whistles every night in Macon when they heard I got another Japanese plane, and put the numbers up in the *Macon Daily Telegraph*, where I'd been a paper boy. And Katherine would wake up and hear those sirens going and say, 'I wonder if number twelve will get Scotty.'" His final score of "kills" was twenty-two. "My last day in combat was my best day in the world," he nods. "I got four bombers that one day. I was hit once," he says,

and that gave me the title for the book. They hit my armor plate with a cannon shell over Hong Kong on a day when we attacked twenty-eight airplanes with our eight. We got nineteen, but they got behind me and hit my armor plate with a cannon shell—the armor plate behind the pilot's seat—and it sounded like the airplane's coming apart when that happened. The armor saved my life, but the shell knocked rivets from the armor into my back. And when I got back to Kweilin—we lived in a cave at Kweilin, we had no hospital—Dr. Fred P. Manget, who was raised in Macon, he had me put up there on a table and began to take these rivet heads out without benefit of anaesthetic and no liquor. And to keep me conscious, I didn't know what he was doing, a big Chinese held this arm; but he was countin' the pulse, and he would nod at the doctor if it was time to stop. And he nearly drove me crazy. "You shoot the guns, you fly the fiji," that's a fighter plane in Chinese, "You destroy the barbarian, you come back alone."

And I said, "Yes, I'm alone, goddammit, I'm a fighter pilot." And there was a quiet you could cut with a knife, and Dr. Manget, this missionary, steps out and holds up this last rivet head and drops it in a tin trash can and says, "Oh no, son, you're not alone or you wouldn't come back from this." And through tears in my eyes I saw "God is my co-pilot" in the darkness of this cave.

God Is My Co-pilot was the first of fifteen books he has published. The movie version had its world premiere in 1945 at the Grand Opera House in Macon. The old war hero pauses and gazes at a plane coming in for a landing. "Macon has been so nice to me since I was a little boy that I didn't even consider retiring in this area. Because it's like you don't want people to find out, people who really like you, to find out that you got an Achilles heel somewhere."

As to his age, he shrugs, "I figure I make a million dollars a week by the people I meet around here, so I don't feel old. I'm very fortunate, I don't have any problems. The only way I even feel like I'm old is my mouth gets dry when I talk. Now I run when I ought to walk. I walked the Great Wall from one end to the other in 1980 and wrote a book about it. And things like that, if you keep moving these muscles you'll have 'em."

He points out some memorabilia and photos in his office and then confides, "This museum saved my life. Old people don't have a purpose in life, and this museum gives me a purpose."

General Scott squints up at the sky and declares, "I'm waiting for a day like yesterday was, well this was just about good enough at midday. But tomorrow I'm going to sixty thousand feet in an F-15 and take a picture of the museum from ten miles above it, to show Macon, I think, and Perry, where Sam Nunn is from, and Fort Valley, where my Katherine is from. There's the Air Force insignia on top of this building, a beautiful thing up there. This, to my mind, is the most striking museum in the whole world. As we cut the ribbon I said, 'This is better than the Louvre in Paris.' I knew it would be good, but I didn't know it would be this good.'"

Maybe you were there when the undulating pink amoebic shapes danced across the sky while heliotrope lights exploded in the fragrant, smoky blackness and a blinding stream of electric notes skirled out into the night—to be answered by the distant echo of a bellowing cow.

You might have seen the longhaired, shirtless boy in overalls and a blissful smile doing a slow, stoned, purely private, barefoot, boogie-shuffle-step in the red Georgia dirt. You might have even *been* that boy, and you could have come from anywhere, you and forty thousand others—from California, Oregon, Michigan, New York. In July 1970, the *Hippoisie* from all over, with every corrupt thing they carried, descended like a malignant wave on a gone-bust racetrack outside the tiny (population 1,368) town of Byron for what became the legendary Byron Pop Festival—and nothing seems to have been quite the same since.

Terry Deese, now a middle-aged major in the Peach County Sheriff's office, remembers, "I was at a church softball game, on the team. It was a Saturday afternoon. The preacher came out and called us all inside. Said we should immediately go home to our families. Said, 'The hippies have taken over Vinson Valley.'"

Terry, then sixteen, says that in the face of this threat, "A couple of us got in a car to see what was going on. From Byron north it was solid people. It was the dawn of a new era. We didn't know what drugs were. It opened a door for us."

In the wake of this historic Southern Woodstock, horrified Byron-ites passed ordinances, "to keep it from ever happening again," says Terry, "plus the clean-up took months." Today Byron, in Peach County, takes pride in the thirty-foot wide peach—visible to travelers on

I-75—that advertises the Peach Outlet Mall, not far from where each June they hold the Peach Festival with annual prizes for the "largest peach cobbler."

Today the old racetrack lies vacant. Just behind it is a trailer park, populated mostly by Mexican field workers who move with the seasons. But the current outrage to the mores of greater Byron is Cafe Erotica, the new strip joint that promotes itself on I-75 billboards all the way from the state line. "The citizens don't want it, they're fighting it," says Terry. "They picketed it for months. But now a new joint has branched off, the Neon Cowboy. Totally nude. The girls, I think, are out of Florida."

Peach is Georgia's freshest county, having been sliced off the northwestern corner of Houston in 1924. Houston itself was originally a huge county when it was created in 1821, then gave up portions of itself to form all or part of Upson, Crawford, Macon, Pulaski, Bibb, and finally Peach. But the town of Elberta remains in Houston. Elberta was named for the peach that was named for the wife of Samuel Rumph, who tinkered with nature in the 1870s and came up with a flavorful peach of remarkable size and texture, which, by 1900, made Houston the largest peach growing county in America—and which, because of its eventual economic impact, gave Georgia the nickname of "Peach State."

Perry was the first official town in Houston in 1824 and was named for Commodore Oliver Hazard ("We have met the enemy and they are ours") Perry, hero of the War of 1812. Today, while agriculture and its peripheral industries are still strong here, and while Warner Robins up the road certainly counts for a lot, the Number One source of Perry's prosperity is tourism. Hence its downtown area is now dolled up in the style of Williamsburg.

Perry's self-descriptive slogan is the "Crossroads of Georgia," thanks to its being the intersection point of I-75 and highways 41, 341, and the Golden Isles Parkway. As a consequence of all this traffic, Perry, with a population just under ten thousand, now boasts of its vast Georgia National Fairgrounds and Agricenter, a major regional gathering point, which, since opening in 1990, has had nearly three million visitors attending livestock shows, dog, horse, flower and antique shows, rodeos, musical events, square dances, proms, carnivals, even family reunions.

According to Perry's most prominent favorite son, U.S. Senator Sam Nunn, the hub around which so much of the city's tourist trade has been built is the nationally known New Perry Hotel, a three-story Federal-ish structure with six white columns flanking the entranceway. The New Perry, on Main Street, was built on the site of the old Perry in 1925, when U.S. 41 was paved from Tennessee to the Florida line. Mrs. Yates Green, who, with her late husband, has managed the

JUST PEACHY

How do you make the world's largest peach cobbler? Combine 1,500 pounds of peaches, 350 pounds of sugar, 150 pounds of self-rising flour, 90 pounds of margarine, and 32 gallons of milk to make the five-by-ten-foot dessert served during Fort Valley's annual Georgia Peach Festival in June.

—Betsy Braden and John Braden

hotel for half a century, says, "Perry has gotten too big for me, but there's no other hotel like this anywhere." She reflects on the many famous people who've stayed here. I myself recall hearing of when Lash Larue, the cowboy star, stayed overnight, allegedly too drunk to hear himself being serenaded beneath his window on a ukelele by pig-tailed, eight-year-old Laurie Anderson, daughter of the local judge and former mayor.

"I remember so well growing up here," says Senator Nunn. "You know, when I think about Perry I think about the summer evenings, the front porches of so many homes where people sat out. I think about the church on Sunday night."

Senator Nunn reflects on the changes that have transformed his hometown and Georgia just within the course of his lifetime. "I was born in 1938," he says, "and when I think of 1938, that was an eventful year. Cotton was eight cents a pound; the *Progressive Farmer* magazine began that year pushing kudzu very, very hard as a soil conservation practice—but all things don't work out. The big economic issue of the day was the equalization of rail rates. Back then the rail rates from the North were very cheap—they could bring their goods down very cheaply—and those in the South trying to ship North had to pay through the nose. Finally, after Governor Ellis Arnall brought a suit to the U.S. Supreme Court, we got equal rail rates and that had a whole lot to do with the industrialization of Georgia and the South.

"Not long after I was born," he says, "Perry's sons marched off to war. As they say, they left as boys and came back as men. And they came back to a different world—where horses and mules were no longer dominant, where farm machinery was really prevalent everywhere, and where automobiles were becoming a fixture in every garage. It was also a world that had started to air condition itself. Air conditioning probably had as much to do with changing the South as rail rates. So we've undergone radical change in every direction.

"I learned something else growing up in Perry that we've all learned in the last thirty or so years. I learned that black people have the same fears, the same pains, hopes, aspirations, dreams, the same family ties as white people. I learned in a period of great tension—and in this case it was racial tension—that there's no substitute for communication. There's no substitute for people sitting down and talking to one another. We were able to do that here. And to this day I believe that the communication—which we continued—helped make sure that Perry was not the place where racial tension grew into violence. Those were valuable lessons I learned here. And I continue to learn from Perry. I continue to get my inspiration here. I continue to have my conscience pricked by this community."

Just off one of Perry's Interstate exits, on Sam Nunn Boulevard, stands Kimberly Barbecue, a small, modern, brick building with none of the rustic atmospherics typical of such establishments. The floor is carpeted for one thing, and the decor is bright and neat. It's near the 10 P.M. closing time, but Kimberly stands beside the counter and directs one of his young employees in a firm but fatherly way. He is a lean man in his mid-fifties, quite tall, wearing a black suit and professorial gold-rimmed glasses. "There's a piece of paper under those chairs," he points. "You can pick it up by hand, won't hurt you. Then go wash your hands."

Kimberly has been in business here since 1969. "We're right on the edge of our black community," he notes. "This area here was carved out of a black community. But the thing is, we're on the beaten path and we run a respectable service. We don't have people standing on the corner. The community respect us, we respect the community. It's time that we all work together."

He remembers the time his place was jammed with journalists from everywhere who descended on Perry in 1970 for the first public stirrings of a civil rights demonstration march that erupted here and moved all the way up to Atlanta. "Those were turbulent years," he shakes his head. "I was here. Yes, sir. I'm native, I was spawned here. I came out of something little better than apartheid. And I've seen the changes."

He says that Perry itself "within the last five or so years has come into the twentieth century. It was too small, too backward in the area of housing, fair housing, jobs. People who were in a superior position were in control. Now I attend city council meetings and am on a first-name basis with the members. It's a town that depends upon how you live, how you think, how you work, how you respect yourself. We're like any town. So, I would recommend it. In fact, when I'm out of the state, the Department of Industry and Trade should owe me a lot of money, 'cause I advertise Perry, Georgia, wherever I am."

Kimberly is firmly proud of the barbecuing skills he learned from his father. "I had some good teachers. So you eat it, you critique it, you say the man does it with wisdom, which is passed down," he smiles. "I was also taught the customer is always to be treated with royalty. I look upon people, especially young people, as future customers at some point. That's what the big companies do. They look beyond this into the year 2010 to see what the market's going to be."

He looks over at one of his two young employees attending to a table. "Push it back towards the wall. Gotta have that tablecloth *square*. People look at your place when they come in, son."

Just down from Kimberly's are most of the motels that allow Perry to boast of roughly thirteen hundred rooms for overnight lodging. One of these motels advertises itself as Under American Management. The rest around here—and seemingly most of the motels throughout

Middle Georgia, in these closing years of the twentieth century—are operated by individuals who are naturalized citizens or legal aliens from India.

A little Road Music:

Here's a farm beyond Perry where one can actually come eye-to-eye with tall, unearthly birds. When the cowboys at the Black Diamond Ranch hold a roundup, what they round up is emus. And ostriches. And rheas. Ratites all. Ratites are large flightless birds from Australia and Africa that produce meat, leather, oil, and fancy feathers; and the industry that raises and produces the birds themselves is now where the poultry industry was forty years ago. And growing.

Here's a painting in a dean's office at Fort Valley State College depicting Mt. Rushmore, with the old familiar faces replaced by Martin Luther King, Malcolm X, Harriet Tubman, and Thurgood Marshall.

Fluffs and wads of cotton, spilled from fast trucks, line the shoulders of the two-lane highways, like roadside snow.

Sign in front of a handsome brick house just off the highway in Dodge County:

FOR SALE
Due To Rattlesnakes.

And here is one of the South's more ornate and aesthetically pleasing monuments to the unconquerable spirit of our warrior past: Hawkinsville's Confederate Memorial, standing at the right shoulder of Hawkinsville's similarly elegant 1841 courthouse and backed by the broadest, biggest magnolia tree that the Lord allows. There's one of these stone tributes somewhere in just about every county seat in Georgia, but few are as nice as this: The common rebel, in this version, leans on his rifle atop a tall stone column whose lower third is carved with the image of a Confederate flag drooping from a broken standard. Flanking the spire are statues of Generals Lee and Jackson. "Comrades," it says, and beneath that, a stone plaque: "To Our Confederate Soldiers." The base of this monument is ringed with flowering plants and in front today is a fresh holly wreath with a red-and-white bow and ribbons saying "Season's Greetings."

Pulaski County was hewn from land the Creeks ceded in 1805. It became a county in 1808 and was named for a Polish nobleman, Count Casimir Pulaski, who was killed in Savannah during the Revolution. Hawkinsville, which became the county seat in 1836, was named for Benjamin Hawkins, an Indian agent and later politician, who helped open up Central Georgia to settlement.

At present about thirty-seven-hundred people are settled in Hawkinsville itself, and they seem determined to make a healthy comeback—if not to the days when Hawkinsville was a vital cotton ginning center and riverport on the Ocmulgee for barges and steamboats, at least to a level of sustainable growth.

"Hawkinsville is definitely growing; our business is up," declares Chuck Southerland, publisher of the *Hawkinsville Dispatch & News,* a weekly that consists largely of gossip columns. As for current local issues, "Well," he says, "there's a new school superintendent come to town tryin' to change the curriculum, who's got a lotta people stirred up. Where he come from they did it that way and it seemed to work." The newspaper office is a block down the street from the city's onetime movie house, a well-made, large-capacity theater that's been dark for a full decade now. "It folded due to cable TV, VCRs, home movies and such," he shrugs, "just like in every small town."

There are at least two major local features for which Hawkinsville simply has no competition. One of these is the City Hall and Auditorium, or "Old Opera House," as it is called. Built in 1907, it is one of three such vaudeville opera houses left in Georgia—the other two being in Columbus and Macon. Oliver Hardy, a native Georgian, often played here in his pre–Stan Laurel days and stayed overnight up at the hotel his aunt ran, just across from the courthouse. In properly dramatic fashion, this old theater—a really nice one with a semicircular balcony and a large array of theatrical effects—was saved by the skin of its teeth, just as the wrecking ball was about to swing, by some local preservationists in 1976 and has since had a major facelift and gone on to host concerts by major symphony orchestras and jazz bands, stage plays, and numberless presentations.

The other thing that's distinctively Hawkinsville is harness racing. Harness racing started here in the 1880s when the men would wager on the speed of their buggies and the women would come out to watch the contest. Ten years later the town became a stop on the grand racing circuit. In the 1930s horse trainers began wintering their horses in Hawkinsville. And today the fine art of harness racing is honed almost year-round at the modern, city-built Hawkinsville Horse Training Center outside town.

Each October trainers bring their horses, several hundred of them, to the center and work throughout the winter on improving their performances—as trotters or pacers, the two styles of gait that define Standardbred harness racehorses—until the steeds are ready to travel up North for a summer of racing on the big-money tracks. The horses' period of training is officially complete by the time of the annual Hawkinsville Harness Horse Festival on the first weekend in April, and upwards of ten thousand spectators and interested parties come out to watch what are essentially out-of-town tryouts, or professional debuts, to let the trainers see what they can expect from the objects of their affections.

Harness racing at Hawkinsville

But this is early November, work-out season, and out on the race-course at dawn today is a single horse named Anu coming around the far curve, trussed up in the elaborate leather lacing that links the horse to the lightweight two-wheeled sulky with its goggled, red hel-meted jockey perched aboard. There is no other sound in the still air except the syncopated beat of Anu's trotting gait, now coming around the near curve, the horse legs clipping along and the sulky wheels slicing with exquisite symmetry through a light, knee-high fog that lingers on the morning track.

From Hawkinsville, on horseback, you can reach Eastman within a couple of hours. Dodge became a county in 1870, about the time the lumber business began to boom in Georgia. It was carved out of Pu-laski County and was named not for a statesman or military hero but for one William E. Dodge, a New York industrialist and developer of the first lumbermill towns in the state. His folks later went on to make cars. Eastman was named for one of his business cronies.

Dodge built the first courthouse here in Eastman, which was certainly nice of him. But on the other hand it should be remembered that his Dodge Land and Lumber Company, which came into the state in 1868, laid claim, through questionable deeds, to over 300,000 acres of the finest longleaf yellow pine in the world—on land that in-cluded the present counties of Telfair, Dodge, Laurens, Montgomery, and Pulaski. For this they paid less than ten cents an acre.

Meanwhile, according to the State of Georgia, there were local resi-dents, farmers, who had valid titles and had paid taxes on that same land for forty years. The Dodge Company appealed to the Republican-controlled federal courts and was awarded all the lands it had seized since the Civil War.

As the company proceeded to evict the settlers, a regional war erupted. A Dodge superintendent was assassinated in 1890. Others died in response. Unable to locate an assassin, federal authorities developed a conspiracy case against any individuals who had ever criticized the Dodges. Ultimately, sheriffs, mayors, state representatives, and others were found guilty and sent to the Ohio State Penitentiary.

Not satisfied, in 1894 the Dodge Company launched a giant conspiracy case against almost four hundred landowners, a case that was not settled until 1923. In the end, many of the lots were returned to their original claimants. But by that time the timbering operations of the Dodges and others had completely depleted the great stands of longleaf yellow pine trees, the largest sawmill in the South had burned to the ground, and there was nothing left to exploit.

So the Dodges forgot about their Central Georgia namesake county and concentrated on the automobile business. But they left bad blood. People still speak of it.

Since that time, Dodge County, and Eastman in particular, has been identified with the candy empire created by Williamson Sylvester Stuckey—an empire that, at its height, extended to more than three hundred profitable stores on major highways and interstates all across the country. Had one myself.

I remember Eastman from 1966, when I lived here as speechwriter and campaign strategist for W. S. (Billy) Stuckey Jr.'s first campaign for Congress, representing Georgia's "Bloody Eighth" Congressional district—of which Dodge and most of these other counties are still a part.

In 1966, Eastman was associated with one industry: Stuckey's. Today there's not a trace of the grand old name, once synonymous with "pecan log roll." The original store on Highway 23/341 is now a restaurant, the candy plant has different owners, and the elegant Stuckey's Carriage Inn, the flagship of a small fleet of such inns, lies in rubble on the roadside.

Stuckey stores still exist out in the land, but Stuckey's is now headquartered in Washington, D.C., where Billy Stuckey has continued to live after serving five terms in Congress. As for the sad fate of the Carriage Inn: "People came from all over to carry away a piece of rock or rubble as a memento," nods Orene Burns, Billy's octogenarian aunt. "If it hadn't been for Stuckey," she says, "so many people wouldn't have had anything."

Orene seems resigned to the commercial intrusions upon Eastman. "But honey, some of our beautiful homes burned to make way for some of these things. One beautiful colonial home burned to put a filling station in. You know, those sooty filling stations have ruined everything. Can't keep your draperies clean no matter what you put up."

Indeed, the dominant new sights along the thoroughfares of Eastman now include: Hardee's, McDonald's, Pizza Hut, and Texaco; Fina, Chevron, Exxon, and Revco; Piggly Wiggly, Pizza Inn, Huddle House, and KFC; Dairy Queen, Chic-King, Wal-Mart, and three motels managed by Indians—each one representing another advance of civilization as we know it, yet another commercial step along the road leading towards every place becoming pretty much like everyplace else, and nowhere in particular. Eastman does, however, have an unusual new church, built on land donated by Billy Stuckey—the St. Mark Catholic Church, smack in the heart of Baptist country, with a priest who is black and a swelling membership consisting mostly of Mexican field workers.

Julia Roberts, editor of the *Times-Journal Spotlight*, takes a whimsical view of the good old days in Dodge. "There's no telling how many bodies that old Ocmulgee River could cough up," she says. Currently she's concerned about a by-pass being built on the Golden Isles Parkway which will go around Eastman. With I-75 far to the west and I-16 to the east, poor Eastman will be off the beaten track from anywhere. "That bypass is going to kill our little town if it is used."

Many of the little towns around here "have sort of dried up," she says. "Roddy, Empire, Plainfield, Chauncey. They try to keep things going, and most have branch banks, but see, these little satellite communities no longer have schools. They're all right here in Eastman. Looking down the road they could become ghost towns. But we all could. I believe within ten years, maybe less, we won't know our little towns like Eastman like we know 'em today, because they're branching out from the downtown areas to the Wal-Marts and the shopping centers.

"We are, however, literally surrounded by prisons," she says, then shrugs. "Only good thing I can say about it is that it has brought a lot of new jobs."

Tucked away in Eastman's new industrial park are two prison facilities. The first is the Eastman Regional Youth Detention Center, which holds juveniles from fourteen surrounding counties who are awaiting trial. It is operated by the state's Department of Children and Youth Services.

The second, run by the Department of Corrections, is the Eastman Youth Development Facility, a benign-sounding name for an impregnable state-of-the-art prison for hard-core young offenders from thirteen to twenty years old who have assaulted inmates or guards in other prisons and who are held here in solitary cells under "close security," the next thing to maximum security. It is surrounded by a patented climb-proof metal fence that rises twelve feet in a high, inward-curving arch, with the last four feet made of minimesh and a line of razor wire along the edge.

Warden Wayne Peacock, a wiry and intense man in his mid-fifties, dark-haired with dark-tinted glasses, is proud of what he and his staff have accomplished at the YDF since it opened in 1993. "There's not another facility like this in the world," he says. "It's as much like an adult prison as a youth facility can be. A lot of states and other countries have sent observers here to learn about doing what we're doing. This is a treatment center. The kids we got here are the worst of the worst. We've got 'em in education, counseling, phys ed, and work adjustment. It's a semi-boot camp, one kid to a cell, escorted everywhere, supervised twenty-four hours a day. It's more structured than anything they've ever had in their lives."

He says the YDF, currently with ninety-seven inmates, has had an impact on every kid who's passed through here—in terms of undoing some of the damage from their dysfunctional families. "We've got 'em doing what they're told. Our whole thrust here is to get 'em to do right because they want to, wanting to do a good job. Why do you want to do a good job? Because it feels good to do a good job, it pleases you, gives you a good feeling.

"That's what we do with these kids. We bring 'em in and test 'em and scare the hell out of them, and then we prescribe what level of school they should be on and plug 'em in. Someone comes in here with a third grade level in reading, when he makes ninety or a hundred in a math test we give him a certificate and pat him on the back and brag on him, and they like that. So that's what our whole program is based on—positive reinforcement."

Warden Peacock says prisons in Georgia are "definitely a growth business." He points to a map of the other facilities within these twenty-six counties: In this county there's the Dodge Correctional Institution in Chester and the Milan C.I., then there's the Telfair C.I. in Helena, the Pulaski C.I. for women in Hawkinsville, the Wilcox C.I. in Abbeville, the Johnson C.I. in Wrightsville, and the Treutlen Boot Camp in Soperton. Bibb County has the Central C.I., the Macon Transitional Center, and the Macon Diversion Center. And up in Baldwin County, portions of the once-vast Central State Hospital in Milledgeville have been converted into five separate state prisons.

Outside, a group of young felons is counting military cadence. He says it costs about fifty thousand dollars to keep a prisoner here for a year. "The Department of Corrections has been most supportive of us in putting together a program based on the idea of discipline and making people feel good about doing good."

If Rhine, Georgia, were a person instead of a very small town, it probably would have served some of its life in prison. Rhine, named by settlers of German descent in the 1880s, is known far and wide as "the meanest place there is."

For whatever reason, probably aided by the one-time profusion of moonshine stills in the area, people from Rhine have always had the reputation of being prone to easy aggravation—and willing, at the drop of nothing at all, to back up their words with gunplay.

One local character legendarily adept with the firearm was "Old John" Stuckey (no relation to the Eastman Stuckeys) who, even after an accident landed him in a wheelchair, always carried a rifle and a pistol, with which he managed to shoot and kill his own son in a fit of drunken ire.

Rhine once had two cotton gins, a grist and flour mill, a nearby sawmill, a railroad depot, and bus service. Today it has a small array of stores and shops necessary for a population of fewer than five hundred; a branch bank; a cafe; several residential yards jammed with old cars, some of which are for sale; a couple of filling stations; a Methodist church; a Baptist church; and something called Delton Hilliard's Snake Show. Here, in Belvin's Appliance, Furniture and Monument Company, owner Lucile Conley, along with the local postmaster and a furniture salesman, is eager to disabuse anyone of the notion that Rhine today is anything at all like the way it has always been.

"We got that reputation as a gunslinging, mean town, where everybody was afraid to come through here, afraid to stop at our filling stations," says Mrs. Conley, "but it's not really like that. We've got a wonderful spirit of cooperation and community here. We come together better than anyplace in the world." The other two agree completely. "Yeah," says the postmaster, "we can talk about each other here, but you can't."

A mile-long bridge west of Rhine traverses the Ocmulgee and delivers you into another age, or at least into a county that seems pretty much the way it was in Gene Talmadge's time. Wilcox is considered 100 percent rural inasmuch as its two largest towns, Abbeville—the county seat, which does have a lovely courthouse—and Rochelle, have populations of 907 and 1,510, respectively—not quite enough to qualify as urban. Whereas only 1.2 percent of all Georgians are rural farm dwellers, here in Wilcox 11.4 percent of the citizens live and work on their farms.

The old one- and two-horse farms of the Roosevelt era, however, are increasingly rare. As one farmer put it, "There are not many small family farms left because an individual now farms thousands of acres. Has to. You need a lot of land to keep the machines busy. Can't have fifteen or twenty acres and have a mechanical cotton picker. A tractor nowadays costs seventy-five to a hundred thousand dollars. Forty years ago you got a tractor for three thousand. Also, successful farm-

Cotton gin house and bale press, circa 1900

ers now have computers that tell 'em the correct amount of seeds per acre and every other thing. It's highly technical now."

Dooly County was created at the same time as Houston County, after the Creek Nation signed the Treaty of Indian Springs in 1821. Long before that, in 1540, DeSoto may have passed through these lands, then continued his exploratory treasure-seeking trek north.

The original Dooly, Georgia's twenty-second county, was an enormous expanse, later carved up to form Crisp County, most of Pulaski, and parts of Wilcox, Turner, Worth, and Macon. Dooly was named for Col. John Dooly, a hero of the Revolution who was foully murdered. Its county seat was originally called Centerville until someone came up with the inspired notion of naming it after the Austrian city of Vienna. (It is, however, known as Vy-anna in Georgia.)

Vienna, with a population of twenty-eight hundred, presides like an architectural apparition of yore, virtually unchanged over the past century since its courthouse was constructed. Its honored native son, whose bust graces the town square, is the late, once-powerful U.S. senator Walter F. George, architect of the NATO alliance, who resigned from the Senate in 1955 rather than run against Herman Talmadge.

Three-quarters of Dooly's ten thousand inhabitants live in rural circumstances. Almost half are black, and together the black and white farmers here are said to produce more cotton than any other county in Georgia. Peanut production is huge, but there are also corn, soybeans, wheat, oats, rye, sorghum, and pecans.

Ten miles south of here—the second exit off I-75—is Cordele, the seat of Crisp County. Crisp was named for Congressman Charles Crisp of Americus, who became Speaker of the U.S. House of Representatives. Cordele was founded in 1888 as a railroad junction and named for Cordelia Hawkins, whose father was president of the Savannah, Americus and Montgomery Railroad.

Cordele clearly casts its lot with the modern age by displaying a Titan ICBM in plain sight of the highway. The 110-foot missile, a relic of the early sixties, rests on "Confederate Air Force Pad No. 1" beside a filling station and manages to lure off the interstate a steady stream of tourists whose trade is vital to Cordele's economy. Agribusiness is the chief component of the general economy, and Cordelians are eager to advertise their town as "The Watermelon Capital of the World."

Darren Drevik, publisher of the *Cordele Dispatch,* says Cordele, with eleven thousand citizens, "is as close as you can come to the idyllic small town." The town is at least large enough to merit a daily newspaper, though he points out that it is the smallest daily in Georgia, with 5,125 subscribers.

The interstate traffic is a blessing, he says, because it brings people through, but it also inspires sharp-eyed, fast-buck types from elsewhere to set up strip joints similar to Cafe Erotica up in Byron. One such establishment just went under because, he says, "Here in the Bible belt it's kinda hard to get local clientele to come out to a nudie bar."

Cordele is more than half black, yet, according to Drevik—and this seems generally true throughout the rest of central Georgia at this juncture in history—there are no traces of racial strife or stress or prejudicial posturings in the ongoing life of Cordele and Crisp. "There's a spirit of inclusion here," he says, pointing to white support of black political officeholders. "I think somehow we've figured out that diversity can be a strength rather than a weakness."

If Drevik had his druthers he would make Cordele "more aggressive and progressive. I think it's afraid to grow. Too many people see development as something that could destroy their way of life and are threatened by change."

The most dramatic evidence of change over the past year has been the draining of Lake Blackshear, just west of town, as a result of a broken dam on the Flint River caused by the great flood of 1994. The great sweeping lake is presently reduced to a huge, strange, tree-ringed depression covered with grassy vegetation and a meander of water twining through it like an open ditch.

Down U.S. 41, past the dying town of Arabi, consisting mostly of cotton wagons resting under sheds, and into Turner County: The highway winds between pecan groves, large fields of unpicked cotton, tall stands of longleaf pines, and vagrant spreads of nearby wiregrass. And masses of migrating birds. Here's a huge swirl of small starlings high up in the air, wheeling, pouring, flexing, and expanding like the flow of an amoeba.

Ashburn is both the county seat and "The Peanut Capital of the World." Near the Ashburn exit on I-75 is the Big Peanut Monument, and a Peanut Museum, promising to display peanuts past present and future, is under construction in the heart of town. And yet:

"Worth County *actually* has the title of peanut capital because their county's so big," allows Ben Baker, editor-publisher-general manager of the *Wiregrass Farmer,* "but Turner County grows more peanuts per acre than anyplace else in the state of Georgia."

Turner is pretty small, he says, "but it has more farmland under current tillage; more land per square mile is farmed here than anyplace else in the state. We are the most agriculturally intensive county in Georgia."

Ben, a bright, round-faced twenty-seven-year-old with a thin moustache, was faced with the options of becoming a mechanic, a farmer, or a writer, until his farmer father took him aside and told him how hard it was. So now he writes about farmers.

"Farmers are the most independent persons in the nation," he declares. "You're not going to find anybody that's more stubborn, more proud and, as a general rule, smarter than a farmer. People will look at a farmer and say, 'He's just a farmer, he doesn't know anything.' I'll take any farmer out here that's been at this ten, twenty years and match him against an MIT physicist, as far as doing mathematical equations. The farmer does equations in his head *every day.* He may not know *why* something happens but he can tell you *how* it happens and what's going to happen when it does happen. They're smart. Common sense. They know more than people give 'em credit for. For generations back my family farmed."

Ben says Ashburn retains much of its character as "a very religious community, with lots of Irish and Germanic descendants here." They are hard-working, they're conservative, they vote Democratic, and for local entertainment they happily attend big gospel sings at the civic center. But he shakes his head over the town's eighty-two-hundred inhabitants: "We're losing population slowly."

Irwin was another giant county when it was laid out as Georgia's nineteenth and named for Gov. Jared Irwin, a Revolutionary War hero who also gave his name to the original county seat, Irwinville. Irwinville later lost out as county seat to Ocilla, but it is forever etched in the hearts of Civil War buffs as the site of Jeff Davis's capture by Federal troops a month after Lee's surrender at Appomattox.

There's a Jefferson Davis Memorial Park in Irwinville, but it's closed for repairs. Nonetheless, President Davis's fateful trek through middle Georgia is worth remembering:

Jefferson Davis and an escort of officers and cabinet members, with over $300,000 in gold and silver from the Confederate Treasury, fled Richmond, Virginia, in early April of 1865. By May 4, in Washington, Georgia, they convened the Confederate government for a final time, and dissolved. Meanwhile, Pres. Andrew Johnson, regarding Davis responsible for Lincoln's assassination, offered $100,000 in gold for his capture.

In the hope of making his way to Mexico, Davis and twenty men with three wagons fled to Sandersville, then crossed the Oconee and reached Dublin on May 7, where Davis was reunited with his family. They then traveled through what is now Dodge County, were ferried across the Ocmulgee, and camped near Abbeville on May 9.

The following day, not knowing that two separate columns of Union cavalry were hot on their trail, the Davis party proceeded to a point a mile north of the village of Irwinville and camped in a pine grove beside a stream.

At about two o'clock on the morning of May 10, the First Wisconsin and the Fourth Michigan cavalries, coming from different directions, came upon the camp and began shooting—at each other.

Davis came out of his tent in the early mist to see a soldier on horseback drawing a bead on him. Davis intended to rush the horseman, unseat him, and flee, but just then his wife rushed forward and threw her arms around her husband's neck, telling the soldier to shoot her instead. At this, Davis surrendered. "God's will be done," he said, then sat upon a log by the campfire. In moments, a Michigan colonel rode up and said, "Well, old Jeff, we've got you at last."

From here Davis was escorted to Macon, then to Savannah, and finally to prison at Fortress Monroe, Virginia. But he came back to Georgia twenty-two years later, to Macon in 1887, where, though frail, he drew a crowd of fifty thousand in what was his last public appearance. On that occasion, he rose from his chair at the sight of a torn battle flag, reached over the rail and drew it to him to kiss its folds. This act, they say, drew open tears from the thousands who witnessed it.

As for the Confederate gold and silver the Davis party brought from Virginia, it was never recovered; its existence and whereabouts remain a mystery. And so it rests today—maybe—buried somewhere here in Central Georgia.

Benjamin Harvey Hill was a Confederate and then a U.S. Senator, and in 1906 the state carved a county out of Irwin and Wilcox and named it for him, Ben Hill. The county is younger than its county seat, Fitzgerald, which was established in 1896 by P. H. Fitzgerald, an Indianapolis publisher and Union Civil War veteran who bought the land in the sunny South and laid out a town intended as a colony for other Union veterans. Soon Confederate vets joined the endeavor, with the result that the north-south streets on the east side of town are named for Southern generals while those on the west are for Northern generals. The drives are named for warships, like the *Monitor* and the *Merrimack,* and there used to be a Lee-Grant Hotel—all of this, as they say here, symbolizing "an enduring unity born of the respect which brave men hold for each other."

Today Fitzgerald and Ben Hill are both success stories with a good balance between agriculture and manufacturing. Lyman Brewer, just retired from the Delco-Remy Battery plant, says, "We've got a diversified economy so that if one industry shuts down it doesn't completely cripple us. Here in Fitzgerald we make railroad cars, jet engine parts, textiles, sportswear—such as many of the 1996 Olympic uniforms—plus wood products and much more. Out in the county they grow peanuts, cotton, corn, tobacco, soybeans, and lots of pine trees."

Lyman and his wife Margie run the Dove's Nest Christian Bookstore and are pleased with the variety of religious denominations represented here, including a Roman Catholic church and a Jewish synagogue. "We *are* in the middle of the Bible Belt," he points out, "and people do talk about the devil here. Unfortunately he's real active in the community too."

Fitzgerald is extraordinarily tidy, with attractive houses and big columned mansions and condominiums, all with well-manicured lawns. It is a prospering, growing place, according to Gerald W. Pryor, well-dressed editor and publisher of the weekly *Herald-Leader.* "There was a boom in the seventies, a slump in the eighties, but now we're really bringing in new industries and even some tourist trade to see the unique town itself and the Blue and Grey Museum in the old railroad depot."

Hogue Smith is a slight, energetic eighty-year-old with an amiably cantankerous twinkle in his blue eyes. He used to be in the lumber business but is now a prominent real estate broker in Fitzgerald, and he's irked at farmers: "I wonder," he confides, leaning forward at his desk, "why the farmers wield so much power—'cause they're not many of 'em. I say they've been ridin' our back long enough. Farmers, gettin' all these payoffs, allotments, allowances, living high on the hog—and me paying for it. I don't like it. Never have and never will. Nobody was paying *me* in the lumber business. Nobody was going to pick up *my* tail if I went busted."

He shakes his head. "That's what infuriates me about the federal government. This is the way you make sorry, good-for-nothing people.

He'll always expect something. Truth is, they just about *won't let* a farmer go under now. I say let 'em root, hog, or die."

Beards of Spanish moss, drooping from the hardwoods that still have their leaves, wave in the cool November wind. Back from the road, overgrown farmers' houses, bowed in the center, lean toward earth in a state of protracted collapse.

The Osierfield Grocery is a low brick building that faces the railroad tracks in Osierfield, near the border of Ben Hill and Irwin Counties, on the Irwin side. A tall Texaco sign on the corner looms over a single fuel pump. The grocery shares the building with an identical space next door, which is vacant. In front a sign says: "Open 7AM. Cold Beer."

The Osierfield Grocery is the last thing left to be open or closed in this once high-toned town—which, as it presently stands, is about twenty-five aging citizens away from being a total ghost. Down the street is the husk of a larger, more ornate brick building, partly smashed in, with no roof and tall weeds growing out the windows. Past this are two utterly rusted trailers and a shed full of old cars and broken farm vehicles.

Mary Denton, a slim, pleasantly attractive woman with iron gray hair, sits alone behind the counter with her Siamese cat dozing beside her on a stool. The two top shelves behind her are lined with vintage soda pop bottles.

Mary speaks with affection. She says that Osierfield was developed before Fitzgerald and was originally laid out in city blocks. "A man who just died, Esbon Faulkner, who was eighty-five, he owned a bank, a cotton gin, a commissary. He's the last one who could have told you the real story of Osierfield," she nods.

"There were section houses for the turpentine still, a railroad depot. They even said there was a hotel here, a blacksmith shop, a broom factory. It was a thriving little place at one time. A post office. Schools and stores.

"All you have now is farmers, a handful of farmers who come through. It's just a farming section, and we're just about a ghost town. There are very few kids anymore, five kids. I live at the old schoolhouse. I took my mother's house when she went into a nursing home. I haven't got anyplace else to go. I did live in the store, in an apartment in the back.

"But I just won't close it down. It keeps hanging on. It's one of the few places left where people come down to sit and chew the fat, sit around that heater on those big buckets. All the men come have breakfast with me every morning. Honey buns and Co-colas. Four farmers come in every morning.

"Twenty-five years ago this was a prospering place. Hundreds of people, just a few colored people's families."

A big CSX diesel roars through Osierfield with two quick toots of its whistle. "The train used to stop here twice a day and drop mail," she says softly. "Times have changed. I liked those times back then. Carnival shows with rides and clowns would stop here, right beside this building. There were lots of children 'round here then. All that's gone now. Isn't it funny how places like this just fold up?" she smiles. "Hurry back!"

From Osierfield, as the crow files, Douglas is twenty-one miles and a whole world away. Here in "dynamic Douglas," county seat of the almost equally dynamic Coffee County, they've got the industrial development game honed down to a fine tooth. Those here would have you know that the first settlers came into these parts around 1854 from the Carolinas and Virginia and immediately set about farming the land while energetically building churches, schools, stores, and commercial institutions—*and their descendants are still at it!*

"Douglas isn't a sleepy hollow," says Sid Cottingham, a tall, red-haired attorney in his forties who grew up here, went away for college and law school, and finally determined that, unlike most young people from small towns, he would come back to this place of his origin like a prodigal son and invest his own bright future in the future of Douglas.

"Now everybody comes back to Douglas," he says, driving through the town and its outskirts, pointing out the industrial parks, the $13 million high school, the site for the $30 million hospital, the new regional library, the high-tech plant that makes components for jet aircraft engines, the textile manufacturer, the big poultry processor. "And here's Fleetwood Mobile Homes," he points, "the largest mobile home builder in the country. They have nine plants here. Within twenty-five miles is the largest concentration of mobile home construction in the country. More even than in Texas. For us, it's just one part of the pie."

A seriously big part of the pie are the giant Wal-Mart Distribution Center and Wal-Mart Dispatch Center, source of eleven hundred jobs. "I see Douglas as a regional trade center. I know some of these other towns feel a bit of jealousy, but what's good for Douglas is good for this whole area. That Wal-Mart Center draws employees from seven counties."

Sid, whose father was a professor at South Georgia College here in Douglas, is an unabashed lover and booster of his hometown and spearheaded the renovation of the Coffee County courthouse. In the courthouse are pictures of Gen. John Coffee, an Indian fighter and hero of the Creek War, and Stephen A. Douglas of Illinois, who was popular, during the time this town was founded, for his debates with Abraham Lincoln.

Douglas is a handsome, growing town of thirteen thousand, not overly concerned with dwelling on an antebellum past. It is concerned right now with its own industrial momentum. Not, however, to the exclusion of agriculture. Agriculture is a $150 million business in Coffee County—more than half of which is covered with forest and timberland. Of the county's thirty-two thousand citizens, 64 percent are rural dwellers, perhaps living around or near the other communities of Ambrose, Broxton, or Nicholls. The farmers here grow row crops, peanuts, poultry, hogs, and enough tobacco to make this the number-one tobacco market in the state. And they also grow cotton.

"Ten years ago," says Ralph Evans, president of the Coffee County Gin Company, "there were maybe nine hundred acres planted in cotton. This year we got eighteen thousand acres planted." He speaks over the whooshing whine of his ultramodern Feed Master cotton gins whirring away. His family's been in this trade for seventy years. He says an old cotton gin could process thirty-five hundred bales in a year. This gin can do that in a week. And, much to his exasperation, construction has begun in Douglas for yet another high-speed ginning company like this.

Meanwhile, Max Lockwood, former president of the chamber of commerce and an industrial hustler extraordinaire, is content with no less than heading up a grandiose statewide effort to develop the corridor surrounding the entire 364-mile length of U.S. 441, which runs from the North Carolina border to Florida and passes right through "dynamic" Douglas. Max is pleased that "Coffee is already the fastest growing county in South Georgia" and hopes to speed it up.

A mere fifteen miles south of Douglas, on 441, one enters the more languorous latitudes of Atkinson County, with its principal towns being Willacoochee on the west, famous for its nondescript No Name Bar, and the county seat of Pearson, population 1,714. A railroad line crosses west to east through Pearson, roughly parallel with the four-lane called Corridor Z, or U.S. 82, which runs to Brunswick.

Here, among the byways and bayous and backwoods possum crossings, one finds Sid Strickland, a retired banker in his late sixties. "I consider us a diamond in the rough. We got some natural resources, fresh water close to the surface, super weather, good work force, lotta pride, discipline in our young people, and good highways." Unfortunately nobody around here is really trying to do anything about it.

Mr. Strickland's enthusiasm for natural resources extends to his keeping a pet, full-grown alligator named Elmer, which he and his wife raised in the pond behind his house from the time it was hatched.

A mechanical cotton picker, 1990s

When some small children recently moved into the neighborhood, he was compelled to move the creature to a more distant body of water. He shows the photo of the eight-foot Elmer securely tied to a ten-foot stepladder in preparation for the trip to his new digs.

Jeff Davis became a county in 1905, when cotton was booming and farmers were coming from everywhere and the esteemed Mr. Davis himself was by then properly deceased and could legally have a county named after him. Hazlehurst was the name of the civil engineer who surveyed the route of the railroad that came through here.

Hazlehurst today has tattered mansions standing beside ranch-style dwellings and lots of open spaces where people set up boiled peanut stands and vegetable stands. Hazlehurst on a Saturday afternoon feels fairly squashed by the bright sun, even in late fall: gospel music harmonies on the local radio; people home from their jobs in the timber mills, textile mills, plastic plants; a police car idly cruising the community with "Hazlehurst: The Industrial City" emblazoned on its doors.

Big logging trucks grind up and down the highway through Lumber City in Telfair County, on up past the community of Scotland, just south of McRae, where the widowed Mrs. Margaret Shepherd, daughter of Eugene Talmadge and sister of Herman, presides alone with her dog at the six-columned red-brick colonial house called Sugar Creek, of which her father was once the Wild Man. She grows pine trees here, as does most everyone else. Not much interested in politics today.

McRae is minimally aggressive and not especially concerned, like the three-legged dog that took five minutes to sniff his way across

Main Street. There's a "Liberty Square" with a one-twelfth-scale version of the Statue of Liberty and monuments to fallen local soldiers; and the chamber of commerce displays a reminder that McRae is the home of George Washington Perry, who caught the world's record largemouth bass—twenty-two pounds four ounces—in 1932.

Eddie Selph, a banker in McRae, points out that Wheeler County, just east of here, is "very sparsely populated. It's mostly timberland, not much tax base. They're good solid people but it's a doggone poor county. Among the poorest in the state. Montgomery is pretty poor too."

Wheeler was named for a Confederate cavalry leader, and its county seat, Alamo, home to 855 souls, was named for *the* Alamo out in Texas. Unfortunately, few people have known that Georgia has ever had an Alamo to remember; but the brick courthouse here, with columned facades on all four sides, is worthy of recall.

Montgomery is among the smallest counties, mostly forested, with 99 percent of its seven thousand citizens dwelling in the country. "Economically," as an elder resident put it, "it's a poor county, but it's a pretty aristocratic county as far as the families and the people who are still living on the same land and that sort of thing." Little Ailey is an architecturally pretty town of six hundred, and Mount Vernon, the county seat almost next door, is truly about as tranquil as the human mind can imagine. Mount Vernon, named for George Washington's estate, boasts a Baptist institution of higher learning, Brewton-Parker College. On the avenue in front of the campus is an electronic sign with the image of a cow, wearing glasses, beside the words: "MOOOOve Ahead With B.P.C." and a telephone number.

Soperton, the seat of Treutlen County, calls itself "The Million Pine City." A million pines and twenty-eight hundred people in a county of seventy-five hundred, about a third African American and over half rural-dwelling. This relatively tiny county was created in 1917 and named for John Treutlen, the first governor after Georgia became a state. Soperton is the home of the Gillis family, of state governmental fame, including legendary James L. Gillis, former highway commissioner, who paved things pretty nicely here and elsewhere around the state.

The most exciting event for Soperton in recent weeks was sending its entire fire brigade to do battle with a big hotel fire in Swainsboro, up in Emanuel County, eighteen miles away. One could see the blaze clear to Soperton.

This fire consumed a significant piece of Swainsboro's heritage: The Durden Hotel, which had stood across the street from the Emanuel County Courthouse since 1895, caught fire under "suspicious circumstances" and burned down to a hunk of rubble just a few months short of its one-hundredth birthday. In a spirit of middle Georgia solidarity, fire-fighting units converged on Swainsboro from Meeks, Normantown, Vidalia, Wadley, Sandersville, Louisville, Dellwood, Kite, Norristown, Adrian, Dublin, Nunez, Garfield, Oak Park, Soperton, Ohoopee, Tennille, South Thomson, Riddleville, South Toombs, Treutlen County, Washington County, Cedar Crossing, Mount Vernon, Emanuel County Forestry, Twin City, and the Montgomery Correctional Institution.

Swainsboro is a neat, no-nonsense town of some seventy-three hundred in a county of twenty-four thousand. It bills itself as "The Metal Working Capital of Georgia," and as "Where Mainstreets Meet," on account of being at the intersection of U.S. highways 1 and 80. It is also the home of East Georgia College, a part of the state university system.

James Morgan, eighty-one, former owner and editor of the *Blade,* the local weekly, is a world traveler who has continued coming home to Swainsboro. He has cataloged slides from everywhere he's been, and most recently he's been cataloging his new books. He bid for, and won, all the books that the local library wanted to get rid of, not knowing how many there were. Now he's wound up with over six thousand volumes, the shelves for which consume three full rooms of his office. One room is nothing but history and biography, another is all fiction.

Mr. Morgan is working on the upcoming Pine Tree Festival, an annual event for the past half century. "This is longleaf pine country," he explains. "That's the basis of the economy of this strip of land. We've got rolling hills and reasonably good agricultural land, but not *real* good. It's really best for the growing of pine trees, grows pine trees faster than anyplace in the world. A hundred zillion longleaf pines. Also we've got good underground water, almost anywhere here you can dig down and get irrigation.

"This county was sort of an afterthought in 1812. It was really second-rate country, not even any Indians. Just pine trees and mosquitoes and rattlesnakes. Still got all three of 'em. Slowed down the mosquitoes at least."

Wrightsville is "The Friendliest Town In Georgia," as it says on the municipal water tower, above the image of two clasping hands. "I wouldn't swap it for noplace else to live," smiles city clerk Jewell Parker, who runs the office while longtime, part-time mayor Willis Wombles sells insurance.

There is the Johnson C.I. just outside town, and there are a few small clothing factories, but the county itself is 100 percent rural, and consequently rather peaceful. The county was named in 1858 for Herschel Johnson, a governor; but Wrightsville's rightful claim to fame is as "the Home of Herschel Walker," the tailback Heisman Trophy winner from the University of Georgia.

To get to the fine brick house that Herschel Walker bought for his parents and considers home, one must go eight or so miles outside Wrightsville on a rural road and look for Herschel Walker Drive. But there is no such drive. Must be a trick. Eventually, one finds a two-story brick house with a big lawn that might fit the description. As it happens, the man out in the yard today on a riding lawnmower, wearing a baseball cap with FBI on it, is Herschel's father, Willis, while mother Christine is gathering pinestraw.

Mrs. Walker laughs about the FBI hat. "Herschel gave him that when we was out at Philadelphia last year. He's really retired, from MacIntyre Industries, a chalk mine."

She says they go out of town quite often, "But we always want to come back home. We love the peoples around here and everybody know everybody and everybody's cooperating, and we seem to like it here.

"Herschel don't get home very often, but he loves it. Oh, he loves it. One time we, we had two tragedies in our family. We talked about maybe selling and moving away and he said, 'Momma, that's home.' He loves home, 'cause he was born when we was living right down the road from here."

Is there a Herschel Walker Road?

"Well," she says, "used to be this," indicating the drive leading up to the house. "Used to be a sign out there. But I think my husband disagreed with that. He said, 'I think it should be Willis Walker Road.' So the sign is no longer there."

A flock of birds flies across the face of the Laurens County courthouse, which, with no traditional clock tower, looks more like a massive, white-columned mansion perched in the busy center of a town of seventeen thousand. It stands back-to-back with the equally large federal courthouse here in the heart of Dublin, our own "emerald city," so named because of the earliest Scots-Irish settlers who came here from the mountains of Virginia and North Carolina in the 1780s.

Straight out the main avenue is the Dublin–Laurens County Museum, red brick with columns; the city hall is another four-columned plantation house; then comes the Presbyterian Church, with columns; a columned U.S. post office; Adams Funeral Home, with columns; Farmers Furniture, a columned mansion; the red-brick, columned Laurens County Library; and a two-story, white-columned mansion serving as the office of a law firm.

This is the law office of Wash Larsen, sixty-five, a third-generation Dublin attorney currently practicing with his daughter. Former representative to the General Assembly and grandson of a congressman, he is a legendarily effective trial lawyer. He looks like a bit like Walter Matthau.

"The columns in Dublin are not antebellum," he states in his slow, deep voice.

They were built around the turn of the century. Far and away, the period of most rapid growth in Dublin and Laurens County was from 1890 to 1920—until the boll weevil arrived about 1918, out of Mexico. The area grew tremendously. That old six-story building downtown was built in 1912, at the same time that type of building was built in Atlanta, the Flatiron Building. Now it's an empty old building.

In terms of the boll weevil's impact, there were sixty-five thousand acres of cotton produced in this county before it arrived and eighteen thousand the next year. Seven banks were here when the boll weevil arrived and five years later, by 1924, there was not a bank left.

As for today, he says, "Dublin is in a better position than most small towns. A good mix of industry, a significant medical community, it's the largest community on I-16 between Macon and Savannah. There was a right significant little railroad hub here, but now there's no passenger service. Freight trains stop. Many places in the county were once important stops on the railroad. Brewton was larger than Dublin at one time. Now there's one store, a virtual ghost town. And Lovett, there's not even a store left in Lovett."

Dublin is certainly safe from ghost status for the imaginable future. If such a fate should ever appear on the horizon, at least everyone would hear about it through the pages of the *Courier Herald,* a daily newspaper with thirteen thousand subscribers, edited by DuBose Porter, who also represents Dublin in the General Assembly.

Alan Thomas, clerk of the Superior Court of Laurens County, says, "What's happening now is a lot of our young people go off and get their education and come back as professionals—'course a lot of them leave, too. But those who return start businesses. In the last twenty years our county has increased 30 percent in population, contrary to most rural counties in the state of Georgia."

In Dublin and neighboring East Dublin, "the population is twenty thousand. With forty thousand in the county, that means half our population is now living in the main metro area." Along with the urbanization of Laurens—which is among the largest pieces of territory constituting a county in the state—has come, he says, "Crime. Crime often tied with drugs. It's like Atlanta's problems on a smaller scale."

And yet there is still the fact that "I can leave here and be hunting in fifteen minutes." Thomas, fifty-three, moved here to raise his children. "There is such a thing as a rural virtue," he maintains. "I think a child that has an opportunity to be outside, to experience a rural environment—where you can be exposed to animal life, wildlife—

perhaps brings out a gentle side to us and an appreciation for nature that a lot of children who are reared inside a metropolitan area don't get. My wife is a teacher who has taught in big cities and she says the temperament here is different in these children."

Northwest out of Dublin you get into Twiggs County, with its seat of Jeffersonville, and then Wilkinson County, whose seat is Irwinton. Both of these are totally rural counties with a fifty-fifty split of blacks and whites. And these two—together with Washington County, to the east—constitute the Kaolin Kounties. Sixty percent of the world's kaolin, nearly 7 million tons, is produced in Georgia. Right here.

We all know what kaolin, or "china clay," is: the chalky residue of crystalline rocks deposited from fifty to a hundred million years ago when the Atlantic seashore lapped on the outskirts of Macon and Augusta and left the rich fall line when it finally receded.

We all know what kaolin is used for: Aside from those who eat it, kaolin goes into paper coatings, plastics, latex paints, medicines (Kaopectate), toothpaste, vinyl wire insulation, printing inks, fiberglass and nylon, rubber tires, cosmetics. On and on. The industry will gladly send you a kaolin-coated brochure, for free. That may be some consolation to those citizens who complain that the industry pays disproportionately small fees to extract this valuable public resource.

The communities scattered throughout these counties are about as elemental as settlements can be. Patternless scatters of simple houses and mobile homes, most with drooping lines of wash, discarded old tires with weeds growing through the center, here and there some stores, a school. And every stretch of railroad line and mile of highway bears the almost constant grumbling traffic of tank cars, hopper cars, box cars, bulk trucks, tank trucks, and tractor-trailer rigs, bearing our kaolin on to higher purposes.

Toomsboro, in Wilkinson County, hopes to make something else of itself as the home of the "Swampland Opera," a sort of rawboned Grand Old Opry without the glitz, free of charge. And indeed there are tiny signs of recognition by an outer world that has hitherto overlooked these profoundly isolated claybog precincts almost completely.

Leaving Atlanta in ruins, General Sherman began his March to the Sea in two divergent columns, to broaden his swath of destruction. The left wing started toward Augusta but then swung south to smite the capital at Milledgeville. The right wing appeared headed to Macon but dodged eastward just above it and moved across the lower part of what is now Jones County. And it was here, at Griswoldville, between Macon and Milledgeville, that the only serious infantry action took place between Atlanta and the Atlantic.

Old Governor's Mansion, Milledgeville

In the wake of the army's rampage through the country, the Union general left a rear guard of some fifteen hundred men arrayed along the crest of a hill east of Griswoldville. Late on the afternoon of November 22, 1864, these hardened soldiers were surprised to see a heavy column of Confederate infantry moving in their direction. But they were shocked when the troops formed for attack and marched straight at them across the field.

The veteran bluecoats blasted the attacking line, which pulled back and then marched forward again, uphill in close formation, into another infernal hail—which made them pull back again only to regroup and come forth a third and a fourth time, some say as many as seven Pickett-style charges before retreating.

When the victorious Federals went out to gather booty they were unanimously horrified to see that the six hundred dead and dying attackers they had coldly mowed down were almost entirely old men and young boys.

Twenty miles away, the Union troops from the left wing entered Milledgeville that same afternoon, followed the next morning by Gen. William Tecumseh Sherman himself, who slept that night in the governor's mansion, freshly abandoned by Gov. Joe Brown.

According to legend, owing to a promise made to a fellow Freemason, Sherman went easy on Milledgeville—destroying only the armory, the prison, and a few practical things—and left all the architectural showplaces intact upon pulling out after two days.

There's still some residual outrage here that he quartered his horses in St. Stephen's Episcopal Church and that rowdy Union officers assembled in the Hall of Representatives in the State Capitol Building and, after a mock debate, repealed the ordinance of secession. But such is the fate of a proud capital city, and Milledgeville was Georgia's for sixty-four years, from 1804 until Atlanta won the title in 1868.

Baldwin County was created in 1803 and named for Abraham Baldwin, signer of the U.S. Constitution and "father" of the University of Georgia. Gov. John Milledge gave his name to the county seat and also gave most of the original land in Athens to the university.

Milledgeville, on the Oconee River, like Washington, D.C., was designed and laid out as a seat of government. The central streets are arrayed in a neat checkerboard grid, and, thanks to Sherman—and thanks to the fact that the city went into an economic slump after the war and therefore had no reason to tear down old things to build new ones—Milledgeville today looks, in part, like something out of an antebellum time warp.

"Greetings from historic Milledgeville," Flannery O'Connor, Georgia's greatest novelist, wrote to a young friend, "where the ladies and gents wash in separate tubs. Are you sure you haven't caught anything; what I mean is, the blood disease and all, what I mean is there are certain advantages to being stiff-necked? Unadaptability is often a virtue. If I were in Japan, I would be pretty high by the time I left out of there as I wouldn't have washed during the trip. My standard is: when in Rome, do as you done in Milledgeville."

There are traditions and there are traditions. And they will probably be forever upheld by the graduates of Georgia Military College, a military prep school whose campus occupies the buildings of the Old Capitol, and whose cadet corps is named Old Capitol Guard Battalion. These are the kinds of kids who would have fought at Griswoldville.

Another institution occupying a downtown campus is Georgia College, the fourth-largest senior college in the University System of Georgia. The president has his office in the Old Governor's Mansion, and many of the faculty live around Lake Sinclair, just outside town.

Still another institution, for which the name Milledgeville once came to sound like a threat, is Central State Hospital, originally established in 1842 as the Georgia Lunatic Asylum. Its thousand acre "campus," which held a peak of 12,205 patients in 1964, now treats some 1,800 and is still the county's largest employer. The space vacated by one-time mental patients has now been converted into five separate, high-security state prisons. The state, says the mayor, Dr. James Baugh, owns eighteen thousand acres of Baldwin that can't be taxed or used for any local development. "So we're stuck."

But the scions of the old families and traditional residents are paying more attention to their historical structures as potentially lucrative objects of tourist curiosity. The city has the state's best-preserved display of Federal-style architecture, enhanced by Greek Revival,

Classic Revival, and Victorian houses abiding side by side throughout the historic district. People are buying them and fixing them up—and sometimes falling prey to their ghosts . . . and their secrets.

Caron and her husband bought a ninety-six-year-old house last year, and now Caron is almost too dizzy to walk. It seems the place was infested with bats. In fact, an accumulation in the walls of fifty years' worth of bat guano, and the chemicals rising from it, had reached such a level of toxicity that Caron soon succumbed to disruptions in her inner ear that led to a perpetual state of vertigo.

Caron has a fine-boned, faintly ethereal face, with black hair worn close, almost in the style of a flapper. She frequently wears black and walks with a gold-handled black cane. She says she often strolls among the tombstones in Memory Hill. This is the thirty-acre cemetery designed in 1804 as part of the original town—the second-oldest planned cemetery in the state of Georgia.

Memory Hill is an intersection in time, a place to push the fragile boundaries between worlds, especially on a bright, clear, cold night like this, with all the stars in sharp relief. Louis Andrews, eighty-five, has devoted much of his life to the preservation of this place and knows a good many of the silent residents, both the ones who rest quietly and the ones whose ghosts flow among the cemetery's ancient cedars, live oaks, cypresses, and magnolias. He doesn't care to come here at night.

Flannery O'Connor is here, and Carl Vinson, and almost every mayor of Milledgeville, plus governors, congressmen, Confederate soldiers, mental patients, and slaves. The bodies of so many people with tales still in their bones: of fading farms, the chronicles of forgotten towns, the many erected and eroded monuments to our fathers' pretentions, of ghosts that won't let go.

The wind rustles the leaves with a phantomic murmuring, and suddenly there is a stirring in the treetops, and a small "Hoooo." Then a different, deeper "HOOOOO." And now, with a faint rustling, a large light-hued owl leaps from a cypress limb, spreads its large wings in the light of the stars, then rises and glides quietly down the slope, toward the swift stream behind Memory Hill that feeds into the mighty Oconee River, which flows into that great Atlantic Ocean, which brought everyone here to begin with.

Betsy Braden # TOURING CENTRAL
and John Braden # GEORGIA

Central Georgia is both a gentle region and one of constant skirmishing between man and nature for control of this fertile heartland where agriculture, timber, and related industries underpin the economy. The most populous city numbers 120,000 people. The second in size contains 21,000. Only five towns have over 10,000; only six, 5,000 or more. Many seem no bigger than a fist. Most are rooted in the nineteenth or the early twentieth centuries. Their legacies—columned grandeur, frame bungalows, brick emporia stretched along meandering riverbanks or ramrod-straight railroad tracks—may be faded now, even abandoned; but they are appealing, nostalgic, inviting.

Life here is simple. The taproots of religion and civility run deep. Baptist spires are as prevalent as pine trees, with Methodist hard on their heels. Families bow heads for grace before meals.

Life is slow—the speech; the pace; progress; early to bed, early to rise, natural in a region whose clock follows the sun and the seasons. Winter days seldom hit the freezing mark, but the summer sun gets scorching hot. Torpor embraces the land; even the cicadas don't bother to buzz and nobody's fool enough to work up excess sweat.

Life is casual and easygoing. Nobody dresses up except for church, weddings, funerals, the country club. Travel directions seldom include a street name but do give lots of "red lights." (Traffic signals in rural Georgia talk are never green or yellow.) Should the local museum be locked, the fellow pumping gas next door probably knows where to find the staff—who in one town doubles as the probate judge. Or likely he'll hand over the key himself. Everybody knows everybody, and everybody knows every*thing* about everybody. They gossip and bicker, but they care, even about strangers. These people have twenty-four hours in a day, just like everyone else, yet there's always time to point out the right path, explain how a thing is done, lend a hand, chew the fat.

The South is ritualistic, and traditions die hard. A Confederate monument guards every other courthouse square. Rockers sit on wide porches. Sunday dinner—lunch, actually—is inviolable. This is deep-fried country, where food staples are fried chicken, shrimp, catfish,

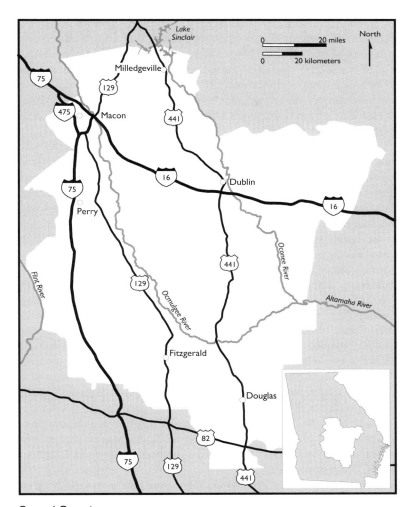

Central Georgia

okra, onion rings, green tomatoes, and hushpuppies. Vegetables are slow-cooked and salty, and the iced tea is sweet. Dining out means rib shacks, barbecue joints, and luncheonettes, where portions are big and prices are low.

This bounty is home grown in a land divided into vast timber tracts, wide river basins, and small farms. The soil yields a cornucopia of peaches, peanuts, pecans, corn, cotton, sorghum, soybeans, mushrooms, tobacco, watermelons, kiwi, cantaloupes, wheat, oats, rye, sweet potatoes, and sweet Vidalia onions. Dairy and beef cattle graze in pastures. Catfish swim in lakes and rivers. Poultry and swine are big business. Those who think peaches grow in cans and berries sprout in green plastic baskets at the grocery store can pull off the road and head for the fields to pick their own fruit and corn, watch cotton ginning and peanuts boiling. Many places open their gates to the public. The spring planting and autumn harvest seasons occasion local celebrations, as do July Fourth and county fairs. Spring and autumn also are the prettiest seasons. Flowers and fruit trees blossom from March through May, and leafy shawls bedeck pecan groves. Peanuts "bloom" and cotton "bolls" in August, September, and October.

Not everyone is tied to the land. Increasing diversification into manufacturing and light industry has lessened dependency on agriculture. It has spawned a variety of jobs from the aircraft industry to a huge Wal-Mart distribution center; and produced everything from air conditioners, blue jeans, and costume jewelry to fluorescent lighting, lawnmowers, vinyl products, scoreboards, and school buses.

Central Georgia has its nuances and contradictions, of course, but mostly it's pretty straightforward. Too many travelers tend to zip right through, seeing but not knowing. How many are aware that the racks of dried gourds around outlying houses are birdhouses for the purple martins that eat the pesky mosquitoes so prevalent below Georgia's infamous "gnat line"? How many people who spy smoke over a wheat field know that the farmer is clearing—in the quickest way—the remnants of his last crop (and its pests) so he can coax a second harvest from his field?

The best advice for the traveler through Central Georgia is to slow down, savor the land, look into people's back yards, and discover the real Georgia.

This twenty-six-county Central Georgia region covers a vast area, yet its gateway of Macon is only ninety miles and ninety minutes from Atlanta via I-75. A straight shot from Atlanta to Fitzgerald, for instance, takes three hours.

The tours in this section follow main federal and Georgia highways through Central Georgia to and from popular destinations such as the Georgia coast, Savannah, the Okefenokee Swamp, and Florida. They avoid interstates, and, if at all possible, so should the explorer. The tours cover the larger cities and towns along the routes because these usually hold more interest, but visitors should also veer from these paths to explore less traveled byways.

For organization, the tours begin in Macon or Milledgeville, but they can easily be traveled in reverse or randomly to towns and areas that sound appealing. Lodgings, dining options, and activities may be limited, however, or may not suit particular tastes and budgets. Cordele, Douglas, Dublin, Macon, Milledgeville, Perry, Swainsboro, and Warner Robins offer the greatest choice of amenities. Fitzgerald, Hawkinsville, McRae, Milledgeville, Perry, and Vienna have small-town ambience. Fitzgerald, Macon, Milledgeville, and Perry combine the best of both. Maps of Macon and some of the other cities are available locally.

Within the region are several major outdoor recreational areas such as state parks, and most towns maintain a park or recreation complex with swimming pool, playground, and perhaps a tennis court and public golf course.

Museums of local history or other specialties are interesting even though they may be quite small or eccentric. They are important to the communities and represent a great deal of time, interest, and effort. Many survive only through the efforts of volunteers and therefore may be open at odd hours.

TOUR ONE: MACON, GATEWAY TO CENTRAL GEORGIA

Situated on the fast-moving Ocmulgee River, **Macon** in Bibb County has been a home place for more than ten thousand years. Within the grounds of Ocmulgee National Monument, vestiges remain of Early Mississippian habitation. The reconstructed earthlodge, one of eight grass-covered mounds, caps an original clay floor packed hard more than a thousand years ago.

The site contrasts sharply with modern-day Macon, where impressive government, commercial, and residential structures are concentrated in a fifty-square-block downtown. Since its founding in 1823, Macon has emerged as the gateway and largest city of the state's heartland. It is a regional center for business, education, culture, and shop-

Ocmulgee National Monument

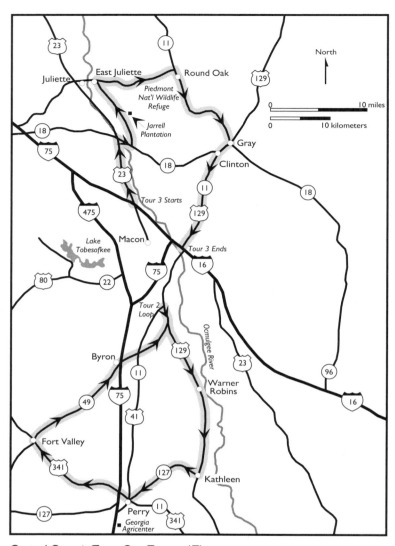

Central Georgia, Tours One, Two, and Three

ping, with museums, theaters, sightseeing and historical attractions, motels, restaurants, and after-hours entertainment.

Macon is not, however, a metropolis like the state capital ninety miles to the north. It is a gentle place of church steeples, twilight carriage tours, police on bicycles and horses, minor-league baseball games, flower-planted medians, and acres of trees: pine, oak, magnolia, dogwood, and the 170,000 Yoshino cherry trees that veil Macon in palest pink during the annual Cherry Blossom Festival in March. Close-in suburbs encompass four college campuses whose programs and young people enrich community life. One of the institutions, Wesleyan College, is a United Methodist institution chartered in 1836 as the first college in the world to grant degrees to women.

Three walking or driving tours lead through Macon's architectural wealth, a mix of antebellum, Victorian, and early-twentieth-century mansions and modest cottages within a relatively compact area. The Italianate grandeur of the 1859 Hay House makes it one of the most splendid houses in the South. Among others open to the public are the Old Cannonball House (1854), which took an indirect hit during the Civil War and still displays the offending missile, and the Sidney Lanier Cottage (1840), where Georgia's most famous poet was born. The cottage is headquarters of the Middle Georgia Historical Society. Lanier material and memorabilia are in this house and also at Wesleyan College. Notable too are the 1836 Woodruff House (now owned by Mercer University) that crowns Coleman Hill, the restored 1884 Grand Opera House, the 1889 Steward Chapel African Methodist Episcopal Church where Dr. Martin Luther King Jr. spoke in 1957, and the Tubman African American Museum. Altogether, more than two thousand acres of Macon's downtown neighborhoods are listed on the National Register of Historic Places.

If architecture is Macon's skin, music is its soul. In earlier days great musical figures such as Count Basie, Cab Calloway, and Bessie Smith performed at the Douglass Theater. Later, Lena Horne, James Brown, Little Richard Penniman, Otis Redding, and the Allman Brothers Band polished their acts prior to achieving stardom. The graves of Duane

Hay House, Macon

"From Africa to America," a mural by Wilfred Stroud, Tubman African American Museum, Macon

Allman and band member Berry Oakley at historic Rose Hill Cemetery regularly attract devotees.

The state plans to enshrine its rich musical legacy in Macon in the Georgia Music Hall of Fame. Other plans call for a pedestrian plaza to link the complex with the renovated 1913 Douglass Theater, the Tubman African American Museum, and the 1916 Terminal Station where the downtown welcome center is the focal point for tourist inquiries, sightseeing tours, and literature.

Eons ago, the Atlantic Ocean covered this part of Georgia, and one of the most unusual exhibits at the Museum of Arts and Sciences is the fossilized skeleton of a 40-million-year-old, yoke-toothed whale that was discovered in the vicinity. Children and parents alike enjoy the museum's live animal shows, planetarium, and nature trails. For sport, the Macon Braves play Class A baseball mid-April through Labor Day, and nearby Lake Tobesofkee provides three recreational areas. Fresh edibles, including that old southern staple, hot boiled peanuts, stock the state farmer's market on the city's outskirts.

Because of its concentration of amenities, Macon is a natural base for excursions to surrounding sites and towns. Refer to tours two and three for sightseeing "loops."

TOUR TWO: SOUTHERN SIGHTSEEING LOOP

From Macon, take U.S. 129 to Warner Robins, U.S. 129/Ga. 127 to Perry, U.S. 341 to Fort Valley, and U.S. 49 to Byron. Return to Macon via Ga. 49 to U.S. 129, or I-75 north.

World War II and the military created **Warner Robins**. In short order, the town grew from fifty souls into a busy city bunched around Robins Air Force Base, an enormous installation that is one of Georgia's largest single industries. The Museum of Aviation is adjacent to the base. The mammoth complex—100,000 square feet and expanding—is impressive for both aviation buffs and the uninitiated. An F-15 Eagle dominates the three-story rotunda where photomontages give a three-dimensional effect. Films and several dozen exhibits complement another eighty aircraft and missiles, among them America's first fighter jet (F-80 Shooting Star), the fastest known plane in the world (SR-71 Blackbird), a Soviet MiG, a P-51 Mustang, and a B-52 Stratofortress. National Hot Rod Association drag races draw fans to Warner Robins every weekend January through November.

While Warner Robins is a twentieth-century strip city, **Perry**, seat of Houston County, is an older community. A walking and driving tour winds through the renovated downtown and venerable neighborhoods such as the boyhood street of Georgia's longtime senator, Sam Nunn. Suburban Cranshaw's One Horse Farm and Day Lily Garden invites visitors to wander and picnic among the hundreds of hybrid lilies growing in manicured plots.

The Georgia National Fairgrounds and Agricenter just off I-75 (exit 42) hosts a constantly changing parade of horse, livestock, flower, dog, car, and antiques shows as well as rodeos and concerts. Most are open to the public and are announced at the marquee or the Perry Welcome Center at the same exit.

Peach County, named with good reason, claims only 21,000 residents but 617,000 peach trees. A full 65 percent of all Georgia peaches grow here. Orchards stretching to the horizon are breathtaking with blossoms at the end of March and heavy mid-May through the summer with the fruit that gives Georgia the nickname the Peach State.

During the May–September harvest season, Lane Packing Company (on Ga. 96 between Fort Valley and I-75) entices visitors with homemade ice cream and fresh-baked cobblers. A self-guided tour leads onto a catwalk, below which people and machines deliver, dump, hydro-cool, wash, dry, sort, box, and cover the fruit in a nonstop cacophony.

At Big 6 Farm, three siblings and their spouses converted the old Zenith Elementary School into a peach-packing plant and their parents' first home next door into an office. No jams, jellies, or peach ice cream are to be found at this smaller, more sedate operation, but visitors can mingle with the crew and try their hands at grading the fruit. October through December, the plant processes pecans. Peach County has seventy-three thousand pecan trees and an annual peanut crop of more than a million pounds. Big 6 Farm is reached by taking U.S. 341

northwest from Fort Valley toward Roberta for seven miles and turning left at the Big 6 sign; it's another mile to the plant.

Fort Valley, "the Peach City," is the location of Fort Valley State College, a traditionally African American college that has historically been significant to central Georgia for the agricultural research and improvement stemming from its land-grant status. The college's old central quad typifies a small southern college campus.

Manufacturing bolsters the local economy considerably. With a week's notice, one may tour the Blue Bird Body Company, the world's largest producer of school buses. Free, hour-long tours of sister facility Blue Bird Wanderlodge, maker of exclusive recreational vehicles, take place Monday through Friday at 10 A.M. and 2 P.M.

Blooming November through March, camellias brighten bleak winters in the deep South. They are profuse at Massee Lane Gardens, four miles south of Fort Valley on Ga. 49. Hundreds of camellia bushes, a Japanese garden, and seasonal dogwoods, roses, azaleas, narcissus, daffodils, and day lilies spread their beauty over ten acres. The adjacent headquarters of the American Camellia Society display the world's largest collection of Edward Marshall Boehm porcelains.

Most folks hurry through **Byron** toward the Peach Festival Outlet Center at I-75 (exit 46) and miss a five-minute detour into nineteenth-century America. From the commercial strip of Ga. 42, a turn onto Ga. 42N, Main Street, leads to the restored 1870 depot-cum-museum, an antiques shop, and a cluster of old homes.

TOUR THREE: NORTH FROM MACON

From Macon, take U.S. 23 north to Ga. 18, turn right, cross the Ocmulgee River, and drive north on Jarrell Plantation Road. For the Hitchiti Nature Trail, about half a mile before the Jarrell Plantation, turn right onto Hitchiti Road just before the bridge over Falling Creek. From the Jarrell Plantation, drive north on Jarrell Plantation Road to the dead end at the Round Oak–Juliette Road. For Juliette, turn left. For the Piedmont National Wildlife Refuge visitor center, turn right and drive about five miles. To Gray, continue east on the Round Oak–Juliette Road to Ga. 11 at Round Oak. Turn right (south) to Gray. In Gray, Ga. 11 merges with U.S. 129 to Clinton (Old Clinton).

Youngsters sing about Old McDonald and his farm, but at the old John Fitz Jarrell Plantation, they can see, touch, and smell the real thing—a spartan, hardscrabble farm that was worked by the same family for a hundred years, ending in the 1940s. The 1847 cabin, steam-powered mill complex, and numerous outbuildings once were the nucleus of a five-hundred-acre, forty-five-slave spread. Through family artifacts and special seasonal demonstrations, the state historic site allows a look at just how tenacious and self-sufficient early planters had to be.

Main house, Jarrell Plantation State Historic Site

It's quite a hike around the Jarrell Plantation, but anyone wanting more exercise can take the three-mile path through the Hitchiti (HITCH-i-tee) Nature Trail, part of the Oconee National Forest. Explanatory brochures should be in an information box at the trailhead. If not, they may be available at the U.S. Forest Service research station half a mile farther on.

The Piedmont National Wildlife Refuge was established in 1939 to demonstrate that depleted land—in this instance, soil severely eroded and undernourished by more than 100 years of cotton farming—could again support native flora and fauna. Loblolly pine forests and hardwood groves now cover its thirty-five thousand acres, and streams and beaver ponds attract migrating waterfowl. Best sightings are late November through January; spring bird migration occurs March and April, and fall migration peaks in September and October.

Along walking trails (one equipped with a photography and observation blind) and a wildlife drive, hundreds of species of birds, mammals, lizards, turtles, snakes, frogs, and toads can be glimpsed. The endangered red-cockaded woodpecker is most likely to show itself during the May/June nesting season. The best times, in general, to observe wildlife are early morning or at dusk. Fishing is permitted at some ponds during summer months. A visitors' center, open year-round except federal holidays, provides orientation, exhibits, and printed guides.

The smaller Bond Swamp National Wildlife Refuge recently was created adjacent to the Piedmont NWR but currently is not accessible to the public.

TOUR FOUR: PARALLELING I-75 ON U.S. 41

From Macon, follow U.S. 41 due south.

South of Perry, U.S. 41 winds in tandem with the Norfolk Southern Railway. The occasional blast of a diesel's horn heightens the nostalgia of the rural scape, clapboard churches, and modest brick towns huddled in the lee of peanut silos. **Byromville** is a tidy little place on Ga. 230 southwest of Unadilla.

Vienna (vy-AN-na) is a Victorian time capsule wrapped in the summer in fuchsia-blossomed crape myrtles. The National-Register-listed Dooly County courthouse, erected in 1891, dominates a square ringed with a post office, luncheonette, and antiques shops. Houses and buildings ranging from Queen Anne and Greek Revival to Craftsman fill a thick photographic and historical guide available from merchants. One of the more modest residences belonged to the late Walter F. George, a U.S. senator from 1922 until 1957 and architect of the North Atlantic Treaty Organization (NATO). Tours of his early, white-frame law office, now a small museum, may be arranged weekdays through the Dooly County Chamber of Commerce. Personnel there can also advise on pick-your-own produce farms and processing plants.

Cotton is king in Dooly County, and during the fall and winter ginning season Coley's Gin gives free, informal tours. November's pecan harvest occasions a flurry of activity at Ellis Brothers Pecans where, through Christmas, weekday visitors can witness shelling, cleaning, bagging, and candy making.

Methodist gospel singing fills the open-air tabernacle each June at the historic Dooly County Campground. Over at Pig Jig Village, mouth-watering aromas waft over one- and two-story shacks during the annual Big Pig Jig barbecue championship of Georgia in October. County officials hope to open a Georgia Cotton Museum/Dooly Welcome Center at I-75 and exit 36.

The state farmer's market on the way into **Cordele** stocks all manner of fresh fruit and produce from late May through September. Naturally there's a watermelon or two—or two million! That's how many pounds Crisp County produces annually, enough to crown the county seat of Cordele the Watermelon Capital of the World. Even a seed-spitting contest is part of the fun and competition during the annual two-week Watermelon Days Festival in July. As an area hub, Cordele has grown dramatically in the past few years. Consequently, fringe development has left downtown looking a little neglected. Community efforts are remedying that, however, along with a district-wide listing on the National Register of Historic Places. A walking and driving tour skirts twenty-three buildings erected between the town's founding in 1888 and 1913. East Eleventh, Twelfth, Thirteenth, and Fourteenth Streets constitute a well-maintained neighborhood of older homes.

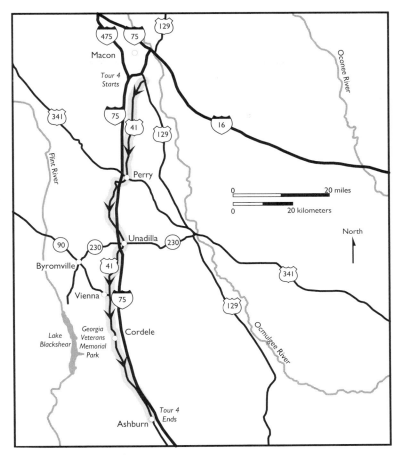

Central Georgia, Tour Four

Georgia Veterans Memorial State Park, ten miles west of Cordele, commemorates the men and women who fought America's wars. Cannons, tanks, and planes from World War I through Vietnam complement the military theme, as do a space to fly model airplanes and an indoor collection of artifacts. In addition to cottages and camping, the thirteen-hundred-acre park has a swimming pool, beach, and golf course. All nestle within the eighty-mile shoreline of Lake Blackshear, a giant aquatic playground formed by the damming of the Flint River. The lake emptied when the dam broke during the flood of July 1994.

A mile south of Cordele on U.S. 41 to Ashburn, a marker commemorates a mass performed on April 1, 1540, by priests in Hernando DeSoto's expedition. In a search for fabled treasure, DeSoto, his army, and the religious entourage may have trekked near or through present-day Dublin, Abbeville, Gordon, Milledgeville, and Macon.

Ashburn touts itself as the "Peanut Capital of the World." The Golden Peanut Company, reputedly the world's largest peanut processing plant, stores its supply in a 20-million-pound facility in the heart of town. Agents at the Turner County Cooperative Extension Service can arrange excursions at planting, harvesting, and shelling seasons.

In Ashburn, Turner County government has operated from the same impressive brick and stone courthouse since shortly after the county was created in 1905. Of the vintage homes on quiet, shady side streets, thirty-three are mentioned in a walking and driving guide. The two showiest houses stand at the northern outskirts, on U.S. 41.

TOUR FIVE: IN SHERMAN'S FOOTSTEPS

From Milledgeville, take Ga. 22 southwest to Gray and Clinton, Ga. 18 southeast to Gordon, and Ga. 57 southeast to Irwinton, Toomsboro, Wrightsville, and Swainsboro.

Milledgeville is one of the most picturesque and historically intact towns in Georgia. It was designed as a capital city—Georgia's fourth—and founded in 1803 when stately federal architecture was coming into full flower. Neither the Civil War nor twentieth-century development has obliterated its character and ambience.

Milledgeville functioned as Georgia's political center from 1803 to 1868, even though officials delayed until 1807 the erection of a proper statehouse and the first legislative session there. The Old Capitol Building, a Gothic structure that was twice rebuilt following fires, now serves Georgia Military College and contains a small museum of early town and school days.

Age has only embellished the beauty of the pink-stuccoed Old Governor's Mansion (1838), a National Historic Landmark long regarded as one of America's most perfect examples of Greek Revival architecture. The first two floors, laid out around a rotunda capped by a fifty-foot-high domed ceiling, are open to the public. Union general William T. Sherman slept in the mansion on the night of November 23, 1864, during his March to the Sea. Historical markers on the courthouse lawn describe the panic that preceded the arrival of thirty thousand soldiers and the havoc that followed.

The two-hour trolley tour offered on Tuesday and Friday mornings is an entertaining and enlightening way to see the historic area. It is the only means of entering the 1825 Stetson-Sanford House, headquarters of the Old Capitol Historical Society. Several of the many other points of interest on three tours—the trolley tour, a walking and driving tour, and a Black Heritage tour—are open to the public. They include the handsome 1887 Baldwin County courthouse; the 1830

Marlor House and Arts Gallery; the 1890 Sallie Ellis Davis House, proposed to be an African American heritage museum; Georgia College's Museum and Archives of Georgia Education; and the columned brick buildings of Georgia College, founded in 1889. A former student sculpted the six-and-a-half-foot-long hot dog, complete with ketchup, mustard, mayonnaise, and bun, that identifies the college's art department.

A more famous alumna, author Flannery O'Connor, grew up in Milledgeville. After being diagnosed with lupus she returned, lived thirteen years at Andalusia, the family farm, and wrote *Wise Blood, The Violent Bear It Away,* and other fiction before her death in 1964 at age thirty-nine. She is buried in Memory Hill Cemetery, only a few blocks from the 1820s house where her family lived. O'Connor's mother donated mementos from Andalusia, manuscripts, and memorabilia to furnish the Flannery O'Connor Room at the Georgia College library.

The underlying theme of forty-five-acre Lockerly Arboretum on Milledgeville's southern edge is education and conservation. Walking and driving trails of colorful conifers, flowers, and shrubs wind through the horticultural laboratory.

Lake Walmead, a world-class water-skiing lake, hosts a number of tournaments, while fifteen-hundred-acre Lake Sinclair offers aquatic activities of all kinds. The U.S. Forest Service operates a campground and recreation area with a beach and bathhouses.

The town of **Gray** spreads around the beautifully restored 1905 Jones County courthouse, listed on the National Register of Historic Places. An antiques business in the town's oldest house, circa 1900, permits a peek at original light fixtures and corner fireplaces.

Hard-core Civil War buffs might make the ten-mile detour to **Round Oak** (north of Gray on Ga. 11), the scene of the July 1864 Battle of Sunshine Church. There Confederates bested a Northern cavalry raiding party. In retribution, Sherman's troops burned the church during the March to the Sea. The present chapel dates to 1880.

From Gray, four-lane U.S. 129 runs the scant two miles to **Clinton,** but a more inviting introduction lies along the Old Clinton Road. Leaving Gray, turn right off U.S. 129 on Washburn Street at Hardee's, then make a left on Old Clinton Road behind the hardware store.

The road immediately narrows into a lane (albeit paved) that must appear much as it did in 1808 when Clinton was settled on Georgia's western frontier. The population surged, northeastern immigrants built fine, New England–style homes, and by 1833 Clinton was a booming county seat with many dozen houses, stores, and businesses. Old Clinton now consists of lofty oaks and pines, meadows, and only the occasional house.

As early as the 1850s, the "new" town of Macon twelve miles away had sapped Clinton's economic strength. On November 19, 1864,

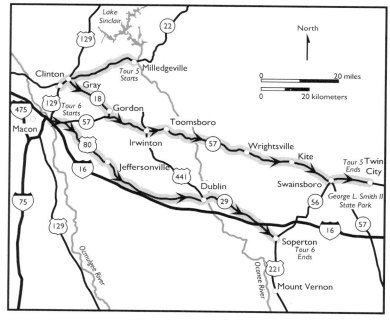

Central Georgia, Tours Five and Six

some twenty thousand of Sherman's Savannah-bound army and five thousand head of cattle overran the town. To fend off heavy Confederate harassment they fortified Clinton and, upon withdrawing five days later, left one-third in ashes. (These tempestuous times are re-lived during April's Old Clinton War Days.) After the war, Clinton's citizens rejected the new railroad. It moved through nearby Gray, which prospered; the county seat followed in 1905.

No further development marred Clinton's appearance, so that even though many buildings have disappeared, the town today is a prime example of an early-nineteenth-century county seat. On the Old Clinton Road, an orientation map of the National Register neighborhood shows extant structures: three houses from 1810, a dozen later houses and offices that are private dwellings, and a fairly large cemetery. "The Park," a private, twenty-acre garden, blooms spring and fall with more than 100,000 bulbs. The Old Clinton Historical Society (see appendix) provides literature and permission to wander its grounds and to tour the restored McCarthy-Pope House.

A one-two punch from Federal forces in July and November of 1864 destroyed the town of **Gordon**. It revived, and its citizens persevere thanks to the clay known as kaolin, an ingredient of paper, plastics, paint, and many other products. Georgia produces 60 percent of the world's supply. Deposits are concentrated along the fall line between Macon and Augusta. The smokestacks and sheer bulk of the New Jersey–based Engelhard plant are Gordon's defining feature. The only other highrise landmark is a clip joint—a barber shop in the base of the 1923 concrete tower that provided water for the railroad's steam engines. At **Ivey Station**, a few miles northeast of Gordon on Ga. 243, Charles Ivey is said to have grown Georgia's first watermelons, in the 1850s, with seeds ordered from abroad. Toward Irwinton, Federal officers commandeered the 1861 Ramah Church on Ga. 57 as their headquarters.

In **Irwinton**, the seat of Wilkinson County, "the boys [Sherman's troops] had a good time last night. Wrecked town; recovered valuables," wrote a soldier in his diary. The Wilkinson County courthouse was among the buildings torched; the present brick structure dates to 1924.

The Union Church, so called because Methodist, Baptist, and Presbyterian congregations shared the premises, crowns a small hill at the turn onto Ga. 57. Built in the mid-1850s, it drew duty during the Civil War as a field hospital, a granary, and a warehouse for Federal plunder. Though the church became inactive in 1950, the building was restored in 1966 and is occasionally left unlocked for visitors.

Small **Toomsboro** springs to life and more than doubles its population each Saturday afternoon when the Swampland Opera cranks up. Since 1978, singers, pickers, and fiddlers have belted out six hours of country, gospel, and bluegrass music while the audience wanders in and out of the fan-cooled brick building where Ford autos once held the floor. Scenes from *Wise Blood*, the movie based on the Flannery O'Connor novel, were filmed in the old general store awaiting restoration across the street. The town is off Ga. 57 to the northeast on Ga. 112 (Milledgeville Highway). Hungry opera-goers can either grab a hot dog at the show or chow down on fried catfish at a lakeside restaurant several miles distant, but they'll have to sleep in Milledgeville, twenty-three miles north.

Wrightsville claims the imposing 1895 Johnson County courthouse, a small but prosperous business district, and enough nineteenth-century houses and historic spots to fill a walking and driving brochure. Yet the town's biggest boast is Heisman Trophy winner Herschel Walker, the University of Georgia running back who received the coveted award for collegiate football's best in 1982. "Transition," Earl Thorp's 1939 New Deal relief, is in the post office.

Early settlers around tiny **Kite** made their living in turpentine, moonshine, cotton, and corn. All four, and more, are represented in the Grace Elliott Museum in an 1891 building above the headquarters of the Kite Homemakers Club. A sign just south of the intersection of Ga. 57 and U.S. 221 marks the site, and someone at either of the neighboring houses or the one behind the museum can provide the key.

Swainsboro, eleven miles north of I-16, grew up at the intersection of transcontinental U.S. highways 1 and 80, so promoters call it "the Crossroads of the South." Within the county seat of Emanuel County are an arts center in a former church and the campus of East Georgia College. A 1939 New Deal mural, "Experimenting with the First Model of the Cotton Gin," by Edna Reindel, decorates the lobby of the federal courthouse.

For an evening out, the locals favor McKinney's Pond, a dining and recreation area with weekend entertainment, and Coleman Lake, with more of the same. The latter, twenty miles north of Swainsboro on an Ogeechee River backwater studded with moss-hung cypress, also has camping and a few cabins. By taking U.S. 1 to the designated turnoff, visitors can traverse the Old Savannah Road, blazed in 1777 from Savannah to Georgia's then-western frontier at what is now Milledgeville. An alternate route, Ga. 56, passes through **Summertown**, a community established in the 1850s by well-to-do families in adjoining Burke County who were seeking a summer refuge from malaria. Today's crossroads was incorporated in 1906.

George L. Smith State Park lies eleven miles east of Swainsboro, through the Victorian town of **Twin City**. In addition to a large fishing lake, hiking trails, and camping, the thirteen-hundred-acre park encompasses Watson Mill (1880), a grist mill located inside one of the state's few remaining covered bridges. From Swainsboro, Ga. 57S, the Wiregrass Trail, is a direct route to the Georgia coast.

TOUR SIX: DAWDLER'S ROUTE FROM MACON TO SAVANNAH

From Macon take U.S. 80 southeast through Jeffersonville and Dublin. From Dublin take Ga. 29 to Soperton and U.S. 221 to Mt. Vernon. Turn east on U.S. 280 and continue to Savannah.

Locals joke ruefully that the greatest threat in traveling I-16 between Macon and Savannah is death by monotony. Off the beaten path, however, older, narrower highways and bucolic views break the boredom: pastures of contented cows and the occasional antebellum house and "Get Right With God" sign.

Jeffersonville provides a small-town interruption of the gently rolling fields, omnipresent pines, and lucrative kaolin mines. Twiggs County's stark, white, 1903 courthouse gazes over a small populace.

Richland Baptist Church is on a pleasant, half-hour side trip along seldom-traveled terrain. Constituted in the early 1800s and later abandoned, the church was restored in the 1950s and listed on the National Register of Historic Places. The annual service on the first Sunday in October is the only chance, without a prior appointment, to see the original slave balconies and the ground-floor divider that separated

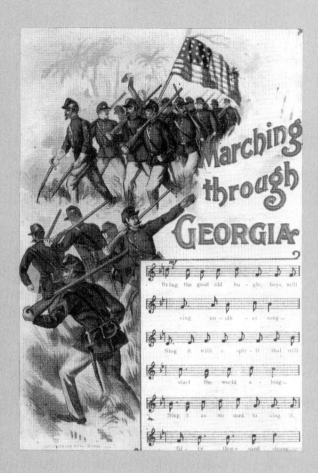

SHERMAN'S MARCH TO THE SEA

The Civil War had been raging for more than three years when Atlanta surrendered on September 2, 1864, following a summer-long siege. Although a key Confederate city and distribution point for men, munitions, and supplies had fallen, fighting continued in other military theaters. Moreover, the middle Georgia "breadbasket" still was capable of producing food to sustain rebel forces, and the South's spirit remained undaunted.

William Tecumseh Sherman, the uncompromising Union general who masterfully executed the flanking strategy that won Atlanta, set his next objective: to bring the Confederacy decisively to its knees.

With one move he would achieve three-fold results: demoralize the entire civilian populace; convince them of the North's power to prevail; and punish Georgians, who he believed were not suffering enough for the "sin of secession." He would march his army across Georgia to Savannah and the Atlantic Ocean, scorching the earth and dividing the state.

"This movement is not purely military or strategic but it illustrates the vulnerability of the South. They don't know what war means. . . . The utter destruction of its roads, houses and people will cripple their military resources. . . . I can make this march, and make Georgia howl."

Sherman divided his troops into two armies, or wings, each composed of two corps. Gen. Henry Slocum commanded the left wing, the old Army of the Cumberland. Gen. O. O. Howard led the right wing, the reorganized Army of the Tennessee. They would advance east on multiple routes twenty to forty miles apart, weaving through Georgia's countryside. "Bummers" would forage provisions for troops and livestock. Squads would demolish the railroad, and to prevent its being rebuilt, they would burn the ties to heat the metal rails and twist them around tree trunks, leaving in their wake heaps of "Sherman's neckties."

On November 14 and 15, Sherman left Atlanta with sixty-two thousand soldiers, two thousand artillerymen, five thousand cavalrymen, ten thousand cattle, twenty-five thousand horses and mules, twenty-five hundred supply wagons, and six hundred ambulances. The columns moved forward virtually unimpeded. The left wing took the "northerly" route through Decatur, Stone Mountain, Lithonia, Conyers, Social Circle, Covington, Rutledge, Madison, Eatonton, Milledgeville, Sandersville, Tennille, Louisville, Bartow, Waynesboro, Millen, Springfield, and Ebenezer.

The right wing proceeded through Jonesboro, Lovejoy, Stockbridge, McDonough, Jackson, Indian Springs, Monticello, Hillsboro, Round Oak, Clinton, Irwinton, Gordon, McIntyre, Toomsboro, Oconee, Wrightsville, Midville, Millen, Scarboro, Statesboro, Summerville (now Summertown), Canoochee, Oliver, Blitchton, Eden, and Pooler.

Although troops were prohibited from raping, burning, and pillaging, orders were routinely ignored or disobeyed. At each stop, the Yanks ate and drank their fill, stole what they could, and destroyed what remained, leaving little or nothing for the defenseless civilians whose land and homes they trampled. By the time the armies reached Savannah on December 10, they had devastated a path sixty miles wide and three hundred miles long.

—Betsy Braden and John Braden

men from women. At other times, solitude wraps the simple frame structure and adjacent cemetery. The route to the church follows Ga. 96 west from Jeffersonville, crosses I-16 (exit 8), makes an immediate right onto a paved road, and continues for 2.2 miles. A far hardier trek leads to the geographic center of Georgia in a Twiggs County swamp near Savage Creek. Most folks make do with photographing the official state marker in front of Old Marion Baptist Church on the Jeffersonville-Bullard road one mile northeast of I-16.

Forty-nine historic or otherwise interesting buildings—all contained in a walking tour—enhance **Dublin**. Many of them line two blocks of Jackson Street, anchored at one end by the Laurens County courthouse and a federal building and at the other by the 1904 Carnegie Library, now the Dublin-Laurens Museum. Jackson Street merges into Bellevue Avenue, a wide and busy thoroughfare lined with turn-of-the-century houses that are, literally, traffic-stoppers.

Both the railroad and the Oconee River, transportation routes that contributed to the city's early growth, run through Dublin. Ten thousand years ago, an unidentified mound-building culture settled along the river's banks, leaving a handful of four- to five-foot mounds. With a little effort and directions from chamber of commerce or museum personnel, it's possible to visit the sites north and south of the city.

Any self-respecting town named Dublin celebrates St. Patrick's Day in grand style. Festivities in Georgia's wee bit of Ireland begin the first day of March, peak with a parade on March 17 (or the closest Saturday to it), and eventually subside towards the end of the month. Later in the year, on the last Thursday in July, the county Cooperative Extension Service sponsors a free farm tour that culminates in a fresh country meal of produce grown by local farmers.

At exit 17 from I-16 to Ga. 29 sits the restored Old Blackville Post Office (1888–1904) and the Million Pines Visitor Center in an 1845 cabin. The visitors' center provides a short driving tour and information on seasonal tobacco, Vidalia onion, cotton, and manufacturing operations. Six miles to the south in **Soperton**, magnolias frame the 1920 National Register courthouse of Treutlen County. Across the street, in the ninety-year-old Fowler-Lawton House, are the beginnings of a local history museum. A look around the area explains why the visitors' center and the city of Soperton are called "Million Pines" for the southern slash pines that are a staple of the pulpwood industry.

A short side trip on U.S. 221 east from McRae leads to Mount Vernon and Ailey, sleepy neat villages of Montgomery County. The county courthouse in Mt. Vernon was built in 1907 and completely renovated in 1992. Inside, antique cases display historical, county-related items donated by citizens during America's Bicentennial. The pine-log Cooper-Conner House, reportedly one of the oldest structures in the state, is being preserved on the campus of Brewton-Parker College, a private, four-year institution.

TOUR SEVEN: GOLDEN ISLES PARKWAY

From Macon, take U.S. 23/129 Alt. southeast to Cochran. Continue on U.S. 23 southeast to Eastman, where the highway becomes U.S. 23/341 southeast to McRae and Hazlehurst.

Like snow, cotton bolls surround **Cochran** in early fall. March brings the tender blush of peach blossoms, followed by the golden blooms of the canola fields. Also in March, the twelve-acre "front yard" of Dogwood Manor blazes with the myriad colors of thousands of mature azaleas, camellias, and dogwoods. Visitors may drive through the private grounds on U.S. 129 Alt./Ga. 26 two miles south of town. Those "in the money" at the turn of the century commissioned houses on Beech and Cherry Streets near the 1914 Neoclassical Revival Bleckley County courthouse; 406 Beech was the town's first two-story house and probably is the oldest. Also notable are residences on Dykes, East Dykes, and Dohl Streets. A 1940 New Deal relief, "The Little Farmer" by Ilse Erythropel, graces the post office.

Cochran's population is augmented from September to May by students attending Middle Georgia College, one of the oldest two-year institutions in the United States (1884). The 1890 Ebenezer Hall, furnished in Victorian style, can be toured through arrangement with the college's alumni affairs office.

Longstreet, an antebellum cotton plantation community six miles northwest of Cochran, has been proposed as a National Register Historic District. Active congregations worship at the 1843 Evergreen Baptist Church and the Longstreet Methodist Church, established shortly after the War of 1812.

In the vicinity, Barksdale Bobwhite Plantation offers hunting for quail, pheasant, and chukar (an imported Indian partridge), guided hunts, and an eleven-station sporting clays course. Bobwhite was built on the grounds of old Longstreet Plantation. Ocmulgee Wildlife Management Area contains thirty-six thousand acres of undisturbed woodland. The Cochran Speedway, a three-eighths-mile dirt track, operates Saturdays, May through September.

Bleckley County and neighboring Pulaski County are collaborating on a ten-mile "Rails to Trails" project that would take hikers, bikers, and horseback riders past cotton and peanut fields and the site of a former Uchee Indian village.

Travelers who grew up in pre-interstate highway, unairconditioned years remember bright yellow "Five Miles Ahead—Stop at Stuckey's" billboards that for weary families signaled a bathroom stop, a break

Bobwhite quail, the state's official game bird

from the heat, and pecan log rolls and other sweet treats! Georgia had more than its share, for the Stuckey family launched the roadside empire from their native **Eastman**. Stuckey remains a household name, although now it is owned by the Standard Candy Company, which happens to be one of the world's largest purchasers of pecans. Groves of graceful pecan trees are an attractive sight in the countryside.

The 1872 Eastman-Bishop-Bullock Home, Eastman's oldest residence, has been restored as a house museum and is open by appointment through the Dodge Historical Society. A city driving tour includes the 1908 Dodge County courthouse and the 1885 Shorter Chapel AME, the city's oldest church building. The post office displays a 1938 New Deal mural, "Georgia Lumbermen Receiving Mail by Star Route Wagon," by Arthur E. Schmalz.

A. G. Williamson founded Orphans Cemetery and named it to honor himself and his five brothers, who were orphaned in the 1870s. A Carrara marble baldachin and lifesize statues of A. G., his wife, and a nephew—sculpted in Italy from photographs—top Williamson's mausoleum. It is one of seventeen entries, most of them churches, in a county-wide driving tour developed by the Dodge Historical Society, as was the city tour.

A number of inviting ponds and lakes distinguish Eastman's environs. One, a large fishing lake with picnic area, is open to the public, as is the resort Jay Bird Springs.

North of McRae on U.S. 441, Little Ocmulgee State Park straddles the Little Ocmulgee River that divides Wheeler and Telfair Counties. Spanish moss, in a departure from its usual kinship with live oaks,

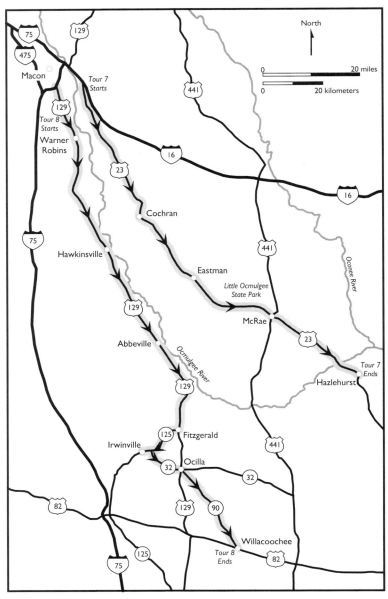

North

0 _____ 20 miles

0 _____ 20 kilometers

75

129

475

Macon

Tour 7
Starts

441

16

129

Tour 8
Starts

Warner
Robins

23

16

Cochran

441

75

Hawkinsville

Eastman

Little Ocmulgee
State Park

Oconee River

129

McRae

Abbeville

Ocmulgee River

23

Tour 7
Ends

Hazlehurst

129

125

Fitzgerald

441

Irwinville

32

Ocilla

32

82

129

90

125

Willacoochee

Tour 8
Ends

82

75

Central Georgia, Tours Seven and Eight

voluptuously drapes magnolias and pine trees. The tall pines have large cones like those at General Coffee State Park in Douglas. Within the grounds are a children's playground, a nature trail, a swimming pool, fishing lake, tennis courts, motel and restaurant, cottages, and camping.

In downtown **McRae**, a diminutive and distinctive Miss Liberty reigns over the intersection of U.S. 23/341 and U.S. 441/319/280. The local Lions Club created her in honor of the New York Harbor statue's 1986 centennial. Carrying out the freedom theme, she shares Liberty Square—actually a linear slice of city block—with the old city fire bell that was refinished to replicate Philadelphia's 1776 model.

Another bit of whimsy marks the grave in McRae of Eugene Talmadge, Georgia governor in the thirties and forties and the father of former Georgia governor and longtime U.S. senator Herman Talmadge. It is an eight-foot-tall miniature of the facade of the family mansion a few miles outside town. McRae has many beautiful houses on streets radiating from Third Avenue (U.S. 319/441). The 1880 McRae Baptist Church is interesting, and farther out College Street in Helena the 1892 red-brick auditorium of Old South Georgia College acts as a cultural center.

Eight miles from the confluence of the Ocmulgee and Oconee Rivers to form the Altamaha, **Hazlehurst** is the Jeff Davis County seat. Notable are the recently renovated courthouse of stuccoed concrete and the "Big House" at the Village Inn Motel. Built at the turn of the century, this mansion now is a restaurant. A nearby antiques shop affords a vicarious glimpse into the interiors of yesteryear. Every Friday night, Circle Double S holds a tack sale and registered horse auction.

TOUR EIGHT: MACON TO THE COAST

From Macon, follow U.S. 129 south to Warner Robins, Hawkinsville, Abbeville, and Fitzgerald; Ga. 125 southwest to Irwinville; Ga. 32 southeast to Ocilla, and Ga. 90 southeast to Willacoochee. To continue to the Georgia coast via Waycross and the eastern entrances to the Okefenokee Swamp, travel east on U.S. 82.

Hawkinsville, astride nine major highways and the Ocmulgee River, clocks in as Georgia's raciest city. Temperate winters, modern facilities, and fast red Georgia clay ovals have since the 1920s lured equine owners from the northern United States and Canada to the "Harness Horse Capital of Georgia." From October through March, as many as five hundred standard-bred horses, their grooms, and trainers quarter at the track. The transients deck out in colorful racing silks for the annual Harness Horse Festival in April. The public may view daily practice races.

History peppers Hawkinsville. Downtown stand the fine 1874 Pulaski County courthouse, the restored 1907 Old Opera House, and "Katie," an 1880s LaFrance engine touted as one of the oldest steam-powered fire pumpers in existence. Gracious churches and houses, such as the circa 1825 Taylor Hall, the county's oldest house, fill adjacent streets. A walking and driving tour gives a complete rundown.

Georgia and kiwi usually aren't spoken in the same breath, but as chance, or Mother Nature, would have it, Hawkinsville lies in a narrow swath that is climatically correct for growing the exotic fruit. Double Q Farms, eight miles west of Hawkinsville on Ga. 26, hosts pick-your-own picnics the last week in October, followed by harvesting and jam-making in November.

U.S. 129 and the 350-mile-long Ocmulgee River flow side by side to **Abbeville**, once an important steamboat stop on the Macon-Savannah waterway route. The 1903 Wilcox County courthouse rises an impressive three stories. It faces a stone likeness of a Confederate soldier. Several markers describe the closing days of the administration of Jefferson Davis, president of the Confederate States of America (1861–65), as he fled Union troops.

For more than thirty years, the county has supplied the entree for the Wild Hog Bar-B-Que Supper that feeds members of the Georgia General Assembly as they convene in Atlanta each January. Small wonder, then, that Abbeville stages the annual spring Ocmulgee Wild Hog Festival. With hog calling, greased pig chasing, hog dog baying, and real downhome barbecue (of hogs rounded up from the swamps bordering the Ocmulgee River), it's a good day to sample the local flavor.

Anyone in the mood to bag a prebarbecued pig can sign up for controlled hunts at Addison Wild Boar Hunting (no Georgia hunting license required). Spectators can take in operations at the Pitts Cotton Gin Company, the Pineview Peanut Company, and Doster Peanut Warehouse in Rochelle.

Fitzgerald, like Milledgeville, is one of those prosperous, progressive, and appealing towns with enough friendly ways and slow-motion charm to make the visitor want to linger or even live there. Still, something isn't quite right about the wide avenues, landscaped medians, profusion of architectural styles, and neatly kept National Register neighborhoods: Grant, Sherman, and Sheridan Streets; Logan, Meade, and Hooker. What are these Yankee names doing on street signs deep in Dixie, in a town not ten miles from the place C.S.A. president Jefferson Davis spent his last night of freedom before capture by Yankee cavalry? It's a story worth telling, for Fitzgerald may be the only town in the South that quit fighting the Civil War long before it was fashionable to do so.

About twenty-five years after the conflict ended, a prominent Indianapolis newspaper publisher and pension attorney conceived the idea of a warm-weather colony where aging Union veterans could live comfortably. A combination of circumstances brought Georgia to P. H. Fitzgerald's attention. He settled on fifty thousand acres in timber-growing territory, sold stock in the venture nationwide, and by 1895 had lured immigrants. Within a year they had cleared a forest and built a town—celebrating with a parade in which the Blue and the Gray marched as one behind the Stars and Stripes. Descendants have mingled peacefully ever since. The Blue and Gray Museum in the former railroad depot chronicles this history and displays an eclectic collection of local and Civil War memorabilia. It opens weekday afternoons, April through September. (By the way, an equal number of streets are named for Confederate commanders.)

Turning a run-down 1950s movie theater into a cultural advantage, Fitzgerald renovated and enlarged the Grand Theatre into an active performance venue. The Main Street–Fitzgerald office next door serves as an information center and guide to crop-picking and other operations. In outlying Ben Hill County the privately owned, 1860s Dickson Farmhouse is open for tours.

Jefferson Davis may not carry much weight in Fitzgerald, but **Irwinville** is another matter. A pine clearing on the town's outskirts was the scene of his capture by Union cavalry in the early hours of May 10, 1865. They had pursued Davis and his eight-man military escort since shortly after his April 2 flight from the Confederate capital of Richmond, Virginia, with a bounty on his head. Davis had intended to cross the Mississippi River, regroup the rebel forces there, and maintain enough military clout to convince the United States to guarantee the South's cherished "state's rights" in exchange for reunification.

The escape route led to Washington, Georgia, on May 4, and thence to Sandersville, Ball's Ferry, Dublin (where he met his wife and daughters), Abbeville, and, finally, Irwinville.

Within the Jefferson Davis Memorial Park and Museum, a National Register site, a granite memorial and bronze bust mark the exact spot where Davis was taken prisoner. The stump of the tree under which he and his entourage camped is on exhibit, along with period weapons, portraits, photographs, and paper money. (During the war, each state, some cities, and even larger plantations printed their own.) An annual June pilgrimage and picnic honor the Confederate leader.

Moss-draped oaks frame Crystal Beach, a summer playground that revolves around a thirty-acre freshwater lake, dotted with slides and water rides, that fills a five-thousand-year-old limestone sink. The naturally occurring white sand beach, ninety feet deep in some places, reminds us that the waters of the Atlantic Ocean once lapped a shore as far inland as Macon.

A tranquil laziness suffuses the rural countryside on the short ride to **Ocilla**, the seat of Irwin County. Personnel at Ocilla Gin are willing, with a little notice, to explain cotton ginning. At Paulk Vineyards, eleven miles east on Ga. 32 to Douglas, peaches and nectarines hang ready for picking in May and June, scuppernongs and muscadines, from mid-August through September.

At **Willacoochee**, on the western fringe of Atkinson County, a little searching reveals a rare, wood-burning turpentine still once used to process pine resin. The McCranie family operated it from 1936 until 1942, when newer steam-driven stills put it out of business. The family-owned complex was restored and preserved with state help as an example of Georgia's premier position in the naval stores industry in the twentieth century. Although the site is unstaffed and unmarked, visitors and picnickers are welcome to stop by. (A cabin and shed are private.) The wood-fenced compound is just outside Willacoochee's western city limit, on the north side of U.S. 82. In Willacoochee, a T-33 jet stands in front of the Masonic Lodge. Pearson, the county seat, is east of Willacoochee on U.S. 82.

TOUR NINE: PRE-INTERSTATE TIME WARP ON OLD U.S. 441

From North Carolina, U.S. 441 enters Georgia's northeast corner and winds through Clarkesville, Commerce, Athens, Madison, and Eatonton before reaching the Central Georgia region. To continue to the Georgia coast via Waycross and the eastern entrances to the Okefenokee Swamp, travel east on U.S. 82. To Fargo, the western entrance to the Okefenokee Swamp, and Florida, continue south through Pearson on U.S. 441.

Between McRae and Douglas, U.S. 441 passes close to Broxton Rocks Preserve, a geological aberration in Georgia's flat, alluvial coastal plain. Sandstone outcroppings and other features form a haven of unique habitats for plants rarely found in the southern United States. The Atlanta-based Nature Conservancy of Georgia, which owns the environmentally fragile 778 acres, conducts quarterly guided tours.

Douglas is a thriving distribution center and the locale of South Georgia College. Two National Register districts, downtown and residential Gaskin Avenue, provide turn-of-the-century atmosphere and architecture. Gargoyles atop the Coffee County Bank, catercorner to the 1940 courthouse, and the Martin Centre, a restored 1950s movie palace cum cultural hall, are among driving tour landmarks.

One figurative step away from urban Douglas brings rural life into full focus. Coffee County auctioneers rattle off $25-million worth of tobacco at public auction from July to September. Lott's Grist Mill grinds corn and wheat into meal, grits, or flour using a small grinder from the 1920s and sells five-pound bags. Quail Ridge organizes quail hunts, October through March. A big tom turkey struts his stuff at Pioneer Village, the centerpiece of General Coffee State Park five miles east of Douglas on Ga. 32. Original log cabins, smokehouse, tobacco

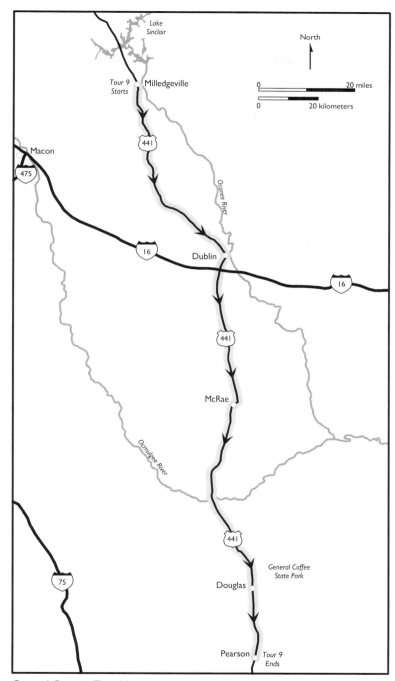

Central Georgia, Tour Nine

barn, corncrib, syrup boiler, and a moonshine still confiscated in a nearby county form a working farm circa 1910. The fifteen-hundred-acre park also harbors a preserve for the threatened gopher tortoise and the endangered but harmless indigo snake, nature trails, a swimming pool, camp sites, cabins, and two cottages. On an arbor, Cherokee roses, Georgia's distinctive state flower, bloom in March and April.

SOUTHWEST GEORGIA

Lee W. Formwalt

A GARDEN OF IRONY AND DIVERSITY

"S - L - O - O - O - O - W" is the response you'll often get when you ask a Southwest Georgian to describe life in this region of the state. And that will mean "slow" in a positive sense. Much of Southwest Georgia is the antithesis of hectic, fast-paced, urban America with its glitzy technology, its impersonal way of life, its rat-race pace, and its crime. Residents of Morgan, Donalsonville, Quitman, and most Southwest Georgia communities extol their lack of crime. They can tell when visitors from Albany or a bigger city are in town—they'll lock the car! In these small communities, everyone knows everyone else. There's no need to lock the car—or more likely, the pickup truck—or the house. Many folks still leave their keys in the ignition. When a stranger shows up, folks know about it, and soon.

One of the things that struck three exchange students from Germany, Brazil, and Colombia at Grady County's Cairo High School was how fast word spreads in small-town Southwest Georgia. At the local drugstore in Morgan, the Calhoun County seat, townspeople gather for coffee and, abiding by the honor system, place their thirty cents in the cup by the pot. When visitors enter another Calhoun County town, they are greeted by a sign proclaiming, "Welcome to Leary, the City where everybody is somebody." And it could probably add, "where everybody knows everybody." State statistics verify the residents' claims about the lack of crime. All but three of the region's twenty-four counties boast a lower property crime rate than the state average, and two-thirds have a lower violent crime rate.

Travelers find the small-town atmosphere of many Southwest Georgia communities inviting. But it can also be frustrating. Southwest Georgians may never bother to learn street names or the direction their roadways run. There's no need to, since everyone in town knows where most stores and public buildings and many residences are located. When a longtime resident of Fort Gaines was asked the location of the county extension agent's office, she could not give a street name, but said to "go about a block up and turn and it's about halfway down with the curtains in the windows." When queried further, she apologized that she didn't know the street name, but "everyone gives directions by 'one street up' or 'two streets over.'" Another resident giving "typical Fort Gaines directions" to a private home on Troup Street explained, "It's the house on the corner with steps up to it with paint peeling."

The warm, easygoing ambiance in Southwest Georgia towns occasionally exhibits a dark side. While people may feel safe because everyone knows everyone, they lose a certain amount of privacy in such an environment. And the word that can spread so fast in these towns may not always be the truth. Rumors and gossip can, at times, sap the very strength of the small town. A recent Clay County administrator, who holds a doctorate and had earlier worked as a college administrator in Atlanta, left his county post when he became the victim of "character assassination." He explained, "I have . . . dealt with most of the local 'characters' and have tried not to be offended when I have been cussed at or fussed at." But when he was accused of being a "crook" and taking kickbacks from a state senator, the "rumors, innuendo and out-and-out lies" were too much, and he resigned.

The small towns, like Georgetown, Ty Ty, and Stockton, that dot the Southwest Georgia landscape do not provide the amenities modern Georgians have come to expect in the late twentieth century. For these they go to the region's major urban centers, Albany and Valdosta. Although Albany is much the larger of the two, each has a senior institution of higher education (Albany State College and Valdosta State University), a military base (Marine Corps Logistics Base and Moody Air Force Base), well-developed commercial and industrial sectors, and a spacious shopping mall. The Georgia license plates (indicating county of registration) on vehicles at the Albany Mall suggest that its attraction is far and wide. Residents of places like Baker and Calhoun Counties, which have no national or regional chain stores or restaurants, come to Albany to shop, to eat out, or to see a movie at a theater. Although some Albanians regard their community as a backwater compared to Atlanta or Savannah, most Southwest Georgians see Albany and even Valdosta as major metropolitan areas with all the sophistication and advantages as well as the problems they expect to find in the modern American city. Albany has become so urbanized that many of its citizens forget that their city's and region's economy is based largely on agriculture.

Although the importance of agriculture has diminished in some regions of Georgia, it remains central to the economy of the southwestern part of the state. Travel anywhere in the region outside of downtown Albany and Valdosta, and you will see the evidence of agriculture's importance. In most counties you will find cotton, corn, and peanuts (on the Early County courthouse square, citizens actually erected a monument to the peanut); in the eastern part of the region tobacco flourishes; and in the south vegetables dominate. Around Albany are omnipresent pecan trees (the largest concentration of the trees in the nation), and scattered about are cattle and some dairy herds. Throughout the region, but especially in the southwestern counties, are large mechanized pivot irrigation systems that keep the crops green during even the driest of droughts. In late spring the large combines enter the fields to harvest the winter wheat, rye, and oat crops. In June the watermelon harvest begins, followed quickly by peaches. The next month, farmers of flue-cured tobacco start bringing their crop to market. By late summer and fall the cotton and peanut fields buzz with activity. Crop dusters swoop down from the skies to apply the last of the pesticides or, in the cotton fields, the defoliants that will kill the green leaves to facilitate mechanical picking. Peanuts are unearthed and exposed to the sun before they are picked for processing. Once the cotton foliage loses its color and drops to the ground, the two- or four-row mechanical pickers descend on the brown and white fields, removing the fluffy white bolls and leaving rows of denuded stalks in their wake. By November, the mechanical shakers have invaded the pecan orchards. These machines with a long arm extending from the front grab the trees and literally shake the trunks so that any remaining nuts will fall to the ground. Meanwhile, wheat farmers begin planting their winter grain crops, and the annual cycle begins anew.

Although the type of crops and their cultivation have changed over time, the importance of farming has remained unchanged throughout the region's recorded history. Even in the prehistoric period, agriculture was a key element in the life of American Indians who resided here before the Europeans and Africans arrived. The last of those Indians, the Lower Creeks, had an economy based on hunting and farming. They practiced riverine agriculture in the rich bottomlands along rivers and streams. The Creeks grew three major crops: corn, beans, and squash. Hominy, the hulled kernels of corn, was a staple of their diet. From cracked hominy they made corn bread and a thin soup called sofki. The Indians' corn diet was one of the most prominent elements of their culture that southern whites and blacks later absorbed.

The southern affinity for corn was just part of a two-way process of European–Native American acculturation that also involved the Indians' adoption of Old World crops and farming techniques into their own agriculture. According to anthropologist Charles Hudson, Europeans introduced fruit trees, including peach, fig, and orange, into the Southeast, and the Lower Creeks established a Georgia tradition when they planted a number of peach orchards in Southwest

Georgia. Two other European products they adopted were honey and melons, especially watermelons, another regional mainstay.

Hunting was also a major source of food for the Creeks. As with modern Southwest Georgia sportsmen, the game the Creeks hunted most was the white-tailed deer. Not only was venison a large part of their diet, but deerskins were important articles of trade with Europeans.

As the Lower Creeks absorbed European items into their material culture, they depended more on the white traders, who deliberately strengthened that dependency over time. Traders acquired Indian land by getting the Creeks into debt and then arranging to take land in payment. When the new federal government was established in 1789, it too practiced this strategy. Pressure to negotiate for the complete removal of Indians from Georgia increased after the development of the cotton gin in 1793 led white Georgians to desire Indian lands for cotton fields. When Gen. Andrew Jackson negotiated the end of the Creek civil war in 1814, he insisted that they cede to the United States 22 million acres of land in central and southern Alabama and southern Georgia. Despite the obvious unfairness of the Treaty of Fort Jackson, it was ratified, and most of present-day Southwest Georgia was transferred from Creek control to the U.S. government and then to Georgia. The few Creeks left in Southwest Georgia moved to West Central Georgia, Alabama, and Florida. Eventually, the federal government forced the Creeks to move to the trans-Mississippi Indian territory (modern Oklahoma) in the 1830s.

The Georgia government moved quickly to open the new lands to settlement. In late 1818 the ceded land was divided into three counties—Appling, Irwin, and Early—and each was divided into land districts and land lots. All of Early and most of Irwin included twenty of today's twenty-four Southwest Georgia counties. The remaining four counties were created out of later cessions. After the surveys, the Georgia government gave away the land lots to state residents through a lottery system.

These earliest settlers in the recently vacated Creek lands entered a stretch of the Coastal Plain divided by the southwesterly flowing Flint River, which joins the Chattahoochee at the extreme southwest corner of the state. There the two rivers form the Apalachicola River, which empties into the Gulf of Mexico. Much of the land on the northwest side of the Flint is red lime soils, the "reddest soils in the eastern Coastal plain" and "the strongest and most fertile soils in this part of the country." Similar soils are found in the Tallahassee Red Hills area, the northern part of which stretches into the southernmost part of Southwest Georgia. On the red soils grew oak, hickory, and other hardwoods, as well as pines. The hardwoods were difficult to clear, but the reward was fertile lands for cotton. Much of the land on the southeast side of the river was lighter and sandier, like much of the Coastal

Plain soils. Here grew magnificent stands of virgin longleaf pine in vast, parklike stretches of wiregrass. The pines were easier to clear than the hardwoods to the west, but the soil lacked the accumulated organic matter of the red soils and produced a poorer yield of cotton.

As settlers moved into Southwest Georgia, wealthy slaveholding planters were attracted to the more expensive fertile soils in the extreme south and to the west of the Flint. Ordinary farmers with few or no slaves gravitated to the cheaper sandier soils east of the river. Enough cattlemen and farmers migrated to Southwest Georgia that by 1825 four new counties were carved out of Early and Irwin. Although many settlers moved into the region with their families, single and ambitious young men also came. Like West Central Georgia at this time, the southwestern part of the state was a frontier with all the violence and instability associated with it. A decade after the first settlers of Lowndes County arrived, English traveler and writer Charles Latrobe described the inhabitants as cursing, ignorant, "muzzy," "hotbrained," and "disorderly . . . intemperants" who lacked "any thing like propriety and good taste."

Planters who migrated to the region from Central Georgia and elsewhere bought up land lots and began assembling plantations. They brought in gangs of slaves to clear the land and plant, cultivate, and pick cotton. By 1850, enslaved blacks outnumbered whites in Lee and Thomas Counties. Ten years later, a third of Southwest Georgia's coun-

Steamboat, near Bainbridge, 1910

Georgia Northern Railway Company, Brooks County, 1899

ties were predominantly black, with another third between 45 and 50 percent black. Only the wiregrass counties, where largely subsistence farmers scratched out a living in the sandy soil, had few slaves.

Cotton planters needed access to northern and European markets for their product, and the transportation infrastructure of early Southwest Georgia was limited. Until the railroads arrived in Albany and Thomasville in the last antebellum years, the Chattahoochee and Flint Rivers and poorly maintained roads were the major means of export. Planters floated their bales on barges and steamboats down to Apalachicola, Florida. Thomas County farmers sent their cotton by road to Tallahassee and then by rail to St. Marks and later Port Leon. From the Gulf ports the cotton went to New Orleans or the Atlantic ports. An ambitious Connecticut-born merchant and land speculator saw the need for a local trading center on the Flint to handle this new and bustling business. In 1836, Nelson Tift (1810–91) and his partners established the town of Albany, which would develop into the entrepôt of the region. Eventually over the next century and a half Albany would have its competitors—especially Valdosta and Thomasville at the turn of the century—but it won out in the end and remains today the urban center of the region.

During the last two antebellum decades, planters and their slaves as well as small farmers and laborers poured into Southwest Georgia. This population explosion led to the creation of new counties, more than doubling the number of local government units in the region. The rich cotton lands of the northwestern part of the region attracted the greatest number of new settlers, especially planters and their slaves. The newly established Dougherty County, with Albany as its government seat, stood out among the rest with the most large plantations (a thousand acres or more) and major planters (slaveholders with fifty or more slaves) in the region. In 1860, Dougherty paid the highest per capita taxes, which were based on slave property, in the entire state. The enormous investment in antebellum cotton plantations by local and absentee planters pointed Southwest Georgia down the road to a cotton monoculture, especially in the northwestern counties where cotton production increased 172 percent in the 1850s at the expense of other crops and livestock. Although cotton production increased in the southern counties, the rate was more moderate and not at the expense of other crops and stock. Planters and farmers in counties like Decatur, Thomas, and Lowndes continued to plant rice and to increase corn and swine production at moderate rates similar to that of cotton production. In fact, it was at this time that the more agriculturally diversified southeastern counties of the region significantly expanded their production of sugar cane, laying the basis for their later reputation in syrup making.

The huge influx of African slaves that inevitably accompanied the cotton boom in Southwest Georgia laid the basis for the region's race relations, the repercussions of which residents still feel today. Many white Southwest Georgians still look back wistfully to the days of antebellum slavery as the region's golden age. There were no race problems back then. "Life on these big Southwest Georgia plantations was ideal," reflected octogenarian Adelaide E. Jackson of Albany. "The planters raised everything required to feed man and beast, and the times were times of plenty. Their families had everything the heart could wish for. Ah, those were, in truth, 'the good old times'!" Those sentiments expressed in 1907 are still repeated at family gatherings and when local Sons and Daughters of the Confederacy meet to talk about the past. The failure of many whites to perceive the brutality of a forced labor system on which "the good old times" depended reinforces the wall of division between the races today.

Former slave Clayborn Gantling of Dawson recalled seeing "slaves sold in droves like cows. . . . Mothers and fathers were sold and parted from their chillun; they wuz sold to white people in diffunt states. I tell you chile, it was pitiful." The recollections of another former slave in Terrell County became the basis for one of the best-known fictional accounts of slavery written in this century. African American writer Margaret Walker learned about slavery in the Dawson area from the many stories her grandmother told. These tales plus years of research in various archives and in Dawson itself went into the making of *Jubilee* (1966). Walker's great-grandparents, Vyry and Randall Ware, are the central characters of her novel. When Dr. Walker went to Dawson in 1953 to research her great-grandfather's property records (he was one of the few free blacks in town) in the Terrell County courthouse, she took her husband's advice and hired a local white attorney to undertake the task. Courthouse officials, who regularly denied local African Americans the right to register to vote, probably would not have looked kindly on this black outsider who wanted to examine the court's official documents. Walker's best-selling novel is not without its faults. There are minor historical errors suggesting a lack of detailed knowledge about mid-nineteenth-century Southwest Georgia, but her portrayal of slavery in the region rings true. Walker's characters also shed light on the important family bonds that existed in the slave community where the family was such a fragile institution. The role of the underground African American church and its veiled attacks on slavery are clearly delineated, as is the significant role of the slave preacher in the character of Brother Ezekiel. All the roots of postemancipation institutions can be seen in the enslaved black community.

Emancipation in Southwest Georgia was a revolutionary act. Planters could not imagine how agriculture in their region would function without slave labor. Everyone "knew" that blacks would not work without compulsion. The whip or the threat of it, not wages, was what made the antebellum plantation system successful. Yet most whites reluctantly accepted the fact that they had lost the Civil War, that slavery was abolished, and that some type of free labor system would have to be developed in the place of slavery.

Most freedmen dreamed of running their own small farms with complete control over their own labor. But it soon became clear that they were not going to get their forty acres and a mule. Many blacks, however, refused to sign contracts to work for wages in gangs under white overseers, and eventually sharecropping emerged as a compromise solution. Black sharecroppers would rent small farms from white planters in exchange for a third or a half of the crop and work without direct daily supervision.

In the meantime, the former slaves tried to rebuild and strengthen their families and communities, which had been devastated by slavery and the war. The family continued its significant role as supporter, nurturer, and prime socializing force for its members whether they were immediate or distant kin. As African Americans in Southwest Georgia struggled to strengthen and keep their families together, they established their own churches and schools, which became important foundations of the black community.

The most revolutionary activity by African Americans during Reconstruction, however, was their determination to secure political rights. Blacks questioned what protection they could be guaranteed if they could not elect the officials who made the laws or run for political office themselves. Southwest Georgia whites were horrified at the idea of black voters and elected officials. They abhorred the thought of ignorant, lazy former slaves, just one step removed from savagery, governing the region. Since 1865 both violence and the law have been used to prevent and then to minimize African American political influence.

One of the earliest examples of black political organization in Southwest Georgia occurred in Dougherty County in early 1866 when a group of Wilkes County blacks rented a plantation and established a chapter of the Equal Rights Association (ERA). This black voting rights organization evolved into the Loyal League, which laid the groundwork for the black-supported Republican party in the Albany area. By the time congressionally mandated elections for a state constitutional convention were held in late 1867, African American men throughout Southwest Georgia were registered to vote, and a majority of Republican delegates were elected.

The white response to black voting in 1867 was to boycott the elections, but that action simply insured a greater Republican majority in the state constitutional convention, which produced a document guaranteeing blacks the right to vote. When the ratification election was held in April 1868, whites changed their tactics and campaigned vigorously for rejection of the new constitution. Although the results were much closer, Republicans still carried the day. Later that year in the regular fall congressional and presidential election campaign, Southwest Georgia whites, determined not to lose again, resorted to violence and fraud. When several hundred African Americans and a few white Republican leaders marched to Camilla to attend a Republican political rally, some white Mitchell Countians ambushed them as they entered the courthouse square. Nine marchers were killed, and nearly forty were wounded. News of the Camilla Massacre flashed over telegraph wires and was reported in newspapers across the nation. The massacre is still a sensitive topic in Mitchell County. There is no memorial on the courthouse square; after the event's 125th anniversary passed unnoticed in 1993, several African Americans attempted to plan a commemoration in 1994, but it never materialized.

Violence was used throughout Southwest Georgia to intimidate African Americans and keep them from voting in 1868. Whites organized rifle clubs and, hiding behind their Ku Klux Klan disguises, terrorized politically active blacks. On election day itself, poll managers in Baker County simply refused to accept any Republican ballots. In Albany, election managers pocketed or altered Republican ballots; others replaced them with Democratic ones. The result was a Democratic victory even in places like Dougherty County, where black Republicans outnumbered white Democrats four to one.

Election fraud was a Southwest Georgia tradition that was to last another hundred years. In 1962, when Georgia abolished the county unit system, a young Sumter County peanut farmer decided at the last minute to run for the state senate. In a short campaign, Jimmy Carter canvassed the region well, and the election was close. In Quitman

County, the local political boss supervised the voting, literally. In his book on the 1962 election, *Turning Point: A Candidate, a State, and a Nation Come of Age* (1992), Carter describes the outright cheating and fraud in Georgetown, the Quitman County seat, that stole the election from him. Carter eventually got the fraudulent votes tossed out and was seated in the Georgia senate.

The violence and fraud in Southwest Georgia in 1868 led to federal intervention. Eventually, however, a combination of economic coercion and the old standbys, violence and fraud, reduced black Republican strength and participation throughout much of the region. In his memoirs, *I Can Go Home Again,* Blakely native Judge Arthur G. Powell describes the effectiveness of the Colomokee Nine, an Early County group organized to keep African Americans from voting in the 1880s: "At one election . . . the members had appeared at the precinct in baseball suits, and each of them carried a baseball bat. They used for the ball the head of any Negro who tried to vote." When the state passed voter reform (i.e., disfranchisement) legislation after the turn of the century, African American voting in Southwest Georgia practically ceased. By 1915 there were only twenty-eight blacks registered to vote in Albany.

The conditions in which Southwest Georgia African American sharecroppers and tenants lived around 1900 were similar to those in the Third World today. Their diet, education, and way of life were substandard. They were often at the mercy of their landlords, some of whom looked for any pretext to break their contracts and kick them off the farm. Lynching, too, was a very real threat in the late nineteenth and early twentieth centuries. In 1899 whitecappers in Early and Miller Counties launched a campaign of killing blacks and burning black property "to produce entirely white counties." Between 1880 and 1930, Southwest Georgians lynched 122 African Americans, including two women.

A major player in the campaign against southern lynching was the National Association for the Advancement of Colored People, founded in 1910. After Walter F. White joined the NAACP national office staff in 1918, he made numerous trips throughout the South investigating lynchings and race riots. One result was a novel, *The Fire in the Flint,* written at the behest of H. L. Mencken and published by Alfred A. Knopf in 1924. White set his story in a flourishing South Georgia town he called Central City, "situated in the heart of the farming section of the State, with its fertile soil, its equable climate, [and] its forest of pine trees." White knew Southwest Georgia well, and the reader can find traces of several of the region's towns in his Central City. His description ("Drowsy, indolent during the first six days of the week, Central City awoke on Saturday morning for 'goin' t' town' day with its

Cooking class in 1928 at Georgia Normal and Agricultural College, which later became Albany State College

bustle and excitement and lively trade") reminds the reader of W. E. B. Du Bois's depiction of Albany a quarter-century earlier in *Souls of Black Folk:* "Six days in the week the town looks decidedly too small for itself, and takes frequent and prolonged naps. But on Saturday suddenly the whole county disgorges itself upon the place, and a perfect flood of black peasantry pours through the streets."

In *The Fire in the Flint* White tells the story of a young black physician, a Central City native who went north for his medical training and returned to improve the health of his people without getting involved in the "race question." He learns quickly, however, that a black man in Southwest Georgia cannot avoid such matters. Like other black professionals who would like simply to practice in their fields, he ends up assisting those who were facing blatant discrimination. In the end, after alienating the local white merchants, landlords, and Ku Klux Klan, he is lynched.

Like the Central City physician in White's novel, African American doctors, lawyers, and businessmen could not ignore the plight of the poor black farmers who were often cheated and discriminated against by the local white elite. In Thomasville, Valdosta, and Albany some responded by organizing local chapters of the NAACP in 1918 and 1919. NAACP representatives took affidavits and advised local blacks of their legal choices. Local whites viewed the NAACP, which opposed segregation and fought for political equality, with deep distrust, if not outright hatred. In those Southwest Georgia counties with the highest lynching rates (Brooks, Early, Decatur, Mitchell, and Lee) and with few or no middle-class blacks, African Americans did not establish local chapters of the NAACP until after World War II.

It is ironic that in counties where white hostility to the NAACP hindered chapter formation until the post–World War II era, fifteen divisions of Marcus Garvey's Universal Negro Improvement Association (UNIA) were established in the 1920s. Garvey's black separatist ideology called for decolonization of Africa and establishment of a "strong and powerful Negro nation" there. Garvey's insistence on strong racial pride, belief in developing separate black economic institutions, and opposition to miscegenation formed the basis for most versions of the black power movement in the twentieth century. The Garveyite movement appealed to the poor and powerless, who viewed his back-to-Africa plans as the solution to the problem of living in a racist society controlled by whites.

The primarily middle-class NAACP opposed Garvey's back-to-Africa movement and rejection of integration. In those rural South Georgia counties with little or no black middle class and no NAACP, black tenant farmers were attracted to Garvey's ideas and formed local divisions of the UNIA. Nearly half of the thirty-four divisions in Georgia in 1926 were in Southwest Georgia. Worth County, where tenant farmers complained of regular abuse by landlords, had five divisions, while Mitchell and Echols Counties each had two. Divisions were often located in tiny communities like Ty Ty, Ray City, or Haylow. Even in counties with no UNIA divisions, like Terrell, Randolph, and Thomas, supporters sent money and letters of support that were published in the organization's weekly, the *Negro World*. Although white landlords strongly resisted the NAACP, they may have been less likely to oppose the UNIA, because it encouraged separation of the races.

While most white Southwest Georgians were known for their conservative attitudes about race, agriculture, and life in general, their willingness, however grudging, to experiment with new crops during critical periods in their history often saved them from impending economic disaster. For Southwest Georgia's first century after Indian removal, cotton dominated the regional economy. The Civil War briefly interrupted cotton production, but it resumed and expanded after Reconstruction. As the railroads and lumber companies cleared the piney woods east of the Flint River, cotton production spread rapidly into the wiregrass counties. In the forty years between 1859 and 1899, cotton production increased by over 1,000 percent in Colquitt and Berrien Counties and by over 500 percent in Worth County. All but four other counties in Southwest Georgia increased their cotton production, if by somewhat more modest amounts, during the same period. In the easternmost counties of Echols, Lowndes, and Berrien, the short-staple upland cotton grown throughout the region was largely replaced by long-staple Sea Island cotton usually grown in coastal Georgia. Because Sea Island cotton grew slowly and had lower yields, growing it could be risky. The gamble, however, was outweighed by the higher prices its long, silky fibers fetched, and for several decades farmers in eastern Southwest Georgia produced thousands of bales each year.

While most farmers concentrated on cotton, more progressive voices in the region warned of the dangers of a cotton monoculture and urged agricultural diversification. Editors of the *Valdosta Times*, the *Thomasville Times-Enterprise*, and the *Albany Herald* encouraged farmers to try other crops. Counties east of the Flint River, like Thomas, Colquitt, and Lowndes, had always been more diversified than those to the west. By the turn of the century, sugarcane, watermelons, and pears grew alongside Sea Island cotton. Even in the heart of the northwestern cotton counties, the campaign for diversification was making strides. In the 1890s, planters in Dougherty, Lee, and Mitchell Counties began growing pecans and eventually developed the three-county region into the "pecan capital of the world."

The greatest incentive to diversification came in the post–World War I era when Southwest Georgia was hit by the double blow of the boll weevil and the agricultural depression of the 1920s. If the weevil didn't destroy the cotton crop, the market did. Cotton prices dropped from thirty-five cents per pound in 1919 to seventeen cents the following year. Many farmers could not adjust to the shock, and a number of them simply quit and moved to town. A number of African American tenant farmers boarded the train and headed north to New York, Chicago, and other industrial centers. Throughout Southwest Georgia in 1925 fewer farmers were cultivating fewer acres than they had five years earlier. Nearly half the farm owners in Miller, Mitchell, and Berrien Counties, and over half in Lee, mortgaged their farms.

Southwest Georgia farmers who decided to stick it out had to look to other crops to replace their longtime moneymaker. Many Southwest Georgians had been growing peanuts, or ground peas, for livestock feed since the turn of the century. In many cases they planted them between rows of corn, pulled enough for domestic consumption, and turned loose the hogs to root up the rest. Pine-belt farmer D. T. Sapp noted in 1911 that "mules will quit eating any feed to eat groundpeas." The devastation of the boll weevil led many Southwest Georgians to consider peanuts for a new cash crop. The peanut butter industry had taken off around 1904, and a wartime shortage of seed oil increased the demand for peanut oil. By 1916, the Tifton Cotton Oil Company was advertising for peanuts for its newly installed peanut crushing machinery. As farmers started growing peanuts for market, Southwest Georgians established shelling plants and warehouses.

At the turn of the century South Georgia farmers grew "shade tobacco" for wrapping cigars.

Another potential cash crop that attracted the attention of Southwest Georgia farmers east of the Flint River was tobacco. Some tobacco had been grown in Southwest Georgia before the Civil War, and around the turn of the century cigar factories operated in Thomasville and Valdosta. In the 1920s, farmers started growing tobacco for the commercial market, which had expanded significantly as cigarettes became more popular. One farmer felt comfortable with tobacco as a substitute for cotton because, unlike the cantaloupes promoted by northerner C. H. Strangward in Worth County, tobacco came from Virginia and North Carolina and "had a comfortable ring of being a true 'southern' crop like cotton. . . . He could rest comfortably knowin' he wasn't becomin' a damn yankee for tryin' it." Growing and curing quality tobacco, however, were difficult at first. The Georgia Southern & Florida Railroad, which connected Macon and Valdosta along a route parallel to I-75 today, arranged for experienced tobacco-growing demonstrators from North Carolina to come to South Georgia and train farmers in growing and curing the flue-cured tobacco. Within a couple of years, South Georgia growers mastered the art. In 1925, a tobacco market was established in recently created Cook County, and over the next seven years five large tobacco warehouses were built in Adel.

When the Great Depression followed the 1929 stock market crash, Southwest Georgia farmers were further pressed economically. Cotton, still their most important crop, dropped to five cents a pound. In response, Franklin Roosevelt's New Deal farm program established the basic outlines of federal farm policy under which most Southwest Georgia farmers still operate today. The government paid farmers to restrict production and to plant soil-conserving crops instead of staples. Today, production of the region's three major crops—cotton, peanuts, tobacco—is still restricted, although through separate and somewhat different programs. The result is the same: Crop prices are propped up, and the farmer can make a decent living. The New Deal programs did not assist all farmers. The wealthier third could afford to take some of their land out of production and still have enough land on which to grow a profitable crop. Southwest Georgia tenants and small farmers, however, were increasingly squeezed off the land. Planters no longer needed as many tenants when they accepted government payments to take land out of cultivation. Small farmers didn't own enough land to make the system profitable for themselves, and so many of them sold out.

The trend toward fewer and larger farms continues unabated to the present. The average size of Calhoun County's 1,378 farms in 1924 was 64 acres; in 1987, its 127 farms averaged 906 acres. Those Southwest Georgia counties with the fewest and the largest average-sized farms are in the antebellum cotton lands to the west of the Flint River, while the counties with the largest number of farms and the smallest average-sized farms are in the former wiregrass or piney woods. More typical of the latter region is Berrien County with its 477 farms that average 273 acres.

Mechanization of Southwest Georgia's farms was a slow and gradual process. Tractors were a rare sight in some of the region's counties in the 1920s. In 1924, Echols had none and Baker only one; Miller and Berrien had nine each. Conservative Southwest Georgians did not take quickly to modern technology. Radios, which had recently come on the market, were even scarcer than tractors. Only five radio sets could be found on farms in Brooks, Lowndes, or Berrien Counties. There were none in Echols and Baker and all of fourteen on Dougherty County farms. But the changes brought on by the New Deal, including the decline in tenantry, led farmers to invest in tractors and other mechanized equipment.

Still, in the late 1940s, a young white farmer starting out in Berrien County would rent a one-horse farm (thirty to forty acres) for a half-share of the crop. His mule would pull the plow as he prepared the land to plant ten to fifteen acres of cotton, two or three acres of tobacco, and the rest in corn and other vegetables. When it came time to pick the cotton, he would probably hire African Americans to help. Over in Dougherty County, white farmer John Ed Wooten rented one-horse farms out to black families who lived in the small wooden tenant houses that can still be seen dotting the landscape. These black and white tenants, however, were the last of a dying breed. Several years

Water fountains in the Dougherty County courthouse in Albany, 1962

later Wooten and other landowners bought tractors and stopped contracting with tenant families. The replacement of tenants with tractors was largely completed in Southwest Georgia by the 1950s and early 1960s.

It is no coincidence that the revolution in race relations in mid-twentieth-century Southwest Georgia accompanied the contemporary agricultural revolution. As African American tenants moved off the plantation and the farm to the towns and cities, they moved from an environment of strict racial control to one with less white domination. The civil rights movement began in the cities, and the first Southwest Georgia city to experience a severe challenge to the Jim Crow system was the biggest and most progressive trade center in the region, Albany. The movement in Southwest Georgia had its roots in both the city and countryside. During the Second World War and immediately after, Southwest Georgia blacks launched a wave of NAACP organizing and chartered chapters in nine new counties, including such dangerous places as Brooks, Early, and Mitchell Counties, which had some of the highest lynching rates in the region, if not the state.

African Americans in post–World War II Southwest Georgia still lived "behind the veil" of strict segregation. In *The Negro Revolt*, Valdosta native Louis E. Lomax described how the southern racial caste system had isolated blacks from the American mainstream and contributed to the development of an African American culture complete with its own schools, churches, and fraternal organizations. The perennial desire to gain more control over their own lives led some middle-class blacks, like the Rev. E. James Grant in Albany, to organize voter registration drives in the 1940s and 1950s. Others petitioned local governments to make improvements in the infrastructure of African American neighborhoods. Streets in the black sections of towns remained unpaved long after those in white neighborhoods had been resurfaced with asphalt. In 1961, Albany witnessed the intersection of some of these local efforts with those of three young Student Nonviolent Coordinating Committee (SNCC) workers—Charles Sherrod, Cordell Reagon, and Charles Jones—who had originally come to Southwest Georgia to conduct a voter registration drive in Terrell County. But "Terrible" Terrell was too difficult to break into, so they went to nearby Albany to help raise the consciousness of its black community.

The SNCC workers talked with students and others in Albany, encouraging them to challenge the establishment and its policies of segregation. From the start, the SNCC workers faced opposition from whites as well as from conservative African Americans. Divisions in the black community would continue to plague civil rights efforts throughout 1961 and 1962. Yet at important moments, Albany's African Americans rose above the divisions. They did so in mid-November 1961 when the major black improvement organizations in town formed the Albany Movement and selected as their president Dr. William G. Anderson, a young black osteopath. Mass meetings were called, protestors marched, and by mid-December, over five hundred demonstrators had been jailed. The leaders decided to call in Dr. Martin Luther King Jr. to keep the momentum going and to secure greater national publicity for the cause. King arrived in Albany expecting to give a speech and return to Atlanta. Instead he stayed and marched and was arrested and jailed.

Convinced that city officials had agreed to certain concessions, King accepted bail only to discover that the white leadership refused to consider any of the movement's demands. King returned to Albany the following summer for sentencing on the convictions related to the December marches. He and Ralph Abernathy refused to pay their $178 fines, instead choosing the alternative punishment of forty-five days in jail; but before much of the sentence could be carried out, a representative of the white establishment anonymously paid their fines, and they were released against their will.

King decided to stay and carry on his effort to desegregate the city. He brought in his Southern Christian Leadership Conference (SCLC) staff to coordinate the campaign. He had a formidable opponent in Albany police chief Laurie Pritchett. Pritchett ostensibly practiced the nonviolence that King preached, ordering his officers to avoid brutality and name-calling, at least when the TV cameras and news reporters were present. When Ku Klux Klan members from outlying counties came to Albany, the police chief persuaded them to disperse quietly. Prepared for the waves of marchers King encouraged, Pritchett had them arrested and sent off to jails in the surrounding counties, including "Bad" Baker, Mitchell, and Lee.

In the end, King ran out of willing marchers before Pritchett ran out of jail space. At one point in July 1962 violence flared in Albany as frustrated blacks threw rocks and bottles at the police. King was saddened as his nonviolent attempts turned violent. He was further frustrated as fewer volunteers showed up to march and get arrested after the violence. Once again King got himself arrested, and once again he was let go. By early August it was clear that King had proved himself ineffective in bringing about change in Albany. He had failed to desegregate the city—but he learned some important lessons that he and the SCLC would carry to Birmingham.

From King's perspective the Albany Movement was a failure. He admitted as much, but African Americans in Albany disagreed. Because King failed did not mean that the movement failed. SNCC field secretary (and later Albany city commissioner) Charles Sherrod remarked, "Now I can't help how Dr. King might have felt, or . . . any of the rest of them in SCLC, NAACP, CORE, any of the groups, but as far as we were concerned, things moved on. We didn't skip one beat." In fact, two months after King left Albany, the success of black voter registration efforts led to African American businessman Thomas Chatmon securing enough votes in his election for a city commission seat to force a run-off election. And the following spring, the city commission removed all the segregation statutes from its books.

The challenge to the white power structure in other parts of Southwest Georgia followed in the wake of the Albany Movement. The civil rights movement developed sooner in some counties than others, and its form varied from county to county. In conservative Echols County, however, according to a former resident, "there was *no* civil rights movement." For Echols County African Americans, the movement was a distant event happening as if in a foreign country, much the way Melissa Fay Greene described McIntosh County in *Praying for Sheetrock*.

The civil rights movement has gone through several stages in Southwest Georgia. Once the segregation laws were challenged and overturned, movement leaders turned next to school integration in the late 1960s and 1970s. In the 1980s efforts shifted to politics and the attempt to end at-large voting in city and county elections; in the 1990s

Civil rights march, Albany, 1962

civil rights leaders have refocused on education and practices like tracking (grouping students by academic ability), which persist in the region.

School integration was a divisive issue once the Jim Crow statutes and ordinances were wiped off the books. The first steps were taken in the late 1960s with "freedom of choice" plans that allowed students to choose their schools. In her story "Making Beliefs" (*Going Through the Change*), Janice Daugharty provides a vivid insight into the thoughts and fears of those young African Americans chosen to be the first to integrate. Set in Swanoochee (a thinly disguised Echols) County, her tale follows young Willie from the time he has a "feeling that he's about to be singled out without any say-so" along with Nelline through their first two days in the white school. As the white principal brings the two children into the school, he warns them, "Y'all don't make no trouble and ain't nobody gone make none back, you hear?" "*Oh, man! I ain't gone make it,* thinks Willie." When they get to the classroom, the principal jerks Willie's head and says, "'You people's been itching to intergrate. Now intergrate.' Students at their desks laugh." The teacher clearly resents her two new pupils. At lunchtime she says, "Now children, . . . I want you to take note how these people . . . eat free. While taxpayers, hard-working people like me and your parents, have to eat baloney for lunch."

After the Willies and Nellines made it through their first year or two in Southwest Georgia's white schools, court-ordered integration required many school boards to sit down and devise the busing necessary to achieve it. Suddenly, white parents in many Southwest Georgia counties became enthusiasts of private education and established white academies. Some thirty years later a number of these schools still flourish in the region. At the same time, the Board of Regents of the University System of Georgia established a new junior college in Albany to meet the needs of its residents for higher education close to home. No one considered at the time the possibility of enhancing the campus of Albany State College, the city's historically black senior college, as a way to meet the higher education needs of white Albany-area residents.

The civil rights revolution has made significant changes in Southwest Georgia. Lynchings and legal segregation are things of the past. Blacks and whites work together and attend school together, but rarely do they pray or play together. The way we work and the way we educate our young may be easier to change than our attitudes. There is a lot more racial harmony today than there was thirty years ago, but much division remains. Churches remain largely segregated, not by law, but by volition. When the black Catholic churches in Albany and Valdosta were closed and merged with the larger white churches, few African Americans remained in the Catholic congregations. Country clubs remain segregated, although a few have accepted token blacks. When several middle-class black families move into a formerly all-white neighborhood, the real estate agents begin their campaign to change it into a "black" neighborhood. Even local historical societies are not immune to racial division. Since 1983, historical societies in Lee, Calhoun, Baker, and Seminole Counties have published county histories that largely ignore the African American past; this lapse is especially regrettable since three of the four counties were predominantly black for most of their history.

The demographic history of Lee County dramatically illustrates some of the recent developments in Southwest Georgia race relations. In 1930, Lee County was the heart of the region's Black Belt. With African Americans comprising 77.9 percent of the county's population, Lee had the highest black population percentage in the state. Sixty years later, blacks comprise a mere 19.3 percent of Lee's population. The big turning point came in the 1960s. Between 1930 and 1960, Lee's population declined, largely as a result of blacks leaving. In August 1962, at the time of the Albany Movement, the Shady Grove Baptist Church was firebombed four days after SNCC workers had conducted a voter registration meeting there. The Lee County sheriff investigated and concluded that lightning had caused the blaze. Lee County blacks continued to leave in the 1960s, but now large numbers of whites, many from neighboring Dougherty County, moved in. In the 1970s, the black population declined by 10 percent, while the white population grew at the rate of 124 percent. Lee was becoming

Dougherty's bedroom community as whites abandoned the latter's integrated schools attended by growing numbers of blacks. White flight continued to increase the percentage of whites in Lee County in the 1980s and 1990s. A Lee County Chamber of Commerce was established and began touting its "superior" (i.e., whiter) school system.

Meanwhile community leaders in Albany and several other larger Southwest Georgia cities began in the 1990s to address the issues of race that had previously been swept under the carpet. The Albany–Dougherty Chamber of Commerce helped establish and supports the Coalition for Diversity, which touts the advantages of a diverse and multicultural work force and community. BASE Network, a group of African American professionals, built a memorial in downtown Albany to celebrate the Albany Movement. The citizens of Dougherty County voted in 1994 for a 1 percent sales tax, $750,000 of which is allocated for the renovation of the Old Mt. Zion Church into a civil rights movement museum. And supporting all of these efforts is the *Albany Herald,* which in the early 1960s campaigned vigorously against Martin Luther King Jr. and black Southwest Georgians' struggle to destroy segregation.

While white Southwest Georgians railed against the federal government's efforts to end segregation, they welcomed the federal largesse that accompanied the establishment of military bases in the region. Turner Air Force Base in Albany and Moody Air Force Base in Valdosta were established at the beginning of World War II, and the Marine Corps Logistics Base was built in Albany fifteen years later during the Cold War. It is ironic that the military bases that Southwest Georgians welcomed were the first institutions in the region to require desegregation of their facilities. Yet it was easy to overlook and excuse the distasteful federal policies when one took into account the economic impact of the bases. Today, Moody and MCLB are the largest single employers in Lowndes and Dougherty Counties. When Turner closed in the early 1970s, the economic impact was felt in the Albany area for years.

Southwest Georgians' ambivalent attitude toward the federal government is also prevalent among the region's farmers and businessmen. Farmers gripe about the overregulation of agriculture, the numerous rules and regulations that govern what land can be planted and with what. They decry the federal welfare policies that keep African Americans in a state of dependency, yet they willingly accept what may be called agricultural welfare: price supports and federal payments to grow soil-conserving trees and keep land out of production. Businessmen gladly sign government contracts that bring capital into the region through building and highway construction projects. In their next breath, however, are the standard complaints about OSHA rules or environmental regulations. Cook County entrepreneur John L.

Williams notes, "At times, running a business in the '90's gets hairy—Government at every level, every federal agency is anti-business. They are growing and growing and growing and are nothing more than parasites on the nation's doers."

Southwest Georgia's industrial sector has grown significantly in the last half century. Local chambers of commerce as well as the Southwest Georgia Chamber of Commerce aggressively recruit new industry. Yet much of the region's industry is agriculturally related or located here because of the available natural resources. Bobs Candies, the world's largest manufacturer of candy canes, started in Albany by making pecan candies. M&M/Mars, manufacturer of Snickers candy bars, opened its plant in Albany because of the easy access to peanuts. Procter & Gamble's Albany paper products plant draws on the region's timber supply. One of Miller Brewing Company's largest breweries is in Albany because of the large quantities of excellent water there. Outside Albany, the same holds true. In Sylvester, self-styled peanut capital of the world, Worth County's Beatrice Hunt Wesson plant produces all the company's Peter Pan peanut butter. Peerless Manufacturing Company in tiny Shellman produces peanut farming equipment; Decatur County's Engelhard Corporation mines the attapulgite clay found in the Attapulgus area; and Lowndes County's Southern Bag Corporation depends on local timber. Industries unrelated to farming or to local natural resources prosper in Southwest Georgia (e.g., mobile home manufacturer Destiny Industries in Moultrie, bearing manufacturer Torrington Company in Cairo, and Delco-Remy in Albany), but economically they have been dwarfed by agriculture and those industries related to agriculture and local natural resources.

The most radical changes in the history of Southwest Georgia farming have occurred in the last half of the twentieth century. Corn typifies the continuity and change in the region's agriculture. It continues to be grown throughout the region, but its productivity has soared. In 1925, Southwest Georgia farmers produced between 9 and 12 bushels of corn per acre. In 1992, they grew between 67 and 150 bushels an acre. In 1925, most Southwest Georgia counties grew several hundred thousand bushels of corn; in 1992, nearly two-thirds of the counties produced between 1 and 2.7 million bushels. Six of the top ten corn-producing counties in the state are in Southwest Georgia.

Tobacco and peanuts, which became important cash crops in the 1920s, remain mainstays of the region's agriculture, although the future of both may not be very bright. Produced under the government-controlled allotment system, tobacco, which grows well in the sandy soils of the wiregrass, is raised in every Southwest Georgia county east of the Flint River. Five of them are among the top ten tobacco-producing counties in the state. Farmers are reluctant to abandon to-

Peanut harvest

bacco because of the comparatively high prices it brings at the market. In the early 1990s, Cook County farmers devoted five times as many acres to peanuts as to tobacco yet at market received about the same amount of money for each. Health concerns, however, have led to proposals for increasing the cigarette tax and banning smoking in the workplace, both of which would limit the market for American tobacco. Southwest Georgia farmers feel under attack even at home. When the Brooks County School Board proposed a ban on smoking and chewing tobacco on school grounds in 1994, tobacco farmers appeared before the board and persuaded it to make an exception, at least for high school football games.

Peanuts, Georgia's number-one row crop from 1965 until 1994, have dominated much of Southwest Georgia agriculture for most of this century. Nine of the top ten peanut-producing counties in the state are in Southwest Georgia, where every county but Echols grows the crop. Federal price supports keep peanuts as one of the region's most profitable crops. In 1993, the net return for peanuts per acre was $507, compared to $202 per acre for cotton, $101 for soybeans, and $65 for corn. Without price supports, peanut farmers' income would drop substantially. When Congress writes a new farm bill every five years, Southwest Georgia farmers lobby their congressmen and senators to retain the supports. Just in case they lose those supports, peanut farmers are usually looking for an alternative crop to replace or supplement the goobers.

In the mid-1990s that alternative was cotton. Relatively little cotton was grown in Southwest Georgia in the 1970s. In 1987, however, the federal government began a comprehensive boll weevil eradication program that has largely eliminated the insect obstacle to cotton production. In the meantime the market for cotton improved significantly. Peanut farmers, aware that cotton was a good rotation crop for peanuts, were willing to expand cotton production. By 1993, cotton was on the road to regaining its crown as king in Southwest Georgia. Eight of the top ten cotton-producing counties in the state were in the region. Decatur County led the state with 925 pounds of lint per acre. The cotton revolution happened suddenly for many counties. Between 1979 and 1984 no cotton was grown in Dougherty County; in 1993 it had the twelfth-highest average yield in the state. In neighboring Lee County, cotton acreage increased from 64 acres in 1983 to nearly 18,000 in 1994. Much the same change occurred across the region. Once again, travelers on Southwest Georgia's roads can see miles and miles of the fluffy white bolls before harvest. And once the picking has begun, a relatively new sight appears in the harvested fields—large loaf-shaped modules of compressed and covered seed cotton. Storing the cotton in modules allows the farmer to bring his crop to the gin when it is convenient rather than when it is picked. Despite the five new large state-of-the-art cotton gins, costing several million dollars each, that opened in Southwest Georgia in 1994, the region's gins were overwhelmed as they attempted to remove the seed from and process the largest cotton crop in the state since 1937. As modules stacked up outside gins running around the clock in late 1994, new gins were being constructed, and Southwest Georgia farmers, learning of the latest cotton prices (89.6 cents a pound on the New York Cotton Exchange) and having made cotton the number-one row crop in the state for the first time in thirty years, prepared to plant even more of the white gold in 1995.

Although cotton, peanuts, and tobacco are the agricultural stars in the region, farmers in several Southwest Georgia counties make most of their money growing vegetables. In Brooks, Colquitt, Decatur, and Seminole Counties, vegetables bring in the most money. Farmers in these mostly southern counties of the region began growing vegetables when Florida farmers cut back because of water problems in their state. Vegetables, produced for both the fresh market and canning, are a risky crop since the market can be volatile. A farmer can make lots of money one year and lose his shirt the next. Still, Southwest Georgia farmers take the risk each year. As a result, Georgia is the number-five tomato producer in the country. Because tobacco, like vegetables, is labor intensive, tobacco farmers are already accustomed to hiring large numbers of temporary laborers and are planting vegetables. Most recently Latinos, usually Mexicans, have supplied that labor. Some vegetable farmers practice plasticultural farming. Tomatoes, peas, beans, squash, cabbage, peppers, and other vegetables are planted in raised beds covered with plastic. Running beneath it down the middle of the beds are drip tubes through which crops are irrigated and fertilized. Plasticulture generates phenomenal yields, but it is very expensive to set up and not yet widespread. The "green industry" (turf, ornamentals, flowers, trees, and greenhouses) has grown significantly since the early 1980s. Lanier County, home of Patten Seed Company, is the region's largest producer of turf grass, the primary vegetative covers on home lawns, golf courses, and athletic fields. In the 1940s, Lawson L. Patten grew coastal Bermuda grass sprigs that were very drought tolerant and began selling them to farmers in Texas. Eventually, Patten Seed Company developed markets for turf as well as forage grasses across the country and around the globe. Most of the turf grass counties are east of the Flint River. In the nursery industry, Grady is the one Southwest Georgia county that stands out from the rest. Its more than eleven hundred acres devoted to raising young trees, shrubs, and other high-value crops are worth more than $40 million. Like the other types of "green industry," the greenhouse industry is concentrated in the eastern counties of the region. Colquitt, Grady, and Tift are the leaders growing transplants in greenhouse trays for sale to farmers, especially those practicing plasticulture.

Colquitt is also a regional leader in livestock production. The transformation of the cattle industry since World War II has been remarkable. Today's "glossy-haired," fat, purebred beef cattle winter-grazing in lush fields contrast sharply with the grade Jersey cows that were pastured on wiregrass and broomsedge a half-century ago to provide beef and milk to farm families.

One of the region's newest forms of farming is aquaculture, the commercial production of fish. The flood of July 1994 devastated the state's largest catfish farm, on Pineland Plantation in Baker County. The Flint River inundated Pineland's forty-four ponds, and a million mature catfish, worth about $500,000, swam down the river. This unexpected stocking provided anglers on Lake Seminole with some of the "best catfishing . . . in years."

A number of factors account for the huge increase in productivity by Southwest Georgia farmers in the late twentieth century. One is irrigation. Southwest Georgia sits on one of the largest underground water supplies in North America. Limestone aquifers, huge natural reservoirs rapidly replenished by rainfall, yield an enormous supply of water. Groundwater from Dougherty County's Radium Springs, the largest natural springs in the state, flows at the rate of seventy thousand gallons a minute. Much of Southwest Georgia lies above the Floridan aquifer. The farther southwest in the region, the closer the aquifer is to the surface. Wells in extreme Southwest Georgia penetrate less than a hundred feet to reach water; above Albany, the water is two hundred feet and more below the surface.

Since 1975, Southwest Georgia farmers have significantly increased irrigation. A whole infrastructure has been established facilitating the sale, installation, and service of center pivot mechanized irrigation systems. The top eight counties in the state with irrigated acreage are in the region. The two in the extreme southwest corner of the state are first in number of irrigated acres (Decatur, over eighty-nine thousand) and in percentage of irrigated acres (Seminole, over 37 percent). The cost of an irrigation system can be staggering. Each one- to two-hundred-foot section of pipeline and truss rod can cost five thousand dollars or more. It is not uncommon to see systems with six or more sections in Southwest Georgia fields.

Irrigation systems are but one of the huge expenses faced by Southwest Georgia farmers today. An average-sized two-hundred-horsepower tractor cost $70,000 in 1994. The latest four-wheel-drive large tractor was $100,000. The most commonly used peanut harvester started at $35,000, while the latest four-row cotton picker cost $165,000. Fertilizers and pesticides are also expensive. An application of pesticide can cost $200 an acre. These costs alone have made farming prohibitive for many, and each year sees a reduction in the number of farmers and farms. The remaining farmers are forced to increase their efficiency. Many of them use personal computers in their management practices. One government farm expert noted that the seventy-five active farmers in Randolph County in 1994 produced as much as three hundred had in the 1940s and 1950s. The survivors have been called "super-farmers," sharp businessmen who can increase their yields and cut their costs enough to have a profit margin.

Black farmers, who were historically poorer than their white colleagues, have had even greater difficulty staying in business. The highest percentages of black farmers are in the predominantly black counties of Quitman and Clay (16 and 18 percent), but elsewhere in Southwest Georgia, they range from none in Echols County to 13.6 percent in Lowndes County. The Federation of Southern Cooperatives, organized to help farmers, especially African Americans and women, who have limited resources, provides financial, production, and marketing advice. Using laptop computers, FSC experts bring computer models to their clients' farms to assist them in such things as crop selection.

Always looking for new crops or products that will market well, some Southwest Georgia farmers have recently turned to canola and chickens. Canola can be grown for edible and industrial purposes. The edible canola produces a seed crushed for its oil, which has a lower fat content than other vegetable oils. The industrial canola produces laurate, a key ingredient in soaps and detergents.

While only a few Southwest Georgia farmers are trying canola, more are moving into the number-one agricultural product in the state—

poultry. Recently, two major chicken processors established plants in Southwest Georgia: Cagle in Camilla and Cargill (bought by Tyson in late 1995) in Dawson. Farmers interested in raising broilers build two to four chicken houses (forty by five hundred feet) and install computer-driven equipment. The chicken-processing company supplies chicks and feed to the farmer, who keeps them until they are ready for processing. The chicken farmer does not own the chickens or the feed but gets a check every eight weeks for raising the chickens under the company-dictated controlled environment. One observer compared it to a McDonald's franchise. The chicken farmer uses the litter produced by the chickens as fertilizer for his crops. The chicken industry not only benefits the farmer but also provides jobs in the processing plants, hatcheries, and rendering plants. Many Southwest Georgia farmers see chickens, like cotton, as a major growth area in the future.

Another area in which Southwest Georgia farmers are expanding production is timber. After the Civil War the industry began here in earnest in the vast stretches of piney woods or wiregrass east of the Flint River. Immense stands of virgin longleaf pine were opened up by the railroads, and naval stores operations and lumber mills flourished. Many towns started out as sawmill villages and turpentine camps. Once the pines were tapped out for the gum, they were cut for lumber or pulpwood. Farmers moved in on the cleared lands and planted cotton, corn, and other crops. Naval stores and lumbering, however, remained an important part of the southeasternmost counties, particularly Echols, Lowndes, Lanier, and Berrien.

Connecting the Okefenokee Swamp to Lanier and Echols Counties are the "flatwoods" that Echols County native Janice Daugharty describes in her first novel, *Dark of the Moon:* "Woods so flat and swampy you can't see out, can't see in, or into one another's doings. You go to walking and happen up on your neighbors: people shock-eyed and dark, like they've taken on the color of the swamp." Echols has always had a small population, below three thousand for most of this century. For several decades it was the least populated county in the state. When the naval stores industry took off in the late nineteenth century, blacks migrated to the county to take the low-paying, labor-intensive jobs collecting gum from the pines to be distilled into turpentine. In the 1940s and 1950s, the vast majority of Echols blacks worked in turpentine, a much dirtier job than logging and pulpwood, which employed the county's whites.

It was in the forests of Echols and Lowndes that John W. Langdale and his son, Harley Langdale Sr., built a turpentine and timber empire. The Langdales operated twenty-five turpentine stills by the late 1930s and worked almost 3 million trees for naval stores. Harley's sons, including W. P. "Billy" Langdale, now run the Langdale Company, which owns much of Echols County and is one of the largest forest products manufacturers in the country. Recently the state named state highway 133, which connects Albany and Valdosta—the latter the headquarters of the Langdale Company—the Billy Langdale Parkway.

More than 93 percent of Echols County is in timberland, making it the number-one forest products county in Southwest Georgia. Close behind it is Quitman County, which has more than 85 percent of its land in timber. These two counties rank among the state's top ten with the highest percentage of timberland.

Between Echols County in the east and Quitman County in the west lie the region's famous quail plantations, hunting resorts in the Tallahassee Red Hills that reach into southern Thomas and Grady Counties and on the red lime soils on the northwest side of the Flint River in the Albany area. In these areas the state's most productive antebellum cotton plantations were first established. The quail plantations' origins can be found in the 1870s when the Thomasville area developed a reputation for its healthy climate (due largely to its vast longleaf pine forests) and wealthy northerners who suffered from a variety of illnesses, especially pulmonary tuberculosis, came to Thomasville. Once residents learned of the contagious nature of the disease, they discouraged consumptive patients from visiting. The town's reputation, however, had been established, and the former health resort became a winter resort for wealthy businessmen and their families who wished to escape the freezing conditions of the North.

The late nineteenth century also saw the development of the modern shotgun and the perfection of sporting dogs through breeding and training. This combination of developments resulted in northerners buying Thomasville-area plantations specifically for hunting. A number of these big businessmen were associated with the Standard Oil Trust in one way or another. Pebble Hill Plantation, south of Thomasville and now open to the public, was purchased by Howard M. Hanna, a director of Standard Oil, in 1896.

By the 1920s most of the plantations available for quail hunting in the Thomasville-Tallahassee area had been purchased, and potential buyers looked to the closest area with similar conditions—sixty miles or so to the north around Albany. Beginning in the 1920s, Robert W. Woodruff, Judge Robert Bingham, Lewis S. Thompson Jr., and others began purchasing cotton plantations in Baker and Dougherty Counties and consolidating them into quail plantations. Many of the new owners had connections with Standard Oil and the Thomasville-area plantation owners. A recent novel by Shellman native Sonny Sammons (*The Keepers of Echowah*, 1995) is set on a quail plantation thirty miles northwest of Albany. Like many shooting plantation owners, Echowah's fictional Colonel O'Hearn usually visited his place when he entertained fellow businessmen from the North.

Hunting quail, Dougherty County

Some of Southwest Georgia's hunting plantations became associated with scientific research to help eradicate disease in the area and to study the ecology in an effort to improve the quality of quail hunting. Soon after Coca-Cola president Robert W. Woodruff purchased Ichauway Plantation in the late 1920s, he learned about the widespread incidence of malaria in the region. At first, he provided free quinine for plantation and area residents. When that proved ineffective, he turned to Thomasville internist Roy A. Hill, who recommended a synthetic drug, atabrine. Together with help from biologist Dr. Melvin H. Goodwin and Dr. W. Elizabeth Gambrell of Emory University, an effective program of malaria control was established at Ichauway and made available to all Baker County residents. By the late 1930s, malaria rates had plummeted, and Woodruff encouraged Emory University and the U.S. Public Health Service to establish a full-fledged field station at Ichauway to study malaria control and elimination of hookworm and pellagra. The field station, which closed in 1957, not only improved the quality of health in Baker County but also served as a model for what eventually became the Centers for Disease Control in Atlanta.

Twenty years after the field station closed, Emory University–trained physician James Hotz, on whose story the hit movie *Doc Hollywood* is based, found himself two counties north of Baker in Leesburg, a community that had not had a doctor in ten years. Hotz established the private, nonprofit Albany Area Primary Health Care, with three clinics in Lee, Dougherty, and Baker Counties. Designed to provide health care to those who can least afford it, the program is supported by sliding-scale patient fees, a federal grant, and a commitment by Albany specialists to provide free surgery or therapy when needed. When Robert Woodruff heard about Dr. Hotz and his program, he had a $1 million medical clinic built in Newton for the people of Baker County.

In addition to medical research and support, Southwest Georgia plantations have been the sites of important ecological research. Several plantation owners in the Tallahassee Red Hills of south Thomas and Grady Counties supported the work of Herbert Stoddard in using prescribed, or controlled, burning to renew lands and improve hunting. Henry L. and Genevieve Beadel, owners of Tall Timbers Plantation in northern Leon County, Florida, and Ed and Betty Komarek, owners of Birdsong Plantation in southern Grady County, were all keen observers of natural history and frequently met with Stoddard at Sunday gatherings at Birdsong. In 1958, Beadel established a research station at Tall Timbers and provided that the plantation would become a private nonprofit research facility after his death in 1963. Since then the original twenty-eight hundred acres have expanded through gifts to nearly four thousand contiguous acres, including two hundred in Grady County. Although fire ecology is an important part of the Tall Timbers research effort, scientists here also study the longleaf pine forests, bobwhite quail, wild turkey, songbirds, rare and endangered plants, and endangered species, such as the red-cockaded woodpecker. The Komareks transformed their plantation, on which many scientific studies had been performed, into the Birdsong Nature Center in 1986. Birdsong is one of Southwest Georgia's best-kept secrets. Hidden away in extreme southern Grady County, it offers nature trails and Betty Komarek's famous bird window through which numerous species may be observed.

Southwest Georgia's newest research center, the Joseph W. Jones Ecological Research Center, is located on Ichauway Plantation in Baker County. When Robert Woodruff died in 1985, he left his plantation to the Woodruff Foundation, which established the center and named it for Jones, Woodruff's close friend and associate. Ichauway has "one of the most extensive, unbroken tracts of longleaf pine upland forest and undisturbed wiregrass understory remaining in the United States," which will be the subject of long-term research. In addition, Ichauway includes twelve miles of the Flint River and over fourteen miles of the Ichauwaynochaway Creek, an aesthetically and ecologically valuable Coastal Plain whitewater stream. Both aquatic and forest ecosystem management are major subjects of research at Ichauway.

The most famous of Southwest Georgia's research centers is the University of Georgia Coastal Plain Experiment Station (CPES) in Tifton. The CPES started out in 1919 with one employee and 206 acres. It has since grown to five hundred employees in 1990 and six thousand acres in 1993. CPES researchers have developed numerous varieties of peanuts, cotton, grasses, and other crops grown in Georgia and throughout the world. Early design work on the peanut combine was done at CPES, and in the 1980s CPES researchers developed the hull scrape method for assessing peanut maturity. The method, used throughout Southwest Georgia, saves peanut farmers as much as $23 million a year. The most famous scientist at CPES is plant geneticist Dr. Glenn Burton, who came to Tifton in 1936. Among his accomplishments are the development of coastal Bermuda grass that enables cattle to live on fewer acres and gain weight more rapidly; hybrid food grains that prevented major famine in India's Green Revolution in the 1960s; and turf grasses used on some of the most exclusive golf courses in the world. An octogenarian who does not let age slow him down, Burton was still working at CPES in 1994.

The twenty-four counties of Southwest Georgia are often perceived by outsiders as a distinct and unified block in the southwest corner of the state. Although geographically Albany appears to be the center around which the region revolves, Southwest Georgia is not a cohesive whole but rather a collection of subregions whose foci, in some cases, are not even in Georgia, but instead in bordering Alabama and Florida.

Residents of Quitman and Clay Counties in the northwest view Eufaula, Alabama, as their urban center. This orientation is especially true in the Quitman County seat of Georgetown. Residents of Fort Gaines in Clay County similarly cross the river and drive the fourteen miles to Abbeville, Alabama, to the closest fast food franchise—Hardee's. In order to avoid the predominantly black Clay Elementary School, some white students attend the Abbeville Christian Academy. For their shopping and entertainment, Clay Countians usually go to either Eufaula or Dothan, Alabama.

The southern tier of Southwest Georgia counties has always been oriented to Florida. The earliest settlers traveled to the Gulf coast to get salt, a scarce commodity, by boiling sixty-gallon drums of seawater on the beach and collecting the residue. Until the railroad arrived in Thomasville in 1861, cotton was shipped out through Gulf ports. Today, Tallahassee is the major urban center for Decatur, Grady, Thomas, and Brooks Counties. As a university town with a population of 125,000, Florida's state capital has more to attract Southwest Georgians than any Georgia city south of Atlanta. Culturally, African Americans in extreme South Georgia share more with North Florida blacks than with blacks in the Albany area. The Twentieth of May, commemorating the emancipation of blacks in the Thomasville-Tallahassee area by federal troops on May 20, 1865, is still celebrated on Pebble Hill Plantation in Thomas and Grady Counties as well as in northern Florida's Leon County.

In eastern Southwest Georgia, the completion of the southern leg of I-75 in 1963 drew those counties much closer to Tifton and Valdosta. Exits in those towns and in Adel have flourished on the trade of tourists passing through the region. As Tifton and Valdosta grew, they attracted more trade from the surrounding counties. Even in little Adel, largely as a result of entrepreneur John L. Williams's aggressive efforts, a factory outlet mall with restaurants and gas station was established. No one traveling I-75 can miss Williams's King Frog Restaurant, King Frog Factory Outlet, or the Factory Stores at Adel at exit 10.

As diverse and divided as Southwest Georgia is, church is one thing that nearly every community champions as a major priority. One of the first questions asked of newcomers to the region is, "Do you belong to a church?" From the beginning, the church—usually Baptist or Methodist—was one of the earliest institutions established in a community. In many Black Belt counties, slaves outnumbered their masters in the usually biracial churches. After emancipation many black Baptists and Methodists broke away to form new African American churches, like First African Baptist in Bainbridge, Macedonia Baptist in Valdosta, Bethel AME in Albany, and St. Luke CME in Thomasville.

Southwest Georgia's religious life was further diversified when immigrants moved into the region and established their own churches. In Albany, German and Irish immigrants established St. Teresa's Catholic Church before the Civil War. The church, constructed in 1859, still stands and is one of the oldest Catholic churches in the state in continuous use. In Valdosta, several Lebanese Catholic families became the basis for St. John the Evangelist Catholic Church, established in 1927. The most recent Catholic immigrants to Southwest Georgia are Latino migrant workers, mostly Mexicans, who harvest the tobacco and vegetable crops in the region. Farmers report that the Latinos are industrious workers who save their hard-earned wages to send to their families in Mexico. White attitudes seem to change, however, once the immigrants settle in the region. Local whites complain about Latinos at the supermarket: "They go to talking that Spanish and you don't know what they're saying. Some of them can talk American, but they don't want you to know what they're saying." One Southwest Georgia writer, who has called the Latinos the "new niggers," suggests that in places like Echols County, they have replaced the African American at the bottom of the social scale. Local churches—Catholic and Protestant—have established missions to minister to the migrants' physical and spiritual needs.

Not all immigrants to the region have been European or Christian. Recently arrived Asians have established Chinese restaurants in Albany, Camilla, and Donalsonville. Jews from Germany, Poland, Hungary, and other places first migrated to Southwest Georgia in the antebellum era. Many started out as peddlers before settling down as merchants or craftsmen in the towns. Albany's Jewish congregation was formally chartered in 1876, and eventually congregations were established in Valdosta and Bainbridge. Aware of the anti-Semitic threat of organizations like the Ku Klux Klan, Jews in Southwest Georgia assimilated quickly. Aside from the Star of David, the exterior of the Albany synagogue looks no different from a Baptist or Methodist church. Recent Jewish newcomers are sometimes surprised at how assimilated Southwest Georgia Jews have become. One elderly descendent of an old Jewish family in Albany recently professed shock at some visiting Atlanta Jews who wanted to wear their yarmulkes and prayer shawls to a service.

While some Southwest Georgians are cautious about acknowledging religious and ethnic diversity, even fewer recognize sexual diversity. Not until 1994 did the *Albany Herald* mention the existence of a gay community in the region's largest city; as it would be for most of the state, such notice was unusual. A gay man in Albany said there was no difference between being gay in Southwest Georgia and elsewhere, but he warned, "the smaller the town and the more rural the area, the more careful you have to be."

Although Southwest Georgia is not famous for its cultural life, the region has made some important contributions in music, art, and literature. Trumpet-playing band leader Harry James (1916–83), rhythm-and-blues musician Ray Charles (1930–), and composer Wallingford Riegger (1885–1961) were born in Albany, and singer Ray Stevens grew up there. Former Cairo resident Mickey Thomas is a vocalist for the band Starship (formerly Jefferson Starship, and before that Jefferson Airplane). But Southwest Georgia's most significant contribution is in African American music, and its most important exponent is Dr. Bernice Johnson Reagon, another Albany native. Reagon grew up in the black Baptist churches that her father, Rev. Jessie Johnson, pastored. She says: "The first music I heard was in church. The sound I make is Southwest Georgia. The harmonies are Southwest Georgia. The sound I hear in my head as a composer is Southwest Georgia." Reagon was active in the Albany Movement where music played a crucial role in stirring African Americans to action. She and her future husband, SNCC field secretary Cordell Reagon, joined Albanian Rutha Mae Harris and Charles Neblett in forming the SNCC Freedom Singers, who toured the country singing many of the freedom songs first composed in Albany and raising money for the movement. Eventually Reagon went on to earn her Ph.D. in history and serve as a curator at the Smithsonian Institution. She formed Sweet Honey in the Rock, an a cappella group that has recorded and performs a variety of songs. In 1994 for National Public Radio she produced and narrated *Wade in the Water,* a twenty-six-part series on black sacred music.

The power of Southwest Georgian African American music was reiterated by Dr. Mary Nell Morgan of Empire State College: "For the African Americans in this country, the message is in the music."

Concluding a lecture on W. E. B. Du Bois at Albany State College, as only a native Southwest Georgia African American could, she sang a cappella "Climbing Jacob's Ladder" and, like the civil rights singers thirty years ago, altered the words to fit the current situation.

Several writers have written novels and short stories about Southwest Georgia. Current fiction writers of note include Harry Crews, Janice Daugharty, and O. Victor Miller. Although Crews is a southeast Georgia native, his *A Feast of Snakes*, set in a south Georgia town with an annual rattlesnake roundup, could easily have taken place in Whigham, the Grady County town that features such an event. Daugharty and Miller, both Southwest Georgia natives, share with Crews his ability to capture the peculiar speech patterns of this region. Writing authentic dialect is a difficult task. According to Crews, "You either do it with idiom—get a flavor of the speech, the dialect, . . . [or] by syntax, the placing of the words, and by phonetically spelling a key word." Thus "There's enough business in this town for everybody" would become "It's enough bidness for everbody." In explaining how his books come about, Crews stated, "I just wonder about the tiniest little stupid-assed thing, and I look at it and I think, 'Hmmm, damn, why would people do that?' But they did."

Both Daugharty and Miller, newcomers on the literary scene, have demonstrated their mastery of dialect and their ability to write prose that comes alive. In his story "The Lost Cause" (*One Man's Junk*, 1994), Miller has Darby, a northern transplanted factory worker out of work in Albany, "trying to speak cracker, which is about as natural on him . . . as a sidesaddle on a hog." "Mo," he discovers, means "I am going to," as in "Mo whip your ass." At the Lost Cause, a local redneck bar, Calvin, who lost his hand in an industrial accident and wears a hook in its place, is at the bar alongside Darby. The bartender narrates: "Then, real quick, I hear this noise sounds like somebody jerking his fist out of a five-gallon bucket of axle grease—schulck—and a bucktooth bounces on the bar. I realize that Calvin's tried to push Darby's face out of his, forgetting the hook, which goes in Darby's mouth and latches on to his tongue. Calvin sees what he's done and tries to jerk the hook back, yanking Darby's tongue out about a yard. Darby's eyes are showing more white than a pickled egg, and tears squirt. His arms are flapping. He squats and stands back up, cawing like a crow. 'Gah, gah, gah!'"

Daugharty's command of the Southwest Georgia idiom is masterful. In *Dark of the Moon*, Merdie Lee asks if someone "might could give us a lift." Expressions like "blue dozen," "wall-eyed mad," "swigging cocoalers," and "chester drawers" reveal Daugharty's intimate knowledge of the folk of Southwest Georgia. She has Merdie's mama explain the reaction of flatwoods folk to the government's anti-tick program: "Way back the gover'munt took a notion to make us dip our cattle

HOW'S THAT AGAIN?

The state's roadside signs make interesting reading. Travelers as well as longtime residents of Georgia may find it odd that the name of the county seat frequently seems more appropriate to some county other than the one it serves. Lumpkin, the town, is not in Lumpkin County but is the county seat of Stewart County, many, many miles to the southwest of Lumpkin County, whose seat is Dahlonega. Macon is the county seat of Bibb County, while Oglethorpe is the seat of Macon County. The seat of Oglethorpe County, in turn, is Lexington. Similar examples are readily obvious from even a casual glance at a list of Georgia county and town names. And then there are other curious place-names, like the one in the photograph above.

—Steve Gurr

for ticks in vats they built, and I can't say we liked it. Took all day on mule and horseback just to round up a little drove of cows. Some was knowed in these parts to dynamite a dip vat."

Violence, tragedy, and suffering are common in the works of Crews, Daugharty, and Miller, whose stories focus more on lower-class whites than on other Southwest Georgians. Says Crews: "Suffering is pretty much more or less with us in greater or lesser degrees." Violence is all too common: "There's more men in the South that's been killed over fence lines and bird dogs than anything else." And yet the region is also known for its gentility: "Manners are what protect us from ourselves and protect us from each other."

The violent side of life is not the subject of Thomas County first-grade teacher Bailey White's writing. Popularly known for her National Public Radio essays on the more sedate side of rural Southwest Georgia, White has published some of these and other essays in *Mama Makes Up Her Mind and Other Dangers of Southern Living* (1993). Anyone who has been to a rural fair will recognize her description:

> Out on the midway, slack-jawed women amble, their giant rumps packed into tight nylon pants like two shoats in a sack, and little stringy-haired children run around eating food made entirely of poisons. Hawkers with rotting snaggle teeth peddle dusty stuffed animals with polyester fur in shades of pink and purple just invented in this decade. . . . There's that unmistakable smell of humans in the subtropics. A woman squats down and feeds her baby something bright red on a stick. Another mother smacks her little girl on the side of the head because she's whining. My fellowmen.

Bailey White's storytelling is part of a great Southwest Georgia tradition. Go anywhere in the region and you'll find someone willing to tell a story. In Miller County, they say "Northerners tell stories and call it therapy. Southerners tell stories and call it swappin' lies." Uncle Charlie, in Sonny Sammons's *The Keepers of Echowah*, admits, "I never have been one to let the truth interfere with a good story. Any story worth telling is worthy of embellishment." Mariella Glenn Hartsfield, a humanities professor at Bainbridge College, studied the folktales of Grady County that she heard growing up and as an adult. In her *Tall Betsy and Dunce Baby: South Georgia Folktales* (1987), she categorizes and analyzes many of these tales. When the Baker County Historical Society assembled a county history, they included a chapter called "Rumors, Legends, Tall Tales, Characters and Such."

A recent development in Southwest Georgia storytelling has been the transformation of the tales into theater. First to do this successfully were the Miller County residents who conducted a series of taped interviews with older residents—white and black. They hired a playwright to turn the oral history and tales into a musical. The result was *Swamp Gravy*, named after the gravy or soup made from fried fish drippings, onions, tomatoes, and anything else that was available. *Swamp Gravy*, then, is a potpourri of Miller County's past, and a delightful blend it is. The musical, which opens with the line, "You've got a story, and I've got a story; we've all got a story to tell," is Georgia's official folk life play. All performers are Miller County residents who have traveled around the state and to Florida to give performances. After the success of *Swamp Gravy*, residents in nearby Seminole County organized an arts council and created their own folklife musical, *Cornerstone*. In the meantime Mariella Hartsfield and Jacque Wheeler have transformed Hartsfield's collection of Grady County tales into a musical, *Tall Betsy and the Cracker Barrel Tales*. Efforts to disseminate Southwest Georgia literature and culture have resulted in the publication of *Swamp Gravy: Folk Tales from South Georgia* and two literary reviews, *Snake Nation Review*, published quarterly in Valdosta, and *Flint River Review*, published annually in Albany.

While hundreds of residents attend musicals and other cultural events, thousands turn out for Friday night high school football games, in many counties the social event of the week. The income from the gate at football games often pays for many, if not all, of the other South Georgia high school sports programs. According to the national media, the Valdosta Wildcats are the winningest high school football team in the nation. Valdostans take their football so seriously that football coaches in other parts of Georgia facetiously claim that at birth a boy in Valdosta is given a packet containing a Wildcats T-shirt and a toy football. Boys start playing in the midget league in elementary school and move on to middle school football, which hones their skills for high school. So successful has Valdosta High School been that the city has been called "Winnersville, U.S.A.," and will be the location of the new National High School Football Hall of Fame.

Southwest Georgians have always been proud of their sports. They have produced, among others, two Olympic gold medalists, both of them African American women: Albany's Alice Coachman in track (1948) and Cairo's Teresa Edwards in basketball (1984, 1988, and 1992). New York Mets third baseman Ray Knight and his wife, professional golfer Nancy Lopez, make Albany their home.

Southwest Georgia's only minor league baseball team is the Albany Polecats. The city's first minor league team was the Albany Cardinals, part of the Georgia-Florida League that lasted from 1935 to 1959. In 1992 minor league baseball returned with the Polecats, a Class A expansion team in the South Atlantic League. An affiliate of the Montreal Expos, the Polecats received a lot of attention when they chose the team name. Polecat hats with the skunk mascot, Pepper the Polecat, are a collector's item in other parts of the country.

Southwest Georgia has made its mark in the world of diving competition with the 1993 opening in Moultrie of the Moose Moss Aquatic Center, the only competitive diving complex in Georgia that meets the U.S. Diving Association's standards. In 1994, the Phillips 66 National Outdoor Diving Championships were held in the facility, which contains a tower with four platforms and eight springboards.

The National Hot Rod Association's largest drawing dragway in the southeast is the U.S. 19 Racetrack. Tim Pafford of Lanier County is the owner-manager-announcer at the newly renovated dragstrip south of Albany. Competitions on Friday and Saturday nights may draw two to three hundred entrants.

Another interesting competition in the region is team penning. A team-penning organization formed in Dawson in 1994 holds its competition at the Terrell County 4-H Pavilion and Horse Arena. At one end of the arena is a small herd of cattle, each cow with a number affixed to it. Three numbers are called out to a team of three horseback riders, who are given one-and-a-half minutes to enter the herd, cut out the three designated cattle, move them down to the end of the arena, and put them in a free-standing pen.

Team penning may be just catching on in Southwest Georgia, but for many in the region the favorite sports are as old as the region itself—hunting and fishing. While most hunters' favorite targets may be deer or quail, dove and turkey are also popular. One quarry that few Southwest Georgians shoot anymore is mistletoe. In past generations during the holiday season, it was common to shoot the plant out of its host tree with a shotgun so it could be used for Christmas decorations.

The American Indians referred to the warm half of the year as the "time of the snake," and Southwest Georgia hunters are usually very careful about the reptiles. One of the region's greatest concentrations of snakes, according to naturalist Jim Fowler, can be found in the area around Albany. Rattlesnakes and water moccasins are the two most common poisonous serpents in the region. Local weekly newspapers frequently carry pictures of five- and six-foot rattlesnakes killed by hunters, farmers, and others and warn their readers, "Snakes Are Crawling!"

Even more popular than hunting in Southwest Georgia is fishing. According to the *Albany Herald* lifestyles market analysis, "the only activity that is engaged in more frequently than fishing in South Georgia is owning a dog." The region's numerous ponds, lakes, and streams provide ample opportunity for the casual angler as well as the tournament competitor. Lake Seminole and Lake Walter F. George (known as Lake Eufaula in Alabama) are two of the most popular fishing spots in the region. Southwest Georgia fishing, however, was severely interrupted along with most other aspects of life in the region in July 1994 when the worst natural disaster to hit the state devastated the region.

The flood of 1994 took almost everyone in Southwest Georgia by surprise. As Tropical Storm Alberto stalled over central Georgia, he first spoiled Fourth of July picnics and family gatherings. Like an unwanted guest, he would not leave, instead dropping unheard-of levels of rain over Central and South Georgia that caused a five-hundred-year flood, a disaster, in Victor Miller's words, "of biblical magnitude when graveyards yawn[ed], burping caskets and bodies from saturated graves." By the time the Flint River crested at nearly forty-three feet in Albany, the worst-hit community, twenty-three thousand residents had been forced to evacuate twenty-three square miles of Dougherty County that were under water. Bridges connecting the two halves of Albany were shut down. The Albany State College campus was inundated; nearly every building suffered serious damage, finally estimated at $40 million. The swirling chocolate-colored waters showed no mercy, not even to the dead. More than four hundred caskets in the city's cemeteries were unearthed, and rescuers had to secure them before they floated downriver. As a result of a breach in Lake Blackshear Dam, Blackshear became lakeless. Weeks later, seven thousand Albanians made homeless by the flood were still in shelters. South of Albany, the Baker County seat of Newton, a tiny town of nine hundred, was engulfed by water that rose twenty-one feet above flood level. Two hundred houses were swamped; sixty of them and the downtown were ruined beyond repair. Months after the flood, residents were still pessimistic about the town's future.

Dougherty County suffered the greatest damage in the flood of 1994: $99.4 million in damage to residential, commercial, and other structures, 62,502 tons of flood debris dumped in landfills, 4,907 unemployed as a result of the flood, $80 million in home and small business loans issued by the Small Business Administration. In the city of Albany alone, the total cost of flood recovery projects (not including Albany State College) has been estimated at $125 million. The impact of this disaster will be with the residents of Southwest Georgia for years to come. But with every tragedy comes some good. Old dilapidated housing in the poorer sections of Albany will be replaced; the rebuilt Albany State campus will have new and refurbished buildings; and fishing in the Flint River and Lake Blackshear will be better than ever. Another positive development that emerged from the tragedy was a refreshing unity in this often racially divided region. Black and white worked together to rescue, to resuscitate, to repair. A large step toward racial harmony was made in the shadow of the worst natural disaster in the state's recorded history.

The floodwaters have receded, and reconstruction proceeds apace. Driving through much of Southwest Georgia, a traveler sees few remnants of the flood. Although some farms suffered damage, most were not seriously affected. The traveler through the region notices what he noticed before 1994: the importance of agriculture. If he turns on the TV in his motel room in the early morning, he may see a farm show. In addition to the usual advertisements for headache and hemorrhoid relief, she may see a commercial for the latest herbicide, pesticide, or fertilizer.

A visitor to Southwest Georgia should stop in its towns and sit down and talk with some of the folk. In most places, she'll feel right at home and witness communities that cherish values that seem to have disappeared elsewhere. Family is important in Southwest Georgia. One of the biggest reasons for hotel room rentals on the weekends in Albany is African American family reunions. People study their families here; they have built large genealogical collections in Moultrie at the Ellen Payne Odom Genealogy Library and in Albany at the Dougherty County Central Library's Genealogy Room.

People are friendly and respectful in small-town Southwest Georgia. Older adults are addressed as Mr. or Mrs. or Ms. with "sir" and "ma'am" used frequently. But they can also be direct when it comes to political or social issues, and the contrast can sometimes startle the listener. When the visitor moves on to the next town or gets ready to leave the region, the road will take him through the farms that make this region what it is. He'll see the graceful white birds next to, or even on, the cattle as he drives by. Locals call them cow birds; the ornithologists call them cattle egrets. They consume the insects stirred up when the cow moves. If the traveler steps out of the car to admire the countryside, he should avoid the occasional dirt mounds that are home to thousands of fire ants. If he gets bitten by one of them, he'll remember Southwest Georgia in a painful way for several days. It is this land—with its ants and egrets, its cotton and corn, its peanuts and vegetables, its cattle and pecans, and its black and white residents—that makes this region of Georgia the slow-paced, yet diverse, place it is.

Fred C. Fussell

TOURING
SOUTHWEST
GEORGIA

Even though it is more than a hundred miles from Randolph, Terrell, and Lee Counties in the north to Thomas, Brooks, and Echols Counties in the south, Southwest Georgia changes little in climate, culture, and topography from north to south. To the untutored stranger, the South Georgia landscape might even seem tedious and dull. Flat-land agriculture and pine-tree forestry are the principal, and sometimes only, substantial economic activities within extensive sections of the region.

Traditional culture in Southwest Georgia is tied to agriculture. Crops of seemingly endless fields of cotton, corn, wheat, tobacco, peanuts, sweet potatoes, and pine trees, along with fenced lots and broad pastures for the keeping of hogs, sheep, chickens, honeybees, mules, and cattle, create the essence of the Southwest Georgia farmscape.

For many decades, thousands, even millions, of road-weary vacation travelers bound for Florida have withstood the long, hot trip through the roadside farmlands and the small one-street towns of south Georgia. They trudge impatiently along, yearning for the beaches and the resort hotels of their destinations. On crossing over the Georgia state line into Florida, they roar with celebration, as if crossing from darkness into light.

While stopped for gas or for a cooling drink, the road-weary travelers may sometimes gaze with bleary-eyed interest at the Georgia people whom they see in the towns or fields. The travelers may wonder, "Who are they? Why do they live here in this hot place? How can they stand it here, day after day, year after year? How can they possibly endure?"

Southwest Georgia was once the beloved land of native southern tribespeople. Parts of these hot lands were among the last in Georgia to be taken from the Indians—Yuchis, Creeks, Hitchitees, Seminoles—who for centuries had farmed the rich fields beside the rivers, hunted

537

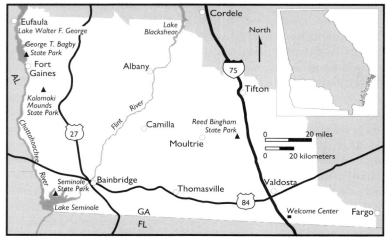

Southwest Georgia

and gathered in the wild pine and oak forests, and fished in the dark waters of the swamps and creeks that abound throughout the land.

Much later, as industrial America prospered, the region became a warm winter retreat and playground for privileged northerners who acquired grand expanses of unregimented forests of freeborn pine trees and prairies of wiregrass and who created great hunting reserves in which to ride on horseback after hounds and to follow, shotguns in hand, after bird dogs.

And even though the people who are seen by the passing Florida-bound vacationers know of this, they know much more. The real people of south Georgia, black and white, are bound by life in the small steaming towns and in the fields and swamps and woods—and deep down within themselves, they like it.

Sitting up in trees, they hunt deer. They fish for bream and catfish in farm ponds using two-dollar bamboo poles and baits of cricket and worm. From high on the elevated stools of ten-thousand-dollar bass boats they fish with spinning reels for monsters hidden deep in rivers and sinkholes. They ride around on the weekend in pick-up trucks, drinking canned beers drawn from Styrofoam coolers. They sometimes chew tobacco, and when they do they spit. They boil and eat peanuts pulled up from a neighbor's field, and they stay up all night to cook pork barbecue and talk. They put Tom's Toasted Peanuts down inside bottled Coca-Colas and then eat and drink at the same time. They go to church every Sunday morning, eat out sometimes at the town cafe for Sunday dinner, and swim in the creek on Sunday afternoon. They sit still on a quilt on the ground in the park for a summer's night symphony performance, and on rainy days they hang out at juke joints and listen to rhythm and blues, country, gospel, bluegrass, and rock. They run twice over rattlesnakes and play blues guitar, bottleneck style. They eat collard greens, cornbread, haslet, cheese grits, fried squash, pickled eggs, and pork chops. They run uptown for a minute. They watch the sky a lot and talk to each other about the hot weather and about if it will or won't rain. They love watermelons, homemade peach ice cream, banana pudding, fried chicken, potato salad, and tomato sandwiches. They eat pizza. They attend PTA meetings, and some go to meetings of the historical society and the garden club. They watch school plays, graduation, and high school football. They go to family reunions and pay dues to the Masonic Hall, the Kiwanis Club, and the burial club. They clean off cemetery lots, swat gnats and mosquitoes, plant vegetable gardens, watch professional wrestling on TV, and play church league softball—and they like it.

There is a distinctive beauty, found only in Southwest Georgia, that endures in the deep waters of the limestone sinks and in the slowly meandering, tannin-stained streams; in the moccasin- and mayhaw-filled bogs, and in the fields of corn and peanuts. That beauty endures also in the people and in the towns that are often indifferently passed up by the apathetic tourist.

Now is the time to put aside the urge to glide blindly by. The traveler who offers an inquisitive mind and an adventurous appetite to Southwest Georgia will be rewarded with a memorable experience and the discovery of a culture that is not to be found elsewhere. In Southwest Georgia, the table is set. Take your place! Get it while it's hot!

Grave shelter, Thomasville Cemetery

TOUR ONE: A CIRCUIT OF SOUTHWEST GEORGIA

From Tifton, travel west via U.S. 82 to Sylvester and Albany. From Albany travel north via U.S. 19 to Leesburg. From Leesburg travel west via Ga. 32 to Dawson, then U.S. 82 to Cuthbert and Georgetown. From Georgetown travel south via Ga. 39 to Fort Gaines and Blakely. From Blakely travel south via U.S. 27 to Colquitt. From Colquitt travel southwest via Ga. 91 to Donalsonville. From Donalsonville travel south via Ga. 39 to Seminole State Park. From Seminole State Park travel east via Ga. 253 to Bainbridge. From Bainbridge travel east via U.S. 84 to Cairo, Thomasville, Quitman, and Valdosta. From Valdosta travel northeast via U.S. 221 to Lakeland. From Lakeland travel north via U.S. 129 to Nashville and Alapaha. From Alapaha travel west via U.S. 82 back to Tifton.

Tifton is a great place to begin a tour of Southwest Georgia, for it truly typifies the region, setting the tone and pace with its strong agricultural orientation, its variety of outdoor recreational facilities, and its distinctive cultural flair. Less than two blocks from the major interchange at I-75 and U.S. 82, Tifton restaurants serve foods that are to be found only in these parts of Southwest Georgia. Aside from the ready-sweetened iced tea that is a standard mealtime beverage in cafes and at home, patrons of locally owned and operated restaurants can expect to find menus listing such distinctive items as deep fried quail and channel catfish served with hushpuppies, cole slaw, pickles, sliced onions, and a local favorite, cheese grits! Even a few of Tifton's fast-food restaurants serve cheese grits.

Tifton, the county seat of Tift County, has been described as the hub of South Georgia. The eight-block downtown shopping and commercial center includes a large historic district, with over fifty restored shop and store buildings. Abraham Baldwin Agricultural College, just west of I-75 on the north side of Tifton, is a major factor in both the educational and cultural aspects of the entire Southwest Georgia region. The college's Arts Experiment Station along with the University of Georgia Coastal Plain Experiment Station and the Rural Development Center have been historically, and are today, leading factors in the academic, agricultural, cultural, and commercial development of the region.

The Georgia Agrirama, north of Tifton on I-75, is the official state living history museum. It features ninety-five acres of farmland, period buildings, and a series of interpretive programs that accurately depict South Georgia as it existed nearly a hundred years ago. Costumed artisans and interpreters demonstrate a wide variety of skills and workways, from wood stove cookery to blacksmithing. Vintage buildings that have been moved and restored on the museum grounds include a one-room schoolhouse, several farmhouses, a saw mill, a steam-powered cotton gin, a water-powered grist mill, and a Masonic lodge. A gift shop in a restored country store features locally produced traditional crafts and such indigenous food products as water-ground corn meal, sugar cane syrup, hominy grits, crackling bread, honey, and roasted peanuts. Annual special events at Georgia Agrirama include a Black Heritage Celebration, a Folklife Festival, an old-fashioned Independence Day Celebration, a County Fair on Labor Day, a Political Rally, a Winter Homecoming, and many seasonal demonstrations such as cotton ginning, cane grinding and syrup making, sheep shearing, planting and harvesting, Christmas festivities, and square dances. The Agrirama office has information on specific dates.

The Georgia Peanut Festival, held in late October, is the event of the year in **Sylvester**, and peanuts and peanut-related products are the lifeblood of Worth County. There is an annual Peanut Parade; a barbecue to honor peanut farmers; peanut cuisine; the Goober Gala, an annual dance; the Worth County Fair, arts and crafts at Possum Poke; and numerous other elements of celebration, all of which culminate in the selection of a new queen at the Miss Georgia Peanut pageant. Possum Poke, the former winter residence of Michigan's early-twentieth-century governor Chase S. Osborne, is located at Poulan, a few miles east of Sylvester. Osborne, who was a friend of poet Robert Frost, was instrumental in organizing the North Atlantic Treaty Organization (NATO). A WPA mural painted in 1939 by Chester J. Tingler and titled "Cantaloupe Industry" can be seen at the Sylvester Post Office on Main Street.

With its population of over ninety-one thousand, the city of **Albany**, the seat of Dougherty County, is the industrial and commercial "big city" of the Southwest Georgia region, yet an agricultural commodity—the pecan—is touted by promoters of the town as its identifying product. Albany is home to many cultural amenities that might be expected only in a city that is larger. It has a worthy art museum, two colleges, a symphonic orchestra, a community theater and performing arts center, a museum of science and history, an eleven-thousand-seat civic center, a planetarium, and a zoo. The Albany Museum of Art, 311 Meadowlark Drive, includes in its holdings one of the premier collections of African ethnic art in the Southeast. The museum's changing exhibition schedule focuses on contemporary American art, particularly that of the South.

Albany State College, 504 College Drive, is a senior unit of the University System of Georgia. The school offers over forty fields of study for its student population of twenty-one hundred. Albany State, one of three historically black public colleges in Georgia, suffered $40 million in damages from the great flood of July 1994. The state university system, however, quickly committed resources to rebuild the institution. Darton College, 2400 Gillionville Road, is a two-year community college of the state university system.

Roadside signs, Albany

Chehaw Park, on Philema Road, is an eight-hundred-acre public use area of woodlands, lakes, campsites, and playgrounds. Chehaw Park is the site of the Chehaw National Indian Festival, an event held annually in May at which Pan-Indian pow-wow style dancing, Southeastern Indian stomp dancing, Native American foods and crafts, and primitive woodland skills are demonstrated. Also in Chehaw Park is a replica of a late-eighteenth-century Creek Indian town, including a Tcokofa or winter council house, a square ground, and a chunkey yard. Replicas of family housing units, garden plots and fields, and other features typical of a Creek settlement are planned for the site. Chehaw Wild Animal Park is a one-hundred-acre component of

Chehaw Park at which native and exotic wildlife in natural environmental settings is exhibited. There are a petting zoo, performances by trained elephants, an aviary, and an area for interpretive programming. Adjacent to Chehaw Park is Lake Chehaw, an impoundment of two major tributaries of the Flint River—Kinchafoonee and Muckalee Creeks. At the nearby Georgia Power Company Lake a plant produces electrical energy for approximately twenty-eight hundred houses in Albany. The lake is open for fishing, canoeing, and boating. The Municipal Auditorium (1915) on Pine Avenue, renovated in 1990, is listed on the National Register of Historic Places.

The Bridge House, 112 North Front Street, was the toll office for the wooden bridge that crossed the Flint River here. Commissioned to be built in 1857 by Nelson Tift, founder of Albany, the upper level of the two-story brick house has a theater that features hand-painted scenic decorations created by artists imported from New York. During the Civil War, the building was used as a pickling plant for the Confederacy. The Bridge House was constructed by ex-slave Horace King of Girard, Alabama (see West Central tour).

The Union Passenger Station, 100 Roosevelt Avenue, is the central element of a series of facilities operated by the Thronateeska Heritage Center. The area around and including the old depot is the site of the Museum of Science and History, the Wetherbee Planetarium and Discovery Center, the Fryer-Merrit House, the Jarrard House, and other related historical and cultural exhibition elements. The museum exhibits housed inside several rooms of the renovated train station interpret an eclectic assemblage of Indian artifacts, natural history specimens, and historical memorabilia.

Although rhythm and blues musician Ray Charles grew up in Florida, he was born in Albany in 1930, where he lived until he was about six years old. It was not until he and his family moved away from Georgia that he developed glaucoma and became blind. Charles, whose career as one of America's most popular singers began to soar in 1955 following the release of "I've Got a Woman," has recorded dozens of hits. He also wrote "Georgia," the state's official song. Tradition in Albany has it that Charles's first job as a musician took place there at the Continental Room in the basement of the Jackson Hotel near the Municipal Auditorium.

The Old St. Theresa Church, located at 317 Residence Avenue, is one of the two oldest Catholic churches in Georgia. Begun in 1859 from bricks made by slaves and in use since 1860, it was a hospital during the Civil War. The church was recently restored, and mass is celebrated each Wednesday at noon.

In 1961, local African American citizens, determined to change the prevailing system of racial segregation and discrimination, organized the Albany Movement. In December of that year, they invited Dr. Martin

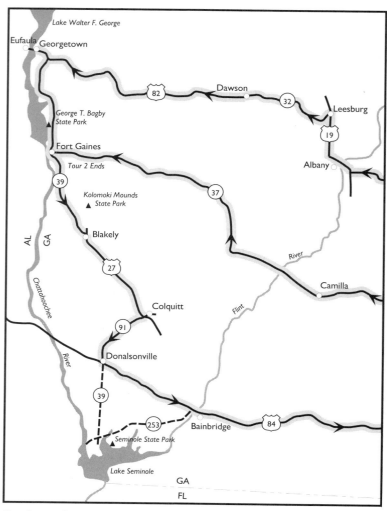

Southwest Georgia, Tours One and Two

Luther King Jr. to the city to address a mass meeting. During a march of protest, he and others were arrested and jailed. King's involvement in the Albany Movement brought national attention to the Southwest Georgia city. Most of the mass meetings in 1961 and 1962 were held at the Shiloh Baptist Church, 325 Whitney Avenue, and at the Mount Zion Baptist Church across the street. The Mount Zion Church building is being renovated to become the Mount Zion–Albany Civil Rights Museum. In 1993, the Albany Civil Rights Memorial and Park was dedicated at the corner of Highland Avenue and South Jackson

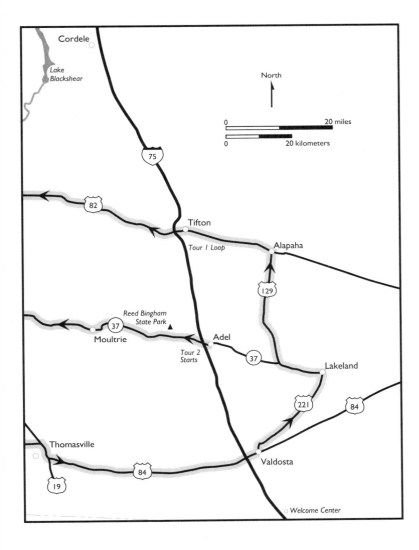

Street. The memorial consists of a fountain surrounded by four up-right black marble slabs upon which is engraved a detailed chronology of events of the Albany Movement and a quotation from a speech by Dr. King concerning the plight of African Americans in Albany. Adjacent to the park are the offices of the *Albany Southwest Georgian*, the African American newspaper that was the only reliable local source of media information for blacks during the civil rights movement.

Lee County is one of the most rapidly growing counties in the state as its southern section has become the expanding, largely white, suburb of Albany. **Leesburg**, the county seat, was incorporated in 1872. Both the county and the town are named for Henry (Lighthorse Harry) Lee, Revolutionary War hero and father of Confederate general Robert E. Lee.

Peanut-butter manufacturing is an important industry in **Dawson**, the county seat of Terrell County. The Cinderella Company, one of several large manufacturers of peanut butter in Southwest Georgia, has its plant here. Historically, Dawson has been a quiet center for the self-perpetuation of traditional African American music. Even though much has been made of his connection with Macon, the great soul musician Otis Redding (1941–1967) was born in Dawson, the son of a Baptist minister, and spent his early childhood here. Folk singer Bessie Jones, who achieved a measure of fame in the 1960s and 1970s as the lead vocalist for the Georgia Sea Island Singers, was by birth a native of Dawson, and many of the traditional games and songs that she recorded were, in fact, learned during her childhood in Terrell County. **Parrott**, almost a ghost of a little town, is located about twelve miles northwest of Dawson, via Ga. 520. The nearly empty picturesque streets and buildings of Parrott have been used occasionally as sets for the filming of motion pictures.

The **Cuthbert** Historic District, in Randolph County, features thirty-five examples of nineteenth-century domestic and commercial architecture, reflecting periods and styles ranging from antebellum plantation plain and Greek revival to Victorian Gothic. Andrew College, on U.S. 82 a few blocks west of the Cuthbert town square, served as a Confederate hospital during the Civil War.

The Fletcher Henderson House, at 1016 Andrew Street, built in 1888, was the residence of Fletcher Henderson Sr., an educator whose son, Fletcher Henderson Jr., became one of the greatest jazz musicians in the history of American music. He played with such other jazz and blues greats as Gertrude "Ma" Rainey (see West Central tour), Louis Armstrong, and Thomas Dorsey (see Northwest tour). Henderson is buried at Greenwood Cemetery on Hamilton Avenue. Other twentieth-century notables from Randolph County are professional football greats Pat Summerall, Cuthbert; and Roosevelt "Rosie" Grier, who was born at Punkin' Town, a tiny community north of Cuthbert on U.S. 27. In Cuthbert's Greenwood Cemetery, where Fletcher Henderson is buried, are the graves of twenty-four Confederate soldiers who died at Hood (Andrew College) Hospital. They are commemorated with an unusual monument—a ground-level, life-sized full figure marble sculpture of a Confederate soldier.

An Italian-born artist, Carlo Ciampaglia, painted a New Deal mural in 1939 at the Cuthbert post office. The painting, titled "Last Indian Troubles in Randolph County—1836," depicts a skirmish between a contingency of the United States Army, led by Andrew Jackson, and the native Creek Indians. The Cuthbert home of Sylvester Toney Jr. is an example of artistic expression far different from that of Ciampaglia in the Cuthbert post office. Toney has decorated his house, his yard and surrounding fence, and even his automobiles with a colorful array of found materials that range from wildly whirring plastic windmills atop poles to military-like formations of toy dolls stationed at the corners of the fences that surround the clean-swept yard.

The 1891 jail house in **Georgetown**, county seat of Quitman County, with its twelve-inch-thick brick walls and its iron-barred windows, is fairly typical of jails constructed in county seats throughout Southwest Georgia. The jail yard, now open, was originally enclosed with a tall, thick, wooden wall. The Union Methodist Church was built in 1867 by a congregation that had first gathered thirty years earlier in a hewn log church house. The original hand-fashioned pine benches are still in use in the church's sanctuary. The nearby cemetery contains graves that date back as early as the 1850s. At the north end of the main street in Georgetown is a locally famous barbeque restaurant called Sam's. Georgetown is located directly across the Chattahoochee River, via the Ernest Vandiver Causeway, from Eufaula, one of the major centers of tourism and historic preservation in Alabama. The Eufaula area offers a host of picturesque glimpses into its past, when the architecturally rich river town was an agricultural and commercial center for the cotton kingdom.

(For Fort Gaines, see tour two.)

Kolomoki Mounds State Historic Park in Early County is one of Georgia's most important archaeological sites. The mounds are a National Historic Landmark. The ruins include seven earthen mounds, all built nearly a thousand years ago by southern American Indians at a crossroads of trade for the entire southeastern quadrant of the North American continent. The great temple mound at Kolomoki is the oldest, and one of the largest, in Georgia. The park includes a visitor center with exhibits interpreting the culture that occupied the site and built the mounds. Camping, swimming, boating, fishing, and picnic facilities are available.

The Early County courthouse in **Blakely** was built 1904 to 1905. Each facade of the building is fronted with a set of four solid Georgia granite columns that support porticos. On the courthouse square is an original Confederate flagpole, erected in 1861 and still standing. A monument on the town square pays homage to the peanut, a longtime and important cash crop in the region. The U.S. post office, located at the corner of South Main and Liberty Streets, displays a 1938 New Deal mural by artist Daniel Putnam Brinley. "The Land Is Bought from the Indians" depicts the signing of a document declaring a cession of lands from the native tribespeople to the Georgia settlers. Nine miles southwest of Blakely, off Ga. 62 on Old River Road, the Coheelee

Creek Covered Bridge, constructed in 1891, is the most southerly surviving covered bridge in the United States. In spring and summer, the woods surrounding the bridge abound in native wild flowers including dogwood, redbud, sweet shrub, native azaleas, and mountain laurel. An impressive series of waterfalls is west of the bridge.

The George W. Andrews Lock and Dam, about fifteen miles southwest of Blakely via Ga. 62, is the central of three such structures that lie on the Chattahoochee River between the Gulf of Mexico and the head of navigation at Columbus. The others are the Walter F. George Lock and Dam near Fort Gaines and the Jim Woodruff Lock and Dam at the Florida border.

Miller County's Spring Creek Park is a great place to see the legendary mayhaw trees in their natural habitat. The mayhaw (*Crataegus aestivalis*) is a locally common small tree of the hawthorne family. In spring, it produces a red fruit that resembles apples but is the size of cranberries. These trees grow near many of the numerous limestone sinks, river swamps, wet woods, and pond margins around Southwest Georgia. The mayhaw's natural tartness produces an unusually flavorful jelly. The town of Colquitt stages an annual Mayhaw Festival at Spring Creek Park in celebration of the local fruit and the jelly that local cooks produce from it. *Swamp Gravy* is a participatory theater production based upon locally collected folkways. Billed as Georgia's official folk life play, *Swamp Gravy* is a theatrical presentation of family stories, tall tales, regional history, and traditional music. The Colquitt–Miller County Chamber of Commerce provides information on performance schedules.

Seminole State Park, sixteen miles south of the town of **Donalsonville**, lies on the shores of Lake Seminole, in Seminole County in the extreme southwest corner of Georgia. The park features fishing, boating, camping, a beach area, and an unusual natural study area called the Gopher Tortoise Trail, a 2.2-mile-long path that winds through the natural habitat of the protected *Gopherus polyphemus* (and those of approximately two hundred other species of native flora and fauna). The park contains a marker commemorating the historically important site of Santa Cruz de Sabacola El Menor, a seventeenth-century Spanish mission to the Christianized Indians of the Lower Chattahoochee Valley. The site of the mission now lies buried beneath the waters of Lake Seminole. The Jim Woodruff Lock and Dam, positioned at the narrow point where the states of Alabama, Florida, and Georgia join, creates the lake and five-hundred-mile-long shoreline of Lake Seminole. The dam is situated at the confluence of the Flint and Chattahoochee Rivers, where they join to create the Apalachicola River. Tours of the Woodruff Dam powerhouse are available. Lake Seminole is one of the most highly regarded fishing lakes in North America. Anglers can expect to encounter sizable populations, and specimens, of large mouth,

NEW DEAL ART IN GEORGIA

During the Roosevelt years of the 1930s and early 1940s, American artists decorated the public buildings of the nation with murals and sculptural reliefs that reflected the local or national scene. In Georgia thirty-five of these works are extant; they are particularly rich in depictions of the state's agricultural traditions and can be found, primarily in post offices, from Adel to Commerce, from Cuthbert to Swainsboro. These works are visual reminders of the social ideals of the New Deal as well as graphic illustrations of an important movement in the history of American art, the American Scene.

The works in Georgia were sponsored by a federal government program known as the Section of Painting and Sculpture, later the Section of Fine Arts. Under the direction of the Treasury Department from 1934 to 1943, the Section was responsible for the embellishment of public buildings, thereby offering employment and commissions to unemployed or underemployed artists, who suffered particularly from the effects of the Great Depression.

Post office art in Georgia from this period was commissioned through competitions by the Section for federal buildings and should not be confused with the better-known Federal Art Project under the Works Progress Administration (WPA). The Section used local juries of prominent townspeople to select artists, who entered the competitions by presenting sketches of their ideas for murals or sculptures. The Section urged artists to seek the opinions of local residents and demanded a realist, "American" style in the execution of the work. The works in Georgia represent a visual catalogue of a way of life in the state with subjects ranging from agricultural labors to festivals, industrial workers in Rockmart, railway development, the local countryside in Pelham and Cornelia, downtown Rome, and early local postal service as well as historical scenes of treaties and battles with American Indians.

—William U. Eiland
Director, Georgia Museum of Art

Overleaf: Detail of "The Two Rivers" by Peter Blume, located in Rome

striped, and white bass, catfish, crappie, bream, and during spawning season, even salt-water mullet.

Bainbridge, in Decatur County, is located near the head of navigation on the Flint River. There is conjecture that the Spaniard Hernando DeSoto traveled through there in 1540 on his famous exploration of the Southeast. In 1765, the site of present-day Bainbridge was a Creek Indian town called Pucknawhitla. By 1790 a settlement, Burgess Town, had been established as a trading center, and, by 1817, a U.S. Army post called Fort Hughes was built. In 1824, the name of the settlement was changed, for the final time, to Bainbridge, named in honor of Commodore William Bainbridge, commander of the USS *Constitution*.

Bainbridge College, a two-year unit of the University System of Georgia, was established in 1973. It primarily serves students who commute from surrounding rural communities. The Bainbridge British Brass Band, created by college president Ed Mobley, brings local citizens and visitors to the downtown park for music and picnics. The college archives hold a notable collection of manuscripts including the papers of the late governor of Georgia S. Marvin Griffin (1907–82), who was a native.

The Bainbridge–Decatur County Chamber of Commerce distributes a driving guide of historical sites along the Flint River basin south of Bainbridge. Two parks in Bainbridge, Earle May Boat Basin Park and Cheney Griffin Park, afford boaters access to the Flint River and Lake Seminole. On the first weekend in May, the Riverside Artsfest, held on the banks of the Flint River, celebrates the art, history, and culture of a different state each year.

A visit to Jack Wingate's Lunker Lodge can open a door to the remarkable history, folklore, and down-home cuisine of Decatur County. Signs lead to Wingate's from Ga. 97 south of Bainbridge—or local people can point the way. The walls and ceiling of the restaurant are virtually jammed with artifacts from local American Indian sites, riverboat days, mule and cotton agriculture, and other assorted odds and ends, any of which may prompt proprietor Wingate to spin a colorful yarn from local history or legend. The wonderfully prepared and leisurely served Wingate fare of deep-fried catfish, coleslaw, sliced Spanish onions, fried potatoes, hushpuppies, and sweetened iced tea goes ever so well with overheard tales of Indian wars, gigantic alligators, and monster bass.

Attapulgus, twelve miles south of Bainbridge via U.S. 27, is an important site for an extensive mining operation of an absorbent clay called fuller's earth. Decatur County is the nation's leading producer of the mineral, historically a vital element in the wool hat manufacturing industry but now a primary ingredient in cat litter.

Climax, nine miles east of Bainbridge on U.S. 84, is so named for its location on the crest of the highest point of elevation along the railroad line connecting the Chattahoochee River and the Georgia coast at Savannah.

Besides being the self-proclaimed collard capital of the world and the birthplace of baseball's Jackie Robinson, **Cairo** (KAY-roe) is the home of an enormous pickle processing industry and the site of a major producer of sugar cane syrup. A light corn syrup produced in Cairo is a standard ingredient in the kitchens of cooks throughout the South. The Roddenbery Public Library in Cairo is an excellent community facility. A New Deal mural in the Cairo post office at 203 North Broad Street, painted in 1938 by Paul Ludwig Gill, is titled "Products of Grady County."

The Grady County community of **Calvary** was founded by a group of North Carolinians who, while searching the deep South for a "nature's garden spot" in which to settle, found the landscape to their liking and remained there. Mule Day, the first Saturday in November, is a community celebration that includes a mule beauty pageant, a plowing contest, a tobacco-spitting contest, a greased-pig chase, a rooster sailing, barbecue, a fish fry, and a variety of other equally compelling activities.

Each year on the last Saturday in January, the town of **Whigham**, six miles west of Cairo, is the site for the annual Rattlesnake Roundup. At what may be the strangest celebratory event in Georgia, hundreds of snakes are hunted and captured. The venomous creatures are driven from their underground burrows when the hunters spill small amounts of gasoline into them through short lengths of plastic water hose. There is a competition to determine who can catch the biggest snake. After the serpents are rounded up, some are killed, skinned, and prepared for the pot. Deep-fried rattlesnake steaks are available for those who have an appetite for the unusual.

The Lower Muscogee Creek Tribe, one of the few groups of American Indians recognized as such by the state of Georgia, is located near Whigham at the tribal town of **Tama**. The Creeks host an annual powwow and festival there on the weekend following the Fourth of July.

Thomasville, a town of twenty thousand, seems bigger. Situated in a geographic region called the Tallahassee Red Hills and characterized by rich, red, fertile soil, pine forests, and a generally warm climate, the area around Thomas County contains much of the few remnants in North America of old-growth longleaf pine forests. Today fewer than twenty-five-hundred acres of such forests remain—only three square miles.

The warm climate and the bountiful woodlands surrounding Thomasville have supported human culture for many centuries. But the heyday for local culture, at least in recent times, can be pinpointed as that of the so-called Thomasville Hotel Period, which began in the 1880s and continued for about three decades afterward. This was a time when hundreds of well-to-do Americans from colder climates of

Lapham-Patterson House,
Thomasville

the Northeast and Midwest flocked to warmer cities in northern
Florida and southern Georgia to vacation during the winter months.
Thomasville became one of the most popular of these southern resort
towns, and the descendants of those who came there remain today a
crucial element in the culture of the region.

Thomasville's Broad Street, the center of a picturesque downtown
shopping and commercial district, features long rows of nineteenth-
century storefronts that invite a casual morning or afternoon stroll.
Two attractive drugstores have working period soda fountains, and a
nearby billiard parlor, to spare its more genteel clientele sight of the
games of pool underway inside, serves hot dogs to passersby from a
front window. The three-hundred-year-old Thomasville Great Oak (it
sprouted about 1685) is an enormous specimen of live oak (*Quercus
virginiana*). The main trunk of the giant tree at the corner of Monroe
and Crawford Streets exceeds twenty-four feet in circumference, and
the limbs spread over fifty yards. The Lapham-Patterson House on
North Dawson Street is one of the most architecturally entertaining
houses in the Southeast. Built by Chicago shoe manufacturer Charles
W. Lapham in 1884, this extravagant three-level house is furnished

with no fewer than forty-five exit doors, all to assuage the builder's great fear of becoming hopelessly trapped inside a burning building. He had witnessed the great fire of 1871 in his native Chicago and, as a result, developed a lifelong phobia of fire. Not one room in the house is built square, or even rectangular. Each room has at least five walls, and some have more than six. The Lapham-Patterson House has the distinction of being one of only several houses in the entire nation whose designation as a National Historic Landmark is based primarily on unique architectural features. It is open to the public as a state historic site.

The Thomas County Historical Museum, 725 North Dawson Street, besides its excellent collection of historical materials interpreting local history, has a possibly unique feature, at least for Georgia—an intact late-nineteenth-century bowling alley. The Thomasville Cultural Center is a regional center for the visual and performing arts. It is housed in a renovated school building that dates to 1915. Events scheduled at the center include exhibitions of art, plays, performances of music, and workshops on a variety of crafts.

Since 1922 Thomasville, "City of Roses," has hosted a nationally known rose festival. Championship rose growers, horticulturists, and rose lovers know the city for its ornamental roses and the demonstration Rose Test Garden at 1842 Smith Avenue. The State Farmers Market in Thomasville is one of the largest in the southeastern United States and, in season, offers an impressive variety of fresh fruits and vegetables for sale, along with such regional specialties as mayhaw jelly and Vidalia onions.

In 1877, Henry O. Flipper, a native of Thomasville, was the first black graduate of the United States Military Academy at West Point. Flipper is buried in the north section of the old cemetery in Thomasville. His grave site is prominently designated with an interpretive historical marker.

In December 1864, five thousand Union prisoners were brought to Thomasville from the Confederate prison at Andersonville (see West Central tour), where it was feared that Sherman's army would launch a raid to free the incarcerated prisoners-of-war. No such raid occurred, so they were returned to Andersonville Prison several weeks later, after Sherman's army had captured Savannah. A historical marker on Wolfe Street denotes the location of the Thomasville Prison Camp where the Union prisoners were held.

Box Hall, Hollywood, Millpond, Melrose, Inman, Winstead, Pebble Hill: Those are the names of only a few of the over seventy woodland plantations located near Thomasville. Pebble Hill, one of the grander as well as the oldest of them, is open for public viewing. Visitors are welcome to wander leisurely through several of the plantation gardens and outbuildings—the carriage house, the kennels, the log schoolhouse, the old tennis courts, the cemetery, and the stables. Tou the interior of the main house are more closely regulated and limited to groups of six adults and teenagers, on a first-come ba The Thomasville Tourism Authority publishes a well-planned and informative printed guide for a walking and driving tour of the remarkable architecture in Thomasville and the surrounding countryside. The guide includes useful information on many of the historic buildings and an informative glossary of architectural terms defining various styles and periods as they occur in and around Thomasville. **Quitman**, the seat for Brooks County, lies on U.S. 84, about fifteen miles west of I-75, between Valdosta and Thomasville. The Old Library Building, on Culpepper Street, houses the Historical Museum and Cultural Center. The main street of the town features a fine collection of early-twentieth-century storefronts and commercial buildings little changed from their original appearance. Townspeople joke that they have always been "too poor to tear them down, rebuild them, or even cover them up with new facades." Of particular interest is the Brooks County courthouse, begun in 1859, delayed by the Civil War, and completed in 1864. One of a few antebellum county courthouses left standing in Georgia, it is constructed of brick manufactured locally from native clay. The Quitman city hall (1888) on East Screven Street was originally an opera house. Betty Sheffield, a native of Quitman who was a famous gardener and horticulturist, has been internationally recognized for her work in developing new varieties of camellias, including many that bear her name. In 1981, the United States Postal Service issued a commemorative stamp illustrating the Betty Sheffield Supreme Camellia. The same flower was used as a subject by porcelain artist Edward Marshall Boehm. The Sheffield Camellia Garden, located on North Court Street, contains at least forty varieties of the flowering shrub. Quitman's Historical Museum and Culture Center provides a self-guided driving tour of the commercial and residential architectural wealth of the town.

Valdosta is a pivotal city in the economic and cultural makeup of extreme south central Georgia. Its location on I-75, only fifteen miles north of the Florida state line, has enabled the town to take full advantage of the economic boosts provided by the thousands of tourists and vacationers who pass through each day. Apart from the usual commercial clutter typical at major interstate interchanges everywhere in America, exit 2, south of Valdosta, is the site for a collection of over a hundred factory-direct outlet stores that offer reduced prices on merchandise ranging from jeans to books. Along with these very commercial aspects of the region, Valdosta has a side that offers a full range of opportunities for both resident and visitor.

One of Valdosta's most impressive landmarks is the Crescent, a Neoclassical house built in 1898 by Col. W. S. West, a United States

Tobacco in the field

senator from Valdosta. The house is distinctive for its huge, crescent-shaped front porch, the roof of which appears to be supported by a row of thirteen massive white columns. The thirteen columns, one to represent each of the thirteen original American colonies, are actually made of a thin metal, painted white. The front roof is in reality cantilevered and requires no support from huge porch columns below. The Lowndes County Historical Society and Museum, located in the former Carnegie Library building at 305 Central Avenue, exhibits an eclectic collection of objects from Valdosta and Lowndes County's prehistoric, pioneer, industrial, architectural, Confederate, and agricultural past. The society's collections include extensive genealogical holdings pertaining to local families. Included are exhibits and biographical materials on the western gunfighter John Henry (Doc) Holliday, legendary associate of Wyatt Earp and participant in the infamous Gunfight at the O.K. Corral. He was a native of Griffin but lived in Lowndes County from 1864 to 1872.

Within the limits of the city of Valdosta is a one-square-mile reserve known as Remerton, which is a town within the town. Remerton was established in 1899 as a village for employees of the Strickland Cotton Mill. It now has a population of approximately seven hundred living along its ten miles of streets. The row houses on Remerton's Baytree and Plum Streets have been restored and are the focus of a newly developed art and craft retail center. Valdosta State University is notable for its Spanish Mission style architecture and beautifully planted and maintained grounds of its campus. The university art department regularly schedules faculty and traveling exhibitions. Valdosta is home of the Valdosta High School Wildcats, the winningest high school football team in the history of the sport. The National High School Football Hall of Fame is scheduled to open here in 1996.

Monthly exhibitions of artistic works by national, regional, and local artists are a standard feature at the Lowndes/Valdosta Arts Commission, 1204 N. Patterson Street. The commission presents an active series of programs ranging from local bluegrass bands to nationally known pianists and string quartets.

The Grand Bay Wildlife Management Area consists of wooded forests and wetlands that create an array of natural wildlife habitats in which a variety of animals, including white-tailed deer, foxes, bobcats, turkeys, raccoons, rabbits, and others, abound. Boating, hiking, fishing, canoeing, camping, and other outdoor activities are available at the park.

Hahira (hay-HIGH-rah) is an interesting little village located seven miles north of Valdosta via I-75 or U.S. 41. The unusual name, a part of the town's charm, is said to have originated from that of an African village called Hairaairee, which was described enthusiastically by a visiting Englishman to an early Lowndes County planter. The planter took the name for his plantation. In turn, the first post office in the area was located on the plantation, so it took the name Hahira and thus did the community and the town. There are several alternate stories explaining the origin of the name.

Hahira today is active with commercial interests that center on the annual tobacco auction and the production of honey and bee-keeping supplies and equipment. The town is a major center for the production and world-wide shipment of queen bees. Annually during the first week in October, the community celebrates its honeybee connection by staging the Hahira Honey Bee Festival. Public tobacco auctions occur in Hahira from mid-July through early October at the downtown auction barn, one of eleven such markets in Georgia. Approximately 5.2 million pounds of tobacco are sold there annually, or about 186,000 pounds a week. Free tours of the tobacco auction and warehouse are available, and visitors are welcome to observe a tobacco auction in progress. Another local festival, the Great Hahira Pick-in, celebrates the preponderance and popularity of bluegrass music in south Georgia and occurs annually on the last weekend in April.

Twenty miles southeast of Valdosta via Ga. 94 is Echols County, the eastern border of which is defined by Suwannoochee Creek, a major tributary of the Suwannee River, which flows from the western edge of the great Okefenokee Swamp to the Gulf of Mexico. Echols County is unique in Georgia in that there is not one incorporated city or town in the entire county. Although the community of Statenville is the location of the county courthouse, there is no city—at least not officially.

The town of **Lakeland**, in Lanier County, lies directly between the Alapaha River and a natural body of water known as Banks Lake, a reserve that includes the Banks Lake National Wildlife Refuge. Banks

Lake consists of a mixture of open water and marshes in which pond cypress (*Taxodium ascendens*) is the dominant vegetation. According to representatives of the National Wildlife Management office at the Okefenokee National Wildlife Refuge, which oversees the Banks Lake Refuge, Banks Lake is the site of one of the premier stands of pond cypress in the eastern United States. A body of open water within the refuge is available for fishing.

The old county jail in **Nashville** was the site of the last hanging to occur in Berrien County. The old jail was replaced by a new one in 1965. Berrien was the last county in Georgia to do away with open-range cattle grazing.

TOUR TWO: A DAY IN THE SOUTHWEST GEORGIA MIDLANDS

From Adel travel west via Ga. 37 to Moultrie, Camilla, Morgan, and Fort Gaines.

Cook County is neatly bisected by I-75 and U.S. 41, which are parallel as they traverse the county from north to south. The Cook County Historical Society in **Adel** is housed in the former Adel Methodist Episcopal Church building, an ornate white frame structure built in 1901. The Adel–Cook County Chamber of Commerce has its offices in the Jim Paulk–Sowega Building, popularly known as the Watermelon Building. This unusual commercial building was built in 1931 as headquarters for the Sowega Melon Association, a south Georgia cooperative formed to market the important regional crop of watermelons. The exterior of the building is decorated with green watermelon motifs. The U.S. Post Office on Parrish Street in Adel contains the New Deal mural "Plantation Scene," painted in 1941 by Alice Flint.

In April 1994 the Cook County Exchange Club staged the first annual Longleaf Yellow Pine Festival, celebrating the importance of timber and timber products to the local economy. On Cook County's western border with Colquitt County, about eight miles west of the Cook County seat of Adel, is Reed Bingham State Park. Its fresh-water lake is a major location for boating and water-skiing in the area. The park exhibits native plant and animal life along the Coastal Plains Nature Trail. A series of natural habitats for such wildlife as Canada geese, bald eagles, gopher tortoises, alligators, and others is a feature of the trail. Reed Bingham State Park is the site of a winter roost for hundreds of American vultures (*Cathartes aura* and *Coragyps atratus*), known widely as buzzards. The park hosts the annual Buzzard Day Festival, staged the first Saturday of each December, to celebrate the arrival of the birds for the winter. Bingham State Park offers full tent and trailer camping facilities, boat ramps, fishing and swimming, and family and group picnic sites.

Moultrie is located twenty-four miles west of I-75 via Ga. 37. The Colquitt County courthouse, built in 1902, is a central downtown landmark. The Ellen Payne Odum Genealogy Library, in a wing of the public library, is a treasure for genealogists, especially those of Scottish ancestry. The collection provides information on Scottish clans and Native American tribal groups, specifically Cherokee and Creek, as well as less specialized records. The Colquitt County Arts Center, 401 Seventh Avenue SW, includes an art exhibition area as well as an ambitious slate of dance programming ranging from ballet to clogging. The work of visionary artist O. L. Samuels can be seen in the arts center offices. The Colquitt County Farmer's Market is a place where the visitor can take advantage of the wealth of produce grown in the Colquitt County area.

The Mitchell County courthouse square in **Camilla** was the site of the 1868 "Camilla Massacre," when local whites fired upon several hundred African Americans marching into town for a Republican political rally. Several blacks were killed, and many more were wounded. Annually on the second weekend in May, Camilla hosts the Gnat Days Summer Celebration, a festival meant to "honor" the gnat. Gnats are small, pesky, flying insects distantly related to mosquitoes. They are a summer scourge, loathed by South Georgia residents from Americus to Valdosta. The festival features the usual arts and crafts vendors, cruises on the Flint River, a gnat market, and a gnat run.

At **Pelham**, nine miles south of Camilla, a New Deal mural painted in 1941 by Georgina Klitgaard and titled "Pelham Landscape" can be seen at the U.S. Post Office on Mathewson Street. Also there is a signpost that has attracted local and regional attention for many years now. The tall post is an exaggerated directional highway sign that informs the traveler of the general direction and distances to perhaps as many as fifty cities around the world—Saigon, Mexico City, New York, Tokyo, and so on.

Newton, the county seat of Baker County, is located about twenty miles southwest of Albany on Ga. 91. Its old courthouse, after having endured two destructive floods—first in 1925 and recently in 1994—in 1995 was granted state funds for restoration. A notable battle occurred near there in 1836 between a contingency of the Georgia State Militia and Creek Indians at Chickasawhatchee Swamp. A large area of Chickasawhatchee Swamp, located in the northern section of the county, is now a wildlife management area. Pineland Plantation, originally owned by black planter Burton Powell, is known for its active program in aquaculture. During the 1994 flood, it lost millions of fish from its farm ponds.

A few miles south of the town of **Edison**, the seat of government for Calhoun County, near the town of **Arlington**, is the historic Nancy Springs. The abundant supply of clear, fresh water of the springs,

Brown Chapel AME Church, Fort Gaines

which was so attractive to early settlers of the region, is now bottled and sold all around. At nearby **Morgan**, Taylor's old cotton gin, now abandoned, stands as a ghostly symbol of the past importance of cotton to the county's culture and history.

The town of **Fort Gaines** is among the oldest settlements in Southwest Georgia. In 1814, a fort situated to protect the western frontier was constructed by the United States on a high bluff overlooking the Chattahoochee River and the lands to the west. In 1818, this frontier outpost was incorporated into the land holdings of the state of Georgia, and an active community has functioned there ever since, making Fort Gaines one of the oldest continuously occupied towns in the Southeastern United States. The Fort Gaines Frontier Village and Park, located on the bluff, is a collection of reconstructed log houses and related outbuildings representative of an early historical period of the town. A monumental painted wood sculpture, the portrait bust of nineteenth-century Creek Indian leader Otis Micco, stands in the southwest corner of the park. In 1816, the Creek people who had originally occupied the lands where Fort Gaines is located were forced by Andrew Jackson's army to remove to Spanish Florida. Immediately to the north of Frontier Village is the site of an original Confederate gun emplacement. From this spot, it is easy for the visitor to understand why this bluff has been selected over the years as a site for settlement, cannons, and fortifications. The panoramic view of the river and the lands to the west is spectacular. In Fort Gaines, the New Park Cemetery features a circa 1880 gazebo. This white frame, latticed pavilion sits atop an earthen temple mound constructed in prehistoric times by native people. Additional points of interest in Fort Gaines include the Dill

House; the Toll House, at which people crossing the Chattahoochee River in the 1820s paid a fee for passage by ferry; and the Pioneer Cemetery, located on Carroll Street. A Fort Gaines Historic District driving tour is available from the Clay County Economic Development Council.

George T. Bagby State Park, four miles north of Fort Gaines on Ga. 39, is furnished with a lodge equipped for group meetings and conferences. In addition, Bagby State Park offers the visitor a restaurant, lodging, access to boating and fishing on Lake Walter F. George, pool and beach swimming, and three hundred acres of woodlands with marked walking trails. Nearby is Sandy Creek Park, a lakeside public access area furnished with rest rooms, a swimming beach, and picnic tables. Lake Walter F. George (Lake Eufaula in Alabama) is a large impoundment of the Chattahoochee River. The lake begins near Fort Gaines and stretches upstream all the way to Columbus. Two miles north of Fort Gaines on Ga. 39 is the Lake Walter F. George resource manager's office, which houses an interpretive center featuring displays and printed materials to assist visitors. Tours of the lock and dam as well as the related electrical power plant can be scheduled. The lock and dam are among the largest in the eastern United States. The massive power plant contains four generating units with a total installed capacity of 130,000 kilowatts. The contact for tour appointments or additional information is the Lake Walter F. George resource manager.

SOUTHEAST GEORGIA

Whit Gibbons

THE SPIRIT OF SOUTHEAST GEORGIA

It all started a long time ago, about 50 million years to be inexact, during the Late Cretaceous. The band of sand that now catches the morning sun on the banks of the Savannah River and stretches southwestward to the Florida line was different then.

Today, the sandy land is flat, or sometimes rolling, the perfect habitat for pine trees with all their products, from turpentine to pulp wood, red straw to saw timber. Today, the morning sun brightens near-white sandbars as it passes over big rivers and smaller streams, the perfect place for experiencing pristine nature. The sun's last view each day in this region of Southeast Georgia is the biggest swamp it will cross in its journey across the rest of the country, the perfect swamp in which to marvel at the natural world with a mixture of trepidation, fascination, and contentment.

Today, an overland traveler using either back roads or major highways can readily experience these seventeen counties, which cover 8,628 square miles. County sizes range from Ware, the largest county in Georgia, with 906 square miles, to Evans with 186 square miles. Traveling southwest from Jenkins County, or from the Savannah's riverbank counties of Screven and Effingham, one crosses the floodplains of the Ogeechee, Altamaha, and Satilla rivers and ends up in the Okefenokee region. Depending on the route, one could be east of the swamp in Charlton County, or west in Clinch County in the eastern third of the Suwanee River basin.

This low country covers parts of the habitats the famous botanist Roland Harper, in the 1930 publication *The Natural Resources of Georgia,* called the Rolling Wire-grass Country and the Flat Pine Lands. The region is also referred to as the Atlantic Coast Flatwoods.

But back in the Cretaceous, this land now known as Southeast Georgia had no sand hills, no Altamaha River, no Okefenokee Swamp. American alligators and wood storks, longleaf pine and cypress trees

Mosasaur skeleton, Georgia Southern University Museum

were absent. On the other hand, the giant lizard-like, ocean-dwelling reptiles known as mosasaurs thrived, because 50 million years ago the region was covered with water—salt water.

Today we know mosasaurs only by their fossils, as represented by the twenty-seven-foot-long reconstructed skeleton in the Georgia Southern Museum on the university campus in Statesboro. Another legacy of a relatively recent ocean past is that nowhere in the region can you find a county seat with an altitude more than 260 feet above sea level. The highest is in Statesboro (Bulloch County) at 258, the lowest in Nahunta (Brantley County) at 65.

Over millions of years, as the waters gradually receded during the Eocene Epoch and into the present, the ancient beaches moved south, past Millen, past Statesboro, and on past Folkston. The ancient coastal sand dunes and ocean bottom left plenty of sandy terrain, some undulating, some flat. Forested sandhills and flatwoods are dominant topographical features of the region today. As the ocean waters retreated, the fresh waters found their natural courses from the uplands, inexorable courses that carried the Pleistocene rainwaters toward the great sea that would later become distinguishable as the Atlantic Ocean and Gulf of Mexico. Today, the consequences of these natural etchings of the landscape have names—the Ogeechee, Altamaha, and Suwanee Rivers, as well as many others. During the Eocene and then again in the Pleistocene, they were just anonymous waterways carrying the biological wealth of eons to the sea.

Over the millennia, as the comings and goings of ice ages changed climate and sea levels, terrestrial life began to inhabit the former ocean sands, and the rivers teemed with freshwater forms. The contest between salt water and fresh, between sand and land continued for millions of years, and still does. But the margin of the biological tournament has moved south to Florida and to a more eastern Georgia coast. The natural freshwater and terrestrial habitats of Southeast Georgia won the battle. Mosasaurs had lost out long before.

Spawned by wave action behind an offshore sandbar in the Pleistocene ocean, the Okefenokee depression lay insignificant and silent beneath the sea for most of the last quarter million years. Once on land, exposed to air and fresh water, the depression took on a new life as the largest freshwater swamp in North America. Overlying the former ocean sands that form the base of the depression are the remains of thousands of years of organic debris in the form of peat. In some places the peat looks like land, but beneath is water. When one walks on such terrain, the name "trembling earth" takes on a vivid meaning.

THE FIRST SOUTHEAST GEORGIANS

New species evolved in the natural habitats, and immigrant species arrived from other regions. The land and waters of the recently created geological landscape were rich in biodiversity. And then, several centuries after the Wisconsin Ice Age, long after the sea had dropped to its lowest level, the North American continent welcomed, or at least accepted, the arrival of a new species—humans.

The earliest human inhabitants, American Indians, may have qualified as a keystone species, defined in the book *Keeping All the Pieces* as any kind of plant or animal that controls the character of an ecological system. No doubt the American Indians altered the landscape to some degree, but no more so than other keystone species modify the habitats they live in. Some believe they reduced the understory in pine forests with their intentional use of fire to drive game animals for hunting. Some American Indians farmed on a small scale and maybe even dammed a few small streams to establish fishing holes. The American Indians probably reduced the number of American bison, a mammal whose numbers were far fewer than their counterparts on the western plains but that nonetheless once roamed the savanna-like flatwoods of Southeast Georgia. But the American Indians functioned in a system of sustainability, an approach favored by small population sizes and more elementary tools and weaponry.

With the coming of the men and women from Europe, the forests, streams, and swamps of Southeast Georgia were destined to change further, in a far bigger way. Armed with implements of agriculture and war, these new immigrants were prepared to accept any challenge that land, water, forest, or other people might offer. But as these people shaped the land through agriculture, industry, and community development, likewise did the land and its wildlife guide the directions to be taken. Just as people shape the land, the land shapes the people. Such has been the story of Southeast Georgia.

In the spirit of continental conquest and a heritage of Christianity, the early settlers took what they could from the land and from other humans, though the region is not noted for warfare. Such a distinction is reserved for other regions. Based on written records, in the seventeen southeastern Georgia counties not now favored by ocean front, combat was, with few exceptions, restricted to that between individuals. Undoubtedly, some fighting or bullying existed for which no records exist. For example, Creek Indians were known to have inhabited the areas now known as Evans County and Wayne County in the late 1700s. Their absence today suggests that someone encouraged them to leave. The Seminole Indian war hero Osceola and his braves lived in the Okefenokee before being driven toward the Everglades by General Jesup and the American militia.

General Sherman scrawled his signature across Southeast Georgia in 1864. The Confederate prison Fort Lawton, near Millen, and another at Blackshear in Pierce County, give testament that there were two sides in the War between the States. But for the most part, the region was spared the kinds of wars popular in history books, perhaps because men have fought few military battles for possession of a big swamp, sweet-tasting onions, or pine trees.

Another struggle continued, however, for all new settlers. The major challenge was how to become a beneficiary of the land rather than a rival. In the tradition of Americans, from colonial to modern times, many Southeast Georgians operated with an attitude of dominion over all other creatures. This prevailing attitude was further fueled when any species had biological attributes capable of augmenting the well-being or welfare of humans or was perceived as being potentially harmful. The alligator fit both categories and therefore qualified as a victim of a land ethic contending that any natural resource can be exploited if it benefits or harms humans.

ALLIGATORS

Alligators lived in the Okefenokee Swamp and basked along the Altamaha River long before any humans had ever seen the area, let alone named the region Georgia. America's largest reptiles inhabited the coastal marshes and inland waterways as they do today, tracking the fresh waters through the ages, as the aquatic habitats moved landward or seaward in response to rising or falling sea levels. The fossil record suggests that ancestors of the alligator, looking little different from today's descendants, prowled the coastal margins while mosasaurs swam in the sea.

Alligator hunters with the day's catch, May 1912

Alligators had inherited the southeastern Georgia region over geologic time, through evolutionary change in response to environmental remodeling. But by the time Lyons was chartered as the seat of Toombs County in 1897, alligators were being rapidly subdued by humans, not the American Indians of the region, most of whom had been subdued themselves, but by the new residents, the progeny of European colonizers.

In the Okefenokee Swamp, the backwaters of the Altamaha, and other wetlands throughout Southeast Georgia, alligators were confronted by an assailant unknown in their evolutionary history, a new predator—the hide hunter. Beginning in the nineteenth and on into the twentieth century, the hunters came at night in boats, looking for the red or yellow eyes reflected in the light of a burning pine knot or, in later years, a carbide lantern. With guns or axes they killed, selecting alligators that would make the best skins to bring back to camp and leaving dead in the swamp those that were too small or imperfect for skins. For perhaps the only period in their history, the ruling reptiles at the top of the food chain in southern wetlands had become the prey. Shoes and purses made from the skins of the once great predator-turned-prey became status symbols. Expensive and synonymous with high class, the finished products were sought in the marketplace by the elite, thus encouraging further slaughter in the swamps.

Few if any Okefenokee hide hunters themselves got wealthy; they simply served as suppliers for tanners, distributors, and retailers. City people outside the great swamp made the profits. The big losers, along with the alligators themselves, were the hide hunters and other inhabitants of southeastern Georgia's swamps. But they probably got to eat a lot of 'gator tail, which even today is considered fine eating in many parts of the South, where alligator harvesting is regulated by the states.

One must be careful in today's age of environmental awareness not to judge too harshly the actions of former inhabitants of, or even visitors to, the region and their assault on the land and its native wildlife. Environmental chauvinism is an easy trap. Assuming the self-righteous position that overexploitation of the alligator as a natural resource was an evil that could have been foreseen and should have been avoided may be popular with some today. Hindsight judgments are seldom complicated by the constraints of foresight. And at the time, anyone could see that plenty of alligators were available for the taking. And take the hide hunters did.

Some might attribute the actions of the people toward their environment and natural resources to the drive of a primitive behavior that is rare today. Such an interpretation shows a misunderstanding of human nature. Embedded traits such as avarice and greed are often indistinguishable from self-preservation. Such qualities do not change with culture. Some people will always be skillful at taking more than their share.

Nonetheless, regardless of whether the people should have known better, toward the middle of the twentieth century, a major ecovoid could be felt in the Okefenokee Swamp. A part of the environment was missing. The alligator had seemingly vanished, for those remaining were shy and cautious of the two-legged creatures that floated on wood in the water. Today if you visit the Okefenokee Swamp, or for that matter almost any of the swamps, rivers, or lakes in Southeast Georgia on a cool, sunny day, you're likely to see an alligator. Of course there's no such thing as a cool day during a southeastern Georgia summer, where daytime temperatures average above ninety degrees Fahrenheit (thirty degrees Centigrade), so you might have to search for alligators at night. And if you find yourself in a swamp after dark, you'd better have a flashlight and a good sense of direction, lest you end up spending more time with an alligator than you care to.

Alligators continue to shape the mindset and culture of the Okefenokee region. They are respected as a tourist draw and offer a sense of well-being that the natural communities of swamps and rivers remain in a functional state. Georgians view these giant reptiles as a tribute to the character of the southern half of the state. Native Georgians take pride in having alligators as part of their environmental scenery. In one sense the alligator continues to be an exploited natural resource, exploited for its value in attracting tourists eager to see one.

Canoeing in the Okefenokee

Alligators get people's attention, through fear or fascination. One might even wonder which is more interesting, the alligators themselves or people's attitudes toward them. Numerous legends and tall tales can be expected to develop about a reptile that can reach a length of fifteen feet, or even nineteen feet if one accepts an early record in Louisiana, and can kill and eat a full-grown deer. But some foundation of truth can be found for each tale.

Will alligators attack humans? A few spectacular reports keep alive an awareness that alligators can be highly dangerous, causing serious injury if not death. But unprovoked attacks by alligators on humans occur rarely, if ever. Because a mother alligator has a strong maternal instinct, she will attack a person who appears to be a threat to her eggs or babies. At every stage of development of the young, the mother alligator is the paragon of proper parenting. She begins by building a large nest of grasses and brush on shore in which she deposits the eggs. When the young hatch and enter the water, she guards them from any potential danger. If hatching young have problems digging out of the nest, the mother may crawl from the water onto land, open the nest, and gently carry the babies in her mouth to the water. If necessary, she will even crack open the hard-shelled eggs in her mouth so the babies can escape, unharmed.

The powerful protective instinct induces mother alligators to remain in the vicinity of their nests after egg laying. Thus, an intruder, whether raccoon, possum, or person, approaching an active alligator nest may suddenly be confronted by an enormous, hissing reptile emerging from the water and charging overland. Few reports exist of how far a watchful mother alligator will go to defend her young from a human intruder. In some instances she may retreat, if you stand your ground and do not molest the nest or pick up a baby. Considering the cost of the consequences of misjudgment, few people stay around long enough to find out exactly what the outcome would be. The Okefenokee Swamp has served as a potential testing ground of this behavior for some time, and still does.

As far as other attacks by alligators go, some are unexplained. In many of these cases the reptile causing the problem is believed to have been provoked in some way, although perhaps unwittingly. Normally, an unharassed alligator is shy, slow, and peaceful. Based on the evidence, Georgia's alligators no longer consider humans a menu item, if they ever did. However, some may have attacked a crouched person splashing at the water's edge, mistaking the individual for smaller prey. Although definitely different from some of their Old World cousins, the crocodiles, which are uncontested man-eaters, big alligators should be viewed—and approached—with caution.

Alligators love dogs like Georgians love barbecue. Many of the reported alligator attacks on boats in the Okefenokee occurred when a dog was aboard—a clear signal to the denizens of the swamp that a 'gator meal was being brought into their natural habitat. Such reports occurred when the swamp was an open no-man's-land without rules about not bringing dogs along on an excursion. South Georgians know that alligators consider a dog a small prey animal, and small prey are meant to be eaten. Consequently, most Southeast Georgians accept the alligators' place in the natural world and let them lead their lives accordingly, especially when it comes to dogs.

A few simple rules for visitors to Georgia to observe about alligators are based on common sense. For example, anyone with common sense would know to keep a safe distance from a large animal with big teeth, powerful jaws, and a long, strong tail capable of swiping a small crowd of grown men off a sandbar. Feeding, teasing, or even getting near alligators in the wild could result in an accident. Approaching nesting areas or picking up the babies, no matter how cute they are, is not advisable when dealing with a large animal that is extremely protective of its eggs and young.

Alligators in Southeast Georgia build their nests on land and usually lay their eggs in June. The young hatch and take up their home in the water with the mother in September, usually staying with her at least a year. Alligators have their place in nature, and we have ours. If our paths cross it behooves the human participants in the encounter to keep a watchful eye.

If you visit a swamp or lake in Southeast Georgia, make sure your children know and follow the rules about alligators just as they follow the rule of not walking onto a highway. Living around and watching alligators can be an uncomplicated activity. But don't try to become a part of their world or encourage them to become part of ours.

THE OKEFENOKEE SWAMP

Whether you want to see alligators and other magnificent wildlife or not, any visitor to Georgia should make the Okefenokee a target. If for no other reason, you can say you've been to the environmental hub of the region. The swamp symbolizes the historical contest between humans and the environment. The battle over, both have won, with a few casualties on each side. But today the Okefenokee Swamp still has most of its wild creatures, save a few, such as panthers, ivory-billed woodpeckers, and Carolina parakeets. An enthusiastic spirit toward wildlife and wild nature itself, openly characterized in southern Georgians, resurfaces in anyone who enters the Okefenokee Swamp.

Georgia, not Florida, claims the Okefenokee Swamp. Most of the six hundred to eight hundred square miles (people argue about the boundaries of a swamp) of wilderness lie west and inside of the southeastern corner of the state, where Charlton and Ware Counties lay claim to the biggest portions. The formal demarcation of the Okefenokee National Wildlife Refuge and Wilderness Area, as it is officially known but seldom called by natives of the region, spills over into Brantley County on its northeast side and Clinch County to the west.

With a tail wind from a late autumn cold front, a crow could probably fly the forty miles from Waycross on the north end of the swamp to Moniac on the south in less than half an hour. Boat travelers might take three days, or longer if the water's down and there are many shaking peat layers to cross on foot. Air and water, interspersed with islands and freshwater prairies, are the only ways to get from one town to the other in anything resembling a straight line, because no roads go from either side of the Okefenokee Swamp to the other. The greatest highway penetration into the swamp is found on the fifteen miles of blacktop road leading from Fargo to Stephen C. Foster State Park, less than halfway across the short axis of the Okefenokee.

The watershed from which the Okefenokee Swamp collects its water is immense, almost fifteen hundred square miles. Most of the water entering the swamp comes from rainfall, either on the swamp itself or on the uplands of the watershed. Southwest Georgia's average annual precipitation, mostly as rainfall and a little bit as snow, ranges from forty-five to fifty-five inches. About half the rain falls during the summer months. The contribution from spring-fed waters to levels in the Okefenokee is trivial compared to rainfall and runoff. The swamp is relatively shallow, average water depths being about two feet and maximum depths generally less than eight. Trail Ridge on the eastern edge, presumed to be a remnant of the ancient sea, serves as a barrier to water flow in that direction.

The Okefenokee Swamp is one of Georgia's greatest environmental endowments, one that rivals North America's mountains, oceans, or upland forests in scenic beauty, albeit an inner beauty best appreciated when one enters and becomes a part of the swamp. Some did just that. The Chessers were one of several families of swamp inhabitants who joined the swamp and lived off it, beginning in the mid-1800s. The last Chesser left in the late 1930s after the Okefenokee Swamp was declared a federal preserve. The swamp could sustain families and small communities and did so for nearly a century. One who knew how to take advantage of the bounty in a swamp always had plenty to eat.

In the early 1900s, less sustainable practices arrived in the form of the timber industry, from Philadelphia. Drawn to the ancient forests of enormous cypress trees that gave the swamp its character, the tree cutters took most of them, but not all. Today, some of the old trees still remain, and throughout the swamp, where conditions are suitable, replacements fill the former ecovoid. Today a visitor in one of the larger cypress stands can experience the same sense of the diminutive that one feels in a redwood forest or when looking at the stars from a deserted beach.

A century ago people looked on the land as a place to survive, to get food, clothing, shelter. The Okefenokee provided all of these for those who chose to make it their home and knew how to do so effectively. Its value for survival, however, came not from annual crops on a large scale as could be found on the uplands or in a sustainable commerce such as would be found at a port city or mining town. Early inhabitants of the Okefenokee surely valued also the natural beauty that surrounded them.

That beauty still engulfs those who enter the Okefenokee, and its expressions are many. Effect on the human psyche and influence on society need not always come through immensity, as with cypress trees, or perceived threats of violence and fear of the unknown, as with alligators and snakes. Natural beauty itself probably influenced the attitudes of some in the Okefenokee during the settling days of Southeast Georgia. Even the most pragmatic of people were surely charmed in the swamp by some of the carnivorous plants.

Plants that capture and digest animals are found in many parts of the world, mostly in highly acidic habitats low in nutrients. The Okefenokee waters qualify for this situation as a consequence of the organic acids produced by decaying vegetation. To survive under such conditions, plants must have mechanisms to compensate for the low availability of nutrients such as nitrogen and phosphorous. What better way than to have them delivered, packaged in the form of insects?

SWAMP TALK

Many colorful expressions heard in the Okefenokee have their roots in Old English or Scottish expressions preserved and passed on by early settlers from the British Isles. Many of the sayings are common throughout Georgia and southern Appalachia. A few are unique to the swamp. This sampler comes from Francis Harper's journals in *Okefinokee Album*.

addled
> mentally weak or crazy, a term applied to both people and animals

batteries
> small swamp islands

blowed off
> the doleful howl of exhaustion and despair of a dog that has given up an unsuccessful chase

blowsey
> untidy, unkempt, referring to hair or clothes

blue whistler
> a turpentine barrel with a sixty-gallon capacity

biggity
> tense with anger

branch
> small stream or creek

calaberment
> loud noise made by an animal

catheads
> a popular name for biscuits

chivaree
> a serenade by musicians on a special occasion, such as a wedding

common
> pleasant or likeable

cow house
> barn

cracklins
> pork skin that has been fried until crisp, often an ingredient in cornbread

croker sack
> burlap bag used for seed

evening
> any time between noon and dark

flinder
> to harass or bother

fresh, freshet
a sudden heavy rain that causes streams to overflow their banks

gallberry child
a child born out of wedlock, also called a "wood's colt"

gower
to stare

hobbiedehoy
an irresponsible young person

jerk up
reprimand, the censuring of a wayward church member by the congregation

jower
quarrel

light'ood
fat pine wood, used for lighting fires, light-wood or kindling

passel
can mean either a large or small group of something, usually "a whole passel"

pinder
peanut, from the African word *pinda*

prairie
the open marshes of the Okefenokee, usually covered with water and aquatic vegetation

progue
to prowl or explore

pull-bone
wishbone or "pully-bone" of a chicken

scrimptious
a small amount

shim-shacking
loafing, kidding, dilly-dallying, or wasting time

shivers
splinters of wood

strand
swampy area such as a small branch or creek

toll
to entice or lure

wallet
a leather pouch used to carry corn or ammunition

working
a day set aside by the church for cleaning the church building, grounds, and graveyard

Several distinct kinds of carnivorous plants live in the Okefenokee, and each lures and captures its prey in its own way. The pitcher plant uses a highly effective pitfall trap, a vertical tube looking not unlike a trumpet with the wide end up. The tube is only a few inches high in some species, up to three feet tall in others. Downward-pointing hairs around the lip of the tube assure that a careless bug making a misstep will disappear over the edge and soon become part of the plant world. An enzymatic liquor at the bottom of the flask digests the carcass. The plant absorbs the newly acquired nitrogen and phosphorous.

Some carnivorous plants may have gone unnoticed or been ignored by the practical-minded Chessers or other Okefenokee Swamp inhabitants, but surely all were aware of the pitcher plants, as would anyone be who visits today. As with the cypress, tupelo gum, and many other big trees, botanical features other than flowers are what bring the pitcher plants to the attention of visitors. An array of hundreds of trumpet-like columns of green, yellow, or brown in shallow water or on a floating mat would capture anyone's attention.

Sundews and butterworts are less well known to the casual observer in the Okefenokee. These innocent-looking little plants capture prey with a form of sticky trap that probably smells good to an insect. An insect landing on the leaves quickly discovers its feet are stuck in glue. Digestion proceeds on the surface of the leaf, and to ensure that the insect stays for dinner, sundew plants have tiny tendrils that slowly close around the captive.

Bladderworts are probably the least familiar of the carnivorous plants, although their small white or yellow flowers can be seen on the surface of many pools where the body of the plant is floating. Prey capture by bladderworts is fascinating, qualifying as one of the most amazing feats of any plant. Floating at the water's surface, each slender branch is armed with thousands of special, air-filled trapping devices called bladders. When a small, aquatic creature brushes against one of the hair triggers on the outside of the air-filled bladder trap, a tiny door snaps inward, in less than one-four-hundredth of a second! The helpless victim is sucked inside in front of a miniature wave of water. The door immediately slams shut, but now the prey is inside the bladder chamber. The digestive process begins immediately. The bladder trap is no larger than a drop of water; hence it preys primarily on small insects, such as mosquito larvae and protozoans.

A fantastic thought always comes to mind about carnivorous plants—what if they got as big as the cypress trees? The Okefenokee Swamp natives may have had such stories.

Among the impressions of people who have heard of, but not been to, the Okefenokee are those of the animal life. Snakes and alligators come readily to mind, as do bears and panthers. But the panthers are gone now, as is true for this species almost everywhere in the remain-

Great egrets feed on a variety of fish species and in southern Georgia may raise three to four young per nest.

ing wilds of eastern North America. So are the gray wolves that once inhabited the Southeast, the migrating passenger pigeons whose numbers were measured in millions, and the Carolina parakeets, North America's only native parrot.

But rather than dwell on the missing, let us revel in the species that remain. Among the mammals: the otter and mink, bobcat and bear, flying squirrel and cottontail. Virtually all the wading birds and waterfowl native to the southeastern United States can be found in the swamp at one time or another, including the federally endangered wood stork. Some are seasonal, like the buffleheads and ruddy ducks that arrive in winter, or the purple gallinules and yellow-crowned night herons that are more likely to be present during the warm months. Many impressive ones, such as the stately great blue heron, the wood duck whose male in breeding plumage looks like a brightly painted work of art, and the sandhill crane whose in-flight bugling is a true call of the wild, make their homes in the Okefenokee year round. During spring the smaller migratory birds, some of which winter in tropical America, bring the Okefenokee alive with their sounds as well as their appearances.

The thirty-six species, representing fourteen families, of freshwater fishes reported from the swamp are not an exceptionally high species diversity compared to the lakes and streams of the surrounding countryside. But the fishes, like all creatures and plants in the Okefenokee, live in a special environment by modern standards, a natural habitat not only healthy now but destined to remain so with continued environmental protection.

No species of plant or animal is endemic to the Okefenokee; every species is found somewhere else outside the swamp. But today the natural biodiversity is far less affected than the many despoiled and pillaged habitats in other areas for which human progress can be credited, or discredited, depending on one's point of view. The Okefenokee is more than Georgia's greatest natural treasure, as some have called it; the great swamp, wisely set aside for generations of the future, is a virtual trove of biological wealth and riches. One would have to go a long way to find a wildlife paradise that can compare with the Okefenokee Swamp.

THE PINEY WOODS

Outside the Okefenokee in Southeast Georgia one can find other swamps and river bottomlands that look like swamps. But on the higher ground, still of relatively low elevation and covered with sand from the Pleistocene, one begins to find pine trees. The early settlers saw bigger trees and a different composition of pine species than is seen today, but the general scenery was much the same—tall pines with an understory of one of two types.

In the true pine flatwoods, also known as lowland forests, in which the soil is wetter and more organic than at slightly higher levels, the dominant tree is slash pine. Slash pine is a fast-growing tree that can reach heights of more than 135 feet; it has been planted commercially in much of the region by the timber industry for pulpwood and lumber production. The understory of a lowland pine forest is characteristically short palmettos and gallberry. Gallberry is an evergreen shrub, found in a variety of habitats and much valued as the origin of honey produced in domestic beehives, now and a century ago.

Where the sandhills were highest and driest, a different pine and understory assemblage was present—the longleaf pine-wiregrass community. Some say that American Indians who lived in this dominant terrestrial ecosystem of longleaf pine and wiregrass put their own stamp on the landscape by periodically setting fires to the ground covering of wiregrass beneath the pine forests. With the right circumstances, a fire could drive deer and other game to a favored killing spot for the waiting hunters.

This was already a classic fire climax community, with frequent summer fires being a natural phenomenon. So with or without the aid of American Indians, fires normally swept through at intervals of less than five years, with wiregrass and pine needles serving as tinder.

Clearly, any species of plant or animal persisting in such an environment with periodic burning would need to be fire adapted. Many of the native animals, such as snakes and salamanders, are fossorial; that is, they have adapted to living or retreating beneath the ground's surface in times of danger. The tall, widely spaced, and thick-barked longleaf pines are resistant to the low-to-the-ground fires. Fire is a natural event in the life of a longleaf pine forest, and rather than being an environmental disaster, it is essential to prevent the invasion of hardwoods. Some wiregrass even requires fire for assured germination.

Such pine forests are also home to the red-cockaded woodpecker, a federally listed endangered species that builds nest cavities exclusively in old, but still living, pine trees. The preferred trees are those that are at least half a century old and infected with red heart disease, a condition caused by a fungus that softens the wood, thus making it more suitable for a woodpecker to chisel a hole.

Red-cockaded woodpeckers have endured forest fires for centuries by remaining safely in their cavities. Their decline throughout their range, and their listing as endangered, is attributed to events far more devastating to a tree-dwelling bird than something as trivial as a natural forest fire. The birds' decline was probably initiated with the removal of pine forests across the South. Early forestry practices, and a few that continue into the late twentieth century, removed most of the economically suitable trees, including old ones with red heart disease.

Today red-cockaded woodpeckers influence operations in the timber industry in southern Georgia and other areas because of the birds' protected status. The only way to assure the welfare of the woodpeckers, where they still occur, and permit them to expand to their former range is to have an environmentally sensitive forest management plan. Such a plan includes not removing the oldest trees in a pine forest and not harvesting all the younger trees that are on their way to becoming old.

Environmental regulations that protect natural habitats may have delayed or prevented some enterprises. But in most, if not all, instances these were situations that would have allowed short-term profits for a small minority of people, often including profiteers from outside the region. There is little evidence of long-term job loss as a result of protecting the environment. The people of a region can truly benefit when they achieve the best use of the land and natural ecosystems. And the people of Southeast Georgia have a splendid opportunity for keeping or recovering high-quality environments while fulfilling the needs for recreation, tourist activities, and other sustainable commerce.

Although similar in appearance to what the American Indians and first European colonizers of the region saw, the pine forests of Southeast Georgia are no longer the same as in earlier times. The lowland pine forests were dominated by slash pine, but on the occasional higher and drier ground, longleaf pine was present. Today, many of the high ground areas have slash pine, even those where longleaf held jurisdiction in earlier times. The reason is a sound one economically. Slash pine, which is a common native species in the region, grows faster than longleaf pine. The putative soundness of modern commercial interests has outweighed any instincts to preserve the natural forests.

Regardless of present-day forest management practices, many of the big pine trees of southern Georgia had been floated down the Altamaha River after an excessive removal period in the 1800s. One must wonder if regional folk were mostly the losers, economically as well as environmentally. City people outside the region, as in the port city of Darien at the mouth of the river, made some of the profit from logging activities. And one account in *A History of Georgia,* edited by Kenneth Coleman, tells of a company in Maine, quite a journey from Georgia in those days of 1834. The company cleared longleaf pine stands in southern Georgia from more than a thousand square miles!

While the magnificent pine forests were being removed for major profit by those from other regions, the local populace was able to make a living cutting the trees and setting up a few sawmills. Any of them could pretty much live and work where they wanted to, and the land and trees were there to be exploited. Presumably these early loggers did not realize that today's generation would have preferred a more moderate approach. Few virgin pine forests are left today, although some still exist on a small scale, and the pine forests on commercial paper company lands and other areas still have the atmosphere of what the region was like before men with saws paid a visit.

Pines turned a profit for some, and still do, in another manner that did not involve cutting down trees—turpentine production. People have used naval stores for centuries and for many purposes, such as to seal the seams of wooden ships and to thin paints. Thus, the vast forests of slash and longleaf were an opportunity to the European newcomers. The industry of turpentine production got a major boost in the early 1900s when a University of Georgia chemist, Charles H. Herty, presented a new way to extract turpentine.

The Georgia pine forests came into their own, with the state leading the nation in turpentine production at the time of the Great Depression. Southern Georgia was still making the most of its natural resources, this time in a manner that was a bit more sustainable because the tree was not removed. The only commercial turpentine distillery in America is found today in Appling County in the town of Baxley. Ironically, it is owned by a Dutch company.

Turpentiners collecting resin

Trees have provided jobs for two centuries in Southeast Georgia, but flowers provide a visual delight. Visit the area at any time of the year and you will find flowers in bloom. Most plants flower in spring and summer, ranging from the tiny chickweeds with white flowers the size of a thumbtack to the mighty magnolias with fragrant white flowers that can cover most of a dinner plate. The bright orange flowers of trumpet vines, climbing high on trees and fence posts, are ever evident. Through the hot summer and into autumn, yellow, white, and purple composites, enhanced by a plethora of legumes, enliven the roadsides with color.

The Cherokee rose, Georgia's state flower, with its five white petals, is guaranteed to bloom in spring and, under some conditions, in autumn. No doubt more than a few native Georgians have wondered why on earth the Georgia Federation of Women's Clubs, in 1916, would pick an introduced, oriental plant as their state flower. One reason is that the climbing rose vines are a tribute to the Cherokee Indians who distributed the plant throughout the state.

THE MYSTERY TREE OF THE ALTAMAHA

Few plants bloom in winter, but among those that commonly do is the shrub known as sasanqua, a form of camellia. A close kin of sasanqua is one of the most mysterious plant species ever found in North America. Known as *Franklinia*, this species of plant performed one of the most unusual disappearing acts known to botany.

Franklinia, like sasanqua and the camellias, belongs to the tea family and can be purchased from horticultural companies. Botanical history would be made if it were to be discovered growing in the wild, for *Franklinia* is more than simply a variety of pretty-flowered tree produced in horticultural greenhouses. The species is the last representative of a plant, an entire genus, that has disappeared from the wild within the past two centuries.

In the late 1700s, the explorer William Bartram traveled throughout the wild bottomland forests of southeastern Georgia. He reached only the edge of the Okefenokee but spent many days on the Altamaha River and in its forested margins. According to his detailed natural history records of the region, in the autumn of 1765 he discovered a new plant, one with white flowers like its close kin the loblolly-bay (*Gordonia lasianthus*) that was common in the region.

In his journals, Bartram reported discovering a small grove of trees growing along the southern reaches of the Altamaha River. He found these strange trees with white flowers nowhere else. He returned to the same grove in 1773, by which time botanists had recognized the species as rare and unusual. Bartram then collected seeds and sent them to England for identification. He also gave the species its scientific name, *Franklinia alatamaha*, in honor of Benjamin Franklin and after an earlier spelling of the Altamaha River.

Although only William Bartram had collected the seeds, other explorers also found the grove of trees during the next two decades. Here the mystery begins. Since the late 1700s, no one has been able to relocate the site of the rare *Franklinia* trees. Did an entire species of tree become extinct in the wild between the time of Bartram's travels and the early 1800s? No one can be sure, and botanists still search the Altamaha's floodplain forests for the lost grove.

An unexpected turn of events began to unfold with the seeds that Bartram had collected. After he sent them across the Atlantic to England, they were sent back across the ocean and ended up in Philadelphia. The remarkable part of it all is that they were viable! Seedlings were produced, the stock survived, and today one can buy *Franklinia* as a horticultural plant—but no one has yet found it again in its undomesticated state.

We may never know the origin of or find an explanation for the mysterious disappearance of the species from the wilds of Southeast Georgia, though botanists tend to speculate. Some postulated that English tea growers brought the plant to the New World as a new crop. Perhaps Bartram discovered the last relict of an abandoned crop venture. Some theorized a route of introduction via American Indians or European explorers who brought the plant from high-elevation rain forests of tropical America. Indeed, horticultural *Franklinia* trees seem to thrive in cool temperatures at mid latitudes in North America. Even the English do not seem likely candidates for planting trees in the middle of a forest, however, so this explanation is a bit unlikely. Furthermore, no one has rediscovered the plant anywhere in the wild—in Europe, Asia, tropical America, or the bottomlands of the Altamaha. For the past two centuries, botanists have seen only those raised by horticulturists.

The answer to the puzzle of the missing grove of trees of Southeast Georgia may have a simple explanation, albeit one of high improbability. The species may have been hovering near extinction from natural events when Bartram stumbled into the last grove left on earth. Had Bartram arrived two decades later, this relict population would never have been recorded. The odds on finding the last survivors of a species are less than those of winning the Georgia lottery. But people do win, so it could have happened.

Was *Franklinia* a plant species clinging to the last strand of existence and saved only by serendipity, by timely human intervention? Is it really gone from the wild forever? Could the silent, secret darkness of the Altamaha River's wild swamps and bottomlands still be hiding the last vestige of a near-extinct species? Does the answer lie within an early morning drive away from the lights and action of Metropolitan Atlanta, followed by a long, wet walk through the heart of the Altamaha River floodplain?

A wet walk it would be to get there, but if the river isn't in flood stage, you would find it dry once you reached *Franklinia*'s habitat, the hammock. *Franklinia* may be gone from Southeast Georgia, but a few hammocks remain, characterized by sandy soils that are deep, dry, and nutrient poor. Botanically, the hammock habitats are dominated by evergreen broadleaf trees such as live oaks, laurel oaks, magnolias, and American holly.

Today, two conditions must be met for one to have a worthwhile visit to a hammock in Southeast Georgia. One prerequisite is an elevated sand ridge surrounded by moist habitat. Charles Wharton, in his book *The Natural Environments of Georgia*, credits Roland Harper with an early observation on how hammock plant communities kept their botanical composition. Harper had noted that these upland broadleaf evergreen habitats he called hammocks were common on islands and peninsulas, where natural fires were infrequent. Thus the hardwood trees could persist without extensive invasion by pine trees.

The second criterion, and the one most important for appreciating the visit, is that the hammock still be in a natural state; that is, destructive logging has not removed the trees. Once hammocks have been cleared of the trees and other vegetation that give them their character, they have been used as pastures, for residential housing, and even for commercial plantations of slash pine. What remains of these vestiges of Georgia's natural heritage today would best serve as reminders of the region's environmental bounty, not as places for more fields, houses, or pine trees. Fortunately, one such hammock, protected by the state, is guaranteed to Georgia's residents and visitors. Big Hammock Natural Area, on a sand ridge along the Altamaha River in Tattnall County, serves as a lasting reminder of the allure and enchantment of natural beauty one can discover in a bottomland river swamp.

THE SNAKES

As the alligator serves as keystone species and symbol to the swamplands, rattlesnakes set the mood for terrestrial habitats of the region. Snakebite befell characters in two of the better literary contributions to emerge from the minds and pens of Southeast Georgia writers. A heroine in the Pulitzer Prize–winning *Lamb in His Bosom*, by Caroline Miller of the town of Baxley in Appling County, survives the bite of a canebrake rattler. *Feast of Snakes,* by Harry Crews, a native of Bacon County, features the most magnificent rattlesnake of them all, the eastern diamondback, biggest rattlesnake in girth and length in North America. Canebrakes are not small either, record lengths for the species being over six feet.

People who think they have dominion over the serpents that crawl on their bellies should think again, at least in the terrestrial habitats of Southeast Georgia. Thoughts of these two snakes dominate the minds and control the actions of blackberry pickers, roadside cleanup crews, and even lovers taking a moonlight stroll through piney woods. Many Southeast Georgians dare not venture into tall vegetation. When considering who has the upper hand, rattlesnakes or Georgians, one would certainly have to consider the possibility that rattlesnakes prevail.

Most Georgians have yet to learn proper appreciation for snakes of any sort, but they most certainly have a healthy respect for rattlers. The respect is similar to the kind Georgians had for William Tecumseh Sherman's troops when they held the high hand in Jenkins County and continued to move southeastward toward Savannah. Small wonder. Yankees and big rattlesnakes were capable of killing a full-grown, healthy man. And rattlesnakes still can, if their needle-pointed fangs hit the right vein and inject two tablespoons full of the amber venom. A ground-traveling gray squirrel struck by a big rattler is unlikely to scurry back up the live oak tree it calls home. Evidence for this assertion comes from the many canebrakes and diamondbacks, shot or road-killed, that the curious have slit open in search of an explanation for the snake's swollen belly. A gray squirrel is often found to have been the snake's last meal.

Snakes have guided the paths of many a Georgian, in the southeastern region and statewide. The influence of snakes was no doubt

The eastern diamondback rattlesnake, the largest and most dangerous poisonous snake in Georgia, is found in the southern third of the state.

evident as early as 1734, soon after the Lutheran Salzburgers settled the town of Ebenezer in Effingham County. Upon losing the first child or adult from the bite of a big rattler, trod upon in innocence, the Salzburgers undoubtedly changed their attitudes toward their newfound sanctuary. Trepidation for the at-hand dangers that lurked beneath the palmettos and gallberry bushes would have temporarily replaced the fears of religious persecution they were trying to escape in their native Austria. Clearing brush around dwellings, outbuildings, or other points of congregation such as the Jerusalem orphanage built in 1737 and the Jerusalem Lutheran Church built in the late 1760s became standard practice—not to gain a scenic view but to ensure that the lurking snakes with the whirring sound had no places to hide. None close by, at least.

Leave the high ground and head for the swamp, and rattlers become infrequent. Southeast Georgians learned quickly that someone walking in swamp water need not be in constant fear of treading on the gray serpent with the black velvet chevrons or the brown monster with the yellow-rimmed diamonds. Instead one kept a constant eye open for their replacement—the dread cottonmouth, the water moccasin.

Anyone walking along southeastern rivers, swamp margins, and especially in the deep swamp itself must pay attention. Even the most swamp-wise Georgia trapper might overlook a cottonmouth with its coiled, camouflaged muddy-colored body of brown or black. The "no trespassing" sign of the cottonmouth is the open-mouthed display showing the pure white lining. This "don't-tread-on-me" signal of the killer with no rattles has been said to look like a white swamp flower with a pair of cat eyes. Such is the cottonmouth's greeting to the alert traveler.

A mouth lined with cotton was a good sign. It meant you were still enough inches away to step back and not get bitten; and although some cottonmouths get real possessive about the little plot of mud beneath their coil and will not retreat, they will not attack. The last thing any North American venomous snake wants to do is bite something too large to eat, especially a human. If snakes gave thought to the issue, they would consider man to hold dominion.

No summer goes by in Southeast Georgia without one hearing tales about water moccasins. Sometimes they fall out of trees into boats; sometimes they crawl into boats; and often they get shot from boats, along river banks, around lakes, or in swamps. One intriguing aspect of water moccasin stories is that the snakes being referred to are most often not poisonous; they are not cottonmouths, only harmless water snakes. They may look and act mean; nevertheless, they are nonvenomous creatures.

These impersonators of the cottonmouth die by the hundreds each year throughout Georgia and other southern states because people, perhaps with good intent, think they are killing cottonmouths. Considering the advent of more enlightened attitudes about native wildlife and its importance on an ecosystem level, a little environmental education about water snakes in Southeast Georgia is in order, for many residents as well as visitors. Education serves more than one purpose. In the case of cottonmouth versus water snake, people will benefit from knowing they have nothing to fear from a water snake—the snakes too will benefit.

Because of their color patterns of brown, black, and copper, water snakes are often confused with venomous species. Countless harmless snakes have been killed, with someone returning as a hero, having supposedly rid the world of a copperhead or cottonmouth. Pick up any big water snake improperly, and you'll get snakebit for sure, and probably bleed. But the rows of tiny teeth really do little more than scratch.

The brown water snakes, common along big rivers, are ugly customers in appearance and behavior. If picked up, they proceed to bite at one end and spray a foul-smelling musk from the other. To add to their image of being dangerous, some water snakes get enormous. A pregnant brown water snake can be over five feet long and almost as big around as a softball. Despite appearances, as unpleasant as they may seem, the aquatic snakes of Georgia are harmless, except for the cottonmouth.

All Georgians should view this rich biodiversity of their snake fauna—forty species—with pride. No greater abundance of such herpetofaunal wealth can be found anywhere in the state than in Southeast Georgia, including all six venomous species native to the southeastern United States. Besides the two big rattlesnakes and the cottonmouth, the copperhead, the pygmy rattler, and the rare and beautiful coral snake are also native to the region. In spite of this seemingly dangerous array, one must remember that the other thirty-four species are as harmless as a Georgia white-footed mouse.

Selecting the grand prize among the snakes of Georgia is no easy task, not one most Georgians indulge in. But if they did, perhaps the indigo snake, the largest snake in North America, reaching a length of almost nine feet, would be the winner. This snake is indeed magnificent, especially in sunlight where its iridescent sheen has the look of blue steel. Despite its majesty, the indigo snake is on a downward spiral, due in great part to habitat loss.

The indigo snake is protected wherever it occurs in the Southeast, having been declared a federally threatened species during the last quarter of the twentieth century under the Endangered Species Act. Due to the legal status of the species, land development must contend with the aura of litigation associated with the federal protection. Ironically, this nonvenomous species may have shaped land development in parts of southern Georgia more so than the venomous ones. Most people fear lawyers more than rattlesnakes.

Indigos are at home in the villages of gopher tortoises, whose underground tunnel-homes they share in the winter, along with diamondbacks, cottontail rabbits, and a host of other guests. Wherever indigos are found, they need large tracts of land to forage for the terrestrial vertebrates that constitute their prey. A blacktop highway through indigo habitat assures a steady drain on the population. It takes an eight-foot-long snake a while to cross a road, whether or not a pickup truck is coming.

Some might choose the eastern king snake as the snake to represent the region. King snakes might win the pretty prize in a snake beauty contest, but they would never win Miss Congeniality. The king of snakes gets its name for its perceived role as a cannibal, readily dining on other snakes as well as rats, mice, and lizards. The knowledgeable farmer of Southeast Georgia leaves the king snake be. Immune to pit viper venom, a king snake would as soon eat a rattlesnake, copperhead, or cottonmouth as a harmless water snake. Woe to the five-foot canebrake that meets a six-foot king snake coming through the piney woods.

Georgians may be fearful of almost all snakes—and there are a lot of them in this state—but only a half-dozen species tip the danger scale. The majority are completely harmless, and the rest will bite but have no venom. Even a bite from a coachwhip, rat snake, or water snake, all of which have big mouths and lots of tiny teeth, seldom merits any more attention than a rinsing with soap and water first chance you get.

Still, fear of snakebite rides everywhere with the timid in the fields, woods, and wetlands of Southeast Georgia. The informed know that outsiders' chances of even seeing a snake are slim, unless they know where to look. Unfortunately, too few people even in Georgia know that the dangers from venomous snakebite are vastly overrated throughout the Southeast. Not that rattlesnakes or cottonmouths can't kill a person, for they have certainly done so. But compared to the hazards of everyday living, such as driving a car on a public highway, snakebite should be a long, long way down on the worry list.

Although the early inhabitants of Georgia knew more than those of us today about some aspects of nature, modern inhabitants are better apprised about what to do in the rare event someone gets bitten by a snake. Forget the folk remedies. No cutting. No tourniquets. No whiskey. The best thing to have with you if you are bitten by a poisonous snake is a set of car keys and someone to drive you, at a safe speed, to the nearest emergency treatment facility. Let the physicians deal with the treatment. Harmless as most snakes are, some can be dangerous, and most people cannot always differentiate between the two kinds. So snakes continue to mold the behavior of Southeast Georgians who tread in their domain.

Besides snakes and alligators, the other reptiles (sixteen species of turtles and a dozen lizards), as well as amphibians (twenty-two frog and nineteen salamander species), give the region one of the richest assemblages of such animals in North America. Although they make up a diverse and impressive array of vertebrate species in the woods and wetlands of southern Georgia, reptiles and amphibians (collectively known as herpetofauna) are perhaps the most maligned of Georgia's wildlife. The sundry collection of species is a natural heritage that all Georgians should, and some do, take pride in. Yet all of the herpetofauna have taken a frightful beating over the last few decades.

The uninformed still kill snakes; basking turtles are still used for target practice; salamanders are still used for fish bait. In addition, millions of reptiles and amphibians die each year on public highways, although most drivers are unaware of their contribution to the roadkill tally.

Reptiles and amphibians are natural phenomena that shape the character of the Southeast Georgia landscape. They serve as barometers of the change in public attitudes about wildlife protection. More and more people accept and appreciate the key environmental role native herpetofauna play as critical links in the intricate food web of which all organisms are a part. The environmentally informed realize that these animals are as important to the workings of natural ecosystems as species such as the white-tailed deer and bobwhite quail, which are considered "practical" wildlife, directly useful to humans. Many view intentional destruction of reptiles and amphibians as inexcusable, whether through calculated killing of individual animals or as a consequence of destroying their habitat.

RATTLESNAKE ROUNDUPS

One of the more controversial phenomena in the way people treat snakes occurs annually in Claxton, a Southeast Georgia town known also for its fruitcakes. The event is a rattlesnake roundup, an activity viewed by some as an environmental atrocity and by others as a way to get some tourists and revenue into a small town once a year. Still others simply look forward to a good time seeing old friends and catching rattlesnakes.

In preparation for a roundup, the participants gather in early spring at a site with plenty of rattlesnakes. As at a fishing rodeo, by capturing the largest or the most rattlesnakes, individuals compete for recognition as the best snake collector. A criticism of rattlesnake roundups is that the people of a region have part of their natural wildlife destroyed or removed without the user paying a fee or having any limits imposed. Others counter this argument by insisting that the users do pay, with a cash flow into the community through commercial routes.

A broader environmental complaint is that rattlesnakes are not the only wildlife affected. At one time a primary capture technique known as "gassing" was used. Gasoline fumes are forced into a burrow or crevice through a plastic hose. If the weather is still cool, most snakes are in underground burrows or retreat to them when alarmed. When the gasoline fumes pervade the burrow, out come the inhabitants. Or, at least some of them. Unfortunately, some die while still in the burrow, and a few do so after they crawl out. And not just rattlesnakes. Gopher tortoises, indigo snakes, and gopher frogs are among the species that seek winter sanctuary in holes beneath the sands of Southeast Georgia. All three species have entered the spotlight of federal protection because of their declines in all or parts of their geographic ranges. To their credit, some rattlesnake catchers in Georgia will tell you they no longer use gasoline as a collecting technique because of the potential harm to the animals, regardless of what the laws might be.

The snakes captured at a rattlesnake roundup may be sold or bartered among the participants. Their use may be as pets, or for skins, meat, or curios. Special events are held, including a contest to see who can put a half dozen or so diamondback rattlers into a sack the fastest, by hand. Some visitors to the annual rattlesnake roundup at Claxton admit they come mainly in hopes of seeing someone get bitten—sort of like going to a stock car race in hopes of seeing a wreck.

The original reason for having a rattlesnake roundup may have been founded on a biblical interpretation of the Garden of Eden—that snakes are evil and meant to be destroyed. Another more practical, although equally unjustified, reason given is that poisonous snakes should be removed from areas of high concentration to reduce the danger of snakebite to humans and domestic animals. Aside from their being a form of entertainment, the reason for rattlesnake roundups today, whether stated or not, is primarily commerce, citizens using the environment to their own best advantage and creating a form of posterity for themselves.

People who have had pets, livestock, relatives, or friends bitten or killed by a diamondback might understandably be unsympathetic to recommendations that we should protect such a species. Few people, especially southern legislators, would be eager to strike out on a campaign to protect an animal that can not only kill a person but also has a rather poor endorsement by the Bible. Although protecting potentially lethal animals is a difficult concept for some to accept, others think the time has come to consider the idea of developing guidelines to preserve even dangerous animals like rattlesnakes.

THE HERITAGE OF SOUTHEAST GEORGIA

The products of a culture can be measured in many ways. Paintings, literature, and music can provide enduring statements about a region and are often but expressions of the natural world around the artist. Novels of the southeastern region of Georgia portrayed the hard life of agricultural folk trying to wrench their calories and vitamins from a stingy soil of sand. Books exclusively on the natural habitats of the region, primarily of the Okefenokee Swamp, present a kinder picture of resourcefulness and deep appreciation for the natural world.

Natural history books written more than half a century apart emphasize the persistence of natural beauty and biodiversity of the swamp ecosystem. A classic work on the life history of frogs of the Okefenokee was written by Albert Hazen Wright and published in 1932, whereas the most complete and comprehensive work on fishes of the Okefenokee, by Joshua Laerm and Bud Freeman, was published by the University of Georgia Press in 1986. Del Presley's book *Okefinokee Album,* compiled from the writings of the famous naturalist Francis Harper, gives an inside account of the great swamp and of the self-reliant families who inhabited it. In art and music the contributions from southeastern Georgia have been more meager, but not less than might be expected for such a sparsely populated region, a rural land averaging fewer than seventeen thousand people per county.

In 1990, the most heavily populated area, Toombs County, claimed sixty-five people per square mile. Fewer than eight people per square mile lived in Clinch County. By comparison, DeKalb County in the greater Atlanta area could boast more than two thousand people per square mile. In Southeast Georgia you do not have to know a special place to go if you want to escape into solitude. You can go practically anywhere. If you want to be around people, you are likely to encounter two highly valued features of the low population density: a community spirit and traditional southern hospitality, a disappearing style in many parts of the South.

As with art, the commerce and industry of a region are also inexorably entwined with the natural world's offerings. Port cities must have navigable waters; farming communities must have proper climate and soils; mining towns must have minerals or ore. Natural resources in the mineral line assured the persistence of some locations in other states (such as iron and coal in Birmingham), as well as Georgia (such as gold in Dahlonega). Southeast Georgia had few ore and minerals in quantities large enough to draw a crowd, but a handful of communities gained national reputations. The Ludowici clay that underlies the sand in Long County was distinctive enough to develop a red roofing tile industry, and the particular qualities of the soils in Toombs and Candler Counties produce Vidalia onions, which some say are the sweetest onions in the world.

Despite the lack of focus on centers of commerce in response to specific circumstances of geology, topography, or climate, the entire region is heir to a legacy that can last indefinitely. The major natural resources of the southeastern portion of Georgia inland from the coast are the vast terrain of pine forests underlain with sand, the big swamp known as Okefenokee, and the long, undammed Altamaha River and its sisters, the Ogeechee and Satilla, that run roughly in parallel with it to the sea. Associated with each of these natural scenes is the diversity of wildlife, the greatest natural resource of all.

The southeastern United States has a natural heritage to be proud of, and part of this heritage resides in Southeast Georgia. Using the natural habitats of a region as an environmental showcase is the ideal model for sustainability. Economic effort, therefore, should rely on natural resources in a manner that secures equal profit in succeeding generations. Southeast Georgia has such an opportunity.

Some might say the area would have developed in an economically more prosperous fashion had it not been for the capriciousness of nature toward the farming communities. Nature gives little foreshadowing of next year's droughts or floods, of impending malaria outbreaks, of corn or tobacco blights. Natural catastrophes, some might call them environmental curses, bestowed upon the early settlers of any region can turn prospects for success into assured failure. Maybe if the full story were known, the settlers of Southeast Georgia got some bad breaks. Maybe that's why southern Georgians can claim few big towns, let alone big cities.

But then again, maybe the people of Southeast Georgia did not want such a claim. For they still have something that metropolitan areas have lost forever. They still have natural environments that now are priceless. No one can build an Okefenokee Swamp. Dams would have to be removed to create a river in the Southeast as long and free-flowing as the Altamaha. And one must have the sands that long ago lay beneath a former ocean to have pine forests with wiregrass as a carpet.

All of these natural settings show the marks of human progress and the signs of environmental healing. Millions of pine trees were removed by lumbering, but millions still remain. The Okefenokee Swamp lost its alligators to hide hunters and big trees to the timber industry, but some portions remain pristine, and all are slowly recovering. The Altamaha has a nuclear power plant along its west bank in Appling County, but still no dams.

With this perspective, the visitor to Southeast Georgia has much to anticipate, in a region where the contrast of wildness and calmness in nature blends with human progress. This relatively unpopulated, mostly rural tract has become a rarity compared to the heavily populated urban meccas of industry and commerce in many sections of Georgia and the United States. In Southeast Georgia the natural environments still have much to offer and still shape the way people think, how they live, and what they do.

Delma E. Presley

TOURING SOUTHEAST GEORGIA

Anyone who travels in southeastern Georgia quickly discovers that this is a land of sand. Visible on almost every curbside, it is the stuff of unpaved roads. Somehow farmers manage to grow abundant crops in it. Many rural homeowners still take pride in front yards of sand—neatly swept and grassless. In north Georgia rocks and red clay form the banks of rushing streams, but in South Georgia white sandbars transform gentle bends of rivers into freshwater beaches.

The reason for all the sand here is that the entire region once was covered by the prehistoric sea. Despite centuries of erosion by wind and water, the land very much resembles an ocean floor, but without the water. For good reason geologists include Southeast Georgia as part of the Coastal Plain.

The landscape rises and falls gently as a consequence of ancient drainage patterns that formed a multitude of rivers. American Indians and subsequent European settlers bestowed on them euphonious names: Savannah, Ogeechee, Canoochee, Ohoopee, Altamaha, Satilla, and Suwannee. All carry water to the Atlantic Ocean. An exception is an ancient expanse of water that would not drain because a sand ridge of dozens of miles created a natural dam. The result is that priceless ecological treasure known as the Okefenokee Swamp.

A major geographical feature of the region is the Altamaha River. The uppermost boundary of the mighty river's drainage basin begins in northeastern Georgia's corner and extends to downtown Atlanta. Although only 140 miles in length, the Altamaha empties more water into the Atlantic ocean than any other river in the southeastern United States. Swollen by winter's rains, some of its swamps extend the river beyond five miles in width. The Altamaha is one of a handful of undammed major rivers in America. Between April and October, its waters recede and reveal hundreds of sandbars with white sand beaches bordered by willows.

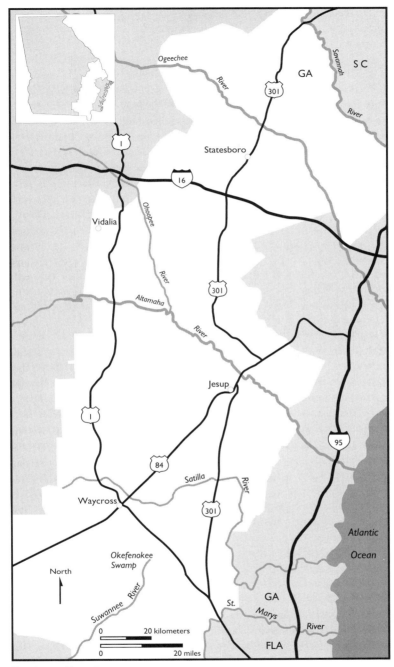

Southeast Georgia

The southeastern region is refreshingly natural. It lies between two population centers: Macon, in central Georgia, and Savannah, on the coast some 170 miles to the east. Its seventeen counties and respective county seats clearly reflect the state's agricultural heritage. The two most populous counties, Bulloch and Ware, have fewer than fifty thousand residents each; the county seats, Statesboro and Waycross, each have populations of approximately twenty thousand. Most of the towns in the region are in the five-thousand-and-under category. Although some boast of thriving industries that enhance local economies, the dominant economic influence is farming. The fields and forests, as a slogan has it, produce jobs.

What the traveler sees in southeastern Georgia, therefore, is a slice of rural America. The colorful ingredients of this slice are bits and pieces of a culture tangibly related to nature. It is a relaxed relationship—a way of life—reinforced by local tradition.

Now in this part of Georgia, one tradition that will not die is good cooking. While several restaurant chains operate in the region, local restaurants offer menus that cater to local tastes. Southeast Georgians enjoy vegetables throughout the year, and other foods that have universal appeal in the region are fried fish and barbecued pork and chicken. True barbecue is cooked slowly in a pit or smokehouse, usually adjacent to the restaurant. The tempting, rich aroma of sweet oak and hickory smoke that envelopes the simmering and tender pork ribs and shoulders is unforgettable.

After visiting small towns and communities, the traveler grows accustomed to long, straight roads that quietly stretch into horizons of green. Here and there farmers have sculpted some of the sand hills and rich river valleys into landscapes that produce bountiful crops of soybeans, corn, peanuts, wheat, cotton, and tobacco. Farmers also create ponds liberally throughout this area, providing freshwater bream, catfish, and bass as well as reservoirs for irrigation.

Occasional groves of pecan trees divide the neat fields bordered by dense pine forests. As one approaches the rivers and their swamps, the pines relinquish to cypress and hardwoods: sweet bay, gum, poplar, tupelo, and oak. Colorful blossoms abound in early spring months: March and April feature a pink and white extravaganza of azalea and dogwood blossoms; in May and early June the white magnolia flower emits a pleasantly sharp and sweet aroma. Often flowering trees are on the grounds of white-washed wooden churches. These neat buildings resemble houses, because people of the frontier built not temples but houses of worship or houses of God.

During the spring and summer months, many farmers provide pick your own gardens. Strawberries and raspberries ripen in April and May. From late April until June Vidalia onions are available in most of the counties in the region. Tomatoes, beans, and other garden vegeta-

In the spring roadside stands display Vidalia onions and other local produce.

bles are harvested from June until August. Watermelons and canta-loupes are abundant in June and July. Blueberries can be picked from June through August. Peanuts are harvested twice: In June and July they are gathered before maturity for boiling; in August and September they are harvested as mature plants and sold in the shell. Green pea-nuts, boiled in salt water, are favorite snacks in the region and can be purchased at most convenience stores and vegetable stands, and pea-nuts roasted in the shell usually are plentiful.

Depending upon the starting point, there are at least four tours that introduce Southeast Georgia: From Sand Hills to the Salzburgers (tour one), the Coastal Plain (tour two), Wiregrass Trail to the Coast (tour three), and the Heart of Southeast Georgia (tour four).

TOUR ONE: FROM SAND HILLS TO THE SALZBURGERS

Exit I-16 at Metter; north on Ga. 121 to Millen; east on Ga. 21 to Syl-vania to Springfield; four miles south of Springfield, Ga. 275 to Ebe-nezer (then on to Savannah via Ga. 21).

This pleasant route to the Savannah area carries one through several communities dotting Southeast Georgia's sand ridges. Destinations on this tour include Metter, Millen, Sylvania, and New Ebenezer. Each traces its settlement to rivers or railroads. Between Sylvania and New Ebenezer are several communities and the town of Springfield, with origins tied to the Central of Georgia Railroad. Local history slowly unveils itself as one moves from the charming Metter, incorporated in 1903, to New Ebenezer, settled by persecuted Lutherans who fled Ger-many for the colony of Georgia in 1734.

Driving southeast on I-16 between Macon and Savannah, the traveler exits at Ga. 121N. The rustic welcome center is a restored commissary (store) that served lumber workers in the 1930s. Its back porch faces a mirror-like lake filled with lilies and edged with moss-draped trees. One enters **Metter**, the Candler County seat, through the South Metter National Register Historic District, a collection of late nineteenth- and early twentieth-century Victorian- and Craftsman-style residences. Tree-lined avenues provide unhurried access to a park-like downtown shopping area.

Local stores and shops in Metter offer glimpses of everyday small-town life, especially two drug stores whose soda fountains are reminiscent of the 1940s and 1950s. An appealing attraction in the vicinity is a three-acre park, Guido Gardens, which features quiet waterfalls, graceful fountains, winding brooks, several gazebos, and a little chapel open for prayer and meditation throughout the day and night. The lovely public retreat is adjacent to the radio and television production studios for "The Sower" devotionals. Welcome center staff can give easy directions to the Charles C. Harrold Nature Preserve, home of a rare native plant, *Elliotia racemosa* (Georgia plume), originally observed by William Bartram in Southeast Georgia in the 1770s. Deeded to the Nature Conservancy in 1964, the preserve encompasses classic sand hill formations.

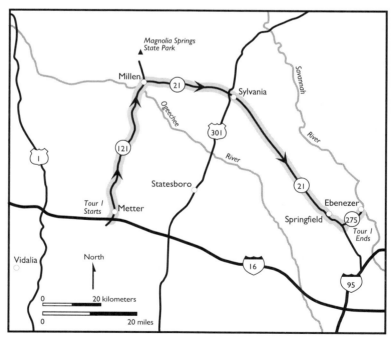

Southeast Georgia, Tour One

Southeast Georgians call Ga. 121, the road from Metter to Millen, the Woodpecker Trail. The name is especially appropriate, because no towns or commercial centers exist near the thirty-mile corridor through pine forests and sand hills; but woodpeckers of several varieties, including the large pileated woodpecker, and other forms of wildlife thrive in this environment.

The Canoochee River and its tributaries and swamps provide Candler County with abundant fish and wildlife, as the Ogeechee River does for Jenkins County. Before one enters the county seat, Millen, the road bed runs through a mile of river bottom and swamp. North of town on Ga. 121 is Magnolia Springs State Park, a testimonial to an unspoiled environment that characterizes much of southeastern Georgia. The Georgia Department of Natural Resources maintains an area of approximately a thousand acres of rolling sand hills and forest. Each day some nine million gallons of crystal-clear water gush from the springs. Recreational opportunities include hiking on nature trails, water skiing, two swimming pools, boat and canoe rentals, and tent and trailer camping. Cottages with modern conveniences can be rented at reasonable rates. Day trippers can take advantage of numerous picnic tables, many beneath shelters.

Magnolia Springs also offers two unique educational opportunities. Camp Lawton was built by the Confederacy as a prison camp. Remnants of the ten-thousand-acre camp are visible, and the park staff offers interpretation of the rise and fall of this Civil War site. The Bo Ginn National Fish Hatchery and Aquarium raises approximately three million fish each year in twenty-seven ponds. The hatchery specializes in propagating species that declined in population in the latter half of the twentieth century: striped bass, shad, short-nose sturgeon, and red drum. Visitors can observe these and other species in twenty-six aquariums.

Downtown **Millen**, the Jenkins County seat, has a charming museum and welcome center in a restored railroad depot, open weekdays. Exhibits and artifacts tell the story of a community whose fortunes have been tied to farming and related activities. Chamber of commerce staff are eager to direct travelers to sites in the region, especially historic Big Buckhead Church, established in 1787, and Birdsville Plantation (private), both of which are National Register properties. The plantation, built in phases between 1800 and 1850, closely resembles its original plan.

The nineteen-mile drive from Millen to **Sylvania** carries the traveler through sand hills, trees, and farmlands to the county seat of Screven County. Sylvania's downtown is filled with handsome masonry buildings that reflect the attractive small-town architecture of the 1920s and 1930s.

Civic clubs in the town and county jointly host a series of festivals to focus attention on arts, crafts, foods, and a way of life. The first week of April is devoted to the Livestock Festival, perhaps the largest civic event of the year. Farmers and cattlemen take great pride in animals judged and awarded prizes by experts in animal husbandry. Cooking demonstrations, beauty pageants, and a circus round out the week. Other notable events of regional interest are the Summer Celebration on the first Saturday in August; the Sampler, devoted to arts and crafts, on the third Saturday in September; and Christmas Open House on the first Thursday evening in December.

The chamber of commerce in the heart of downtown Sylvania can direct travelers to local sites, including the historic Seaborn Goodall House in an early county seat at Jacksonborough. Interpreted and maintained by the Daughters of the American Revolution, the house faces the Old Quaker Road that connected the colonial cities of Savannah and Augusta. The structure's style is often called plantation plain, although it bears some Federal style details. The house witnessed many notables of American history who traveled this road: naturalists John and William Bartram and John Abbot, as well as Pres. George Washington.

The road from Sylvania to New Ebenezer is a typical Southeast Georgia straight shot. Parallel to the Ogeechee and Central of Georgia Railroad tracks, Ga. 21 runs southeasterly along the sand ridges of the Savannah River valley. Some inviting communities along the way are **Newington**, **Shawnee**, and **Springfield**, the seat of Effingham County. **Guyton's** Victorian-style houses recall a prosperous town in the early twentieth century. A delightful four-mile side trip begins at a right turn in Newington on Ga. 24. The destination is a picturesque village known as Oliver, located on Screven County's southern boundary line. Several turn-of-the-century houses and handsome churches stand beneath giant trees draped in Spanish moss. Store owners in Oliver sometimes recount local history, especially tales of activities of Sherman's soldiers as they rested before advancing toward Savannah near the end of the Civil War. In the mid-1990s, one particularly friendly store owner displayed this intriguing and inviting sign in his window: "I Ain't Mad at No Body."

The entrance to **New Ebenezer**, Ga. 275, is a well-marked left turn four miles south of Springfield on Ga. 24. For five miles the paved roadway cuts through pine forests and fields, then ends abruptly at a picturesque bend of the Savannah River, the state's eastern boundary line. A collection of buildings, including a museum, rental cottages, and a retreat center, has been designed to complement the stately Jerusalem Lutheran Church.

The building and grounds bear testimony to traditions of Salzburgers who arrived in the infant colony of Georgia in 1734. (Salzburgers were Lutherans from Salzburg, Austria, who were exiled to Augsburg, Germany, in the early 1700s.) After finding an earlier site unsuitable for habitation (Old Ebenezer), the Salzburgers established New Ebenezer in 1736. Since that time Lutheran worship and Salzburger traditions have continued. They used locally produced bricks to construct the church in 1769, and its steeple ascends to a lofty peak upon which rests the replica of a swan (one of Martin Luther's favorite symbols for the church). The church has an active congregation and holds weekly Sunday school and morning worship. Members of the Salzburger Society point out that the first Sunday school and the first orphanage in Georgia were introduced at Ebenezer. The church is Georgia's oldest building still intact and in use.

To visit the church building and grounds is to experience the state's colonial history firsthand. A large graveyard provides evidence that over two thousand people once lived on farms nearby. The museum's exhibits explain that battles and skirmishes from the Revolutionary and Civil Wars took place on these grounds. The Lutherans' continuing influence can be found in names of streets and businesses in Springfield and in descendants of Salzburgers who are scattered throughout Effingham and adjoining counties. Their rural mailboxes bear Salzburger names, and the distinctive swan weathervane of Ebenezer Church is replicated atop their homes and barns. Each Labor Day a festival sponsored by the Georgia Salzburger Society includes demonstrations of colonial crafts, games, and foods.

This tour began in what once was called the backcountry (Metter, Millen, and Sylvania). The communities and culture here are legacies of the men and women of the frontier who migrated into Georgia from the Carolinas during the late eighteenth and early nineteenth centuries. New Ebenezer, on the other hand, reminds one of the social and religious struggles that many immigrants had experienced in England and in Europe. It is fitting that the tour ends less than twenty miles from Savannah, established only a year before the Salzburgers settled this area.

TOUR TWO: THE COASTAL PLAIN

U.S. 301 enters Georgia north of Sylvania and continues to the Florida line via these stops: Sylvania, Statesboro, Claxton, Glennville, Ludowici, Jesup, Nahunta, Folkston. At Folkston take Ga. 121 and 121 Sp. to the Suwannee Canal Recreation Area. Visitors who prefer to make Waycross a destination may take an alternate tour, using a portion of the Woodpecker Trail: at Claxton, take U.S. 280 west to Bellville, then travel south via Ga. 169 and Ga. 121 through Mendes and Surrency to Blackshear, and follow U.S. 84 west to Waycross (see tour four).

Many who use this route are on their way to Florida and wish to avoid the heavy traffic and boredom of I-95. U.S. 301 is a scenic and well-

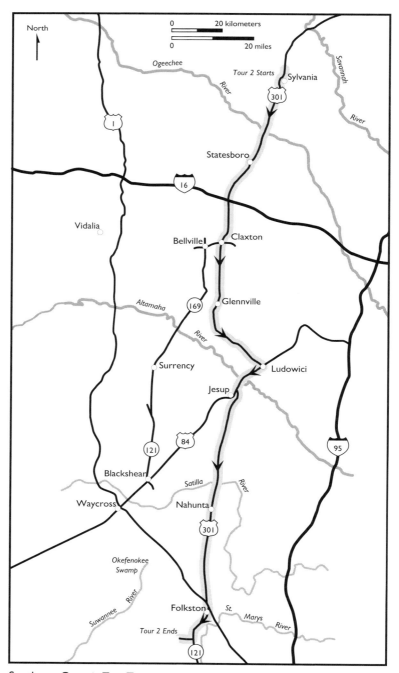

North

0 20 kilometers

0 20 miles

Ogeechee

River

Tour 2 Starts

Sylvania

301

Savannah

River

1

Statesboro

16

Vidalia

Bellville

Claxton

Altamaha

169

Glennville

River

Surrency

Ludowici

Jesup

84

121

95

Blackshear

Satilla

River

Waycross

Nahunta

301

Okefenokee
Swamp

Suwannee

River

Folkston

St.

Marys

River

Tour 2 Ends

121

Southeast Georgia, Tour Two

maintained highway with numerous passing lanes and four-lane segments. The welcome center on U.S. 301 north of **Sylvania** is within sight of the Savannah River, which separates Georgia from South Carolina. The staff provides current information about festivals, exhibits, and special events in Southeast Georgia. The traveler should forgo the U.S. 301 bypass in order to visit this charming town (see tour one). The road south to Statesboro traverses the Ogeechee River Valley. Like most bottomlands of Southeast Georgia, it has been well used by farmers. The canebrakes and swampy areas provide an abundant harvest of game and fish. Boaters have easy access to a "scenic and natural river" at a paved ramp and parking area, Dover Landing.

Much of **Statesboro**'s charm can be credited to a bypass that routes commercial traffic around the downtown area. The perfect beginning place for the traveler is the Statesboro Convention and Visitors Bureau on South Main Street. The building has information about the history of Bulloch County as well as a gift shop with local crafts and food items. Aficionados of small-town architecture will enjoy the walking tour of downtown. There are six National Register Historic Districts in Statesboro. Genealogists will find well-catalogued information about rural South Georgia families at the Brannen genealogical collection at the Statesboro Regional Library.

Georgia Southern University, a regional member of the state university system with some fourteen thousand students, offers numerous attractions, athletic events, and educational opportunities for the general public. An especially popular Youth Arts Festival takes place on the second weekend of March each year. The Georgia Southern Museum features exhibits on the natural history of Georgia's coastal plain, including fossil remains of many extinct creatures, a twenty-six-foot mosasaur skeleton, and the skeleton of the oldest whale ever discovered in North America. Traveling exhibits and hands-on activities appeal to many visitors, as does a collection of American Indian artifacts. The museum manages the Herty Nature Preserve and Nature Trail and a museum store.

The Georgia Southern Botanical Garden on ten secluded acres east of the campus on Ga. 67 introduces native flora of southeastern Georgia, unusual plants, a nature trail marked with educational signs, year-round vegetable and herb gardens, and a gift shop. The Eagle Sanctuary and Lamar Q. Ball Jr. Raptor Center, near the entrance to the campus on Ga. 301, consists of four acres of natural habitats for bald eagles and other native raptors such as falcons, owls, and hawks. Scheduled for completion in 1996, the center will offer educational presentations by a registered falconer and exhibits for visitors of all ages. A restoration of a turpentine still can be found in **Portal**, on a side

Splitting rails, Altamaha River Festival, Baxley

trip on U.S. 80 to the western end of Bulloch County. Besides the still complex, there are interesting stores, houses, and a cotton gin.

From Statesboro to **Claxton**, U.S. 301 is mostly four lanes. Before entering Claxton, it crosses the Canoochee, another scenic and natural river ideally situated for canoeing and bank fishing at the landing and picnic area near the highway. The county seat of Evans County, Claxton was a railroad town before it became a vital agricultural center. Visitors to Claxton during the annual Rattlesnake Roundup on the second weekend in March will find arts, crafts, entertainment, and educational demonstrations about snakes and wildlife. Two commercial bakeries in Claxton sell fruitcake all over the world. Giving a lasting impression of turn-of-the-century small-town life in southeastern Georgia, **Daisy**, just four miles east of Claxton on U.S. 280, is a photogenic small town whose residents have restored several charming municipal and commercial buildings.

Travelers who take the alternate tour (below) to visit the Okefenokee Swamp Park in Waycross will find another attractive small town, **Bellville**, three miles west on U.S. 280. The Anderson House, one of several Victorian-style homes here, is open for lunch. Nearby is a relic from the mid-nineteenth century: the Tattnall Campground, a large open-air meeting house, or tabernacle, consisting of a very large roof, pews, and podium. During the second week of August each year, United Methodist churches host protracted services (see Northeast Georgia tour) each evening, featuring group singing and "old-time" preaching. One cannot easily forget the structure's striking setting beneath tall pines and majestic oaks.

The alternate route begins in Bellville and continues south on Ga. 169 and Ga. 121 via Surrency and Blackshear (Woodpecker Trail). An advantage of this route to Waycross is the opportunity to visit a Vidalia onion farm as well as a significant natural area on the Altamaha River. The entrance to the farm is on Ga. 169 south of **Bellville**. With over a thousand acres in cultivation, Bland Farms is the world's largest grower and shipper of Vidalia sweet onions. Because the owners have developed a "controlled atmosphere" for storing the onions, they can ship them during most of the year, although onion season begins near the end of April and continues through July. In September the Blands begin planting seed beds for next spring's crop. Visitors may see the operation, including the grading and packaging of this world-famous onion.

Continuing toward Blackshear and Waycross on Ga. 169/121, the traveler will find a serene nature trail maintained by the Department of Natural Resources, the Big Hammock Natural and Wildlife Areas. "Hammock" is a term for a raised piece of land in the area of a swamp. The entrance is a paved road that runs east, one mile north of a bridge. There are two reasons to visit this passive recreational area maintained by the Georgia Department of Natural Resources. It is the site of a colony of rare plants first observed by William Bartram who explored the Altamaha at the time of the American Revolution. The *Elliotia racemosa*, Georgia plume, survives in this densely wooded area. Also, an extremely secluded entrance to a "dead river" swamp of the Altamaha is located at the end of the one-lane dirt and gravel road that meanders down a steep bluff immediately before the bridge. While a boat or canoe would permit one to explore the swamp-like environment, the area gives the car-bound traveler the opportunity to view the Big Hammock.

At **Blackshear**, county seat of Pierce County, the traveler will drive nine miles west on U.S. 84, a divided highway, before reaching Waycross (tour four). Pierce County was named for Franklin Pierce, the fourteenth president of the United States.

The traveler who leaves Claxton on the main tour route, U.S. 301S, will pass through Glennville (tour three), Ludowici (tour three), Jesup, Folkston, and smaller communities. As the highway crosses the Altamaha River north of Jesup, it rises above the spreading swamplands and hardwood trees, reaching a high bluff on the southern side of the river. Wayne County maintains a scenic picnic area and public boat landing to the right of the bridge. There one can observe the strong currents of the largest river in the southeastern United States. Nearby is a marker for Doctortown, the location of a major Civil War skirmish involving Sherman's troops as they marched to the sea.

Several lakes also offer recreation and entertainment. Lake Kennerly sponsors water skiing competition and lessons; Lake Grace

Installation of irrigation system, Pierce County

offers entertainment each weekend; Cherokee Lake is used primarily for fishing. The traveler who arrives in **Jesup** around the middle to the end of March will be amazed at the colorful combination of dogwood and azalea blossoms throughout the town. The Dogwood Festival, the third weekend in March, includes several special events for the public. On the third Saturday of each October, Jesup and Wayne County sponsor the Altamaha River Heritage Festival, which focuses on regional foods and always begins on the river with a spirited canoe race.

Residents have preserved several important buildings in Jesup. A good place to begin is the visitors center in a railroad caboose (fittingly, because Jesup's origins are tied to the railroad). The center provides information about restaurants, motels, a bed-and-breakfast inn, and a walking tour of Jesup. Nearby is the Wayne County Heritage Center, built in a restored railroad section house. The museum introduces the history and folklore of the Altamaha River Valley through artifacts and exhibits dating to the period of the early Native Americans. Of particular interest are items found at Fort James, a military outpost in the late 1700s, on the Altamaha. The area's colonial past is also memorialized by a New Deal mural. Painted in 1938 by the Canadian artist David Hutchison, the work is entitled "General Oglethorpe Concludes a Treaty of Peace and Amity with the Creek Indians—May 18, 1733." The mural hangs in the Wayne County Library on Sunset Boulevard.

Fifty-five miles of relatively straight U.S. 301 separate Jesup from Folkston. Since traffic is usually light, the traveler stopping alongside the road can hear some sounds of nature: birds, tree frogs, and squirrels. An especially good place to listen is near the public landing on the Satilla River as it passes beneath U.S. 301. The river's white sand contrasts with the mineral-enriched dark water. Much of the wildlife of Brantley County is the result of the Rayonier Wildlife Management Area, almost twenty thousand acres of forests, river valleys, and swamps in the northeast section of the county.

In **Waynesville**, on U.S. 82, the Satilla River Vacation Land has camping and swimming facilities. Another popular form of recreation takes place each Saturday evening throughout the year except for four Saturdays between December 20 and January 20. At the Satilla Creek Raceway on Ga. 32 near Hortense, novice and experienced racers gather to participate in "kart" racing on a track sanctioned by the World Karting Association. Before leaving Brantley County, the traveler might enjoy sampling produce at a vegetable stand in the county seat of **Nahunta**.

Folkston is the last town the traveler encounters on U.S. 301 before entering Florida. This county seat of Charlton County originated as a railroad stop, and the town's early depot now serves as the headquarters for visitors, as well as the chamber of commerce. The Okefenokee Festival on the second Saturday in October is a tribute to the Okefenokee Swamp as well as to the resourceful people who settled in and around the swamp as early as 1820. A parade, a road race, an arts and crafts fair, and a "Tour de Swamp" bicycle race are key events on this day. All who participate in the festival are invited to an open house at Chessers Island (see below).

The road to Chessers Island takes one near the historic Sardis Church, a weathered wooden structure standing in rustic dignity beneath moss-draped trees. Nearby is Traders Hill Recreation Park—thirty-two acres of white sand, tall pines, spreading oak trees, camping facilities, and picnic shelters near the bank of the picturesque St. Marys River which begins in the Okefenokee. On the opposite side of the river is the state of Florida.

Eleven miles south of Folkston is the Suwannee Canal Recreation Area, one of three public entrances to the Okefenokee National Wildlife Refuge. This fascinating natural area is part of a seven-hundred-square-mile swamp in southeastern Georgia and northern Florida. Visitors can rent boats and canoes for travels into the quiet and beautiful Okefenokee. Although alligators are quite visible, the shy creatures usually flee at the slightest human noise. Even so, they can be quite dangerous and should be avoided at all times. The U.S. Fish and Wildlife Service operates an interpretation center where exhibits and dioramas afford fascinating glimpses of this home to great blue herons, American wood storks, red-cockaded woodpeckers, sand hill cranes, robins, hawks, owls, bald eagles, and dozens of other birds. Boardwalks and towers permit visitors to observe typical swamp environments.

Before ending the tour, the traveler should visit the Chesser Family Homestead within the refuge. The U.S. Fish and Wildlife Service has preserved the family home of Tom Chesser, a descendant of the Chessers who settled an island in the swamp in the 1850s. Until the late 1930s, when the swamp became a national wildlife refuge, the Chessers lived and worked on the island named for their family. Today descendants of the original Chessers who are on the staff of the refuge take pleasure in discussing farm and family life in the Okefenokee before and after the Civil War. Usually someone is working on a quilt, making soap, or grinding corn as the Chessers have done for generations. The Folkston entrance to the swamp is the only one to feature an Okefenokee farm on its original site. By ending the tour at a typical farm house, the traveler is able to learn about the people who once called the swamp home.

TOUR THREE: THE WIREGRASS TRAIL TO THE COAST

Leave I-16 at Ga. 57 at Aline and continue southeast to the Land of the Golden Isles, through the communities of Cobbtown, Collins, Reidsville, Glennville, Ludowici, Townsend. Beyond Townsend the highway intersects with I-95 near historic Darien.

Travelers who choose this trail may be en route to one of the coastal counties or islands, because many Atlantans have found that Ga. 57 is the shortest of many routes to the Golden Isles. Local governments of Tattnall and Long Counties persuaded the Department of Transportation to designate the seventy-nine miles of highway from I-16 to I-95 as the Wiregrass Trail. They are eager for travelers to stop, because they are convinced that towns like Reidsville, Glennville, and Ludowici have much to offer. Once off the interstate highway, travelers may find this pleasant journey through farmlands, forests, and interesting small towns as rewarding as the destination itself.

One of the unique features of this region is that it retains much of the natural beauty and charm that attracted early settlers, many of them Scots. Anglers, canoeists, and campers who discover the Ohoopee River, with its distinctive dark waters, white sand, and moss-covered cypress, agree that the environment is unmatched among the rivers of Georgia.

Those who travel this way will have an opportunity to experience the Altamaha River, which parallels the Wiregrass Trail. Its swamps and tributaries provide nesting and feeding for many endangered species of birds and animals.

The exit for Ga. 57 south is marked "Wiregrass Trail." The twenty-mile segment from the interstate to Reidsville passes through three small towns: Aline, Cobbtown, and Collins. **Cobbtown** reached its

EARLY DAYS IN THE OKEFENOKEE

Neighborhood picnic, Suwanee Lake, 1929

Family baptism in Billys Lake, 1921

Making cane syrup in the "syrup shed," Chessers Island

The Lee family home on Billys Island, 1912

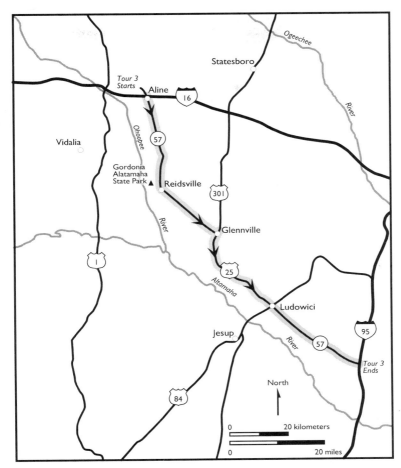

Southeast Georgia, Tour Three

height of commercial activity in the 1920s when it was a center for traveling salesmen and cotton brokers. Some of the buildings now standing echo this era. **Collins**, a small railroad center in the early twentieth century, also bears evidence of an earlier prosperity. Several turn-of-the-century houses have generous front porches and pressed tin roofs. Another attractive community located six miles from Collins on Ga. 292E is **Manassas**. Some handsome houses are here, as is a typical rural post office of the 1920s. An intriguing bit of local history is that in the 1890s some 250 Croatan or Lumbee Indians lived here. They had moved to Manassas from Robeson County, North Carolina, and their mission was to harvest pine resin for once-active turpentine distilleries. Most of Manassas has been nominated as a National Register Historic District.

Near the entrance to **Reidsville**, county seat of Tattnall County, is the Gordonia-Alatamaha State Park, featuring picnicking, swimming, fishing, boating, paddle-boating, camping (tent and trailer), a nine-hole golf course, and a miniature golf range. The park owes its name to a significant regional plant, the *Franklinia alatamaha*, or Lost Gordonia. Bartram discovered the plant in the 1770s and named it for his good friend Benjamin Franklin. (The only *Franklinia* in cultivation today are offspring of cuttings propagated by the Philadelphia Arboretum.)

Reidsville converted a National Register property, the Alexander Hotel, into its welcome center. Built in 1892, the two-story structure has Victorian elements and has a pressed-tin roof. A charming wooden structure, it is complete with a rambling picket fence. On the second weekend in October Reidsville hosts a hobby and craft show. Near the hotel is the Tattnall County courthouse (1902).

Reidsville's somewhat larger sister is **Glennville**, where a historic public school building has been turned into a new museum to introduce the land and the people of the region. The town's population and commercial activity have increased as a result of the large number of personnel at nearby Fort Stewart Military Reservation. Farmers in the Glennville area have capitalized on the Vidalia onion market. On the second Saturday of each May, the town hosts the Glennville Sweet Onion Festival. From April through June, Bland Farms (tour two) invites visitors to see their large harvesting and sorting operations. Sweet onions are readily available in Glennville from April through July. The traveler who ventures to this onion farm is just a stone's throw from the Big Hammock Natural and Wildlife Areas on the Altamaha River (alternate tour two).

The Altamaha provides a serene environment for naturalists, birdwatchers, and anglers. Freshwater species of fish include large mouth bass, redbreast, bluegill, shellcracker, crappie, and catfish (both channel and flathead). The river's distinctive features—sandbars, dead rivers, and swamps—should be experienced firsthand and can be at a fish camp that rents boats and cabins. It is located between Glennville and Ludowici near historic Beard's Bluff, a fortification during the American Revolution. The entrance from U.S. 301S is the first road to the right after one leaves Tattnall County.

Ludowici is the seat of Long County and the county's only incorporated area. In the early twentieth century, the Ludowici Brick and Tile Company employed hundreds of people to produce a distinctive clay roofing material, Ludowici tile. The clay came from the region, but William Ludowici may have learned the manufacturing techniques in his native Germany. The roofing tiles were especially popular among contractors in booming Florida. Many homes in Ludowici still display these distinctive roofs. To keep the memory alive, the town has roofed several information shelters with the tile, and the library offers a special exhibit about Ludowici tile. Beyond this community the Wiregrass Trail (Ga. 57) cuts through twenty-five miles of pine forests and sand hills that resemble dunes and beaches of the ancient sea.

Those who travel the Wiregrass Trail have an unparalleled opportunity to retrace a significant portion of William Bartram's travels in coastal Georgia, for the region he described closely parallels portions of today's Wiregrass Trail. Bartram provided a remarkable glimpse into the Altamaha River Valley in his classic work *Travels Through North and South Carolina, Georgia, East and West Florida*. He carefully documented the natural features of the region, including some now-extinct plants. His book also thoughtfully depicts the people with whom he lived and conversed, including European settlers and American Indians.

Remarkably, if Bartram were to revisit this region today, he would find relatively few changes as far as the river valley is concerned. Only one industry, located on the south side of the river near Jesup, is within eyesight or earshot of the modern traveler. The "Bartram corridor" is refreshingly undeveloped for an uninterrupted stretch of twenty-five miles between Ludowici and I-95, save for Townsend, a tiny community located near the interstate highway.

In addition to running parallel to Bartram's travels in the Altamaha River valley, the larger Wiregrass Trail also encompasses much of the flora and fauna he described. The tour ends at I-95 a few miles above Darien, the first stop in the Land of the Golden Isles.

TOUR FOUR: THE HEART OF SOUTHEAST GEORGIA

Exit I-16 at Soperton; south on Ga. 15 to Vidalia; continue on Ga. 15 to U.S. 1, which on the way to the Okefenokee Swamp passes through Baxley, Alma, Dixie Union, Waycross; follow U.S. 82E or U.S. 1 to the entrance to the Okefenokee Swamp Park on Ga. 177. From Waycross take U.S. 84 west to Homerville; take U.S. 441 south to Fargo; follow Ga. 177 east to Stephen C. Foster State Park.

A number of main roads, including U.S. 1 and U.S. 280, lead to Toombs County and its two major towns, Vidalia and Lyons. Although Vidalia is the larger of the two, Lyons is the county seat. Both are approximately fifteen miles south of I-16.

The name **Vidalia** has been immortalized by the famous sweet onion that is grown abundantly in Toombs and nearby counties. During the last of April and the beginning of May each year, visitors join local residents in a ten-day celebration, the Vidalia Onion Festival, that includes farm tours, golf tournaments, music, food booths, and an arts and crafts fair. Vidalia also has year-round amenities. The

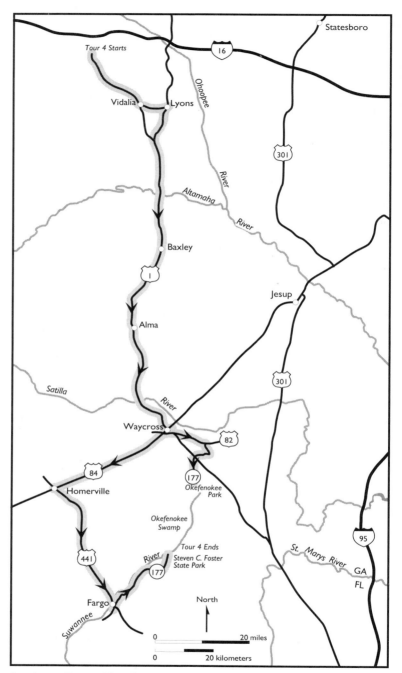

Southeast Georgia, Tour Four

Altama Museum of Art and History has several significant collections, including twenty-four first edition, hand-colored prints by John James Audubon, and a sizable collection of Staffordshire porcelain. Genealogical researchers know Vidalia as the home of a large compilation of historical materials and manuscripts, the Ladson Genealogical and Historical Library.

Travelers to Vidalia will find several antique shops and over forty acres of parks and picnic areas. An itinerary for visitors to the downtown area should include three houses listed on the National Register of Historic Places: the Brazell House (1911, location of the Altama Museum of Art and History), the Peterson-Wilbanks House (1916, neoclassical architecture), and the Leader and Rosansky House (1903), all three on Jackson Street. The municipal building displays a small New Deal mural, "Town Store and Post Office" (1938), by Daniel Celentano.

The five-mile drive from Vidalia to **Lyons** passes through a popular shopping and restaurant district. A New Deal relief, "Wild Duck and Deer," by the Italian artist Albino Manca, was installed in the post office on North State Street in 1942. Antiques and collectibles can be found in several stores. For a number of years the Preread Bookstore (open Wednesday through Saturday) has attracted travelers. The historic Lyons depot serves as a local museum and tourist information center. A roadside sign outside Lyons calls attention to the city limits of **Santa Claus**.

Fewer than twenty miles south of Lyons on U.S. 1, the ribbon of highway once again weaves through green forests that frame blue skies on the horizon. Occasional clumps of wiregrass surround the trunks of flourishing pine trees. Seldom does any man-made structure disturb this pastoral scene. The road runs gently over sand hills that grow in size as the traveler encounters something unique to this section: the backwater swamps of the Altamaha River, formed by the confluence of the Oconee and Ocmulgee Rivers twenty-five miles upstream from the U.S. 1 bridge. The Altamaha is the end of Toombs County and the beginning of Appling. On the Appling side, facing west, is Piney Bluff, a steep cliff fringed with pines and gum trees. To the east, however, huge concrete funnels force steam upward, forming momentary clouds. The lonely giant structure seems out of its element.

In fact the great river itself made possible this Georgia Power Company nuclear plant. Edwin I. Hatch Nuclear Plant Visitors Center's attractive exhibits provide a historical overview of the river whose depth and breadth provided the only feasible means of transporting a giant reactor to its destination. The center also introduces for visitors of all ages the process of making and distributing electricity.

Plant Hatch provides a picnic and observation area on the south side of the river next to the bridge near Piney Bluff. Here one can observe swift waters whose currents once carried Indian dugouts to the region of "Tama" near the coast. (Altamaha is said to mean "the way to Tama.") Georgia Power is one of only two industries located anywhere near the banks of the entire river. (The other is at Jesup, some fifty miles downstream.) These exceptions notwithstanding, the river both appears and runs now as it always has—freely and wild. The state's Bullard Creek Wildlife Management Area plays a major role in maintaining the natural environment in Appling and Jeff Davis Counties.

The "plain people" who settled Appling County and its county seat, **Baxley**, in the early nineteenth century knew secrets of the forests, swamps, and river. The best introduction to these not-so-simple folk is *Lamb in His Bosom* (1936), the first Pulitzer Prize–winning novel by a Georgian. The author was Caroline Miller, whose home in downtown Baxley has been restored as a private residence. The town also has renovated a historic school building, which is now the Appling County Heritage Center, a museum and interpretation center for the history of the Altamaha River Valley and Appling County. A room in the center introduces the author, rural Georgia in the early 1900s, and the people about whom Caroline Miller wrote with compassion.

While agriculture and forest products are important components in Appling County's economy, only a few remnants of the naval stores industries remain. At one time gathering pine resin and distilling turpentine provided employment for hundreds of workers. The naval stores tradition continues in Appling County today in a manufacturing plant owned by Axso Noble Coatings, a company with headquarters in Holland. In fact, the plant in Baxley is said to be the only commercial turpentine distillery in the United States. Visitors can arrange a tour. Outside the distillery, in the pine forests along the byroads of Southeast Georgia, visitors can see trees that have been slashed and tapped to gather resin. At times the pungent scent of fresh resin permeates the air.

Seventeen miles south of Baxley on U.S. 1 is **Alma**. Local signs refer to Alma–Bacon County. The county is Bacon, and its only town is the county seat, Alma. Alma was a railroad stop for locomotives that steamed to and from major cities in Florida. A modern industrial park in Alma is comprised of several major manufacturing companies. The scenic Satilla River provides boating and fishing.

The very best time to visit Alma is the last weekend in June. Then the town literally shuts down and hosts the annual three-day Blueberry Festival, highlighted by craft demonstrations, food booths, a parade, entertainment, and, naturally, blueberry picking. Travelers who arrive in July will find several pick-your-own blueberry farms catering to visitors. The blueberry's importance to Bacon County is manifest in the logo of the Chamber of Commerce: three blueberries glistening in the center of a sunburst.

The entrance to **Waycross**, thirty-two miles south of Alma on U.S. 1, runs parallel to a railroad track. As the road and track continue to the heart of town, the traveler realizes that the railroad runs toward a giant intersection of rail lines. Much of the town's early activity had to do with its crucial position in the transportation industry. The Okefenokee Heritage Center has assembled an impressive collection of steam engines, railroad buildings, and artifacts that bring to life the vital era of rail transportation. The visitor who begins a tour of Waycross at the Heritage Center will find other exhibits about Native Americans and early settlers. Near the Heritage Center is a museum dedicated to the role of southern forests in the economy and culture of Georgia and the nation. Southern Forest World provides hands-on exhibits and audiovisual educational programs. The visitor has a rare opportunity to climb stairs inside a giant loblolly pine tree.

Waycross is the seat of Ware County. According to a slogan used by the local chamber of commerce, Waycross is "the largest city, in the largest county, in the largest state east of the Mississippi." Much of the county consists of the Okefenokee National Wildlife Refuge.

The most popular attraction here is the Okefenokee Swamp Park, a privately administered entrance to the swamp. Located a dozen miles from town on U.S. 1 south, the park provides several interpretive demonstrations of wildlife. The alligator zoo allows visitors to view the reptiles in a natural habitat. Guided boat tours take visitors on a trip into the swamp, explaining history and wildlife along the way. The park also has restored a typical swamp farmstead, complete with cabin, outbuildings, and a well sweep.

Nearby Laura S. Walker State Park has camp sites and picnic shelters scattered in secluded spots throughout the park. Visitors may enjoy fishing and water skiing on the large freshwater lake and hiking a well-marked nature trail. There is also a large swimming pool. The endangered red-cockaded woodpecker nests within this spacious park.

Another site worth visiting is immediately south of Waycross—Obediah's Okefenok. Here is the restored, authentic 1850s homestead of "The King of the Okefenokee," Obediah Barber, who died at the age of 84 in 1909. It is an excellent example of the everyday life of early pioneers who established self-sufficient farm operations in the Okefenokee prior to the Civil War. (Tour two includes another restoration near Folkston on Chessers Island.) The staff here can enthrall visitors with tales about the man who stood over six-and-one-half-feet tall and who was the father of twenty children. One story tells of how he once single-handedly killed a menacing bear without benefit of a firearm. There is also a small zoo of local animals, both domestic and wild.

Travelers who have come this far should spend time inside the Okefenokee itself. To reach the southwestern entrance, one must travel from Waycross to Homerville to Fargo. **Homerville**, roughly halfway to Fargo, is a good stopping place. The seat of Clinch County is an attractive South Georgia town nestled among the tall pines that cover 97 percent of the land. That is a lot of pine trees, considering that Clinch County is one of the largest counties in Georgia.

Residents refer to Homerville as "a honey of a place," because honey production is a major business enterprise here. South Georgians are familiar with the unmatched rich, sweet, and aromatic honey that can be purchased in Homerville. Bees obtain nectar from the gallberry and other native plants of the Okefenokee to produce a distinctive honey that has little in common with clover or orange blossom honey. Another delicacy associated with Homerville since 1936 is barbecue, cooked in a log kitchen near the heart of downtown.

Visitors often come to Homerville specifically to use the extensive collections of the Huxford Genealogical Society. The library, open to the public, has large holdings for those whose roots are in Georgia and other eastern states, a microfilm library with resources for the entire United States, and a large collection of genealogical magazines and local history books. The society also provides instruction in using genealogical materials. A popular attraction in Homerville is the Timberland Jubilee Festival during the first weekend in October each year. The event features timber exhibits, arts, crafts, foods, and entertainment.

The entrance to the Stephen C. Foster State Park is twenty-eight miles south of Homerville on U.S. 441. This southwestern entrance to the Okefenokee is remote. However, it is the best entrance for those who wish to penetrate the swamp to observe its natural environment. Highways in the Okefenokee region are both straight and flat, unlike the undulating roads through the sand hills of Southeast Georgia. Shortly before reaching the park's entrance, the traveler crosses the Suwannee River, popularized by the nineteenth-century composer for whom the park is named. Campers and picnickers may wish to purchase supplies in the small town of Fargo before entering the park.

The Georgia Department of Natural Resources maintains the park, air-conditioned efficiency cottages, tent and trailer sites, picnic tables, and day shelters. An interpretive center introduces numerous bird, mammal, reptile, and amphibian species. It also provides a brief history of the people who once lived on secluded islands within the Okefenokee before it became the Okefenokee Wildlife Refuge in the 1930s.

The reason to travel here, of course, is to explore the swamp. It is possible to use twenty-five miles of waterways via motorboats, canoes, or johnboats that can be rented for day trips. The explorer soon recognizes the distinctive environments of the Okefenokee. Dark expanses of water, framed with moss-festooned cypress and cypress knees, mirror tall trees and clouds. Lily pads seem to float freely, providing temporary homes for small turtles, frogs, and insects. Areas called prairies appear to be fields of tall grass. Some of the peat islands float and shake when people walk on them. (Tradition says that Okefenokee means "land of the trembling earth.") For those who do not wish to venture into the swamp waters, the park has developed a one-half mile Trembling Earth Nature Trail that covers some of the swamp's unique environments.

Playing the role of tourist sometimes degenerates into plodding well-beaten paths. Hoping to see the prescribed sites, tourists retrace the familiar. Travelers, on the other hand, visit places, meet people, and experience the environment. The final destination of the Heart of Southeast Georgia Tour, like the Coastal Plain Tour, is the Okefenokee Swamp. This tour, however, does not stop at the edge. Rather, it allows one to get close to the vital center of the great swamp. Certainly it is off the beaten path. Yet one who takes time to venture into the Okefenokee will begin to understand why many regard it as a natural wonder of the modern world. While southeastern Georgia may not have another swamp like this one, it does hold a healthy share of natural areas, small towns, and people—all of which can enrich the one who "sees what he sees."

COASTAL GEORGIA

James Kilgo # TIDEWATER HERITAGE

Across the Savannah on I-95, south into Georgia. If you don't stop, you can make it to Florida in less than two hours. The country on the left is the coast—a level plain ten miles wide that disintegrates on its seaward edge into marsh, inlet, and island.

The interstate highway is not a natural boundary, but it is an old one. When Gen. James Oglethorpe arrived at Yamacraw Bluff, the present site of Savannah, in 1733, he found an Indian trail leading south to the mouth of the Altamaha. Two years later Highland Scots established the village of Darien, and the trail became a thoroughfare. Two hundred years after that it was paved over and called U.S. 17, a major route for Northerners seeking the winter sun. When the folks in Washington decided to connect the eastern United States with Disney World, they ran a straight, four-lane chute alongside old 17. Sun-baked and broad, I-95 offers little scenery to distract air-conditioned motorists and their families. They can drive across Georgia without noticing a thing. From the air the traffic resembles opposing columns of ants, intent and undeviating.

A light plane at five thousand feet is not a bad vantage point for an overview of what those tourists miss: the shaded city of Savannah, snug against the winding river; the salt marsh coastline, green or brown depending on the season, and veined with silver creeks; and then, as your plane flies south, the chain of barrier islands, live oak dark in the shining sea. Their names, read from a map, sound like an incantation: Tybee, Wassaw, Ossabaw, St. Catherines, Blackbeard, Sapelo, St. Simons, Jekyll, and Cumberland.

No other state can claim such a coastline. Not only does it consist entirely of islands, but most of them, because they remained until recently in private ownership, seem almost as wild today as they were when the first Europeans beheld them 450 years ago. The key word here is _almost_. What keeps even the most natural of the islands from being pristine is history. From the first Spanish explorer in 1525, the Georgia coast has been the scene of repeated attempts at development: Franciscan missions, colonial towns and the forts to protect them, rice fields, cotton fields, slave cabins, and the mansions of millionaires. Fragments of these efforts lie all about—some preserved, most swallowed up in vegetation and returning to the earth—but whether they are visible or not, the coast everywhere resonates with history. It is steeped in its past.

Having never lived on the Georgia coast, I cannot speak with the authority of a native, but travel writing, as it's called, has its own advantages, for both writer and reader, notably the fresh point of view. Yet I am not a total stranger either. With roots in the low country of South Carolina, I have felt at home strolling through the shaded squares of Savannah or walking the broad, white beach of Sapelo, and the accents of the people have sounded friendly to my ears. But most hospitable of all has been that spirit of the past which hangs like a gauzy atmosphere upon the land, as palpable as the heat and humidity.

In *Praying for Sheetrock* Melissa Fay Greene says of the Georgia coast, "Coastal people understand history personally, the way religious people do, the way ancient people did. They own history in a way lost to most Americans." I agree. Let others tout the recreational opportunities of the islands or write the natural history of the salt marsh. I will speak of ghosts—the glimmering presence of those whose lives and deaths hallowed the places where they lived.

GUALE AND THE SPANISH MISSIONS

On the wall of our den here in the Georgia Piedmont hangs a large oil canvas by June Ball of a Sapelo Island landscape. A gifted interpreter of the coastal scene, Ball has depicted the burning air, the dazzling sugar-white sand of Nannygoat Beach, the deep green, shadowed live oak forest that stands inland from the dunes. So palpable is the shimmering atmosphere that the painting often becomes for me a portal, and I find myself knee-deep in surf, facing the dunes and the dark forest beyond—the very scene beheld by Spanish explorers when the first lumbering galleons wallowed along the coasts of the off-shore islands.

What they found when they landed—and land they did, on island after island—was a jungle wilderness, zooming with biting flies, crawling with ticks and chiggers, and, for most of the year, steamy hot. Many of the islands are still that way, or that way again. Wassaw, Ossabaw, St. Catherines, Blackbeard, Cumberland, and much of Sapelo have reverted from intensive agriculture to a wild, pre-agrarian state, or at least to a close approximation of such, making it easy for the visitor to imagine what the Spaniards found.

Though each of the islands is ecologically unique, they share a common geological history, a plant and animal life, and weather. Wherever the Spaniards landed, the beach was wide and white, the tall, wind-sculpted dunes fringed with sea oats. Behind the dunes lay a sandy trough where yucca grew and prickly pear, yaupon holly, saw palmetto, and stunted wax myrtle trees. Here and there along this inner zone lay brackish lagoons, feeding grounds for egrets and herons, ibises and woodstorks, anhingas and gallinules. On higher ground to the west stood the ancient forest, park-like groves of live oaks with massive, twisting limbs that touched the ground and lifted again in a muted, cathedral light, or gloomy stands of slash pine where the ground was hidden by saw palmetto so dense that the explorers could not see their feet or hear, because of the rustle of the stiff, fan-shaped fronds, the warning buzz of a diamondback. Spanish moss and yellow jasmine hung all about; alligators basked in still ponds; and deer bounded away, disappearing with a flash of tail down narrow green aisles. After two or three miles, the company emerged from the shadows of the forest, as the poet Sidney Lanier would do several hundred years later, and beheld a sunny expanse of rippling salt marsh, a vast green meadow that stretched away to the mainland miles to the west.

Though it has been widely believed that Spain's interest in the New World was limited to conquest and gold, the purpose of the missions along the southeastern coast was to secure territory for permanent settlement. The thrust was military, but the enemies were France and England, not native America. In fact, Spanish policy forbade making war on the Indians, and for good reason: Spain hoped to "civilize" them into good Spanish citizens. To accomplish that aim, they had first to convert them to Christianity. Hence the Jesuit and later the Franciscan priests who went out with the soldiers.

The natives they found on the sea islands called themselves Guale, a name for both themselves and their land, which extended from the mouth of the Ogeechee south to the Newport River and included the islands of Ossabaw and St. Catherines. Evidence from archaeology shows that the Guale were a Muskogean people, related by language to inland tribes whose descendants would become the Creek confederation. From early reports, the Muskogeans were a handsome people who supported themselves by hunting, fishing, gathering, and to some extent planting. They lived in round huts of wattle and daub built around a central plaza. The capital of Guale, situated on St. Catherines, was probably such a town.

Little was known about the Spanish missions and their impact upon native culture until the last quarter of the twentieth century, when two major discoveries revealed much of that encounter. The first was the excavation of the mission Santa Catalina de Guale on St. Catherines by a team from the American Museum of Natural History. Until then it was known only that the Spanish established missions on several of the islands—St. Simons, Sapelo, and St. Catherines for sure—but none had been located. In the mid-1970s archaeologist David Hurst Thomas from the Museum of Natural History came to St.

Catherines. By tedious and painstaking labor, he and his team eventually found what they were looking for—indisputable evidence of a seventeenth-century Franciscan mission, Santa Catalina de Guale.

The second discovery was made by a young anthropologist named John Worth. Searching through archives in Spain, he came upon a trove of seventeenth-century documents, written by Franciscans, relating the story of Santa Catalina. Combined with Thomas's findings, these documents allow scholars to understand for the first time what happened on the Georgia coast when Europeans encountered Indians.

Though Lucas Vasquez de Ayllon attempted a colony as early as 1526 (probably on Sapelo, Thomas believes), the mission efforts originated out of St. Augustine in the 1570s. The usual method began with an audience between Franciscans and the mico or cacique of an Indian town. If the mico embraced the faith, his people followed, and the Spaniards went to work on the mission. Early attempts at Santa Catalina antagonized the natives, but in 1605 the Bishop of Cuba baptized Guale caciques, and the following year 286 Indians converted to Christianity. The mission, as John Worth explained to me, would have been built alongside the Guale town according to a template prescribed by the Royal Ordinances of Philip II—"a direct attempt," Thomas says, "to transplant a 'civilized' way of life upon America's wilderness." The remains of that mission are what Thomas and his crew found when they began digging in 1979. "Our excavations," he writes,

> demonstrate the degree to which Philip II's Ordinances were used to plan Georgia's first known European settlement. Public buildings were laid out along a rigid pattern, as stipulated by Ordinance 110. At Santa Catalina, a rectangular plaza defined the center of the complex (Ordinance 112), flanked on one side by the mission church (Ordinance 124 . . .), on the other by a friary (Ordinances 118, 119, 121). The plaza was surrounded by (and separated from) the Guale *pueblo;* "in the plaza no lots shall be assigned to private individuals; instead they shall be used [only] for the building of the church and royal houses" (Ordinance 126). Housing in the *pueblo* consisted of rectangular buildings, perhaps separated by "streets." Native American structures were apparently built as an extension of this initial gridwork.

One could hardly express more clearly the dominant fact of the European presence in the New World: a rigid form, paradigm of the western sense of order and control, imposed upon a culture and a landscape—a culture, moreover, that lived, as far as we can tell, in harmony with its environment.

The inevitable question is why did the Guale submit to Spanish authority? The minute they were baptized they entered not only the Kingdom of Heaven but the Spanish Empire as well, becoming colonial citizens subject to the rule of the church as well as to such secular institutions as the labor draft, which required that one-fourth of the single male population, as chosen by the caciques, go each year to work in the fields around St. Augustine. While this system was not slavery—the natives were paid in beads and trinkets—it surely must have been an unwelcome disruption of their natural rhythms.

Among the answers given are, first, obedience to the cacique, who had converted in order to strengthen his power among his people, and second, the appeal of the highly esteemed religious medals and other paraphernalia available to converts. While these motives may well have been at work, however, it appears that many of the American Indians living and working within the shadow of Santa Catalina were devout Christians. Though we cannot tell exactly what they understood Christianity to be, records show that in times of conflict with unconverted Indians, they remained loyal to the friars, and when they died they were buried in holy ground, recipients of the sacraments.

My efforts to visit St. Catherines in the summer of 1994 were unsuccessful. The Noble Foundation, which owns the island, is wary of publicity. I suppose I should be glad of that. Because of their vigilance, St. Catherines remains today, I'm told, the wildest, most unspoiled of Georgia's barrier islands. I wouldn't have seen much anyway, I learned later, not of the Santa Catalina dig. That project is completed, the site covered over with sand—no different in appearance from dozens of other clearings between marshland and forest on any of several islands with which I am familiar.

So I content myself with June Ball's painting. The scene is Sapelo, true, but it might be St. Catherines. She has painted there, and who is to say that remembered impressions of that island did not affect her perception of the landscape of Sapelo? Whether or not, I can make it St. Catherines when I want to and just as easily imagine, beyond the live oak trees, on the unseen side of that unseen island, a busy mission town. In the long rectangular plaza, naked bodies, copper-skinned, the flash of sun from the mirrors of Spanish armor, long brown robes that sweep the flat, sandy ground. In my vision the people seem content. Some of the Guale, in fact, are clothed in rags of European dress—a hat here, pantaloons there—and the shadow of a towering cypress cross falls upon them all.

I don't know what to make of that scene: On the one hand, an ancient aboriginal culture regulated by streets and squares, rules and rituals; on the other, the disease-stricken natives dying in Christ, as the Church says, decked out in their medals of confirmation, requesting burial in consecrated ground.

When David Hurst Thomas uncovered the bones of these people, he found, lodged among ribs, skulls, and femurs, the medals they had

worn with such delight. Thomas was concerned at first about offending biological descendants, were any to be found, but records show
that after the fall of Santa Catalina in the 1680s—a fall precipitated by
the British presence in South Carolina and not by hostile Indians—a
few Guale allowed themselves to be absorbed by the Yamasee people;
others followed the friars to St. Augustine. When the Spaniards departed Florida in 1763, the eighty-three Indians who lived at the mission—including perhaps descendants of the Guale—went with them.

Thomas turned next to the Church, contacting the Bishop of Savannah, first as to the propriety of excavating what once was holy ground
and second as to the ultimate disposition of Indian remains. The
Bishop approved the dig. The Church was interested in learning more
about this early mission effort to the natives of Georgia. And when
that part of the dig was completed in 1984, the Bishop came to St.
Catherines to reconsecrate the mission cemetery, interring again the
remains of the faithful.

SAVANNAH

The historic district of Savannah is a two-square-mile museum of Old
South architecture. You may drive through it if you like, but it is designed for a slower pace. Better to park your car and walk. Start at Forsyth Park, on the southern edge, and head north up Bull. The street
will remind you of a tunnel, straight and narrow, with a roof of inter-
twining live oak branches. One block and you enter a small square.
Enclosed by a hedge of azalea, carpeted with fescue, it feels like a
green room, intimate and inviting. This is Monterey, so named, according to a marker, to commemorate the Battle of Monterey, in which
young men from Savannah fell, but the shaft of marble in the center
honors Count Casimir Pulaski, the Polish general killed in the Battle
of Savannah, fighting for American independence.

Monterey Square has a nineteenth-century, small-town charm that
you don't expect to find in an age of Portman towers and six-lane
thoroughfares. And there are twenty more of them, though few if any
as lovely as this. Twenty more, plus Forsyth Park and the Colonial
Cemetery, laid out in a grid of mathematical precision, elegantly landscaped, lovingly restored. If the historic district reminds you of a
movie set, that's because you've seen it several times on the screen.

The restoration and preservation of Savannah is a story of victory
for the good guys—triumph over those interests that are always willing to barter the past—the irreplaceable heritage of a place—for a
quick and temporary buck. If you wonder how Savannah managed to
save so much while other towns and cities failed, turn to the left. You
will be facing two houses of two of the people most responsible. The
handsome red brick mansion is Mercer House, so called because it

Forsyth Park, Savannah

was built by the grandfather of Johnny Mercer, though the songwriter himself never lived there. In recent years it was the home of the notorious Jim Williams, whose lurid story is the subject of *Midnight in the Garden of Good and Evil*, by John Berendt. An antiques dealer from middle Georgia, Williams came to Savannah just as the preservation movement was gathering steam. Soon he was buying and restoring dilapidated houses in the historic district. Mercer House was his final and crowning achievement. But it was Williams's next-door neighbors, Leopold and Emma Adler, whose energy and vision had helped invigorate the movement to begin with.

Like many fine old neighborhoods throughout the South, the residential area of downtown Savannah by the 1950s had become a slum. Great Regency and Greek Revival houses of nineteenth-century factors and cotton brokers had been cut up into tenements, and prostitutes worked the narrow streets. The squares, worn bare of grass, turned muddy or dusty depending on the weather, and the city cut fire lanes through those that lay along major traffic arteries. About the only feature not destroyed was the grid design of streets and squares.

The idea of restoring and preserving such an appalling ruin might have daunted the most idealistic crusader, but a small group of citizens established the Historic Savannah Foundation and took on the task one property at a time. In an article written for the magazine *Antiques* in 1967, Leopold Adler says that the foundation saved the Davenport House in 1954 and soon thereafter the Owens-Thomas House. What he does not tell is the story of his rescue of Marshall Row—a building of Savannah gray brick row houses on Oglethorpe Avenue— a feat that he initiated by a dramatic eleventh-hour intervention. John Berendt cites that action as the real beginning of historic preservation in Savannah. By 1968, as a result of the efforts of Historic Savannah, eight hundred buildings had been saved from the wrecking ball.

As you walk north on Bull toward Madison Square, the work of the preservationists seems complete. The narrow old houses stand crowded and close to the sidewalk, their pastel facades often cracked and stained, but they observe a patrician decorum. You are welcome to walk our streets, they seem to say, and please feel free to pause and admire us, but don't forget that you are tourists, and do respect our privacy. There may be a small, exquisite garden behind that ficus-covered wall, but it is for the pleasure of the house.

The tourists are easy to spot. By their tentative expressions they look as though they are walking through a museum. And I, indistinguishable from the crowd, approach Madison Square, looking up the barrels of the twin antique cannons that guard it against invasion from the south. That's where the Spanish were when Oglethorpe landed on Yamacraw Bluff in 1733. A small plaque at the base of the cannon on the right catches my eye. I am standing on the spot, I read, at which the original road to Darien commenced; the Yamasee cacique Tomochichi showed Oglethorpe the way.

Tomochichi should be honored as one of the founders of the Georgia colony. Without his assistance and support, it is doubtful that Oglethorpe's venture would have succeeded. Ninety years old when he and Oglethorpe met on the bluff, the old cacique was still tall enough to impress observers, and he was in full command of his powers. The lower Savannah was Yamasee country, but there was room on the bluff for the British. Oglethorpe in turn promised peaceful trade with Tomochichi's people. Communicating through Mary Musgrove, a woman of mixed blood, the two leaders became not only allies but close friends. When Oglethorpe returned to England, Tomochichi and his entourage accompanied him. They received a royal welcome, and Tomochichi's nephew was given a gold watch.

Madison Square, however, honors Revolution hero Sergeant Jasper, a young South Carolinian who like Pulaski died in the Battle of Savannah. A fine bronze statue portrays the soldier at the instant he received his fatal wound.

I continue north, cross busy Liberty Street, and enter another square. History is coming at me from all sides, buildings and markers, more than I can assimilate. I plop down on a park bench. I have figured out by now that the name of the square has nothing to do with the person honored by the monument or statue in the center. This is Chippewa, so called to commemorate a battle fought in Canada in the War of 1812. But the bronze statue in the middle is that of General Oglethorpe, just as he must have appeared on the February day in 1733 when he first stood right here on Yamacraw Bluff.

The statue, considered the finest in Savannah, is the work of Daniel Chester French, the noted sculptor who carved the marble Lincoln in the Lincoln Memorial. His Oglethorpe is magisterial, an eighteenth-century gentleman-soldier, standing like a man fully confident of his ability to found a colony. From his pedestal he looks south, commanding the town he designed, and a palmetto frond bends beneath his heel—a nice touch.

A wino lies sprawled on a bench to my left—one of Savannah's homeless—and across the square an old man is feeding squirrels. On this sultry summer morning he wears a coat and tie, but his trousers are mid-calf length, full and loose, like clown pants. He reaches into what looks like a gym bag for another handful of peanuts. If that thing is full he could feed every squirrel in Savannah. But he doesn't like pigeons. He keeps poking at them with his cane.

James Edward Oglethorpe was a wealthy officer, unmarried and in his early thirties when he became a trustee of the Georgia Colony, which at the time was no more than a charter granted by the Crown to a group of entrepreneurs. England was glad to establish a presence in the disputed territory between Carolina and Spanish Florida. The trustees were interested in the colony's producing such commodities as wine and silk. But Oglethorpe, perhaps more enthusiastically than his partners, envisioned an opportunity for the poor among his countrymen to escape debt-ridden lives by farming small tracts in a tightly organized community. To that end, he successfully encouraged the forbidding of slavery in Georgia, not because he opposed the institution on moral grounds but because he attributed to it an indolence among whites that he had noticed in Charles Town. He also outlawed rum. Georgians were expected to stay sober and to work hard. He intended to be on hand to see that they did.

He brought over the first shipload himself—114 men, women, and children—and dropped them off at Port Royal while he scouted the Savannah River country for a site. After securing the assistance of Tomochichi's Yamasees, Oglethorpe returned for his people, and then, back at Yamacraw Bluff, he put his design into action.

That design consisted of not only rules and regulations but also a plan for laying out the town. No sooner did he land than he transferred the design from paper to the pine-covered bluff. A drawing made that year by Peter Gordon, one of Oglethorpe's officials, provides an excellent view of the bluff as it must have appeared after a few months' labor: a large flat clearing in the forest marked off in a grid of streets and squares. In each block and around each square are narrow lots, some seventy-five of which are already occupied by houses, though Oglethorpe himself lived in the tent that appears in the foreground throughout his first stay in Georgia.

The Gordon drawing makes clear what you do not see as you walk the shaded streets of the historic district—that the design of the town is a projection of its author's neoclassical and military mind, his obsession with order. An anthropologist named Kathleen Deagan has described the old Spanish mission plan as a "rigid organization of space by a formal sixteenth-century template." That description applies just as well to Oglethorpe's plan for Savannah two hundred years later. In fact, the two designs may well have had the same source. David Hurst Thomas writes, "Like the urban planners of Savannah, Spanish visionaries turned to the classics; both, for instance, drew upon the ancient writings of Vitruvius."

I like to imagine Tomochichi and his people watching from the shade as Oglethorpe's workers laid out the streets and squares. No telling what they thought—those round-house people—but however they viewed the project, the plan worked well for the colonists, and Savannah grew steadily, easily expanding the grid according to the original pattern as more and more people arrived.

The wino continues to slumber on the bench to my left, oblivious to the founder's stern supervision, but the old man who was feeding squirrels is gone. I get to my feet. Students cross the square, bearded and grubby looking, and earnest young joggers, decked out in bright designer colors, weave through them. A man is sitting on a bench to my right, his face hidden behind a newspaper. Another man on an adjacent bench calls a question to him about the day's events.

Two blocks north, and I enter Wright Square, its center dominated by an ornate monument—marble columns rising at each corner from a base, upon the sides of which are depicted scenes of early railroading. Erected in the 1880s, it commemorates one of the movers and shakers of Victorian Savannah, William Gordon, founder of the Central of Georgia Railroad. The monument stands upon the unmarked grave of Tomochichi.

You hear different versions of the story. Some sources say that the grave had been vandalized long before the Gordon monument was erected, or that the city believed it had. But Emma Adler told me that they had to remove the mound above the Indian's grave in order to build the monument. In either case, the city discovered too late that Tomochichi's remains did in fact lie beneath the center of the square. William Gordon was no doubt an important man, a key figure in the economic recovery of Georgia after the Civil War, and I'm sure he deserves a monument. But there are other squares in Savannah. Here I would prefer a fine bronze of Tomochichi, the Yamasee cacique, lordly atop a marble shaft, looking from the center of Wright Square south toward the figure of his English friend. Instead, there is a granite boulder on the southeast corner. Placed by the Colonial Dames in

1891, it acknowledges the role played by Tomochichi in the founding of the colony.

FANNY KEMBLE AND THE BUTLER PLANTATIONS

Head south out of Darien on old 17, cross the Darien and Butler Rivers, arms of the Altamaha, and there on your right, rising out of a low marshy field, stands a square brick chimney, seventy-five feet tall. If you're not driving too fast to stop for the roadside marker, you'll learn that the chimney is all that is left of a steam-powered rice mill on the Pierce Butler plantation Butler Island; that Pierce Butler was married to the famous English actress Fanny Kemble; and that "during a visit here with her husband in 1839–40 [actually 1838–39] Kemble wrote her *Journal of a Residence on a Georgian Plantation,* which is said to have influenced England against the Confederacy." That was not all, nor by any means the worst, that was said by southerners about Fanny Kemble's book. It was still being reviled in South Carolina a hundred years after its publication.

By fortuitous event, I'm on my way to see Fanny Kemble, or an incarnation of her, on a stage in Brunswick. A drama called *An Audience with Fanny Kemble*—a one-woman performance featuring an actress named Sandi Shackleford—is being staged tonight in a Brunswick theater—Fanny's natural habitat—and I happen to be in town for the occasion.

After her southern sojourn in 1838–39, Fanny never returned from her Philadelphia home to Georgia. She wanted to, even insisted—she was anxious to make corrections in her journal—but her husband and his brother John—absentee owners of eight hundred slaves—forbade it. She had caused too much of a stir the first time. According to Malcolm Bell in his superb study *Major Butler's Legacy,* John argued that her presence on the plantation "was distressing to herself, an annoyance to others, and a danger to the properties."

Now, after 150 years, she's back, and coastal Georgia, black and white, has turned out to see her. The curtain opens upon a Victorian parlor, circa 1848, a time in Fanny's life when her husband has not only divorced her, against her will, but has also embarrassed her by a published statement justifying his action. Fanny is on hand tonight to defend herself.

Ms. Shackleford, with her dark curls massed high on her head, bears such a striking resemblance to pictures of Fanny Kemble that I immediately suspend disbelief. She is Fanny Kemble, and her words are Fanny's words.

Those words—and many more—are available to the reader in a recent paperback edition of the *Journal.* An introduction by John A. Scott explains that when Fanny began taking notes during her residence at Butler Island, she had no intention of publication. Though a moderate abolitionist under the influence of her friend William Ellery Channing, she believed, even years afterward, that publication would violate the circumstances under which she visited the plantations—as the master's wife. By the outbreak of the Civil War, however, Fanny was long since divorced, and the issue of slavery was about to be decided by arms. The *Journal* appeared in 1863, first in England, then in New York. While it hardly affected international diplomacy, it fanned flames both north and south.

The response of southerners for many years was what it has always been to outsiders who bring to southern practices and problems a sense of moral superiority. Fanny Kemble was denounced as a meddling woman who presumed to stand in judgment on matters with which she had only passing acquaintance. To make things worse, they said, she distorted and exaggerated, as Harriet Beecher Stowe did in that dreadful book of hers. How could a foreigner with a strong anti-slavery bias even pretend to present a fair and balanced view? The question is still debated, but in any discussion of the validity of her report, one should remember that the Butler plantations—Butler Island and Hampton Point on the north end of St. Simons—were not typical. Perhaps no single plantation was. There were great variations within the system, depending upon the size of the operation, its location, its major crop, and the attitude of the master. In any case, the Butler plantations seem to have come short of the standard for basic humane treatment of slaves, and the biggest reason appears to have been that the Butlers from the beginning managed their Georgia properties from Philadelphia.

At the time of the Butler family visit, Pierce and his brother John had recently inherited the plantations from their grandfather Maj. Pierce Butler, though they had to change their surnames to do it. Major Butler, an Irish immigrant, had acquired through marriage into a prominent South Carolina family the means to purchase land and slaves, first in his wife's state, then in Georgia. The rice produced on these plantations made him wealthy. He fought in the Revolution, represented South Carolina at the Constitutional Convention, and served as one of the first senators from that state. As he grew older, he spent more and more time at his Philadelphia residence, leaving Butler Island and Hampton Point to the supervision of a man named Roswell King.

King was by most accounts a harsh taskmaster, as was his son Roswell Jr. who succeeded him. The Butlers forbade the breaking up of families by sale, but otherwise the Kings were left to their own devices. They relied heavily on the lash as a means of discipline and, in the interests of profit, withheld some of the meager amenities that might have brought a bit of relief from the misery of working on a rice plantation.

Today you can drive from Darien to Butler Island in less than five minutes, crossing the Darien and Butler Rivers on Highway 17. When the Butler party arrived at Darien on December 3, 1838, there was no road south across the Altamaha estuary. They went by boat, landing at Butler Island almost exactly where U.S. 17 crosses the river, within the shadow of the steam mill chimney.

Fanny describes the landing: "As we neared the bank, the steersman took up a huge conch, and in the barbaric fashion of early times in the highlands, sounded out our approach. A pretty schooner . . . lay alongside the wharf, which began to be crowded with Negroes, jumping, dancing, shouting, laughing, and clapping their hands . . . and using the most extravagant and ludicrous gesticulations to express their ecstasy at our arrival." Fanny was baffled by such a demonstration, but after a few days at the plantation, she began to understand that "this species of outrageous flattery is as usual with these people as with the low Irish, and arises from the ignorant desire, common to both races, of propitiating at all costs the fellow creature who is to them as Providence—or rather, I should say, a fate—for 'tis a heathen and no Christian relationship."

Though Fanny was sickened by the conditions of the slaves she encountered, the natural beauty of the Georgia coast delighted her eye. Butler Island itself was merely a vast rice field, ditched and diked, that lay below the level of the tidal rivers to the north and south, and the general impression of the winter landscape was dismal at first. But she admired the evergreen shrubs that grew along the dykes, and she was pleased by the rich variety of unfamiliar birds. More than anything else, she was captivated by the light: "But then the sky—if no human chisel can yet cut breath, neither did any human pen write light; if it did, mine should spread out before you the unspeakable glories of these Southern heavens, the saffron brightness of morning, the blue intense brilliancy of noon, the golden splendor and rosy softness of sunset."

Unfortunately, the natural scene was all she found to rave about. The only residence for white people on the island was the overseer's cottage—a plain house of three rooms to accommodate not only the overseer but also the Butlers, their two infant daughters, and their Irish nurse. After describing the house in detail, Fanny says, "Such being our abode, I think you will allow there is little danger of my being dazzled by the luxurious splendors of a Southern slave residence." The plantation itself, consisting entirely of rice fields and swamp, afforded no opportunity for Fanny's favorite pastime, horseback riding, so she had to content herself with walking the dykes that lay in a grid upon the island, and with rowing, which she turned to with eagerness.

But it was the slaves who commanded her attention. Their most appalling feature was the most apparent—they were filthy and they smelled bad. Fanny quickly came to understand that their indifference to hygiene was not a natural tendency but one of the degrading effects of bondage: "A total absence of self-respect begets these hateful physical results. . . . Well-being, freedom, and industry induce self-respect, self-respect induces cleanliness and personal attention, so that slavery is answerable for all the evils that exhibit themselves where it exists—from lying, thieving, and adultery, to dirty houses, ragged clothes, and bad smells."

The worst of these conditions she found in the infirmary. With no light from its shuttered windows and little heat from a stick or two in the fireplace, it was a cold, dank, dirt-floored building where women lay about in various degrees of misery, covered only by rags of filthy blankets and virtually unattended. Horrified, Fanny set out immediately to improve the situation. But she soon discovered that that was not a simple task. Demanding of one sick woman why she made no attempt to clean her sick child, Fanny was told that by the time the women completed their tasks in the field, they were too exhausted to do anything but collapse and go to sleep. In great indignation Fanny reported the woman's complaint that night to her husband and the overseer only to find next morning that the woman had been flogged for lying to the mistress. Before the month was out, Fanny wrote: "It is hopeless to attempt to reform their habits or improve their condition while the women are condemned to field labor; nor is it possible to overestimate the bad moral effect of the system as regards the women, entailing this enforced separation from their children, and neglect of all the cares and ties of mother, nurse, and even housewife, which are all merged in the mere physical toil of a human hoeing machine."

Yet slowly her efforts bore fruit. By the middle of February, when she and her family left Butler Island for Hampton Point, she was able to report greater cleanliness in the infirmary and among the children.

Hampton Point, a cotton plantation, was in some ways an improvement over Butler Island. The house, though far from grand, was roomier, and the higher ground allowed for horseback riding. But the slaves, Fanny thought, were even more degraded than those on Butler Island. The plight of the women, to whom naturally she had more access, was particularly distressing. During the time of old Major Butler, new mothers were granted a four-week convalescence following childbirth, but after his death the Kings reduced that period to three and in some cases to two weeks. As a result, many women never fully recovered, and infant mortality was high. Fanny was confronted constantly by ill effects of that policy, but soon after removing to Hampton Point, her husband forbade her to bring to him any more of the people's complaints. By her sympathy, he argued, Fanny was encouraging them to lie, and worse, to conceive false hopes for relief. Nothing could be done.

Of all the cruelties Fanny recorded, none was more outrageous than the report she heard of three black women who were delivered at about the same time of mulatto babies, two of whom were sired, allegedly, by Roswell King Jr.: "It was not a month since any of them were delivered, when Mrs. K[ing] came to the hospital, had them all three severely flogged, a process which *she* personally superintended, and then sent them off to Five Pound—the swamp Botany Bay of the plantation . . .—with further orders to the drivers to flog them every day for a week." Unable to change the system that permitted such atrocities, Fanny began to long for home. Her powerlessness before the misery of the slaves was more than she could bear.

There was one matter, however, that she did insist on changing—the religious life, or lack thereof, among the people. To her dismay, she learned early in her sojourn that the Kings had all but forbidden religious activity, and that at a time when more and more slaveholders were reacting to abolitionist criticism by attending to the spiritual needs of the slaves. The overseer at Butler Island, a Mr. O—, had had a man flogged for allowing his wife to be baptized, and a neighbor on St. Simons, Mrs. Fraser, "gave me a very sad character of Mr. King. . . . As for my care for the moral or religious training of the slaves, that, she said, was a matter that never troubled his thoughts; indeed, his only notion upon the subject of religion, she said, was that it was something *not bad* for white women and children."

Toward the end of her stay, Fanny obtained permission from her husband to conduct a sort of religious service for the people at Hampton Point. Many came, filling the large parlor, and listened quietly as Fanny read to them from the scriptures. What she did not tell her husband was that secretly she was trying to teach some of them to read.

The veracity of Fanny Kemble's *Journal* has often been challenged. Skeptics cite several willful misrepresentations as evidence of unreliability throughout, and even her own daughter Frances Leigh published a book after the war that contradicted her mother's report. So what are we to make of Fanny's *Journal*?

Fanny Kemble was a highly intelligent person. She was fully aware of the effects of prejudice on her view of plantation conditions, and she had an active enough sense of irony to see herself as their planter neighbors saw her. Of a conversation with a doctor from Darien, "who is a shrewd, intelligent man . . . with much kindness of heart and cheerful good temper," she says, "I have already tried the latter by the unequivocal expressions of my opinion on the subject of slavery, and, though I perceived that it required all his self-command to listen with anything like patience to my highly incendiary and inflammatory doctrines, he yet did so." And later, "so suggestive . . . a woman as myself is, I suspect, an intolerable nuisance in these parts." Moreover, she was willing to represent the views and practices of more beneficent slaveholders, while allowing that the Butler slaves "are generally considered well off." Finally, though, the issue for her was a matter of religious conscience: "The more I hear, and see, and learn, and ponder the whole of this system of slavery, the more impossible I find it to conceive how its practicers and upholders are to justify their deeds before the tribunal of their own conscience or God's law."

When the curtain closed on our "audience with Fanny Kemble," I found myself in the crowded lobby—I, a descendant of slaveholders, the African Americans in the audience surely descended from slaves, some possibly from Pierce Butler slaves. I could not guess what thoughts were going through their heads any more than they could guess what I was thinking.

The night following the performance I set out from the motel where I was staying to join a group on Sea Island looking for loggerhead turtles coming up onto the beach to nest, but not knowing St. Simons as well as I later would, I failed in the dark to turn where I should have and eventually found myself at the gates of Hampton Point Plantation. The narrow blacktop road meandered through a live oak forest. In places the road split to accommodate an ancient tree, and curtains of Spanish moss shone spooky gray in my headlights. Even so, I glimpsed from time to time, well back from the road, lighted mansions of the rich, plantation style, with deep front verandas. I was in an exclusive development, and I was lost—in the very woods, among some of the very trees, where Fanny had ridden her stallion Montreal, to the scandal of her proper neighbors. I was, in fact, on Fanny Kemble Drive, for the third time in ten minutes, until I turned once again on Pierce Butler Circle. By the time I found my way back out of that labyrinth, it was too late for the turtles.

MIDWAY

South out of Savannah on old 17 or north from Darien, thirty minutes either way, and you come upon a church standing in a grove of pine and oak. It is obviously different from the white frame churches that you usually see along southern highways. A plain, though stately, chalk-white meeting house, it looks as though it might feel more comfortable in a Massachusetts village than sweltering here on the Georgia coast. Even its name—Midway Congregational—sounds foreign to people who are mainly Baptist, Methodist, or some brand of Pentecostal.

At the entrance to the grounds stands a squadron of historical markers. One of them explains. Midway was founded in 1754 by descendants, sure enough, of Massachusetts Puritans; they had come to South Carolina a generation before and then moved on to Georgia. In spite of their New England roots, most of them became cotton plant-

Midway Congregational Church

ers and slaveholders, but their Puritan heritage exerted an influence on their community that lasted as long as the church did, until 1865, and maybe longer.

The original structure was burned by British troops during the Revolution, and with good reason from their point of view. The transplanted Yankee stock of Midway was a breeding ground for Revolutionary War leaders. Dr. Lyman Hall, one of Georgia's three signers of the Declaration of Independence, was a member of Midway, as were young Daniel Stewart, who attained the rank of brigadier, and Gen. James Screven, who died in an engagement one mile south of here. Georgia counties were named for each of those men, and the county of their origin, in honor of their service, was designated Liberty.

The achievements of Midway people were not limited to that generation. From its founding to the end of the Civil War, four future governors went out from the church, as well as six congressmen, two university chancellors, six professors, including the famous LeContes, four authors, and various ministers, scientists, doctors, and lawyers. Among the ministers who served the church were the fathers of Oliver Wendell Holmes and Samuel F. B. Morse.

I obtained a key from the museum next door—the biggest key I've ever seen—and turned the antique lock.

The Puritan heritage of Midway is even more apparent inside than out. The walls and windows are plain, and an austere light falls upon the gated pews. White columns support a gallery designed for the use of slaves, and the elevated pulpit communicates as effectively with the upper level as with the pews below.

I take a seat on a hard bench and find myself looking up, trying to imagine a minister. The one who comes to mind is Charles Colcock Jones. Though he has no marker at the gate—he was a member of Midway but never its minister—he is as widely known perhaps as any of those who do, having entered southern history with the publication of Robert Manson Myers's monumental work, *The Children of Pride*.

That book is an edition of letters written by the Jones family— twelve hundred out of a collection of approximately seven thousand—mostly to each other, between 1854 and 1868. Nothing I have read—neither fiction nor history—has imparted to me so strong a sense of the impact of the Civil War upon a southern community. The Reverend and Mrs. Jones and their three children wrote to each other two or three times a week. Often the younger Charles wrote to each parent within the space of a day or two, and each parent wrote to him. And not brief notes. Many of the letters must have run to fifteen or twenty pages of hand-cramping script, requiring several hours to compose. The result—even the portion that Myers includes—presents a large and exceedingly detailed canvas of plantation life on the Georgia coast during the mid-nineteenth century.

The Joneses defy the stereotype of the southern planter family. The father, Charles C. Sr., was a Princeton-educated Presbyterian clergyman who resigned from the pulpit, though not from his calling, to manage the three plantations he had inherited and to minister to the spiritual needs of his slaves. Myers says in his prologue that Jones was "a man of radiant Christian character." Mary—a sensible, well-educated person herself—was her husband's first cousin and co-owner of the plantations and the slaves. Charles Jr. in 1854 was completing legal studies at Harvard, Joseph was a medical student in Philadelphia, and Mary Sharpe, soon to be married to a young Presbyterian minister, was living with her parents.

Nor did the Joneses' three homes approach the grandeur of Greek Revival mansions. In keeping with the Puritan heritage of the community, Montevideo, a few miles south of Midway, Maybank, over on the marsh, and Arcadia were all plain-style plantation houses, comfortable but utterly unpretentious. Though the Joneses maintained a gracious lifestyle, it was disciplined and sober, befitting the decorum of a manse rather than a manor.

The modern reader of *The Children of Pride* must wonder that a minister of Jones's intellect and education could justify slavery much less own and manage slaves himself. All we can tell from the letters is that Jones addressed the question; an 1856 letter from a friend in Kentucky thanks him for his "article on slavery." Unfortunately, Myers makes no reference to that item in the prologue; he doesn't even discuss the matter. The reader may infer, however, from comments scattered throughout the correspondence, that Jones defended slavery on scriptural grounds; that he embraced a benevolent paternalism, regarding Africans as children in need of discipline and spiritual instruction; and that he believed slaveholders had been given a divine mandate to lead their charges in the way of salvation.

No one took that responsibility more seriously than he himself. By 1854 Jones had produced two volumes—*Catechism of Scripture Doctrine and Practice* and *The Religious Instruction of the Negroes in the United States*—that were used so extensively in the South that he had become known as "the Apostle to the Blacks." While these books emphasized, no doubt, St. Paul's injunction to slaves to obey their masters, Jones's principal aim was the spiritual salvation of black people. To that end, he not only wrote books but ministered to "the servants," as he called them, by teaching, preaching, and tending the sick. Though sick himself for the last ten years of his life, he rode from plantation to plantation in all seasons, exhausting himself in the effort. When a slave fell ill, Jones hastened to the bedside, more in the role of minister than master. Writing to Charles Jr. of the death of a "servant," Mary Jones said, "You know the tenderness of your father's feelings, and his ceaseless anxiety when the servants are sick."

The plantation life of the Joneses, like that of thousands of others, came to an end with the Civil War. The old preacher died in the spring of 1863, while both sons were away in uniform, and when Sherman invaded the coastal region in the winter of 1864, the widow Mary Jones and her pregnant daughter had to stand by without protection as Union soldiers repeatedly ransacked the house, insulting the women and the slaves alike, and stripping the place of every morsel of food. In the midst of this terror, Mary Sharpe Jones Quarterman gave birth to a daughter.

Sherman's army left the Joneses with a roof over their heads—three roofs, in fact—but that was all. Desperate that spring to get both food and money crops in the ground, Mary Jones found it impossible to farm with free labor. To her consternation, former slaves refused to work, and many left the plantation for what looked to them like a better life in Savannah.

In a letter to her daughter, who had moved to New Orleans, the widow wrote:

The management of the place *has truly been astonishing!* Mr. Quarterman told me he believed *Henry* was the person who stole the cotton. . . . My heart is pained and sickened with their vileness and falsehood in every way. I long to be delivered from the race. . . . You can have no idea of their deplorable state. They are

perfectly deluded—will not contract or enter into any engagement for another year, and will not work now except as it pleases
them. I know not from day to day if I will have one left about me
or on the place.

To us, the irony of that complaint is almost amusing. Without realizing it, Mary Jones is acknowledging that she is the one in bondage
now, a slave to the refusal of "her people" to continue in slavery.

After a frustrating year, she gave up the effort to manage her plantations. Though only sixty years old, she was in poor health, and two
of her children had moved far away—Mary Sharpe with her husband
to New Orleans, Charles to a law practice in New York City. In January 1868 she "closed up her life at home" and went to New Orleans,
leaving the three Jones houses to deteriorate and finally to fall in
upon themselves.

A paper mill now stands upon the site of Montevideo; Arcadia is a
pine plantation, its endless rows of trees producing pulpwood for the
mill; and out on Colonels Island not a brick is left to indicate the site
of Maybank. I drove past the paper mill and the pine plantation on a
hot day in June, turned right at Midway Church, and headed east,
looking for something called Seabrook Village.

The brochure describes it as an "African American living history
museum [where] you can actually sit in the historic one-room Seabrook School the way children did at the turn of the century."

Though early on many of the Midway planters taught slaves to read
in order to facilitate their religious education, the state of Georgia soon
outlawed slave literacy. The Reverend Jones's catechism was designed
for "the oral instruction of Africans." Even after Reconstruction, the
white South did little if anything to promote black education and in
many instances actively opposed it. Because the forbidden often seems
particularly desirable, former slaves in the years following the war
demonstrated a strong determination to go to school. They were aided
throughout the South by often zealous northern missionaries, but the
freedpeople of the Midway-Sunbury community—as elsewhere—preferred to staff and to administer their schools themselves. Hence Seabrook.

A one-room frame building constructed around the turn of the century by the people of Sunbury Baptist Church, Seabrook served the
rural black community until the late 1940s. For the next fifty years it
stood abandoned, slowly succumbing to the elements. Then, in 1990,
a local resident, descendant of the Jones-Stevens family connection,
envisioned restoration. It would not be an easy task. Indeed, at times
it seemed impossible, but by the concerted effort of a growing number
of enthusiastic supporters, white and black, directed by a professional

preservationist, the building was dismantled and reconstructed on a nearby site.

By the time of my visit it stood complete, supported at the corners by oak stumps, as it had been originally, and gleaming with a coat of whitewash. Scattered about the spacious grounds were other period structures—a corncrib and a residence, the type of tenant house still common in the South during my childhood but almost entirely replaced today by mobile homes and brick ranch-styles.

My guide unlocked the door to the school, and we entered its single room—as unadorned and functional as the sanctuary of Midway Church, though here the function was education. The blackboards were original, my guide explained, uncovered in the process of renovation. Fifty-year-old arithmetic could still be seen, but the desks, she said, were replicas, built to the specifications of the memories of the people who had occupied them as children. I sat down, trying to absorb the spirit of the place, the hunger to learn, despite having to walk miles in any weather, and that after the morning chores were done, and then sit for the rest of the day on these hard boards.

Today's generation, of both races, would do well to remember their grandparents' experience, I thought, sounding like the proverbial grandfather myself. But not simply to realize how fortunate they are. It has been said many times that we begin to discover who we are only by remembering our past, but here at Seabrook African Americans can look upon the tangible evidence of a community's commitment to education, and they can come in and sit at these desks.

There is no way of knowing whether the Puritan emphasis on learning that sent so many white sons of Midway to Harvard, Princeton, and Yale had any appreciable effect on the determination of the former slaves and their children to acquire education for themselves. But as we were leaving, my guide gave me a verbal picture that rendered the question pointless. When reconstruction of the school was complete, she said, the Seabrook Foundation held a whitewash party. Scores of people turned out, of all ages and both races—descendants of Midway planters and descendants of Midway slaves—to celebrate their mutual legacy.

HOG HAMMOCK

I went to Sapelo Island for the first time in 1968, a year after I moved to Georgia. With little idea of what the island was or meant, I wangled an invitation to participate in the annual Sapelo Christmas Bird Count. On the Friday after Christmas I arrived at the dock at Meridian, and with twelve or fourteen other bird-watchers—all of them veterans of Sapelo—I boarded the *Sapelo Queen* for the thirty-minute ride across the gray waters of Doboy Sound.

The Julienton River, which flows into Sapelo Sound

The fact that Sapelo was inaccessible except by boat made it seem a special place. By the time we arrived at Marsh Landing, I had learned the general facts: that the island had been owned until a few years before by the late tobacco heir R. J. Reynolds Jr.; that the University of Georgia Marine Institute, where we would be staying, was located on the south end; and that the rest of the island was virtually uninhabited except for a small black community called Hog Hammock. In those days I was more interested in birds than I was in history or in the African American presence on a barrier island. The only black people I saw were preparing and serving our food in the kitchen, and I didn't talk with them. Through many subsequent birding trips, Hog Hammock remained for me an unseen place, somewhere on the island.

But interests change. In 1993 I was back for the bird count, for the first time in twenty years, though I had visited the island a number of times in other capacities. I arrived at the dock two hours early, the only person there. Soon a couple joined me in the waiting room—African American, neatly dressed, and, from the way they talked, well-educated. Outsiders, I figured, northerners probably, here to visit relatives. We spoke to each other, but that was all. Presently, a fourth person came along, an apparently blind woman escorted by a young man who guided her into the waiting room and helped her get settled. "There are three people in here with you," he told her as he was leaving.

"Black or white?"

"Two black, one white."

I could tell from her speech that she was a Sapelo woman. It resembled what most people call Geechee or Gullah, virtually interchangeable terms for the same West Africa–influenced dialect, though Geechee is preferred on the Georgia coast, Gullah in South Carolina. In both states the dialect has been all but extinguished by television. What this woman was speaking might have been a hundred years old.

To my surprise, the well-dressed man spoke to her: "This is Charles, Louise."

I could not understand all that Louise said in response, but it was clear that she knew who the man was, and she was glad to learn that he and his wife were there. The three of them fell to chatting, mostly about residents of the island.

Charles all the while was working hard at removing a fishhook tangled in a ball of fishing twine. At a break in the conversation I introduced myself. He was Charles Hall, he said, born and raised on Sapelo until he left the island for high school in Brunswick. From there he went to Morehouse and from Morehouse to graduate school in the North, where he received a doctorate in physical therapy. He had been practicing for a long time in Ohio, but more and more often in recent years he had been coming home to Sapelo.

The name Hall rang a bell, but I couldn't place it.

In the twenty-seven years that I had been coming to Sapelo, Hog Hammock had become well known in academic circles as a field laboratory for anthropologists, linguists, folklorists, historians, and sociologists. It was my impression that the community was a real living history village, not a restoration like Seabrook, but, though I had become keenly interested in African American culture on the barrier islands, I had kept my distance from Hog Hammock, assuming that the residents had had enough of academics.

Now here was Dr. Hall with no trace that I could detect of Sapelo in his talk, coming home from Ohio to see his people and to fish. I asked him what the greatest changes were from the Sapelo of his youth to the island as it is today. Pretty much the same, he said, as those that have occurred throughout the rural South—a greater degree of homogenization into the mainstream of American society through television, automobiles, land, and education. And far fewer people in Hog Hammock now.

Was that good or bad, net gain or loss?

"Some of both," he said.

I learned that weekend that several residents of Hog Hammock offered "bed-and-breakfast" accommodations—well-equipped mobile homes parked in their yards. On a weekend in June I returned to Sapelo as a guest of George and Lulu Walker. By chance my visit coincided with the publication of a book called *Sapelo's People* by my University of Georgia colleague, the historian William McFeely. I spent most of the weekend shut up in the Walkers' air-conditioned trailer reading Bill's book, fully aware of the irony.

The author insists that *Sapelo's People* is not "a history of Sapelo"; rather, he says, it is "a meditation on race." Even so, it *contains* history, and a great deal of it. For McFeely is fascinated, as I am, with the antecedents of these people. We know that Thomas Spalding owned slaves, as many as five hundred at one time; we know that Emancipation and Reconstruction caused upheaval and dispersion among the freedpeople; and we know that Hog Hammock has been owned for many years by the folks who live there. But who are they? Are they descendants of Spalding's slaves? George Walker owns a fine brick house and several acres of land. How did he and others acquire property on an island such as Sapelo? And how have the residents survived as an intact community through 130 years? McFeely finds answers to these questions.

One available source is *Drums and Shadows*, a collection of interviews with coastal African Americans undertaken by the Georgia Writer's Project in the late 1930s. That work came along just in time. Katie Brown, "one of the oldest dwellers on Sapelo," remembered her grandmother's stories of *her* father, Belali Mohamet, who had been brought from Africa. Probably the original of the old Muslim in the film *Daughters of the Dust*, Belali "wuz bery puhticluh bout duh time dey pray and dey bery regluh bout duh hour. . . . Dey bow tuh duh sun an hab lil mat tuh kneel on. . . . Belali he pull bead and he say, 'Belambi, Hakabara, Mahamadu.'" Another Belali descendant, Shad Hall—that's where I'd heard that name; the picture of Shad Hall's face is one of the most memorable photographs in *Drums and Shadows*— recalled his grandmother Hester, who "say she kin membuh duh house she lib in in Africa. She say it was cubbuh wid palmettuh an grass fuh roof, an de walls wuz made uh mud."

Many sources confirm Shad Hall's and Katie Brown's stories about their great-grandfather: that he was probably an educated adult at the time of his capture, that he spent time as a slave in the West Indies where he may have learned the cultivation of long-staple cotton, that he brought to Sapelo with him a wife and many grown children, and that he served until the end of his long life as a driver on Spalding's plantation. By the time of the Civil War the blood of this almost-legendary patriarch ran in the veins of many of the slaves on Sapelo.

McFeely does an excellent job imagining the transition from life in Africa to slavery on a sea island cotton plantation. But he is more interested in history than he is in folklore. He does not mention, for example, the legend of the flying Africans—the persistent and widespread story that there were slaves who, unable to accept the conditions of their new lives, simply picked up and flew back to where they had come from. This is the image that Toni Morrison converts into a powerful symbol in her novel *Song of Solomon*. I was excited to discover Shad Hall referring to it in the *Drums and Shadows* interview: "Doze folks could fly too. Dey tell me deah's uh lot uh um wut wuz bring heah un dey ain much good. Duh massah wuz fixin tuh tie um up tuh whip um. Dey say, 'Massuh, yuh ain gwine lick me,' and wid dat dey runs down tuh duh ribbuh. Duh obesheeuh he sho tought he ketch um wen dey get tuh duh ribbuh. But fo he could get tuh um, dey riz up in duh eah an fly away. Dey fly right back to Africa. I tink dat happen on Butler Ilun."

Some think it happened on St. Simons—not flight but the tragic incident of Ibo Landing in which a large group of newly arrived Africans waded into the tidal river and drowned rather than accept bondage in a strange land.

When war broke out, slaves flew in other ways. With the Union navy patrolling the offshore waters, so many slaves attempted to gain the security of Yankee gunboats that the Spaldings decided to move the people far inland. By then, the Spaldings left at home were two women, daughters-in-law of the late Thomas, one already a widow. Alone, these women undertook the formidable task of marching hundreds of people from the coast to Baldwin County, 150 miles west. Those who were too young or too old and infirm to walk were left behind to fend for themselves.

Baldwin County, as it turned out, lay directly in the path Sherman would take in his fiery march to Savannah. At least some of the Spalding slaves must have increased the throng of "contrabands," as the former slaves were called, that followed the Yankees to the sea. In any case, many of them returned, freedpeople, to the island of their former bondage, there to be reunited with lost family members, some of whom had earlier escaped and recently trickled back.

Despite their bitter experience in that place, Sapelo was home to them, and they meant to claim the land and restore the community they had known before the war. That dream was realized briefly in Sherman's Field Order No. 15, by which abandoned lands on the coastal islands as well as a thirty-mile-wide strip of mainland (the section that lies for the most part within the hard edge of I-95) were granted in forty-acre allotments to the freedpeople. Under the administration of Gen. Rufus Saxton and his assistant, a northern black man named Tunis Campbell, hundreds of former slaves were located and relocated on St. Catherines and Sapelo Islands.

They set to work immediately cultivating garden patches. Campbell had them build a schoolhouse and a church, the First African Baptist. A community began to emerge, a people free for the first time to make decisions for themselves.

The dream of autonomy, grounded in the institutions of landownership and education, did not last long. Saxton was replaced by Gen.

Davis Tillson, a man supportive of the interests of the planters, and he honored the claims of the Spaldings. Campbell survived for another year on Sapelo, advising the people against entering into labor contracts, but by 1867 he too was gone, along with all blacks who were not natives of the island.

Like Mary Jones, the Spaldings discovered quickly that the profitable management of a free labor force was not an easy matter. McFeely says, "As far as I can determine, after the war no Spalding made money on a crop of Sapelo cotton." By 1885 the Spalding heirs had sold much of the island, and by the end of the century, McFeely continues, "the only relic of the once lordly clan was Sarah Spalding McKinley, who, having moved back from Milledgeville for a time, returned . . . to become the island's postmistress."

The freedpeople, meanwhile, were still in pursuit of the dream denied them by the policies of General Tillson. In 1871 three Sapelo men somehow scraped together a down payment on a thousand acres at Raccoon Bluff, which they subdivided into thirty-three-acre plots and sold to former Spalding slaves—not quite forty acres and a mule but closer to that ideal than most nineteenth-century blacks ever came. By the end of the century Raccoon Bluff was the dominant community on the island.

It was not a prosperous one. The people subsisted on what they could grow—vegetables and hogs—and the crabs, oysters, and fish they gathered from tidal creeks. They attended the First African Baptist Church and sent their children to the island school. If not prosperous, they were independent, shaping their lives both as individuals and as a community, doing for themselves.

Then in 1911 the last of the Spaldings, together with several other owners, sold the greater part of the island to Howard Coffin of the Hudson Motor Company. One of many northern millionaires who discovered wintering grounds in the South around the turn of the century, Coffin was a man who liked to make things run. He restored the dilapidated South End House of Thomas Spalding and put the island into production, cutting down forests and building an oyster canning factory. Life in the Sapelo communities remained for the most part unaffected, but the people went to work for Coffin, and once again the island had a master.

Sapelo changed hands again in 1934 when Coffin sold it to tobacco heir Richard J. Reynolds Jr. In 1950 Reynolds set aside the northern half of the island for a game preserve, but Raccoon Bluff stood in his way. Residents were descendants and heirs of former slaves who had bought the ground they lived on, and many were reluctant to move. To solve the problem, Reynolds offered to swap them parcels in Hog Hammock and houses with plumbing and electricity. Even so, some, like the famous basket-maker Allen Green, refused to budge. But Reynolds held economic power over the black community, and eventually the Sapelo people, even Green, were concentrated in Hog Hammock.

Hog Hammock does not strike the visitor as a planned community. No grid here. As I followed a sandy road, side-stepping mud puddles from a recent shower, the road led me where it wanted to go, not in a straight line but bending back and forth, digressing past yards and weedy fields, through groves of live oaks. The houses were often mobile homes, like the one where I was staying, or painted cinder block, or brick. They occurred in a flat landscape, widely spaced and random, like wild plants, expressive of some dynamic of community, or communal life, not apparent to me.

Several months after that visit, I learned of the recently formed Sapelo Island Cultural and Revitalization Committee. Its president was a man named Ben Hall, brother of Charles. I reached Ben Hall by phone—an educated voice on the other end, a thoughtful, articulate man.

Like his brother, Mr. Hall had left Sapelo as a boy and, until a month ago, had lived and worked in Tennessee as a biological technician with the Department of Interior. Retired, he had come home to his native island and immediately gone to work to protect and preserve what he called "the integrity of Hog Hammock."

"What is the greatest threat to that integrity?" I asked.

The answer was complicated, but it began with the attrition of the Hog Hammock population. "No young people," Mr. Hall said. "Only two teenagers on the island."

I remembered twenty-five years ago, when the early boat to "the other side" was filled with school children. Now there is little reason for a young adult with a family to stay on the island, and many reasons for him or her to seek education and opportunity on the mainland, as the Hall brothers had done. The Department of Natural Resources and the Marine Institute have only so many jobs to offer, and many of those are menial.

As people move away, land becomes vulnerable to developers and speculators. Many are drooling over the small parcels that often become available when a resident dies. If heirs live far away, they may be eager to sell. Ben Hall dreads the nightmare possibility of condos going up in Hog Hammock.

"We are trying to create economic incentives for young people to come back," Mr. Hall said.

Already underway is a clam and crab project. With the support and assistance of both the DNR and the Marine Institute, Hog Hammock residents are "planting" clams and, while the clams mature, harvesting soft-shell crabs. They anticipate a self-sustaining business that will provide a living for five workers.

"If we can show young people that they can make a living on the island, Hog Hammock may survive. That's the only way you're going to fight off the speculators," Mr. Hall explained.

Before hanging up, I asked Mr. Hall how he and Charles were related to Shad Hall.

"He was our great uncle."

I remembered that face in *Drums and Shadows* and the stories Shad Hall told of his great-grandfather Belali Mohamet and the flying Africans.

Like their legendary ancestors, Ben and brother Charles have picked up and flown back to the place they came from. With other residents of Hog Hammock, descendants too of Belali, they have committed themselves to the preservation of their community.

THE BIG HOUSE

Like most of the barrier islands, Sapelo has its big house. The first time I saw it, twenty-five years ago, I thought, incredible: such extravagance, way out here, hidden in this offshore wilderness; I thought, how costly it must have been to haul such materials from the mainland; and I wondered why. Whoever built it must have sought isolation, but what kind of person creates such grandeur for his own solitary pleasure?

The house is not an antebellum Greek Revival manor. Rather, it reminds you of Hollywood in the 1920s. Coming up the avenue from the beach, you first catch glimpses of white through the live oak shade and the curtains of Spanish moss. Closer, you see a cruciform reflecting pool adorned with statues of nymphs. The pool leads the eye to a columned veranda. On either side wings extend so far that the house appears to be of one story, low and flat roofed, though in fact it has two. Through the front door you enter a large, dark, elegantly paneled room—bookshelves and fireplace. In the room beyond is a swimming pool.

From the 1960s until 1994 the Big House was maintained and operated by the University of Georgia Marine Institute. I had an opportunity twice to stay there for a weekend. Both times I was fascinated by the evidence throughout of extraordinary wealth. Again I wondered what kind of person would consider himself worthy of a private barony the size of Manhattan.

Antebellum planters—Thomas Spalding here on Sapelo, the Butlers and Coupers on St. Simons, the Nightingales and Staffords on Cumberland—were never vexed by that question. As far as they were concerned, the islands were rice paddies and cotton fields, a place to work and live. When, after the war, they found it impossible to farm with free labor, they put the islands up for sale.

Lawn party at Mistletoe Cottage, Jekyll Island, circa 1900

There's a story of an old Confederate veteran who was asked by his grandson years after the war if it was really true that the Yankees had won; the old man answered, "It's too soon to tell, son, too soon to tell." By 1890, though, the outcome was clear. Wealthy northern industrialists and financiers came down to Georgia, bought up and occupied the land ravaged by Sherman. They were especially attracted to the islands, mostly uninhabited and reverting to wilderness.

Among the most famous of these winter retreats was the Jekyll Island Club. Organized in 1885 by Newton Finney, an in-law of the du Bignon family who had owned Jekyll before the war, the club listed among its members J. P. Morgan, William Rockefeller, Vincent Astor, Joseph Pulitzer, James J. Hill, and William K. Vanderbilt. These men and others built what they called "cottages" on Jekyll, some as grand as the house on Sapelo. These are open to the public now—you can walk the tile and parquet floors and marvel at the opulence—but during the club's heyday—1885 to 1945—the island was a private, closely guarded winter playground of the crowned heads of American industry and finance.

The members of the Jekyll Island Club apparently enjoyed social activity—playing together with their own kind—but other millionaires sought solitude. In the early 1880s Thomas Carnegie, brother of Andrew, was buying up large tracts of Cumberland Island just to the south of Jekyll; the Wannamakers purchased Ossabaw; and in 1911 Hudson Motors magnate Howard Coffin acquired Sapelo.

According to Buddy Sullivan, whose book *Early Days on the Georgia Tidewater* is one of the most professional local histories I have read, Coffin and his wife Matilda "took the peace and solitude of Georgia's coast to their heart." Well and good, but twenty thousand acres of wilderness is a large and complex responsibility. When the deal was closed in June 1912, the *Savannah Morning News* announced that Coffin "acquires a veritable paradise, blessed with exquisite natural beauty, needing only the hand of man to transform it into one of the most delightful spots on earth."

Whatever the paper meant by "delightful," Coffin had the transforming hand. He also had vision, energy, and money. Coastal historian Burnette Vanstory writes, "the rehabilitation of Sapelo satisfied the urge to construct and develop that was a leading force in Howard Coffin's nature, while the peace, privacy, and serenity of the island brought relaxation and escape from the outside world."

The challenge was to accomplish transformation without destroying the natural beauty of Sapelo. He started on what remained of the old Spalding seat—South End House—which had been damaged by Union gunboats almost fifty years before and more recently used as a hunting lodge. At first Coffin was content to make it comfortable for his wife and their guests, but after World War I, he tore it down to its thick tabby foundations and rebuilt it according to a picture of the original—low and solid to withstand hurricane winds, vast to accommodate an indoor pool, a bowling alley, and other recreational facilities. Meanwhile, he was working to make the island productive. He constructed and cleared land—mature, second-growth forest—and sold timber; he brought in a large herd of cattle; and he started an oyster cannery to provide work for black residents.

After 1921 most of the labor was directed by Coffin's young cousin Alfred "Bill" Jones, who had discontinued his studies at the University of Pennsylvania to recover from tuberculosis. Jones was as captivated by the charm and beauty of the barrier island as the Coffins had been and decided right away to become a full-time resident of Georgia.

While Jones worked, Coffin entertained. Virtually a full-time resident himself, he invited to Sapelo, among other distinguished guests, President and Mrs. Calvin Coolidge, Charles Lindbergh, who landed his airplane on the Sapelo airstrip, and without fanfare in 1932 the lame-duck president, Herbert Hoover.

As the decade of the 1920s closed, Howard Coffin looked around for new fields to transform. Though he valued the privacy of his Sapelo retreat, he was conscious of a population that was growing increasingly affluent and, because of the machine he himself had designed and marketed, mobile. Not wanting the public on Sapelo, he bought a part of St. Simons called Long Island, changed its name to Sea Island, and put Bill Jones in charge. With Coffin's financial support Jones built the Cloister, one of the great resort hotels of its time, and developed Sea Island. Then came the Great Depression. Like many others, Coffin lost huge amounts in his investments. With the death of Mrs. Coffin in

1932, he appeared to lose interest in both Sea Island and Sapelo. Two years later he sold Sapelo to Richard J. Reynolds Jr.; three years after that, depressed and alone on Sea Island, he took his life.

Reynolds owned Sapelo until his death in 1963. During the three decades of his tenure, he renovated the Big House to suit the tastes of a succession of wives, moved the black residents to Hog Hammock, and in the early fifties, at the request of University of Georgia ecologist Eugene Odom, gave consent and support to the University of Georgia Marine Institute. After Reynolds's death, his widow sold the northern half of the island to the state. A few years later Georgia bought the rest, except for Hog Hammock.

By the time of Reynolds's death, the owners of the islands were finding it increasingly difficult to hold onto their domains. For some, taxes and maintenance had become prohibitively expensive; for all pressure was mounting to meet in some way the interests of the public. The people of Georgia, for the first time comfortable enough to take their families on vacation, looked to the coast. Only Jekyll, now a state park, and St. Simons were accessible. Developers were eyeing the other paradises, licking their chops. At the same time, preservationists and conservationists, fired by Eugene Odom's discovery of the vital necessity of healthy marshland, were demanding that the islands be protected from development. In view of the ecological catastrophe of the Florida and South Carolina coastlands, they realized that Georgia had been incredibly fortunate to have had the millionaires. Whether the owners were deemed selfish or not, the result of their control was thus far the preservation of thousands of acres of coastal wilderness. Wassaw, Ossabaw, St. Catherines, Blackbeard, Sapelo, and Cumberland were still inaccessible except by boat, their ecology still relatively undamaged. The fight was on to keep them that way.

CUMBERLAND

A windless night on the beach of Little Cumberland, tattered clouds backlighted by the moon, a plague of sand gnats. We head south on foot, four of us, looking for turtles—the great loggerheads that emerge from the surf, heaved ashore by the waves, to deposit their slick, pingpong eggs in the dry dunes. Having never witnessed that spectacle, I have to rely on the reports of others, none better than Herman Melville's. The turtles, he writes, are as "heavy as chests of plate, with vast shells medallioned and orbed like shields . . . newly crawled forth from beneath the foundations of the world."

No flashlight, little talk, we march on, our eyes taking in more and more of the dark beach, searching for a crawl. Up ahead a shape at the water's edge but darker than the water, undefined but moving. We stop. The shape continues to move but makes no progress beyond the utmost reach of the waves. We approach. A racing wavelet breaks

Dunes on Cumberland Island

against her, flooding around her. She labors, struggling to go, but she seems anchored to the wet sand.

The beam of a flashlight hits her encrusted shell. She is huge. For how many decades, I wonder, has this old mama been coming ashore on Little Cumberland? In the play of the light, we spot her problem. Her left front flipper, at the joint, is wrapped tight with yellow ski rope, around and around. The flesh has swollen about the rope; it is necrotic and maculate.

The light hits her old face. She is weeping.

I know. I know. The tear ducts run constantly to discharge salt from her system, but this mother, her primal urge thwarted, is simply crying.

The people I'm with are scientists. They are angry. I can afford a more anthropomorphic response. I want to grieve with her.

One of the scientists asks if anyone has a knife. Someone has, a heavy sheath knife, I don't know why.

It takes a long time to saw through the hard plastic coils of ski rope, but the turtle is patient. She continues to weep but doesn't complain.

Cut through at last, the rope is pulled free from the swollen meat. The four of us, gripping her shell at its four corners, walk her with quick little steps into the water. We release her to the surf, consign her to the sea, and at least one of us prays that the salt water in which she lives will heal her injured flesh.

It is 1980. I am standing before the ruins of Dungeness, trying to get a photograph. Stone walls rise against an overcast sky, a shell as gaunt as any bombed European castle. I want a shot of the whole thing, but I can't find a point of view. Though reduced to ruins, Dungeness is still too grand for my single lens reflex.

The name originated with Oglethorpe, the old grid maker, who, according to legend, came down to Cumberland in the 1730s and built a hunting lodge. Fifty years later, Gen. Nathanael Greene bought the property and designed a great house to be called Dungeness. It would be constructed upon or near the site of Oglethorpe's camp. Though Greene died before construction began, his widow carried out his plans, building on the slight elevation of a prehistoric oyster shell mound a four-story mansion with tabby walls six feet thick. For sixty years Greene descendants lived and entertained in their sea island castle, but the Civil War destroyed that way of life, and during Reconstruction the great house burned.

History repeated itself with uncanny accuracy ten years later. Thomas Carnegie of Pittsburgh bought as much of the island as he found available and immediately drew up plans for a new Dungeness to be built upon the ruins of the former. But like his predecessor Nathanael Greene, Carnegie died before construction was completed, leaving his widow to finish the work.

I try to merge the ruins with a guidebook photograph of the gaudy Carnegie mansion, tiered like a wedding cake with four towering chimneys, Italianate terraces, and walled garden pathways. I cannot superimpose that image upon the skeleton before me. But the skeleton is enough to invoke a scene of privilege that rivals the show of royalty—grand balls, hunting parties, children in sailor suits riding ponies on the lawn.

Ruins of Dungeness, Cumberland Island

Three generations of Carnegies enjoyed this semitropical fairyland. But by 1950 Dungeness was abandoned in favor of more practical houses on the island. On a dark night in 1959 vandals came ashore on the south end and set the empty mansion ablaze. Newspaper accounts said you could see the light of the conflagration from as far as St. Marys.

John McPhee wrote a book back in the seventies called *Encounters with the Archdruid*, a third of which recounts a weekend he spent on Cumberland several years before. The reason for his visit was to meet the major antagonists in a fight over the future of the island. In one corner was Charles Fraser, a native of Liberty County and developer of Sea Pines Plantation on Hilton Head. In the other was David Brower, founder of the Sierra Club.

Fraser had his eye on Cumberland. In fact, by the time of that visit he had his hands on it as well, a death grip around the midsection of the island—three thousand acres purchased from Carnegie heirs more interested in money than in the natural integrity of Cumberland. Brower had come to appraise the potential for destruction, McPhee to write about the confrontation. Their airplane landed on the strip that Fraser had already cut, a scar in the jungle. Sam Candler, whose family owned a large section on the north end, met them. Though opposed to Fraser's plans, he would be their guide.

What Fraser had in mind was a highly controlled, exclusive development to be called Cumberland Oaks. In view of the possibilities, it was not a bad idea. Carnegie progeny had become so numerous by the 1960s that they had gone to court to get their titles straight. Some of them owned land they couldn't afford to keep, McPhee says, and developers knew that. Though the island probably resembled more closely than any other place the country as it was found by sixteenth-century Spaniards, development seemed inevitable. If so, Charles Fraser, with his experience, his understanding, and his aesthetic sense, seemed to be the best man for the job.

Nevertheless, many of the Carnegies viewed Fraser as the archvillain and began to cooperate with each to oppose him, "galvanized... into unanimity," as one of them reportedly said. At the time of McPhee's visit, they were proposing a Cumberland Island National Seashore. That suited Fraser just fine, as long as the National Park Service surrounded his property, preventing cheaper, more destructive development. The founder of the Sierra Club was forced to agree. If the island had to be developed, Fraser's plan was best. Still, Brower preferred a national park. Thus the two seeming antagonists discovered a wary respect for each other.

It was Brower's interests that won in the end, as everyone can see, but ironically it was Fraser's plans that served as catalyst for the victory. The Carnegies sold to the Park Service. Fraser succumbed to the pressure of those who, in his opinion, loved trees more than people, the druids, and the Park Service bought his three thousand acres too.

At the end of his essay, McPhee says: "for three days we had roamed an island bigger than Manhattan and had seen no one on its beach and, except at Candler's place and Greyfield, no one in its interior woodlands. In the late twentieth century, in this part of the world, such an experience was unbelievable . . . a privilege made possible in our time by private ownership. . . . No one," he predicted, "was ever to be as free on that wild beach in the future as we had been that day."

Three or four years later. A friend from Little Cumberland takes me on his boat one November day over to the Candler dock. We bring along a little four-wheel Honda, and I am to spend the day alone on the beach looking for migrating peregrine falcons, though I fear that I am a couple of weeks too late.

I grew up on the beaches of South Carolina. I have been to Sapelo. But I have never seen anything like the beach of Cumberland. At low tide its width is greater than a football field, and it stretches before me, unbroken by any structure for as far as I can see. But the feature that silences me is its emptiness. Not a soul in sight. I put on sunglasses against the winter glare and still the dunes are as white as hills of powdered sugar.

It takes a long time to cover the twenty miles to the south end and back. At one point three wild horses up ahead vanish by some path among the dunes. I see deer and pig tracks, flocks of sandpipers, gulls, terns, and pelicans, and rafts of scoters beyond the surf. I sit a spell and watch an elegant little kestrel hunting from a silvered snag of driftwood. But not a peregrine do I spy. That's all right, I'm thinking as I head back north. I have been witness all day to the same beach beheld by Spanish explorers 450 years before, exactly the same except for stranded lightbulbs and bottles. Like McPhee, I know it will never happen again, not to me. The Park Service has already taken control of the island, and it will not be long now before they open the doors. The next time I come back I'll be the public.

I stop to sit another spell, try to take hold of the day with both hands, but there is no way to save it. I haven't even brought a camera, sensing its inadequacy. All I can do as the sun drops down the western sky is say thank you.

I start the four-wheeler, annoyed by its noise. Is that a vehicle up there? Sure enough, far up ahead, a car of some kind is driving north. Park Service, I guess, and begin to rehearse my story. Then I see that the vehicle is stopped. By the time I reach it, its occupants have piled out, anticipating me. They are not Park Service. They are the public, two men, two women.

We greet each other.

"What's up ahead?" a man asks.

I'm not sure I understand. "Just what you see," I say.

"You mean just *this?*" asks a woman.

"Yes ma'am."

"Y'all don't have any facilities yet? No place to eat or use the rest room?"

"*Y'all?*"

Then I realize. They think I'm Park Service. I am wearing an olive shirt with a Georgia Ornithological Society patch sewn on the shoulder, and binoculars hang from my neck. That must be it.

"No," I say, "not a thing. We like it the way it is."

Buddy Sullivan

TOURING COASTAL GEORGIA

Coastal Georgia, comprising six mainland counties paralleled by a strand of barrier sea islands that bask in a sub-tropical environment, is amazingly diverse in human history and culture. To the uninitiated traveler entering the region for the first time, however, it is the natural beauty of the coast that captures the imagination. Here, one's visual horizons stretch broadly across the expanses of tidal salt marsh that weave through the sea islands—Tybee, Wassaw, Ossabaw, St. Catherines, Sapelo, St. Simons, Jekyll, and Cumberland—to the open sea. These low-lying islands, each distinct in its identifying characteristics, and the mainland are crowned with dense stands of live oak, cedar, pine, and palmetto. Sea oats and wax myrtle fringe the beaches, protecting the fragile sand dunes from the pounding surf rolling in from the Gulf Stream seventy miles offshore. Winds, waves, and currents continually shape and reshape the sea islands.

The fourteen barrier islands along Georgia's one-hundred-mile coastline protect the verdant, green-and-gold salt marshes against the furies of the winter northeasters and the tropical storms of summer and fall. Six-to-nine-foot tides are the norm along this crescent of the southeastern coast, known variously as the Georgia Bight, or Atlantic Embayment, which curls southward from Cape Hatteras, North Carolina, to Cape Canaveral, Florida. The tides flood the marshes twice daily, thus perpetuating one of the most ecologically sensitive areas of the world. Georgia's marshes (*Spartina alterniflora*), protected from development by state legislation enacted in 1968, comprise about 28 percent of all the salt marshes along the U.S. eastern seaboard. The marshes' nutrients sustain a variety of shellfish, such as shrimp, blue crabs, oysters, and clams, that inhabit Georgia's numerous bays, sounds, rivers, and estuaries.

West of the marshes is the sandy, low-lying plain of the mainland, penetrated by numerous tidal salt water rivers and creeks, which empty into the larger estuaries between the barrier islands. Great forests of live oak draped with Spanish moss and grapevine fringe the mainland coast. Behind them are vast stands of pine timber—largely longleaf and loblolly—and in between are sand hills and cypress swamps bordering the larger rivers that empty fresh water from Geor-

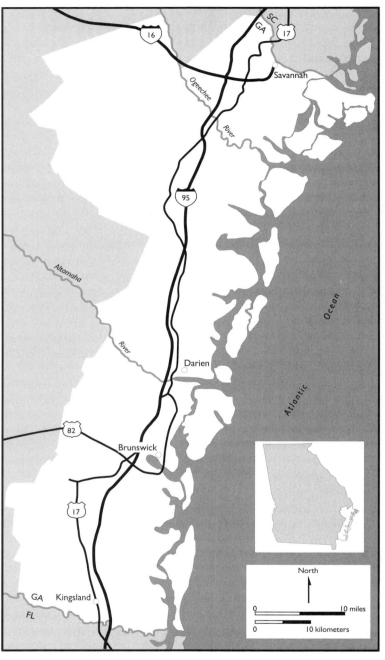

Coastal Georgia

gia's uplands into the tidal bays near the sea. The names of the rivers—Savannah, Ogeechee, Altamaha, Satilla, and St. Marys—are synonymous with the history of Georgia's coast. In the eighteenth and nineteenth centuries they were the great commercial highways flowing from the interior to the coast, and along them grew towns, including the economic centers of Savannah, Sunbury, Riceboro, Darien, Brunswick, and St. Marys.

Georgia's coast has been populated over the centuries by a wide diversity of human occupants. First were the Native American members of the Guale Mocama provinces, who lived on the mainland. Spanish friars followed to build the chain of missions along the coast. Then came English freebooters, followed by the colonists and Scottish Highlanders of James Edward Oglethorpe. Antebellum planters cultivated rice along the great rivers near the sea and long-staple cotton on the sea islands, enormous operations that based their existence on the legions of black slaves who labored on the great plantations. Timbermen in the 1880s and 1890s rafted millions of board feet of yellow pine down the rivers to the great sawmills of Savannah, Darien, and Brunswick. In the early years of the twentieth century, hardy commercial fishermen turned their small, fragile craft to the sea for its abundant harvests of shrimp and oysters.

Georgia's six coastal counties, from north to south, Chatham, Bryan, Liberty, McIntosh, Glynn, and Camden, are transected by two major conveyors, Interstate 95 and U.S. Highway 17. The latter is by far the more picturesque and historic, and along this route (with several side trips along outlying roads) the Georgia coastal tour will pass, from north to south, from Savannah to St. Marys. The tour almost necessarily begins in the richly historic city of Savannah, the early repository of much of coastal Georgia's heritage and the first town to be established in what was to be England's thirteenth and last North American colony.

TOUR ONE

Savannah and Chatham County

Savannah, the seat of Chatham County, is the economic, business, transportation, and cultural center of coastal Georgia and is among the busiest seaports on the U.S. east coast. Chatham County, created in 1777, is named for William Pitt, Earl of Chatham, an American colonial rights advocate. The city has a unique variety of nineteenth-century architecture, colonial cemeteries, and a far-reaching preservation movement that has been in the national forefront for decades. The entire historic downtown is a National Historic Landmark, as are several individual sites within the district. Savannah's 1990 population of 153,000 makes it one of the largest cities in Georgia and, historically,

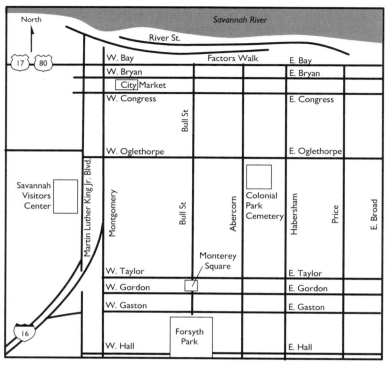

Coastal Georgia, Tour One

one of the most culturally diverse. Its popular St. Patrick's Day parade is the nation's second-largest.

Originally laid out by James Edward Oglethorpe, it was the first planned city in North America. Oglethorpe landed at Yamacraw Bluff, sixteen miles up the Savannah River from the Atlantic Ocean, on February 12, 1733. With Col. William Bull, a South Carolinian, he built Savannah around a plan of city squares that now number twenty-one. The heart of the city's historic district is suitable for walking, driving, or horse-drawn carriage tours. Architecture of the Historic and Victorian districts progresses through Georgian Colonial, Classical Revival, Greek Revival, and Victorian. A notable feature is the distinctive, soft-hued brick known as Savannah gray.

Early in the colonial period Savannah became an important commercial hub and the governmental center for the royal colony from 1754 until the Revolution. One of the most important battles of the Revolutionary War was fought at Savannah in September 1779 when occupying British forces repulsed a combined French and American assault. This military campaign signified Savannah's strategic importance during times of war, a factor that contributed to the construction of two brick masonry fortifications near the city, Fort Jackson, in 1808, and Fort Pulaski, in 1829.

After the Revolution, Savannah became an agricultural and commercial center. Large rice plantations developed along the Savannah River a short distance upriver from the city, and it was at one of these, the Mulberry Grove plantation of Gen. Nathanael Greene (1742–86), that Eli Whitney invented the cotton gin in 1793. Savannah's commercial greatness flourished in the first half of the nineteenth century when the city became a center for the shipment of cotton, rice, and naval stores. The port thrived on its river trade from the interior of Georgia, and ships from all over the world came to load cargoes at wharves along the present-day River Street waterfront. During the early 1840s, the Central of Georgia Railroad opened between Macon and Savannah, allowing the city to become the state's primary export center and further dominate the agricultural market. Other events during this period added to Savannah's growth as a major city. In 1819, the SS *Savannah* sailed from the city and became the first steamship to cross the Atlantic. In 1825, the Marquis de Lafayette visited Savannah during his celebrated American tour.

Savannah was an important Confederate shipping center early in the Civil War, but with the fall of Fort Pulaski in 1862, the city was sealed off from its vital link with the sea by the Union Navy. Two years later, in December 1864, the city fell to Gen. William Tecumseh Sherman's forces at the end of the March to the Sea. Because Sherman did not burn Savannah, much of its historic antebellum architecture survives.

Savannah recovered from the war again to become a prosperous commercial center. It took the national lead in the export of cotton and naval stores during the last three decades of the nineteenth century. The port continued to thrive after 1900 as Savannah became a naval stores manufacturing and shipbuilding center for Liberty ships during World War II. Now Savannah's port is a leader in the shipment of containerized cargo, and the growing volume of ocean-going traffic has led to constant expansion of the harbor and its facilities.

Savannah Historic District, West Side

Whether entering Savannah from the west along I-16 by automobile or embarking on a tour of the city's historic district from one of the downtown area's outstanding hotels or bed-and-breakfast inns, the visitor should begin with an orientation at the Savannah Visitors Center at 303 Martin Luther King Jr. Boulevard. The center provides maps, brochures, and information on the city's wide variety of excellent restaurants, cultural amenities, overnight accommodations, entertainment, and recreation. It is here also that many bus, trolley, and carriage tours of the downtown historic district originate. (Sightseers walking or driving around the city should keep in mind that the riverfront is to the north.)

Adjacent to the visitors' center is an essential stop, the Savannah History Museum, which provides excellent exhibits and overviews of the city's history in a building that was originally the passenger station of the Central of Georgia Railway. There is an 1890 steam locomotive here and a cotton exhibit featuring an antique cotton gin.

Nearby, the Historic Railroad Shops, the nation's most complete and best-preserved antebellum railroad manufacturing and repair facilities, are now a museum operated by the Coastal Heritage Society. Thirteen of the original structures on the site begun in 1850 are still standing. The roundhouse, dominated by a 125-foot-tall brick smokestack, operated from 1852 to 1963. It was also on this site, in 1779, following a long siege, that the allied French and American forces unsuccessfully attacked British forces occupying Savannah.

By following Jones Street west of M. L. King Boulevard for several blocks to West Boundary Street, then south on West Boundary to Cohen Street, one will arrive at the Old Jewish Burial Ground, established in 1773 by Mordecai Sheftall. This plot, according to a marker outside the walls of the burial ground, was established on Crown lands granted Sheftall to be used "as a Place of Burial for all persons whatever professing the Jewish Religion." The entire area was the site of the Siege of Savannah in 1779, and the cemetery was a rallying point.

At 41 M. L. King Boulevard is an imposing three-story brick house designed by architect William Jay and built about 1818 in the Classical Revival style for Savannah business leader William Scarbrough. For almost a century, this building housed the West Broad Street School for African American children, the first black public school in Savannah, established in 1878.

On nearby Montgomery Street, facing Franklin Square, is the First African Baptist Church (present structure, 1861). This historic center of African American religion, thought to be one of the oldest black congregations in America, was begun by a slave, Andrew Bryan, in 1788. Later, Bryan was ordained as the first pastor of the church, which he served until his death in 1812. Members who split from First African Baptist formed First Bryan Baptist Church, 575 West Bryan Street, in 1832. An original frame structure was replaced in 1873 by the present brick edifice.

Across Franklin Square the area between West Bryan and West Congress Streets is the City Market, a restored section of shops and restaurants. At the foot of M. L. King Boulevard near the Savannah River (see historic marker), the Confederate evacuation of Savannah occurred in December 1864.

Savannah River Front and Bay Street

At the intersection of M. L. King Boulevard and Bay Street, a right turn to the east leads to the intersection of Whitaker and Bay, where parking is available near the Hyatt Regency Hotel. Historic points along Bay Street and River Street, which parallels Bay at the foot of the bluff along the Savannah River, are a short walk east. At Bay and Jefferson Streets in the park, a historic marker describes the Confederate evacuation of Savannah in December 1864.

The traditional landing site of James Edward Oglethorpe and his English colonists in 1733 is near the present Hyatt Hotel location. About 114 colonists sailed with Oglethorpe in late 1732 on the ship *Anne*, landing at Charles Town in January 1733. Proceeding south to the Savannah River, Oglethorpe and his party landed here on February 12 at Yamacraw Bluff, where he entered a peaceful agreement with the local chieftain, Tomochichi, with Mary Musgrove, a mixed-blood American Indian, acting as interpreter. Oglethorpe laid out Savannah into squares starting at this point.

The buildings facing Bay Street, with their lower rear entrances acessible from River Street below the bluff, are on Factor's Walk, which runs along much of the length of Bay Street but is most distinct on Bay between Whitaker and Abercorn Streets. These red-brick and stucco buildings once housed large cotton and rice exporting factorages and were the headquarters for Coastal Georgia's wealthiest merchants during the nineteenth century. The cobbled streets and retaining walls along the bluff at Factor's Walk were constructed of ballast stone unloaded from sailing ships entering the harbor to load cotton

River Street, Savannah

and rice. Many of the multilevel buildings between the river front and Factor's Walk now house shops and restaurants. The Ships of the Sea Museum (503 East River Street) has an impressive collection of ship models and nautical memorabilia. River Street runs for nine blocks and features restored cotton warehouses and a river promenade where one may view large ships entering or departing the harbor.

At 1 West Bay Street, at the head of Bull Street, is the Savannah City Hall, built in 1905 of gray brick. From a point on the river behind this structure the SS *Savannah* sailed on May 22, 1819, for Liverpool, England, becoming the first steamship to cross the Atlantic Ocean.

The U. S. Customhouse at 3 East Bay was begun in 1848 and completed four years later. Here in 1859–60 the famous case of the slave ship *Wanderer,* which had illegally landed slaves from Africa, was heard before U. S. District Judge James Moore Wayne. Nearby are the Washington Guns of the Chatham Artillery, presented by Pres. George Washington after his 1791 visit to Savannah. Several of these cannon were captured at Yorktown in 1781 when Lord Cornwallis's British army surrendered.

On Bay, at the head of Drayton Street, is the Savannah Cotton Exchange, completed in 1887 to the design of the Boston architect William Gibbons Preston. This brick structure was the center of business activity when exports of two million bales of cotton a year made Savannah the leading cotton port on the Atlantic.

On the waterfront at the east end of River Street, the Waving Girl Monument honors Florence Martus (1868–1943), who lived on nearby Elba Island. She became known by sailors around the world between 1887 and 1931 as she waved a handkerchief by day and a lantern at night to greet ships arriving at and departing from Savannah's harbor. At the east end of Bay, near the Pirates' House Restaurant, is Trustees' Garden, which was the scene of early colonial agricultural experiments in growing flax, hemp, indigo, olives, medicinal herbs, and mulberry trees needed for silk production.

South of Bay, West of Bull Street

Walking is the preferred transportation in Savannah, but if visitors prefer to travel by automobile through the remainder of the Savannah Historic District, street parking is usually available near the squares.

Johnson Square, one block south of City Hall on Bull Street, is named for South Carolina governor Robert Johnson, who assisted the Georgia colonists. Laid out by William Bull, the square has been the scene of speeches by such personages as Pres. James Monroe (1819), the Marquis de Lafayette (1825), Henry Clay (1847), and Daniel Webster (1848). Maj. Gen. Nathanael Greene, Revolutionary War commander and associate of George Washington, is buried here. Nearby is Christ

Episcopal Church, where in an earlier structure the first congregation of the Georgia colony was organized in 1733 and among whose early ministers was John Wesley, who arrived as an Anglican missionary in 1736. Some of the outer walls of the Greek Revival structure date to 1838. The interior of the church was rebuilt in 1898.

Two blocks south of Johnson Square is Wright Square, laid out in 1733 and later named for James Wright, last royal governor of Georgia. The Tomochichi boulder honors the Yamacraw chief who befriended Oglethorpe and the colonists when they arrived in 1733.

Two blocks west of Wright Square are Telfair Square and the Telfair Academy of Arts and Sciences at Barnard and State Streets. The academy, the legacy of Savannah philanthropist Mary Telfair (1789–1875), opened in 1885 as the first public art museum in the Southeast. Built in 1818 to the design of William Jay for Alexander Telfair, this structure is perhaps Savannah's best-known example of Regency architecture. Also on Telfair Square is the Trinity United Methodist Church, completed in 1850, the oldest center of Methodism in Savannah.

Two blocks south of Telfair Square is Orleans Square, where a fountain is dedicated to the contributions of early German immigrants. East along West Hull Street, Chippewa Square was laid out in 1815 to commemorate the battle in Canada fought in the War of 1812. Dominating the square at 23 Bull Street is the First Baptist Church, a Greek revival structure built in 1833 to the design of Elias Carter. In Chippewa Square is one of Savannah's most recognizable monuments, Daniel Chester French's bronze of General Oglethorpe, the founder of the Georgia colony.

One block north of Chippewa Square along Bull Street, at the corner of Bull and Oglethorpe Avenue, is the Independent Presbyterian Church, organized in 1755. The original church (1819) was destroyed by fire in 1889. The present edifice is a replica built in 1891 with William G. Preston as architect. One of the most notable members of this church was Lowell Mason, a composer of sacred music and organist of the church in the 1820s.

On the northeast corner of this intersection is the Wayne-Gordon House, birthplace of Juliette Gordon Low (1860–1927), founder of the Girl Scouts of America. Acquired and restored in 1953 by the Girl Scouts of America, the house is a public memorial to the founder of Girl Scouts and a national program center for the Girl Scouts.

South on Bull Street is Madison Square, laid out in 1837 and named in honor of Pres. James Madison. Prominent here are a monument to Sgt. William Jasper, killed during the attack on British forces at Savannah in 1779; the St. John's Episcopal Church, built in the Gothic Revival style in 1853; and, on the southeast corner of the square, the administration building of the Savannah College of Art and Design (SCAD), the former Savannah Volunteer Guards armory constructed in 1892. The college has acquired and restored many other buildings in the historic district. Opposite the northwest corner of Madison Square is the Green-Meldrim House, one of the finest examples of Gothic Revival architecture to be found in the South. The stuccoed brick mansion, designed by John Norris and built in 1856 by Englishman Charles Green, was the headquarters of Gen. William T. Sherman during the Union occupation of Savannah in the winter of 1864–65. From here Sherman sent a famous telegram delivering the city of Savannah as a Christmas present to Pres. Abraham Lincoln. The house is open to the public.

Monterey Square, to the south along Bull Street, was laid out in 1847 to commemorate an American victory during the Mexican War. Prominent here is the monument to Count Casimir Pulaski, the Polish patriot who served the American cause in the Revolution and was killed in the siege of 1779. An imposing structure on Monterey Square is the synagogue of the Congregation Mickve Israel. The oldest congregation now practicing Reform Judaism in the United States was founded in 1733 at Savannah by a group of Jews largely of Spanish-Portuguese extraction. The congregation built the first Jewish synagogue in Georgia in 1820 and the present synagogue in 1878. Its museum is open for limited hours.

One block south on Bull is Forsyth Park, which links Savannah's Historic and Victorian districts, being laid out in 1851. Within the park's twenty acres are a white fountain modeled in 1858 after a similar structure in the Place de la Concorde in Paris; a Spanish-American War memorial; and, in the center of the park, an imposing monument to the Confederacy, built in 1875 to honor Southern war heroes. Opposite the northwest corner of Forsyth Park (501 Whitaker Street) is Hodgson Hall, built in 1876 as a gift from Margaret Telfair Hodgson and Mary Telfair as a memorial to William B. Hodgson, noted scholar. The building is the home of the Georgia Historical Society, founded in 1839, Georgia's oldest historical organization, and one of the oldest in the United States. It is the repository of books, documents, and manuscript collections related to the history of Georgia, particularly Savannah and the coast, and is open to researchers.

South of Bay, East of Bull Street

Reynolds Square, near the head of Abercorn Street, was laid out in 1733 and is named for Georgia's first royal governor, John Reynolds. Its most prominent feature is the Pink House (23 Abercorn Street), one of Savannah's oldest and most historic structures. The stucco Pink House was built in 1789 as the home of Savannah rice factor James Habersham. It later was the Planter's Bank, the first state bank of Georgia, and is now a well-known Savannah restaurant and pub.

Balcony, Richardson-
Owens-Thomas House,
Savannah

South on Abercorn Street two blocks is Oglethorpe Square, laid out in 1734. Across from the square's northeast corner (124 Abercorn) is the Richardson-Owens-Thomas House, built in 1819 for Richard Richardson, a prominent Savannah banker and cotton factor. This is another superb example of English Regency architecture attributed to William Jay. It was here that the Marquis de Lafayette stayed during his 1825 visit to Savannah. The house is now operated by the Telfair Academy of Arts and Sciences and is open to the public.

Two blocks east of Oglethorpe Square at 324 East State Street, opposite the north side of Columbia Square, is the Isaiah Davenport House. Davenport, a noted architect, contractor, and shipbuilder, completed the Georgian brick mansion in 1820. The Historic Savannah Foundation restored the house, open to the public as a living history museum reflecting the lifestyles of a middle-class Savannah family in the 1820s. Also in Columbia Square is the location of the Bethesda Gate, a colonial entrance into the town, established in 1757 by royal governor Henry Ellis.

Near Abercorn Street's junction with Oglethorpe Avenue are several points of interest. Famed poet and novelist Conrad Aiken (1889–1973) was born at 228 East Oglethorpe Avenue.

Colonial Park Cemetery, established in 1750, dominates a large section between Oglethorpe Avenue on the north and East Perry Street on the south. Among the early Georgians buried here is Button Gwinnett, one of Georgia's three signers of the Declaration of Independence.

South of Colonial Park Cemetery on Abercorn is Lafayette Square, named for the Marquis de Lafayette. Two prominent structures here are the Cathedral of St. John the Baptist and the Andrew Low House (329 Abercorn Street), headquarters of the National Society of the Colonial Dames of America in the State of Georgia. The classical mid-nineteenth-century mansion is open to the public. Just off the square, at 207 East Charlton Street, is the childhood home of Georgia author Flannery O'Connor (see Central Georgia tour).

Two blocks southeast of Colonial Park Cemetery (502 East Harris Street) is the Beach Institute African-American Cultural Center, a structure completed in 1867 by the American Missionary Association as the first black Freedmen's Bureau school in Savannah. The best-known alumnus of the school was Robert S. Abbott, who in 1905 founded the *Chicago Defender,* one of the nation's most influential black newspapers. The center now sponsors black art exhibitions and other cultural activities. Massie Heritage Interpretation Center, near Calhoun Square at 207 East Gordon Street, occupies an original building of Georgia's oldest chartered school system.

A good side trip at this point, the end of the Savannah square tours, is about three miles east of downtown Savannah via the President Street extension (U.S. 80), to Old Fort Jackson on the Savannah River. This original brick masonry fort was begun in 1808, manned during the War of 1812, and enlarged from 1845 to 1860. During the Civil War, it was the primary site for Confederate river defenses of Savannah's seaward approaches. Operated by the Coastal Heritage Society, the site features a museum and living history demonstrations.

TOUR TWO

Savannah Environs, South

Wormsloe State Historic Site is reached from downtown Savannah by traveling south on Abercorn Street to Montgomery Crossroad, left to Skidaway Road, right and south to a traffic light. On the Isle of Hope, Wormsloe was a colonial plantation established by Noble Jones, a physician and carpenter who arrived on the first boat with Oglethorpe in 1733. The Jones family was linked continuously with Wormsloe for more than two centuries. The name Wormsloe comes from Jones's cultivation of mulberry trees to support silk production. On the site are the tabby ruins of his fortified colonial home, Fort Wimberly, built in 1741 overlooking the Skidaway River. In addition to the tabby ruins, the site has an interpretive museum with eighteenth-century colonial artifacts and year-round living history demonstrations.

Also in this area, on Ferguson Avenue, is Bethesda, the oldest orphanage in America, opened in 1740 by George Whitefield and James

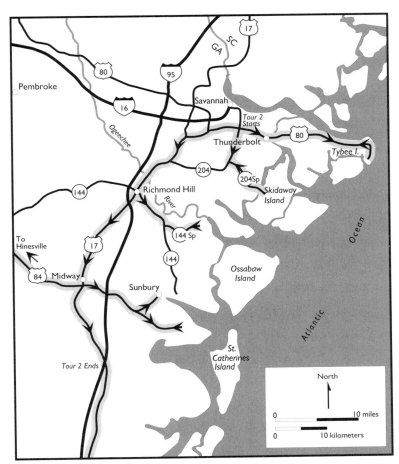

Coastal Georgia, Tour Two

Habersham. Bethesda has a small museum telling its history. By proceeding on Ferguson Avenue to its junction with Diamond Causeway, one can reach **Skidaway Island** across a bridge over Skidaway Narrows, part of the Atlantic Intracoastal Waterway. A short distance farther is the entrance to Skidaway Island State Park, which has camping, hiking, swimming, and other recreational activities including an interpretive nature trail through the salt marshes and upland forest. The Skidaway Institute of Oceanography overlooks the Wilmington River on the north end of the island. Here the University of Georgia Marine Extension Service operates the only public saltwater marine aquarium on the Georgia coast. One may view many species of fish, sharks, and sea turtles. The service conducts regular marsh and barrier island studies and field trips.

Savannah Environs, East

From downtown, Abercorn Street leads south, and a left turn at the junction with Victory Drive, a palm-lined twin thoroughfare built in the 1920s as a memorial to the Savannah soldiers of World War I, leads three miles east to the small fishing community of **Thunderbolt**. On the way to Thunderbolt, Victory Drive passes Grayson Stadium, the home of the Savannah Cardinals, the minor-league baseball farm team of the St. Louis Cardinals. Picturesque Thunderbolt lies beside the Wilmington River, where shrimp boats and pleasure craft are docked and fresh seafood is available in various restaurants and packing houses. Also in Thunderbolt is Savannah State College, chartered as a land-grant state college for African Americans in 1890 and now a unit of the University System of Georgia. Just north of Victory Drive, on Bonaventure Road along the river, is historic Bonaventure Cemetery.

This drive proceeds east across the bridge over the Wilmington River and continues past the junction with U.S. 80 across Whitemarsh Island, Turner Creek, and Wilmington Island. U.S. 80, known locally as Tybee Road, crosses the Bull River, which connects the Savannah River with Wassaw Sound to the south, and McQueen Island. Near the approaches to Tybee is a turnoff (left) to Fort Pulaski National Monument on Cockspur Island. Open daily, Fort Pulaski is an outstanding example of the nineteenth-century brick masonry fortifications constructed along the southern U.S. coast. Built on massive pilings sunk deep into the salt marsh and mud, the fort was begun in 1829 and was overseen by a young engineer recently graduated from West Point, Lt. Robert E. Lee. Federal batteries of rifled cannon, sited under the cover of darkness near Lazaretto Creek on Tybee Island, reduced Fort Pulaski so effectively after thirty hours of bombardment that the Confederate commander, Col. Charles H. Olmstead, was forced to surrender. There is a museum, and regular living history demonstrations take place at the site.

Tybee Island is across Lazaretto Creek. On the north end of this small resort and residential island are Fort Screven and the Tybee Lighthouse. Fort Screven, constructed in 1875, became an active army outpost and battery in 1898 prior to the Spanish-American War. The site served as an artillery and infantry training ground during World Wars I and II, being commanded for a time by Gen. George C. Marshall. Fort Screven was closed in 1945.

The 145-foot-high Tybee Lighthouse was built in 1791, partially destroyed by retreating Confederate forces in 1862, and rebuilt to its present configuration in 1867. One of two operable lights on the Georgia coast, it guides shipping through Tybee Roads at the approaches to the Savannah River. The Tybee Museum and the lighthouse are open for tours. Hotel and restaurant facilities are available along the beach.

TABBY

Tabby is a building material refined by Thomas Spalding and utilized by nineteenth-century plantation owners, many of whom adopted his architectural ideas. Spalding's formula for tabby combined equal parts of oyster shell, sand, water, and lime, which is acquired by extracting the residue from burned oyster shells. The shells, which served as a binder for tabby, were gathered from creek banks or from the Indian mounds on the coastal islands.

—Buddy Sullivan

Bryan County

Any tour of coastal Georgia proceeding south from Savannah should ideally follow the picturesque route of U.S. 17 and its various arms that extend along the coast as state highways.

Before the Civil War, the Ogeechee River basin on the southern edge of Chatham County and the northern section of Bryan County was the scene of extensive rice cultivation operations. The huge Bryan County rice plantations, with their large slave populations, made this area vital to the Confederate war supply effort and thus an early target of Union military strategy. The traveler proceeding south along U.S. 17 toward the Ogeechee River into Bryan County will see state historical markers that detail the considerable Civil War military activity in this section.

Bryan County, named for colonial planter Jonathan Bryan, was created in 1793. The county seat is Pembroke. Just south of the Ogeechee River on U.S. 17, **Richmond Hill** is located on the former site of Ways Station, a depot on the Savannah and Gulf Railroad, which opened through the region in the 1850s.

Beginning in 1925, Detroit automaker Henry Ford developed Ways Station as a planned community. He acquired enormous tracts of land in the Bryan County area and built a winter home on the Ogeechee River on the former site of three antebellum rice plantations. Under Ford's expertise, many educational, social, and religious facilities and programs were developed for the people of the area, black and white alike. Many of the structures associated with the Ford era in Richmond Hill are still standing. By turning left at the traffic light in Richmond Hill to Ga. 144, the traveler can cross the lands of the former rice plantations and observe some of the Ford-era structures, none of which is presently open to the public. One of these, a former kindergarten building, houses the Richmond Hill Heritage Society, which sponsors a small museum of memorabilia in the building and conducts periodic tours of some of the buildings associated with Henry Ford.

Ford's efforts resulted in the first real steps toward providing quality education for blacks of the area. This was realized with the construction of the George Washington Carver School, a modern, consolidated school for black children. In 1937, the large eighteen-room Community House was built in Ways, on Ga. 144 near the Catholic church. The Community House provided the young women of the area with a place to expand their "social horizons" through instruction in the homemaking arts. Ford also established a trade school for the young people of the area and an adult education program.

Eight miles southeast of Richmond Hill is Fort McAllister State Historic Park, where there are tent and trailer camping, picnic areas, boat launching facilities, a marina, a nature trail, and excellent recreational fresh and salt water fishing. At the historic site an interpretive museum and a number of restored earthwork fortifications mark the site of Fort McAllister, built in 1862 by the Confederates defending the Ogeechee River opposite Genesis Point to protect the river plantations and the southern flank of Savannah. During 1862 and 1863 the fort successfully withstood repeated Federal naval assaults from the river by armored ironclad vessels mounting fifteen-inch guns, but it fell to Union troops under Major Kilpatrick in December 1864. With the fall of Fort McAllister, the Ogeechee River was unobstructed to the Union supply ships, and Sherman's forces successfully breached the "back door" to Savannah. The delta's booming rice economy never recovered after the war, although planting continued on a small scale until 1887 when a hurricane destroyed many of the dikes, canals, tidegates, and other plantation equipment.

About a half-mile west of the Ga. 144 junction with U.S. 17, the Georgia Department of Natural Resources operates the Richmond Hill Fish Hatchery, previously known as the Henry Ford Fish Hatchery. This tract is the scene of the cultivation of bass, bream, crappie, and various other species.

Liberty County, Midway, and Sunbury

Five miles south of Richmond Hill, Liberty County is one of the most historically rich Georgia counties. Created in 1777, it was the "cradle of liberty" in the years before and during the American Revolution and homeplace of an unusually large number of people involved in the formation of the American republic. Liberty County's seat of government is **Hinesville**, several miles west of U.S. 17. Hinesville is the home of Fort Stewart and the 24th Infantry Division. The fort is one of the largest military reservations in the nation, being established in 1940 preparatory to the U.S. buildup for World War II. A military museum at Fort Stewart features the story of the 24th Infantry, including its important role in the 1991 Persian Gulf War. Information and admission procedures are available at the post gate just off U.S. 84 in Hinesville. Many of Liberty County's points of interest are situated along and east of U.S. 17, however, and it is in this area that the tour of this section will concentrate.

U.S. 17 leads the traveler directly into the small town of **Midway**, established in 1752 by Puritan descendants of the English colony begun at Dorchester, Massachusetts, in 1630. They came from South Carolina and established themselves along the Medway and Newport Rivers, about ten miles from the sea and roughly midway between Savannah and Darien. In 1754, they organized the Midway Congregational Church and built a wooden frame house of worship facing the road to Sunbury. British forces burned this structure in 1778. The present clapboard Midway Church, built of cypress timber and held together by hand-wrought nails, was completed in 1792. It features a high pulpit and elevated galleries for the slaves from the area plantations. The names, dates, and inscriptions on the tombstones in the cemetery across the highway are a vivid testimony to Liberty's rich and enduring legacy, particularly during the nineteenth century. A tour of the museum beside the church is a good introduction to that legacy.

About six miles east of Midway from U.S. 17's junction with U.S. 84/Ga. 38 (at the light) is the site of Dorchester Village, settled in 1843 by settlers from Midway and Sunbury and named for the Dorchesters in England, Massachusetts, and South Carolina, homes of the ancestors of the Midway settlers. Dorchester Presbyterian Church near here was built in 1854.

Ga. 38 leads to Fort Morris Historic Site, at which is located an interpretive museum with exhibits and displays depicting the history of Fort Morris and the "dead town" of Sunbury. Periodic living history demonstrations are held here. Fort Morris was a Revolutionary War fortification built to defend the port of Sunbury. It fell to the British in 1779, and Sunbury was burned. The earthwork redoubts of another fort built on the site in the War of 1812 can be seen today. Just past the entrance to Fort Morris is the old Sunbury Cemetery, where virtually all the burials occurred before the Civil War. With the rapid development of Savannah after the Revolution, once-prosperous Sunbury began to decline in importance and by 1860 was completely deserted.

From Fort Morris, three barrier islands can be seen across the Medway River and the intervening salt marshes: Ossabaw, St. Catherines, and Colonels. Ossabaw, about twenty miles below Savannah, and neighboring St. Catherines, to the south, were the hunting islands of the local branch of the Creek Indian nation, the Guale (WAHL-ee).

On St. Catherines Island in 1566, the Spanish, under Florida governor Menendez de Aviles, established a large Jesuit mission-presidio that later became a Franciscan mission. Archaeological investigations on the island in the 1980s revealed considerable evidence of Spanish religious and military activity dating to the sixteenth and seventeenth centuries.

In the nineteenth century, both Ossabaw and St. Catherines were the scene of extensive agricultural operations, particularly in the cultivation of Sea Island cotton, and numerous slaves populated both islands. Arrangements for a visit to Ossabaw Island must be made with the Brunswick office of the Georgia Department of Natural Resources, which manages it for the state. St. Catherines is privately owned and is not open to the public.

In 1773 naturalist William Bartram visited Colonels Island, a marsh island between the Liberty County mainland and St. Catherines, and noted its Indian shell mounds in his *Travels Through North and South*

Carolina, Georgia, East and West Florida. The island, reached by Ga. 38E, was later the home for a number of prosperous Liberty County planters prior to the Civil War. Extensive cotton cultivation took place on the island, which is now a recreational and residential community where boat launching and fishing facilities are available.

Near Fort Morris (follow signs) is the restored Seabrook Village, a living history museum of early twentieth-century African American culture, including restored homes, churches, and a school. There are interpretive tours of this site.

West on Ga. 38 through Midway, past the junction with U.S. 17, is an important center of African American heritage, the old Dorchester Academy. With the assistance of the American Missionary Association, the Freedmen's Bureau started a school for black children on this site in 1870 on one acre of land. Later named Dorchester Academy, by 1917 it had eight frame buildings and housed over three hundred students. The academy closed in 1940 with the construction of a consolidated black public school at Riceboro. In 1948, the American Missionary Association converted the structures of Dorchester Academy into a community center that became associated with the growing civil rights movement in the 1950s and 60s. Workshops sponsored by the Southern Christian Leadership Conference were held at Dorchester Academy, and Dr. Martin Luther King Jr. held a planning retreat here in 1962 to prepare for his successful 1963 Birmingham Campaign.

Back in Midway, a right turn at the light leads south along U.S. 17 into McIntosh County.

TOUR THREE

McIntosh County and Sapelo Island

U.S. 17 crosses the South Newport River into McIntosh County, created from Liberty County in 1793 and named for the McIntosh family, which was prominent in the formation of the Georgia colony and the movement for independence. Across the South Newport bridge is Memory Park, site of the "Smallest Church in America," tiny Christ's Chapel. In 1950, Mrs. Agnes Harper built the little chapel as a place for travelers to rest and worship.

Beyond the chapel, a paved road to the east travels six miles to the Harris Neck National Wildlife Refuge. Managed by the U.S. Fish and Wildlife Service, the refuge has a network of roads by which one may travel to view many species of birds, particularly migrating waterfowl, such as nesting wood storks and great egrets. The refuge is on the north end of Harris Neck, scene of colonial land grants dating back to the 1750s and extensive cotton plantations in the nineteenth century. During World War II, land that had been given to freed blacks was taken from their descendants for an army airfield. After the war,

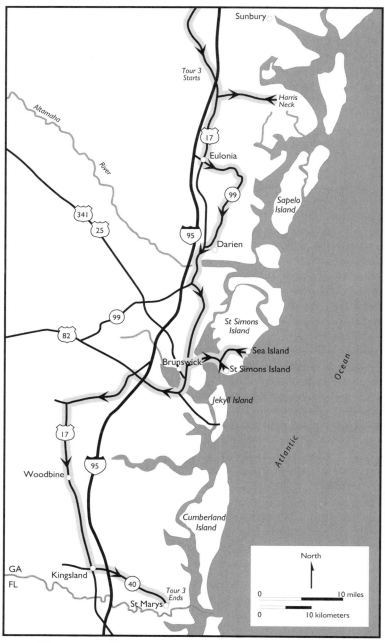

Coastal Georgia, Tour Three

Sorting the day's catch, Eulonia

instead of being returned to those owners, the tract was designated a federal wildlife refuge. Its roads are the concrete runways and parking aprons of the airfield.

At Eulonia Ga. 99 proceeds from U.S. 17 east to **Crescent**, a small community named for the bend in the Sapelo River. Here one may take a side road to Belleville, where shrimp boats are docked. Just off Ga. 99 east of Crescent, on a high bluff overlooking Creighton Island across the salt marshes, is the site of the old Baisden Bluff Academy where the children of prominent local citizens attended classes in the early nineteenth century. In another two miles, the Valona Road travels east to the small fishing community of **Valona**, established in the 1890s. Here shrimp trawlers dock at packing houses along Shell-bluff Creek.

A short distance south on Ga. 99 a sign marks the turnoff to the Sapelo Island ferry dock. Here the Sapelo Island Visitors Center offers exhibits and interpretive displays that focus on the ecology of the Georgia barrier islands and the history and African American culture of state-owned **Sapelo Island**. Tickets for guided day trip tours of Sapelo via the island ferry may be purchased at the center. Space is limited, and reservations can be made through the visitors' center.

Sapelo Island contained the plantation of Thomas Spalding from 1802 until his death in 1851. Spalding refined the Sea Island cotton and sugar industries and designed and built his octagonal tabby sugar manufactory on Barn Creek in 1809. The ruins of this structure are still visible. In 1810, Spalding built South End House, constructed of thick tabby walls designed to withstand the worst of hurricanes (which it did in 1824). The restored house is on the guided island tour.

When Spalding's slaves on Sapelo were freed after the Civil War, they established several settlements on the island, one of them **Hog Hammock**. Tour visitors will be able to see Hog Hammock, which is home to about seventy residents, many of them descendants of slaves. This is one of the few surviving sites on the south Atlantic coast of African American culture associated with the barrier sea islands.

Later owners of Sapelo were Howard E. Coffin, chief engineer of the Hudson Motorcar Company and founder of the Cloister resort on nearby Sea Island, and tobacco heir Richard J. Reynolds. The state of Georgia now owns much of the island. The University of Georgia uses old farm and dairy buildings on the south end of the island as a marine research laboratory. The Marine Institute has been the scene of significant ecological research associated with the salt marshes and estuaries and now functions as a vital element of the Sapelo Island National Estuarine Research Reserve.

Off the northeast end of Sapelo is Blackbeard Island, an unpopulated national wildlife refuge that was a government live oak timber reserve and yellow fever quarantine station in the nineteenth century. It is accessible only by chartered boats, which may be hired at the mainland fishing community of Shellman Bluff at the western end of Sapelo Sound. Eighteen miles off Sapelo is Gray's Reef, a National Marine Sanctuary that is ideal for sport fishing and diving. The limestone outcropping on the seabed of the Atlantic is Georgia's only natural reef.

South of Valona on Ga. 99 is the quiet, oak-shaded residential community of **Ridgeville**, known historically as The Ridge. A mile farther is St. Andrew's Cemetery, originally the Spalding family plot. Many people associated with local history are buried here, including Thomas Spalding.

Darien

Two miles south is **Darien**, a small fishing community and the seat of McIntosh County. This second-oldest planned town of Georgia was settled by Scottish Highlanders as a military outpost under James Oglethorpe in January 1736. The Highlanders established a permanent town and were instrumental in saving the new Georgia colony from Spanish invasion in 1742. At the intersection of U.S. 17 and Ga. 99 is the pink marble Highlander Monument, a memorial to the Scots.

The Darien welcome center provides walking tour brochures of the historic district, which extends from the waterfront for several blocks on either side of U.S. 17. The self-guided tour takes only about two hours.

Except for the tabby waterfront ruins and the two-story Strain building on West Broad Street, all the buildings in Darien were constructed after the Civil War. The town was burned in June 1863 by Federal troops stationed on nearby St. Simons Island. Despite Darien's remarkable growth as a center for the export of cotton, rice, and timber during two distinct boom eras before and after the Civil War, the town's population has never exceeded two thousand residents. In the early 1900s, after overcutting of the forests along the Altamaha River ended the timber and sawmill boom for Darien, the town began to rely on commercial fisheries as an economic mainstay.

Near the welcome center is the site of Fort Darien, laid out by Oglethorpe for the Highlander forces in 1736 on a high bluff overlooking the river. Farther west are waterfront tabby ruins that are the remains of cotton factorages and warehouses built about 1815 to 1820. Sawmills developed along the riverfront after the Civil War as Darien became one of the leading pine timber ports on the southern coast from about 1870 to 1910.

Darien has a number of historic churches, among them the First Presbyterian Church, home of the oldest Presbyterian congregation in Georgia; the First United Methodist Church; St. Andrew's Episcopal Church; and St. Cyprian's Episcopal Church, a tabby structure built by former Butler Island slaves in 1876 and named for a martyred African saint.

One mile east along the paved road from the Darien welcome center is the Fort King George State Historic Site. A museum of local history interpreting the Indian, colonial, Scottish, and sawmilling periods and a replica of a twenty-six-foot square, two-story gabled cypress blockhouse built here in 1721 are attractions. The fort was the first English settlement on land that is now the state of Georgia and for seven years was garrisoned by British soldiers from His Majesty's 41st Independent Company. The soldiers endured many hardships in the hostile coastal environment, and many of their dead rest in graves in the cemetery near the fort. Living history demonstrations and cannon firings are regularly held at the fort.

Also on this site, called Lower Bluff, are ruins from two eras of Darien sawmilling. A steam sawmill that operated on the site from 1818 until 1905 became the leading timber business on the Georgia coast. After a merger made the company the leading pine timber concern in the world, Darien exported a record 112.5 million linear board feet of yellow pine timber in the peak year of 1900. Up to eighty sailing vessels at a time loaded timber and lumber and deposited ballast rock in the marshes along the local waterways.

South of the welcome center U.S. 17 crosses the Darien River bridge and the northern portion of the expansive Altamaha River delta. Ten miles upriver was the site of Fort Barrington, a colonial outpost built in 1760. Here in 1765 the naturalist John Bartram of Philadelphia found the rare evergreen shrub known as the Lost Gordonia

(*Franklinia alatamaha*). Also on the Altamaha is the Lewis Island Game Management Area, managed by the Georgia Department of Natural Resources. Lewis Island, much of which is inundated during spring tides and freshets, is the site of one of the few remaining stands of virgin cypress in Georgia.

Just south of Darien U.S. 17 crosses the Butler River to **Butler Island**, which was the nineteenth-century rice and cotton plantation of Maj. Pierce Butler of Philadelphia. He was the largest slaveholder in tidewater Georgia, with a thousand slaves working two plantations. Butler Island was the leading rice plantation south of the Savannah River, shipping over two million pounds of rice annually during the peak years of the 1850s. Slave mortality was high on rice plantations, for their cultivation required hot, grueling work in malarial waters. The grounds and river dikes of Butler Island are open to the public with the most noticeable structure being the brick rice mill chimney built by slave labor in the 1850s.

Butler's grandson, Pierce Mease Butler, inherited the holdings in 1836. In the winter of 1838–39, the younger Butler and his wife, Frances Anne Kemble, visited the Butler Island plantation, and she compiled her *Journal of a Residence on a Georgian Plantation*, published in England and America in 1863.

Butler Island and the adjoining delta islands of Generals, Champneys, and Broughton are managed by the Georgia Department of Natural Resources as the twenty-six-thousand-acre Altamaha Waterfowl Management Area, where managed duck hunts are conducted on a seasonal basis. This second-largest waterfowl management area east of the Mississippi River is a refuge to alligators, bobcats, raccoons, herons, egrets, ducks, and other wading birds. The area is ideal for recreational fishing and bird-watching, especially from October through April when the former rice fields are flooded to attract migrating waterfowl.

Glynn County

Glynn County, which begins about two-and-a-half miles south of Darien, was created in 1777 and named in honor of John Glynn, a member of the British House of Commons who defended the American cause of independence. The Altamaha delta on the Glynn County side of the river is also rich in nineteenth-century rice plantation culture. Tabby ruins west of U.S. 17 are the remains of a sugar mill built by Robert Grant at Elizafield Plantation in the early 1800s. West of Elizafield were the great rice plantations of Hopeton and Altama. In 1832 Hopeton was reported to be the best-managed and most efficient of any plantation in the South.

Near the intersection of U.S. 17 and Ga. 99 is the entrance to Hofwyl-Broadfield Plantation State Historic Site, where an excellent museum interprets the complexities of nineteenth-century rice cultivation, the slave labor system, and Georgia tidewater plantation life. Visitors may view actual rice fields, dikes, irrigation ditches, canals, and tidegates, all of which made a rice plantation one of the engineering marvels of its day. Also at Hofwyl is a frame plantation house built in 1851 by George Columbus Dent and his wife, Ophelia Troup Dent. Five generations of the same family lived on the plantation until a descendant willed Hofwyl to the State of Georgia in 1973. Living history programs at the site interpret the rice culture, and several African American history programs are held here during the year.

Six miles south of Hofwyl, a traffic light marks the entrance to the Federal Law Enforcement Training Center, on the site of the former Glynco Naval Air Station. In 1942, Glynco, just north of Brunswick, was opened by the U.S. Navy as an airship base for anti-submarine warfare. The facility continued to be used after the war as a blimp base. Its two airship hangars were at one time said to be the largest wooden structures in the world.

Brunswick

Five miles farther south is **Brunswick**, the seat of Glynn County. A good point to begin a tour of the Brunswick historic district is the visitors' center at the intersection of U.S. 17 and the causeway to St. Simons Island. An interesting exhibit on the grounds of the visitors' center is a replica of a World War II Liberty ship, ninety-nine of which the Jones Shipyards at Brunswick constructed from 1942 through 1944.

Immediately south of the visitors' center on U.S. 17 is a live oak tree called the Lanier Oak. It was here, overlooking the salt marshes toward Glynn County's sea islands, that legend says Sidney Lanier composed his poem "The Marshes of Glynn" in 1874. A historical marker notes the site and is a good place to stop for the expansive vistas of the marshes and tidal mud flats. Here one may better understand the quiet beauty of Georgia's salt marshes, which inspired Lanier to write that "Somehow my soul seems suddenly free/From the weighing of fate and the sad discussion of sin,/By the length and the breadth and the sweep of the marshes of Glynn."

Brunswick is Georgia's second-leading seaport behind Savannah. Containerized cargo and imported automobiles are off-loaded at the Mayor's Point and Colonels Island terminals. Brunswick is also the scene of considerable pulp-paper milling and commercial seafood activities, including the harvesting and processing of shrimp and blue crabs.

Part of the World War II effort, Jones Shipyards, Brunswick

The city's original street names, which reflect a decided English influence, were all retained following the colonies' independence from the mother country. The streets were named in the 1771 survey for the Dukes of Gloucester and Newcastle, for King George, Lord Mansfield, and General Monk, with additional English influence being reflected in the names of Prince, Norwich, London, Reynolds, and Union Streets, along with Hanover, Wright, and Queens Squares on the south end of the city. Glynn Academy, the second-oldest chartered public school in Georgia, opened in Brunswick in 1788.

In the nineteenth century the city prospered as a seaport and rail center and from the 1880s to the early 1900s ranked second only to Savannah in world leadership for the export of naval stores products, timber, and lumber. In the early 1900s, Brunswick was the world leader in the production of railroad ties, creosote products, and other naval stores. Later in the twentieth century, Brunswick developed as a resort city. In the 1950s Brunswick was prominent in the processing of seafood, particularly shrimp and crabs. Many Portuguese and Greeks migrated here from the north Florida coast in the 1920s and began the shrimping industry.

The Old Town Brunswick historic preservation movement on the south end of the city has been one of the most successful in the southeast. Much of Brunswick's Victorian-style architecture has been preserved through this effort. A good example of the Old Town movement is the Mahoney-McGarvey House, a Victorian residence built in 1891 at 1709 Reynolds Street opposite the old Glynn County courthouse. The Old Town section of Brunswick is a National Register District. Downtown Brunswick is the site of several excellent examples of varied architecture, including the former city hall building at 1227 Newcastle Street, a Romanesque brick structure built in 1891; and the old Glynn County courthouse at G and Union Streets, constructed in 1907. Wright Square at the intersection of Norwich and George Streets was Brunswick's public cemetery until the 1850s.

About a mile north of the downtown area, on Norwich Street, is Selden Park, a public park built on the site of the Selden Normal & Industrial Institute. This was considered one of the outstanding African American schools in Georgia when it opened in 1903 to serve the young people of the Brunswick area. Named for Dr. Charles Selden, who purchased the land for the school, it closed in 1933. Glynn County acquired the land for a public park that is popular for family outings, picnics, and recreation.

St. Simons and Jekyll Islands

From the visitors' center on U.S. 17, the F. J. Torras Causeway crosses a series of bridges, tidal rivers, and salt marshes to reach **St. Simons Island**, second-largest and most developed of Georgia's barrier islands. A left turn at the first light on Sea Island Road and another left at the entrance to Epworth-by-the-Sea lead to a large United Methodist center that draws people of all denominations from throughout the South for educational and spiritual retreats. The Arthur J. Moore Methodist Museum, named for a beloved bishop, has a heavily used

Annual "Blessing of the Fleet," Brunswick

research library. Epworth is built at Gascoigne Bluff, the grounds of the former Hamilton Plantation. Here can be seen the restored ruins of several tabby slave cabins. Historical markers describe the development of large sawmills along Gascoigne Bluff in the 1870s and 1880s when St. Simons Island was a lumbering center.

Turning left from Epworth, continuing along Sea Island Road, and looking north across the marsh at Dunbar Creek, the traveler can see Ebo Landing, where, in May 1803, West African slaves being transported from Savannah to St. Simons drowned as they were being unloaded. Legend is that as their sailing vessel neared the shore, rather than submit to slavery, an Ebo chieftain led his tribesmen into the water, resulting in many tragic deaths. The survivors were taken to Cannon's Point Plantation on St. Simons and to Sapelo Island.

Frederica Road, to the left at a traffic light, proceeds several miles to the Fort Frederica National Monument. Gen. James Edward Oglethorpe established the fort in March 1736 to protect the southern flank of the new Georgia colony from incursions from the rival Spanish in Florida. At the peak of its influence in the mid-1740s, Frederica was the most elaborate British fortification in North America.

The town of Frederica rapidly grew around the fort as Oglethorpe encouraged craftsmen, artisans, shopkeepers, and their families to settle there. Walking the grounds reveals the excavated tabby foundations of many of the homes of these original town settlers, the layout of some of the streets, the town gate and moat, a portion of the barracks building, and the tabby ruins of the King's Magazine where gunpowder was stored in a brick-lined vault. After the British victory at the Battle of Bloody Marsh, the regiment disbanded, and many settlers left for other parts of the colony or England. In 1758 a fire swept through Frederica, and the town was never rebuilt.

A visitors' center makes available a film of the site, artifacts, exhibits, brochures, and guides. Viewing the film and exhibits and walking the grounds of the fort can take at least two hours. Lime burnings (burning oyster shells to extract lime for the making of tabby) and other interpretive programs are held on a periodic basis at Fort Frederica, open daily.

A visit to Christ Episcopal Church, adjacent to Fort Frederica National Monument, is an option either before or after visiting the fort. With the arrival of the first settlers to Frederica in 1736, the congregation of this church was established where John Wesley preached under the live oak trees. Anson Phelps Dodge Jr., whose family operated the prosperous St. Simons lumber mills on the island, provided funds to build the present Christ Church edifice in 1884. In the church cemetery many of the leading citizens of St. Simons are buried, beginning with the early nineteenth century and including plantation owners and their families, wealthy cotton and lumber merchants, and busi-

Fort Frederica National Monument, St. Simons

ness and political figures, all associated with the sweeping panorama of coastal Georgia history.

By turning left at the fork of Frederica Road after leaving Christ Episcopal Church, one may travel about five miles to the north end of St. Simons, where some of the tabby ruins of Hampton Point Plantation can be seen. Also known as Butler's Point, this tract was the large Sea Island cotton plantation of Maj. Pierce Butler. It is now a fashionable residential district and golf resort.

The traveler should return along Frederica Road to the first stop light, which is the intersection with the Sea Island causeway (at the stables), turn left, and travel one mile to **Sea Island**. Here the automotive pioneer Howard Earle Coffin of Detroit and Sapelo Island developed the world-famous Cloister. The resort's Spanish-Mediterranean architecture reflects the styles along the lower southern coast and Florida in the 1920s. Designed by Addison Mizner of Palm Beach and Boca Raton, the Cloister has been visited over the years by presidents, kings, queens, and dignitaries from around the world. Also on Sea Island are the residences and summer cottages of some of the most affluent families in the southern United States.

To the left at the Sea Island intersection, Frederica Road travels two miles to a light at the intersection of Demere (DEM-er-y) Road. To the left, signs point to the Bloody Marsh Battlefield Monument, another left just off Demere Road. In 1742 a force of British regulars and Scottish Highlanders under Oglethorpe ambushed a much larger force of Spanish grenadiers who were marching up the Military Road for an attack upon Frederica. This small battle, though insignificant tactically, proved to be one of the most important strategic outcomes in North America during the first half of the eighteenth century, for it preserved Britain's hold on its southernmost colony and ended the threat of further invasion attempts on Georgia by the Spanish based in Florida.

Demere Road travels on south to the St. Simons Lighthouse and the Museum of Coastal History. Operated by the Coastal Georgia Historical Society, this museum and exhibits interpret the history of Brunswick, St. Simons Island, and the local lighthouse. Tour highlights are the climb up a winding stairwell to the top of the St. Simons Light, 104 feet above the ground, and the magnificent views of the ocean, waterways, and islands. James Gould built the first lighthouse on this site in 1810. It was destroyed in the Civil War. The present tower and the adjoining brick Victorian lighthouse keeper's residence (which houses

St. Simons Lighthouse and Museum of Coastal History

"Beating the Rice," Georgia Sea Island Festival

the museum) date to 1872. The U.S. Coast Guard operates the St. Simons light as it guides shipping into the Brunswick port through St. Simons Sound.

The village of St. Simons is adjacent to the lighthouse. Here are a concrete public fishing pier, restaurants, shops, boutiques, and souvenir outlets. Each August, the Sea Island Festival at Neptune Park honors the African American heritage of the barrier islands and coastal mainland of South Carolina, Georgia, and upper Florida through traditional crafts of basket, quilt, soap, and fishnet making; low country foods such as smoked mullet, barbecued ribs, and shrimp boils; and the songs and other folk traditions that make up the enduring legacy of the Gullah-Geechees of tidewater Georgia. The cultures of coastal Georgia and the Windward Rice Coast of Africa are referred to locally as the "Gullah-Geechee Connection." The Gullah language combines elements of English and West African speech. The Gullahs began in low-country South Carolina, and Geechee usually refers to the Georgia coastal areas.

King's Way travels from the village to a traffic light where a turn to the left leads through huge live oaks to the Sea Island Golf Club, on the site of the nineteenth-century Retreat plantation. Here are tabby ruins of Retreat's slave hospital, barns, and other structures. This plantation of Thomas Butler King and his wife, Ann Matilda Page King, was one of the most prosperous on the Georgia coast during its heyday.

After touring St. Simons Island, the traveler can return to the mainland, take U.S. 17 south, and cross the Brunswick River to the turnoff to **Jekyll Island**, the barrier island directly south of St. Simons. On Jekyll are resort hotels, restaurants, public beaches, and golf courses.

Attendants at the approach to the island collect a small fee and hand out brochures, maps, and other information.

Named for a financial backer of the Georgia colony, Jekyll Island was the colonial plantation of Major William Horton, who grew hops and barley and operated Georgia's first brewery in order to supply ale for the British regiment at nearby Frederica. Tabby foundation remains mark the site of the brewery on the north end of Jekyll. A Frenchman, Christophe Poulain du Bignon, who also owned part of Sapelo Island, acquired Jekyll (then Jekyl) in 1792. He developed farming operations and was one of the leading cotton planters of the region. At a small tidal creek on the north end of Jekyll, the schooner-yacht *Wanderer* in 1858 illegally landed 490 slaves from Africa.

The highlight of a visit to Jekyll is a tour of the Millionaire's Village in the Jekyll Island Club Historic District on the west side of the island fronting on the Intracoastal Waterway (to the left just past the toll booth). In 1886, the du Bignon family sold their holdings to the newly formed Jekyll Island Club of New York City. The island was to be a winter retreat for a hundred of the wealthiest, most affluent of America's business, industrial, financial, and social elite. According to the *New York Times* of April 4, 1886, the Jekyll Island Club "is going to be a swell club, the creme de la creme of all, in as much as many of the members are intending to erect cottages and make it their Winter Newport." A 1904 publication referred to the Jekyll Island Club as the "richest, the most exclusive, the most inaccessible Club in the world."

The large, turreted Jekyll Island Clubhouse (now a commercial hotel) in 1887 was followed by a number of private cottages. Members included such luminaries as Joseph Pulitzer, William Rockefeller, J. Pierpont Morgan, Vincent Astor, William K. Vanderbilt, Edwin Gould, Henry Kirke Porter, Richard Crane, and Walter Jennings. The club season usually ran from early January through March. Jekyll was the scene of the first transcontinental telephone call, made in 1915 on a hookup between Alexander Graham Bell in New York, his assistant Thomas A. Watson in San Francisco, and Theodore N. Vail, the president of the American Telephone and Telegraph Company, on Jekyll Island.

The 240-acre Jekyll Island Historic District, operated by the Jekyll Island Authority, represents one of the most ambitious historic preservation projects in the southeastern United States. Information and tour tickets are available on Stable Road at the museum orientation center, housed in the restored club stables. At the center are photographic exhibits and displays about the Jekyll Island Club and a video presentation. A two-hour tram tour includes visits to several cottages, and a summer architectural tour explores other cottages and Faith Chapel (1904). The chapel's Tiffany windows are considered the best in the state.

The growth of south Florida as the preferred winter retreat for the nation's wealthy and the onset of World War II, which severely reduced the force of available local labor needed to maintain and manage the facility, led the Jekyll Island Club to disband in 1942. Five years later, the state of Georgia purchased the island from the club trustees for a state recreational park.

On the mainland, U.S. 17 leads south to Camden County. Those wishing to visit the Okefenokee Swamp can follow U.S. 82 west toward Waycross.

Camden County

Camden County was laid out in 1777 and named in honor of Charles Pratt, the Earl of Camden, a member of Parliament who was sympathetic to the American colonial cause. During the 1980s and early 1990s, Camden was one of the fastest-growing counties in the southeastern United States because of the development of the huge King's Bay Naval Submarine Base.

U.S. 17 passes through **Woodbine**, seat of Camden County. Founded in 1893 when the Seaboard Air Line Railroad was constructed through the section, it is the site of the former Woodbine rice plantation of the early 1800s. Woodbine is the name of the red flowering plant that grows in the area. The town is perhaps best known now for its annual Crawfish Festival held the last Saturday in April each year.

Twelve miles south of Woodbine is **Kingsland**, founded in 1894 as a flag station on the Seaboard Railroad and named for John King, one of Camden County's most prominent original settlers after the American Revolution. This is the last town on U.S. 17 before the highway crosses the St. Marys River into Florida.

At Kingsland, Ga. 40E and Ga. 40 Sp. lead to Crooked River State Park, an outstanding coastal recreational area. Available are cottages, tent and trailer campsites, a swimming pool, picnic shelters, boat launching ramp and marina, and excellent salt water fishing.

Just north of St. Marys is the entrance to the submarine base. Kings Bay is a deep-water inlet that extends into Cumberland Sound and the open sea. Developed by the navy during the 1980s and early 1990s, Kings Bay is the largest submarine base on the U.S. east coast and is the home port of eight nuclear-powered Trident missile submarines. Over ten thousand military and civilian support personnel are stationed at Kings Bay, which has restricted access and no public tours. Near the entrance to Kings Bay are the tabby ruins of a sugar mill built in 1825 by John H. McIntosh.

At the end of Ga. 40 is **St. Marys**, which, like the rest of Camden County, owes its recent phenomenal growth to the rapid development of the nearby submarine base. The town grew from about two thousand residents in 1980 to over eight thousand ten years later. St. Marys, founded in 1787, grew into an important seaport because of its position near the mouth of the St. Marys River. It was also the southernmost town in the United States when Florida was still a Spanish possession. St. Marys was a timber exporting center in the nineteenth century and a major stop on the Georgia-Florida inland waterway steamboat routes before and after the Civil War. In the early 1900s, a motorized train trolley operated between St. Marys and Kingsland to the west. In the 1930s, the well-known cartoonist Roy Crane visited St. Marys and was so intrigued by the old trolley system that he incorporated it into the storyline of his comic strip *Wash Tubbs*, which featured the antics of Wash and Captain Easy. Thus the famous "Toonerville Trolley" conceived in the sleepy Georgia coastal town of St. Marys gained national notoriety.

Some of the more historic attractions in St. Marys include the Presbyterian Church, on Osborne Street, the oldest church structure in the town, which was built in 1808 as a community worship center. It was incorporated as the Independent Presbyterian Church in 1818. Orange Hall, across from the Presbyterian Church at the corner of Osborne and Conyers Streets, is open to the public. The three-story Greek Revival house was begun in 1829 and completed by 1837 by Horace S. Pratt, pastor of the St. Marys Presbyterian Church. Because Orange Hall also serves as the St. Marys visitors center, it is a good first stop on a walking tour of the historic town. A self-guided walking tour brochure is available at the center. Guided tours are also available. The Methodist Church of St. Marys was built prior to the Civil War for a congregation established in 1799. Just east of St. Marys is Point Peter, where the British built Fort Tonyn in 1776 as a means of controlling the lower Georgia coast during the Revolution.

St. Marys is the access point to the **Cumberland Island National Seashore**, operated by the National Park Service. From the Cumberland Island visitor center at the waterfront, a ferry departs for the island several times daily, making possible half-day and all-day visits. There are no bridges to the island, nor are there vehicles for public use or concession facilities. Visitors on foot may view the ruins of Dungeness mansion on the south end of the island, the old Greene-Miller family cemetery, and the wild horses that roam the south end.

Cumberland, the largest and southernmost of the coastal Georgia chain of sea islands, is ideal for hikers who wish to enjoy a remote barrier island experience. The island is largely unpopulated and features an unspoiled maritime forest, a pristine beach almost twenty miles long, many walking trails, and primitive campgrounds. A developed campground, Sea Camp, near the ferry landing, has shower and restroom facilities and access to the beach. For information about camping on Cumberland, call or write Cumberland Island Na-

Feral horses, Cumberland Island

tional Seashore. The private Greyfield Inn provides overnight or weekend accommodations on the island.

Cumberland was the site of a sixteenth-century Spanish garrison and was later the scene of extensive live oak timbering operations for shipbuilding, particularly the construction of wooden warships of the early U.S. naval fleet. The island's owners included Thomas Carnegie, of Pittsburgh, whose mansion, Dungeness, burned in 1959 and left ruins visible to island visitors. His widow, Lucy Carnegie, ran Cumberland Island for many years after her husband's death. About 1900, other members of the family built several impressive residences that still stand.

In 1972, the National Park Service of the U.S. Department of the Interior established the Cumberland Island National Seashore. The south end of the island was opened to the public in 1975, with the beginning of regular ferry service to and from the mainland. The Carnegie family wished the National Park Service to preserve and interpret the natural and historic aspects of Cumberland and to encourage active participation in outdoor recreation in a natural environment.

SOURCES OF INFORMATION

BASIC SOURCES

Georgia Department of Industry, Trade, and Tourism: In addition to the annual official travel guide *Georgia on My Mind*, the department can provide a variety of specialized publications and information. Many of their materials are available at Georgia Welcome Centers. Georgia Department of Industry, Trade and Tourism, P.O. Box 1776, Atlanta, Georgia 30301; 1-800-847-4842 (toll free) or 404-656-3590.

Georgia Department of Natural Resources, Parks, Recreation and Historic Sites Division: *Georgia Parks on My Mind* brochure includes list of state parks and historic sites, facilities, addresses, phone numbers, and information on overnight accommodations. Georgia Department of Natural Resources, 1352 Floyd Tower East, 205 Butler Street, SE, Atlanta, Georgia 30334; 404-656-3530.

Georgia Department of Transportation (DOT): Official State Highway Map. Includes maps of roads and highways, mileage charts, a selection of city and town maps, phone numbers for State Patrol and other state and federal agencies that provide services of interest to travelers, and other valuable information. Approximate mileage can be calculated by using figures between mileage points marked on the map. The maps are available from the DOT map office or from state welcome centers. Georgia Department of Transportation, 2 Capitol Square, SE, Atlanta, Georgia 30334; 404-656-5267.

Phone Books: Consult a telephone directory for local information, government agencies, emergency numbers, and helpful "where to find" hints.

FOR MORE INFORMATION

Arts and humanities

Georgia Council for the Arts, 530 Means Street, NW, Atlanta, Georgia 30318; 404-651-7920.

Georgia Humanities Council, 50 Hurt Plaza, SE, #440, Atlanta, Georgia 30303; 404-523-6220.

Georgia's natural setting

Georgia Conservancy, 1776 Peachtree Street, NW, #400 South, Atlanta, Georgia 30309; 404-876-2900.

National Wildlife Refuges: U.S. Department of the Interior Fish and Wildlife Division; 404-679-7319.

Nature Conservancy of Georgia, 1401 Peachtree Street, NE, Atlanta, Georgia 30309; 404-873-6946.

State Wildlife Management Areas: Georgia Department of Natural Resources Wildlife Resources Division, 2070 U.S. Highway 278, SE, Social Circle, Georgia 30279; 770-918-6416.

History and historic sites

Georgia Department of Archives and History, 330 Capitol Avenue, SE, Atlanta, Georgia 30334; 404-656-2350.

Georgia Historical Society, 501 Whitaker Street, Savannah, Georgia 31499; 912-651-2128.

Georgia Trust for Historic Preservation, 1516 Peachtree Street, NW, Atlanta, Georgia 30309; 404-881-9980.

National Archives Atlanta Branch, 1557 St. Joseph Avenue, East Point, Georgia 30344; 404-763-7477.

National Sacred Harp Foundation, c/o Hugh McGraw, 1010 Waddell Street, Bremen, Georgia 30110 (write ahead to arrange a tour).

Old Clinton Historical Society, P.O. Box 341, Gray, Georgia 31032; 912-986-3384.

Local historical organizations.

Local communities: Consult local or area chambers of commerce, welcome centers, or visitors' bureaus.

Laws and regulations pertaining to alcoholic beverages: Local ordinances vary.

Laws and regulations pertaining to operating motor vehicles: Georgia State Patrol; 404-657-9300, or local stations.

Statistics about Georgia: The *Atlas of Georgia*, listed in the bibliography, is available in a computer version as the *Interactive Atlas of Georgia*. The Atlas Project, Institute of Community and Area Development, 1234 South Lumpkin Street, Athens, Georgia 30602-3552; 1-800-524-8527 or 706-542-3350.

Wildlife, hunting, and fishing regulations and maps: Georgia Department of Natural Resources (address above); fishing information, 404-656-4817; hunting information, 404-656-3522; licenses, 770-414-3333.

COUNTIES AND COUNTY SEATS

	County	Seat	Created	Postal ZIP Code
1	Appling	Baxley	1818	31513
2	Atkinson	Pearson	1918	31642
3	Bacon	Alma	1914	31510
4	Baker	Newton	1825	31770
5	Baldwin	Milledgeville	1803	31061
6	Banks	Homer	1858	30547
7	Barrow	Winder	1914	30680
8	Bartow	Cartersville	1832	30120
9	Ben Hill	Fitzgerald	1906	31750
10	Berrien	Nashville	1856	31639
11	Bibb	Macon	1822	31208
12	Bleckley	Cochran	1912	31014
13	Brantley	Nahunta	1920	31553
14	Brooks	Quitman	1858	31643
15	Bryan	Pembroke	1793	31321
16	Bulloch	Statesboro	1796	30458
17	Burke	Waynesboro	1777	30830
18	Butts	Jackson	1825	30233
19	Calhoun	Morgan	1854	31766
20	Camden	Woodbine	1777	31569
21	Candler	Metter	1914	30439
22	Carroll	Carrollton	1825	30117
23	Catoosa	Ringgold	1853	30736
24	Charlton	Folkston	1854	31537
25	Chatham	Savannah	1777	31402
26	Chattahoochee	Cusseta	1854	31805
27	Chattooga	Summerville	1838	30747
28	Cherokee	Canton	1830	30114

29	Clarke	Athens	1801	30601
30	Clay	Fort Gaines	1854	31751
31	Clayton	Jonesboro	1858	30236
32	Clinch	Homerville	1850	31634
33	Cobb	Marietta	1832	30060
34	Coffee	Douglas	1854	31533
35	Colquitt	Moultrie	1856	31768
36	Columbia	Appling	1790	30802
37	Cook	Adel	1918	31620
38	Coweta	Newnan	1825	30263
39	Crawford	Knoxville	1822	31050
40	Crisp	Cordele	1905	31015
41	Dade	Trenton	1837	30752
42	Dawson	Dawsonville	1857	30534
43	Decatur	Bainbridge	1823	31717
44	DeKalb	Decatur	1822	30030
45	Dodge	Eastman	1870	31023
46	Dooly	Vienna	1821	31092
47	Dougherty	Albany	1853	31701
48	Douglas	Douglasville	1870	30134
49	Early	Blakely	1818	31723
50	Echols	Statenville	1858	31648
51	Effingham	Springfield	1777	31329
52	Elbert	Elberton	1790	30635
53	Emanuel	Swainsboro	1812	30401
54	Evans	Claxton	1914	30417
55	Fannin	Blue Ridge	1854	30513
56	Fayette	Fayetteville	1821	30214
57	Floyd	Rome	1832	30161
58	Forsyth	Cumming	1832	30130
59	Franklin	Carnesville	1784	30521
60	Fulton	Atlanta	1853	30303
61	Gilmer	Ellijay	1832	30540
62	Glascock	Gibson	1857	30810
63	Glynn	Brunswick	1777	31520
64	Gordon	Calhoun	1850	30701
65	Grady	Cairo	1905	31728
66	Greene	Greensboro	1786	30642
67	Gwinnett	Lawrenceville	1818	30245
68	Habersham	Clarkesville	1818	30523
69	Hall	Gainesville	1818	30501
70	Hancock	Sparta	1793	31087
71	Haralson	Buchanan	1856	30113
72	Harris	Hamilton	1827	31811
73	Hart	Hartwell	1853	30643

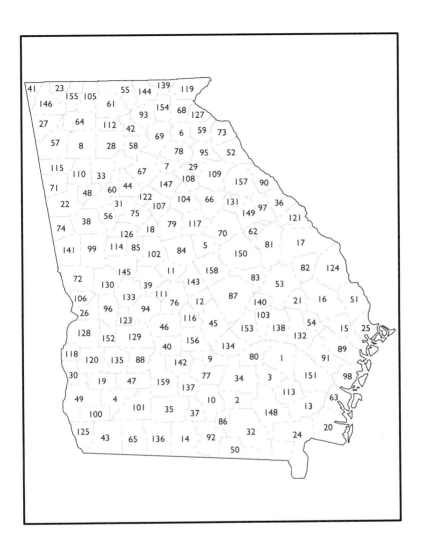

74	Heard	Franklin	1830	30217
75	Henry	McDonough	1821	30253
76	Houston	Perry	1821	31069
77	Irwin	Ocilla	1818	31774
78	Jackson	Jefferson	1796	30549
79	Jasper	Monticello	1807	31064
80	Jeff Davis	Hazlehurst	1905	31539
81	Jefferson	Louisville	1796	30434
82	Jenkins	Millen	1905	30442
83	Johnson	Wrightsville	1858	31096
84	Jones	Gray	1807	31032
85	Lamar	Barnesville	1920	30204
86	Lanier	Lakeland	1920	31635
87	Laurens	Dublin	1807	31021
88	Lee	Leesburg	1825	31763
89	Liberty	Hinesville	1777	31313
90	Lincoln	Lincolnton	1796	30817
91	Long	Ludowici	1920	31316
92	Lowndes	Valdosta	1825	31601
93	Lumpkin	Dahlonega	1832	30533
94	Macon	Oglethorpe	1837	31068
95	Madison	Danielsville	1811	30633
96	Marion	Buena Vista	1827	31803
97	McDuffie	Thomson	1870	30824
98	McIntosh	Darien	1793	31305
99	Meriwether	Greenville	1827	30222
100	Miller	Colquitt	1856	31737
101	Mitchell	Camilla	1857	31730
102	Monroe	Forsyth	1821	31029
103	Montgomery	Mount Vernon	1793	30445
104	Morgan	Madison	1807	30650
105	Murray	Chatsworth	1832	30705
106	Muscogee	Columbus	1825	31908
107	Newton	Covington	1821	30209
108	Oconee	Watkinsville	1875	30677
109	Oglethorpe	Lexington	1793	30648
110	Paulding	Dallas	1832	30132
111	Peach	Fort Valley	1924	31030
112	Pickens	Jasper	1853	31043
113	Pierce	Blackshear	1857	31516
114	Pike	Zebulon	1822	30295
115	Polk	Cedartown	1851	30125
116	Pulaski	Hawkinsville	1808	31036
117	Putnam	Eatonton	1807	31024
118	Quitman	Georgetown	1858	31754

119	Rabun	Clayton	1819	30525
120	Randolph	Cuthbert	1828	31740
121	Richmond	Augusta	1777	30901
122	Rockdale	Conyers	1870	30207
123	Schley	Ellaville	1857	31806
124	Screven	Sylvania	1793	30467
125	Seminole	Donalsonville	1920	31745
126	Spalding	Griffin	1851	30223
127	Stephens	Toccoa	1905	30577
128	Stewart	Lumpkin	1830	31815
129	Sumter	Americus	1831	31709
130	Talbot	Talbotton	1827	31827
131	Taliaferro	Crawfordville	1825	30631
132	Tattnall	Reidsville	1801	30453
133	Taylor	Butler	1852	31006
134	Telfair	McRae	1807	31055
135	Terrell	Dawson	1856	31742
136	Thomas	Thomasville	1825	31792
137	Tift	Tifton	1905	31794
138	Toombs	Lyons	1905	30436
139	Towns	Hiawassee	1856	30546
140	Treutlen	Soperton	1918	30457
141	Troup	LaGrange	1825	30240
142	Turner	Ashburn	1905	31714
143	Twiggs	Jeffersonville	1809	31044
144	Union	Blairsville	1832	30512
145	Upson	Thomaston	1824	30286
146	Walker	LaFayette	1833	30728
147	Walton	Monroe	1818	30655
148	Ware	Waycross	1824	31501
149	Warren	Warrenton	1793	30828
150	Washington	Sandersville	1784	31082
151	Wayne	Jesup	1803	31545
152	Webster	Preston	1853	31824
153	Wheeler	Alamo	1912	30411
154	White	Cleveland	1857	30528
155	Whitfield	Dalton	1851	30720
156	Wilcox	Abbeville	1857	31001
157	Wilkes	Washington	1777	30673
158	Wilkinson	Irwinton	1803	31042
159	Worth	Sylvester	1853	31791

BIBLIOGRAPHY

This bibliography is intended to be an introduction for readers seeking more detailed information about Georgia, past and present. Beginning with selected items from the original guide and Phinizy Spalding's 1990 update, it adds many of the works consulted or recommended by writers of essays and tours in the *New Georgia Guide*. No attempt was made to provide here an exhaustive listing of sources; rather the compilers hope to provide a relatively brief list of some of the more readily available recommended publications, including some fiction, which in turn will lead the interested reader and traveler well beyond this selected listing.

The most detailed views of Georgia are found in the many local studies, county histories, family and corporate biographies, and an impressive volume of genealogical works. These constitute notable sources for further consideration. The journals, magazines, and agencies mentioned in the bibliography offer helpful reviews and notices of the most current relevant publications in topics related to Georgia, its land, people, and history.

GENERAL SOURCES ON GEORGIA

Bachtel, Douglas, and Susan R. Boatright, eds. *The Georgia County Guide*. 12th ed. Athens: University of Georgia Cooperative Extension Service, 1993.

————. *The Georgia Municipal Guide*. 2d ed. Athens: University of Georgia Cooperative Extension Service, 1993.

Brinkley, Hal E. *How Georgia Got Her Names*. Rev. ed. Lakemont, Ga.: CSA Printing, 1973.

Coleman, Kenneth, and Charles Stephen Gurr, eds. *Dictionary of Georgia Biography*. 2 vols. Athens: University of Georgia Press, 1983.

Doster, Gary, ed. *From Abbeville to Zebulon: Early Post Card Views of Georgia*. Athens: University of Georgia Press, 1991.

Georgia Historical Markers. Helen: Bay Tree Grove, 1973.

Goff, John H. *Place Names of Georgia: Essays of John H. Goff*. Edited by Francis Lee Utley and Marion R. Hemperley. Athens: University of Georgia Press, 1975.

Hemperley, Marion R., and Edwin L. Jackson. *Georgia's Boundaries: The Shaping of a State*. Athens: Carl Vinson Institute of Government, 1993.

Hepburn, Lawrence R., ed. *Contemporary Georgia*. Athens: Carl Vinson Institute of Government, University of Georgia, 1987.

Hodler, Thomas W., and Howard A. Schretter, eds. *The Atlas of Georgia*. Athens: Institute of Community and Area Development, 1986.

King, Spencer B., Jr. *Georgia Voices: A Documentary History to 1872*. Athens: University of Georgia Press, 1966.

Krakow, Kenneth K. *Georgia Place-Names*. Macon: Winship Press, 1975.

Southerland, Henry deLeon, Jr., and Jerry Elijah Brown. *The Federal Road through Georgia, the Creek Nation, and Alabama, 1806–1836*. Tuscaloosa: University of Alabama Press, 1989.

Spalding, Phinizy, ed. *Georgia: The WPA Guide to Its Towns and Coutryside*. Columbia: University of South Carolina Press, 1990.

Vanishing Georgia. Athens: University of Georgia Press, 1982. Reprint, Brown Thrasher Books, 1994.

Works Progress Administration. *Georgia: A Guide to Its Towns and Countryside*. Athens: University of Georgia Press, 1940.

ARCHEOLOGY AND INDIANS

Anderson, William L., ed. *Cherokee Removal: Before and After*. Athens: University of Georgia Press, 1991.

Cook, Jeannine, ed. *Columbus and the Land of Ayllón: The Exploration and Settlement of the Southeast*. Darien: Darien News, 1993.

Coulter, E. Merton. *Georgia's Disputed Ruins: Certain Tabby Ruins on the Georgia Coast*. Chapel Hill: University of North Carolina Press, 1937.

Foreman, Grant. *Indian Removal: The Emigration of the Five Civilized Tribes of Indians*. Rev. ed. Norman: University of Oklahoma Press, 1953.

Hudson, Charles M. *The Southeastern Indians*. Knoxville: University of Tennessee Press, 1976.

Kelly, A. R. *A Preliminary Report on Archaeological Explorations at Macon, Ga*. U.S. Bureau of American Ethnology, Bulletin 119. Washington: Government Printing Office, 1938.

Malone, Henry Thompson. *Cherokees of the Old South: A People in Transition*. Athens: University of Georgia Press, 1956.

Of Sky and Earth: Art of the Early Southeastern Indians. Exhibition catalogue. Editor and curator, Roy S. Dickens Jr. Atlanta: High Museum of Art, 1982.

Swanton, John Reed. *Early History of the Creek Indians and Their Neighbors*. Washington: Government Printing Office, 1922.

Walker, Charles O. *Cherokee Footprints*. 2 vols. Canton, Ga.: Privately published, 1988–89.

Winn, William W. *The Old Beloved Path: Daily Life Among the Indians of the Chattahoochee River Valley*. Eufaula, Ala.: Historic Chattahoochee Commission, 1992.

Worth, John E. *The Struggle for the Georgia Coast: An 18th-century Spanish Retrospective on Guale and Mocama*. With an introduction by David Hurst Thomas. New York: American Museum of Natural History, 1995; distributed by University of Georgia Press.

Wright, J. Leitch, Jr. *Creeks and Seminoles: The Destruction and Regeneration of the Muscogulge People*. Lincoln: University of Nebraska Press, 1986.

ARTS AND FICTION

Burns, Olive Ann. *Cold Sassy Tree*. New York: Ticknor & Fields, 1984.

Burrison, John A. *Brothers in Clay: The Story of Georgia Folk Pottery*. Athens: University of Georgia Press, 1983.

———, ed. *Storytellers: Folktales and Legends from the South*. Athens: University of Georgia Press, 1991.

Carr, Virginia Spencer. *The Lonely Hunter*. Garden City, N.J.: Anchor Press / Doubleday, 1976.

Cobb, Buell E. *The Sacred Harp: A Tradition and Its Music*. Athens: University of Georgia Press, 1989.

Crews, Harry. *A Feast of Snakes*. New York: Macmillan Company, 1976.

Dickey, James. *Deliverance*. Boston: Houghton-Mifflin, 1970.

Fitzgerald, Sally, ed. *The Habit of Being: Letters of Flannery O'Connor*. New York: Farrar, Straus and Giroux, 1988.

Gournay, Isabelle. *AIA Guide to the Architecture of Atlanta*. Athens: University of Georgia Press, 1993.

Griffin, Louis Turner, and John Erwin Talmadge. *Georgia Journalism, 1763–1950*. Athens: University of Georgia Press, 1951.

Hartsfield, Mariella Glenn. *Tall Betsy and Dunce Baby: South Georgia Folktales*. Athens: University of Georgia Press, 1987. Reprint, Brown Thrasher Books, 1991.

Harris, Corra. *A Circuit Rider's Wife*. New York: Doubleday, Page & Co., 1916.

Harris, Joel Chandler. *Told by Uncle Remus: New Stories of the Old Plantation*. New York: McClure, Phillips & Co., 1905.

Killion, Ronald G., and Charles T. Waller. *A Treasury of Georgia Folklore*. Atlanta: Cherokee Publishing Company, 1972.

Linley, John. *The Georgia Catalog: Historic American Buildings Survey*. Athens: University of Georgia Press, 1982.

Loveland, Anne C. *Lillian Smith: A Southerner Confronting the South.* Baton Rouge: Louisiana State University Press, 1986.

Miller, Caroline. *Lamb in His Bosom.* New York: Harper & Brothers, 1933.

Patterson, Tom, ed. *St. EOM in the Land of Pasaquan: The Life and Times and Art of Eddie Owens Martin.* Jargon Society, 1987.

Rosenbaum, Art. *Folk Visions and Voices: Traditional Music and Song in North Georgia.* Athens: University of Georgia Press, 1983.

Ruppersburg, Hugh, ed. *Georgia Voices.* Vol. 1, *Fiction* (1992). Vol. 2, *Nonfiction* (1994). Athens: University of Georgia Press.

Wade, John Donald. *Augustus Baldwin Longstreet; a Study of the Development of Culture in the South.* New York: Macmillan Company, 1924.

Walker, Alice. *The Color Purple.* New York: Harcourt, Brace, Jovanovich, 1982.

Walker, Margaret. *Jubilee.* Boston: Houghton Mifflin, 1966.

White, Bailey. *Mama Makes Up Her Mind and Other Dangers of Southern Living.* Reading, Mass.: Addison-Wesley, 1993.

White, Walter F. *The Fire in the Flint.* New York: Alfred A. Knopf, 1924.

CONTEMPORARY TOUR BOOKS AND GUIDES

Bailey, Sue C., and William H. Bailey. *Cycling Through Georgia.* Atlanta: Susan Hunter, 1989.

Boyd, Brian. *The Chattooga: Wild and Scenic River.* Conyers: Fernbank Press, 1990.

Davis, Ren and Helen. *Atlanta Walks: A Guide to Walking, Running and Bicycling Historic and Scenic Atlanta.* Atlanta: Peachtree Publishers, 1988.

De Vorsey, Jr., Louis, and Marion J. Rice. *The Plantation South: Atlanta to Savannah and Charleston.* Touring North America Series. New Brunswick, N.J.: Rutgers University Press, 1992.

Georgia Conservancy. *The Georgia Conservancy's Guide to the North Georgia Mountains.* 2d ed. Edited by Fred Brown and Nell Jones. Atlanta: Longstreet Press, 1991.

Georgia Conservancy. *A Guide to the Georgia Coast.* Rev. ed. Edited by Gwen McKee. N.P.: Georgia Conservancy, 1988.

Georgia Department of Industry, Trade and Tourism, Tourist Division; Georgia Department of Natural Resources, Office of Historic Preservation; and Georgia Civil War Commission. *Crossroads of Conflict: A Guide for Touring Civil War Sites in Georgia.* Atlanta, 1995.

Harman, Harry, and Jeanne Harman. *Georgia at Its Best.* Nashville: Rutledge Hill Press, 1988.

Homan, Tim. *The Hiking Trails of North Georgia*. Atlanta: Peachtree Publishers, 1987.

Jordan, Robert H., and J. Gregg Puster. *Courthouses in Georgia*. Norcross: Harrison Co., 1984.

Kahn, E. J., Jr. *Georgia from Rabun Gap to Tybee Light*. Atlanta: Cherokee Publishing Company, 1978.

McCarley, J. Britt. *Atlanta Is Ours and Fairly Won: A Driving Tour of the Atlanta Area's Principal Civil War Battlefields*. With a readers' guide by Stephen Davis and Richard M. McMurry. Atlanta: Atlanta Historical Society, 1984. Reprint, Atlanta: Cherokee Publishing Co., 1989.

Miles, Jim. *Fields of Glory: A History and Tour Guide of the Atlanta Campaign*. Nashville: Rutledge Hill Press, 1989.

―――. *To the Sea: A History and Tour Guide of Sherman's March*. Nashville: Rutledge Hill Press, 1989.

Milt, Harry, Karen S. Bentley, and David C. Jowers. *The North Georgia Mountains: A Comprehensive Guide to Sightseeing, Shopping, Activities, Restaurants, and Accommodations*. Atlanta: Cherokee Publishing Company, 1992.

O'Briant, Don. *Looking for Tara*. Atlanta: Longstreet Press, 1994.

Ockershausen, Jane. *The Georgia One-Day Trip Book*. McLean, Va.: EPM Publications, 1993.

Rhyne, Nancy. *Touring the Coastal Georgia Backroads*. Winston-Salem, N.C: John F. Blair, 1994.

Schemmel, William. *Country Towns of Georgia*. Castine, Maine: Country Roads Press, 1994.

―――. *Georgia Off the Beaten Path*. 2d ed. Chester, Conn.: Globe Pequot Press, 1993.

Schwartz, Janet, and Denise Black. *Ethnic Atlanta: The Complete Guide to Atlanta's Ethnic Communities*. Atlanta: Longstreet Press, 1993.

Winterberger, Suzanne, and Bill Tomey. *Sideways Atlanta: A Field Guide to Offbeat Attractions in "The City Too Busy to Hate."* Edinboro, Pa.: Creative Intelligence Agency, 1995.

HISTORY

Andrews, Eliza Frances. *The War-Time Journal of a Georgia Girl, 1864–1865*. New York: Appleton, 1908. Reprint, Macon, Ga.: Ardivan Press, 1960.

Bartley, Numan V. *The Creation of Modern Georgia*. 2d ed. Athens: University of Georgia Press, 1990.

Branch, Taylor. *Parting the Waters: America in the King Years, 1954–63*. New York: Simon and Schuster, 1988.

Bryan, Thomas Conn. *Confederate Georgia*. Athens: University of Georgia Press, 1953.

Cash, W. J. *The Mind of the South*. New York: Alfred A. Knopf, 1941.

Coleman, Kenneth. *The American Revolution in Georgia: 1763–1789*. Athens: University of Georgia Press, 1958.

———. *Colonial Georgia: A History*. New York: Charles Scribners' Sons, 1976.

———, et al. *A History of Georgia*. Athens: University of Georgia Press, 1991.

Coulter, E. Merton. *A Short History of Georgia*. Chapel Hill: University of North Carolina Press, 1933.

Dittmer, John Avery. *Black Georgia in the Progressive Era, 1900–1920*. Urbana: University of Illinois Press, 1977.

Futch, Ovid L. *History of Andersonville Prison*. Gainesville: University of Florida Press, 1968.

Hornsby, Alton, Jr. *Chronology of African-American History*. Detroit: Gale Research, 1991.

Jackson, Harvey H., and Phinizy Spalding. *Forty Years of Diversity: Essays on Colonial Georgia*. Athens: University of Georgia Press, 1984.

Jones, Charles C., Jr. *The History of Georgia*. Boston: Houghton, Mifflin & Co., 1883.

Lane, Mills, ed. *Marching Through Georgia: William T. Sherman's Personal Narrative of His March Through Georgia*. New York: Arno Press, 1978.

———. *The People of Georgia: An Illustrated Social History*. Savannah: Beehive Press, 1975.

Lawrence, Alexander A. *Storm over Savannah*. Athens: University of Georgia Press, 1951.

Spalding, Phinizy. *Oglethorpe in America*. Chicago: University of Chicago Press, 1977.

White, George. *Historical Collections of Georgia*. New York: Pudney & Russell, 1854.

Woodward, C. Vann. *Tom Watson, Agrarian Rebel*. New York: Macmillan: 1938. Reprint, Oxford University Press, 1963.

LOCAL STUDIES

Allen, Frederick. *Secret Formula: How Brilliant Marketing and Relentless Salesmanship Made Coca-Cola the Best-Known Product in the World*. New York: Harper Business, 1994.

Bell, Vereen. *Swamp Water*. Boston, 1941.

Bonner, James, C. *Milledgeville: Georgia's Antebellum Capital*. Athens: University of Georgia Press, 1964.

Braden, Betsy, and Paul Hagan. *A Dream Takes Flight: Hartsfield International Airport and Aviation in Atlanta*. Athens: University of Georgia Press, 1989.

Cashin, Edward J. *Colonial Augusta*. Macon: Mercer University Press, 1986.

Crimmins, Timothy J., and Dana F. White, eds. "Urban Structure, Atlanta." *Atlanta Historical Journal* 26 (Summer/Fall 1982).

Garrett, Franklin. *Atlanta and Environs: A Chronicle of Its People and Events*. Vols. 1 and 2. 1954. Reprint, Athens: University of Georgia Press, 1969. For vol. 3, see Martin, Harold H.

———. *Yesterday's Atlanta*. Miami, Fla.: E. A. Seemann Publisher, 1974.

Ginn, Edwin H. *Recollections of Glynn*. 2d ed. Brunswick, Ga.: Brunswick–Golden Isles Chamber of Commerce, 1990.

Harper, Francis, and Delma E. Presley. *Okefinokee Album*. Athens: University of Georgia Press, 1981. Reprint, Brown Thrasher Books, 1990.

Hickson, Bobbie Smith. *A Land So Dedicated*. Perry, Ga.: Houston County Library Board, 1976.

Jones-Jackson, Patricia. *When Roots Die: Endangered Traditions on the Sea Islands*. Athens: University of Georgia Press, 1987.

Kyle, F. Clason. *Images: A Pictorial History of Columbus, Georgia*. Norfolk: Donning Company, 1986.

Leigh, Jack. *The Ogeechee: A River and Its People*. Athens: University of Georgia Press, 1986.

Lupold, John. *Columbus, Georgia: 1828–1978*. Columbus: Columbus Sesquicentennial, 1978.

Lyon, Elizabeth Anne Mack. *Atlanta Architecture: The Victorian Heritage, 1837–1918*. Atlanta: Atlanta Historical Society, 1976.

Margeson, Hank, and Joseph Kitchens. *Quail Plantations of South Georgia and North Florida*. Athens: University of Georgia Press, 1991.

Martin, Harold H. *Atlanta and Environs: A Chronicle of Its People and Events*. Vol. 3. Athens: University of Georgia Press, 1987. For vols. 1 and 2, see Garrett, Franklin M.

Mason, Skip. *Going Against the Wind: A Pictorial History of African-Americans in Atlanta*. Atlanta: Longstreet Press, 1992.

McCash, William Barton, and June Hall McCash. *The Jekyll Island Club: Southern Haven for America's Millionaires*. Athens: University of Georgia Press, 1989.

McFeely, William S. *Sapelo's People*. New York: W. W. Norton & Co., 1994.

Miller, Wilbur. *Revenuers & Moonshiners: Enforcing Federal Liquor Law in the Mountain South, 1865–1900*. Chapel Hill: University of North Carolina Press, 1986.

Miller, Zell Bryan. *The Mountains Within Me*. Toccoa: Commercial Printing Company, 1976.

Morrison, Mary Lane, ed. *Historic Savannah*. Savannah: Historic Savannah Foundation and Junior League of Savannah, 1979.

Reynolds, Hughes. *The Coosa River Valley: From DeSoto to Hydroelectric Power.* Cynthiana, Ky.: Hobson Book Press, 1944.

Rogers, William Warren. *Pebble Hill: The Story of a Plantation.* Tallahassee: Sentry Press, 1979.

Rozier, John, ed. *The Granite Farm Letters: The Civil War Correspondence of Edgeworth and Sallie Bird.* Athens: University of Georgia Press, 1988.

Schmier, Louis E. *Valdosta & Lowndes County: A Ray in the Sunbelt.* Northridge, Calif.: Windsor Publications, 1988.

Shivers, Forrest. *The Land Between: A History of Hancock County Georgia to 1940.* Spartanburg: Reprint Co., 1990.

Sibley, Celestine. *Dear Store.* Garden City: Doubleday, 1967.

Sullivan, Buddy. *Early Days on the Georgia Tidewater: The Story of McIntosh County and Sapelo.* Brunswick: McIntosh County Board of Commissioners, 1990.

Teal, John, and Mildred Teal. *Portrait of an Island.* 1964. Athens: University of Georgia Press, Brown Thrasher Books, 1981.

Thomas, David Hurst. *St. Catherines: An Island in Time.* Atlanta: Georgia Humanities Council, 1988.

Thomas, Frances Taliaferro. *A Portrait of Historic Athens and Clarke County.* Athens: University of Georgia Press, 1992.

Thompson, K., ed. *Touching Home: A Collection of History and Folklore from the Copper Basin, Fannin County Area.* Orlando: Daniels Publishers, 1976.

Thurmond, Michael L. *A Story Untold: Black Men and Women in Athens History.* Athens: Clarke County School District, 1978.

Vanstory, Burnette. *Georgia's Land of the Golden Isles.* Athens: University of Georgia Press, 1981.

Walker, Turnley. *Roosevelt and the Warm Springs Story.* New York: A. A. Wyn, [1953].

Watkins, Floyd C., and Charles Hubert Watkins. *Yesterday in the Hills.* Chicago: Quadrangle Books, 1963. Reprint, Athens: University of Georgia Press, Brown Thrasher Books, 1982.

Wigginton, Eliot. *Sometimes a Shining Moment: The Foxfire Experience.* Garden City, N.Y.: Anchor Press, 1985.

Williams, David. *The Georgia Gold Rush: Twenty-Niners, Cherokees, and Gold Fever.* Columbia: University of South Carolina Press, 1993.

NATURAL SETTING

De Vorsey, Louis, Jr., ed. *DeBrahm's Report of the General Survey in the Southern District of North America.* Columbia: University of South Carolina Press, 1971.

Duncan, Wilbur. *Wildflowers of the Southeastern United States.* Athens: University of Georgia Press, 1975.

English, John W. *Brown's Guide to the Georgia Outdooors*. Atlanta: Cherokee Publishing Company, 1986.

Gibbons, Whit. *Keeping All the Pieces: Perspectives on Natural History and the Environment*. Washington: Smithsonian Institution Press, 1993.

Hatcher, George, ed. *Georgia Rivers*. Athens: University of Georgia Press, 1962.

Johnson, A. H. Hillestad, et al. *An Ecological Survey of the Coastal Region of Georgia*. Atlanta: National Park Service, 1974.

Laerm, Joshua, and B. J. Freeman. *Fishes of the Okefenokee Swamp*. Athens: University of Georgia Press, 1986.

Leigh, Jack. *The Ogeechee: A River and Its People*. Athens: University of Georgia Press, 1986.

Randklev, James. *Georgia: Images of Wildness*. Englewood, Colo.: Westcliffe Publishers, 1992.

Wharton, Charles. *The Natural Environments of Georgia*. Atlanta: Georgia Department of Natural Resources, 1978.

POLITICS AND ECONOMICS

Anderson, William. *The Wild Man from Sugar Creek: The Political Career of Eugene Talmadge*. Baton Rouge: Louisiana State University Press, 1975.

Bonner, James C. *A History of Georgia Agriculture, 1732–1860*. Athens: University of Georgia Press, 1964.

Brooks, Robert Preston. *The Agrarian Revolution in Georgia, 1865–1912*. Madison: University of Wisconsin Press, 1914. Reprint, Westport, Conn.: Greenwood Press, Negro Universities Press, 1970.

Carter, Jimmy. *Turning Point: A Candidate, a State, and a Nation Come of Age*. New York: Time Books, 1992.

Georgia Agricultural Statistical Service. *Georgia Agricultural Facts*. Athens, 1994.

Fite, Gilbert C. *Richard B. Russell, Jr., Senator from Georgia*. Chapel Hill: University of North Carolina Press, 1991.

Hoffman, Charles, and Tess Hoffman. *North by South: The Two Lives of Richard James Arnold*. Athens: University of Georgia Press, 1988.

McGill, Ralph. *The South and the Southerner*. 1963. Reprint, with a foreword by Eugene Patterson, Athens: University of Georgia Press, Brown Thrasher Books, 1992.

McMath, Robert C. *Populist Vanguard: A History of the Southern Farmers' Alliance*. Chapel Hill: University of North Carolina Press, 1975.

Phillips, Ulrich Bonnell. *Life and Labor in the Old South*. Boston: Little, Brown and Company, 1929.

Range, Willard. *A Century of Georgia Agriculture, 1850–1950*. Athens: University of Georgia Press, 1954.

Raper, Arthur. *Preface to Peasantry; a Tale of Two Black Belt Counties.* Chapel Hill: University of North Carolina Press, 1936.

Smith, Julia Floyd. *Slavery and Rice Culture in Low County Georgia, 1750–1860.* Knoxville: University of Tennessee Press, 1985.

SOCIAL AND CULTURAL

Bacote, Clarence A. *The Story of Atlanta University: A Century of Service.* Atlanta: Atlanta University, 1969

Bell, Malcolm, Jr. *Major Butler's Legacy: Five Generations of a Slaveholding Family.* Athens: University of Georgia Press, 1987. Reprint, Brown Thrasher Books, 1989.

Berendt, John. *Midnight in the Garden of Good and Evil.* New York: Random House, 1994.

Byers, Tracy. *Martha Berry: the Sunday Lady of Possum Trot.* New York: G. P. Putnam's Sons, 1932.

Carter, E. R. *The Black Side: A Partial History of the Business, Religious and Educational Side of the Negro in Atlanta, Georgia.* Atlanta: N.p., 1894.

Cobb, Buell, Jr. *The Sacred Harp: A Tradition and Its Music.* Athens: University of Georgia Press, 1989.

Covington, Dennis. *Salvation on Sand Mountain: Snake Handling and Redemption in Southern Appalachia.* Reading: Addison-Wesley, 1995.

Coulter, E. Merton. *College Life in the Old South.* New York: Macmillan Company, 1928.

Crews, Harry. *A Childhood: The Biography of a Place.* 1978. Reprint, Athens: University of Georgia Press, 1995.

Dinnerstein, Leonard. *The Leo Frank Case.* 1968. Reprint, Athens: University of Georgia Press, Brown Thrasher Books, 1987.

Du Bois, W. E. B. *The Souls of Black Folk.* Vintage ed., 1990.

Duncan, Russell. *Freedom's Shore: Tunis Campbell and the Georgia Freedmen.* Athens: University of Georgia Press, 1986.

Dyer, Thomas G. *The University of Georgia: A Bicentennial History, 1785–1985.* Athens: University of Georgia Press, 1985.

Georgia Writers' Project. *Drums and Shadows: Survival Studies Among the Georgia Coastal Negroes.* 1940. Athens: University of Georgia Press, Brown Thrasher Books, 1986.

Greene, Melissa Fay. *Praying for Sheetrock.* New York: Addison Wesley, 1991.

Hunter-Gault, Charlayne. *In My Place.* New York: Vintage Books, 1993.

Inscoe, John C., ed. *Georgia in Black and White: Explorations in Race Relations of a Southern State, 1865–1950.* Athens: University of Georgia Press, 1994.

Joyner, Charles. *Remember Me: Slave Life in Coastal Georgia*. Georgia Humanities Council Publication. Athens: University of Georgia Press, 1989.

Kuhn, Clifford, Harlon E. Joye, and E. Bernard West. *Living Atlanta: An Oral History of the City, 1914–1948*. Atlanta and Athens: Atlanta Historical Society and University of Georgia Press, 1990.

Lewis, David L. *King: A Critical Biography*. New York: Praeger 1970.

McMath, Robert C., Jr., Ronald H. Bayor, James E. Brittain, Lawrence Foster, August W. Giebelhaus, and Germaine M. Reed. *Engineering the New South: Georgia Tech, 1885–1985*. Athens: University of Georgia Press, 1985.

Myers, Robert Manson, ed. *The Children of Pride*. New Haven: Yale University Press, 1972.

Orr, Dorothy. *A History of Education in Georgia*. Chapel Hill: University of North Carolina Press, 1951.

STANDARD AND HISTORIC TRAVEL AND DESCRIPTION

Bartram, William. *Travels through North and South Carolina, Georgia, East and West Florida*. Reprint, New York: Barnes & Noble, 1940.

Grant, C. L., ed. *The Letters, Journals, and Writings of Benjamin Hawkins*. 2 vols. Savannah: Beehive Press, 1980.

Kemble, Frances Anne. *Journal of a Residence on a Georgia Plantation in 1838–1839*. Edited by John A. Scott. Reprint, Athens: University of Georgia Press, Brown Thrasher Books, 1984.

Longstreet, Augustus Baldwin. *Georgia Scenes*. New York: Harper & Brothers, 1897.

Miller, Paul W., ed. *Atlanta: Capital of the South*. New York: Oliver Durrell, 1949.

White, George. *Statistics of the State of Georgia*. Savannah: W. Thorne Williams, 1849.

FOR FURTHER CONSIDERATION

The following organizations publish a variety of materials about the state:

 Atlanta History Center, Atlanta
 Foxfire, Mountain City
 Georgia Department of Archives and History, Atlanta
 Georgia Historical Society, Savannah
 Georgia Trust for Historic Preservation, Atlanta
 Institutions of the University System of Georgia

See especially:

Atlanta Historical Society. *Atlanta History: A Journal of Georgia and the South*. Before 1987, *The Atlanta Historical Journal*.

Foxfire Fund. *Foxfire.*

Georgia Department of Archives and History. *Directory of Georgia's Historical Organizations and Resources.* 1996.

———. *Georgia Official and Statistical Register.* Published semiannually.

Georgia Department of Community Affairs. *The Georgia Courthouse Manual.* Atlanta, 1992.

Georgia Department of Education. *Georgia Bibliography: County History.* Compiled by Hazel Purdie. 2d ed. Atlanta, 1979.

Georgia Department of Industry, Trade and Tourism. *Georgia on My Mind.* Atlanta, yearly.

Georgia Historical Society. *Georgia Historical Quarterly.*

———. *Georgia Historical Quarterly Index to Volumes 1–60 (1917–1976).* Edited by Tracy D. Bearden. Savannah, 1991.

Georgia Journal. Atlanta.

Georgia Office of Historic Preservation. *African-American Historic Places and Culture: A Preservation Resource Guide for Georgia.* Atlanta, 1993.

———. *Preserving the Legacy: A Tour of African-American Historic Resources in Georgia.* Atlanta, 1993.

Georgia Review. University of Georgia, Athens.

Georgia Trend. Atlanta.

Many of these publications, and others, are increasingly available electronically on the Internet.

CONTRIBUTORS

Betsy Braden and **John Braden** are Atlanta-based writers and photographers whose travel articles and photographs appear in regional, national, and international publications and guidebooks. They have traveled in sixty-two countries and thirty-three states and write frequently about Georgia. They are the authors of *Atlanta Access,* a guide to the city.

Jane Cassady, a North Carolinian by birth, moved to Athens to attend the University of Georgia, where history and preservation made a lasting impression on her. Working as a historic preservation planner opened her eyes to the diversity of the state and its wealth of resources.

James C. Cobb is a native of Hart County, Georgia. He attended Hart County High School and received his A.B., M.A., and Ph.D. degrees from the University of Georgia. He has written widely on the relationship between the economy, society, and culture in the American South. In addition to numerous articles, his publications include *The Selling of the South: The Southern Crusade for Industrial Development, 1936–1990*; *Industrialization and Southern Society, 1877–1984*; and *The Most Southern Place on Earth: The Mississippi Delta and the Roots of Regional Identity*. He holds the Bernadotte Schmitt Chair of Excellence in History at the University of Tennessee, Knoxville.

Timothy J. Crimmins is chair of the Department of History and director of the Program in Heritage Preservation at Georgia State University. Coeditor of *Urban America: A Historical Bibliography* and *American Life/American People*, with Dana F. White he also coedited the "Urban Structure, Atlanta" special issue of the *Atlanta Historical Journal* (Summer/Fall 1982).

Thomas G. Dyer teaches higher education and history at the University of Georgia, where he earned M.A. and Ph.D. degrees in history. For seven years he was the editor of the *Georgia Historical Quarterly*. He is the author of a history of the University of Georgia and other books. A native of Missouri, he has lived in Athens for twenty-five years.

Lee W. Formwalt, professor of history, Albany State College, received his Ph.D. in history from the Catholic University of America. He is coeditor of several volumes of the *Papers of Benjamin Henry Latrobe* and editor of the *Journal of Southwest Georgia History*. He has published numerous articles on Southwest Georgia and has an interest in the socioeconomic history of nineteenth-century Dougherty County, Georgia.

Fred C. Fussell, born in Phenix City, Alabama, lives in Columbus, Georgia. Since the late 1960s, he has studied the traditional folk culture of the Deep South, particularly that of the Lower Chattahoochee River Valley of Georgia and Alabama. He has been director of interpretive programming for Westville, the living history museum at Lumpkin, and chief curator of the Columbus Museum. He is folklorist for the Historic Chattahoochee Commission and program director for the Festival of Southeastern Indian Cultures at Columbus College.

Whit Gibbons, professor of ecology at the University of Georgia's Savannah River Ecology Laboratory, has published over 150 scientific articles and written six books on herpetology and ecology. An environmental advocate, he has written numerous articles on the environment for encyclopedias, popular magazines, and newspapers.

Steve Gurr, native of Ellaville, Georgia, is emeritus professor of history at Gainesville College. Coeditor with Kenneth Coleman of the *Dictionary of Georgia Biography,* he has served on the boards of the Georgia Trust for Historic Preservation and the Georgia Historical Society. Gov. Zell Miller appointed him to the board of the Georgia Historical Records Advisory Board. He divides his time between Gainesville and Ellaville.

William Hedgepeth, an actual native Atlantan, is a former *Atlanta Journal* reporter and later a senior editor at *Look, Saturday Review, Intellectual Digest,* and other publications. A political speechwriter and consultant, he is the author of several books, including *The Hog Book*, and has written for television and movies at Universal Studios in Hollywood.

Mary Hood is a native Georgian. She is the author of two short story collections—*And Venus Is Blue* and *How Far She Went*—and a novel, *Familiar Heat*. In the spring of 1996 she held the Grisham Chair at the University of Mississippi, Oxford. Her honors include the Flannery O'Connor Award for Short Fiction and the Whiting Award.

John C. Inscoe, born in western North Carolina, is associate professor of history at the University of Georgia and editor of the *Georgia Historical Quarterly*. He is the author of *Mountain Masters: Slavery and the Sectional Crisis in Western North Carolina*, coeditor of *Ulrich Bonnell Phillips: A Southern Historian and His Critics*, and editor of *Georgia in Black & White: Explorations in the Race Relations of a Southern State, 1865–1950*. A recent project is a study of the Civil War in southern Appalachia.

James Kilgo, who was born and grew up in Darlington, South Carolina, is professor of English and director of creative writing at the University of Georgia. He is the author of two collections of nonfiction narratives, *Deep Enough for Ivorybills* and *Inheritance of Horses*.

Delma E. Presley is the director of the Georgia Southern Museum in Statesboro. A native of Toccoa, Georgia, he is the author of essays and articles about the literature and culture of the South. His books include *Okefinokee Album* (with Francis Harper), *Dr. Bullie's Notes: Reminiscences of Early Georgia and of Philadelphia and New Haven in the 1800s*, and *The Glass Menagerie: An American Memory*.

Buddy Sullivan is a native of Coastal Georgia, a graduate of LaGrange College, and the author of several books about the history of the coast, including *Early Days on the Georgia Tidewater: The Story of McIntosh County and Sapelo*. For eight years he was editor of the *Darien News* in McIntosh County, and since 1993 he has been resident manager of the Sapelo Island National Estuarine Research Reserve, where he continues his historical research and writing.

Jane Powers Weldon, from Calhoun in northwestern Georgia, graduated from Wesleyan College and Emory University, where she studied southern literature. She is a writer, editor, and publication consultant in southern literature and culture for organizations including university presses, museums, historical societies, government, and membership groups.

Dana F. White, professor of urban studies at Emory University, writes widely about Atlanta history. He is coeditor of *Olmsted South: Old South Critic/New South Planner* and author of *The Urbanists, 1865–1915*. With Timothy J. Crimmins, he has collaborated on the design of museum exhibitions and television productions about Atlanta's history and development.

Philip Lee Williams is the author of seven published novels, including *Blue Crystal*. He has also published poetry, short stories, and essays in numerous magazines around the country. His novels have been translated into Swedish, Japanese, French, and German. He lives near Watkinsville, Georgia.

William W. Winn, editorial page editor of the *Columbus (Georgia) Ledger-Enquirer*, has been writing about Georgia and his native South for thirty years. His work has appeared in *American Heritage, Atlanta Magazine, Rolling Stone, Argosy,* and many other magazines. His *The Old Beloved Path: Daily Life Among the Indians of the Chattahoochee River Valley* was published by the Historic Chattahoochee Commission.

Photo Credits

Page 20: Kennesaw Mountain National Battlefield Park. Georgia Department of Industry, Trade and Tourism.

Page 25: Weighing cotton, Milledgeville, 1934. Kenneth G. Rogers Collection, Atlanta History Center.

Page 36: Prison labor, Gwinnett County, 1920. Vanishing Georgia Collection, Georgia Department of Archives and History.

Page 41: Eugene Talmadge at a campaign rally, 1942. Kenneth G. Rogers Collection, Atlanta History Center.

Page 47: Sawmill scene, Swainsboro, 1935. Vanishing Georgia Collection, Georgia Department of Archives and History.

Page 56: Martin Luther King Jr., Vine City rent demonstration, Atlanta, 1966. William B. Wilson Collection, Atlanta History Center.

Page 68: Country store scene. Photograph courtesy of James C. Cobb.

Page 78: Rosa Lee Carson and Fiddlin' John Carson, LaGrange, 1925. Photograph courtesy of Gene Wiggins.

Page 80: Blacksmith's shop near Covington, 1940s. Kenneth G. Rogers Collection, Atlanta History Center.

Page 86: Olympic banners, Atlanta. Georgia Department of Industry, Trade and Tourism.

Page 96: Hamilton Holmes, Charlayne Hunter-Gault, and Jesse Jackson, Athens, November 1992. Photograph by Rick O'Quinn, University of Georgia Office of Public Information.

Page 101: Nobel Laureates of Literature, Atlanta, April 1995. Photograph copyright ACOG, 1995.

Page 113: Artifacts from Etowah Indian Mounds State Historic Site. Georgia Department of Industry, Trade and Tourism.

Page 119: "Guiding Light," by Cherokee artist Donald Vann. Copyright 1989 by Native American Images, Austin, Texas.

Page 121: Chickamauga National Battlefield Park. Georgia Department of Industry, Trade and Tourism.

Page 125: Peacock Alley, 1940. Vanishing Georgia Collection, Georgia Department of Archives and History.

Page 129: Justice of the Peace, Dade County, 1940s. Kenneth Rogers Collection, Atlanta History Center.

Page 131: Sacred Harp singing, Holly Springs. Photograph by Maggie Holtzberg, Georgia Council for the Arts Folklife Program.

Page 133: Howard Finster, Pennville, 1980. Photograph by Margo Newmark Rosenbaum.

Page 141: Yarn Dyer, Cartersville. Georgia Department of Industry, Trade and Tourism.

Page 143: Barnsley Gardens, Woodlands. Georgia Department of Industry, Trade and Tourism.

Page 149: Cloudland Canyon. Georgia Department of Industry, Trade and Tourism.

Page 152: Rock City "billboard." Courtesy of See Rock City, Inc.

Page 156: Supreme Court Building, New Echota State Historic Site. Georgia Department of Industry, Trade and Tourism.

Page 157: Dining room, Vann House, Spring Place. Georgia Department of Industry, Trade and Tourism.

Page 159: Resaca Confederate Cemetery. Vanishing Georgia Collection, Georgia Department of Archives and History.

Page 160: Laurens Hillhouse, 1892. Vanishing Georgia Collection, Georgia Department of Archives and History.

Page 169: Rafting on the Chattooga River. Photograph by James D. Strawser, University of Georgia Cooperative Extension Service.

Page 171: Outing at Tallulah Gorge, circa 1900. Vanishing Georgia Collection, Georgia Department of Archives and History.

Page 181: Moonshiner's arrest, 1890s. Reproduced from "Moonshining in Georgia," *Cosmopolitan* magazine, 1897.

Page 184: Vegetable peddler, Gainesville, early twentieth century. Vanishing Georgia Collection, Georgia Department of Archives and History.

Page 194: Old Sautee Store. Photograph by Hank Margeson.

Page 198: The Eller Brothers, Upper Hightower, 1979. Photograph by Margo Newmark Rosenbaum.

Page 199: Pottery shop of Cleator Meaders, Jr. Photograph by Maggie Holzberg, Georgia Council for the Arts Folklife Program.

Page 200: The Hewell family, Gillsville, 1993. Photograph by William F. Hull, Atlanta History Center.

Page 209: Amicalola Falls. Photograph by James D. Strawser, University of Georgia Cooperative Extension Service.

Page 210: Gold Museum, Dahlonega. Georgia Department of Industry, Trade and Tourism.

Page 215: Atlanta Motor Speedway. Georgia Department of Industry, Trade and Tourism.

Page 218: Sautee-Nacoochee Mound. Photograph by Hank Margeson.

Page 223: Traveler's Rest. Vanishing Georgia Collection, Georgia Department of Archives and History.

Page 229: Bobby Jones and Ty Cobb. Kenneth Rogers Collection, Atlanta History Center.

Page 235: Decatur Street railroad station, 1893. Vanishing Georgia Collection, Georgia Department of Archives and History.

Page 236: Tom Moreland Interchange. Georgia Department of Industry, Trade and Tourism.

Page 239: The Atlanta Braves. Georgia Department of Industry, Trade and Tourism.

Page 243: Movie premiere of *Gone with the Wind*, December 1939. William B. Wilson Collection, Atlanta History Center.

Page 256: Rich's "Pink Pig." Courtesy of Rich's.

Pages 262–63: Atlanta in the mid 1990s. Photograph by Kevin C. Rose, Atlanta Convention and Visitors Bureau.

Page 280: *Metropolitan Frontiers: Atlanta 1835–2000*. Atlanta History Center.

Page 281: Herndon Home. Georgia Department of Industry, Trade and Tourism.

Page 282: Atlantic Center and High Museum of Art. Georgia Department of Industry, Trade and Tourism.

Page 287: Stone Mountain Memorial Carving. Georgia Department of Industry, Trade and Tourism.

Page 289: The Fox Theatre. Georgia Department of Industry, Trade and Tourism.

Page 305: R.E.M. Photograph by Keith Carter. Copyright 1994 Warner Bros. Records, Inc.

Page 310: Eatonton. Photograph by Barbara McKenzie.

Page 316: Hancock County courthouse, Sparta. Georgia Department of Industry, Trade and Tourism.

Page 319: Wildflowers. Georgia Department of Industry, Trade and Tourism.

Page 324: Robert Toombs House, Washington. Georgia Department of Industry, Trade and Tourism.

Page 331: Arch, University of Georgia, Athens. Office of Public Information, University of Georgia.

Page 332: Morton Theater, Athens. Photograph by Wingate Downs.

Page 339: Elder's Mill Covered Bridge, photographed circa 1975. Vanishing Georgia Collection, Georgia Department of Archives and History.

Page 345: Rock Eagle, Putnam County. Photograph by James D. Strawser, University of Georgia Cooperative Extension Service.

Page 348: Riverwalk, Augusta. Georgia Department of Industry, Trade and Tourism.

Page 351: Masters Golf Tournament, Augusta. Georgia Department of Industry, Trade and Tourism.

Page 355: Rock House. Georgia Department of Industry, Trade and Tourism.

Page 361: Franklin Delano Roosevelt at Warm Springs. Kenneth Rogers Collection, Atlanta History Center.

Page 364: Peach blossoms. Georgia Department of Industry, Trade and Tourism.

Page 374: Andersonville National Cemetery. Georgia Department of Industry, Trade and Tourism.

Page 377: Mill workers' home. Vanishing Georgia Collection, Georgia Department of Archives and History.

Page 383: Hog killing. Photograph by Fred Fussell.

Page 387: Gourd birdhouses. Photograph by Fred Fussell.

Page 399: Produce stand, Senoia. Georgia Department of Industry, Trade and Tourism.

Page 409: Roosevelt's Little White House. Georgia Department of Industry, Trade and Tourism.

Page 412: Fort Benning. Georgia Department of Industry, Trade and Tourism.

Page 413: Pasaquan. Photograph by Fred Fussell.

Page 416: Plains. Georgia Department of Industry, Trade and Tourism.

Page 417: Westville. Georgia Department of Industry, Trade and Tourism.

Page 418: Providence Canyon. Georgia Department of Industry, Trade and Tourism.

Page 427: Gene Talmadge campaigning, 1940s. Vanishing Georgia Collection, Georgia Department of Archives and History.

Page 429: Campaign barbecue, 1950s. Vanishing Georgia Collection, Georgia Department of Archives and History.

Page 431: Downtown Macon. Photograph by Hank Margeson.

Page 435: Museum of Aviation, Warner Robins. Georgia Department of Industry, Trade and Tourism.

Page 439: Peach crop. Georgia Department of Industry, Trade and Tourism.

Page 444: Harness racing at Hawkinsville. Georgia Department of Industry, Trade and Tourism.

Page 449: Cotton gin house and bale press, circa 1900. Vanishing Georgia Collection, Georgia Department of Archives and History.

Page 457: Harvesting cotton in the 1990s. Georgia Department of Industry, Trade and Tourism.

Page 463: Old Governor's Mansion, Milledgeville. Georgia Department of Industry, Trade and Tourism.

Page 469: Ocmulgee National Monument. Macon–Bibb County Convention and Visitors Bureau.

Page 471: Hay House, Macon. Macon–Bibb County Convention and Visitors Bureau.

Page 472: "From Africa to America," mural by Wilfred Stroud, Tubman African American Museum, Macon. Macon–Bibb County Convention and Visitors Bureau.

Page 475: Jarrell Plantation State Historic Site. Georgia Department of Industry, Trade and Tourism.

Page 483: "Marching through Georgia." Postcard courtesy of Gary Doster.

Page 487: Bobwhite quail. Photograph by David E. Scott, University of Georgia Savannah River Ecology Laboratory.

Page 501: Steamboat, near Bainbridge, 1910. Vanishing Georgia Collection, Georgia Department of Archives and History.

Page 502: Georgia Northern Railway Company, Brooks County, 1899. Vanishing Georgia Collection, Georgia Department of Archives and History.

Page 507: Cooking class, Georgia Normal and Agricultural College, 1928. Vanishing Georgia Collection, Georgia Department of Archives and History.

Page 510: Tobacco farmers, 1905. Vanishing Georgia Collection, Georgia Department of Archives and History.

Page 512: Water fountains, Dougherty County courthouse, Albany, 1962. Photograph by Danny Lyon, from *Memories of the Southern Civil Rights Movement* (Chapel Hill: Center for Documentary Photography, 1992), reproduced with permission of the photographer.

Page 515: Civil rights march, Albany, 1962. Photograph by the Albany Police Department.

Page 519: Peanut harvest. Photograph by James P. Strawser, University of Georgia Cooperative Extension Service.

Page 525: Hunting quail, Dougherty County. Photograph by Hank Margeson.

Page 531: "Little River River." Photograph by Mary Hood.

Page 539: Grave shelter, Thomasville Cemetery. Photograph by Fred Fussell.

Page 542: Roadside signs, Albany. Photograph by Hank Margeson.

Page 549: Detail of "The Two Rivers" by Peter Blume, located in Rome. Georgia Council for the Arts.

Page 553: Lapham-Patterson House, Thomasville. Photograph by Fred Fussell.

Page 556: Tobacco in the field. Photograph by Fred Fussell.

Page 560: Brown Chapel AME Church, Fort Gaines. Photograph by Fred Fussell.

Page 566: Mosasaur skeleton, Georgia Southern University Museum. Photograph by Frank Fortune, Georgia Southern University Museum.

Page 569: Alligator hunters with the day's catch, May 1912. Photograph by Francis Harper, from *Okefinokee Album* by Francis Harper and Delma E. Presley (Athens: University of Georgia Press, 1981).

Page 571: Canoeing in the Okefenokee. Photograph copyright Bill Durrence. Courtesy of Wilderness Southeast, Savannah, Georgia.

Page 578: Great egrets. Photograph by David E. Scott, University of Georgia Savannah River Ecology Laboratory.

Page 582: Turpentiners. Photograph by Dan Rahn, Southeast Office, University of Georgia Cooperative Extension Service.

Page 586: Eastern diamondback rattlesnake. Photograph by David E. Scott, University of Georgia Savannah River Ecology Laboratory.

Page 597: Roadside stand. Georgia Department of Industry, Trade and Tourism.

Page 604: Splitting rails, Altamaha River Festival, Baxley. Photograph by Delma E. Presley.

Page 606: Irrigation system, Pierce County. Photograph by Dan Rahn, Southeast Office, University of Georgia Cooperative Extension Service.

Pages 609-610: Early life in the Okefenokee. Photographs by Francis Harper. Several of these photographs and others appear in *Okefinokee Album* by Francis Harper and Delma Presley (Athens: University of Georgia Press, 1981).

Page 629: Forsyth Park, Savannah. Georgia Department of Industry, Trade and Tourism.

Page 639: Midway Congregational Church. Photograph by Robert W. Orchard.

Page 644: Julienton River. Photograph by Robert W. Orchard.

Page 651: Lawn party, Mistletoe Cottage, Jekyll Island, circa 1900. Jekyll Island Authority.

Page 654: Cumberland Island. Georgia Department of Industry, Trade and Tourism.

Page 655: Ruins of Dungeness, Cumberland Island. Georgia Department of Industry, Trade and Tourism.

Page 665: River Street, Savannah. Georgia Department of Industry, Trade and Tourism.

Page 669: Balcony, Richardson-Owens-Thomas House, Savannah. Georgia Department of Industry, Trade and Tourism.

Page 673: Tabby. Georgia Department of Industry, Trade and Tourism.

Page 679: Sorting the day's catch, Eulonia. Georgia Department of Industry, Trade and Tourism.

Page 684: Jones Shipyards, Brunswick, 1943. Kenneth G. Rogers Collection, Atlanta History Center.

Page 685: "Blessing of the Fleet," Brunswick. Photograph by Annie Archbold, Georgia Council for the Arts Folklife Program.

Page 687: Fort Frederica National Monument, St. Simons. Photograph by Robert W. Orchard.

Page 688: St. Simons Lighthouse and Museum of Coastal History. Photograph by Robert W. Orchard.

Page 689: "Beating the Rice," Georgia Sea Island Festival. Photograph by Margo Newmark Rosenbaum.

Page 693: Feral horses, Cumberland Island. Georgia Department of Industry, Trade and Tourism.

INDEX

Aaron, Hank, 286
Abbeville, 424, 447, 448, 452, 477, 489, 491
Abbeville, Alabama, 527
Abbott, John, 600
Abbott, Robert S., 670
Abernathy, Ralph, 513
Abolition of slavery, 16–17, 177
Abraham Baldwin Agricultural College, 540
Accessibility of sites, xxxi
Adairsville, 112, 137, 143
Adams, Alice Wildie, 129
Adams, Darrell, 142
Adel, 527–28, 558
Adler, Leopold and Emma, 629, 632
Adrian, 459
Afghans, "World's Largest Collection of," 217
African American Panoramic Experience (APEX), 279, 288
African Americans (blacks): in Atlanta, 66, 248–50, 257; in Augusta history, 347; churches of (southwest Georgia), 528; and Civil War's end, 20–21, 641–42; community life of, 31–32, 504; in East Central Georgia, 299, 308, 310, 315–16, 317; and Emancipation Celebration (Thomaston), 395; family reunions of (Albany), 536; first to graduate from West Point, 554; and Florida, 527; George Washington Carver School for, 674; and Hahira village, 557; in-migration of, 97, 509; modern sense of involvement of, 95; music of, 155, 529–30; and political process, 21–23, 32, 44, 58, 249; on Sapelo Island, 644–50; in Southwest Georgia (antebellum), 501–2; in Southwest Georgia (farming), 522; and state- flag controversy, 89, 94–95; and state lottery, 84; in West Central Georgia, 366, 379, 402, 405, 406.

See also Civil rights movement; Race relations; Slavery
African-American sites: African American Panoramic Experience Museum (Atlanta), 279, 288; Albany Museum of Art (ethnic art), 541; *Atlanta Daily World* building, 288; Beach Institute African-American Cultural Center (Savannah), 670; Big Bethel AME Church (Atlanta), 288; Butler Street YMCA (Atlanta), 288; of Camilla Massacre, 505, 559; Chubbtown, 132, 146; in Columbus, 405; Dorchester Academy, 677; Ebenezer Baptist Church (Atlanta), 55, 89, 283, 288; First African Baptist Church (Savannah), 664; first black public school in Savannah, 664; Fort Valley State College, 431, 442, 474; Hammonds House Galleries and Resource Center of African-American Art (Atlanta), 285; Haven Church (Waynesboro), 352–53; Laney-Walker District (Augusta), 348; Lucy Craft Laney Museum of Black History, 348; Martin Luther King Jr. Center (Atlanta), 89, 244, 283, 288; Morgan County African-American Museum, 344; Morton Theater (Athens), 332; Noble Hill-Wheeler Memorial Center, 142; Odd Fellows Building (Atlanta), 288; progressive schools in Hancock County, 354; Sallie Ellis Davis House (Milledgeville), 479; SCLC organizing site (Atlanta), 288; Seabrook Village, 642–43, 677; Selden Normal & Industrial Institute (Brunswick), 685; Springfield Baptist Church (Augusta), 348; Steward Chapel AME Church (Macon), 471; "Sweet Auburn" neighborhood (Atlanta), 288; Tubman African American Museum

Altama Museum of Art and History, 615

Ambrose, 456

American Guide Series, xvii

American Indians. *See* Native Americans

American Museum of Papermaking, 282

American Revolution, 7, 300–301; Battle of Kettle Creek, 300–301, 334; Battle of Savannah, 628, 630, 662, 664, 667; and Nancy Hart, 7–9, 228; and Liberty County, 675; Lookout Mountain skirmish, 149; and Sunbury, 676

Americus, 367, 379, 381–82, 411, 414–15

Amicalola Falls, 171, 208

Amicalola Falls State Park, 192, 208

Anderson, Bill, 79, 81

Anderson, Laurie, 440

Anderson, Marian, 405

Anderson, Paul, 222

Anderson, William G., 513

Anderson House, 604

Anderson's Po Folks restaurants, 79

Andersonville, 411; National Prisoner of War Museum in, 381, 414

Andersonville National Cemetery, 374

Andersonville Prison, 373–74, 391–92, 414, 554

Andrews, Benny, 101, 307

Andrews, Eliza Frances, 19

Andrews, George, 101, 307

Andrews, Louis, 465

Andrews, Raymond, 101, 307

Andrews's Raiders, 143, 152, 153, 271

Anna Ruby Falls, 171, 192, 217

Ansa, Tina McElroy, 77, 95–96

Ansley, Thomas, 356

Ansley Park, 284, 290

"Antebellum trail," 304

Anthony's, 281

Antiunionism, 49

Ants, fire, 536

Aonia, 313, 320

Apalachee, 303, 306–7, 343

Apalachicola, Florida, 367, 390, 502

Apalachicola River, 500, 548

APEX, 279, 288

Appalachian mountaineers: appeal of to outsiders, 203; artisans among, 195–97; Asbury on, 173; and Civil War, 176–79; and *Deliverance*, 166–70; early descriptions of, 175; extremes of, 170; and *Foxfire*

magazine, 165–66, 168, 185, 195, 196, 203, 221; and gold rush, 173–74; independent spirit of, 179–80; and modern progress, 184–86; as moonshiners, 180–84; music of, 197–98; Union officer's account of, 178–79; as violent, 179, 180

Appalachian Trail, 158, 171, 191–92, 206, 208; Walasi-Yi Center on, 211

Apple farming, 158, 219

Appling (Columbia County), 328, 336

Appling County, 500, 581, 593, 616, 697

Aquaculture, 521, 559

Aquariums: at Bo Ginn (Jenkins County), 599; in Chattanooga, 151; near Pine Mountain, 409; at Skidaway Institute, 671

Aquifer, Floridian, 521

Arabi, 450

Archaelogical sites, 295; bibliography on, 704–5; Fort Mountain, 109–10, 111, 157; Rock Eagle, 344–45; Singer-Moye Site, 417. *See also* Historic sites

Archibald Smith Plantation Home, 272, 280

Architecture: *AIA Guide to the Architecture of Atlanta*, 267, 267–68, 288; Norman Davenport Askins, 349; of Augusta, 308, 346, 347, 349; of Brunswick, 685; CCC–New Deal period, 211; of Church of Good Shepherd, 350; around Clarkesville, 218; of the Cloister, 687; by Ross Crane (Athens), 332–33; of the Crescent (Valdosta), 556; of The Folly (Columbus, double octagon), 405; of frontier settlement, 334; Greek Revival, 321 (*see also* Greek Revival architecture); of Lapham-Patterson House (Thomasville), 553–54; in Lavonia, 228; in Louisville, 337; in Macon, 431–32, 471; Madison or Washington for, 309, 321, 327; of Meriwether Inn, 359; Oakland Cemetery collection of, 288; of Savannah, 662, 663, 664, 667, 668, 669; of Seaborn Goodall House, 600; in small towns, 321; of Statesboro, 603

Archives, Georgia Department of Archives and History, xxi, xxiii; in Troup County, 396

Arlington, 559

Armstrong, Louis, 332, 546

Armuchee River, 105

Atlanta–Fulton County Stadium, 237, 260, 290; Pascual Perez's attempt to find, 233; and state flag, 89

Atlanta Hawks, 290

Atlanta Heritage Row, 265–66

Atlanta History Center (AHC), 265–66, 277, 279, 280, 283, 286

Atlanta International Museum of Art and Design, 285

Atlanta Journal-Constitution, xxiv, 93; Leisure Guide of, 289

Atlanta Knights, 290

Atlanta Life Insurance Company Building, 288

Atlanta Motor Speedway, 290

Atlanta Museum, 279

Atlanta Negro Voters League, 249

Atlanta Now, 289

Atlanta Preservation Center (APC), 266, 288

Atlanta Symphony Orchestra, xxvii, 100–101

Atlanta Thunder (tennis), 290

Atlanta tour, 265–68; and Atlanta History Center, 265–66; and Atlanta Preservation Center, 266; Campbell's choices for, 283–84; and Martin Luther King Jr. National Historic Site, 266

Atlanta Track Club, 278

Atlanta University, 246

Atlanta University Center complex, 288, 291

Atlantic Center, 282

Atlantic Coast Flatwoods, 565

Atlantic Embayment, 659

Attapulgus area, 518, 551

Audubon, John James, 615

Augusta, 299, 304, 308, 326, 327, 328, 346–52; and American Revolution, 300–301; as anomalous, 315; Confederate war goods from, 370; founding of, 300; and Great Philadelphia Wagon Road, 114; lunch counter desegregation in, 55; musical figures from, 100; in postbellum years, 303; symphony in, xxvii, 308; and time of white settlements, 317; trade with highlands, 185

Augusta Canal, 347, 350

Augusta College, 350–51

Augusta Country Club, 351–52

Augusta–Richmond County Museum, 349

Auraria, 174

Automobile racing: on Atlanta Dragway, 226; at Atlanta Motor Speedway, 290–91; at Cochran Speedway, 486; Dawsonville tribute to, 208; drag racing (Warner Robins), 473; dragway (U.S. 19 Racetrack), 534; dragway (Southeastern International), 138; and moonshiners, 215; at Road Atlanta, 224, 291; stock-car racing (West Central Georgia), 381

Ayllon, Lucas Vasquez de, 626

Babbit, Joel, 86–87

Bachtel, Doug, xxii

Back-to-Africa movement, 508

Bacon County, 39, 75, 585, 616, 697

Bagby State Park, 561

Baggarly Buggy Shop, Senoia, 399

Bagley, Henry C., 190

Bailey-Tebault House, Griffin, 276

Bainbridge, 529, 540, 551; steamboat near, 501

Bainbridge, William, 551

Bainbridge College, 551

Baisden Bluff Academy, 679

Baker, Ben, 451

Baker County, 498, 505, 516, 532, 559, 697; church membership in, 83; health care center in, 525–26; malaria control in, 525; quail plantations in, 524

Baker County courthouse, 559

Baldwin (Habersham County), 217, 219

Baldwin, Abraham, 464

Baldwin County, 447, 464, 647, 697

Baldwin County courthouse, 478

Bale press, 449

Balkans, Southern economy compared to, 240

Ball, June, 624, 627

Ball Ground area, 107, 161

Ball's Ferry, 491

Baltimore, Charles Center of, 251

Banfield, Edward C., 249

Banks, Richard E., 226

Banks County, 226, 697

Banks County courthouse, 226

Banks Crossing, 206, 223, 226–27

Banks Lake, 557–58

Banks Lake National Wildlife Refuge, 557–58

Baptism, family (Billys Lake), 609

Federal Law Enforcement Training
Center, 683
Federal Reserve Bank Monetary
Museum, 282
Federal Road, 115, 157, 158, 161, 412
Federal Writers' Project, xix, xvii, xviii
Federation of Southern Cooperatives,
522
Felton, Rebecca Lattimer, 34–36
Feminism, and Felton, 34–35
Fernbank Forest, 277, 281
Fernbank Museum of Natural History,
281, 283
Fernbank Science Center, 281
Fieldale Farms, xxiv, 219
Fifteenth Amendment, 22
Fine arts, xxvi–xxvii. *See also* Arts,
visual; Literature; Music
Finney, Newton, 651
Finster, Howard, 101–2, 132–33, 148
Fire ants, 536
Fire Baptized Holiness Church and Taxi
Stand, 133
Fire Station Number 6, 288
First African Baptist Church, Savannah,
664
First Baptist Church, Thomson, 317
Fish, commercial production of, 521,
559
Fish Hatchery, Richmond Hill, 675
Fish Hatchery and Aquarium, National,
Warm Springs, 409
Fishing: in Allatoona Lake, 142; in
Altamaha River, 612; in Altamaha
Waterfowl Area, 682; at Amicalola
Falls State Park, 208; at Big Lazar
Creek Area, 410; at Bingham State
Park, 558; in Calhoun area, 155; in
Chattahoochee National Forest, 158;
on Chattahoochee River, 278; on
Colonels Island, 677; at Crooked
River State Park, 691; at Florence
Marina State park, 419; at Fort
McAllister State Historic Park, 675;
at General Coffee State Park, 489; at
George L. Smith State Park, 482; at
Gordon-Altamaha State Park, 612;
at Grand Bay Area, 557; at Gray's
Reef, 680; at Hamburg State Park,
353; at Hard Labor Creek State Park,
343; information on, 696; at James H.
Floyd State Park, 148; on Lake
Chehaw, 543; on Lake Lanier, 214,
278; on Lake Oconee, 341; on Lake
Russell, 219; on Lake Seminole, 521,
548; on Lake Sinclair, 307; on Lake
Walter F. George, 561; at Laura S.
Walker State Park, 617; at Mistletoe
State Park, 336; at Okefenokee
Refuge, 558; at Piedmont National
Wildlife Refuge, 475; at Red Top
Mountain State Park, 142; on Satilla
River, 616; by Southwest Georgians,
534, 538; at Stone Mountain Park,
277; at Unicoi State Park, 217; at
Watson Mill Bridge State Park, 342;
on West Point Lake, 397
Fishing tournaments, on Lake Lanier,
214
Fitzgerald, 452–53, 468, 469, 489,
490–91
Fitzgerald, Ella, 405
Fitzgerald, P. H., 452–53, 491
Fitzpatrick Building, Washington, 323
Five Points area, Atlanta, 250, 252, 287
Flag controversy, 88–90, 94, 95, 179,
322
Flagler, Henry, 360
Flanagan, Thomas Jefferson, 402
Flat Rock, 313
Flat Rock Camp Meeting Tabernacle,
397–98
Fletcher Henderson House, 546
Flint, Alice, 558
Flint River, 363–64, 365, 387, 390,
450, 477, 500, 502, 535, 548
Flint River Review, 533
Flipper, Henry O., 554
Flood of 1994, 521, 534–35, 559
Florence, 411
Florence Marina State Park, 419
Florida, 492
Florida State: and Southwest Georgia,
527; tourists on way to, 537, 623
Floridian aquifer, 521
Floyd College, 146, 147
Floyd County, 132, 417, 698
Floyd County courthouse, 147
Flying Africans, 646–47, 650
Foley, Red, 78
Foliage-viewing: in Northeast Georgia,
205–6, 210, 216; in Northwest
Georgia (Cloudland), 149
Folk Art and Photography Galleries,
285
Folk artists, Leroy Alman, 140; Howard
Finster, 101–2, 132–33, 148; St EOM,
381, 413
Folklife, indigenous, xxvi. *See also*
Foxfire magazine

House (Washington), 323, 324, 335;
Roselawn (Cartersville), 142; Santa
Cruz de Sabacola El Menor
(Donalsonville area), 548; Springer
Opera House (Columbus), 381, 406;
Taylor-Grady House (Athens), 333;
Traveler's Rest (Toccoa), 173, 222–23;
James Vann house (Chatsworth),
128–29, 156, 157; Westville
(19th-century buildings), 381, 412,
416–17; Wormsloe State Historic Site
(Savannah area), 670; in Wrightsville,
481. *See also* African American sites;
Civil War sites; *at* Museums
Historic Wrightsboro, 356
History of Georgia. *See* Georgia history
Hitchcock, Henry, 18
Hitchitee Indians, 386, 537
Hitchiti Nature Trail, 474, 475
Hoard, Dick, 315
Hodchodkee (waterway), 386
Hodgson, Margaret Telfair, 668
Hodgson, William B., 668
Hodkinson, Pete, 192–93
Hoffer, Eric, 260
Hofwyl-Broadfield Plantation State
Historic Site, 683
Hogansville, 375, 397
Hogcrawl Creek, 378
Hog Hammock, 644, 645–46, 648–50,
653, 680
Hog killing, 383
Holliday, John Henry (Doc), 556
Holly Springs, Sacred Harp singing in,
131
Holmes, Hamilton, 51, 96
Homer, 195, 226
Homer the Brave, 238
Homerville, 613, 617–18
Honey: from Homerville, 618; roadside
sale of, 214
Honey Bee Festival, Hahira, 557
Hood, John B., 286
Hood, Mary, 98, 716
Hooker, Joseph, 152
Hoover, Herbert, 652
HOPE program (Helping Outstanding
Pupils Educationally), 84–85, 126
Hopewell, 366
Hornaday, Sarah E., 373
Hornbostel, Henry, 290
Horne, Lena, 405, 432, 471
Horse Creek, 430
Horses: auction of (Hazlehurst), 489; on

Cumberland Island, 692, 693;
harness racing (Hawkinsville),
443–44, 489; horse farms (East
Central Georgia), 318; and Native
Americans, 109; Spaniards introduce,
108; steeplechase, 290, 381
Horseshoe Bend, battle of, 388
Horton, William, 690
Hospitals, in small towns, 313
Hostels, xxxi
"Hotlanta River Expo," 90
Hotz, James, 525, 526
Houghton School, Augusta, 349
House museums, Atlanta area, 279–80
Houston County, 429, 430, 438, 449,
473, 700
Howard, O. O., 484
Howlin' Wolf, 432
Hubert, Zack and Camilla, 354
Hudson, Charles, 499
Hughston, Jack, 379
Huie-Reynolds House, Morrow, 275
Hunt clubs, 381
Hunter, Floyd, 245, 246–47, 249, 253
Hunter-Gault, Charlayne, 51, 96–97
Hunting: Addison Wild Boar
Hunting, 490; at Allatoona Lake,
142; by Creeks, 500; information
on, 696; in Jasper County, 308;
on quail plantations, 278, 486,
524, 526; at Quail Ridge, 492;
in Southwest Georgia, 534; at
Talking Rock Wildlife Management
Area, 158
Hunting dogs competitions,
Waynesboro, 353
Hurricane Shoals Park, 226
Hurt, "Boots," 306, 326
Hutchison, David, 606
Huxford Genealogical Society, 618

*I Am a Fugitive from a Georgia Chain
Gang* (Burns), 38
Ibo (Ebo) Landing incident, 647, 686
Ichauwaynochaway Creek, 526
Ichauway Plantation, 525, 526
*If I Ever Get Back to Georgia, I'm Gonna
Nail My Feet to the Ground*
(Grizzard), 92
Income, personal, 47–48, 122; Atlanta
area contrasts in, 66
Indian Green Corn Ceremonial, 398
Indians. *See* Native Americans
Indian Springs, 484

Marble, in Tate quarries, 161

Marietta, 271; and Atlanta, 234; Bell
Aircraft in, 47; and Civil War, 286;
gay-lifestyle controversy in, 91;
Theatre in the Square in, 91

Marietta-Cobb Museum of Art, 171, 285

Marietta National Cemetery, 271

Marine Corps Logistics Base, 498, 517

Marion County, 365, 386, 413, 700

Marion County courthouse, 413

Marlor House and Arts Gallery,
Milledgeville, 478–79

Marsh, John, 73

Marshall, Daniel, 336

Marshall, George C., 672

Marshall, Thurgood, 442

Marshall Row, Savannah, 629

Marshallville, 414

Marshes, 659, 683

"Marshes of Glynn," 72, 683

MARTA (Metropolitan Atlanta Rapid
Transit Authority), xxx

Martha Berry Museum, Mount Berry, 147

"Marthasville," 239

Martin, Eddie Owens (St EOM), 381,
413

Martin, Harold, xix

Martin Luther King Jr. Center for
Non-Violent Social Change, 89, 244,
283, 288

Martin Luther King Jr. Chapel, 285

Martin Luther King Jr. Historic District,
288

Martin Luther King Jr. National Historic
Site, 266

Martus, Florence, 666

Marvin, Lake, 155

Mary Gay House, 269

Mary Willis Library, Washington, 335

Mason, Charles, 114

Mason, Lowell, 667

Mason, Lucy Randolph, 49

Mason-Dixon Line, 114

Massachusetts Bay Colony, and "City on
a Hill" vision, 246

Massee Lane Gardens, Fort Valley, 474

Massie Heritage Interpretation Center,
Savannah, 670

Masters Golf Tournament, 308, 351–52

Mathis Dam, 188

Matthews, John M., xxii

Matthews House, Washington area, 335

Mayhaw trees, 548

Maysville, 226

Mead, Rufus, 19

Meade, George, 372

Meaders, Cheever, 196

Meaders, Cleator, Jr., 199

Meaders, John Milton, 196

Meaders, Lanier, 196–97, 199

Meaders Pottery, 196, 199

Meadow Garden, Augusta, 349

Meeks, 459

Mehre, Harry, 333

Meier, Richard, 285

Melville, Herman, 653

Member of the Wedding, The
(McCullers), 407

Mencken, H. L., 38, 71–72, 506

Mendenhall, Marmaduke, 342

Mendes, 601

Menendez de Aviles, Pedro, 676

Mennonites, in Macon County, 414

Mentone, Alabama, 148

Mercer, Johnny, 629

Mercer Aircraft Museum, 155

Mercer House, 628–29

Mercer University (previously
Institute), 340, 431, 471

Merchandise Mart, Atlanta, 252

Meriwether County, 365, 366, 367, 384,
390, 395, 700

Meriwether County courthouse, 395

Meriwether Inn, 359–60, 385

Merritt, Bill, 411

Merritt House, Westville, 417

Metro Atlanta, 240–41; tour of, 269–88

Metropolitan Frontiers: Atlanta,
1835–2000, 265, 280

Metter, 597, 598, 601

Micco, Otis, 560

Michael, Moina, 273

Michael C. Carlos Museum, 283, 285

Middle Georgia College, 431, 486

Middle Georgia Pottery, 411

Midnight in the Garden of Good and Evil
(Berendt), 100, 629

Midville, 313, 484

Midway community, 638, 643, 675

Midway Congregational Church, 638,
639, 675–76

Milan Correctional Institution, 447

Milledge, John, 329, 464

Milledgeville, 337, 464–65, 468–69;
Central State Hospital in, 447; cotton
weighing in, 25; and DeSoto, 477;
lynch mob takes Frank from, 37; and
1940s air depot competition, 433;

of Macon, 471–72; of north Georgia, 197–98; Sacred Harp tradition, 130–132, 140, 407, 696, 712; and Schwob School of Music, 381; of Southwest Georgia, 529–30; summer festival of (Chateau Elan), 223; symphony orchestras, xxvi–xxvii; in Valdosta, 557

Music Hall of Fame, Georgia, 155, 432, 472

Muskogulgi Indians, 359, 386

Mussolini, Benito, gift from, 147

Myers, Robert Manson, 640

Myrtle Hill Cemetery, Rome, 146

Myth(s): of Georgia as penal colony, 4; of New South, 34; of Old South, 73; paradise or wilderness as, 105; of slavery, 11

Nacoochee Valley, 176, 193

Nacoochee Valley Historic District, 217

Nahunta, 566, 601, 607

Nancy Springs, 559–60

Nantahala National Forest, 190–91

NASCAR, 215, 290–91. *See also* Automobile racing

Nashville, Georgia, 540, 558

Nashville Agrarians, 72

National Association for the Advancement of Colored People, 506–8, 512

National Fish Hatchery and Aquarium, Warm Springs, 409

National High School Football Hall of Fame, 533, 557

National Infantry Museum, Fort Benning, 381, 411

National Park Service: headquarters of, 288; and King museum, 244

National Prisoner of War Museum, Andersonville, 381, 414

National Recreational Trail, 221

National Science Center, exhibit hall of, 346–47

National Weather Service, in Neese, 304

Native Americans: and Atlanta Braves, 237; bibliography on, 704–5; changed attitudes toward, 325; and Chehaw National Indian Festival, 542; Creek-Cherokee wars, 107–8; and DeSoto, 108–9; and Festival of Southeastern Indian Cultures (Columbus College), 407; forest fires set by, 567, 579; games of, 108, 161;

and Hawkins, 390, 410; history and pre-history of, 295–98, 387–89, 567–68; and Institute for Study of American Cultures, 405; invention of written language (Cherokees), 117; and land hunger after Revolution, 9, 10; mounds built by, 136, 141, 296, 387–88, 417, 419, 469, 485, 547, 560; and names of waterways, 105, 386; in Northwest Georgia, 149; place-names from, 239, 366, 594; as Pleiades, 389; removal of, 10; Santa Cruz de Sabacola El Menor mission to, 548; in Southwest Georgia, 537–38; and Spanish explorers, 109, 386–87, 625–28; trading with Europeans, 106–7, 388, 500; treaties with, 9, 115, 119, 138, 147, 155, 276, 333, 354, 365, 388, 400, 449, 500; and West Central Georgia, 390. *See also* Cherokee Indian Nation; Creek Indian Nation

Native American sites: Ball Ground area, 107, 161; of Battle of Etowah, 146; around Calhoun (Cherokee), 150; Coosa River settlements, 147; Etowah Indian Mounds State Historic Site, 113, 141; Etowah mounds site, 297; Fort Buffington, 280; Hurricane Shoals, 226; at New Echota, 155–56; in Pickens County, 158; John Ross house, 151; Sautee-Naacoochee (burial) Mound, 217, 218; at Toccoa, 222; at Wingate's Lunker Lodge, 551

Nature Conservancy of Georgia, 492, 696

Neblett, Charles, 529

Neese, 304

Nesbit, John, 350

New Corinth, 366

New Deal, 47; and Pine Mountain Valley Community, 382–84; and Southwest Georgia agriculture, 510–11; and Talmadge, 43. *See also* CCC

New Deal art in Georgia, 549–50; in Adel post office, 558; in Blakeley post office, 547; in Cairo post office, 552; in Cochran post office, 486; in Conyers depot, 274; in Cornelia post office, 219; in Cuthbert post office, 546–47, 550; in Eastman post office, 487; in Gainesville federal courthouse, 212; in Greensboro post office, 340; in Lyons post office, 615;

F. D. Roosevelt State Park, 385, 408;
Florence Marina State Park, 419;
High Falls State Park, 277, 392, 393;
Providence Canyon State
Conservation Park, 417–18
Parrott, 546
Partridge Inn, Augusta, 350
Pasaquan, 381, 413
Pataula (waterway), 386
Paternalism: of Jones as slaveholder,
641; of mill villages, 377
Patrick, Michael W., 379
Patsiliga Creek, 386
Patten, Lawson L., 521
Pattison, Abbot, 340
Paulding County, 138, 241, 700
Payne, Billy, 85, 101, 234, 250
Payne, Matthew, 350
Paz, Octavio, 101
Peabody, George Foster, 360, 380
Peach cobbler, largest, 438, 439
Peach County, 423, 437, 438, 473, 700
Peaches, 363, 473; Elberta (Rumph
developer of), 414, 438; Europeans'
introduction of, 499–500; and Fort
Valley, 474; in Talbot County, 410
Peach Festival, 438, 439
Peach Festival Outlet Center, Byron,
438, 474
Peachtree Baptist Church, Atlanta, 100
Peachtree Center, Atlanta, 250, 251–52
Peachtree City, 261
Peachtree Creek, battle of, 287
Peachtree Road (Siddons), 83, 245, 253
Peachtree Road Race, 278
Peachtree Street, Atlanta, 284
Peacock, Wayne, 447
Peacock Alley, 125, 153
Peanuts, 64, 363; Ashburn as capital
for, 451, 478; boiled, 214, 320, 472;
in Central Georgia, 453, 467; and
CPES research, 527; and Dawson,
546; of Dooly County, 449; Festival of
(Sylvester), 541; monument to
(Blakely), 547; from Peach County,
473; and Snickers candy bars, 518; in
Southeast Georgia, 596; in Southwest
Georgia, 499, 509, 511, 518, 519,
538; Sylvester as capital for, 518
Pearce Auditorium, Brenau campus, 212
Pea Ridge (later Buena Vista), 413
Pearson, 456, 492
Pebble Hill Plantation, 524, 527,
554–55

Pecans, 509; and Albany, 499, 541; in
Central Georgia, 467; in Dooly
County, 476; groves of, 487; in
Southeast Georgia, 596
Pecan trees, in Warrenton, 355
Pelham, 559
Pemberton, John, 380, 402, 410
Pemberton Country Home, Columbus,
402
Pemberton House, Columbus, 402
Pembroke, 674
Penfield, 340
Penniman, Little Richard, 78–79,
432, 471
Pennville, 148
People of Atlanta, The (McMahan), 240
Perez, Pascual, 233, 235, 264
Perimeter Center, Atlanta, 251
Perry, 437, 438, 440–41, 468–69,
472, 473
Perry, George Washington, 458
Perry, Oliver Hazard, 438
Peter Pan Peanut Butter, 518
Peters House, Atlanta, 281
Peterson-Wilbanks House,
Vidalia, 615
Phagan, Mary, 36–38
Phenix City, Alabama, 401
Philadelphia, Penn Center of, 251
Philip II (king of Spain), 626
Phillips 66 National Outdoor Diving
Championships, 534
Philomath Historic District, 342
"Phoenix Rising from the Ashes"
(sculpture), 282
Pickens, Andrew, 300
Pickens County, 29, 158, 161, 178, 700
Pickett's Mill, battle of, 137
Pickett's Mill State Historic Site, 137–38
Pick-your-own farms or orchards, 158,
278, 343, 490, 596
Piedmont College, 218
Piedmont National Wildlife Refuge,
474, 475
Piedmont Park, 277, 284
Pierce, Franklin, 605
Pierce County, 568, 605, 606, 700
Pike, Zebulon, 394
Pike County, 365, 394, 395, 700
Pilgrim's Rest, 366
Pillsbury, Emily, 12–13
Pinch Gut Historic District, 349
Pinckneyville Arts Center parks, 279
Pineda, Alonzo Alvarez, 387

Union Manufacturing Company, 341
Union Point, 341
Unions, suppression of, 49
Union Station(s), Atlanta, 234
United Daughters of the Confederacy, 35, 373
Universal Negro Improvement Association (UNIA), 508
University of Georgia, 64, 299, 304–6, 310, 328, 329–33; agricultural experiment station of, 210; antebellum violence in, 14; and Baldwin, 464; blacks admitted to, 51; cattle research farm of, 324; and Elijah Clark, 301; Coastal Plain Experiment Station of, 540 ; iron horse from campus of, 311, 340; Marine Extension Service of, 671; Marine Institute of, 644, 650, 653, 680; and Oglethorpe County, 306, 324–25; Olympic soccer at, 87; and Rock Eagle 4-H Center, 344–45; Rural Development Center of, 540
Upatoi Creek, 386
Upatoi Creek bridge, 412
Upper Hightower, Eller Brothers and Ross Brown in, 198
Upper Trading Path, 114, 354, 355
Upshaw, Berrien K. "Red," 73
Upson County, 365, 394, 395, 438, 701
Upson House, 333
Urban South, The (Heberle), 240

Vail, Theodore N., 690
Valdosta, 498, 555–57; as Albany competitor, 502; and Billy Langdale Parkway, 524; Catholic church integration in, 516; cigar factories in, 510; and high school football, 533, 556–57; interstate commerce to, 527–28; Jewish congregation in, 528–29; Moody Air Force Base in, 517; NAACP in, 507; St. John the Evangelist Catholic Church in, 528; *Snake Nation Review* published in, 533; on tour itinerary, 540
Valdosta State University, 498, 556
Valley, Alabama, 375
Valona, 679
Vanderbilt, William K., 651, 690
Vandiver, Ernest, 48, 50, 59
Vann, James, 128–29, 156
Vann, Joseph ("Rich Joe"), 129, 156
Vann House, 128–29, 156, 157

Vann's Valley, 144, 146
Vanstory, Burnette, 652
Vaudeville houses, 443
Victoria Bryant State Park, 227
Victory Garden, The (PBS), 385
Vidalia, 459, 605, 613, 615
Vidalia onions, 467, 485, 596, 597, 605, 612, 613
Vienna, 433, 449, 468, 476
Views, scenic: from and toward Black Rock Mountain, 220; from bluff on Altamaha, 605; at Buford Dam, 214; at Carter's Dam, 157; at Cloudland Canyon, 149; of Dahlonega, 209; from Dowell's Knob, 362, 378, 408; of fall foliage, 149, 205–6, 210, 216; from Fort Gaines bluff, 560; at Fort Mountain, 111; from Freedom Parkway (Atlanta), 284; of Lake Walter F. George, 413; of mountains (Northeast Georgia), 209, 214, 217, 219; from Russell Highway, 363; from Stone Mountain, 277. *See also* Waterfalls
Villanow, 150, 155
Villa Rica, 136, 138
Vines Botanical Garden, Loganville, 277
Vinson, Carl, 433, 465
Vinson house, 354
Vinson Valley, 437
Violence: in antebellum Georgia, 13–14; of Appalachian highlanders, 167–68, 179, 180; against blacks, 22, 505, 506–7; in Southwest Georgia, 532
Virginia E. Evans/Greene County Historical Society Museum, 341
Virginia-Highland neighborhood, Atlanta, 284, 290
Visual arts. *See* Arts, visual
Vitruvius, 632
Vogel State Park, 192, 210, 211
Voices of the Old South (Gallay), 116
Volleyball tournaments, Atlanta, 290

Wade in the Water (NPR series), 529
Wadley, 459
Walasi-Yi Center, Appalachian Trail, 211
Walcott, Derek, 101
Walden, Phil, 432
Walker, Alice, 57, 76–77, 82, 307, 345
Walker, Christine, 460
Walker, Freeman, 350
Walker, Eli, 238